**Productivity**
Volume 2: International
Comparisons of
Economic Growth

# Productivity
Volume 2: International
Comparisons of
Economic Growth

Dale W. Jorgenson

The MIT Press
Cambridge, Massachusetts
London, England

This book was printed and bound in the United States of America.

Library of Congress Cataloging-in-Publication Data

Jorgenson, Dale Weldeau, 1933–
    Productivity / Dale W. Jorgenson.
        p.   cm.
    Includes bibliographical references and index.
    Contents: v. 1. Postwar U.S. economic growth—v. 2. International comparisons of economic growth.
    ISBN 0–262–10049–5 (v. 1).—ISBN 0–262–10050–9 (v. 2).
1. Industrial productivity—United States. 2. Capital investments—United States. 3. United States—Economic conditions—1945–  4. Industrial productivity—Japan. 5. Japan—Economic conditions—1945–  6. Industrial productivity—Germany (West) 7. Capital investments—Germany (West)—Economic conditions. I. Title.
HC110.I52J668   1995                                              94–22733
338.9—dc20                                                              CIP

# Contents

List of Tables         ix

Preface         xv

List of Sources         xxvii

**1. Productivity and Economic Growth**         **1**

*Dale W. Jorgenson*

1.1  Introduction         1

1.2  Measuring Labor Input         17

1.3  Measuring Capital Input         28

1.4  Measuring Output, Intermediate Input, and Productivity         44

1.5  Measuring Aggregate Output and Productivity         57

1.6  Econometric Modeling of Producing         72

1.7  Conclusion         87

**2. Measurement of Macroeconomic Performance in Japan, 1951–1968**         **99**

*Mitsuo Ezaki and Dale W. Jorgenson*

2.1  Introduction         99

2.2  Basic Accounting Framework for the National Economy         101

2.3  Product and Factor Outlay for the Producing Sector         109

2.4  Income, Outlay, Saving, and Wealth for the Consuming Sector         130

     Appendix: Data for Consumers' Durables         144

2.5  Measurement of Productivity Change         146

2.6  Concluding Remarks         171

**3. U.S. And Japanese Economic Growth, 1952–1974: An International Comparison**         **179**

*Mieko Nishimizu and Dale W. Jorgenson*

3.1  Introduction         179

3.2  Methodology         181

3.3  Output         184

3.4  Input         188

3.5  Productivity         197

**4   Economic Growth, 1947–1973:  An
     International Comparison**                                        **203**
     *Laurits R. Christensen, Dianne Cummings, and
     Dale W. Jorgenson*
     4.1   Introduction                                               203
     4.2   Methodology                                                210
     4.3   Production Account                                         223
     4.4   International Comparisons                                  239
     4.5   Summary and Conclusions                                    252
     4.6   Appendix                                                   254

**5   Relative Productivity Levels, 1947–1973 :
     An International Comparison**                                    **297**
     *Laurits R. Christensen, Dianne Cummings, and
     Dale W. Jorgenson*
     5.1   Introduction                                               297
     5.2   Methodology                                                299
     5.3   Multilateral Comparisons for 1970                          307
     5.4   Relative Levels of Output, Inputs, and
            Productivity, 1947–1973                                   314
     5.5   Concluding Remarks                                         326
     5.6   Appendix A                                                 328
     5.7   Appendix B                                                 329

**6   Sectoral Productivity Gaps Between the
     United States, Japan and Germany, 1960–1979**                    **333**
     *Klaus Conrad and Dale W. Jorgenson*
     6.1   Introduction                                               333
     6.2   Methodology                                                334
     6.3   Data and Purchasing Power Parities                         338
     6.4   Empirical Results                                          341

**7   Japan—U.S. Industry-Level Productivity
     Comparisons, 1960–1979**                                         **347**
     *Dale W. Jorgenson, Masahiro Kuroda, and
     Mieko Nishimizu*
     7.1   Introduction                                               347
     7.2   Theoretical Framework                                      348
     7.3   An International Comparison of Sectoral
            Patterns of Growth                                        355

7.4    Estimation of Purchasing Power Parity Indexes        365
7.5    International Comparison of Productivity Levels        368
7.6    Conclusion                                                            374

**8    Productivity and Economic Growth in Japan
and the United States**                                            377
*Dale W. Jorgenson*

**9    Productivity and International Competitiveness
in Japan and the United States, 1960–1985**            387
*Dale W. Jorgenson and  Masahiro Kuroda*
9.1    Introduction                                                         387
9.2    Purchasing Power Parities                                    390
9.3    Relative Productivity Levels                                 402
9.4    Conclusion                                                          412
9.5    Appendix                                                            414

References                                                                 419

Index                                                                         455

# List of Tables

| | | |
|---|---|---|
| 1.1 | Aggregate output, inputs, and productivity: Rates of growth, 1947–1985 | 4 |
| 1.2 | Growth in sectoral output and its sources, 1947–1985 (average annual rates) | 10 |
| 1.3 | Contributions of input quality to growth in sectoral output: rates of growth, 1947–1985 | 13 |
| 1.4 | Ratio of self-employed to total employment by age and sex, 1970 | 26 |
| 1.5 | Rates of economic depreciation | 30 |
| 1.6 | Economic depreciation rates: Business assets | 32 |
| 1.7 | Sectoral intermediate input and output: rates of growth, 1947–1969 | 54 |
| 1.8 | Classification of industries by biases of productivity growth | 79 |
| 2.1 | Bird's-eye view of the national economy | 103 |
| 2.2 | Gross domestic product and factor outlay for private sector and government enterprises | 113 |
| 2.3 | Real products and their prices | 116 |
| 2.4 | $\phi_{ij}$ | 118 |
| 2.5 | Factor income = value of input services | 120 |
| 2.6 | Total capital income in each sector and total labor income | 122 |
| 2.7 | Real investment and implicit deflators | 124 |
| 2.8 | Capital stock series | 125 |
| 2.9 | Relative value shares of $K_{ij}$ (1965) | 127 |
| 2.10 | Rates of tax | 128 |
| 2.11 | Rates of return and prices of capital services | 129 |
| 2.12 | Consuming sector, income and expenditure accounts | 136 |
| 2.13 | Income and outlay accounts (data) | 138 |
| 2.14 | Consuming sector, sources and uses of saving and wealth accounts | 141 |
| 2.15 | Saving and wealth accounts (data) | 142 |
| 2.16 | Consumers' durables | 145 |
| 2.17 | Data for labor | 163 |
| 2.18 | Growth rates and divisia indexes | 165 |
| 2.19 | Average rates of growth | 166 |
| 2.20 | Quality indexes of capital, labor and output | 168 |
| 2.21 | Why is the Growth Rate of $K/K^*$ so high? | 169 |
| 3.1 | Output | 187 |

| 3.2 | Capital input | 192 |
| 3.3 | Labor and total factor input | 196 |
| 3.4 | Productivity | 199 |
| 4.1 | International comparisons of growth in total factor productivity | 205 |
| 4.2 | Value share of investment goods product, 1947–1973 | 227 |
| 4.3 | Value share of capital input, 1947–1973 | 228 |
| 4.4 | Value shares of capital stock by asset class, 1970 | 230 |
| 4.5 | Own rate of return to capital in the business sector, 1947–1973 | 234 |
| 4.6 | Annual rates of growth of real private domestic capital input, 1947–1973 | 236 |
| 4.7 | Annual rates of growth of real private domestic labor input, 1947–1973 | 237 |
| 4.8 | Annual rates of growth of real private domestic factor input, 1947–1973 | 238 |
| 4.9 | Annual rates of growth of real gross private domestic product, 1947–1973 | 240 |
| 4.10 | Annual rate of growth of total factor productivity | 241 |
| 4.11 | Average annual growth rates of real product, real factor input, total factor productivity, real capital input, and real labor input | 243 |
| 4.12 | Value share of capital input and contributions of growth in real capital input, real labor input and total factor productivity to growth in real product | 246 |
| 4.13 | Average annual growth rates of quality of capital stock, capital stock, quality of hours worked, and hours worked | 251 |
| 4.A.1US | Gross private domestic product and factor outlay, 1970, United States (billions of dollars) | 262 |
| 4.A.2US | Private domestic capital input, 1947–1973, United States | 263 |
| 4.A.3US | Private domestic labor input, 1947–1973, United States | 264 |
| 4.A.4US | Gross private domestic product and factor input, 1947–1973, United States (constant dollars of 1958) | 265 |
| 4.A.1UK | Gross private domestic product and factor outlay, 1970, United Kingdom (billions of pounds) | 266 |
| 4.A.2UK | Private domestic capital input, 1955–1973, United Kingdom | 267 |
| 4.A.3UK | Private domestic labor input, 1955–1973, United Kingdom | 268 |

4.A.4UK  Gross private domestic product and factor input, 1955–1973,
         United Kingdom (constant pounds of 1958)                      269
4.A.1C   Gross private domestic product and factor outlay, 1970,
         Canada (billions of dollars)                                  270
4.A.2C   Private domestic capital input, 1947–1973, Canada            271
4.A.3C   Private domestic labor input, 1947–1973, Canada              272
4.A.4C   Gross private domestic product and factor input, 1947–1973,
         Canada (constant dollars of 1961)                            273
4.A.1F   Gross private domestic product and factor outlay, 1970,
         France (billions of francs)                                  274
4.A.2F   Private domestic capital input, 1950–1973, France           275
4.A.3F   Private domestic labor input, 1950–1973, France             276
4.A.4F   Gross private domestic product and factor input, 1950–1973,
         France (constant francs of 1963)                             277
4.A.1G   Gross private domestic product and factor outlay, 1970,
         Germany (billions of DM)                                     278
4.A.2G   Private domestic capital input, 1950–1973, Germany
         (billions of DM)                                             279
4.A.3G   Private domestic labor input, 1950–1973, Germany
         (billons of DM)                                              280
4.A.4G   Gross private domestic product and factor input, 1950–1973,
         Germany (constant DM of 1962)                                281
4.A.1I   Gross private domestic product and factor outlay, 1970,
         Italy (trillions of lire)                                    282
4.A.2I   Private domestic capital input, 1952–1973, Italy            283
4.A.3I   Private domestic labor input, 1952–1973, Italy              284
4.A.4I   Gross private domestic product and factor input, 1952–1973,
         Italy (constant lire of 1963)                                285
4.A.1J   Gross private domestic product and factor outlay, 1970,
         Japan (trillions of yen)                                     286
4.A.2J   Private domestic capital input, 1952–1973, Japan
         (trillions of yen)                                           287
4.A.3J   Private domestic labor input, 1952–1973, Japan
         (trillions of yen)                                           288
4.A.4J   Gross private domestic product and factor input, 1952–1973,
         Japan (constant yen of 1970)                                 289
4.A.1K   Gross private domestic product and factor outlay, 1970,
         Korea (billions of won)                                      290
4.A.2K   Private domestic capital input, 1960–1973, Korea            291
4.A.3K   Private domestic labor input, 1960–1973, Korea              291
4.A.4K   Gross private domestic product and factor input, 1960–1973,
         Korea (constant won of 1970)                                 292

4.A.1N    Gross private domestic product and factor outlay, 1970,
          Netherlands (billions of guilders)                              292
4.A.2N    Private domestic capital input, 1951–1973, Netherlands          293
4.A.3N    Private domestic labor input, 1951–1973, Netherlands            294
4.A.4N    Gross private domestic product and factor input, 1951–1973,
          Netherlands (constant guilders of 1963)                         295
5.1       Output, inputs, population and productivity relative to the
          United States and labor's share in the value of output, 1970    310
5.2       Decomposition of per capita labor input relative to the
          United States                                                   312
5.3       Capital-labor ratio relative to the United States              315
5.4       Per capita output relative to the United States                316
5.5       Per capita capital input relative to the United States         318
5.6       Per capita labor input relative to the United States           319
5.7       Total factor productivity relative to the United States        320
5.8       Per capita output relative to the 1970 level for the
          United States                                                   322
5.9       Per capita capital input relative to the 1970 level for the
          United States                                                   323
5.10      Per capita labor input relative to the 1970 level for the
          United States                                                   324
5.11      Total factor productivity relative to the 1970 level for the
          United States                                                   325
5.12      Alternative estimates of per capita output relative to the
          United States, 1970                                            326
5.13      Alternative estimates of per capita output and productivity
          relative to the United States, 1960                            327
5.14      Sources of data on educational attainment and earnings         330
6.1       Indexes of total factor productivity (normalized to 1.0 in 1960)
          by industry and country                                        342
6.2       Summary of the results                                         343
7.1       List of industries                                             356
7.2       Average annual growth rates of output, inputs, and productivity
          in Japan and the United States, 1960–1979 (percent per year)   358
7.3       The Japanese price index transformed by the purchasing power
          parity index at 1970 (U.S. price = 1.3670)                     367
7.4       Technology gap between the United States and Japan             369
7.5       Types of technology gap between the United States and Japan and
          expected pattern of technology gap                            372
8.1       Sources of economic growth, Japan and the United States,
          1960–1979                                                      378
8.2       Classification of Japanese industries by biases of
          productivity growth                                            382

| 8.3 | Classification of U.S. industries by biases of productivity growth | 384 |
| 9.1 | List of industries | 393 |
| 9.2 | The Japanese price index transformed by purchasing power parity index at 1970 (United States price = 1.000) | 395 |
| 9.3 | Comparison of trend of value-added price index between Japan and the United States | 396 |
| 9.4 | Comparison of trend of capital input prices between Japan and the United States | 397 |
| 9.5 | Comparison of trend of labor input prices between Japan and the United States | 399 |
| 9.6 | Relative prices of outputs in two energy industries | 400 |
| 9.7 | Annual growth rate of prices | 401 |
| 9.8 | An industrial taxonomy in terms of technology gap | 404 |
| 9.9 | Index of productivity in motor vehicles | 406 |
| 9.10 | Average productivity growth rates in Japan and the United States | 413 |

# Preface

## Dale W. Jorgenson

This volume is devoted to international comparisons of economic growth among industrialized countries and is the second of two volumes containing my empirical studies of economic growth. The first volume, *Postwar U.S. Economic Growth*, shows that investment is the predominant source of U.S. growth since World War II. The objective of this second volume is to compare postwar U.S. experience with the growth of other industrialized countries. The focus is on comparisons among the G-7 countries—Canada, France, Germany, Italy, Japan, the United Kingdom, and the United States.

Investment is the commitment of current resources in the expectation of future returns. The distinctive feature of investment as a source of economic growth is that the returns can be internalized by the investor. The most straightforward application of this definition is to investments that create property rights, such as investments in tangible assets like plant, equipment, and inventories. However, empirical research has broadened the meaning of capital formation to include investment in human capital through education and training. While these investments produce returns that can be internalized, they do not create property rights that can be transferred.

By contrast, the defining characteristic of productivity as a source of economic growth is that benefits generated by higher productivity are external to the activities that create growth. These benefits "spill over" to income recipients not involved in these activities, severing the connection between the creation of growth and the resulting incomes. Since the benefits of policies to create externalities or "spill overs" cannot be appropriated, these policies typically involve government programs or activities supported through public subsidies.

The wide diversity of experiences among industrialized countries provides a badly needed perspective for debates over policies to stimulate future growth of the U.S. economy. My paper "Productivity and Economic Growth in Japan and the United States," reprinted as Chapter 8 below, shows that the Asian model of development exemplified by Japan relies primarily on investment as a source of economic growth. For example, during the period 1960–1979 sixty percent of Japanese economic growth can be attributed to investments in tangible assets, while these investments account for forty percent of U.S. growth.

Investment in tangible assets was especially critical for growth of the Japanese economy during the period 1960–1973, when output grew at more than ten percent annually. However, investment in human capital through upgrading of the education and training of the Japanese labor force was also an important contributor to these double digit growth rates. Although Japan and the U.S. are often portrayed as economic adversaries, postwar experiences in both countries support economic policies that give high priority to capital formation.

This volume also presents assessments of competitiveness among nations that are essential for designing international trade policies. Following the Smithsonian Agreements of 1970, there have been very substantial changes in international competitiveness among industrialized countries. Since the U.S. trade balance has moved from surplus to deficit during this period, it has been natural for economic journalists to assume that U.S. competitiveness has deteriorated. In fact, the U.S. has gained considerably relative to other industrialized countries, where competitiveness is defined in terms of comparisons of product prices in a common currency.

The Smithsonian Agreements replaced the Bretton Woods regime of fixed exchange rates with flexible exchange rates. Subsequent fluctuations in competitiveness have been driven largely by exchange rate changes, especially the steady devaluation of the dollar relative to the German mark and the Japanese yen. An important secondary influence has been the growth of wage rates in other industrialized countries relative to the U.S. In periods affected by increases in petroleum prices, like 1973 and 1979, changes in these prices have further strengthened U.S. international competitiveness.

Since the facts about U.S. gains in international competitiveness are not available from official sources, the business press has been left without an anchor in reality for speculations about the sources of changes in the U.S. trade balance. During the 1980's and 1990's a large literature developed, presenting a broad panoply of mainly fanciful

ideas about the alleged decline in U.S. competitiveness and its relationship to the trade balance. An important role was assigned to the
alleged shortfall in U.S. productivity, relative to that of other industrialized countries.

Readers of the business press are still regularly bombarded with
anecdotal evidence of the low level of U.S. productivity relative to
Japan and Germany. However, the research presented in this volume
shows that relative productivity levels have been fairly stable since
around 1980 and that Japan and Germany have emerged as productivity laggards, relative to the U.S., with productivity somewhere
between 85–90 percent of the U.S. level. This relationship has been
unaffected by changes in the yen-dollar and mark-dollar exchange
rates and fluctuations of U.S.-Japan and U.S.-German trade balances.

While the growth of productivity in the U.S. has been slower than
that of other industrialized countries for much of the postwar period,
the U.S. began the postwar period with an enormous productivity
advantage over its competitors. Although gains in productivity by
Germany and Japan in the early postwar period were very dramatic,
these gains slowed markedly after 1973. Somewhat paradoxically, relative productivity levels between the U.S. and other industrialized
countries have moved in the opposite direction from changes in international competitiveness since the collapse of the Bretton Woods
regime.

The origin of confusion about international comparisons in the
business media is that these comparisons are not a settled matter
among economists. For decades economists have employed two competing approaches to the analysis of economic growth. National output provides a measure of production and can be used to allocate the
sources of economic growth between investment and productivity.
National income provides a measure of welfare and can be be divided
between current consumption and future consumption through saving. These components of income can identified with alternative uses
of economic growth.

The starting point for my research on international comparisons of
economic growth is a unified system of U.S. national accounts for
income, product, and wealth that I presented in a series of papers with
Laurits Christensen (1969, 1970, 1973a, 1973b). In a paper reprinted in
*Postwar U.S. Economic Growth* Christensen and I (1973a) utilized data
on inputs and outputs from a production account for the U.S. economy to allocate the sources of economic growth between invest-

ment and productivity. We employed data on income, consumption and saving from an income and expenditure account to divide the uses of growth between present and future consumption.

Christensen and I also succeeded in unifying wealth accounts with income and production accounts by introducing a system of vintage accounts for stocks of assets and their prices. These vintage accounts provide the basis for implementing both welfare and production approaches to the analysis of economic growth. Saving is linked to the asset side of the wealth account by capital accumulation equations for each type of asset. These equations provide a perpetual inventory of assets accumulated at different points of time. Prices for different vintages are linked to rental prices of capital inputs through a parallel set of asset pricing equations.

Mitsuo Ezaki and I (1973) constructed a parallel system of national accounts for Japan in a paper reprinted in Chapter 2 below. This paper employed the same conceptual framework as my work with Christensen and presented aggregate accounts for Japan covering the period 1951–1968. These accounts were based on a system of vintage accounts for assets and their prices. Ezaki (1977) updated our results through 1971 and compared our system of accounts with the official national accounts for Japan. Klaus Conrad and I presented a comparable system of accounts for West Germany in our 1975 book, *Measuring the Performance in the Private Economy of the Federal Republic of Germany*, 1950–1973.

After production accounts have been constructed for individual countries, the next problem is to link them. My paper with Mieko Nishimizu (1978), reprinted in Chapter 3 below, presents a methodology for bilateral comparisons of output, input, and productivity. These comparisons require purchasing power parities for outputs and inputs. Purchasing power parities give relative prices at which goods and services produced in different countries can be traded, while exchange rates provide relative prices for trading currencies. Competitiveness is defined in terms of relative prices of goods and services in a common currency, so that measures of competitiveness are obtained by dividing purchasing power parities by the corresponding exchange rates.

Nishimizu and I developed estimates of purchasing power parities for both outputs and inputs for Japan and the U.S., covering the period 1952–1974. These parities are well established for outputs in the official statistics, thanks to the work of Irving Kravis, Alan Heston, and Robert Summers (1982). Levels of output can be compared between countries by using purchasing power parities to express these outputs in a common currency. Unfortunately, outputs are often compared between countries by using exchange rates. These comparisons may be highly inaccurate, since purchasing power parities and exchange rates may differ considerably.

Purchasing power parities available from official sources only deal with the output side of the production account. International comparisons of productivity also require purchasing power parities for inputs. Since labor force composition by characteristics such as age, sex, and educational attainment of workers differs substantially between countries like Japan and the U.S., these differences must be take into account in measuring purchasing power parities for labor inputs. Each type of labor input must be weighted by its marginal product, just as in comparisons over time for a single country.

In both Japan and the U.S. there has been a substantial upgrading of educational qualifications of the labor force and important changes in age and sex composition as well. The measures of labor input employed in official statistics are inappropriate for comparisons over time. For example, the U.S. Bureau of Labor Statistics (1983) employs unweighted hours worked as a measure of labor input. For comparisons over time each component of labor input must be weighted by its marginal product, so that unweighted measures of hours worked are inappropriate for these comparisons.

A similar issue arises for a capital input. Since capital goods differ substantially in marginal productivity, it is necessary to focus on the flow of capital services rather than the stock of capital. Comparisons between countries require purchasing power parities for different types of capital input like those Nishimizu and I have constructed for Japan and the U.S. Each type of capital input must be weighted by its marginal product. The marginal products for different types of capital must be broken down by legal form of organization and class of asset, just as in comparisons over time for a single country.

In order to account for substitutions among different types of capital inputs in comparisons over time for a given country, each capital good must be weighted by its marginal product. Important progress has been made in measuring capital input in the official statistics for the U.S. compiled by the Bureau of Labor Statistics (1983). Unfortunately, the approach implemented for OECD countries by Steven Englander and Axel Mittelstadt (1988) uses unweighted capital stocks.

Productivity comparisons based on these data do not adequately account for substitutions among different types of capital inputs. This results in a highly distorted view of capital as a source of economic growth and a contributor to differences in production levels between countries.

In papers reprinted in Chapters 4 and 5 below Christensen, Dianne Cummings, and I (1980, 1981) extended international comparisons of economic growth and relative levels of economic activity to Canada, France, Germany, Italy, Japan, Korea, the Netherlands, the United Kingdom and the United States. These comparisons covered the period 1947–1973 and included estimates for all nine countries for the period 1960–1973. The methodology for multilateral comparisons was developed by Douglas Caves, Christensen, and Erwin Diewert (1982a, 1982b), generalizing the methodology for bilateral comparisons presented in my paper with Nishimizu.

The key results for international comparisons of economic growth are presented in Chapter 4. During the period 1960–1973, every country except for the United Kingdom grew more rapidly than the U.S. For Japan and Korea annual growth rates were close to ten percent, while growth rates for Canada, France, Germany, Italy, and the Netherlands clustered around five percent. For the U.S. and the U.K. growth rates were around four percent. These variations in growth rates of output are associated with the corresponding variations in growth rates of capital and labor inputs.

Measures of capital and labor inputs based on unweighted capital stocks and hours worked would have resulted in a highly misleading view of the relative importance of growth in input and productivity. For example, growth in hours worked is negative or zero for all five European countries for the period 1960–1973, while measures of labor input are positive. This is due to upgrading of the quality of labor input through substitution of hours with higher marginal productivity for those with lower productivity. Similarly, growth in capital input would be substantially under-estimated by omitting substitution among different types of capital stock.

The comparisons of relative productivity levels presented in Chapter 5 showed that output per capita and productivity converged toward U.S. levels during the postwar period. However, in 1970 the U.S. had the highest levels of output per capita and productivity among the nine countries considered. Only Canada had achieved parity with the U.S. in its capital-labor ratio. Japan's capital-labor ratio was only one-quarter of the U.S., while Korea's ratio was only eleven percent of the U.S. By comparison Japan had attained more than three-quarters of the U.S. productivity level, while Korea had reached more than thirty percent of the U.S. level.

Christensen, Cummings, and I have compared our results for the period 1947–1973 with those of Edward Denison (1967) for the period 1950–1962. Denison employed the concept of income as a basis for productivity comparisons, appealing to the welfare approach to these comparisons. This concept requires data on income and its allocation between consumption and saving and is inappropriate for productivity measurement. These data are provided by the income and expenditure account of the Christensen-Jorgenson accounting system, while productivity comparisons are based on measures of output and input from the production account.

The second stage of my research on international comparisons of economic growth and relative levels of economic activity was to disaggregate the results to the level of individual industries. My 1980 paper on "Accounting for Capital" extended the vintage accounting system I had developed with Christensen to the industry level. For the U.S. this was implemented in my papers with Frank Gollop (1980, 1983) and Barbara Fraumeni (1980, 1986) and our 1987 book, *Productivity and U.S. Economic Growth*. The results are updated and summarized in my paper, "Productivity and Economic Growth," reprinted as Chapter 1 below.

The critical issue in linking productivity to international competitiveness is the definition of output for individual industries. The older literature on productivity measurement, especially that associated with the work of John Kendrick (1973), uses the concept of value added as a measure of industry output. Value added is defined as the difference between the value of output and the value of intermediate inputs. The value added measure of industry output has the convenient property that national product is the sum of industry-level measures of value added. However, by "simplifying" productivity measurements the value added approach severs the connection between productivity and international competitiveness.

One of the important advances in industry-level productivity measurement described in Chapter 1 has been to utilize gross output rather than value added as a measure of product at the industry level. Industry output is especially advantageous for international comparisons, since measures of competitiveness are based on product prices rather than prices of value added. Another advantage of industry output is that intermediate inputs can be treated symmetrically with inputs of capital and labor services in measuring productivity. These important advantages are acquired at some cost, however, since a fully satisfactory implementation requires the integration of interindustry accounts with national income and product accounts for each of the countries involved in an international comparison.

In Chapter 7 Masahiro Kuroda, Nishimizu, and I employed industry-level gross outputs in international comparisons of productivity between Japan and the U.S. For this purpose we developed annual time series of interindustry accounts in current and constant prices for both Japan and the U.S. We supplemented these data by extensive information on capital and labor inputs for both countries. Completion of this arduous task was essential for relating productivity to international competitiveness. In Chapter 6 Conrad and I presented trilateral comparisons for West Germany, Japan and the U.S., using data for Japan from my paper with Kuroda and Nishimizu and U.S. data from my book with Gollop and Fraumeni. A more extensive discussion is provided by Conrad (1985).

After measures of output have been constructed for individual industries, the next problem is to link the results for different countries. This requires purchasing power parities for outputs at the industry level based on producers' prices rather than the purchasers' prices employed at the aggregate level. Kuroda, Nishimizu, and I have transformed purchasers' prices to producers' prices for Japan and the U.S., using interindustry accounts for both countries to eliminate trade and transportation margins and indirect taxes. A similar approach is employed in the trilateral comparisons involving West Germany in my paper with Conrad.

The second issue that arises in international comparisons of productivity at the industry level is the comparison of labor inputs between countries. Unweighted hours worked are commonly employed for this purpose, but this is highly inappropriate for international comparisons. Hours worked for each type of labor input must be weighted by the corresponding marginal product to capture this substitution. Since the labor force composition of individual industries differs substantially among Germany, Japan, and the U.S. by characteristics such as age, sex, and educational attainment, this is a fundamental issue in comparing labor inputs among the three countries.

The third, and final, issue in comparing productivity at the industry level among countries is the comparisons of capital inputs. Unweighted capital stocks are inappropriate for this purpose, since each type of capital input must be weighted by the corresponding marginal product. Capital stocks differ in composition among Germany, Japan, and U.S. by class of asset and legal form of organization and these characteristics must be taken into account in measures of capital inputs employed in productivity comparisons among the three countries.

The research required for productivity comparisons relevant to international competitiveness poses formidable challenges to economists. These comparisons require a system of national accounts for each country that successfully integrates interindustry accounts with national income and product accounts. Even for Japan and the U.S., two countries with highly developed statistical systems, productivity comparisons have required the development of new data bases for output, and intermediate, capital, and labor inputs. Extending productivity comparisons to Germany poses many additional problems. Finally, data for these countries must be linked by purchasing power parities for inputs and outputs.

An important objective of international comparisons of productivity among Germany, Japan, and the U.S. is to generate data for econometric modeling of producer behavior at the sectoral level. In 1981 Fraumeni and I developed a general equilibrium model of production for the U.S., including econometric models of production for thirty-five industrial sectors. Kuroda, Kanji Yoshioka, and I developed a similar model for thirty-five industrial sectors of the Japanese economy in 1984. Studies presenting models of this type are summarized in my 1986 paper, "Econometric Methods for Modeling Producer Behavior. These papers are reprinted in an accompanying volume, *Econometrics and Producer Behavior.*

In 1990 Kuroda and I updated our paper with Nishimizu and presented new comparisons of competitiveness between Japanese and U.S. industries. This paper is reprinted in Chapter 9. Hikaro Sakuramoto, Yoshioka, Kuroda and I employed the results in constructing a bilateral model of production for Japanese and U.S. industries. This model combined data for both countries in estimating parameters that describe the techology for each industry. This paper is reprinted in the volume, *Econometrics and Producer Behavior.*

An important issue in econometric modeling of producer behavior is the role of economies of scale. For the past decade trade theory has been dominated models of production that incorporate monopolistic competition and economies of scale. Since monopolistic competition uses a zero profit condition, the accounting framework is very similar to the one used in national income and product measurements and interindustry accounting under perfect competition. An implication of monopolistic competition is that economies of scale can generate possibilities for strategic interactions among traders. The question that remains is: Are economies of scale important?

The principal conclusion of the econometric literature reviewed in my 1986 survey paper is that there are two industries in which economies of scale are important. In long distance telecommunications there are sizable economies of scale associated with the indivisibility of such facilities as underwater cables and satellites. These indivisibilities give rise to opportunities for monopoly or, if there is a free entry, monopolistic competition. International telecommunications is an important component of trade in services.

A second industry in which economies of scale are important is the electric utility sector. Again, there are important indivisibilities associated with power generation and transmission facilities. The electric utility sector also plays a role in international trade, for example, between Canada and the U.S. or between France and Germany, but this industry is insignificant for Japanese trade. By contrast, firm level data for manufacturing seems to suggest that economies of scale are not very important. For most industries expansion occurs by increasing the number of manufacturing plants, not by expanding the output of a small number of plants. Under these conditions there is little role for economies of scale.

If there is only a modest role for economies of scale among the determinants of international competitiveness, how should we proceed in constructing econometric models for analyzing the consequences of changes in trade policy? Since economies of scale will be important only for a relatively small range of issues, the best approach is to retain the features of the Heckscher-Ohlin model of trade, especially constant returns to scale. Since growth is a very important focus for trade policy, the Heckscher-Ohlin approach must be implemented within a dynamic setting. Mun Sing Ho and I have developed a model of this type for the U.S. and Kuroda and his colleagues are developing a similar model for Japan.

One of the critical assumptions of the Heckscher-Ohlin theory is that technologies are identical for all countries. That is a very appealing assumption, since it has been difficult find a rationale for failures of countries to achieve the same level of technical sophistication. However, data on relative productivity levels for German, Japanese, and U.S. industries presented in this volume reveal that the assumption of identical technologies is untenable. There is no evidence for the emergence of a regime in which the Heckscher-Ohlin assumption of identical technologies would be appropriate.

Second, product mixes for U.S. and Japanese industries are highly dissimilar, so that the assumption of perfect substitutability of commodities produced in different countries is also inappropriate. John Chipman has suggested that this is the consequence of the relatively high degree of aggregation, even at the two-digit or three-digit level that is practical in empirical trade modeling. We conclude that the appropriate point of departure for econometric modeling of international competitiveness is a model with perfect competition, constant returns to scale, technologies that are not identical across countries, and products of identical industries that are not perfect substitutes.

Could a model with the characteristics I have described be used in the analysis of the issues that motivated interest in international competitiveness in the first place? The answer to this question is definitely in the affirmative. However, changes in competitiveness reflect the evolution of exchange rates, so that the initial approach to these issues must be macroeconomic in character and must deal with the interactions between domestic and international savings and investment balances. There is an obvious role here for macro-econometric modeling, especially in analyzing the relationships between exchange rates and trade balances.

The top priority for future research is better measurement of international competitiveness and relative productivity levels. It is crucial to get the numbers right and the results reported in this volume provide evidence of substantial progress. The initial step is to measure international competitiveness, using purchasing power parities based on OECD and Eurostat data. Second, it is essential to generate relative productivity levels within an accounting framework that includes purchasing power parities for capital, labor, and intermediate inputs, broken down in considerable detail.

I have found that international competitiveness has changed very rapidly under the post-Smithsonian regime of floating exchange rates. The speed of these variations in competitiveness obviously has had a wrenching impact on individual countries. By contrast productivity trends are much more gradual and influence international competitiveness only in the long run. In a period as short as a decade or so, productivity growth is of secondary importance. This is an important conclusion since the absence of detailed information on sources of international competitiveness has produced an intellectual vacuum. Until now this vacuum has been filled by purely speculative ideas with little connection with underlying economic realities.

Productivity measurement requires a system of national accounts that successfully integrates interindustry accounts with national incomes and product accounts. This is one of the most important features of the United Nations (1968) *System of National Accounts*. However, the U.N. system is less successful in integrating capital accounts with those for income flows. For productivity measurement economic researchers must construct data for investment flows, capital stocks, and capital services. These must be linked, using purchasing power parities.

There is a great deal for economists to do in improving economic measurements and using the resulting data in analyzing problems of trade policy. The framework appropriate for this purpose and the results available to date are summarized my paper, "Productivity and Economic Growth," reprinted as Chapter 1. This paper provides a self-contained introduction to the national accounting concepts required for productivity measurement. These concepts are illustrated in detail by empirical studies of U.S. economic growth over the period 1947–1985. The paper also gives a brief summary of alternative econometric approaches for modeling production

I would like to thank June Wynn of the Department of Economics at Harvard University for her excellent work in assembling the manuscripts for this volume in machine-readable form. Renate d'Arcangelo of the Editorial Office of the Division of Applied Sciences at Harvard edited the manuscripts, proofread the machine-readable versions and prepared them for typesetting. Warren Hrung, a senior at Harvard College, checked the references and proofread successive versions of the typescript. William Richardson and his associates provided the index. Gary Bisbee of Chiron Incorporated typeset the manuscript and provided camera-ready copy for publication. The staff of The MIT Press, especially Terry Vaughn, Ann Sochi, and Michael Sims, has been very helpful at every stage of the project. Financial support was provided by the Program on Technology and Economic Policy of the Kennedy School of Government at Harvard. As always, the author retains sole responsibility for any remaining deficiencies in the volume.

# List of Sources

1. Dale W. Jorgenson 1990. Productivity and Economic Growth. In *Fifty Years of Economic Measurement*, ed. E. Berndt and J. Triplett. Studies in Income and Wealth, vol. 54. Chicago, IL: University of Chicago Press. Reprinted by permission of the University of Chicago Press.

2. Mitsuo Ezaki and Dale W. Jorgenson 1973. Measurement of Macroeconomic Performance in Japan, 1951–1968. In *Economic Growth: The Japanese Experience since the Meiji Era*, vol. 1. Tokyo, Japan: Japan Economic Research Center. Reprinted by permission.

3. Dale W. Jorgenson and Mieko Nishimizu 1978. U.S. and Japanese Economic Growth, 1952–1974. *Economic Journal* 88, No. 352 (December): 707–726.

4. Laurits R. Christensen, Dianne Cummings and Dale W. Jorgenson 1980. In *New Developments in Productivity Measurement and Analysis*, ed. J. W. Kendrick and B. Vaccara. Studies in Income and Wealth, vol. 41. Chicago, IL: University of Chicago Press. Reprinted by permission of the University of Chicago Press.

5. Laurits R. Christensen, Dianne Cummings and Dale W. Jorgenson 1981. Relative Productivity Levels, 1947–1973. *European Economic Review* 16, No. 1 (May): 61–94. Reprinted by permission from Elsevier Science Publishers, B.V.

6. Klaus Conrad and Dale W. Jorgenson 1985. Sectoral Productivity Gaps between the United States, Japan, and Germany, 1960—1979. In *Probleme und Perspektiven der Weltwirtschaftlichen Entwicklung*, ed. H. Giersch. Berlin, Germany: Duncker and Humblot. Reprinted by permission from Duncker and Humblot GmbH.

7. Dale W. Jorgenson, Masahiro Kuroda, and Mieko Nishimizu 1987. Japan–U.S. Industry-Level Productivity Comparison, 1960–1979. *Journal of the Japanese and International Economies* 1, No. 1 (March): 1–30. Reprinted by permission from Academic Press.

8. Dale W. Jorgenson 1988. Productivity and Economic Growth in Japan and the United States. *American Economic Review* 78, No. 2 (May): 217–222. Reprinted by permission.

9. Dale W. Jorgenson and Masahiro Kuroda 1990. Productivity and International Competitiveness in Japan and the United States, 1960–1985. In *Productivity in the U.S. and Japan*, ed. C. R. Hulten. Studies in Income and Wealth, vol. 51. Chicago, IL: University of Chicago Press. Reprinted by permission of the University of Chicago Press.

# 1

## Productivity and Economic Growth

### Dale W. Jorgenson

## 1.1 Introduction

The purpose of this paper is to commemorate fifty years of research on economic measurement. I have chosen a theme—economic growth and its sources—that has played a highly significant and continuing role in the Conference on Research in Income and Wealth. Economic growth was a major professional concern of Simon Kuznets, the founder of the conference. During the last quarter of his life Kuznets (1971) devoted much of his prodigious energy and talent to the study of economic growth. A sizable portion of the research on economic growth that I will review first appeared in the conference proceedings, Studies in Income and Wealth. Finally, growth is currently undergoing a dramatic resurgence in interest among economists. This interest is motivated in large part by practical concerns arising from the great slowdown in economic growth that occurred during the 1970s and has continued to the present.

Until very recently the study of sources of economic growth has been based on the notion of an aggregate production function. This concept is one of those masterful simplifications that make it possible to summarize a welter of detailed information within a single over-arching framework. It is also a concept that seems tailor-made for the interpretation of data on output, input, and productivity of the type compiled in national product accounts. At the same time the concept of an aggregate production function is highly problematical, requiring very stringent assumptions on production patterns at the level of individual sectors of the economy. Intuitively speaking, the technology of each sector must contain a replica of the aggregate production function. It will be useful to spell out the assumptions underlying the aggregate production function and their implications in more detail below.

The origins of the concept of an aggregate production function can be clearly identified in the work of Paul H. Douglas and his associates. It is important to distinguish carefully between the notion of an aggregate production function and Douglas's more frequently cited contribution, the linear logarithmic or Cobb-Douglas functional form. Douglas did not make this distinction himself, but the existence of an aggregate production function is implied by the way he used the Cobb-Douglas function. Douglas introduced the aggregate production function in 1928 and pursued its empirical implementation with single-mindedness and determination until his election as U.S. Senator from Illinois in 1948. He returned to the topic after his retirement from the Senate. His last contribution, published posthumously in 1976, appeared almost half a century after his initial paper. Douglas's body of empirical research is one of the major achievements in economic measurement of the first half of the twentieth century.

At first, Douglas and his collaborators worked in isolation, but their work gradually attracted the interest of other economists. The starting point for our discussion of economic growth is a notable but neglected article by the great Dutch economist, Jan Tinbergen, published in German in 1942.[1] Tinbergen's contribution is clearly recognizable as one of the earliest formulations of what I now call the neoclassical theory of economic growth. The supply side of the model was based on an aggregate production function. However, Tinbergen took a critical step beyond the conception employed by Douglas. He added a time trend to the function of capital and labor inputs, representing the level of "efficiency." Tinbergen's work languished in obscurity until the mid-1950s, when it was revived by Stefan Valavanis-Vail (1955). In the meantime the notion of efficiency or total factor productivity was introduced independently by George J. Stigler (1947) and became the starting point for a major research program at the National Bureau of Economic Research.

The National Bureau program involved such pioneers of economic measurement as Moses Abramovitz and Solomon Fabricant and culminated in the epoch-making monograph by John W. Kendrick, *Productivity Trends in the United States*, published in 1961. Kendrick's work focused on the United States and employed an explicit system of national production accounts, including measures of output, input, and productivity for national aggregates and individual industries.

The production account incorporated data on outputs from earlier studies by the National Bureau, especially the work of Kuznets (1961) on national product. The input side employed data from other research work at the National Bureau, including data on capital from Raymond Goldsmith's (1962) system of national wealth accounts. However, much of the data was generated by Kendrick himself. Kendrick's achievement is an important milestone in the progress of economic measurement during the second half of the twentieth century.

The contributions of Douglas and Tinbergen were integrated with the national product accounts generated by Kendrick (1956) in Robert Solow's frequently cited 1957 article, *Technical Change and the Aggregate Production Function*. This article unified the economic theory of production, econometric methods for fitting production functions, and the generation of production accounts at the national level. Solow's work is solidly within the tradition of production modeling established by Douglas and extended by Tinbergen, but it goes beyond this tradition by generating index numbers appropriate to econometric modeling. Solow's approach was instrumental in the further extensions of Douglas's framework by Arrow, Chenery, Minhas, and Solow (1961), introducing the elasticity of substitution as a parameter to be estimated by econometric methods.

An excellent overview of research on sources of economic growth, including alternative data sources and methodologies, is provided by the Rees Report to the National Research Council (1979). Christensen, Cummings, and Jorgenson (1980) and Maddison (1987) have reviewed international comparisons of sources of economic growth among industrialized countries, while Kravis (1976) has surveyed international comparisons of productivity. Griliches (1984), Mansfield (1984), and Nelson (1981) have reviewed research on productivity at the level of the individual firm. Detailed surveys of the literature on productivity have been presented by Kennedy and Thirlwall (1972), Link (1987) and Nadiri (1970, 1972).

### 1.1.1   Sources of U.S. Economic Growth

The conceptual framework developed by Kendrick, Solow, and other pioneers in the study of economic growth can be illustrated by the results presented in table 1.1. At the aggregate level output is represented by the quantity of value added, which is expressed as a func-

**Table 1.1**

Aggregate output, inputs, and productivity: Rates of growth, 1947–1985

| Variable | 1947–1985 | 1947–1953 | 1953–1957 | 1957–1960 | 1960–1966 | 1966–1969 | 1969–1973 | 1973–1979 | 1979–1985 |
|---|---|---|---|---|---|---|---|---|---|
| Value added | .0328 | .0529 | .0214 | .0238 | .0472 | .0360 | .0306 | .0212 | .0222 |
| Capital input | .0388 | .0554 | .0401 | .0229 | .0367 | .0437 | .0421 | .0392 | .0262 |
| Labor input | .0181 | .0251 | .0037 | .0124 | .0248 | .0226 | .0128 | .0219 | .0146 |
| Contribution of capital input | .0145 | .0215 | .0149 | .0083 | .0142 | .0167 | .0149 | .0140 | .0098 |
| Contribution of labor input | .0112 | .0153 | .0022 | .0077 | .0151 | .0140 | .0082 | .0139 | .0089 |
| Rate of productivity growth | .0071 | .0160 | .0043 | .0078 | .0179 | .0053 | .0074 | −.0067 | .0034 |
| Contribution of capital quality | .0058 | .0126 | .0069 | .0016 | .0053 | .0058 | .0054 | .0045 | .0022 |
| Contribution of capital stock | .0088 | .0090 | .0080 | .0067 | .0089 | .0108 | .0095 | .0095 | .0077 |
| Contribution of labor quality | .0039 | .0060 | .0038 | .0084 | .0041 | .0030 | .0018 | .0024 | .0026 |
| Contribution of hours worked | .0073 | .0093 | −.0016 | −.0007 | .0110 | .0110 | .0065 | .0114 | .0063 |
| Rates of sectoral productivity growth | .0088 | .0142 | .0083 | .0112 | .0190 | .0060 | .0097 | −.0012 | .0029 |
| Reallocation of value added | −.0019 | .0007 | −.0044 | −.0021 | −.0021 | −.0007 | −.0023 | −.0053 | .0006 |
| Reallocation of capital input | .0005 | .0003 | .0013 | .0005 | .0009 | .0001 | .0006 | −.0001 | .0009 |
| Reallocation of labor input | −.0003 | .0009 | −.0009 | −.0019 | .0001 | −.0002 | −.0005 | −.0000 | −.0010 |

tion of capital and labor inputs and the level of productivity. Growth rates for the period 1947–1985 are given for output and the two inputs in the first column of table 1.1. Value added grows at the rate of 3.28 percent per year, while capital grows at 3.88 percent and labor input grows at 1.81 percent. The contributions of capital and labor inputs are obtained by weighting the corresponding growth rates by the shares of the inputs in value added. This produces the familiar allocation of growth to its sources: Capital input is the most important source of growth in output by a substantial margin, accounting for 44.2 percent of economic growth during the period. Labor input accounts for 34.1 percent of growth. Capital and labor inputs together account for almost four-fifths of economic growth, while productivity accounts for only 21.6 percent.

The findings summarized in table 1.1 are not limited to the period as a whole. In the first panel of table 1.1 the growth of output is compared with the contributions of the two primary factor inputs and productivity growth for eight subperiods—1947–1953, 1953–1957, 1957–1960, 1960–1966, 1966–1969, 1969–1973, 1973–1979, and 1979–1985. The end points of the periods identified in table 1.1, except for the last period, are years in which a cyclical peak occurred. The growth rate presented for each subperiod is the average annual growth rate between cyclical peaks. The contributions of capital and labor inputs are the predominant sources of U.S. economic growth for the period as a whole and all eight subperiods.

I have found that the contribution of capital input is the most significant source of output growth for the period 1947–1985 as a whole. The contribution of capital input is also the most important source of growth for seven of the eight subperiods, while productivity growth is the most important source for only one, 1960–1966. The contribution of capital input exceeds the contribution of labor input for seven subperiods, while the contribution of labor input is more important only for the period 1960–1966. The contribution of labor input exceeds productivity growth for four of the eight subperiods.

In 1985 the output of the U.S. economy stood at almost three and a half times the level of output in 1947. My overall conclusion is that the driving force behind the expansion of the U.S. economy between 1947 and 1985 has been the growth in capital and labor inputs. Growth in capital input is the most important source of growth in output, growth in labor input is the next most important source, and productivity growth is least important. This perspective focuses attention on the mobilization of capital and labor resources rather than advances in productivity.

The findings just summarized are consistent with a substantial body of research. For example, these findings coincide with those of Christensen and Jorgenson (1973a) for the United States for the period 1929–1969 and the much earlier findings of Tinbergen (1942) for the period 1870–1914. Maddison (1987) gives similar results for six industrialized countries, including the United States, for the period 1913–1984. However, these findings contrast sharply with those of Abramovitz, Kendrick, and Solow, which emphasize productivity as the predominant growth source. At this point it is useful to describe the steps required to go from these earlier findings to the results summarized in table 1.1.

The first step is to decompose the contributions of capital and labor inputs into the separate contributions of capital and labor quality and the contributions of capital stock and hours worked. Capital stock and hours worked are a natural focus for input measurement, since capital input would be proportional to capital stock if capital inputs were homogeneous, while labor input would be proportional to hours worked if labor inputs were homogeneous. In fact, inputs are enormously heterogeneous, so that measurement of input aggregates involves compiling data on components of each input and weighting the growth rates of the components by the corresponding value shares. Capital and labor quality have growth rates equal to the differences between the growth rates of input measures that take account of heterogeneity and measures that ignore heterogeneity. In the Kendrick-Solow approach these components are ignored, since inputs are treated as homogeneous.

The results presented in table 1.1 reveal that the assumption of homogeneous capital and labor inputs is highly misleading. I find that growth in the quality of capital stock accounts for two-fifths of the growth of capital input during the period 1947–1985. This quantitative relationship also characterizes the eight subperiods. For the period as a whole I find that the growth of labor quality accounts for more than one-third of the growth of labor input. The growth in hours worked actually falls below the growth in the quality of hours worked for the period 1953–1960. For the period 1966–1979 the contribution of hours worked accounts for almost two-thirds of the contribution of labor input. The relative proportions of growth in hours worked and labor quality are far from uniform. Although these proportions vary greatly from period to period, there is a decline in the relative importance of labor quality after 1960.

The development of measures of labor input reflecting heterogeneity is one of the many pathbreaking contributions of Edward F. Denison (1961, 1962b) to the analysis of sources of economic growth. Table 1.1 is based on an extension and revision of the measures of labor input presented by Jorgenson, Gollop, and Fraumeni (1987). Hours worked are cross-classified by age, sex, education, and employment status and weighted by wage rates.[2] A total of 160 types of labor input are distinguished at the aggregate level. Denison (1969, 1972) continues to adhere to capital stock as a measure of capital input. This approach ignores the heterogeneity among components of capital input reflected in the growth of capital quality in table 1.1. In this table capital stocks are cross-classified by type of asset and legal form of organization and weighted by rental prices. At the aggregate level a total of 169 components of capital input are measured separately. Assets of different ages are weighted in accord with profiles of relative efficiency constructed by Hulten and Wykoff (1981a).

The point has come where it is necessary to be more precise about the concept of an aggregate production function. In technical jargon the existence of an aggregate production function requires that the technology of each sector is separable in value added and that value added is a function of capital and labor inputs and the level of technology. Moreover, the sectoral value-added functions must be identical for all sectors, while the functions relating labor and capital inputs to their components must also be identical for all sectors. Finally, each component of these input aggregates must receive the same price in all sectors.

The assumptions just enumerated are well known to aggregation theorists and have achieved broader recognition as a consequence of the "reswitching controversy" initiated by Samuelson (1962). The lack of surface plausibility in this set of assumptions has not deterred economists from applying the concept of an aggregate production function in analyzing the sources of economic growth. The obvious question is, why? To attempt to answer this question I can decompose the rate of aggregate productivity growth into its sources at the level of thirty-seven sectors of the U.S. economy. Fortunately, the data for production patterns in these sectors can be generated in a way that avoids the assumptions that underly the aggregate production model. This makes it possible to test the assumptions of the model and assess the importance of departures from these assumptions empirically.

Aggregate productivity growth can be represented as a weighted sum of sectoral productivity growth rates with weights given by ratios of the value of output in each sector to value added in all sectors. In addition, the aggregate productivity growth rate depends on reallocations of value added, capital input, and labor input among sectors. The growth rates of the reallocations are the differences between growth rates of aggregate indexes of value added, capital input, and labor input and the corresponding indexes obtained by weighting each of the components by prices specific to each sector. For example, the index of aggregate labor input involves weighting up the 160 components of labor input. The reallocation of labor input is the difference between this index and an index that separately weights the 5,920 types of labor input, cross-classified by the thirty-seven sectors of the U.S. economy as well as the characteristics of labor input distinguished at the aggregate level.

Reallocations of value added, capital input, and labor input are measures of departures from the assumptions that underly the aggregate production model. Reallocations of value added incorporate differences in value-added functions among sectors and departures from the separability assumptions required for the existence of a value-added function in each sector. Reallocations of capital and labor inputs include differences in capital and labor aggregates among sectors, departures from separability assumptions required for the existence of these aggregates, and differences in prices of individual capital and labor inputs among sectors.

For the period 1947–1985 as a whole the rate of aggregate productivity growth is somewhat lower than the weighted sum of sectoral productivity growth rates. The reallocations of value added, capital input, and labor input are small but not negligible, so that the model of production based on an aggregate production function provides a valuable and useful summary of the data. However, I find that the reallocations, especially the reallocation of value added, are very large for the periods 1953–1957 and 1973–1979. The contributions of the reallocations during the 1973–1979 period contribute to a precipitous drop in the aggregate productivity growth rate.

I have already noted that the growth rate of output in the U.S. economy averaged 3.28 percent per year during the postwar period 1947–1985. During the subperiod 1973–1979 the average growth rate is only 2.12 percent, a decline of 1.16 percent. The contribution of capital input declined by only 0.05 percent per year between the two periods, while the contribution of labor input actually increased by 0.27 percent. The decline in the rate of productivity growth was 1.38 percent, more than the decline in the growth rate of output. In the last panel of table 1.1 I can see that the weighted sum of sectoral productivity growth rates was negative for the period 1973–1979 at 0.12 percent per year. The one percent decline in this sum is almost sufficient to account for the slowdown in U.S. economic growth. The decline in productivity growth at the sectoral level was augmented by a negative contribution of 0.53 percent per year from the reallocation of value added.

My conclusion from table 1.1 is that the aggregate production model used in analyzing economic growth by Denison, Kendrick, Kuznets, Maddison, Solow, Tinbergen, and a long list of others is appropriate for studying long-term growth trends. However, this model is highly inappropriate for analyzing the sources of growth over shorter periods. In fact, the aggregate production model has become a serious obstacle to understanding the causes of the slowdown in economic growth in the United States and other industrialized countries during the period 1973–1979. There is a real danger that the analysis of economic growth will remain wrapped in the straightjacket of the aggregate production model. A disaggregated data set, like that presented in table 1.1, shows that the assumptions underlying this model are clearly inconsistent with the empirical evidence.

### 1.1.2   Sources of Sectoral Growth

The major accomplishment of recent research on the sources of U.S. economic growth is the integration of the growth of intermediate, capital, and labor inputs at the level of individual industrial sectors into an analysis of the sources of growth for the economy as a whole. This integration makes it possible to attribute U.S. economic growth to its sources at the level of individual industries. In table 1.1 the sources of U.S. economic growth are allocated among contributions of growth in capital and labor inputs, changes in productivity at the sectoral level, and intersectoral shifts of outputs and inputs.

The analysis of sources of growth at the industry level is based on the decomposition of the growth rate of sectoral output into the sum of the contributions of intermediate, capital, and labor inputs and the growth of productivity. The contribution of each input is the product

**Table 1.2**
Growth in sectoral output and its sources, 1947–1985 (average annual rates)

| Industry | Rate of output growth | Contributions to growth in output | | | Rate of productivity growth |
| --- | --- | --- | --- | --- | --- |
| | | Intermediate input | Capital input | Labor input | |
| Agriculture, forestry & fisheries | .0192 | .0068 | .0014 | -.0051 | .0161 |
| Metal mining | .0012 | .0067 | .0067 | -.0071 | -.0051 |
| Coal mining | .0078 | .0090 | .0071 | -.0098 | .0015 |
| Crude petroleum & natural gas | .0187 | .0149 | .0160 | .0061 | -.0182 |
| Nonmetallic mineral mining | .0234 | .0099 | .0061 | -.0003 | .0077 |
| Construction | .0308 | .0182 | .0028 | .0086 | .0012 |
| Food & kindred products | .0228 | .0160 | .0010 | .0001 | .0057 |
| Tobacco manufactures | .0033 | .0065 | .0017 | -.0011 | -.0039 |
| Textile mill products | .0201 | .0111 | .0009 | -.0022 | .0103 |
| Apparel & other textile products | .0245 | .0106 | .0012 | .0010 | .0118 |
| Lumber & wood products | .0199 | .0128 | .0039 | -.0014 | .0046 |
| Furniture & fixtures | .0299 | .0150 | .0024 | .0046 | .0078 |
| Paper & allied products | .0318 | .0189 | .0049 | .0034 | .0047 |
| Printing & publishing | .0299 | .0185 | .0040 | .0070 | .0004 |
| Chemicals & allied products | .0457 | .0217 | .0080 | .0041 | .0119 |
| Petroleum refining | .0288 | .0169 | .0021 | .0010 | .0088 |
| Rubber & plastic products | .0453 | .0272 | .0015 | .0083 | .0084 |
| Leather & leather products | -.0150 | -.0118 | .0005 | -.0063 | .0026 |
| Stone, clay & glass products | .0252 | .0142 | .0040 | .0030 | .0040 |
| Primary metals | .0032 | .0038 | .0010 | -.0009 | -.0007 |

**Table 1.2 (continued)**

| Industry | Rate of output growth | Contributions to growth in output | | | Rate of productivity growth |
|---|---|---|---|---|---|
| | | Intermediate input | Capital input | Labor input | |
| Fabricated metal products | .0228 | .0112 | .0035 | .0048 | .0033 |
| Machinery, except electrical | .0398 | .0184 | .0058 | .0058 | .0098 |
| Electrical machinery | .0534 | .0222 | .0057 | .0092 | .0164 |
| Motor vehicles | .0351 | .0233 | .0040 | .0014 | .0064 |
| Other transportation equipment | .0441 | .0273 | .0039 | .0105 | .0024 |
| Instruments | .0505 | .0186 | .0072 | .0123 | .0123 |
| Miscellaneous manufacturing | .0204 | .0090 | .0023 | -.0016 | .0107 |
| Transportation & warehousing | .0223 | .0105 | .0021 | -.0006 | .0103 |
| Communication | .0637 | .0113 | .0223 | .0083 | .0218 |
| Electric utilities | .0543 | .0189 | .0164 | .0043 | .0147 |
| Gas utilities | .0398 | .0285 | .0075 | .0017 | .0020 |
| Trade | .0354 | .0113 | .0074 | .0062 | .0104 |
| Finance, insurance & real estate | .0405 | .0142 | .0118 | .0134 | .0011 |
| Other services | .0388 | .0183 | .0081 | .0137 | -.0013 |
| Government enterprises | .0330 | .0175 | .0081 | .0098 | -.0025 |
| Private households | .0489 | | .0494 | -.0006 | |
| Government, excluding government enterprises | .0316 | | | .0316 | |

of the value share of the input and its growth rate. In table 1.2 the growth rate of output with the contributions of the three inputs and the growth of productivity for the period 1947–1985 is compared. The sum of the contributions of intermediate, capital, and labor inputs is the predominant source of growth of output for thirty-three of the thirty-seven sectors included in table 1.2.

Comparing the contribution of intermediate input with other sources of output growth, I find that this input is by far the most significant source of growth. The contribution of intermediate input exceeds productivity growth and the contributions of capital and labor inputs. If I focus attention on the contributions of capital and labor inputs alone, excluding intermediate input from consideration, I find that these two inputs are a more important source of growth than changes in productivity.

The findings presented in table 1.2 are based on the symmetrical treatment of intermediate, capital, and labor inputs.[3] To provide additional insight into the sources of economic growth at the sectoral level, I can decompose the growth rate of intermediate input into growth of an unweighted index of intermediate input and growth in intermediate input quality. As before, I can decompose the growth of capital input into growth in capital stock and capital quality. Finally, I can decompose the growth of labor input into growth in hours worked and labor quality. In table 1.3 I present this decomposition for thirty-seven sectors for the period 1947–1985.

I find that growth in quality is not an important component of growth in intermediate input. Inferences about the predominant role of intermediate input would be unaffected by the omission of changes in quality. Excluding intermediate input from consideration, however, I find that the relative importance of productivity growth and the contributions of capital and labor inputs would be reversed by using measures that omit changes in input quality. The incorporation of intermediate input is an important innovation in the methodology employed in generating the data presented in tables 1.2 and 1.3. The second major innovation is the measurement of changes in the quality of capital and labor inputs at the sectoral level.

The perspective on U.S. economic growth suggested by the results presented in tables 1.2 and 1.3 emphasizes the contribution of mobilization of resources within individual industries. The explanatory power of this perspective is overwhelming at the sectoral level. For thirty-three of the thirty-seven industrial sectors included in tables 1.2

**Table 1.3**
Contributions of input quality to growth in sectoral output: rates of growth, 1947–1985

| Industry | Average annual rates of growth | | | | | | |
|---|---|---|---|---|---|---|---|
| | Quality of intermediate input | Unweighted intermediate input | Quality of capital stock | Capital stock | Quality of hours worked | Hours worked | Rate of productivity growth |
| Agriculture, forestry & fisheries | -.0004 | .0071 | .0023 | -.0009 | .0020 | -.0071 | .0161 |
| Metal mining | -.0001 | .0068 | .0026 | .0041 | .0013 | -.0083 | -.0051 |
| Coal mining | .0012 | .0078 | .0000 | .0070 | .0012 | -.0110 | .0015 |
| Crude petroleum & natural gas | -.0010 | .0159 | .0007 | .0152 | .0013 | .0048 | -.0182 |
| Nonmetallic mineral mining | .0000 | .0099 | .0001 | .0060 | .0011 | -.0014 | .0077 |
| Construction | .0003 | .0179 | .0005 | .0024 | .0009 | .0077 | .0012 |
| Food & kindred products | -.0005 | .0165 | .0002 | .0007 | .0005 | -.0004 | .0057 |
| Tobacco manufactures | .0005 | .0060 | -.0001 | .0017 | .0006 | -.0017 | -.0039 |
| Textile mill products | .0002 | .0110 | .0004 | .0006 | .0005 | -.0027 | .0103 |
| Apparel & other textile products | .0008 | .0098 | .0002 | .0010 | .0005 | .0004 | .0118 |
| Lumber & wood products | .0008 | .0120 | .0006 | .0033 | .0009 | -.0023 | .0046 |
| Furniture & fixtures | .0000 | .0150 | .0003 | .0021 | .0008 | .0038 | .0078 |
| Paper & allied products | .0000 | .0189 | .0014 | .0034 | .0012 | .0022 | .0047 |
| Printing & publishing | .0001 | .0184 | .0012 | .0028 | .0014 | .0056 | .0004 |
| Chemicals & allied products | -.0004 | .0222 | .0027 | .0053 | .0013 | .0028 | .0119 |
| Petroleum refining | .0020 | .0149 | .0002 | .0019 | .0004 | .0005 | .0088 |
| Rubber & plastic products | .0001 | .0271 | .0005 | .0009 | .0012 | .0071 | .0084 |
| Leather & leather products | .0006 | -.0124 | -.0009 | .0014 | .0005 | -.0068 | .0026 |
| Stone, clay & glass products | .0002 | .0140 | .0010 | .0029 | .0015 | .0015 | .0040 |
| Primary metals | .0002 | .0036 | -.0009 | .0020 | .0008 | -.0016 | -.0007 |

Table 1.3 (continued)

| Industry | Average annual rates of growth | | | | | | |
|---|---|---|---|---|---|---|---|
| | Quality of intermediate input | Unweighted intermediate input | Quality of capital stock | Capital stock | Quality of hours worked | Hours worked | Rate of productivity growth |
| Fabricated metal products | .0000 | .0112 | .0002 | .0033 | .0011 | .0038 | .0033 |
| Machinery, except electrical | .0005 | .0179 | .0006 | .0051 | .0014 | .0044 | .0098 |
| Electrical machinery | .0010 | .0211 | .0002 | .0055 | .0019 | .0073 | .0164 |
| Motor vehicles | .0003 | .0231 | -.0008 | .0048 | .0007 | .0007 | .0064 |
| Other transportation equipment | .0004 | .0269 | .0025 | .0014 | .0018 | .0087 | .0024 |
| Instruments | .0000 | .0186 | .0004 | .0068 | .0021 | .0102 | .0123 |
| Miscellaneous manufacturing | .0001 | .0089 | .0003 | .0020 | .0011 | -.0026 | .0107 |
| Transportation & warehousing | .0004 | .0102 | .0025 | -.0004 | .0007 | -.0014 | .0103 |
| Communication | .0001 | .0112 | .0039 | .0184 | .0018 | .0065 | .0218 |
| Electric utilities | -.0009 | .0198 | .0022 | .0142 | .0008 | .0035 | .0147 |
| Gas utilities | -.0025 | .0311 | .0015 | .0060 | .0007 | .0011 | .0020 |
| Trade | .0003 | .0111 | .0025 | .0049 | .0016 | .0046 | .0104 |
| Finance, insurance & real estate | .0003 | .0139 | .0028 | .0091 | .0022 | .0112 | .0011 |
| Other services | .0002 | .0181 | .0026 | .0055 | .0008 | .0128 | -.0013 |
| Government enterprises | .0000 | .0175 | .0003 | .0079 | .0001 | .0097 | -.0025 |
| Private households | | | .0121 | .0373 | -.0001 | -.0005 | |
| Government, excluding government enterprises | | | | | .0038 | .0278 | |

and 1.3, the contribution of intermediate, capital, and labor inputs is the predominant source of output growth. Changes in productivity account for the major portion of output growth in only four sectors.

### 1.1.3   Summary

The findings on the sources of U.S. economic growth summarized in tables 1.1, 1.2 and 1.3 have been generated by a truly massive empirical research effort. In section 1.2 I describe the sources and methods for construction of data on labor input. These data have incorporated all the annual detail on employment, weeks, hours worked, and labor compensation published in the decennial *Census of Population* and the *Current Population Survey*. Similarly, the data on capital input described in section 1.3 have incorporated all the available detail on investment in capital goods by industry and class of asset and on property compensation by legal form of organization from the U.S. national income and product accounts (NIPA). Finally, the data on intermediate input and output described in section 1.4 have incorporated all of the available annual data by industry from the U.S. national income and product accounts and the U.S. interindustry accounts.

The application of the theory of index numbers to the measurement of labor input requires weighting the components of labor input by wage rates. This was carried out at the aggregate level by Denison (1962b) and implemented for all industrial sectors of the U.S. economy by Gollop and Jorgenson (1980, 1983). Similarly, the measurement of capital as a factor of production involves weighting the components of capital input by rental rates. The conceptual basis for imputing rental prices for capital goods was established by Jorgenson (1963). These rental prices were employed in aggregate productivity measurement by Jorgenson and Griliches (1967). The rental price concept was further elaborated by Hall and Jorgenson (1967). This concept was implemented at the aggregate level by Christensen and Jorgenson (1969) and at the sectoral level by Fraumeni and Jorgenson (1980, 1986) and Gollop and Jorgenson (1980).

The model of capital as a factor of production originated by Walras (1954) was extended to encompass quality change for capital goods and relative efficiencies for capital goods of different vintages by Hall (1971). Hall's methodology generalizes the "hedonic technique" for measuring quality change of capital goods employed by Griliches

(1961b). This methodology has been exploited by Hulten and Wykoff (1981b) in measuring depreciation of capital goods from vintage price data. Griliches (1964), Stone (1956), and Triplett (1983a, 1986) have discussed the rationale for incorporating quality-corrected price indexes into systems of national accounts.

The final step in developing the methodology for analyzing sources of economic growth is to aggregate over individual industrial sectors. This step is critical in integrating the analysis of sources of growth for individual industries into the analysis of growth for the economy as a whole. The methodology for aggregation over sectors originated by Domar (1961) has been generalized by Hulten (1978) and Jorgenson (1980). This methodology was implemented for the U.S. by Fraumeni and Jorgenson (1980, 1986) and underlies the data on aggregate productivity change presented in table 1.1. I describe sources and methods for construction of data on aggregate output, input, and productivity in section 1.5.

At a methodological level the integration of data generation and econometric modeling is an important achievement of recent research on the sources of economic growth. The extensive data development described in sections 1.2, 1.3, and 1.4 is firmly rooted in the economic theory of production. The conceptual basis for the measures of intermediate, capital, and labor inputs in tables 1.1, 1.2, and 1.3 is provided by the theory of exact index numbers employed by Diewert (1976). Diewert showed that the index numbers utilized, for example, by Christensen and Jorgenson (1969) could be generated from the translog production function introduced by Christensen, Jorgenson, and Lau (1971, 1973).

The integration of the analysis of sources of economic growth with econometric modeling of producer behavior has suggested two alternative modeling strategies. The first is based on an aggregate production function, originally introduced by Cobb and Douglas (1928) and developed by Tinbergen (1942) in the form used for the analysis of sources of growth for the economy as a whole. A second strategy for modeling producer behavior is to disaggregate to the level of individual industrial sectors and replace the aggregate production model by a general equilibrium model of production. Models of this type have been constructed for all U.S. industries by Berndt and Jorgenson (1973), Jorgenson and Fraumeni (1981), and Jorgenson (1984b).

The essential idea of the disaggregated approach is to model producer behavior through complete systems of demand functions for inputs into each industrial sector. This approach is a lineal descendant of the general equilibrium models of production introduced by Leontief (1951). By successive steps it is possible to relax the "fixed coefficients" assumption of input-output analysis by making the input-output coefficients functions of the input prices. This approach has the added advantage of relaxing the assumption of value added separability at the sectoral level. Finally, the approach makes it possible to endogenize the rate of productivity growth in each sector by making this growth rate a function of the input prices.

In section 1.6 I review the two modeling strategies outlined above and alternative strategies proposed in the econometric literature. The benefits of the radical simplifications that result from an aggregate production model must be weighed against the costs of departures from the highly restrictive assumptions that underly this model. The limitations of the aggregate production model can be illustrated by an analysis of the slowdown in U.S. economic growth since 1973. An econometric model of productivity growth for all U.S. industries is required for an explanation of the slowdown. In section 1.7 I conclude with a summary of the implications of recent studies of the sources of economic growth for future research on economic measurement.

## 1.2   Measuring Labor Input

The methodology for productivity measurement that underlies the data presented in tables 1.2 and 1.3 is based on a model of producer behavior. The point of departure for this model is a homogeneous production function $\{F^i\}$ for each of n industrial sectors

$$Z_i = F^i\,(X_i,\,K_i,\,L_i,\,T), \qquad (i = 1, 2, \ldots, n),$$

where $T$ is time, $\{Z_i\}$ is output, and $\{X_i\}$, $\{K_i\}$, and $\{L_i\}$ are intermediate, capital, and labor inputs. I can define the shares of intermediate, capital, and labor inputs, say $\{v_X^i\}$, $\{v_K^i\}$, and $\{v_L^i\}$, in the value of output by

$$v_X^i = \frac{p_X^i X_i}{q_i Z_i},$$

$$v_K^i = \frac{p_K^i K_i}{q_i Z_i},$$

$$v_L^i = \frac{p_L^i L_i}{q_i Z_i}, \qquad (i = 1, 2, \ldots, n),$$

where $\{q_i\}$, $\{p_X^i\}$, $\{p_K^i\}$, and $\{p_L^i\}$ denote the prices of output and intermediate, capital, and labor inputs, respectively.

To analyze substitution among inputs I combine the production function for each sector with necessary conditions for producer equilibrium. These conditions are given by equalities between the shares of each input in the value of output and the elasticities of output with respect to that input

$$v_X^i = \frac{\partial \ln Z_i}{\partial \ln X_i} (X_i, K_i, L_i, T),$$

$$v_K^i = \frac{\partial \ln Z_i}{\partial \ln K_i} (X_i, K_i, L_i, T),$$

$$v_L^i = \frac{\partial \ln Z_i}{\partial \ln L_i} (X_i, K_i, L_i, T), \qquad (i = 1, 2, \ldots, n).$$

Under constant returns to scale the elasticities and the value shares for all three inputs sum to unity, so that the value of output is equal to the value of the inputs.

Finally, I can define the rate of productivity growth, say $\{v_T^i\}$, for each sector, as the rate of growth of output with respect to time, holding intermediate, capital, and labor inputs constant

$$v_T^i = \frac{\partial \ln Z_i}{\partial T} (X_i, K_i, L_i, T), \qquad (i = 1, 2, \ldots, n).$$

It is important to note that this definition does not impose any restriction on substitution patterns among inputs. I employ the rate of productivity growth in analyzing changes in substitution possibilities over time.

### 1.2.1   Exact Index Numbers

The production function for each sector listed in tables 1.2 and 1.3 is defined in terms of output and intermediate, capital, and labor inputs. Each of the inputs is an aggregate that depends on the quantities of individual intermediate, capital, and labor inputs

$$X_i = X_i (X_{1i}, X_{2i} \cdots X_{ni}),$$
$$K_i = K_i (K_{1i}, K_{2i} \cdots K_{pi}),$$
$$L_i = L_i (L_{1i}, L_{2i} \cdots L_{qi}), \qquad (i = 1, 2, \ldots, n),$$

where $\{X_{ji}\}$ is the set of $n$ intermediate inputs from the $j$th sector $(j = 1, 2, \ldots, n)$, $\{K_{ki}\}$ the set of $p$ capital inputs, and $\{L_{li}\}$ the set of $q$ labor inputs. Here the production function is separable in intermediate, capital, and labor inputs.[4] If these inputs are each homogeneous in their components, I say that the production function is homothetically separable.[5] The aggregates for each sector are characterized by constant returns to scale.

The shares of the individual intermediate, capital, and labor inputs, say $\{v_{Xj}^i\}$, $\{v_{Kk}^i\}$, and $\{v_{Ll}^i\}$, can be defined in the values of the corresponding aggregates by

$$v_{Xj}^i = \frac{p_{Xj}^i X_{ji}}{p_X^i X_i}, \qquad (i, j = 1, 2, \ldots, n),$$

$$v_{Kk}^i = \frac{p_{Kk}^i K_{ki}}{p_K^i K_i}, \qquad (i = 1, 2, \ldots, n; \ k = 1, 2, \ldots, p),$$

$$v_{Ll}^i = \frac{p_{Ll}^i L_{li}}{p_L^i L_i}, \qquad (i = 1, 2, \ldots, n; \ l = 1, 2, \ldots, q),$$

where $\{p_{Xj}^i\}$, $\{p_{Kk}^i\}$, and $\{p_{Ll}^i\}$ are the prices of individual intermediate, capital, and labor inputs.

Necessary conditions for producer equilibrium are given by equalities between the shares of the individual inputs in the values of the corresponding aggregates and the elasticities of the aggregate with respect to the individual inputs

$$v_{Xj}^i = \frac{\partial \ln X_i}{\partial \ln X_{ji}} \ (X_{1i}, X_{2i}, \ldots, X_{ni}),$$

$$v_{Kk}^i = \frac{\partial \ln K_i}{\partial \ln K_{ki}} \ (K_{1i}, K_{2i}, \ldots, K_{pi}),$$

$$v_{Ll}^i = \frac{\partial \ln L_i}{\partial \ln L_{li}} \ (L_{1i}, L_{2i}, \ldots, L_{qi}), \qquad (i = 1, 2, \ldots, n).$$

Under constant returns to scale, the values of intermediate, capital, and labor inputs are equal to the sums of the values of their components.

The methodology that underlies the data presented in tables 1.2 and 1.3 is based on sectoral production functions of the translog form introduced by Christensen, Jorgenson, and Lau (1971, 1973).[6] Given translog production functions for all sectors, the corresponding price and quantity index numbers can be generated for all three inputs. The growth rate of each input between two periods is a weighted average of growth rates of its components. Weights are given by the average share of each component in the value of the input for the two periods. The corresponding price indexes are defined as ratios of the values of the inputs to the translog quantity indexes. Similarly, the translog index of productivity growth is the difference between the growth rate of output and a weighted average of growth rates of intermediate, capital and labor inputs.[7]

The critical innovation in the methodology that underlies tables 1.2 and 1.3 is to distinguish among components of intermediate, capital, and labor inputs that differ in marginal productivity. For each sector intermediate input is represented as a function of deliveries from all other sectors. Capital input is broken down by class of asset and legal form of organization. Finally, labor input is broken down by characteristics of individual workers such as sex, age, education, and employment status.

### 1.2.2   Data Sources and Methods for Labor Input

A novel feature of the indexes of the quantity of labor input presented in tables 1.2 and 1.3 is that these indexes incorporate data from both establishment and household surveys. Estimates of employment, hours worked, and labor compensation for each industrial sector are controlled to totals based on establishment surveys that underlie the U.S. national income accounts. These totals are allocated among categories of the work force cross-classified by the characteristics of individual workers on the basis of household surveys. The resulting estimates of hours worked and average compensation per hour for each sector provide the basis for the indexes of labor input presented in table 1.2.

For each of the thirty-seven sectors listed in table 1.2 prices and quantities of labor input are cross-classified by the two sexes, eight age groups, five educational groups, and two employment statuses—employee and self-employed. Annual data from 1947 to 1985 on hours worked and average labor compensation per hour are required for 160 components of the work force in each industry. For this purpose employment, hours, weeks, and labor compensation within each sector are allocated on the basis of the available cross-classifications.[8] This methodology makes it possible to exploit all the published detail on labor input from the decennial *Census of Population* and the *Current Population Survey.*

The first step in developing sectoral measures of labor input is to construct employment matrices cross-classified by sex, age, education, and employment status for each year on the basis of household surveys from the *Census of Population* and the *Current Population Survey.* The resulting employment matrices are controlled to employment totals for each sector on the basis of establishment surveys from the U.S. national income and product accounts.[9] Hours worked by workers cross-classified by demographic characteristics are estimated on the basis of household surveys. The resulting estimates are controlled to totals for each industrial sector from the U.S. national accounts.[10] The third step in developing sectoral measures of labor input is to construct labor compensation matrices for each year on the basis of the *Census of Population.*[11] Control totals for annual labor compensation are taken from the U.S. national income accounts.

Average hourly compensation per person for employees is based on data on wage and salary income from the *Census of Population.* Differences in outlay on labor input per person reflect differences in marginal products among workers. However, the cost of labor input from the point of view of the producer also includes supplements. Differences in wage and salary income must be adjusted to incorporate employers' contributions to Social Security and unemployment compensation and other supplements to wages and salaries.

Earnings reported by the census for self-employed workers and income of unincorporated enterprises from the U.S. national income accounts include both labor and property income. Income from unincorporated enterprises can be divided between labor and property components, assuming that after-tax rates of return are the same for corporate and noncorporate business. Labor compensation is distributed among the self-employed on the basis of wage differentials among employees in the corresponding industrial sector. To derive labor compensation per hour worked for each category of labor input, total labor compensation is divided by annual hours worked for each category.

The final step in constructing data on labor input for each of the thirty-seven sectors is to combine price and quantity data, cross-classified by sex, age, education, and employment status, into price and quantity indexes of labor input. To construct an index of labor input for each sector, I express sectoral labor input, say $\{L_i\}$, as a translog function of its 160 individual components, say $\{L_{li}\}$. The corresponding index of sectoral labor input is a translog quantity index of individual labor inputs

$$\ln L_i(T) - \ln L_i(T-1) = \sum \overline{v}_{Ll}^i \left[\ln L_{li}(T) - \ln L_{li}(T-1)\right], \qquad (i = 1, 2, \ldots, n) \,,$$

where weights are given by average shares of each component in the value of sectoral labor compensation

$$\overline{v}_{Ll}^i = \frac{1}{2}[v_{Ll}^i(T) + v_{Ll}^i(T-1)], \qquad (i = 1, 2, \ldots, n; \, l = 1, 2, \ldots, q),$$

and

$$v_{Ll}^i = \frac{p_{Ll}^i \, L_{li}}{\sum p_{Ll}^i \, L_{li}}, \qquad\qquad (i = 1, 2, \ldots, n; \, l = 1, 2, \ldots, q).$$

The value shares are computed from data on hours worked $\{L_{li}\}$ and compensation per hour $\{p_{Ll}^i\}$ for each component of sectoral labor input, cross-classified by sex, age, education, and employment class of workers.

A measure of total hours worked for each sector can be derived by adding hours worked across all 160 categories of labor input within that sector. The quality of labor input is defined as the ratio of labor input to hours worked. Changes in the quality of hours worked represent the differences between changes in the translog quantity index of labor input and changes in an unweighted index of hours worked. Quantity indexes of labor input are presented in table 1.2 for thirty-seven sectors. The corresponding indexes of labor input quality and hours worked are presented for each sector in table 1.3.

Translog index numbers for labor input were introduced for individual sectors of the U.S. economy by Gollop and Jorgenson (1980, 1983). The data on labor input that underly tables 1.2 and 1.3 are cross-classified by sex, age, education, employment status, and sector of employment for a total of 5,920 types of labor input. The growth of labor input can be decomposed to obtain the contributions to change in labor quality of all these characteristics.[12]

## 1.2.3   Alternative Sources and Methods

An overview of issues in the measurement of labor input is provided by the Rees Report (National Research Council, 1979, esp. pp.

122–128). Alternative quantity indexes of labor input and the corresponding price indexes are compared by Denison (1961), Kunze (1979), and Triplett (1983b). To provide additional perspective on the measurement of labor input, it is useful to compare the methodology and data sources that underly the indexes presented in tables 1.2 and 1.3, with those of the Bureau of Labor Statistics (BLS) (1983), Denison (1985), and Kendrick (1983a).[13] My comparative analysis covers both labor hours and compensation. I evaluate the alternative approaches in terms of the data sources and the requirements of the theory of producer behavior. Wherever possible, I test the assumptions implicit in the competing models.

My comparison begins with the measurement of hours. The BLS (1983, pp. 66–68) measure of multifactor productivity employs the same data for hours as the traditional BLS (1973) measures of output per hour. About 85 percent of total hours are based on establishment surveys that collect information on hours paid rather than hours worked. Kendrick (1961a, pp. 382, 496, 503, 515, 559; 1973, p. 156; 1983a, p. 56) and Kendrick and Grossman (1980, p. 25) present a strong case for an hours-worked series but use BLS (1971) establishment data on hours paid for some sectors. As evident from his earliest works, Denison (e.g., 1962b, p. 352) shares Kendrick's view that hours worked are more appropriate than hours paid.[14]

Both Denison and Kendrick attempt to measure hours worked on the basis of the hours-paid series published by BLS. The *BLS Handbook of Methods for Surveys and Studies* (1971) makes clear that separate hours estimates are developed for production and nonproduction workers only in the manufacturing sectors. According to the handbook (1971, pp. 214–215), manufacturing production worker hours are taken directly from the data in the BLS area wage surveys and the study of *Employer Expenditures* (1963) published by BLS. For the nonmanufacturing industries the hours-paid series collected in the census employment survey program relate to nonsupervisory workers only. BLS assumes that these hours apply to all wage and salary workers. BLS does not provide estimates of hours paid for self-employed and unpaid family workers. For these groups, Denison and, for the most part, Kendrick use household survey data on hours worked.

There are important differences in the demographic mix of the supervisory and nonsupervisory occupations and in the average hours worked for different demographic groups. These differences make suspect the assumption that supervisory and nonsupervisory workers in each nonmanufacturing industry are paid for the same average number of hours per week. For example, according to the census of population (Bureau of the Census, 1972, table 5), the 1970 female to male ratio was 0.87 in nonsupervisory occupations in the nonmanufacturing sector and only 0.22 in supervisory occupations. Furthermore, the census (1973a, table 45) data show that female non-supervisory workers in 1970 worked 34.5 hours on average, while their male counterparts worked 41.5 hours.

Given that women work fewer weekly hours than men and are proportionately underrepresented in supervisory occupations, it is highly unlikely that supervisory laborers are paid for the same number of weekly hours as nonsupervisory laborers. A similar analysis could be based on age or education compositions; the evidence suggests that BLS estimates of annual hours paid are biased downward in the nonmanufacturing sectors. Shifts in the demographic composition of the supervisory and nonsupervisory occupational groups over time will bias estimates of productivity growth.

I next compare the Kendrick and Denison approaches to constructing indexes of labor input. Kendrick considers all workers within each industry to be homogeneous. He completely omits the influence of changing labor quality on his measure of each industry's labor input. Admittedly, Kendrick does distinguish between the hours worked by proprietors and unpaid family workers and those worked by wage and salary employees whenever the former group is a "significant fraction" of the particular industry's labor force. Since Kendrick (1961a, p. 261; 1973, p. 12) decided not to weight labor hours from the two employment classes differently, he eliminates any potential effect of changing labor composition.

Kendrick does not attribute any significance to the differences among marginal products of various categories of workers. For Kendrick, the difference in the value of an hour's work by an electrical engineer and a truck driver should be attributed to differences in productivity rather than differences in labor input. Given Kendrick's definition, the appropriate index of labor input for each sector is an unweighted index of hours worked. By contrast, Denison posits that disaggregation by characteristics is essential in measuring labor input. In his view, however, any change in sector of employment does not reflect changes in labor input and should be captured by the measure of productivity growth.

Denison cross-classifies workers by demographic characteristics such as age, sex, and education in deriving indexes of labor input. He uses census data on earnings to construct weights for use in aggregating his education and sex-age hours series in his original *Sources of Economic Growth* (1962b) and his more recent work on productivity (1974, 1979, 1985). The principal problem with using census earnings data to measure marginal products is that reported earnings exclude all supplements to wages and salaries and include the return to capital invested by self-employed workers. Denison (e.g., 1979, pp. 157–158) makes no adjustment to the census data to exclude returns to capital.

As Denison points out, earnings can be used in weighting the components of labor input only if the average earnings for workers cross-classified by education or by age and sex are proportional to the corresponding marginal products. Since supplements, particularly Social Security and unemployment insurance, are charged to employers, reported earnings do not reflect employers' relative labor outlays. If supplements are neglected, only those ratios of hourly earnings among groups of laborers with annual incomes below the lowest base for supplements will be unbiased estimates of relative wages as viewed by employers.

For example, if the average 35–64-year-old male has an annual income above the Social Security or unemployment insurance tax base, while the average 20–24-year-old female's earnings are below either base, then the relative valuation of an average hour's work by males and females based on earnings is clearly upward biased. Supplements add to the employers' outlay for both males and females but, in this example, supplements add proportionately more to the employers' outlay for females than for males. Based on 1969 earnings reported in the decennial *Census* (1973c, tables I and II), employed 35–64-year-old males had mean annual earnings ($10,008) well above either the Social Security ($7,800) or unemployment insurance ($3,000) tax bases in 1969. Females 18–24 years of age, however, had mean labor income of $2,960. Ratios of male (35–64 years old) to female (18–24 years old) hourly wage costs excluding supplements are upward biased estimates of relative labor costs incurred by employers.

The assumption of proportionality between earnings and labor outlay is valid only if the ratio of noncorporate property income to total earnings is constant across sex-age and education groups. If the representative 35–64-year-old male has a larger fraction of his earnings being generated from capital invested in noncorporate enterprises than does the representative 20–24-year-old female, then the earnings-based estimate for the relative valuation of an hour's work by males to an hour's work by females is upward biased. Data measuring the noncorporate property income of workers classified by demographic characteristics are unavailable. However, the reasonableness of Denison's assumption can be evaluated by comparing the distribution of employment in wage and salary versus self-employed activities across sex and age groups.

I refer to data published in the 1970 census to evaluate Denison's assumption. I construct ratios of self-employed persons to total employment in both wage and salary and self-employed activities. The ratios, reported in table 1.4, vary significantly across sex-age groups. For both males and females, the ratios generally increase with age; except for the two lowest age groups, the ratio for males is more than twice the ratio for females. The ratios for older males are considerably higher than the similar ratios for young females. The relevant ratio for 35–64-year-old males is 0.130; the corresponding ratio for 20–24-year-old females is 0.011. Compared to young females, older males apparently allocate a greater proportion of their labor effort to self-employed activities.

Table 1.4
Ratio of self-employed to total employment by age and sex, 1970[a]

| Age | Male | Female |
| --- | --- | --- |
| 14–15 years | .044 | .026 |
| 16–17 years | .016 | .009 |
| 18–19 years | .014 | .005 |
| 20–24 years | .029 | .011 |
| 25–29 years | .052 | .024 |
| 30–34 years | .078 | .033 |
| 35–39 years | .101 | .038 |
| 40–44 years | .114 | .041 |
| 45–49 years | .124 | .045 |
| 50–59 years | .154 | .060 |
| 60–62 years | .166 | .062 |
| 63–64 years | .183 | .073 |
| 65–69 years | .243 | .093 |
| 70–74 years | .300 | .118 |
| 75 years and over | .336 | .133 |

Source: Bureau of the Census (1973b, table 47).
[a] Total employed excludes unpaid family workers.

I infer that earnings for a representative male include a higher percentage of returns to noncorporate capital than do the earnings for a representative female, even after controlling for age. In short, relative earnings are inadequate measures of relative marginal products. The wage and salary income of workers adjusted for supplements is a more appropriate starting point for a measure of labor compensation.

The final issue concerns changes in the pattern of hourly earnings and therefore weights for each labor category. Denison (1974, 1979, 1985) weights by sex-age and education categories but holds weights constant over various subperiods.[15] However, relative wages across industries and among demographic groups have shifted over time due to shifting demand conditions, altered production techniques, and the changing impact of constraints on labor supply. If relative hourly wages are the appropriate estimates of relative marginal products, the labor earnings weights must be allowed to change over time. If the weights are held constant, annual changes in marginal products are not reflected accurately. The resulting estimates of year-to-year productivity change are biased.

The discussion so far has focused on a comparison of data, assumptions, and measurement techniques. I close this section emphasizing an important conceptual difference distinguishing Kendrick's measures of sectoral labor input from the measures presented in tables 1.2 and 1.3. Kendrick (e.g., 1973, p. 146) purposefully defines any growth in sectoral output due to shifts in the demographic composition of the labor force as part of productivity change. For Kendrick, any shift in labor's sex, age, and education mix that leads to greater levels of sectoral output reflects an advance in knowledge and is therefore part of productivity change. I evaluate Kendrick's definition of productivity change in terms of the theory of production in section 1.4.3, below.

The data on labor input presented in tables 1.2 and 1.3 incorporate changes in the composition of labor hours by sex, age, education, and employment status within each of the thirty-seven sectors. The data on labor input in table 1.1 incorporate these shifts for the U.S. economy as a whole. Gollop and Jorgenson (1980) provide a detailed comparison between labor input indexes of this type and those of Kendrick for the period 1947–1973. Quality change is an important component of the growth in labor input. This component accounts for much of the difference between Kendrick's measures of labor hours and the translog indexes of labor input given in tables 1.2 and 1.3.

## 1.3    Measuring Capital Input

The approach to the construction of the data on capital input presented in table 1.2 is strictly analogous to the approach outlined in section 1.2 for data on labor input. Capital services represent the quantity of capital input, just as labor services represent the quantity of labor input. Measures of capital services for depreciable assets are derived by representing capital stock at each point of time as a weighted sum of past investments. The weights correspond to the relative efficiencies of capital goods of different ages, so that the weighted components of capital stock have the same efficiency.

Rental rates for capital services provide the basis for property compensation, just as wage rates provide the basis for labor compensation. Information on rental transactions would be required in order to employ data sources for capital input that are analogous to those I have used for labor input. These data are not available in a readily accessible form, even for the substantial proportion of assets with active rental markets. However, rental values can be imputed on the basis of estimates of capital stocks and property compensation.

Data on rental prices for depreciable assets are generated by allocating property compensation for return to capital, depreciation, and taxes among assets. Depreciation is the decline in value of a capital good with age at a given point in time, so that estimates of depreciation depend on the relative efficiencies of capital goods of different ages. The estimates of capital input presented in table 1.1 incorporate the same data on relative efficiencies of capital goods into estimates of both capital stocks and rental prices.

### 1.3.1    Capital as a Factor of Production

The perpetual inventory method provides the theoretical framework for the measures of capital input presented in tables 1.1, 1.2 and 1.3.[16] The key innovation embodied in the quantity indexes of capital input presented in tables 1.1 and 1.2 is the rental price of capital input originated by Jorgenson (1963, 1965, 1967). This measure of the rental price was employed in the indexes of capital input introduced by Griliches and Jorgenson (1966) and Jorgenson and Griliches (1967).[17] The rental price concept was further developed by Hall and Jorgenson (1967, 1969, 1971). Their approach was employed by Christensen and

Jorgenson (1969, 1970, 1973a, 1973b) to impute rental prices for capital goods that differ in depreciation pattern and tax treatment.[18]

I can refer to the capital goods acquired at different points of time as different vintages. Estimates of the relative efficiencies of capital goods of different ages are derived from a comprehensive study of acquisition prices of assets of different vintages by Hulten and Wykoff (1981a, b, c). I can outline the methodology employed by Hulten and Wykoff by first considering vintage price systems under geometric decline in efficiency with age. Under geometric decline in efficiency, both the rental price of capital services and the acquisition price of a capital asset decline geometrically with age. The rate of decline in efficiency can be estimated from a sample of prices of capital goods of different ages.

The econometric model for vintage price functions gives the price of acquisition of a capital good as a function of the age of the capital good and the time period of observation. This model can be generalized by introducing Box-Cox transformations of the prices of acquisition, the ages of capital goods, and the time period of observation.[19] A further generalization of the econometric model of vintage price functions has been proposed by Hall (1971). This generalization is appropriate for durable goods with a number of varieties that are perfect substitutes in production. Each variety is characterized by a number of attributes that affect relative efficiency. This "hedonic technique" for price measurement was originated by Court (1939) and Waugh (1929) and has been employed, for example, by Griliches (1961b) and studies in the volume edited by Griliches (1971b).[20]

As an illustration, Hall (1971) analyzes a sample of prices for half-ton pickup trucks with characteristics such as wheelbase, shipping weight, displacement, ratio of core to stroke, horsepower, torque, and tire width. Observations of these characteristics are analyzed for pickup trucks produced by Ford and Chevrolet in the United States for the period 1955–1966. With perfect substitutability among pickup trucks of different ages, market equilibrium implies the existence of a vintage price function for trucks. This function gives the price of acquisition of a pickup truck as a function of age and the price of a new truck of the same type, expressed as a function of time. Hall estimates vintage price functions for each category of trucks from annual observations on the prices of used trucks.

Hulten and Wykoff (1981b) have implemented an econometric model of vintage price functions for eight categories of assets in the

United States. In 1977 these categories included 55 percent of investment expenditures on producers' durable equipment and 42 percent of expenditures on nonresidential structures.[21] In the estimation of econometric models based on vintage price functions, the sample of used asset prices is "censored" by the retirement of assets from service. The price of acquisition for assets that have been retired from service is equal to zero. If only surviving assets are included in a sample of used asset prices, the sample is censored by excluding assets that have been retired. In order to correct the resulting bias in estimates of vintage price functions, Hulten and Wykoff (1981b) multiply the prices of surviving assets of each vintage by the probability of survival, expressed as a function of age.

Vintage price functions for commercial and industrial buildings are summarized in table 1.5. For each class of assets the rate of economic depreciation is tabulated as a function of the age of the asset. The natural logarithm of the price is regressed on age and time to obtain an average rate of depreciation, which Hulten and Wykoff refer to as the best geometric average (BGA). The square of the multiple correlation coefficient ($R^2$) is given as a measure of the goodness of fit of the geometric approximation to the fitted vintage price function for each

**Table 1.5**
Rates of economic depreciation

|  | With censored sample correction | | Without censored sample correction | |
| --- | --- | --- | --- | --- |
| Age | Commercial | Industrial | Commercial | Industrial |
| 5 | 2.85 | 2.99 | 2.66 | 2.02 |
| 10 | 2.64 | 3.01 | 1.84 | 1.68 |
| 15 | 2.43 | 3.04 | 1.48 | 1.50 |
| 20 | 2.30 | 3.07 | 1.27 | 1.39 |
| 30 | 2.15 | 3.15 | 1.02 | 1.25 |
| 40 | 2.08 | 3.24 | 0.88 | 1.17 |
| 50 | 2.04 | 3.34 | 0.79 | 1.11 |
| 60 | 2.02 | 3.45 | 0.72 | 1.06 |
| 70 | 2.02 | 3.57 | 0.66 | 1.03 |
| BGA | 2.47 | 3.61 | 1.05 | 1.28 |
| $R^2$ | 0.985 | 0.997 | 0.971 | 0.995 |

Source: Hulten and Wykoff (1981a, table 5, p. 387); commercial corresponds to office and industrial corresponds to factory.

asset. Vintage price functions are estimated with and without a correction for censored sample bias.

The first conclusion that emerges from the data presented in table 1.5 is that a correction for censored sample bias is extremely important in the estimation of vintage price functions. The Hulten-Wykoff study is the first to employ such a correction. The second conclusion reached by Hulten and Wykoff (1981b) is that "... *a constant rate of depreciation can serve as a reasonable statistical approximation to the underlying Box-Cox rates even though the latter are not geometric.* This result, in turn, supports those who use the single parameter depreciation approach in calculating capital stocks using the perpetual inventory method. [Italics in original.]" This finding has been corroborated by Hulten, Robertson, and Wykoff (1989).

Hulten, Robertson, and Wykoff (1989) have tested the stability of vintage price functions during the 1970s. After 1973 energy prices increased sharply and productivity growth rates declined dramatically at both aggregate and sectoral levels, as indicated by the data presented in table 1.1. Baily (1981) has attributed the slowdown in economic growth to the decline in relative efficiency of older capital goods, resulting from higher energy prices. Hulten, Robertson, and Wykoff (1989) find that the relative efficiency functions for nine types of producers' durable equipment were unaffected by higher energy prices: "While depreciation almost certainly varies from year to year in response to a variety of factors, I have found that a major event like the energy crises, which had the potential of significantly increasing the rate of obsolescence, did not in fact result in a systematic change in age-price profiles.[22]

In table 1.6 I present rates of economic depreciation derived by Jorgenson and Yun (1990) from the best geometric approximation approach of Hulten and Wykoff for all assets distinguished by the Bureau of Economic Analysis (BEA) in constructing the U.S. national income and product accounts. Hulten and Wykoff have compared the best geometric average rates with depreciation rates employed by BEA in constructing perpetual inventory estimates of capital stock. The Hulten-Wykoff rates for equipment average 0.133, while the BEA rates average 0.141, so that the two sets of rates are very similar. The Hulten-Wykoff rates for structures average 0.037, while the BEA rates average 0.060; these rates are substantially different.

Hulten and Wykoff (1981b) have summarized estimates of economic depreciation completed prior to their own study. The most

**Table 1.6**
Economic depreciation rates: Business assets

| Assets | Old lifetime | Old depreciation rate | New lifetime | New depreciation rate |
|---|---|---|---|---|
| 1. Household furniture & fixtures | 15 | .1100 | 12 | .1375 |
| 2. Other furniture | 15 | .1100 | 14 | .1179 |
| 3. Fabricated metal products | 18 | .0917 | 18 | .0917 |
| 4. Steam engines & turbines | 21 | .0786 | 32 | .0516 |
| 5. Internal combustion engines | 21 | .0786 | 8 | .2063 |
| 6. Farm tractors | 8 | .1633 | 9 | .1452 |
| 7. Construction tractors | 8 | .1633 | 8 | .1633 |
| 8. Agricultural machinery | 17 | .0971 | 14 | .1179 |
| 9. Construction machinery | 9 | .1722 | 10 | .1722 |
| 10. Mining & oilfield machinery | 10 | .1650 | 11 | .1500 |
| 11. Metalworking machinery | 16 | .1225 | 16 | .1225 |
| 12. Special industry machinery | 16 | .1031 | 16 | .1031 |
| 13. General industrial | 14 | .1225 | 16 | .1225 |
| 14. Office, computing | 8 | .2729 | 8 | .2729 |
| 15. Service industry machinery | 10 | .1650 | 10 | .1650 |
| 16. Communication equipment | 14 | .1179 | 15 | .1100 |
| 17. Electrial transmission | 14 | .1179 | 33 | .0500 |
| 18. Household appliances | 14 | .1179 | 10 | .1651 |
| 19. Other electrical equipment | 14 | .1179 | 9 | .1834 |
| 20. Trucks, buses, & truck trailers | 9 | .2537 | 9 | .2537 |
| 21. Autos | 10 | .3333 | 10 | .3333 |
| 22. Aircraft | 16 | .1833 | 16 | .1833 |
| 23. Ships & boats | 22 | .0750 | 27 | .0611 |
| 24. Railroad equipment | 25 | .0660 | 30 | .0550 |
| 25. Scientific & engineering instruments | 11 | .1473 | 12 | .1350 |
| 26. Photocopy & related equipment | 11 | .1473 | 9 | .1800 |

Table 1.6 (continued)

| Assets | Old lifetime | Old depreciation rate | New lifetime | New depreciation rate |
|---|---|---|---|---|
| 27. Other nonresidential equipment | 11 | .1473 | 11 | .1473 |
| 28. Industrial buildings | 27 | .0361 | 31 | .0361 |
| 29. Mobile offices | 36 | .0247 | 16 | .0556 |
| 30. Office buildings | 36 | .0247 | 36 | .0247 |
| 31. Commercial warehouses | 36 | .0247 | 40 | .0222 |
| 32. Other commercial buildings | 36 | .0247 | 34 | .0262 |
| 33. Religious buildings | 48 | .0188 | 48 | .0188 |
| 34. Educational buildings | 48 | .0188 | 48 | .0188 |
| 35. Hospital & institutional buildings | 48 | .0233 | 48 | .0233 |
| 36. Hotels & motels | 40 | .0247 | 32 | .0247 |
| 37. Amusement & recreational | 31 | .0454 | 30 | .0469 |
| 38. Other nonfarm buildings | 31 | .0454 | 38 | .0370 |
| 39. Railroad structures | 51 | .0176 | 54 | .0166 |
| 40. Telephone & telegraph structures | 27 | .0333 | 40 | .0225 |
| 41. Electric light & power structures | 30 | .0300 | 40 | .0225 |
| 42. Gas structures | 30 | .0300 | 40 | .0225 |
| 43. Local transit | 26 | .0450 | 38 | .0450 |
| 44. Petroleum pipelines | 26 | .0450 | 40 | .0450 |
| 45. Farm structures | 38 | .0237 | 38 | .0237 |
| 46. Petroleum & natural gas | 16 | .0563 | 16 | .0563 |
| 47. Other mining exploration | 16 | .0563 | 16 | .0563 |
| 48. Other nonresidential structures | 31 | .0290 | 40 | .0225 |
| 49. Railroad replacement track | 51 | .0176 | 38 | .0236 |
| 50. Nuclear fuel | — | — | 6 | .2500 |
| 51. Residential structures | — | .0130 | — | .0130 |

Source: Jorgenson and Yun (1990, table 13B, p. 82).

common methodology for such studies is based on vintage price functions.[23] An alternative to the vintage price approach is to employ rental prices rather than asset prices in estimating patterns of decline in efficiency. This approach has been employed by Malpezzi, Ozanne, and Thibodeau (1987) to analyze rental price data on residential structures and Taubman and Rasche (1969) to study rental price data on commercial structures. While leases on residential property are frequently one year or less in duration, leases on commercial property are typically for much longer periods of time. Since the rental prices are constant over the period of the lease, estimates based on annual rental prices for commercial property are biased toward the "one-hoss shay" pattern found by Taubman and Rasche; Malpezzi, Ozanne, and Thibodeau find rental price profiles for residential property that decline with age.

A second alternative to the vintage price approach is to analyze investment for replacement purposes.[24] Coen (1980) compares the explanatory power of alternative patterns of decline in efficiency in a model of investment behavior that also includes the price of capital services. For equipment he finds that eleven of twenty-one two-digit manufacturing industries are characterized by geometric decline in efficiency, three by sum of the years' digits and seven by straight-line. For structures he finds that fourteen industries are characterized by geometric decline, five by straight-line and two by one-hoss-shay patterns. Hulten and Wykoff (1981b) conclude that: "The weight of Coen's study is evidently on the side of the geometric and near-geometric forms of depreciation."

### 1.3.2 Data Sources and Methods for Capital Input

Data on capital input are unavailable for the government sector, excluding government enterprises, listed in table 1.2. For each of the thirty-five private industrial sectors listed in this table, prices and quantities of capital input are cross-classified by four asset classes—producers' durable equipment, nonresidential structures, inventories, and land—and three legal forms of organization—corporate and noncorporate business and nonprofit enterprises.

Data on producers' durable equipment can be further subdivided among the twenty-seven categories listed in table 1.6, while data on nonresidential structures can be subdivided among twenty-three categories listed there. For the thirty-five private industrial sectors listed in table 1.2 annual data from 1947 to 1985 on capital stock and its rental price are required for an average of as many as 156 components of the capital stock. Households and institutions are treated as a separate sector with prices and quantities of capital input cross-classified by producers' and consumers' durable equipment, residential and nonresidential structures, and land.

The first step in developing sectoral measures of capital input is to construct estimates of capital stock by industry for each year from 1947 to 1985. Investment data from the Bureau of Economic Analysis (1987a) for producers' durable equipment and structures are distributed among industries on an establishment basis. Estimates of investment for all sectors are controlled to totals from the U.S. national product accounts. For residential structures investment data are taken directly from the U.S. national product accounts.[25] Investment goods prices from the U.S. national product accounts are employed to obtain estimates of investment in equipment and structures in constant prices.

Estimates of stocks of land by industry begin with estimates of the stock of land for the economy as a whole. Balance sheet data are employed to allocate land among industrial sectors and between corporate and noncorporate business within each sector with the exception of private households and nonprofit institutions. BEA has constructed estimates of inventory stocks in current and constant prices for all sectors. These estimates are consistent with data on inventory investment for the U.S. economy as a whole from the national product accounts. The data are broken down by legal form of organization within each industry.

The second step in developing sectoral measures of capital input is to construct estimates of prices of capital services from data on property compensation. For each asset the price of investment goods is a weighted sum of future rental prices, discounted by a factor that incorporates future rates of return. Weights are given by the relative efficiencies of capital goods of different ages. The same weights are used in constructing estimates of rental prices and capital stocks. For depreciable assets the weights decline with age; for nondepreciable assets the weights are constant.

Differences in the tax treatment of property compensation among legal forms of organization result in differences in rental prices of capital services. Estimates of the rental prices of capital services in the corporate sector include data on the corporate income tax. Data on property taxes for corporate business are also included. Property compensation for corporate business within each industrial sector must be allocated among equipment, structures, land, and inventories. Corporate property compensation is the sum of rental payments for capital services for all four classes of assets.

Similarly, data on property taxes for noncorporate business are included in estimates of the rental prices of capital services in the non-corporate sector. The noncorporate rate of return is set equal to the corporate rate of return after corporate taxes. This assumption makes it possible to allocate noncorporate income between labor and property compensation. Noncorporate property compensation is the sum of rental payments for capital services for all four classes of assets.

To derive prices of capital services for private households and non-profit institutions, the rate of return on owner-occupied housing must be estimated. The rate of return for private households and nonprofit institutions is set equal to the corporate rate of return after corporate and personal taxes. Data on property taxes for private households are incorporated into estimates of the rental prices of capital services used in this sector. Property compensation for households and institutions is the sum of rental payments for all classes of assets.

The final step in constructing data on capital input for each of the thirty-five private industrial sectors is to combine price and quantity data, cross-classified by class of asset and legal form of organization, into price and quantity indexes of capital input. To construct an index of capital input for each industrial sector, I express sectoral capital input, say $\{K_i\}$, as a translog function of its 156 individual components, say $\{K_{ki}\}$. The corresponding index of sectoral capital input is a translog quantity index of individual capital inputs

$$\ln K_i(T) - \ln K_i(T-1)$$
$$= \sum \bar{v}^i_{Kk} \left[\ln K_{ki}(T) - \ln K_{ki}(T-1)\right], \quad (i = 1, 2, \ldots, n),$$

where weights are given by average shares of each component in the value of sectoral property compensation

$$\bar{v}^i_{Kk} = \frac{1}{2} \left[v^i_{Kk}(T) + v^i_{Kk}(T-1)\right], \quad (i = 1, 2, \ldots, n; \ k = 1, 2, \ldots, p),$$

and

$$v^i_{Kk} = \frac{p^i_{Kk} K_{ki}}{\sum p^i_{Kk} K_{ki}}, \quad (i = 1, 2, \ldots, n; \ k = 1, 2, \ldots, p).$$

The value shares are computed from data on capital services $\{K_{ki}\}$ and the rental price of capital services $\{p^i_{Kk}\}$, cross-classified by asset class and legal form of organization. An analogous approach is applied to data for private households and institutions.

A measure of capital stock for each sector can be derived by adding capital stocks across all categories of capital input within that sector. The quality of capital stock is defined as the ratio of capital input to capital stock. Changes in the quality of capital stock represent differences between changes in the translog quantity index of capital input and changes in an unweighted index of capital stock. Indexes of the quantity of capital input are presented in table 1.2 for thirty-six sectors. The corresponding indexes of capital quality and capital stock are presented in table 1.3.

The rental prices introduced by Christensen and Jorgenson (1969, 1970, 1973a, b) were extended to the level of individual industrial sectors by Fraumeni and Jorgenson (1980) and Gollop and Jorgenson (1980). Fraumeni and Jorgenson (1986) have incorporated patterns of relative efficiencies based on the best geometric average (BGA) rates fitted by Hulten and Wykoff. The data on capital input that underly tables 1.2 and 1.3 incorporate differences in depreciation patterns by types of producers' durable equipment and nonresidential structures, differences in tax treatment by corporate and noncorporate business and nonprofit forms of organization, and differences in efficiency by age for an average of as many as 156 types of capital input for each of the thirty-five private industrial sectors. Additional types of capital input are distinguished for consumers' durable equipment and residential structures utilized by private households and institutions.

## 1.3.3   Alternative Sources and Methods

An overview of issues in the measurement of capital input is provided by the Rees Report (National Research Council, 1979, esp. pp. 128–140). The treatment of capital as a factor of production became the central issue in an extended debate among Denison (1957, 1966, 1969, 1972), Griliches (1961a), Griliches and Jorgenson (1966), Hulten (1990), Jorgenson (1968, 1973a, 1980, 1989), Jorgenson and Griliches (1967, 1972a, 1972b), and Kendrick (1961b, 1968, 1973). The debate has been summarized and evaluated by Diewert (1980, p. 480), Katz (1988), Mohr (1988b, c), and Norsworthy (1984a, b). To provide additional perspective on the measurement of capital input I find it useful to compare the methodology and data sources that underly the indexes presented in tables 1.2 and 1.3 with those of BLS, Denison, and Kendrick.

Internal consistency of a measure of capital input requires that the same pattern of relative efficiency is employed in measuring both capital stock and the rental price of capital services. The decline in efficiency affects both the level of capital stock and the corresponding rental price. The estimates of capital stocks and rental prices that underly the data presented in tables 1.2 and 1.3 are based on geometrically declining relative efficiencies with the rates of decline presented in table 1.6. The same patterns of decline in efficiency are used for both capital stock and the rental price of each asset, so that the requirement for internal consistency of measures of capital input is met.

I next describe the methods and data sources employed by BLS, Denison, and Kendrick for estimating capital stocks. I then present their methods and sources for estimating rental prices of capital services and attempt to determine whether the resulting measures of capital input are internally consistent. Denison and Kendrick employ estimates of capital stock for equipment and structures from the BEA capital stock study. The methodology employed by BEA in constructing estimates of capital stock is described by the BEA (1987a), Gorman, Musgrave, Silverstein, and Comins (1985), Musgrave (1986), and Young and Musgrave (1980). These estimates are derived by the perpetual inventory method using investment data based on the U.S. national product accounts. BLS also utilizes the perpetual inventory method to derive estimates of capital stock for equipment and structures from investment data based on the U.S. national product accounts.

The perpetual inventory method for measuring capital input is employed in all four studies that I consider. In this method the sequence of relative efficiencies of capital goods of different ages $\{d(\tau)\}$ enables us to characterize capital stock at the end of each period, say $A(T)$, as a weighted sum of past investments

$$A(T) = \sum_{\tau=0}^{\infty} d(\tau) \, I(T - \tau) \,,$$

where $I(T - \tau)$ is investment in period $T - \tau$ and the weights are given by the sequence of relative efficiencies.

For each asset, the sequence of relative efficiencies of capital goods of different ages enables us to characterize the price of investment goods in each period, say $P_I(T)$, as a weighted sum of future rentals

$$p_I(T) = \sum_{\tau=0}^{\infty} d(\tau) \prod_{S=1}^{\tau+1} \frac{1}{1 + r(T + S)} \, p_K(T + \tau + 1),$$

where $p_K(T+\tau+1)$ is the rental price in period $T+\tau+1$ and the weights are given by the sequence of relative efficiencies $\{d(\tau)\}$. In this expression $r(T)$ is the rate of return on capital in period $T$ and $\prod_{S=1}^{\tau+1} 1/[1+r(T+S)]$ is the discount factor in period $T$ for future prices in period $T+\tau+1$.

Capital goods decline in efficiency at each point of time, generating needs for replacement of productive capacity. The proportion of an investment to be replaced at age $\tau$, say $m(\tau)$, is equal to the decline in efficiency from age $\tau-1$ to age $\tau$

$$m(\tau) = - [d(\tau) - d(\tau - 1)], \qquad (\tau = 1, 2, \ldots, T).$$

I refer to these proportions as *mortality rates* for capital goods of different ages.

I define depreciation as the value that must be recovered in every period to keep wealth intact. Taking first differences of the expression for the price of investment goods in terms of future rental prices, I can express the depreciation on a capital good in period T, say $p_D(T)$, in terms of future rental prices and the mortality distribution $\{m(\tau)\}$

$$p_D(T) = \sum_{\tau=1}^{\infty} m(\tau) \prod_{S=1}^{\tau} \frac{1}{1 + r(T + S)} \, p_K(T + \tau).$$

I begin our comparison of alternative measures of rental prices of capital services with a characterization of the rental price concept. In the absence of taxation the rental price of capital services at time $T$ takes the form

$$p_K(T) = p_I(T - 1)r(T) + p_D(T) - [p_I(T) - p_I(T - 1)],$$

where depreciation, $p_D(T)$, depends on the pattern of relative efficiencies. The value of the services of capital stock is the product of the rental price and the quantity of capital stock

$$p_K(T)A(T - 1) = (p_I(T - 1)r(T) + p_D(T) - [p_I(T) - p_I(T - 1)]) \cdot A(T - 1).$$

Finally, the value of capital services is equal to property compensation, so that I can solve for the rate of return, given data on property compensation

$$r(T) = \frac{\text{Property compensation} - \{(p_D(T) - [p_I(T) - p_I(T-1)])\} \cdot A(T-1)}{p_I(T-1) \cdot A(T-1)}.$$

The first and most important criterion for internal consistency of a measure of capital input is that the same patterns of relative efficiency must underlie both the estimates of capital stock $A(T)$ and the estimates of rental price $p_K(T)$ for each class of assets. Hulten and Wykoff (1981b) have shown that the BGA rates of depreciation provide an accurate description of the decline in the price of acquisition of capital goods with age. The Hulten-Wykoff geometric rates are utilized in compiling estimates of both capital stocks and rental prices for the indexes of capital input presented in tables 1.1 and 1.2.

BLS (1983, pp. 57–59) also employs relative efficiency functions estimated by Hulten and Wykoff. However, BLS does not utilize the geometric relative efficiency functions fitted by Hulten and Wykoff. Instead, BLS has fitted a set of hyperbolic functions to the relative efficiency functions estimated by Hulten and Wykoff. Consistency is preserved between the resulting estimates of capital stocks and rental prices by implementing a system of vintage accounts for each class of assets. Implicitly, this set of accounts includes asset prices and quantities of investment goods of all ages at each point of time. BLS (1983, pp. 57–59) shows that measures of capital input based on hyperbolic and geometric relative efficiency functions are very similar.

For each class of assets Denison's estimates of capital stock are based on a linearly declining pattern of relative efficiency. To derive the method of depreciation appropriate for linearly declining relative efficiencies, I first express depreciation for an asset of age $V$ at time $T$, say $p_D(T, V)$, in the form

$$
\begin{aligned}
p_D(T, V) &= \sum_{\tau=1}^{\infty} m(\tau + V) \prod_{S=1}^{\tau} \frac{1}{1 + r(T+S)} \, p_K(T + \tau) \\
&= \frac{1}{\theta L} \sum_{\tau=1}^{L-V-1} \prod_{S=1}^{\tau} \frac{1}{1 + r(T+S)} \, p_K(T + \tau) \\
&\quad + \left[ 1 - \frac{1}{\theta}\left(1 - \frac{1}{L}\right) \right] \prod_{S=1}^{L-V} p_K(T + L - V).
\end{aligned}
$$

Assuming that the rates of return $\{r(T+S)\}$ and the prices of capital services $\{p_K(T+\tau)\}$ are constant, I obtain the following expression for depreciation on an asset of age $V$

$$p_D(V) = \frac{1}{r\theta L} - \left[ \frac{1}{r\theta L} - 1 + \frac{1}{\theta} \right] \left( \frac{1}{1+r} \right)^{L-V} p_K, \quad (V = 0, 1, \ldots, L-1).$$

Similarly, the value of a new asset is equal to the sum of depreciation over all ages

$$p_I = \sum_{V=0}^{L-1} p_D(V)$$

$$= \frac{1}{r} \left( \frac{1}{\theta} - \left[ \frac{1}{r\theta L} - 1 + \frac{1}{\theta} \right] \left[ 1 - \left( \frac{1}{1+r} \right)^L \right] \right) p_K,$$

so that depreciation allowances appropriate for a linearly declining pattern of relative efficiency are given for each age by the formula

$$\frac{p_D(V)}{p_I} = \frac{\dfrac{1}{\theta L} - r \left[ \dfrac{1}{r\theta L} - 1 + \dfrac{1}{\theta} \right] \left( \dfrac{1}{1+r} \right)^{L-V}}{\dfrac{1}{\theta} - \left[ \dfrac{1}{r\theta L} - 1 + \dfrac{1}{\theta} \right] \left[ 1 - \left( \dfrac{1}{1+r} \right)^L \right]}, \quad (V = 0, 1, \ldots, L-1).$$

The value of depreciation at time $T$ for a linearly declining pattern of relative efficiency is the sum over assets of all ages

$$\sum_{V=0}^{L-1} p_D(T, V) I(T - V - 1)$$

$$= p_I(T) \sum_{V=0}^{L-1} \frac{\dfrac{1}{\theta L} - r \left[ \dfrac{1}{r\theta L} - 1 + \dfrac{1}{\theta} \right] \left( \dfrac{1}{1+r} \right)^{L-V}}{\dfrac{1}{\theta} - \left[ \dfrac{1}{r\theta L} - 1 + \dfrac{1}{\theta} \right] \left[ 1 - \left( \dfrac{1}{1+r} \right)^L \right]} I(T - V - 1).$$

Denison employs linearly declining relative efficiency in measuring capital stock; in fact, he employs three different weighted averages of the straight-line and "one-hoss shay" patterns.[26] For all three weighted averages Denison employs the straight-line method of depreciation. For linearly declining patterns of relative efficiency, depreciation allowances are increasing, constant, or decreasing with age for values of the parameter $\theta$ greater than, equal to, or less than $1 + (1/rL)$, respectively. For the straight-line pattern depreciation allowances are decreasing with age; for the "one-hoss shay" pattern depreciation allowances are increasing with age. Denison's assumption that depreciation allowances are constant is not appropriate for any of his methods of measuring capital stock, so that all three of the resulting measures of capital input are internally inconsistent.

Kendrick (1973, pp. 27–29) employs capital stock estimates based on linearly declining relative efficiencies in allocating property compensation among assets on the basis of "net earnings." Kendrick's measure of net earnings is based on capital consumption allowances from the U.S. national income accounts as an estimate of depreciation. These estimates are based in turn on depreciation allowances for tax purposes and do not reflect a consistent valuation of assets over time or a consistent method of depreciation.

The method of depreciation appropriate for Kendrick's estimates of capital stock based on linearly declining relative efficiencies is the same as that I have given above for Denison with the parameter $\theta$ equal to unity

$$\frac{p_D(V)}{p_I} = \frac{\dfrac{1}{L}\left[1 - \left(\dfrac{1}{1+r}\right)^{L-V}\right]}{1 - \dfrac{1}{rL}\left[1 - \left(\dfrac{1}{1+r}\right)^{L}\right]}, \qquad (V = 0, 1, \ldots, L-1).$$

The value of depreciation at time $T$ for linearly declining relative efficiencies is the sum over assets of all ages

$$\sum_{V=0}^{L-1} p_D(T, V)\, I(T - V - 1) = p_I(T) \sum_{V=0}^{L-1} \frac{\dfrac{1}{L}\left[1 - \left(\dfrac{1}{1+r}\right)^{L-V}\right]}{1 - \dfrac{1}{rL}\left[1 - \left(\dfrac{1}{1+r}\right)^{L}\right]}\, I(T - V - 1).$$

Kendrick (1973) also employs alternative capital stock estimates based on constant relative efficiencies in allocating property compensation among assets on the basis of "gross earnings." Constant relative efficiencies are also utilized by Kendrick and Grossman (1980,

p. 26) and Kendrick (1983a, pp. 56–57). The declining balance pattern of relative efficiencies employed by Kendrick is inappropriate for constant relative efficiencies. The correct method is given by the limit of the formula described above with $\theta$ going to positive infinity

$$\frac{P_D(V)}{p_I} = \frac{r\left(\dfrac{1}{1+r}\right)^{L-V}}{1 - \left(\dfrac{1}{1+r}\right)^L}, \qquad (V = 0, 1, \ldots, L-1).$$

The value of depreciation at time $T$ for constant relative efficiencies is the sum

$$\sum_{V=0}^{L-1} p_D(T, V)\, I(T - V - 1) = p_I(T) \sum_{V=0}^{L-1} \frac{r\left(\dfrac{1}{1+r}\right)^{L-V}}{1 - \left(\dfrac{1}{1+r}\right)^L}\, I(T - V - 1).$$

My conclusion is that neither of Kendrick's two measures of capital input is based on an internally consistent treatment of capital stocks and rental prices of capital services. In estimating capital stocks Kendrick uses straight-line and one-hoss shay patterns of relative efficiency. His weights based on gross earnings ignore differences among assets in rates of depreciation; his weights based on net earnings employ depreciation as calculated for tax purposes, so that neither the depreciation method nor the valuation of assets is consistent over time.

The estimates of capital service prices that underly the capital input indexes presented in table 1.2 incorporate differences in property tax rates among types of assets, differences in the tax treatment of corporate and noncorporate income due to the corporate income tax, and differences between equipment and structures due to variations in the tax formulas for depreciation and the investment tax credit for equipment. BLS (1983, p. 50) employs data on tax depreciation and the investment tax credit and differences in property tax rates among types of assets. However, corporate and noncorporate assets are assumed to have the same capital service prices, so that the effect of the corporate income tax is ignored. Denison and Kendrick ignore differences in property tax rates among types of assets, the effect of the corporate income tax, the tax treatment of depreciation, and the investment tax credit in allocating property compensation among assets.[27]

I have focused the discussion of capital input on the internal consistency of estimates of capital stocks and the corresponding rental prices. However, it is important to emphasize an important conceptual difference between Kendrick's measures of sectoral capital input and the measures I have presented in tables 1.2 and 1.3. Kendrick (e.g., 1973, p. 146) purposefully defines any growth in sectoral output due to shifts in the composition of the capital stock by class of asset or legal form of organization as part of productivity change. For Kendrick, any shift in the mix of capital by depreciation pattern or tax treatment that leads to greater levels of sectoral output reflects an advance in knowledge and is therefore part of productivity change. I evaluate Kendrick's definition of productivity change in section 1.4.3, below.

The data on capital input presented in tables 1.2 and 1.3 incorporate shifts in the composition of the capital stock by class of asset and legal form of organization within an industrial sector. The data on capital input in table 1.1 incorporate these shifts for the U.S. economy as a whole. Gollop and Jorgenson (1980) provide a detailed comparison between capital input indexes of this type and those of Kendrick for the period 1947–1973. Quality change is an important component of the growth in capital input. This component accounts for much of the difference between Kendrick's estimates of capital stock and the translog indexes of capital input given in tables 1.2 and 1.3.

## 1.4   Measuring Output, Intermediate Input, and Productivity

An important innovation embodied in the data on productivity presented in table 1.2 is that intermediate, capital, and labor inputs are treated symmetrically at the sectoral level. The value of output at the sectoral level includes the value of intermediate input as well as the values of capital and labor inputs. All three inputs are employed in analyzing the sources of growth in sectoral output. The industry definitions employed in the U.S. national income accounts are used in measuring output. These definitions are based on establishments within each industry.

A more restrictive methodology for sectoral productivity measurement is based on the concept of value added. Output is represented as a function of intermediate input and value added; value added is represented in turn as a function of capital input, labor input, and time. In the value-added approach intermediate input is not treated symmetrically with capital and labor inputs. The existence of the value added aggregate requires that time and capital and labor inputs are separable from intermediate input. Given the quantities of intermediate input and value added, output is independent of changes in technology.

The methodology for productivity measurement outlined in previous sections treats all three inputs symmetrically. The sectoral models of production do not require the existence of a value added aggregate in constructing an index of productivity growth. The value-added approach is based on more restrictive assumptions but requires precisely the same data. Both the restricted and unrestricted methodologies require prices and quantities of output and intermediate, capital, and labor inputs for full implementation.

### 1.4.1   Sectoral Output, Intermediate Input, and Productivity

I have employed a model of production based on a production function $\{F^i\}$ for each of the $n$ sectors. The production function gives output $\{Z_i\}$ as a function of intermediate input $\{X_i\}$, capital input $\{K_i\}$, labor input $\{L_i\}$, and time $T$. I can specialize this model by introducing a value-added function $\{G^i\}$ for each sector, giving the quantity of value added, say $\{V_i\}$, as a function of capital input, labor input, and time:[28]

$$V_i = G^i(K_i, L_i, T), \qquad (i = 1, 2, \ldots, n),$$

where

$$Z_i = F^i(X_i, V_i),$$
$$= F^i[X_i, G^i(K_i, L_i, T)], \qquad (i = 1, 2, \ldots, n).$$

I say that the production function is neutral with respect to intermediate input, since the substitution of intermediate input for value added is unaffected by changes in technology. If the value-added function is homogeneous of degree one in capital and labor inputs, I say that the production function is homothetically neutral. Homogeneity implies that proportional changes in capital and labor inputs result in proportional changes in value added, so that the value-added function is characterized by constant returns to scale. If the production function is homogeneous of degree one in intermediate, capital, and labor inputs, neutrality of the production function implies homothetic neutrality.

Denoting the price of value added by $\{p_V^i\}$, I can define the share of value added, say $\{v_V^i\}$, in the value of output by

$$v_V^i = \frac{p_V^i \, V_i}{q_i \, Z_i}, \qquad (i = 1, 2, \ldots, n) \, .$$

Necessary conditions for producer equilibrium include equalities between the share of value added and the elasticity of output with respect to value added

$$v_V^i = \frac{\partial \ln Z_i}{\partial \ln V_i} \, (X_i, V_i), \qquad (i = 1, 2, \ldots, n) \, .$$

Under constant returns to scale the elasticities and the value shares for intermediate input and value-added sum to unity, so that the value of output is equal to the sum of the values of intermediate input and value added. Necessary conditions for producer equilibrium also include equalities between the shares of capital and labor inputs in value added and the elasticities of the quantity of value added with respect to those inputs. Conditions for producer equilibrium imply that value added is equal to the sum of the values of capital and labor inputs.

In defining output Kendrick (1973, p. 17) considers whether or not to exclude the value of depreciation from the value of output. At the sectoral level, depreciation could be excluded along with the value of intermediate goods in the measurement of value added. Kendrick considers two measures of productivity, one based on value-added gross of depreciation and the other based on value-added net of depreciation. He associates the gross measure with gross capital stock as a measure of capital input and the net measure with net capital stock as a measure of capital input.

In section 1.3.3, above, I have shown that the selection of an appropriate concept of capital input depends on the relative efficiencies of capital goods of different vintages. Associated with each measure of capital input $A(T-1)$, there is a corresponding measure of depreciation $p_D(T)$. Gross capital stock, as defined by Kendrick, corresponds to the one-hoss shay pattern of decline in efficiency. I have given the corresponding measure of depreciation in section 1.3.3. There is no connection between gross capital stock as a measure of capital input and value-added gross of depreciation as a measure of output. Similarly, there is no connection between net capital stock as a measure of capital input and value-added net of depreciation as a measure of output. For any pattern of decline in efficiency there are corresponding measures of depreciation and capital input. For any measure of depreciation, there are measures of value added both gross and net of depreciation.

Kendrick (1973, p. 18) indicates that he would have preferred to use a measure of output net of depreciation. Kendrick is able to implement an approach based on value-added net of depreciation only at the economy-wide level, where he uses net national product in place of gross national product as a measure of value added. To evaluate Kendrick's approach to the measurement of value-added net of depreciation I can decompose the value of capital input into the value of return to capital, evaluated at the own-rate of return, and the value of depreciation

$$p_K(T)A(T-1)$$

$$= p_I(T-1)\left[r(T) - \frac{p_I(T)-p_I(T-1)}{p_I(T-1)}\right]A(T-1) + p_D(T)A(T-1).$$

As before, I have simplified this expression by ignoring the impact of taxation.

Value added $p_V(T)V(T)$ is the sum of the value of capital input $p_K(T)A(T-1)$ and the value of labor input $p_L(T)L(T)$. Value-added net of depreciation is defined as the difference between value added and the value of depreciation

$$p_V(T)V(T) - p_D(T)A(T-1)$$

$$= p_I(T-1)\left[r(T) - \frac{p_I(T)-p_I(T-1)}{p_I(T-1)}\right]A(T-1) + p_L(T)L(T).$$

Capital stock $A(T-1)$ appears on both the left-hand side, where it is associated with depreciation, and on the right-hand side, where it is associated with the own-rate of return on capital or, using Kendrick's terminology, the net earnings of capital.

Gross value added $\{V^i\}$ can be rationalized as a measure of output by imposing a separability assumption on the production function

$\{F^i\}$ for each sector. This is done by introducing the value-added function $\{G^i\}$ for the sector. Intermediate input is separated from capital and labor inputs and changes in technology by the value-added function. Gross value added is represented as a function of capital input, labor input, and time. If I were to attempt to represent net value added as a function of capital input, labor input, and time, net value added and the list of inputs would both involve the quantity of capital input.

By contrast with net value added, gross value added can be defined, implicitly, as a function of output and intermediate input. The corresponding definition of net value added would involve output, intermediate input, and capital input. I conclude that the quantity of net value added is not an appropriate point of departure for modeling producer behavior. At the economy-wide level only Kendrick's measure of productivity based on gross value added avoids including capital input in the definition of both output and input. Fortunately, only gross value added is used for Kendrick's sectoral aggregates of individual industries, so that his sectoral measures of productivity are free from this defect.

Kendrick and Grossman (1980, pp. 22–25) and Kendrick (1983a, p. 56) have employed measures of output at the level of individual industries based on data from the BEA on gross product originating in each industrial sector. Both studies have dropped the concept of value added net of depreciation employed by Kendrick (1973). This important change in methodology has the advantage over the methodology employed in Kendrick's (1973) study that the problem of including capital input in both net value added and the list of inputs is entirely avoided.[29]

### 1.4.2   Data Sources and Methods for Output and Intermediate Input

Data on output in current and constant prices are available from the Office of Economic Growth of the Bureau of Labor Statistics (1987). In order to evaluate output from the point of view of the producing sector, excise and sales taxes must be subtracted and subsidies must be added to the value of output. The resulting price of output from the producers' point of view is equal to the ratio of the value of output in current prices to the value of output in constant prices.

Data on interindustry transactions published by BEA (1984, various years) must be employed to disaggregate intermediate input by sector of origin. These data are based on industry definitions employed in the U.S. interindustry accounts. In order to bring measures of intermediate input into conformity with industry definitions from the U.S. national income accounts, interindustry transactions must be reallocated among sectors. This reallocation must take into account the reclassifications, redefinitions, and transfers employed in constructing the U.S. interindustry accounts, as discussed by Walderhaug (1973). To construct prices and quantities of intermediate input by sector of origin the value of intermediate input originating in each sector must be deflated by an index of purchasers' prices for the output of that sector. The indexes of producers' prices for the output of each sector are transformed to purchasers' prices by adding sales and excise taxes and subtracting subsidies.

The final step in constructing data on intermediate input for each of the thirty-five industrial sectors is to combine price and quantity data, classified by sector of origin, into price and quantity indexes of intermediate input. To construct an index of intermediate input for each industrial sector, I express sectoral intermediate input, say $\{X_i\}$, as a translog function of its $n$ individual components, say $\{X_{ji}\}$. The corresponding index of sectoral intermediate input is a translog quantity index of individual intermediate inputs

$$\ln X_i(T) - \ln X_i(T-1) = \sum \bar{v}_{Xj} \, [\ln X_{ji}(T) - \ln X_{ji}(T-1)], \quad (i = 1, 2, \ldots, n),$$

where weights are given by average shares of each component in the value of sectoral intermediate outlay

$$\bar{v}^i_{Xj} = \frac{1}{2} \, [v^i_{Xj}(T) + v^i_{Xj}(T-1)], \qquad (i, j = 1, 2, \ldots, n),$$

and

$$v^i_{Xj} = \frac{p^i_{Xj} \, X_{ji}}{\sum_j p^i_{Xj} \, X_{ji}}, \qquad (i, j = 1, 2, \ldots, n).$$

The value shares are computed from data on intermediate input $\{X_{ji}\}$ and the corresponding prices paid by the receiving sectors $\{p^i_{Xj}\}$ for each component of sectoral intermediate input.

An unweighted index of intermediate input for each sector is derived by adding across the intermediate inputs from all originating sectors. The quality of intermediate input is defined as the ratio of the translog quantity index to an unweighted index for each sector. Changes in the quality of intermediate input represent differences between changes in the translog quantity index and changes in the unweighted index. Indexes of the quantity of output and intermediate input are presented in table 1.2 for thirty-five sectors. The corresponding index of intermediate input quality and an unweighted index of intermediate input are presented in table 1.3 for each sector.

To allocate the growth of sectoral output among the contributions of intermediate, capital, and labor inputs and changes in productivity, I construct data on the rate of productivity growth. To construct on index of productivity for each industrial sector, I express sectoral output $\{Z_i\}$ as a translog function of sectoral intermediate input $\{X_i\}$, capital input $\{K_i\}$, labor input $\{L_i\}$, and time $T$. The corresponding index of productivity is the translog index of the rate of productivity growth $\{\bar{v}_T^i\}$

$$\bar{v}_T^i = [\ln Z_i(T) - \ln Z_i(T-1)] - \bar{v}_X^i [\ln X_i(T) - \ln X_i(T-1)]$$
$$- \bar{v}_K^i [\ln K_i(T) - \ln K_i(T-1)] - \bar{v}_L^i [\ln L_i(T) - \ln L_i(T-1)] ,$$
$$(i = 1, 2, \ldots, n) ,$$

where weights are given by average shares of sectoral intermediate, capital, and labor inputs in the value of sectoral output

$$\bar{v}_T^i = \frac{1}{2} [v_T^i(T) + v_T^i(T-1)] ,$$

$$\bar{v}_X^i = \frac{1}{2} [v_X^i(T) + v_X^i(T-1)] ,$$

$$\bar{v}_K^i = \frac{1}{2} [v_K^i(T) + v_K^i(T-1)] ,$$

$$\bar{v}_L^i = \frac{1}{2} [v_L^i(T) + v_L^i(T-1)] , \qquad (i = 1, 2, \ldots, n) ,$$

and

$$v_X^i = \frac{p_X^i X_i}{q_i Z_i} ,$$

$$v_K^i = \frac{p_K^i K_i}{q_i Z_i} ,$$

$$v_L^i = \frac{p_L^i L_i}{q_i Z_i} , \qquad (i = 1, 2, \ldots, n) .$$

The starting point for the construction of data on sectoral productivity growth is a sectoral production account in current prices. The fundamental accounting identity is that the value of output is equal to the value of input. The value of output excludes all sales and excise taxes and includes subsidies paid to producers. The value of input includes all taxes and supplements paid made by producers, as well as the compensation received by the suppliers of each input. Valuation from the producers' point of view is essential for the integration of data on output and input into measures of productivity growth at the sectoral level.

The concept of valuation from the point of view of the producer is used in the sectoral production accounts that underlie tables 1.2 and 1.3. This concept is intermediate between the national accounting concepts of valuation at market prices and valuation at factor cost. The value of output at market prices includes taxes paid by producers and excludes subsidies received by producers. The value of output at factor cost excludes these taxes and includes subsidies. Control totals for the values of output and intermediate, capital, and labor inputs are based on the U.S. national income accounts.

For the government sector, excluding government enterprises, output in tables 1.2 and 1.3 is defined as labor input; for private households output is set equal to an index of capital and labor input. For these sectors productivity growth is zero by definition. Rates of productivity growth for the remaining thirty-five sectors are presented on an annual basis for the period 1947–1985 in table 1.2.

### 1.4.3   Alternative Sources and Methods

An overview of issues in the measurement of intermediate input is provided by the Rees Report (National Research Council, 1979, esp. pp. 140–144). To provide additional perspective on the measurement of output, intermediate input, and productivity I find it useful to compare the methodology and data sources that underly the data presented in tables 1.2 and 1.3 with those of Kendrick and Leontief, who provide alternative estimates of sectoral productivity.[30] In table 1.2 intermediate input is treated symmetrically with capital input and labor input in measuring productivity growth at the sectoral level. The resulting measure of productivity is an index number constructed from data on prices and quantities of output, intermediate input, capital input, and labor input.

The first study of productivity for individual industrial sectors including intermediate input was that of Leontief (1953b). He compared interindustry transactions among fourteen industries for the United States for 1919, 1929, and 1939 in constant prices of 1939. For each industry he tabulated relative changes in the ratios of intermediate inputs and labor input to output; the ratio of capital input to output was simply ignored. Relative changes between 1919 and 1929 and between 1929 and 1939 were weighted by averages of the quantities of inputs for each pair of years to obtain an index of productivity change for each sector. The weights were summed to the average value of input into each sector in constant prices of 1939, excluding capital input. If Leontief's weights had been applied to relative changes in the ratios of individual inputs to output, including capital input, he would have obtained the negative of the translog index of productivity growth presented in table 1.2.

Kendrick (1956, 1961a, 1973) advocates an approach to sectoral productivity measurement based on value added, where value added is defined as the sum of the value of capital input and the value of labor input. Kendrick's approach to productivity measurement is based on the model I have presented in section 1.4.1, above, with output represented as a function of intermediate input and the quantity of value added. The price and quantity of value added are index numbers constructed from data on prices and quantities of output and intermediate input. Value added is represented as a function of capital input, labor input, and time. The corresponding measure of productivity is an index number constructed from data on prices and quantities of value added, capital input, and labor input.

Kendrick combines value added functions for each sector with necessary conditions for producer equilibrium. The rate of productivity growth for value added is an appropriate measure of productivity, provided that output can be represented as a function of intermediate input and value added. In fact, Kendrick (1973, p. 17) does not use value added as a measure of output at the level of individual industries included in his study. He employs output in measuring productivity at the level of individual industries and simply ignores the growth of intermediate input. The resulting rates of productivity growth are measures of the rate of productivity growth for value added only if rates of growth of output and intermediate goods are identical.

To provide further perspective on Kendrick's approach, I represent the accounting identity between the value of output, say $\{q_i \, Z_i\}$, and the sum of the values of intermediate input $\{p_X^i \, X_i\}$, capital input $\{p_K^i \, K_i\}$, and labor input $\{p_L^i \, L_i\}$ in the form

$$q_i \, X_i = p_X^i \, X_i + p_K^i \, K_i + p_L^i \, L_i, \qquad (i = 1, 2, \ldots, n) \, .$$

Value added, say $p_V^i \, V_i$, is defined as the difference between the value of output and the value of intermediate input

$$
\begin{aligned}
p_V^i \, V_i &= q_i Z_i - p_X^i \, X_i \\
&= p_K^i \, K_i + p_L^i \, L_i \, , \qquad (i = 1, 2, \ldots, n) \, ,
\end{aligned}
$$

so that value added is equal to the sum of the values of capital and labor inputs. By employing output $\{q_i Z_i\}$ in place of value added $\{p_V^i V_i\}$ and setting the value of input equal to the sum of the values of capital and labor inputs, Kendrick has omitted on average more than half of the value of sectoral inputs.

The same problem arises in Kendrick's analysis of aggregates over individual industries. For these aggregates Kendrick (1973, p. 22) employs data from the Bureau of Economic Analysis on gross product originating. For approximately fifty per cent of the business economy the data are based on output rather than value added, so that Kendrick's measures of productivity for aggregates over individual industries ignore the growth of intermediate input for half of the industries. The condition required for validity of his measures of productivity growth for aggregates is precisely the same as the condition I have given for individual industries: Rates of growth of output and intermediate inputs must be identical for all sectors.

I can test Kendrick's assumption directly, using the output and intermediate input data presented in tables 1.2 and 1.3. Table 1.7 presents the average annual rates of growth of output and intermediate input in each of thirty-five sectors over the 1947–1969 period, the period analyzed by Kendrick (1973). The ratio of the average annual rate of growth of intermediate input to the corresponding growth rate of output is reported for each sector in the last column of table 1.7. Ratios greater than unity in table 1.7 suggest that Kendrick's measures of productivity growth are upward biased, while ratios less than unity imply downward biased measures. The data in table 1.7 illustrate that Kendrick's assumption is inappropriate and, more importantly, a significant source of bias. Even if one chooses to restrict the sectoral

**Table 1.7**
Sectoral intermediate input and output: rates of growth, 1947–1969

| Industry | Average annual rates of growth | | Ratio of growth of intermediate input to growth of output |
|---|---|---|---|
| | Intermediate input | Output | |
| Agriculture, forestry & fisheries | .0174 | .0173 | 1.0023 |
| Metal mining | .0419 | .0153 | 2.7407 |
| Coal mining | -.0113 | -.0081 | 1.3881 |
| Crude petroleum & natural gas | .0453 | .0381 | 1.1885 |
| Nonmetallic mineral mining | .0515 | .0478 | 1.0775 |
| Construction | .0383 | .0422 | 0.9084 |
| Food & kindred products | .0214 | .0253 | 0.8482 |
| Tobacco manufactures | .0042 | .0075 | 0.5567 |
| Textile mill products | .0266 | .0293 | 0.9060 |
| Apparel & other textile products | .0296 | .0336 | 0.8818 |
| Lumber & wood products | .0242 | .0191 | 1.2706 |
| Furniture & fixtures | .0320 | .0342 | 0.9350 |
| Paper & allied products | .0401 | .0417 | 0.9627 |
| Printing & publishing | .0386 | .0330 | 1.1691 |
| Chemicals & allied products | .0461 | .0625 | 0.7382 |
| Petroleum refining | .0314 | .0406 | 0.7722 |
| Rubber & plastic products | .0538 | .0549 | 0.9804 |
| Leather & leather products | -.0081 | .0000 | 0.0000 |
| Stone, clay & glass products | .0453 | .0390 | 1.1598 |
| Primary metals | .0305 | .0218 | 1.3937 |

**Table 1.7 (continued)**

| Industry | Average annual rates of growth | | Ratio of growth of intermediate input to growth of output |
|---|---|---|---|
| | Intermediate input | Output | |
| Fabricated metal products | .0332 | .0337 | 0.9866 |
| Machinery, except electrical | .0418 | .0359 | 1.1647 |
| Electrical machinery | .0512 | .0620 | 0.8254 |
| Motor vehicles | .0398 | .0434 | 0.9165 |
| Other transportation equipment | .0837 | .0765 | 1.0931 |
| Instruments | .0398 | .0506 | 0.7864 |
| Miscellaneous manufacturing | .0338 | .0371 | 0.9112 |
| Transportation & warehousing | .0326 | .0251 | 1.2998 |
| Communication | .0560 | .0701 | 0.7984 |
| Electric utilities | .0465 | .0647 | 0.7194 |
| Gas utilities | .0964 | .0787 | 1.2245 |
| Trade | .0361 | .0368 | 0.9794 |
| Finance, insurance & real estate | .0553 | .0471 | 1.1751 |
| Other services | .0527 | .0386 | 1.3663 |
| Government enterprises | .0573 | .0344 | 1.6663 |

model of production by postulating the existence of a value-added aggregate, the growth rate of the quantity of value added cannot be measured by the growth rate of output alone.[31]

I have emphasized that Kendrick defines growth in sectoral output due to shifts in the demographic composition of the labor force and shifts in the composition of the capital stock by class of asset or legal form of organization as part of productivity change. However, Kendrick treats growth in sectoral output due to shifts in the composition of input between capital and labor inputs as growth in input rather than productivity change. To eliminate these shifts he weights capital and labor inputs by their marginal products, following the methodology originated by Tinbergen (1942).

It is inconsistent to weight capital and labor inputs by their marginal products without weighting the components of each input by the appropriate marginal products. The theory of production includes both the production function and the necessary conditions for producer equilibrium. These conditions involve the marginal products of capital and labor inputs. They also involve the marginal products of the components of each input. The inconsistency between Kendrick's aggregation of capital and labor inputs and his aggregation within each of these inputs gives rise to substantial biases.

To eliminate biases due to the effects of shifts in the composition of input among intermediate, capital, and labor inputs, these inputs must be weighted by their marginal products, as outlined in section 1.4.2, above. Finally, the components of intermediate input, like the components of capital and labor inputs, must be weighted by the corresponding marginal products. Intermediate inputs account for more than half of the value of inputs at the sectoral level. Omission of intermediate input is a very significant source of bias in Kendrick's measures of productivity growth, as demonstrated by the evidence presented in table 1.7.

In order to assess the biases that arise from using unweighted measures of intermediate, capital, and labor inputs, I have compiled measures of each input with appropriate weights for all components in table 1.2. In table 1.3 I have compiled the corresponding unweighted measures together with ratios between the weighted and unweighted measures that I identify as indicators of input quality. Measures of input quality should be equal to unity for all sectors in all time periods in order to validate Kendrick's definition of productivity change. The data presented in table 1.3 show that Kendrick's definition is inappropriate and the source of very substantial bias in the measurement of productivity.

In section 1.1.2 I have pointed out that intermediate input is the most important source of growth in output at the sectoral level. In effect, Kendrick has set aside the task of measuring this source of sectoral growth by introducing the assumption that intermediate input and output grow at the same rate. This assumption is contradicted by the evidence presented in table 1.7. Similarly, Kendrick has assumed that capital and labor inputs do not change in quality at the sectoral level, setting aside the task of disaggregating these inputs by marginal productivity. This assumption is contradicted by the evidence presented in table 1.3. In this table capital input is disaggregated by an average of as many as 156 individual components in each sector, while labor input is disaggregated by 160 individual components in each sector.

The data on intermediate input, output, and productivity presented in tables 1.2 and 1.3 incorporate changes in the quality of intermediate, capital, and labor inputs. The data on capital and labor inputs in table 1.1 incorporate these changes for the U.S. economy as a whole. Gollop and Jorgenson (1980) provide a detailed comparison between productivity indexes of this type and those of Kendrick for the period 1947–1973. Kendrick's indexes greatly exaggerate the role of productivity change as a source of growth at the sectoral level. Quality change is an important component of the growth of capital and labor inputs at both sectoral and aggregate levels. This component accounts for a substantial portion of the differences between Kendrick's estimates of productivity change and the translog indexes of productivity change given in tables 1.2 and 1.3. However, a sizable portion of these differences can be attributed to Kendrick's omission of intermediate input as a source of growth at the sectoral level.

## 1.5   Measuring Aggregate Output and Productivity

Following Solow (1957) and Tinbergen (1942), our aggregate model of production is based on a production function, say $F$, characterized by constant returns to scale

$$V = F(K, L, T),$$

where $T$ is time, $V$ is value added, $K$ and $L$ are capital and labor inputs. I can define the shares of capital and labor inputs, say $v_K$ and $v_L$, in value added by

$$v_K = \frac{p_K K}{p_V V},$$

$$v_L = \frac{p_L L}{p_V V},$$

where $p_V$, $p_K$, and $p_L$ denote the prices of value added, capital input, and labor input, respectively.

Necessary conditions for producer equilibrium are given by equalities between the value shares of each input and the elasticity of output with respect to that input

$$v_K = \frac{\partial \ln V}{\partial \ln K}(K, L, T),$$

$$v_L = \frac{\partial \ln V}{\partial \ln L}(K, L, T).$$

Under constant returns to scale, value added is equal to the value of capital and labor inputs. Finally, I can define the rate of productivity growth for the economy as a whole, say $v_T$, as the growth rate of value added with respect to time, holding capital input and labor input constant

$$v_T = \frac{\partial \ln V}{\partial T}(K, L, T).$$

The aggregate production function is defined in terms of value added, capital input, and labor input. The quantities of capital and labor inputs are functions of the quantities of their components

$$K = K(K_1, K_2 \cdots K_p),$$

$$L = L(L_1, L_2 \cdots L_q).$$

I can define the shares of the components of capital and labor inputs, say $\{v_{Kk}\}$ and $\{v_{Ll}\}$, in the value of the corresponding aggregate by

$$v_{Kk} = \frac{p_{Kk} K_k}{\sum p_{Kk} K_k}, \qquad (k = 1, 2, \ldots, p),$$

$$v_{Ll} = \frac{p_{Ll} L_l}{\sum p_{Ll} L_l}, \qquad (l = 1, 2, \ldots, q).$$

Necessary conditions for producer equilibrium are given by equalities between the value share of each component and the elasticity of the aggregate with respect to that component

$$v_{Kk} = \frac{\partial \ln K}{\partial \ln K_k} (K_1, K_2, \ldots, K_p), \qquad (k = 1, 2, \ldots, p),$$

$$v_{Ll} = \frac{\partial \ln L}{\partial \ln L_l} (L_1, L_2, \ldots, L_q), \qquad (l = 1, 2, \ldots, q).$$

Under constant returns to scale the value of each input is equal to the value of its components.

### 1.5.1   Aggregation over Sectors

We can also formulate a model of production for the economy as a whole by aggregating over models of production for individual industrial sectors. The purpose of such a model is to integrate the analysis of sources of economic growth for individual industrial sectors presented in tables 1.2 and 1.3 with the analysis for the economy as a whole presented in table 1.1. For this purpose I adopt the restrictive assumption that a value-added function like that defined in section 1.4 above exists for all sectors. It is important to emphasize that this assumption is not used in constructing the data presented for individual industries in tables 1.2 and 1.3. However, this assumption is implicit in the analysis of sources of economic growth for the economy as a whole presented in table 1.1 and all studies at the aggregate level, beginning with Tinbergen (1942).

We can combine sectoral value-added functions for all industrial sectors with market equilibrium conditions for each factor of production to obtain an aggregate model of production. Using this model of production, I allocate the growth of output among contributions of primary factor inputs and the rate of productivity growth in table 1.1. By combining sectoral and aggregate production models I can express the rate of aggregate productivity growth in terms of the rates of sectoral productivity growth and reallocations of value added, capital input, and labor input among sectors.

Aggregate value added $V$ is the sum of quantities of value added $\{V_i\}$ in all industrial sectors. The aggregate model of production includes market equilibrium conditions that take the form of equalities between the supplies of each type of labor $\{L_l\}$ and the sums of demands for that type of labor by all sectors. Similarly, market equilibrium implies equalities between the supplies of each type of capital $\{K_k\}$ and the sums of demands for that type of capital by all sectors.[32] It is possible to distinguish among capital and labor inputs that differ in marginal productivity at the aggregate level as well as at the sectoral level. Deliveries to intermediate demand by all sectors are precisely offset by receipts of intermediate inputs, so that transactions in intermediate goods do not appear at the aggregate level.

The existence of an aggregate production function imposes very stringent requirements on the underlying sectoral models of production.[33] All sectoral value-added functions must be identical to the aggregate production function.[34] In addition, the functions giving capital and labor inputs for each sector in terms of their components must be identical to the corresponding functions at the aggregate level. In essence, the value-added function and the capital and labor input functions for each sector must be replicas of the aggregate functions. The reallocations of value added, capital input, and labor input among sectors presented in table 1.1 provide measures of departures from these assumptions.

Reallocations of value added incorporate differences in value-added functions among industries as well as departures from the separability assumptions required for the existence of a value-added function for each industrial sector. Similarly, reallocations of capital and labor inputs incorporate differences in these aggregates among sectors as well as departures from the separability assumptions required for the existence of the aggregates. If value added and all components of capital and labor inputs were to grow at the same rate for all industries, there would be no reallocations.

The methodology I have outlined for the economy as a whole can be implemented by considering specific forms for the aggregate production function and for capital and labor inputs as functions of their components. I take these functions to be translog in form, so that I can generate a translog index of the rate of productivity growth. The average rate of productivity growth is the difference between the growth rate of value added and a weighted average of growth rates of capital and labor inputs. Similarly, I can generate translog indexes of capital and labor inputs, giving the growth rate of each input as a weighted average of growth rates of its components.

The measures of aggregate output, input, and productivity presented in table 1.1 are derived by explicit aggregation over the industrial sectors listed in tables 1.2 and 1.3. The measure of aggregate productivity growth depends on sectoral productivity growth rates and on terms that reflect reallocations of value added, capital input, and labor input among sectors.[35] Sectoral productivity growth rates are weighted by ratios of the value of output in the corresponding sector to the sum of value added in all sectors.[36] This formula was originally proposed by Domar (1961) for a model with two producing sectors. Each sector is characterized by a Cobb-Douglas production function with output as a function of intermediate input from the other sector, capital input, labor input, and time as an indicator of the level of technology. A closely related approach to aggregate productivity measurement uses sectoral productivity growth rates based on value added rather than output.[37]

Domar's (1961) approach to aggregation over sectors has been extended by Hulten (1978) and Jorgenson (1980) to an arbitrary number of producing sectors without using the assumption that the sectoral production functions are linear logarithmic. Both Domar and Hulten assume that prices of intermediate inputs are the same for producing and receiving sectors and prices of capital and labor inputs are the same for all sectors. Jorgenson allows for differences in prices received and paid among sectors. Under the assumptions of Domar and Hulten the rate of productivity growth for the economy as a whole does not depend on the reallocations of value added, capital input, and labor input among sectors presented in the second panel of table 1.1.[38]

### 1.5.2 Data Sources and Methods for Aggregate Output and Productivity

The starting point for the measurement of aggregate productivity is a production account for the U.S. economy in current prices. The fundamental identity for the production account is that the value of output is equal to the value of input. The value of output and input is defined from the point of view of the producer. Revenue is measured as proceeds to the producing sector of the economy and outlay as expenditures of the sector. The role of an aggregate production account in a complete accounting system for the U.S. economy is discussed by Christensen and Jorgenson (1969, 1970, 1973a, b) and Jorgenson (1980).[39]

The value of output for the U.S. economy as a whole is equal to the value of deliveries to final demand—personal consumption expenditures, gross private domestic investment, government purchases, and net exports—excluding indirect business taxes on output, excise and sales taxes, and including subsidies paid to producers. The value of input includes the value of primary factors of production—capital and labor inputs—including indirect business taxes on input, property taxes, and other taxes on property compensation.

The definition of aggregate output outlined above is intermediate between output at market prices and output at factor cost, as these terms are conventionally defined. The production account for the U.S. economy as a whole includes value added in the thirty-seven sectors listed in table 1.2. These sectors include thirty-five industrial sectors, government, except for government enterprises, and private households and institutions.

As an accounting identity, the value of output is equal to the value of input from the point of view of the producing sector. The value of input includes income originating in business, households and institutions, and government, as defined in the U.S. national income and product accounts. The value of input also includes capital consumption allowances, business transfer payments, the statistical discrepancy, and certain indirect business taxes on property and property compensation. Finally, the value of input includes the imputed value of services of consumers' durables and durables held by institutions and net rent on institutional real estate.

The quantity of value added for each sector is derived by combining price and quantity data on output and intermediate input into price and quantity indexes of value added. To construct an index of value added for each industrial sector, I express sectoral output, say $\{Z_i\}$, as a translog function of sectoral intermediate input $\{X_i\}$ and sectoral value added $\{V_i\}$. The corresponding index of sectoral value added can be written in implicit form

$$\ln Z_i(T) - \ln Z_i(T-1)$$
$$= \overline{v}_X^i [\ln X_i(T) - \ln X_i(T-1)] + \overline{v}_V^i [\ln V_i(T) - \ln V_i(T-1)] \,,$$
$$(i = 1, 2, \ldots, n) \,,$$

where the weights are given by the average value shares

$$\overline{v}_X^i = \frac{1}{2} [v_X^i(T) + v_X^i(T-1)]$$

$$\bar{v}_V^i = \frac{1}{2} [v_V^i(T) + v_V^i(T-1)], \qquad (i = 1, 2, \ldots, n).$$

and

$$v_X^i = \frac{p_X^i X_i}{q_i Z_i},$$

$$v_V^i = \frac{p_V^i V_i}{q_i X_i}, \qquad (i = 1, 2, \ldots, n).$$

The growth rate of value added can be expressed in terms of growth rates of intermediate input and output and the average value shares

$$\ln V_i(T) - \ln V_i(T-1)$$

$$= \frac{1}{\bar{v}_V^i} [\ln Z_i(T) - \ln Z_i(T-1)] - \frac{\bar{v}_X^i}{\bar{v}_V^i} [\ln X_i(T) - \ln X_i(T-1)],$$

$$(i = 1, 2, \ldots, n).$$

The quantity of aggregate value added is the sum of quantities of value added in all industries. Finally, the price of aggregate value added is the ratio of value added to the quantity of value added for the economy as a whole.[40]

In section 1.2 I have described data on annual hours worked and labor compensation per hour, cross-classified by sex, age, education, and employment class of workers. The aggregate model of production includes equilibrium conditions between the supply of each type of labor and the sum of demands for that type of labor by all sectors. The value of each of the 160 labor inputs for the economy as a whole is equal to the sum of the values over all sectors. Labor compensation for the economy as a whole is controlled to labor compensation from the U.S. national income accounts.

Aggregate data on prices and quantities of labor input, cross-classified by sex, age, education, and employment class, but not by industry, underlie the indexes of labor input presented in table 1.1. For the economy as a whole, hours worked and labor compensation for each of 160 categories of the work force are added over all industries. Labor compensation is divided by annual hours worked to derive labor compensation per hour worked for each category. Finally, price and quantity data are combined into price and quantity indexes of aggregate labor input.

To construct an index of labor input for the economy as a whole, I express aggregate labor input $L$ as a translog function of its 160 individual components $\{L_l\}$. The corresponding index of labor input takes the form

$$\ln L(T) - \ln L(T-1) = \sum \bar{v}_{Ll}[\ln L_l(T) - \ln L_l(T-1)] \, ,$$

where weights are given by the average shares of the individual components in the value of labor compensation

$$\bar{v}_{Ll} = \frac{1}{2}[v_{Ll}(T) + v_{Ll}(T-1)] \, , \qquad (l = 1, 2, \ldots, q) \, ,$$

$$v_{Ll} = \frac{p_{Ll}L_l}{\sum p_{Ll}L_l} \, , \qquad (l = 1, 2, \ldots, q) \, .$$

The value shares are computed from data on hours worked $\{L_l\}$ and compensation per hour $\{p_{Ll}\}$ for all components of labor input, cross-classified by sex, age, education, and employment class of workers. A measure of total hours worked for the economy as a whole can be obtained by adding hours worked across all categories of labor input. The quality of aggregate hours worked is defined, as before, as the ratio of labor input to hours worked. Indexes of the quantity of labor input and labor quality are presented for the economy as a whole in table 1.1.

In section 1.3 I have described data on capital stocks and rental prices, cross-classified by asset class and legal form of organization. The aggregate model of production includes market equilibrium conditions between the supply of each type of capital and the sum of demands for that type of capital by all sectors. The value of each of the capital inputs for the economy as a whole is equal to the sum of values over all sectors. Consistent with the treatment of labor compensation, property compensation for the economy as a whole is controlled to property compensation from the U.S. national income accounts.

Aggregate data on prices and quantities of capital input, cross-classified by asset class and legal form of organization, but not by industry, underlie the indexes of capital input presented in table 1.1. For the economy as a whole capital stock and property compensation for each category are added over all industries. Property compensation is divided by capital stock to derive property compensation per unit of capital stock for each category. Finally, price and quantity data are combined into price and quantity indexes of aggregate capital input.

To construct an index of capital input for the economy as a whole, I express aggregate capital input K as a translog function of its individual components $\{K_k\}$. The corresponding index of capital input takes the form

$$\ln K(T) - \ln K(T-1) = \sum \bar{v}_{Kk} \left[ \ln K_k(T) - \ln K_k(T-1) \right] ,$$

where weights are given by the average shares of individual components in the value of property compensation

$$\bar{v}_{Kk} = \frac{1}{2} \left[ v_{Kk}(T) + v_{Kk}(T-1) \right] , \quad (k = 1, 2, \ldots, p) ,$$

and

$$v_{Kk} = \frac{p_{Kk} K_k}{\sum p_{Kk} K_k} , \quad (k = 1, 2, \ldots, p) .$$

The value shares are computed from data on capital stocks $\{K_k\}$ and rental prices $\{p_{Kk}\}$ for all components of capital input, cross-classified by asset class and legal form of organization. A measure of capital stock for the economy as a whole can be obtained by adding capital stock across all categories of capital input. The quality of aggregate capital stock is defined, as before, as the ratio of capital input to capital stock. Indexes of the quantity of capital input and capital quality are presented for the economy as a whole in table 1.1.

### 1.5.3    Alternative Sources and Methods

To provide additional perspective on U.S. economic growth it is useful to compare the sources and methods that underly the analysis given in table 1.1 with those of other studies.[41] For the U.S. economy as a whole Christensen and Jorgenson (1969, 1970, 1973a, b) have presented an analysis of sources of U.S. economic growth similar to that presented in the first panel of table 1.1. Their study covers the period 1929–1969 for the private sector of the U.S. economy.

Christensen, Cummings, and Jorgenson (1978, 1980) have extended the estimates of Christensen and Jorgenson through 1973. Aggregate value added is defined from the producers' point of view, including the value of sales and excise taxes and including the value of subsidies; however, the quantity of value added is measured as an index of deliveries to final demand rather than the sum of quantities of value added over industrial sectors. The quantity of labor input is divided among categories of the labor force broken down by educational attainment, but not by sex, age, employment class, or occupation.

The empirical results of Christensen, Cummings, and Jorgenson (1980) for the period 1947–1973 are very similar to those given in table 1.1. For this period their estimate of the average growth rate of value added for the private domestic sector of the U.S. economy is 4.00 percent per year; by comparison the estimate of the rate of growth for the U.S. economy given in table 1.1 is 3.79 percent per year. The two estimates are not precisely comparable since Christensen, Cummings, and Jorgenson do not include government sectors in their measure of aggregate output.

Christensen, Cummings, and Jorgenson estimate the average growth rate of capital input at 4.26 percent per year for the period 1947–1973; the estimate for this period given in table 1.1 is 4.16 percent per year. These estimates are closely comparable, except that the estimates in table 1.1 include capital input for government enterprises. Christensen, Cummings, and Jorgenson estimate the average growth rate of labor input at 1.62 percent per year, while the estimate presented in table 1.1 is 1.80 percent per year. Finally their estimate of the rate of productivity growth is 1.34 percent per year, while the estimate given in table 1.1 is 1.11 percent per year. Again, the two estimates for labor input and the rate of productivity growth are not precisely comparable since the estimates given in table 1.1 include labor input for the government sectors.

Christensen, Cummings, and Jorgenson (1980) have presented estimates of aggregate productivity growth for Canada, France, Germany, Italy, Japan, Korea, the Netherlands, and the United Kingdom as well as for the United States. Their estimates cover various periods beginning after 1947 and ending in 1973; the estimates cover the period 1960–1973 for all countries. Conrad and Jorgenson (1975) have developed data for Germany for the period 1950–1973, Ezaki and Jorgenson (1973) have presented estimates for Japan for the period 1951–1968 and Jorgenson and Nishimizu (1978) have given estimates for Japan for the period 1952–1974. Christensen and Cummings (1981) have provided estimates for Korea for the period 1960–1973.

Elias (1978) has developed data on a basis that is comparable with Christensen, Cummings, and Jorgenson (1980) for Argentina, Brazil,

Chile, Columbia, Mexico, Peru, and Venezuela for the period 1940–1974. Groes and Bjerregaard (1978) have developed comparable estimates for Denmark for the period 1950–1972. On the basis of the close correspondence between the results for the U.S. economy as a whole given in table 1.1 and those of Christensen, Cummings, and Jorgenson, I conclude that it is appropriate to compare the aggregate results in the first panel of table 1.1 with those for the countries presented in their study and the other studies I have listed.[42]

BLS (1983) has employed private business product as a measure of value added in the U.S. economy as a whole. This measure is obtained from the gross national product by excluding output originating in general government, government enterprises, owner-occupied housing, rest-of-the-world, households and institutions, and the statistical discrepancy. The resulting measure of value added is gross of depreciation. This has the important advantage of avoiding the confounding of measures of output and capital input that I have analyzed in section 1.4.1, above. I have summarized the differences between our methodology for measuring labor and capital inputs and that of BLS in sections 1.2.3 and 1.3.3.

Denison (1985) employs an approach to production based on value added at the economy-wide level. He uses national income as a measure of value added. This measure excludes capital consumption allowances and indirect business taxes. His measure of capital input is based on the net earnings of capital, also excluding business taxes. The prices and quantities of inputs and outputs employed in Denison's measure of productivity satisfy the accounting identity between the value of output and the value of input. However, the corresponding model of aggregate production involves net value added, so that output and inputs are confounded by including capital input in both categories, as I pointed out in section 1.4.1. I conclude that the quantity of net value added employed by Denison is not an appropriate starting point for modeling producer behavior at the aggregate level.[43]

The problem with net value added as a measure of output for the economy as a whole can be traced to the definition of capital consumption allowances introduced by Denison (1957, pp. 238–255). This concept of depreciation is defined by Young and Musgrave (1980, p. 32), as follows: "Depreciation is the cost of the asset allocated over its service life in proportion to its estimated service at each date." Denison (1972, pp. 104–105) refers to this method of allocation as the "capital input method." Within the framework for measuring capital input

presented in section 1.3.1, above, Denison's concept of capital consumption allowances is based on allocating the cost of an asset over its
lifetime in proportion to the relative efficiencies $\{d(\tau)\}$ of capital goods
of different ages rather than in proportion to depreciation $p_D(T)$.

Young and Musgrave (1980, pp. 33–37) contrast the Denison definition with the "discounted value definition" of depreciation $p_D(T)$
employed in the model of capital as a factor of production presented
in section 1.3.1. Among the advantages for the "capital input method"
claimed by Denison (1957, p. 240) and Young and Musgrave (1980, p.
33) is that this definition avoids discounting of future capital services.
In fact, discounting can be avoided in the measurement of depreciation if and only if the decline in the efficiency of capital goods is geometric. In this case the relative efficiencies $\{d(\tau)\}$ decline with the age
of an asset at a constant rate. Capital service prices $p_K(T)$ and investment goods prices $p_I(T)$ decline with age at the same rate and depreciation $p_D(T)$ is proportional to the price of an investment good.

As I have pointed out in section 1.3.3, above, Denison's assumptions about the relative efficiencies of capital goods of different ages
require discounting of future capital services to obtain an appropriate
measure of depreciation. Denison's attempt to avoid discounting
leads him to confuse the relative efficiencies $\{d(\tau)\}$ with decline in the
value of an asset as a basis for measure depreciation $p_D(T)$. This
leads, in turn, to an inconsistency between the assumptions about relative efficiencies utilized in measuring capital input $A(T-1)$ and the
assumptions employed in measuring the rental price of capital input
$p_K(T)$. This chain of inconsistencies and contradictions can be broken
only by replacing the "capital input method" of measuring depreciation introduced by Denison (1957) with the "discounted value definition" presented in section 1.3.3. The "discounted value definition" is
employed, for example, by Christensen, Cummings and Jorgenson
(1980) and BLS (1983).

Denison's (1974, p. 9) "capital input method" of depreciation leads
him to draw an analogy between the consumption of intermediate
goods and capital consumption allowances. Since the consumption of
intermediate goods is eliminated in the course of aggregating over
sectors, but capital consumption allowances are not eliminated by
aggregation, this analogy is inappropriate and misleading. The price
and quantity of capital input are index numbers obtained by weighting each component of capital input by its rental price. Rental prices
depend on differences in depreciation among assets and differences in

the tax treatment of the resulting property compensation. By suppressing these differences Denison greatly underestimates the contribution of capital input to economic growth. A comparison of the capital input measures of Denison (1967) with those of Christensen and Jorgenson (1969, 1970, 1973a, b) is given by Jorgenson and Griliches (1972a). Jorgenson (1989) provides a detailed discussion of Denison's treatment of capital consumption allowances.

Maddison (1987) has recently constructed aggregate growth accounts for the period 1870–1984 for France, Germany, Japan, the Netherlands, the United Kingdom, and the United States. He has divided this period into the subperiod 1870–1913, almost the same as that considered by Tinbergen (1942), and the subperiods 1913–1950, 1950–1973, and 1973–1984. For the period 1913–1984 Maddison gives an analysis of the sources of growth in gross domestic product for all six countries, including hours worked, changes in labor quality, capital stock, and changes in capital quality. His analysis of the sources of growth for the period 1870–1913 includes only hours worked and capital stock, omitting changes in input quality.

Maddison draws on the work of Carré, Dubois, and Malinvaud (1975) for France. This study covers 1913 and the period 1949–1966 on an annual basis and presents an analysis of sources of growth of gross domestic product that includes hours worked, quality of labor input, and capital stock. Maddison utilizes results from the study of Ohkawa and Rosovsky (1973) for Japan, which covers the period 1908–1964 and analyzes the growth of gross domestic product. This analysis incorporates employment, quality of labor input, and capital stock. For the United Kingdom, Maddison employs the work of Matthews, Feinstein, and Odling-Smee (1982). This study covers the period 1856–1973 and gives an analysis of the sources of growth of gross domestic product, including hours worked, quality of labor input, and capital stock. For the United States Maddison utilizes the work of Kendrick (1961a, 1973).

Although Maddison considers the measurement of the quality of capital input by introducing rental prices for individual capital inputs, he rejects this approach and assumes that the rate of growth of capital quality is 1.5 percent per year for the period 1913–1984 for all six countries included in his study. This assumption is not based on empirical data, but Maddison modifies the assumption for the subperiods 1950–1973 and 1973–1984 by an adjustment for changes in the average age of capital goods that incorporates investment data. A more satisfactory approach to the long-term analysis of sources of U.S. economic growth has been presented by Abramovitz and David (1973a, b) for the period 1800–1967. This analysis incorporates the results of Christensen and Jorgenson (1970) for the period 1929–1967 and includes hours worked, quality of labor input, capital stock, and quality of capital input. For the period 1800–1927 the analysis is limited to hours worked and capital stock as sources of growth.

For the U.S. economy as a whole Kendrick (1961a, 1973), Kendrick and Sato (1963), Kendrick and Grossman (1980), and Kendrick (1983a) have employed an approach to the measurement of value added through summation over the growth rates of quantities of value added in all sectors with weights that change periodically. The corresponding estimates of the growth rates of capital and labor inputs are constructed by summing the corresponding quantities over all sectors with weights that depend on property and labor compensation by sector.[44]

Kendrick employs unweighted sums of capital stock and hours worked as measures of capital and labor inputs at the sectoral level. At the aggregate level he employs unweighted sums as a variant of his principal estimates. The differences between the weighted and unweighted measures of capital and labor inputs at the aggregate level are associated with differences in the prices of capital and labor inputs among industries. Since Kendrick's measures of capital and labor inputs at the sectoral level do not incorporate changes in the quality of these inputs, a substantial portion of the differences between his weighted and unweighted measures at the aggregate level is due to unmeasured differences in input quality at the sectoral level.

The measures of value added, capital input, and labor input presented in the first panel of table 1.1 are constructed from unweighted sums of value added, individual components of capital input, and individual components of labor input over all industries. An alternative measure of aggregate value added can be constructed by weighting value added in each industry by the price of value added in that industry. Similarly, alternative measures of aggregate capital and labor inputs can be constructed by weighting individual components of these inputs in each industry by the prices of these components in that industry.

Differences between growth rates of measures of output and input that reflect differences in prices of output and inputs among industries and measures that do not reflect these differences are presented in the second panel of table 1.1. These differences are the measures of reallocations of value added, capital input, and labor input among sectors. The rate of aggregate productivity growth can be represented as a weighted sum of sectoral productivity growth rates and the contributions of the reallocations. If the prices of value added, capital input, and labor input were the same for all industries, the contributions of reallocations to aggregate productivity growth would vanish.

I conclude that capital and labor inputs can be usefully classified by industry in decomposing the rate of aggregate productivity growth between reallocations of value added, capital input, and labor input among sectors and rates of productivity growth at the sectoral level.[45] For this decomposition measures of output and inputs with and without industry as a classification are required. It is important to note that this argument cannot be extended to other characteristics of labor input such as sex, age, education, and employment status. If there are differences in rates of remuneration of individual components of labor input differing in these characteristics, labor input must be broken down by characteristics at both aggregate and sectoral levels. Similarly, capital input must be broken down by type of asset and legal form of organization at both levels.

I have focused attention on the integration of sectoral measures of output, input, and productivity growth with the corresponding aggregate measures. To avoid including capital input in the measure of aggregate output and the aggregate inputs, as implied by Denison's (1962a, b, 1967, 1974, 1979, 1985) measure of output, I present data in table 1.1 that utilize gross value added at the aggregate level. BLS (1983), Christensen, Cummings, and Jorgenson (1980), Kendrick (1984), and the studies utilized by Maddison (1987) also employ gross value added.[46] However, output in these studies is derived from aggregate production data rather than explicit aggregation over industrial sectors. The resulting measures of aggregate productivity growth are not integrated with corresponding sectoral measures, as in the second panel of table 1.1.

The existence of an aggregate production function implies that all sectoral value-added functions are identical. If all sectors pay the same prices for primary factor inputs, the reallocations of value added, capital input, and labor input among sectors have no effect on aggregate output. The contributions of these reallocations can be regarded as measures of departures from the assumptions that underly the aggregate model of production. The data presented in table 1.1 make it possible to assess the significance of these departures. Over the period 1947–1985 the reallocations are very small relative to the growth of capital and labor inputs and productivity growth. Over shorter periods, such as 1953–1957 and 1973–1979, these reallocations are large relative to aggregate productivity growth.[47]

The assumptions required to validate an aggregate model of production are obviously highly restrictive. The evidence presented in table 1.1 suggests that these assumptions are not seriously misleading over a time span as long as the period 1947–1985 that I have considered. Similar evidence for other time periods is lacking. However, it seems plausible that an aggregate production model is an appropriate point of departure for studies of long-term growth like those of Abramovitz and David (1973a, b) for the period 1800–1967, Christensen and Jorgenson (1973a) for the period 1929–1969, Maddison for the period 1913–1984, and Tinbergen (1942) for the period 1870–1914. For shorter periods an aggregate production model can be seriously misleading.

## 1.6   Econometric Modeling of Production

A key innovation in the methodology that underlies the indexes presented in tables 1.2 and 1.3 is the symmetric treatment of intermediate, capital, and labor inputs. Output can be represented as a function of all three inputs and time. Substitution possibilities among intermediate inputs and primary factor inputs can be incorporated explicitly. I have contrasted this approach with a more restrictive model based on the existence of a value-added aggregate within each sector. In this alternative approach output is represented as a function of intermediate input and the quantity of value added. Value added in turn is represented as a function of capital and labor inputs and time.

In section 1.5.1 above, I have pointed out that the existence of an aggregate production function requires the existence of sectoral value-added functions. Furthermore, these value-added functions must be identical for all sectors. These highly restrictive assumptions are appropriate for studies of long-term growth, but can be seriously misleading for shorter periods. To explain important changes in rates of economic growth, such as the recent growth slowdown in industrialized countries, a disaggregated approach is required. It is important to emphasize that a disaggregated approach, based on models of production for individual industrial sectors, is far more costly than aggregate production modeling. However, such an approach is essential in overcoming the limitations of aggregate models of production.

An econometric model based on the symmetric treatment of intermediate, capital, and labor inputs makes it possible to dispense with the value-added approach employed by Kendrick and tested in table 1.7, above. The rate of sectoral productivity growth can be expressed as functions of the prices of all inputs and the level of technology. Models of production for all industrial sectors can be combined to form a general equilibrium model of production. Symmetric treatment of intermediate, capital, and labor inputs makes it possible to integrate the analysis of sources of economic growth with general equilibrium modeling.

### 1.6.1    Sectoral Production Modeling

General equilibrium modeling of production originated with the seminal work of Leontief (1951), beginning with the implementation of the static input-output model. Leontief (1953a) gave a further impetus to the development of general equilibrium modeling by introducing a dynamic input-output model. Empirical work associated with input-output analysis is based on estimating the unknown parameters of an interindustry model from a single interindustry transactions table. These estimates are based on a "fixed coefficients" assumption in modeling demands for all inputs. Under this assumption all inputs are proportional to output.

The first successful implementation of a general equilibrium model without the fixed coefficients assumptions of input-output analysis is due to Johansen (1976). Johansen retained the fixed coefficients assumption in modeling demands for intermediate goods. This form of the fixed coefficients assumption is tested in table 1.7 above. Johansen employed linear logarithmic or Cobb-Douglas production functions in modeling productivity growth and the substitution between capital and labor inputs within a value-added aggregate. Linear logarithmic production functions imply that relative shares of inputs in the value of output are fixed, so that the unknown parameters characterizing substitution between capital and labor inputs can be estimated from a single data point.

In modeling producer behavior Johansen employed econometric methods only in estimating constant rates of productivity growth.

The essential features of Johansen's approach have been preserved in the general equilibrium models surveyed by Bergman (1990), Robinson (1989) and Shoven and Whalley (1984). The unknown parameters describing technology in these models are determined by "calibration" to a single data point. Data from a single interindustry transactions table are supplemented by a small number of parameters estimated econometrically. The obvious disadvantage of this approach is that arbitrary constraints on patterns of substitution are required in order to make calibration possible.

An alternative approach to modeling producer behavior for general equilibrium models is through complete systems of demand functions for inputs in each industrial sector. Each system gives quantities demanded as functions of prices of inputs and output. This approach to the modeling of producer behavior was originated by Berndt and Jorgenson (1973).[48] As in the descriptions of technology by Leontief and Johansen, production is characterized by constant returns to scale in each sector. Output is represented as a function of capital, labor, energy, and materials inputs and time as an indicator of the level of technology.[49]

Under constant returns to scale commodity prices can be expressed as functions of factor prices, utilizing the nonsubstitution theorem of Samuelson (1951). This greatly facilitates the solution of the econometric general equilibrium models constructed by Hudson and Jorgenson (1974) and Jorgenson and Wilcoxen (1990). The nonsubstitution theorem permits a substantial reduction in dimensionality of the space of prices to be determined by the model. The coefficients of the general equilibrium model can be determined endogenously, taking into account prices of primary factor inputs and levels of productivity.

The implementation of econometric models of producer behavior for general equilibrium analysis is very demanding in terms of data requirements. These models require the construction of a consistent time series of interindustry transactions tables. By comparison, the noneconometric approaches of Leontief and Johansen require only a single interindustry transactions table. Second, the implementation of systems of input demand functions requires econometric methods for the estimation of parameters in systems of nonlinear simultaneous equations.

Translog index numbers for intermediate, capital, and labor inputs and rates of productivity growth are employed in the analysis of sources of economic growth presented in tables 1.2 and 1.3. Translog production functions can be used in specifying econometric models for determining the distribution of the value of output among the productive inputs and the rate of productivity growth. In estimating the parameters of these models the quantity indexes of inputs, the corresponding price indexes, and indexes of productivity growth can be employed as data.

Jorgenson and Fraumeni (1981) and Jorgenson (1984b) have constructed econometric models of producer behavior based on the translog functional form for the thirty-five industrial sectors of the U.S. economy included in tables 1.2 and 1.3. Similar models for Japan have been constructed by Kuroda, Yoshioka, and Jorgenson (1984). Production models for all industrial sectors have been incorporated into an econometric general equilibrium model of the United States by Jorgenson and Wilcoxen (1990).[50] The econometric methodology for construction of sectoral models of production is discussed in detail by Jorgenson (1986a).

### 1.6.2    Aggregate Production Modeling

The traditional approach to modeling producer behavior at the aggregate level begins with the assumption that the production function is characterized by constant returns to scale. In addition, the production function is assumed to be additive in capital and labor inputs. Under these restrictions demand and supply functions can be derived explicitly from the production function and the necessary conditions for producer equilibrium. However, this approach has the disadvantage of imposing constraints on patterns of substitution—thereby frustrating the objective of determining these patterns empirically.

The traditional approach was originated by Cobb and Douglas (1928) and employed in empirical research by Douglas and his associates for almost two decades. These studies are summarized by Douglas (1948, 1967, 1976). The principal methodology employed in Douglas's research is based on the analysis of cross-section data for manufacturing industries, treating individual industries rather than plants or firms as observations. The measure of output employed in these studies is based on the value-added model outlined in section 1.4.1 above.

The use of individual industries as observations requires the assumption that the value-added functions for all industries are identical, which is precisely the assumption required for the existence of an aggregate production function. Tinbergen (1942) was the first to formulate the aggregate production function with time as an indicator of the level of technology. This is the form of the production function employed in the analysis of sources of economic growth at the aggregate level.[51]

The limitations of the traditional approach were made strikingly apparent by Arrow, Chenery, Minhas, and Solow (1961, henceforward ACMS), who pointed out that the Cobb-Douglas production function imposes *a priori* restrictions on patterns of substitution among inputs. In particular, elasticities of substitution among all inputs must be equal to unity. The constant elasticity of substitution (CES) production function introduced by ACMS adds flexibility to the traditional approach by treating the elasticity of substitution between capital and labor as an unknown parameter to be estimated by econometric methods. However, the CES production function retains the assumptions of additivity and homogeneity and imposes very stringent limitations on patterns of substitution. McFadden (1963) and Uzawa (1962) have shown, essentially, that elasticities of substitution among all inputs must be the same.[52]

The translog index numbers for capital and labor inputs and the rate of productivity growth for the economy as a whole are employed in the analysis of the sources of economic growth presented in table 1.1. The translog production function can also be used in specifying an econometric model for determining the rate of productivity growth and the distribution of value added between the primary factor inputs. The quantity indexes of inputs, the corresponding price indexes, and the index of productivity growth can be employed as data in estimating the parameters of this econometric model.[53]

The benefits of an aggregate production model must be weighed against the costs of departures from the highly restrictive assumptions that underly the existence of an aggregate production function. Where these assumptions are inappropriate, the econometric approach to general equilibrium analysis outlined above can be employed in analyzing patterns of production for the economy as a whole. This approach is based on sectoral models of production rather than an aggregate production model. Sectoral models are also useful in decomposing aggregate economic growth into sectoral components.[54]

The results presented in table 1.1 show that an aggregate production model is appropriate for studies of long-term U.S. economic growth. However, an aggregate model can be misleading for relatively short time periods, such as the individual business cycles 1953–1957 and 1973–1979. For the period 1947–1985 as a whole the rate of aggregate productivity growth is 0.71 percent per year, while the weighted sum of sectoral productivity growth rates of 0.88 percent per year. The difference between aggregate productivity growth and sectoral productivity growth provides a measure of departures from the stringent assumptions that underly the aggregate production model. This difference is not negligible, even for the period 1947–1985.

Considering the second panel of table 1.1, I can decompose the decline in the aggregate productivity growth rate into the sum of sectoral productivity growth rates and the reallocations of value added, capital input, and labor input. The decline in sectoral productivity growth between the period 1947–1985 and the subperiod 1973–1979 was 1.00 percent per year. This decline is almost sufficient to account for the slowdown in U.S. economic growth. The precipitous fall in sectoral productivity growth was augmented at the aggregate level by a fall in the reallocation of value added of 0.34 percent. I conclude that the assumptions that underly the aggregate model of production failed to hold during the period 1973–1979.

The decline in productivity growth at the level of individual industries can be identified as the main culprit in the slowdown of U.S. economic growth since 1973. To provide an explanation of this decline I must go behind the measurement of sectoral productivity growth rates to identify the determinants of productivity growth at the sectoral level. To illustrate the econometric approach to productivity growth I present a summary of the results of fitting an econometric model to detailed data on sectoral output and capital, labor, energy, and materials inputs for thirty-five industrial sectors of the U.S. economy.

Our econometric study is based on sectoral models of production for each of thirty-five individual industries. Although production functions contain all the available information about producer behavior for each sector, I find it useful to express the sectoral models of production in an alternative and equivalent form. Under constant returns to scale I can introduce price functions for each industry.[55] The price function gives the price of output as a function of the prices of capital, labor, energy, and materials inputs and time, representing the level of technology. Price functions summarize the information about producer behavior contained in the production functions in a more convenient form.

Given the price function for each industry, I can express the shares of each of the four inputs in the industry—capital, labor, energy, and materials inputs—in the value of output as functions of the prices of inputs and the level of technology. I can add to the four equations for the value shares an equation that completes the model. This equation gives the sectoral rate of productivity growth as a function of the prices of the inputs and the level of technology. The equation determining the productivity growth rate is our econometric model of sectoral productivity growth.

Like any econometric model, the relationships determining the value shares of capital, labor, energy, and materials inputs and the rate of productivity growth involve unknown parameters that must be estimated. Included among these parameters are biases of productivity growth. For example, the bias of productivity growth for capital input gives the change in the share of capital input in the value of output in response to changes in technology.[56] It is said that productivity growth is capital using if the bias for capital input is positive. Similarly, it is said that productivity growth is capital saving if the bias for capital input is negative. The sum of the biases for all four inputs must be precisely zero, since the changes in all four shares must sum to zero.

The biases of productivity growth appear as coefficients of time, representing the level of technology, in the four equations for the value shares of the four inputs. Our econometric model for each industrial sector of the U.S. economy also includes an equation that determines the rate of productivity growth. The biases appear with an opposite sign as coefficients of the prices in the equation for sectoral productivity growth. This feature of the econometric model makes it possible to use information about both changes in the value shares with the level of technology and changes in the rate of productivity growth with prices in estimating the biases of productivity growth.[57]

Capital-using productivity growth, associated with a positive bias of productivity growth for capital input, implies that an increase in the price of capital input diminishes the rate of productivity growth. Similarly, capital-saving productivity growth implies that productivity growth increases with the price of capital input. Ho and Jorgenson (1993) have fitted econometric models based on translog price functions to data for all thirty-five industrial sectors. Since our primary concern is with the determinants of sectoral productivity growth, I present a classification of industries by biases of productivity growth in table 1.8.

The pattern of productivity growth that occurs most frequently in table 1.8 is capital-using, labor-saving, energy-using, and materials-using productivity growth. This pattern occurs for eleven of the thirty-five industries. For this pattern the biases of productivity growth for capital, energy, and materials inputs are positive and the bias of productivity growth for labor input is negative. This pattern implies that increases in the prices of capital, energy, and materials inputs diminish the rate of productivity growth, while an increase in the price of labor input enhances productivity growth.

**Table 1.8**
Classification of industries by biases of productivity growth

*Capital using, labor using, energy using, materials saving*
  textile mills; apparel; lumber & wood

*Capital using, labor saving, energy using, materials using*
  agriculture; construction; food & kindred products;
  furniture & fixtures; paper & allied; printing & publishing;
  stone, clay & glass; electrical machinery; miscellaneous
  manufacturing; transportation services; wholesale & retail trade

*Capital using, labor saving, energy using, materials saving*
  nonmetallic mining; tobacco; leather; fabricated metal;
  machinery, except electrical; instruments; communications;
  services; government enterprises

*Capital using, labor saving, energy saving, materials using*
  coal mining; petroleum & coal products

*Capital saving, labor using, energy using, material using*
  finance, insurance & real estate

*Capital saving, labor using, energy using, material saving*
  motor vehicles

*Capital saving, labor using, energy saving, material using*
  metal mining

*Capital saving, labor saving, energy using, material using*
  oil & gas extraction; chemicals; rubber & miscellaneous
  plastics; transportation equipment & ordnance;
  electric utilities

*Capital saving, labor saving, energy using, material saving*
  primary metals; gas utilities

The most striking change in the relative prices of capital, labor, energy, and materials inputs that has taken place since 1973 is the substantial increase in the price of energy. Reversing historical trends toward lower real prices of energy in the U.S., the Arab oil embargo of late 1973 and early 1974 resulted in a dramatic increase in oil import prices. Real energy prices to final users increased by 23 percent in the U.S. during the period 1973–1975, despite price controls on domestic petroleum and natural gas. In 1978 the Iranian revolution sent a second wave of oil import price increases through the U.S. economy. Real energy prices climbed by 34 percent over the following two-year period.[58]

I have now provided part of the solution of the problem of disappointing U.S. economic growth since 1973. Higher energy prices are associated with a decline in sectoral productivity growth for thirty-two of the thirty-five industries included in table 1.8. The slowdown in sectoral productivity growth is more than sufficient to explain the decline in U.S. economic growth. It is important to emphasize that an econometric model of sectoral productivity growth is essential to solving the problem of the slowdown in U.S. economic growth since 1973. An aggregate model of production excludes energy and materials inputs by definition, since deliveries to intermediate demand are offset by receipts of intermediate inputs.

Denison (1979, 1983, 1984, 1985) has attempted to analyze the slowdown in U.S. economic growth using an aggregate model of production and has pronounced the slowdown a "mystery." The results presented in the first panel of table 1.1 appear to bear out this conclusion. The decline in the rate of aggregate productivity growth is more than sufficient to account for the decline in the rate of growth of value added. However, the decline in economic growth is left unexplained in the absence of an econometric model to determine the rate of productivity growth. A model based on an aggregate production function would fail to establish the critical role of the increase in energy prices after 1973, since energy is excluded as an input at the aggregate level by assumption.

In section 1.5.1. above, I have pointed out that the existence of an aggregate production function requires sectoral value-added functions that are the same for all sectors. In section 1.4.1 I have observed that the existence of a sectoral value-added function requires separability between the level of technology and intermediate input. Changes in technology have an impact on sectoral productivity growth only through their impact on value added. An econometric model of productivity growth based on a value-added function for each industry would also eliminate the role of energy prices by assumption. I conclude that the link between energy prices and productivity growth requires a sectoral model of production that treats inputs of energy and materials symmetrically with inputs of capital and labor.

The steps I have outlined—disaggregating the sources of economic growth to the sectoral level, decomposing sectoral output growth between productivity growth and the growth of capital, labor, energy, and materials inputs, and modeling the rate of growth of sectoral productivity growth rate econometrically—have been taken only recently. The results of Ho and Jorgenson (1990) have corroborated those of Jorgenson and Fraumeni (1981) and Jorgenson (1984b). Jorgenson (1984b) has further disaggregated energy between electricity and non-electrical energy. Similar results have been obtained for the Japanese economy, which suffered a far more severe slowdown than the U.S. economy, by Kuroda, Yoshioka, and Jorgenson (1984).[59] Much additional research will be required to provide an exhaustive explanation of the slowdown of U.S. economic growth and the implications for the future growth of the economy.

### 1.6.3   Alternative Production Models

While the rate of productivity growth is endogenous in the econometric models I have outlined, these models must be carefully distinguished from models of induced technical change, such as those analyzed by Hicks (1963), Kennedy (1964), Samuelson (1965), von Weizsäcker (1962), and many others. In those models the biases of productivity growth are endogenous and depend on relative prices. In the model that underlies the results presented in table 1.8 the biases are constant parameters that can be estimated econometrically. As Samuelson (1965) has pointed out, models of induced technical change require intertemporal optimization since technical change at any point of time affects future production possibilities.[60]

The simplest intertemporal model of production is based on capital as a factor of production. In the model presented in section 1.3 myopic decision rules can be derived by treating the price of capital input as a rental price of capital services. The rate of productivity growth at any point of time is a function of relative prices, but does not affect future production possibilities. This greatly simplifies the

intertemporal modeling of producer behavior and facilitates the construction of an econometric model. Given myopic decision rules for
producers in each industrial sector, all of the implications of the economic theory of production can be described in terms of the sectoral
production function or the sectoral price function.

A less restrictive intertemporal model of production generates costs
of adjustment from changes in the level of capital input through
investment. As the level of investment increases, the amount of mar-
ketable output produced from given input levels decreases. Mar-
ketable output and investment can be treated as joint outputs that are
produced from capital and other inputs.[61] Models of producer behavior based on costs of adjustment can be implemented on the basis of
myopic decision rules, provided that accumulated costs of adjustment
can be observed. One approach to measuring these costs is to set
them equal to the difference between the market value of the producing unit and the market value of its capital stock.[62]

As an alternative to myopic decision rules, expectations can be
incorporated explicitly into dynamic models of producer behavior
based on costs of adjustment. An objection to dynamic models of production based on static expectations is that current prices change from
period to period, but expectations are based on unchanging future
prices.[63] An alternative approach is to base the dynamic optimization
on forecasts of future prices. Since these forecasts are subject to ran-
dom errors, it is natural to require that the optimization process takes
into account the uncertainty that accompanies forecasts of future
prices.

Two alternative approaches to optimization under uncertainty have
been proposed. Provided that the objective function for producers is
quadratic and constraints are linear, optimization under uncertainty
can be replaced by a corresponding optimization problem under
certainty.[64] An alternative approach to optimization under uncertainty is to employ the information about expectations of future prices
contained in current input levels. This approach has the advantage
that it is not limited to quadratic objective functions and linear
constraints.[65]

I have considered econometric models of production based on disembodied technical change. Changes in technology affect old and
new vintages of capital goods symmetrically. An alternative approach
is to embody changes in technology in new vintages of capital goods.
The embodiment of technical change was originated by Solow (1957,

pp. 316–317).[66] The index numbers for productivity growth described in sections 1.4 and 1.5 are based on the residual between the growth of output and the growth of inputs. This residual can be interpreted as a measure of the rate of disembodied technical change. Measures of the rate of embodied technical change can also be constructed from data on the residual.[67]

Hall (1971) and Jorgenson and Griliches (1967) have identified embodied technical change with changes in the quality of capital goods. The line of research suggested by Solow's (1960) concept of embodied technical change involves substituting quality-corrected price indexes for existing price indexes of capital goods.[68] Changes in quality can be incorporated into price indexes for capital goods by means of the "hedonic technique" employed by Griliches (1961b) and studies in the volume edited by Griliches (1971b). For example, Cole, Chen, Barquin-Stolleman, Dulberger, Helvacian, and Hodge (1986) have recently developed quality corrections for computer price indexes employed in the U.S. national product accounts.[69]

At both sectoral and aggregate levels I have considered producer behavior under constant returns to scale. This methodology makes it possible to unify data generation, analysis of the sources of economic growth, and econometric modeling of production. The analysis of economic growth and the econometric modeling can be carried out independently. Both employ index numbers of output, inputs, and productivity. Under increasing returns to scale and competitive markets for output and all inputs, producer equilibrium is not defined by profit maximization, since no maximum of profits exists. The analysis of sources of economic growth and the modeling of producer behavior under increasing returns to scale cannot be carried out independently. The implementation of a model of producer behavior under increasing returns to scale requires an econometric approach.[70]

In regulated industries the price of output is set by regulatory authority. Given demand for output as a function of the regulated price, the level of output is exogenous to the producing unit. With output fixed from the point of view of the producer, necessary conditions for equilibrium can be derived from cost minimization. To illustrate the econometric modeling of economies of scale, I can briefly consider examples from the extensive literature on the U.S. electric power industry and the communications industry. An econometric model of electric power generation in the United States has been implemented by Christensen and Greene (1976). This model is based on translog cost functions for cross sections of individual electric utilities in 1955 and 1970. A key feature of the electric power industry in the United States is that individual firms are subject to price regulation. The regulatory authority sets the price for electric power. Electric utilities are required to supply the electric power that is demanded at the regulated price.

Christensen and Greene have employed translog cost functions fitted to data on individual utilities to characterize scale economies for individual firms. For both 1955 and 1970 the cost functions are U shaped with a minimum point occurring at very large levels of output. The cost function for 1970 is considerably below that for 1955, reflecting changes in technology.[71] Gollop and Roberts (1981) have employed translog cost functions for individual firms in analyzing annual data on eleven electric utilities in the United States for the period 1958–1975. They use the results to decompose the growth of productivity between economies of scale and technical change. For the period as a whole economies of scale account for an average of 40 percent of productivity growth, while technical change accounts for the remaining 60 percent. Gollop and Roberts have provided a prototype for the analysis of sources of sectoral output growth in the electric generating industry.

A model with increasing returns to scale has been implemented for time series data on Bell Canada, a regulated firm accounting for more than half of the output of the Canadian telecommunications industry, by Denny, Fuss, and Waverman (1981a). This model is based on cost minimization subject to regulatory pricing constraints. Bell Canada has multiple outputs consisting of different types of telecommunications services. Prices for these outputs are not proportional to marginal costs. Denny, Fuss, and Waverman provide an analysis of sources of growth of productivity for Bell Canada over the period 1952–1976. Economies of scale account for 64 percent of productivity growth, technical change accounts for 20 percent, and nonmarginal cost pricing accounts for the remaining 16 percent.

Given the importance of economies of scale in the electric generating and communications industries, it is interesting to consider the implementation of a model for a whole industry, incorporating economies of scale. Such a model would require an econometric model for each firm, incorporating a panel of annual observations for all firms in the industry, similar to the panel constructed by Gollop and Roberts (1981) for eleven electric utilities.[72] To provide a decomposition of productivity growth for the industry between economies of scale and technical change the model would require an allocation of the growth of industry output among firms.

An important frontier in the econometric modeling of production lies in the disaggregation of sectoral production models to the level of the individual producing unit. For industries with significant economies of scale at this level, it is possible to supplement sectoral models of production with models based on panel data for individual firms and plants. This is already feasible for industries with well-documented production patterns at the level of the individual unit. At present, the required data are available only for regulated industries, such as electricity generation, communications, and transportation. However, the LRD project of the Bureau of the Census will provide a data source that may make it feasible to model production patterns for U.S. industry at the firm or plant level on a broader scale.[73]

The model of "learning by doing" proposed by Arrow (1962) provides an approach to modeling producer behavior with features similar in some respects to increasing returns to scale. This model has been employed in analyzing production from batch-type production processes, for example, in studies of the airframe industry summarized by Alchian (1963). Solow (1967) compares this model to models characterized by increasing returns to scale and provides additional references. Another alternative to the Christensen-Greene model for electric utilities has been developed by Fuss (1977, 1978). In Fuss's model the cost function is permitted to differ *ex ante*, before a plant is constructed, and *ex post*, after the plant is in place.[74] Fuss employs a generalized Leontief cost function introduced by Diewert (1971, 1973) with four input prices—structures, equipment, fuel, and labor. He models substitution among inputs and economies of scale for seventy-nine steam generation plants for the period 1948–1961.

It is worthwhile to consider the data requirements for development of a model of an industry incorporating differences between *ex ante* and *ex post* substitution possibilities. To simplify the discussion I can consider the special case of putty-clay technology with *ex post* "fixed coefficients." Such a model requires a panel of annual observations on individual establishments within an industry. The modeling of substitution possibilities at the establishment level requires estimates of lifetime costs for alternative technologies at the time of construction of each plant. The modeling of subsequent decisions about whether or not to retire the plant requires comparisons of the price of output and variable costs for each plant at every point of time.

I conclude that a wide variety of alternative production models are available for both aggregate and sectoral production modeling. The aggregate production model introduced by Cobb and Douglas (1928) and developed by Tinbergen (1942) in the form used in the studies of sources of economic growth cited in section 1.5 above, retains its usefulness in modeling long-term growth trends. However, the critical empirical evidence provided by the energy crisis of the 1970s has exposed important limitations of aggregate production modeling. These limitations cannot be overcome by introducing additional complexity at the aggregate level.

Sectoral production models are required to explain the slowdown in economic growth in the United States and other industrialized countries that took place after 1973. These models must incorporate inputs of energy and materials along with inputs of capital and labor. The "fixed coefficients" assumptions employed by Leontief and Johansen have been supplanted by econometric modeling of production at the sectoral level. This assumption is also implicit in the value-added models of production employed, for example, by Kendrick (1961a, 1973) and tested in table 1.7 above. The value-added model has also been supplanted at the sectoral level by a model that treats intermediate, capital, and labor inputs symmetrically.

The costs of assembling consistent time series of interindustry transactions tables and disaggregating measures of capital and labor inputs at the sectoral level are very substantial. These costs will continue to be a formidable obstacle to implementing econometric general equilibrium models of production. In addition, a great deal of further testing will be needed to establish the most appropriate specification for such models. However, this work will be essential in assimilating the important new evidence on patterns of production made available by the energy crisis of the 1970s and its aftermath. The new econometric tools that have been developed for modeling production will help to sustain the momentum in empirical research that has characterized the study of sources of economic growth ever since Tinbergen (1942).[75]

The analysis of sources of economic growth is an essential component of any study of economic growth. However, a theory of growth must also include an explanation of the growth in supplies of capital and labor inputs. In the neoclassical model of economic growth presented by Tinbergen (1942), saving generates growth in capital input and population growth generates growth in labor input. These features of the theory of economic growth have been retained in the neoclassical growth models developed by Solow (1956, 1970, 1988).

The theoretical underpinnings of an analysis of growth in factor supplies are to be found in the theory of consumer behavior. For example, the study of saving requires modeling saving-consumption decisions. Similarly, the analysis of labor supplies requires modeling demographic behavior and labor-leisure choices. A theory of economic growth must incorporate the sources of economic growth and the modeling of producer behavior. The analysis of growth of factor supplies and the modeling of consumer behavior are required to complete the theory.

Recent research on economic growth has given considerable emphasis to the analysis of sources of economic growth and the modeling of producer behavior. This has proved to be very fruitful, as suggested by the research I have summarized in this paper. However, the future agenda could usefully give greater attention to growth of factor supplies and the modeling of consumer behavior. This focus characterized the classic studies of economic growth by Goldsmith (1955, 1962), Kuznets (1961, 1971), Machlup (1962), and Schultz (1961).

## 1.7    Conclusion

In this paper I have used the sources of economic growth to illustrate the critical importance of interrelationships between national accounting and economic theory. The link between the two is the econometric modeling of production. The national accountant uses economic theories of production to generate systems of accounts and corresponding systems of price and quantity index numbers. Theories of production are used in determining what the accounts should include and exclude. The econometrician uses theories of production to generate systems of behavioral equations and the statistical methods employed in estimating the parameters of these equations.

The research activities I have mentioned can be carried out in isolation. Accounting systems and the associated systems of index numbers can be developed with no attempt to derive them from an underlying model of producer or consumer behavior. A purely statistical approach of this type can be compared, unfavorably in my view, with the economic approach pioneered by Simon Kuznets and embodied in modern systems of national accounts, like the U.S. NIPA or the United Nations System of National Accounts.

Similarly, econometric studies can be conducted with no attention to accounting methods used in generating the underlying data. However, many of the most interesting problems in econometrics involve the characterization of higher order properties of technology and preferences. As examples, biases of technical change and elasticities of substitution are second-order properties of technology, since they depend on second-order derivatives of price and production functions. The lesson of decades of experience in modeling technology, dating back at least to Arrow, Chenery, Minhas, and Solow (1961), is that econometric estimates of these parameters are highly sensitive to methods of measurement. The best resolution of this problem is to generate accounting systems and econometric models within the same framework. This approach is articulated most fully in Diewert's elegant theory of exact index numbers.

Finally, theories of production can be generated in a form that abstracts from applications. For example, I can contrast the relatively general form of the theory of production presented in Hicks's (1946) *Value and Capital* with the more specific form of the theory presented by Hicks (1963) in *The Theory of Wages*. The concepts of the elasticity of substitution and the bias of technical change, introduced by Hicks (1963), have inspired a whole generation of econometric modelers of production. In section 1.6 I have shown that the bias of technical change is the key to understanding the slowdown in economic growth in industrialized countries since 1973. Clearly, the more specific form of the theory has proved to be better suited to applications.

My conclusion is that the most fruitful approach to research in economic measurement is one that combines national accounting, econometrics, and economic theory. This approach has emerged gradually in the successive volumes that report the proceedings of the Conference on Research in Income and Wealth. In the early days of the conference, econometrics was almost entirely absent, but economic theory and national accounting were represented in the persons of Simon Kuznets and the other founders of the conference. This is not to say that every researcher has to play the role of national accountant, statistician, and economic theorist. Very few of us can combine such diverse talents in the way that Kuznets and many of the founders of the conference did.

We do not have to go all the way back to Adam Smith to appreciate the benefits of a division of labor. Accountants can design systems that are adapted to modeling, econometricians can develop models based on consistent systems of accounts and sound conceptualization, and theorists can choose a level of abstraction appropriate to applications in accounting and econometric modeling. It seems to me that these are the lessons that we, the current generation of participants in the Conference on Research in Income and Wealth, can derive from the experiences of our predecessors of the past half century.

In concluding this paper I would like to emphasize that our final objective remains economic measurement itself. I have used the sources of economic growth to illustrate how our measurements have become more precise and more comprehensive. The view of economic growth that is now coming into focus is very different from the picture based on Douglas's fateful abstraction of the aggregate production function. While this new perspective represents important scientific progress, additional challenges are constantly emerging, even in this much studied area. The research opportunities that have been created are more than sufficient to utilize the combined talents of a legion of national accountants, econometricians, and economic theorists for the next half century and beyond.

## Notes

1. The first English-language reference to Tinbergen's article was by Valavanis-Vail (1955); an English translation appeared in Tinbergen's *Selected Papers* (1942). The article was also cited by Solow (1963a).
2. The initial version of the estimates of labor input presented in table 1.1 were published in Studies in Income and Wealth by Gollop and Jorgenson (1980, 1983). Denison (1985) has continued to publish more highly aggregated estimates of labor input growth. The Bureau of Labor Statistics has initiated a project to develop measures of labor input adjusted for changes in labor quality; see Waldorf, Kunze, Rosenblum, and Tannen (1986).
3. This approach can be contrasted with a more restrictive approach based on the existence of a value-added aggregate within each sector. The value-added approach is utilized by Kendrick (1956, 1961a, 1973, 1983a) and Kendrick and Grossman (1980). These studies exclude intermediate input from consideration. The earlier study by Leontief (1953b) excluded capital input.
4. The concept of separability was introduced by Leontief (1947a, b) and Sono (1961).
5. The concept of homothetic separability was originated by Shephard (1953, 1970). Lau (1969, 1978) has demonstrated that if the production function is homogeneous, separability implies homothetic separability.
6. The translog production function was first applied at the sectoral level by Berndt and Christensen (1973, 1974), using a value-added aggregate. The translog cost function incorporating intermediate input was applied at the sectoral level by Berndt and Jorgen-

son (1973) and Berndt and Wood (1975). Detailed references to sectoral production studies incorporating intermediate input are given by Jorgenson (1986a).

7. Translog quantity indexes were introduced by Fisher (1922) and have been discussed by Christensen and Jorgenson (1969), Kloek (1966), Theil (1965), and Törnqvist (1936). These indexes were first derived from the translog production function by Diewert (1976). The corresponding index of productivity growth was introduced by Christensen and Jorgenson (1970). This index of productivity growth was first derived from the translog production function by Jorgenson and Nishimizu (1978). Earlier, Diewert (1976) had interpreted the ratio of translog indexes of output and input as an index of productivity. Samuelson and Swamy (1974) have provided a comprehensive survey of the economic theory of index numbers.

8. The allocations are based on the method of iterative proportional fitting discussed by Bishop, Fienberg, and Holland (1975, esp. pp. 83–102, 188–191).

9. Establishment surveys count only persons actually at work during the survey week. By using establishment-based estimates of the number of jobs in each sector and assigning to absent workers the average annual hours worked by individuals with comparable characteristics, hours worked for each type of worker can be estimated on an annual basis.

10. Hours worked by workers cross-classified by demographic characteristics are estimated on the basis of household surveys. The resulting estimates are controlled to totals for each sector from the U.S. national accounts. Hours worked for each category of labor input is the product of employment, hours worked per week, and the number of weeks in the calendar year, 52. The concepts employed in these estimates of labor input reflect the conventions used in the *Census of Population* and the *Current Population Survey*.

11. These data provide estimates of average compensation per person rather than average compensation per job. To combine the data with estimates based on jobs from establishment surveys average compensation per person must be converted to average compensation per job. Matrices of weeks paid per year for each category of workers are required for this purpose. Labor compensation is the product of average compensation per person, the number of jobs per person, and the number of jobs. Estimates of average compensation per person and the number of weeks paid per year are based on household surveys, while estimates of the number of jobs are based on establishment surveys.

12. Chinloy (1980, 1981) provides such a decomposition for the U.S. economy as a whole, excluding sector of employment. Jorgenson, Gollop and Fraumeni (1987) present a decomposition for all characteristics of individual workers, including sector of employment.

13. Domar (1962, 1963) has provided reviews of Kendrick (1961a); Abramovitz (1962) has reviewed Denison (1962b) and given a comparison with Kendrick (1961a).

14. In his subsequent works, Denison (1967, 1974, 1979, 1985) begins from an hours-paid series when constructing his hours estimates for wage and salary workers. He converts the average hours paid per job to average hours worked per job, using unpublished BLS ratios of "hours at work" to "hours paid." These ratios, extrapolated from data for the year 1966, were developed by BLS for the 1952–1974 period. Based on the trends in the 1952–1974 series, Denison (1979, p. 155; 1985, p. 64) further extrapolates his hours-worked series back to 1947 and forward to 1982.

15. Denison (1974, p. 187) assumes that the sex-age earnings weights he creates for males and females from 1966 and 1967 data, respectively, and the education weights from 1959 data are constant over and thus representative of all postwar years. Denison (1979, pp. 44–45, 158, 1985) constructs two sets of weights for both sex-age and education cohorts.

16. The model of capital input employed underlying the measures presented in table 1.1 was originated by Walras ([1877] 1954). The relationship between capital stock

and rental prices was first analyzed by Hotelling (1925) and Haavelmo (1960) and has been further developed by Arrow (1964) and Hall (1968). Models of capital as a factor of production are discussed by Diewert (1980), Hulten (1990), and Jorgenson (1973a, 1989). Price and quantity indexes associated with capital as a factor of production are special cases of the index numbers proposed by Hicks (1946). Expositions of Hicks aggregation and references to the literature are given by Bruno (1978) and Diewert (1978, 1980, esp. pp. 434–438).

17. These indexes of capital input have been discussed by Denison (1966, 1969).

18. The resulting indexes of capital input have been discussed by Denison (1972), Harper, Berndt, and Wood (1989), Jorgenson (1980), Jorgenson and Griliches (1972a, b), Katz (1988), Mohr (1986, 1988b, c), and Norsworthy (1984a, b).

19. Hulten and Wykoff (1981b) employ Box-Cox transformations of all three variables and estimate separate parameters for each variable from a sample of capital goods prices.

20. The hedonic technique has been analyzed by Muellbauer (1975) and Rosen (1974). Surveys of the literature have been given by Deaton and Muellbauer (1980), Griliches (1971a, 1988a), and Triplett (1975, 1987).

21. Hulten and Wykoff have estimated vintage price functions for structures from a sample of 8,066 observations on market transactions in used structures. These data were collected by the Office of Industrial Economics of the U.S. Department of the Treasury in 1972 and published in *Business Building Statistics* (Office of Industrialized Economics, 1975). Hulten and Wykoff have estimated vintage price functions for equipment from prices of machine tools collected by Beidleman (1976) and prices of other types of equipment collected from used equipment dealers and auction reports of the U.S. General Services Administration.

22. The Baily hypothesis has also been discussed by Berndt, Mori, Sawa, and Wood (1990).

23. This methodology was first employed by Terborgh (1954). Detailed references to the literature are given by Hulten and Wykoff (1981b), Jorgenson (1989), and Mohr (1988a). Recent applications are presented by Hulten, Robertson, and Wykoff (1989) and Wykoff (1989).

24. This approach was originated by Meyer and Kuh (1957) and has been employed by Coen (1975, 1980), Eisner (1972), and Feldstein and Foot (1974).

25. Tenant-occupied housing is assigned to the finance, insurance, and real estate sector, while owner-occupied housing is assigned to the private household sector.

26. In *Sources of Economic Growth* (1962b, pp. 97–98), Denison employs a measure of capital input for equipment and structures with relative efficiencies constant over the lifetime of the capital good, the one-hoss shay pattern of relative efficiency. In *Why Growth Rates Differ* (1967, pp. 140–141), Denison uses a measure of capital input with relative efficiencies given by an unweighted average of the one-hoss shay and straight-line patterns

$$
d(\tau) = \left|
\begin{array}{ll}
1 - \dfrac{\tau}{2L}, & (\tau = 0, 1, \dots, L-1), \\
0 & (\tau = L, L+1, \dots).
\end{array}
\right.
$$

In *Accounting for United States Economic Growth 1929 to 1969* (1974, pp. 54–55) Denison introduces yet another relative efficiency pattern, based on a weight of one-fourth for straight-line and three-fourths for one-hoss shay patterns

$$
d(\tau) = \left|
\begin{array}{ll}
1 - \dfrac{\tau}{4L}, & (\tau = 0, 1, \dots, L-1), \\
0 & (\tau = L, L+1, \dots).
\end{array}
\right.
$$

The corresponding measure of capital input is employed by Denison in *Accounting for Slower Economic Growth* (1979, pp. 50–52) and *Trends in American Economic Growth, 1929–1982* (1985, p. 65).

For a linearly declining pattern of relative efficiency the mortality distribution can be represented in the form

$$
m(\tau) = \begin{vmatrix} \dfrac{1}{\theta} L & (\tau = 1, 2, \ldots, L-1) , \\ 1 - \dfrac{1}{\theta}\left(1 - \dfrac{1}{L}\right) & (\tau = L) , \\ 0 & (\tau = L+1, L+2, \ldots) , \end{vmatrix}
$$

where $\theta$ is unity for straight-line replacement, positive infinity for one-hoss shay replacement, and two and four respectively, for Denison's two averages of straight-line and one-hoss shay.

27. In *Sources of Economic Growth* (1962b) and *Why Growth Rates Differ* (1967, p. 10), Denison ignores differences in the tax treatment of corporate and noncorporate income. In *Accounting for United States Economic Growth 1929 to 1969* (1974, pp. 267–271) Denison employs separate estimates of corporate and noncorporate capital stock for the nonfarm business sector. He derives weights for these assets from data on corporate and noncorporate income by allocating noncorporate income between labor compensation of the self-employed and property compensation; however, his procedures ignore the effect of the corporate income tax. These procedures are also utilized in *Accounting for Slower Economic Growth* (1979, p. 171) and *Trends in American Economic Growth, 1929 to 1982* (1985, p. 56).

Kendrick (1973, p. 30) allocates noncorporate income between property compensation and the labor compensation of the self-employed. He assumes that the self-employed within each sector receive the same hourly compensation as employees. Kendrick does not separate corporate and noncorporate assets in measuring capital input. This approach is also employed by Kendrick and Grossman (1980, p. 26) and Kendrick (1983a, p.56).

28. The model of production based on value added has been discussed by Arrow (1974), Bruno (1978), Diewert (1978, 1980), Sato (1976), and Sims (1969, 1977). Sato provides references to the literature.

29. de Leeuw (1989) and Denison (1989) have discussed the BEA (1987b) gross product originating data. Denison has proposed an alternative breakdown of aggregate productivity measures by end product.

30. Sectoral models of production have been implemented for the United States by Baily (1982), Fraumeni and Jorgenson (1980, 1986), Gollop and Jorgenson (1980, 1983), Gullickson and Harper (1987), Hall (1986, 1987, 1988), Kendrick (1956, 1961a, 1973, 1983a), Kendrick and Grossman (1980), Leontief (1953b), Massell (1961), Star (1974), Thor, Sadler, and Grossman (1984), and Wolff (1985a). Sectoral models have been implemented for Germany by Conrad (1985), Conrad and Jorgenson (1985), and Frohn, Krengel, Kupier, Oppenlander, and Uhlmann (1973), for Japan by Ezaki (1978, 1985), Jorgenson, Kuroda, and Nishimizu (1987), Nishimizu and Hulten (1978), and Watanabe (1971), for Japan, Korea, Turkey and Yugoslavia by Nishimizu and Robinson (1986), and for the United Kingdom by Armstrong (1974).

The studies of sectoral productivity for Germany by Conrad and Conrad and Jorgenson, for Japan by Jorgenson, Kuroda, and Nishimizu, and for Japan, Korea, Turkey and Yugoslavia by Nishimizu and Robinson are closely comparable in methodology to the study for the United States summarized in tables 1.2 and 1.3. Conrad and Jorgenson provide international comparisons among Germany, Japan, and the United States, including relative levels of productivity by sector in the three countries.

Thor, Sadler, and Grossman (1984) and Jorgenson, Kuroda and Nishimizu (1987) provide international comparisons between Japan and the United States. The methodology of Thor, Sadler and Grossman is based on that of Kendrick and Grossman. Domar, Eddie, Herrick, Hohenberg, Intriligator, and Miyamoto (1964) provide international comparisons among Canada, Germany, Japan, the United Kingdom, and the United States for the period 1948–1960 with separate estimates for as many as eleven sectors within each country. The methodology employed in this study is closely comparable to that of Kendrick (1956, 1961a). Englander and Mittelstadt (1988) have presented international comparisons among twenty OECD countries for the period 1960–1986 for as many as fifteen industrial sectors in each country. Their methodology is similar to that of Kendrick.

31. The data in table 1.7 also provide a test of Leontief's (1951, 1953a) "fixed coefficients" assumption in interindustry analysis. Under this assumption, all intermediate inputs are proportional to output, so that Leontief's (1936) approach to aggregation implies the existence of an intermediate input aggregate. The fixed coefficients assumption implies that ratios of growth of intermediate input to growth of output in table 1.7 must be equal to unity.

32. The derivation of a production possibility frontier from a multisectoral model of production was originated by Debreu (1951, p. 285) and has been discussed by Bergson (1961, 1975), Diewert (1980), Fisher (1982), Fisher and Shell (1972), Moorsteen (1961), and Weitzman (1983). Debreu's (1954, pp. 52–54) definition of aggregate productivity growth has been discussed by Diewert (1976, 1980), Hulten (1973), Jorgenson and Griliches (1967), and Richter (1966).

33. The implications of aggregation over industrial sectors for the existence of an aggregate production function was a central issue in the "reswitching controversy" initiated by Samuelson (1962). This controversy has been summarized by Brown (1980) and Burmeister (1980a, 1980b), who provide extensive references to the literature.

34. This condition for the existence of an aggregate production function is due to Hall (1973) and has been discussed by Denny and Pinto (1978) and Lau (1978).

35. The relationship of aggregate and sectoral indexes of productivity growth was first discussed by Debreu (1954) and Leontief (1953b) under the assumption that prices paid for primary factors of production are the same for all sectors. The relationship between aggregate and sectoral productivity indexes under the assumption that prices of primary factors of production differ among sectors was first discussed by Kendrick (1956, 1961a) and Massell (1961).

36. This generalizes a formula originally proposed by Domar (1961), correcting the procedure introduced by Leontief (1953b). Domar's approach, like Leontief's, is based on the assumption that prices paid for primary factors of production are the same for all sectors. Leontief averages weighted relative changes in ratios of intermediate and labor inputs to output over all sectors. Domar points out that the appropriate measure of aggregate productivity growth is a weighted sum rather than a weighted average. Leontief's approach fails to eliminate deliveries to intermediate demand in the process of aggregating over sectors.

Domar's approach has been discussed by Baumol and Wolff (1984), Diewert (1980), Gollop (1979, 1983), Hulten (1978), and Jorgenson (1980) and has been employed by Fraumeni and Jorgenson (1980, 1986), Nishimizu and Hulten (1978), and Wolff (1985a). One of the curiosities of the literature on productivity measurement is that Leontief's approach has been reintroduced by the Statistical Office of the United Nations (1968), Watanabe (1971), Star (1974), and Ezaki (1978, 1985). Watanabe advocates weights for sectoral productivity growth rates based on the ratio of the value of output in each sector to the sum of the values of outputs in all sectors. Ezaki and Star advocate the use of this same weighting system.

37. This approach was introduced by Kendrick (1956) and has been discussed by Bergson (1961, 1975), Domar (1961), Fisher (1982), Fisher and Shell (1972), Kendrick (1961a), Massell (1961), Moorsteen (1961), the Statistical Office of the United Nations (1968, p. 69, "Value Added and Primary Inputs: The Net System of Productivity Measurement,") and Weitzman (1983). This approach has been employed by Armstrong (1974), Frohn, Krengel, Kupier, Oppenlander, and Uhlmann (1973), Kendrick (1956, 1961a, 1973, 1983a), Kendrick and Grossman (1980), and Massell (1961).

38. Hulten's approach has been implemented for ten sectors of the Japanese economy for the period 1955–1971 by Nishimizu and Hulten (1978).

39. The data that underly tables 1.1 and 1.2 comprise a complete set of U.S. national production accounts for inputs as well as outputs at sectoral and aggregate levels. This system of accounts complements the existing U.S. national accounts for outputs presented by BEA (1986). These accounts can be integrated with the system of national accounts for income and expenditure, capital formation, and wealth outlined by Jorgenson (1980) and implemented by Fraumeni and Jorgenson (1980). The production accounts that underly tables 1.1 and 1.2 can also be combined with systems of national accounts such as those proposed by Eisner (1978, 1985, 1989), Kendrick (1976, 1979), and Ruggles and Ruggles (1970, 1973). Campbell and Peskin (1979) and Eisner (1988) have provided a useful summary and comparison among these accounting systems and give detailed references to the literature. Kendrick's accounting system has been discussed by Engerman and Rosen (1980). Finally, the production accounts can be combined with the system of accounts for the United States proposed by Ruggles and Ruggles (1982). This system integrates income and product accounts, flow of funds accounts, and balance sheets for assets and liabilities.

40. The existence of a value-added aggregate equal to the sum of the quantities of value added in all sectors is an implication of Hicks (1946) aggregation. Further details on Hicks aggregation are given by Bruno (1978) and Diewert (1978, 1980).

41. Models of aggregate production have been implemented for the United States by Abramovitz (1956), Abramovitz and David (1973a, b), Baily (1981), BLS (1983), Christensen and Jorgenson (1969, 1970, 1973a, b), Christensen, Cummings, and Jorgenson (1978, 1980, 1981), Denison (1962a, b, 1967, 1974, 1979, 1985), Fabricant (1959), Jorgenson and Griliches (1967, 1972a, b), Kendrick (1956, 1961a, 1973, 1983a), Kendrick and Grossman (1980), Knowles (1954, 1960), Mills (1952), Norsworthy and Harper (1981), Norsworthy, Harper, and Kunze (1979), Schmookler (1952), Solow (1957, 1960, 1962, 1963a), and Valavanis-Vail (1955).

42. Jorgenson and Nishimizu (1978) have developed methodology for measuring relative productivity levels between countries and applied this methodology to bilateral comparisons between Japan and the U.S. during the period 1952–1974. Caves, Christensen, and Diewert (1982a, b) have developed methodology for multilateral productivity comparisons. Denny and Fuss (1983) have presented an alternative approach. Christensen, Cummings, and Jorgenson (1981) have applied the methodology of Caves, Christensen, and Diewert in deriving estimates of relative levels of productivity for the nine countries analyzed by Christensen, Cummings, and Jorgenson (1978, 1980).

43. Denison (1985) has provided estimates of aggregate productivity for the U.S. economy covering the period 1929–1982. Earlier, Denison (1967) presented comparable estimates at the aggregate level for Belgium, Denmark, France, Germany, the Netherlands, Norway, the United Kingdom, and the United States for the period 1950–1962.

Correa (1970) has given estimates for Argentina, Brazil, Chile, Columbia, Ecuador, Honduras, Mexico, Peru, and Venezuela for the period 1950–1962. Walters (1968, 1970) has provided estimates for Canada for the period 1950–1967; Dholakis (1974) has presented estimates for India for the period 1948–1969; for Japan Kanamori (1972) has given estimates for the period 1955–1968 and Denison and Chung (1976) have given estimates for the period 1952–1971; finally, Kim and Park (1985) have presented estimates for Korea for the period 1963–1982. Bergson (1978) has provided estimates of aggregate productivity for the Soviet Union, France, Germany, Italy, and Japan for the period 1955–1970. All of these estimates are closely comparable in methodology to Denison's estimates for the United States. Bergson (1987) has given estimates of relative productivity levels for Hungary, Poland, the Soviet Union, Yugoslavia, and France, Germany, Italy, Japan, Spain, the United Kingdom, and the United States for the year 1975, extending his earlier study of productivity trends.

Kuznets (1971) has compared Denison's productivity estimates with estimates derived from an analysis of long-term growth trends for Canada, France, Norway, the United Kingdom, and the United States.

44. Beckmann and Sato (1969) and Sato and Beckmann (1968) have compared aggregate productivity estimates for Germany, Japan and the United States. These estimates are based on the methodology of Kendrick and Sato (1963) for the United States. Balassa and Bertrand (1970) have compared sources of economic growth for countries of Western and Eastern Europe, using methods similar to those of Kendrick. Kendrick (1983b) has provided aggregate productivity estimates for Canada, France, Germany, Italy, Japan, Sweden, the United Kingdom, and the United States for the period 1960–1978. Kendrick (1984) has updated these estimates to 1979 and added Belgium to the list of countries.

45. The contribution of changes in the distribution of capital and labor inputs among sectors to productivity growth for the U.S. economy as a whole has been measured by Kendrick (1973) for thirty-four industry groups for the period 1948 to 1966. The contribution of these changes to the rate of productivity growth for the U.S. manufacturing sector has been measured by Massell (1961) for seventeen industry groups for the period 1946–1957. Denison (1985) has measured the contribution of changes in the distribution of capital and labor inputs between farm and nonfarm sectors of the U.S. economy for the period 1929–1982 and of labor input between self-employment and other employment within the nonfarm sector for the same period.

46. Norsworthy (1984b) compares the methodologies employed by Christensen, Cummings, and Jorgenson, Denison, and Kendrick. A detailed comparison of the empirical results of Christensen, Cummings, and Jorgenson (1980) with those of BLS, Denison, and Kendrick is presented by BLS (1983). As I have already pointed out, the concept of net value added used at the aggregate level in Kendrick's (1956, 1961, 1973) early studies was abandoned by Kendrick and Grossman (1980) and Kendrick (1983a). Norsworthy concludes that Denison's (1985) concept of value added net of depreciation has been superseded by value added gross of depreciation as a starting point for studies of productivity at the aggregate level.

47. Gollop (1985) has surveyed the literature on the role of intersectoral shifts.

48. Bergman (1985), Johansen (1976), and Taylor (1975) provide detailed references to the literature on the approach to general equilibrium modeling originated by Johansen. The econometric approach to general equilibrium modeling introduced by Hudson and Jorgenson (1974), is further discussed by Bergman (1990), Jorgenson (1982, 1984a, 1986a), and Jorgenson and Wilcoxen (1990).

49. An important issue in the modeling of producer behavior at the sectoral level is the existence of aggregate inputs, such as the capital, labor, energy and materials inputs. The production function is required to be homothetically separable in the components of each of these aggregates in the approach of Berndt and Jorgenson. The methodology for testing homothetic separability was originated by Jorgenson and Lau (1975). This

methodology has been discussed by Blackorby, Primont, and Russell (1977) and Denny and Fuss (1977). An alternative approach has been developed by Woodland (1978).

Berndt and Christensen (1973) and Norsworthy and Harper (1981) have tested the existence of aggregate capital input. Berndt and Christensen (1974) have tested the existence of aggregate labor input. Woodland (1978) has tested the existence of both capital and labor inputs. Berndt and Wood (1975) have tested the existence of the value-added aggregate discussed in section 1.4. The results of these tests are favorable to the existence of aggregates for capital input, but highly unfavorable to the existence of an aggregate for labor or an aggregate for value added like that employed in Kendrick's (1956, 1961a) studies of sectoral productivity growth.

50. Friede (1979) and Nakamura (1984) have constructed models of this type for Germany, while Longva and Olsen (1983) have constructed such a model for Norway.

51. Early studies of aggregate producer behavior, including those based on the Cobb-Douglas production function, have been surveyed by Heady and Dillon (1961) and Walters (1963). Samuelson (1979) discusses the impact of Douglas's research.

52. The implications of the results of McFadden and Uzawa have been discussed by Solow (1967). Econometric studies based on the CES production function have been surveyed by Griliches (1967), Jorgenson (1974), Kennedy and Thirlwall (1972), Nadiri (1970), and Nerlove (1967).

53. Aggregate models of producer behavior based on the translog functional form have been constructed for the United States by Christensen, Jorgenson, and Lau (1971, 1973) and Jorgenson and Yun (1986). Aggregate models for the United States have also been developed by Hall (1973), Burgess (1974), and Kohli (1981, 1983). Denny and Pinto (1978) have constructed an aggregate model of production for Canada. Conrad and Jorgenson (1977, 1978) have developed aggregate models for Germany.

54. Illustrations of this type of application are provided by the analysis of the impact of alternative energy policies on U.S. economic growth by Hudson and Jorgenson (1974) and the effects of environmental regulation on U.S. economic growth by Jorgenson and Wilcoxen (1990).

55. The price function was introduced by Samuelson (1953).

56. This definition of the bias of productivity growth is due to Hicks (1963). Alternative definitions of biases of productivity growth are compared by Binswanger (1978).

57. Further details on econometric modeling of sectoral productivity growth are given by Jorgenson (1986a).

58. Trends in energy prices since 1973 are discussed in greater detail by Jorgenson (1986b). Bruno (1984) has discussed the impact of higher raw materials prices after 1973. The bias of productivity growth for materials is positive for twenty of the thirty-five industries listed in table 1.8. For these industries an increase in the price of materials is associated with lower productivity growth.

59. Baily (1986), Baily and Chakrabarti (1988), Denison (1983), Griliches (1988b), Jorgenson (1988b), and Romer (1987) have discussed the slowdown in economic growth in the United States. A comparison of the slowdowns in Japan and the United States is presented by Jorgenson (1988a). Giersch and Wolter (1983) and Lindbeck (1983) have analyzed the slowdown in industrialized countries. Baily and Gordon (1988), Englander and Mittelstadt (1988), Maddison (1987), and Wolff (1985b) have provided surveys of the literature on the slowdown in productivity growth in industrialized countries.

60. Surveys of the literature on induced technical change are given by Binswanger (1978), Solow (1967), and Thirtle and Ruttan (1987).

61. Dynamic models of production based on costs of adjustment have been analyzed, e.g., by Lucas (1967) and Uzawa (1969).

62. This approach has been employed in models of investment behavior based on Tobin's (1969) $q$-theory, such as those constructed by Hayashi (1982) and Summers (1981). The literature on econometric models of investment behavior based on Tobin's q-theory has been surveyed by Chirinko (1988). Jorgenson (1973b) has discussed models of investment behavior based on costs of adjustment.

63. Dynamic models with static expectations have been employed by Denny, Fuss, and Waverman (1981b), Epstein and Denny (1980), and Morrison and Berndt (1981). Berndt and Fuss (1986) have surveyed the literature on dynamic models of production.

64. This approach has been developed in considerable detail by Hansen and Sargent (1980, 1981) and has been employed in modeling producer behavior by Epstein and Yatchew (1984), Meese (1980), and Sargent (1978).

65. Pindyck and Rotemberg (1983a, b) have utilized this approach.

66. Models of producer behavior with embodied technical change were developed by Solow (1960, 1962, 1963a, 1964). Solow (1963a) provides a comparison of rates of embodied technical change between Germany and the United States and gives references to the literature. Barger (1969) presents estimates of rates of embodied and disembodied technical change for Denmark, France, Germany, Italy, the Netherlands, Norway, Sweden, The United Kingdom, and the United States for the period 1950–1964.

67. Solow (1960, 1962) has pointed out that separate rates of embodied and disembodied technical change cannot be identified from the residual alone. This point has been elaborated by Denison (1964a, b), Green (1966), Hall (1968), and Jorgenson (1966).

68. An overview of issues in the measurement of aggregate output, including the adjustment of price indexes for quality change, is presented in the Rees Report (National Research Council, 1979, esp. pp. 88–121). Highly preliminary estimates of the impact of these corrections on measures of productivity were presented by Jorgenson and Griliches (1967). Gordon (1990) has provided comprehensive quality corrections for price indexes of producers' durable equipment. Gordon's results have been discussed by Engerman and Rosen (1980).

69. Dulberger (1989) has presented econometric models of computer prices that underly the computer price indexes employed in the U.S. national accounts. Alternative models of computer prices are provided by Gordon (1989). Baily and Gordon (1989) and Triplett (1989) have surveyed the literature on computer price models. Denison (1989) has presented objections to the use of quality-corrected price indexes in the national accounts. Triplett (1990) and Young (1989) have discussed these objections in detail.

70. Econometric studies of economies of scale in the electric generating sector have been surveyed by Cowing and Smith (1978). A review of studies of economies of scale in transportation industries has been presented by Winston (1985). A review of such studies in communications industries has been given by Fuss (1983). Econometric modeling of economies of scale in all three regulated industries has been surveyed by Jorgenson (1986a). Diewert (1981) reviews methods for measuring productivity in regulated industries. Studies of productivity in regulated industries are presented in the volume edited by Cowing and Stevenson (1981).

71. More recently, the Christensen-Greene data base has been extended by Greene (1983) to incorporate cross sections of individual electric utilities for 1955, 1960, 1965, 1970, and 1975. Greene is able to characterize economies of scale and technical change simultaneously.

72. Panel data sets have been constructed for the airline industry by Caves, Christensen, and Trethaway (1984) for the period 1970–1981 and for the railroad industry by Caves, Christensen, Trethaway, and Windle (1985) for the period 1951–1975. In these studies a distinction between economies of scale and economies of density is introduced. Economies of density are defined in terms of the elasticity of total cost with

respect to output, holding points served and other characteristics of output fixed. Economies of scale are defined as the elasticity of total cost with respect to output and points served. Economies of density are important in both airlines and railroads, but neither industry is characterized by economies of scale.

73. A description of the LRD program is provided by McGuckin and Pascoe (1988). Other data bases at the firm level are described by Griliches (1984).

74. A model of production with differences between *ex ante* and *ex post* substitution possibilities was introduced by Houthakker (1955–1956). This model has been further developed by Johansen (1972) and Sato (1975) and has been discussed by Hildenbrand (1981) and Koopmans (1977). Recent applications are given by Bentzel (1978), Forsund and Hjalmarsson (1979, 1983, 1987) and Forsund and Jansen (1983). Fisher (1971), Fisher, Solow, and Kearl (1977), Liviatan (1966), and Solow (1963b) have analyzed the results of fitting "smooth" production functions to data generated from *ex post* fixed coefficients or putty-clay technology. A survey of the literature on putty-clay models and other alternatives to models based on production and cost functions is given by Solow (1967).

75. A detailed survey of econometric methods for modeling producer behavior is presented by Jorgenson (1986a).

# 2

## Measurement of Macroeconomic Performance in Japan, 1951–1968

Mitsuo Ezaki and
Dale W. Jorgenson

### 2.1 Introduction

There are two objectives in the present paper. The first objective is to provide the accounting basis for the theory-oriented empirical researches on macroeconomic performance in the postwar Japanese economy. Economic theories are concerned mainly with economic variables which have their corresponding economic data. The system of economic theories, especially that of macroeconomics, has its firm basis on the social accounting framework. It is impossible to construct the system of macroeconomic theories without reference to the social accounting system. Conversely, the development of social accounting system owes much to the development of economic theories. This close relationship between economic theories and social accounting system does not seem to have been well recognized in the empirical study of the Japanese economy. In this paper, therefore, we will attempt to reorganize the existing Japanese National Income Statistics (NIS) from the point of view of economic theories, especially the theory of production, the theory of consumption, and the theory of general equilibrium, and provide the data for the related economic variables in the producing sector and in the consuming sector. This is the first and (quantitatively) main objective of the present paper.

The second objective is to measure the productivity change in the producing sector based on the accounting framework thus reorganized. Though there have been several attempts to measure the rate of productivity change (or the rate of technical progress) in the Japanese economy, heterogeneity of capital, labor and output has been neglected in most cases. Especially, little efforts have been made on the proper treatment of capital input. This is mainly due to the problem of how to separate social capital input into price and quantity components which is not well established in the present social accounting system. This problem will be solved under the reorganization process of existing National Income Statistics mentioned above. In this paper, therefore, special attention will be paid to the differences in quality among various types of capital, labor and output, and to the use of correctly defined prices of capital services. We will make also some theoretical investigations about the aggregation problem in the measurement of productivity change.

In section 2.2, we will try to summarize and interpret the existing Japanese national accounting system from the point of view of general equilibrium theory. The content of this section will clarify the essential relationships among macroeconomic variables and make it easier to understand the discussions of the subsequent sections. Section 2.3 deals with the producing sector which is defined as private sector plus government enterprises sector. We will construct the product and factor outlay accounts for this sector and investigate in detail the problem of how to separate social capital input into price and quantity components. We will also attempt to separate output into consumption goods component and investment goods component. Section 2.4 deals with the consuming sector which is identified with the private sector. We will construct the income, outlay, saving and wealth accounts for this sector and clarify the basic relationships between the flow variables (income, outlay and saving) and the stock variable (wealth). In section 2.5, we will try to measure the aggregate rate of productivity change in the producing sector based on the data and accounting framework provided in section 2.3. We will investigate two kinds of aggregation problems in the measurement of productivity change, too. One is the problem of sector aggregation which is related with the role of intermediate goods in the measurement of productivity change. Another is the problem of factor and output aggregation which leads to the quality indexes of capital, labor and output as indexes of aggregation bias in the measurement of productivity change. In section 2.6, we will provide the general summary and future prospect of the present paper.

From a methodological point of view, the present paper owes to a great extent to the following three papers which have made the same analysis about the U.S. economy: L.R. Christensen and D.W. Jorgenson (1969, 1970, 1973b). Namely, the first two papers have become the basis of our section 2.3 and the last one is the basis of our section 2.4.

Much of the time and energy in writing this paper has been devoted to the applicational devices and data construction, but the present paper has also its own methodological contributions, which will be found especially in sections 2.2 and 2.5.

Before going to the next section, we must note here that we will adopt the fiscal year (April-March) instead of the calendar year as a time unit in the subsequent tables and discussions. It is because only the data based on fiscal year permit us to allocate the investment series into its components' series and to collect the data for various indirect taxes.

## 2.2    Basic Accounting Framework for the National Economy

In this section, we will attempt to summarize and interpret the existing Japanese national accounting system from the point of view of general equilibrium theory.[1] Note that by the term "general equilibrium theory" we simply mean the supply-demand relations only but not behavioral equations. Here we will also try to investigate the problem of distribution in production which is not well established in the present social accounting system. The content of this section will clarify the essential relationships among macroeconomic variables and prepare the way for the subsequent two sections.

### 2.2.1    General Equilibrium Interpretation of the Existing National Accounting System

Let us consider the Japanese national economy which consists of the following five sectors: households and nonprofit institutions sector ($H$), private business sector ($B$), government enterprises sector ($GE$), general government sector ($GG$) and foreign sector ($F$).[2] In order to simplify the notation and analysis, we assume without loss of generality that there exist in this economy only two kinds of output (consumption goods and investment goods), only a single kind of labor and only a single kind of financial asset. Note that by this assumption we exclude *a priori* the possibility of imported raw materials which the economy cannot produce domestically. In other words, the above assumption implies the fact that all of the imported commodities including raw materials are assumed to be perfectly competitive ones. In case of the financial asset, it is of course possible to separate it into money and other financial asset (bonds, securities, etc.), but this separation is unnecessary for the present purposes. Under the present assumption, the supply-demand relations for flow variables in the economy can be expressed as in table 2.1. Table 2.1 includes also the supplementary tax and stock relations, and shows the bird's eye view of the national economy.[3]

From this table we can derive two types of equality, horizontal type (quantity) and vertical type (value). Namely, reading the table horizontally, we get four equilibrium conditions or ex-post identities for four flow variables (2.2.1–C) to (2.2.1–$\dot{A}$), one tax identity (2.2.1–T) and one initial stock condition (2.2.1–A), i.e.,

$$\Sigma\, C = \Sigma C^* \qquad\qquad\qquad\qquad\qquad\qquad (2.2.1\text{–C})$$

$$\Sigma\, I = \Sigma I^* \qquad\qquad\qquad\qquad\qquad\qquad (2.2.1\text{–I})$$

$$\Sigma\, L = \Sigma L^* \qquad\qquad\qquad\qquad\qquad\qquad (2.2.1\text{–L})$$

$$\Sigma\, \dot{A} = \Sigma \dot{A}^* \qquad\qquad\qquad\qquad\qquad\qquad (2.2.1\text{–}\dot{A})$$

$$\Sigma\, T = \Sigma T^* \qquad\qquad\qquad\qquad\qquad\qquad (2.2.1\text{–T})$$

$$\Sigma\, A = \Sigma A^* \qquad\qquad\qquad\qquad\qquad\qquad (2.2.1\text{–A})$$

On the other hand, reading the table vertically, we obtain five budget restrictions (uses of funds = sources of funds) for five sectors of the economy,[4] i.e.,

$$q_C C_H + q_K I_H + p_L L_H + q_A(\dot{A}_H - \dot{A}^*_H) + (T^V_H + T^A_H)$$
$$= q_C C^*_H + p_L L^*_H + p_A(A_H - A^*_H) \quad \text{(See (2.2.4–H))} \qquad (2.2.2\text{–H})$$

$$(q_C C^U_B + q_K I^U_B) + q_K I_B + p_L L_B + q_A(\dot{A}_B - \dot{A}^*_B) + (T^V_B + T^A_B + T^S_B)$$
$$= q_C C^*_B = q_K I^*_B + p_A(A_B - A^*_B) \qquad\qquad\qquad (2.2.2\text{–B})$$

$$(q_C C^U_{GE} + q_K I^U_{GE}) + q_K I_{GE} + p_L L_{GE} + q_A(\dot{A}_{GE} - \dot{A}^*_{GE}) + T^A_{GE}$$
$$= q_C C^*_{GE} + q_K I^*_{GE} + p_A(A_{GE} - A^*_{GE}) \qquad\qquad (2.2.2\text{–GE})$$

$$q_C C_{GG} + q_K I_{GG} + p_L L_{GG} + q_A(\dot{A}_{GG} - \dot{A}^*_{GG})$$
$$= T^*_{GG} + q_C C^*_{GG} + p_A(A_{GG} - A^*_{GG}) \quad \text{(See (2.2.4–GG))} \qquad (2.2.2\text{–GG})$$

$$(q_C C_F + q_K I_F) + p_L L_F + q_A(\dot{A}_F - \dot{A}^*_F)$$
$$= (q_C C^*_F + q_K I^*_F - T^S_F) + p_L L^*_F + p_A(A_F - A^*_F). \qquad (2.2.2\text{–F})$$

In the actual economy, however, these budget restrictions must be modified to a slight extent due to various transfer payments, which

**Table 2.1**
Bird's-eye view of the national economy

| (Price) Quantity | | Demand H | B | GE | GG | F | Supply H | B | GE | GG | F |
|---|---|---|---|---|---|---|---|---|---|---|---|
| (qc) | C | $C_H$ | $C_B^U$ | $C_{GE}^U$ | $C_{GG}$ | $C_F$ | $C_H^*$ | $C_B^*$ | $C_{GE}^*$ | $C_{GG}^*$ | $C_F^*$ |
| (qk) | I | $I_H$ | $I_B, I_B^U$ | $I_{GE}, I_{GE}^U$ | $I_{GG}$ | $I_F$ | | $I_B^*$ | $I_{GE}^*$ | | $I_F^*$ |
| $(P_L)$ | L | $L_H$ | $L_B$ | $L_{GE}$ | $L_{GG}$ | $L_F$ | $L_H^*$ | | | | $L_F^*$ |
| (qA) | $\dot{A}$ | $\dot{A}_H$ | $\dot{A}_B$ | $\dot{A}_{GE}$ | $\dot{A}_{GG}$ | $\dot{A}_F$ | $\dot{A}_H^*$ | $\dot{A}_B^*$ | $\dot{A}_{GE}^*$ | $\dot{A}_{GG}^*$ | $\dot{A}_F^*$ |
| | T | $T_H^V, T_H^A$ | $T_B^V, T_B^A, T_B^S$ | $T_{GE}^A$ | | $T_F^S$ | | | | | |
| (qA,pA) | A | | | | | | $(A_H - A_H^*)$ | $(A_B - A_B^*)$ | $(A_{GE} - A_{GE}^*)$ | $(A_{GG} - A_{GG}^*)$ | $(A_F - A_F^*)$ |
| (qK,pK) | K | | | | | | $K_H$ | $K_B$ | $K_{GE}$ | $K_{GG}$ | |

H: households and nonprofit institutions sector
B: private business sector
GE: government enterprises sector
GG: general government sector
F: foreign sector
C: consumption goods ($C^U$: intermediate demand for consumption goods)
I: investment goods ($I^U$: intermediate demand for investment goods)
L: labor services (flow)
A: financial assets (flow)   ($\dot{A} = dA/dt$, t = time)
T: tax ($T^V$: income tax, $T^A$: asset tax, $T_S^S$: sales tax ($T_F^S$: tariff), $T_{GG}^*$: total tax revenue; $T^A$ plus $T^S$ is indirect taxes ($T^I$))
A: financial assets (stock), $A^*$: financial liabilities (stock)
K: physical capital stock
q: commodity or asset price
p: service price

are neglected throughout this section.  By summing up all of these five restrictions we get

$$q_C(\Sigma C - \Sigma C^*) + q_K(\Sigma I - \Sigma I^*) + p_L(\Sigma L - \Sigma L^*) + qA(\Sigma \dot{A} - \Sigma \dot{A}^*)$$

$$= (T_{GG}^* - \Sigma T) + p_A(\Sigma A - \Sigma A^*)$$

$$= 0 \quad \text{(from (2.2.1–T) and (2.2.1–A)) .} \qquad (2.2.2\text{–W})$$

This is the aggregate budget restriction which leads to the Walras' Law in the general equilibrium model.[5]

Let us now turn our attention to the fundamental equality in the national accounting system, i.e.,

Expenditure = Value of (Net) Output = Factor Income, and interpret it according to our own framework mentioned thus far.  As is well-known, gross national product (GNP) is defined from the expenditure side in the following way

$$\text{GNP} \equiv q_C(C_H + C_{GG}) + q_K(I_H + I_B + I_{GE} + I_{GG}) + (q_C C_F + q_K I_F + p_L L_F$$

$$+ p_A A_F^*) - (q_C C_F^* + q_K I_F^* - T_F^S + p_L L_F^* + p_A A_F)$$

(GNP defined from expenditure). $\qquad (2.2.3\text{–e})$

By using (2.2.1–C) and (2.2.1–I) we get GNP defined from the output side as follows

$$\text{GNP} = q_C(C_H^* + C_B^* + C_{GE}^* + C_{GG}^* - C_B^U - C_{GE}^U)$$

$$+ q_K(I_B^* + I_{GE}^* - I_B^U - I_{GE}^U) + p_L(L_F - L_F^*) + p_A(A_F^* - A_F) + T_F^S$$

$$= q_C C_H^* + (q_C C_B^* + q_K I_B^* - q_C C_B^U - q_K I_B^U) + (q_C C_{GE}^* + q_K I_{GE}^*$$

$$- q_C C_{GE}^U - q_K T_{GE}^U) + q_C C_{GG}^* + p_L(L_F - L_F^*) + p_A(A_F^* - A_F) + T_F^S$$

(GNP defined from [net] product[7]) . $\qquad (2.2.3\text{–p})$

The more precise concept for the value of output, however, is gross domestic product (GDP) which is defined as GNP less net factor income from abroad, i.e.,

$$\text{GDP} = q_C C_H^* + (q_C C_B^* + q_K I_B - q_C C_B^U - q_K I_B^U) + (q_C C_{GE}^* + q_K I_{GE}$$

$$- q_C C_{GE}^U - q_K I_{GE}^U) + q_C C_{GG}^* + T_F^S . \qquad (2.2.3\text{–p})'$$

In order to get GNP defined from the income side, we define income in each sector in the following way

$$V_H \equiv p_L L_H^* + (q_C C_H^* - p_L L_H) + p_A(A_H - A_H^*) - (T_H^V + T_H^A)$$

$$V_B \equiv (q_C C_B^* + q_K I_B^* - q_C C_B^U - q_K I_B^U - p_L L_B) + p_A(A_B - A_B^*)$$
$$- (T_B^V + T_B^A + T_B^S)$$

$$V_{GE} \equiv (q_C C_{GE}^* + q_K I_{GE}^* - q_C C_{GE}^U - q_K I_{GE}^U + p_L I_{GE})$$
$$+ p_A(A_{GE} - A_{GE}^*) - T_{GE}^A$$

$$V_{GG} \equiv T_{GG}^* + (q_C C_{GG}^* - p_L L_{GG}) + p_A(A_{GG} - A_{GG}^*).$$

(2.2.3–V)

This concept of income is gross in the sense that it includes depreciation on physical capital. Therefore, each $V_j$ (except $V_{GG}$) may be called
"gross income net of taxes in the $j$th sector." By using (2.2.1–L),
(2.2.1–T), (2.2.1–A) and (2.2.3–p), we can easily prove the following
relation

$$\text{GNP} = \Sigma V_j \quad (j = H, B, GE, GG)$$

(GNP defined from income distribution). (2.2.3–i)

The above expression can be rewritten in a slightly different way

$$\text{National Income} \equiv \text{GNP} (\Sigma V_j) - \text{Indirect Taxes} (T_{GG}^* - T_H^V - T_B^V)$$
$$- \text{Depreciation} (\Sigma q_K D_j)$$
$$= (V_H + T_H^V - q_K^D) + (V_B T_B^V - q_K D_B) + (V_{GE} - q_K D_{GE})$$
$$+ (V_{GG} - T_{GG}^* - q_K D_{GG}),$$

where $D_j$ is the quantity depreciated in the $j$th sector. This way of
expression is more in line with the existing national income statistics,
in which the concept of income is that of before income tax and after
depreciation.

## 2.2.2   Distribution in Production (Imputation on Physical Capital)

So far we have been concerned with summary and interpretation of
the existing national accounting system. Now we discuss the problem
of distribution in production which is not well established in the present social accounting system. Distribution in production is closely
related with the production function which has, in general, labor and
physical capital (including land) as its input components, and by the
term "distribution in production" we simply mean the problem of
how to measure the compensation for each factor in production. The
compensation for labor is directly measurable and can be separated

into its price and quantity component through the market for labor services. But the situation is quite different in case of capital due to the lack of explicit market for capital services in almost all cases. Therefore, the essential problem here is the problem of imputation on physical capital, i.e., how to impute the value of output on physical capital and how to separate the compensation for capital into its price and quantity components. The detailed and practical treatment of this problem will be made in the next section. Here we clarify only its basic features under the framework developed so far.

In order to simplify the analysis, we assume that the service price of capital ($p_K$) is common to every sector irrespective of the taxation structure and managerial efficiency. Then we can write the fundamental equality between value of input services and value of (net) output (i.e., distribution in production) in each of the four domestic sectors as follows

$$p_L L_H + p_K K_H = q_C C_H^* \qquad \text{(definition of } q_C C_H^*) \qquad (2.2.4\text{--H})$$

$$(q_C C_B^U + q_K I_B^U) + p_L L_B + p_K K_B = q_C C_B^* + q_K I_B^* - T_B^S$$
$$\text{(definition of } p_K K_B) \qquad (2.2.4\text{--B})$$

$$(q_C C_{GE}^U + q_K I_{GE}^U) + p_L L_{GE} + p_K K_{GE} = q_C C_{GE}^* + q_K I_{GE}^*$$
$$\text{(definition of } p_K K_{GE}) \qquad (2.2.4\text{--GE})$$

$$p_L L_{GG} + p_K K_{GG}' = q_C C_{GG}^* \quad \text{(definition of } q_C C_{GG}^*) \qquad (2.2.4\text{--GG})$$

where $K_{GG}'$ is the quantity of residential structures in the $GG$-sector which is only a part of $K_{GG}$. Note that (2.2.4–H) and (2.2.4–GG) are nothing but the definitions of output in the $H$-sector and in the $GG$-sector respectively, because, according to the Japanese National Income Statistics, $p_K K_H$ is the rental income in the $H$-sector including the imputed value on the owner-occupied residential structures and $p_K K_{GG}'$ is the value of of rental services provided by the general government. Therefore, it is (2.2.4–B) and (2.2.4–GE) that are important as the imputation procedure on physical capital. Note that $p_K$ is defined as the price before depreciation, before income and asset taxes and after sales taxes as can be understood by comparing (2.2.4–B) and (2.2.4–GG) with (2.2.2–B) and (2.2.2–GE) or table 2.1.

By using these imputational equations (2.2.4–H)–(2.2.4–GG), we can rewrite GNP and GDP as follows

$$\text{GNP} = p_L L_H^* + p_K(K_H + K_B + K_{GE} + K'_{GG}) + p_A(A_F^* - A_F)$$
$$+ (T_B^S + T_F^S) \tag{2.2.5–p}$$
$$\text{GDP} = p_L(L_H + L_B + L_{GE} + L_{GG}) + p_K(K_H + K_B + K_{GE} + K'_{GG})$$
$$+ (T_B^S + T_F^S). \tag{2.2.5–p)'}$$

Namely, according to our way of imputation on physical capital, GNP (except as sales tax) as the income concept can be expressed as the sum of income from labor and income from wealth (i.e., income from physical capital plus income from net claims on foreigners). On the other hand, GDP (except sales tax) as the products concept consists of compensation for labor and compensation for physical capital. Sales tax $(T_B^S + T_F^S)$ is considered here as part of the government services which contributes independently to national income and domestic product, because the other taxes $(T_B^V, T_B^A$ and $T_{GE}^A)$ which appear in the production processes are included in the compensation for capital and because the income tax in the $H$-sector $(T_H^V)$ is included in the income from both labor and financial assets. In other words, our imputed price of capital services $(p_K)$ and the market prices for labor and financial services $(p_L$ and $p_A)$ allow for invisible services provided by the general government as far as they are reflected by the asset and income taxes in the private government enterprises sectors. In this context, $p_K$ in the $H$-sector should be considered (or redefined) as the price before asset tax $(T_H^A)$.

There are two problems to be pointed out in relation with the discussions made so far. One is the fact that the physical capital other than residential structures in the general government sector is neglected in the present social accounting system, and the other is the fact that money can also be considered a factor of production in the production function.[8] The first problem is closely related with that of how to evaluate the government services for which there exists no explicit market. The above way of treating government services (symbolized by (2.2.5–p) or (2.2.5–p)') is the most natural solution but it results in the neglect of government physical capital other than $K'_{GG}$ as a substitute for the explicit allowance of sales taxes in GNP. Another solution which we propose here as an example is to regard the general government sector as a producing sector but not as a final demanding sector. In this situation, the $GG$-sector produces its services $(T_{GG}^*$ and $p_K K'_{GG}$ in value) by using labor $(L_{GG})$ and capital $(K_{GG})$ as primary factors and consumption goods purchased from other sectors ($C_{GG} - p_L L_{GG}/q_C$) as intermediate inputs, while the $B$-sector and the $GE$-sector use as intermediate inputs the government services thus produced which are $T_B^V + T_B^A + T_B^S$ and $T_{GE}^A$ in value, respectively. $T_H^V + T_H^A$ is considered here as the value of final demand for government services in the $H$-sector. Then GNP defined from expenditure side must be modified to a slight extent as

$$GNP' \equiv GNP - q_C C_{GG} + (T_H^V + T_H^A), \tag{2.2.6--e}$$

and the imputational equations must be

$$p_L L_H + p_K K_H = q_C C_H^* \qquad \text{(the same as (2.2.4--H))} \tag{2.2.7--H}$$

$$(q_C C_B^U + q_K I_B^U) + p_L L_B + p_K K_B + (T_B^V + T_B^A + T_B^S)$$
$$= q_C C_B^* + q_K I_B^* \tag{2.2.7--B}$$

$$(q_C C_{GE}^U + q_K I_{GE}^U) + p_L L_{GE} + p_K K_{GE} + T_{GE}^A = q_C C_{GE}^* + q_K I_{GE}^* \tag{2.2.7--GE}$$

$$q_C(C_{GG} - p_L L_{GG}/q_C) + p_L L_{GG} + p_K K_{GG} = T_{GG}^* + p_K K_{GG}' \tag{2.2.7--GG}$$

where $p_K$ is the service price of capital after all kinds of taxes. By using these modified equations we get

$$GNP' = p_L L_H^* + p_K(K_H + K_B + K_{GE} + K_{GG}) + p_A(A_F^* - A_F) \tag{2.2.8--P}$$

$$GDP' = p_L(L_H + L_B + L_{GE} + L_{GG}) + p_K(K_H + K_B \tag{2.2.8--P)$'}$$
$$+ K_{GE} + K_{GG}).$$

Namely, in our modified case, GNP as the income concept can be expressed as the sum of income from labor and income from *national* wealth and GDP as the product concept can be expressed as the sum of compensation for labor and compensation for *total* domestic physical capital. This fact guarantees the consistency between the concept of national income and the concept of national wealth, which is the most important merit of our modified formulation. We must, however, note that the effectiveness of our formulation is dependent exclusively on the postulate that the amount (value only) of invisible government services can be measured in terms of tax payments and that the operationality of our formulation is weakened by the difficulty in separating $T_H^V$ and $T_H^A$ from $T_B^V$ and $T_B^A$ in the unincorporated enterprises sector.

Concerning the second problem, i.e., money as a factor of production, we note only the fact that money can be introduced into our production framework by modifying the imputational equations (2.2.4–B) and (2.2.4–GE). Namely, the necessary procedure is to replace $p_K K_B$ and $p_K K_{GE}$ by $p_K K_B + p_M M_B$ and $p_K K_{GE} + p_M M_{GE}$, respectively ($p_M$ = service price of money and $M_j$ = stock of money in the $j$th sector) in (2.2.4–B) and (2.2.4–GE) and to solve the modified imputational equations for $p_K$ and $p_M$.[9] But this procedure will lead to a rather asymmetrical result in the sense that GNP is expressed by the sum of income from labor, income from wealth and income from money existing in the private business and government enterprises sectors only.[10] We will neglect the role of money as a factor of production in the subsequent sections though it is operationally possible to introduce money into our analysis.

## 2.3   Product and Factor Outlay for the Producing Sector

The objective of this section is to provide the product and factor outlay accounts for the producing sector, which is here identified with the integrated private and government enterprises sector (households and nonprofit institutions sector ($H$) + private business sector ($B$) + government enterprises sector ($GE$)). Note that the private business sector can be separated into corporate business sector ($CB$) and noncorporate business sector ($NB$) (i.e., $B = CB + NB$), and this separation will be made in the estimation and data construction of real capital stocks and service prices of capital, which is another objective of the present section. Here we will also try to separate output into consumption goods component and investment goods component based on the product account for the producing sector. Speaking strictly, pure producing sector may be identified with the integrated private business and government enterprises sector (i.e., $B + GE$), but we regard the households sector as a component of our producing sector because the productive activities of the $H$-sector cannot be neglected and the difference in character between households sector and noncorporate business sector is a matter of degree. On the other hand, the general government sector can be neglected from the point of view of productive activities in the ordinary sense of the words and is excluded in our definition of producing sector.

### 2.3.1    Basic Accounting Relationships

Let us begin our discussions with the perspective view of the producing sector based on the accounting framework developed in section
2.2.  The notation and assumptions in this subsection are completely
the same as in section 2.2.

The quantities of (net) outputs in the producing sector are obviously defined as

$$C^* \equiv C_H^* + C_B^* + C_{GE}^* - C_B^U - C_{GE}^U$$
$$I^* \equiv I_B^* + I_{GE}^* - I_B^U - I_{GE}^U \tag{2.3.1}$$

where $C^*$ is the quantity of consumption goods produced (net), and $I^*$
is the quantity of investment goods produced (net). Then, our first
task is to derive fundamental equalities in the accounting system for
the producing sector, i.e.,
Value of Output = Factor Income = Value of Input Services.
As is noted in the previous section, we do not pay attention to sales
tax in our analysis of producing sector and adopt the concept of value
of output after sales tax, i.e.,

$$q_C^* C^* + q_K^* I^* \equiv q_C C^* + q_K I^* - T_B^S , \tag{2.3.2}$$

where $q_C^*$ is the price of consumption goods after sales tax, and $q_K^*$ is
the price of investment goods after sales tax.  In the foreign sector also
we get a similar definitional equation

$$q_C^* C_F^* + q_K^* I_F^* \equiv q_C C_F^* + q_K I_F^* - T_F^S . \tag{2.3.3}$$

In the practical sense or from the point of view of data construction,
this equation should be interpreted as the definition of import quantities, $C_F^*$ and $I_F^*$, under the given $q_C^*$ and $q_K^*$.  Then we get

$$\begin{aligned}
q_C^* C^* + q_K^* I^* &= q_C(C_H^* + C_B^* + C_{GE}^* - C_B^U - C_{GE}^U) \\
&\quad + q_K(I_B^* + I_{GE} - I_B^U - I_{GE}^U) - T_B^S \text{ (from (2.3.2) and (2.3.1))} \\
&= p_L(L_H + L_B + L_{GE}) + p_K(K_H + K_B + K_{GE}) \\
&\quad \text{(from (2.2.4–H), (2.2.4–B) and (2.2.4–GE))} \\
&\equiv p_L L + p_K K \tag{2.3.4}
\end{aligned}$$

which shows the equality between value of output (after sales tax) and value of input services (before asset and income taxes) in our producing sector. We have derived this relation from the supply (production) side but we must derive it from the demand (expenditure) side in order to obtain the data for related variables from the National Income Statistics, i.e.,

$$
\begin{aligned}
q_C^* C^* + q_K^* I^* &= \text{GNP} - q_C C_{GG}^* - (p_L(L_F - L_F^*) + p_A(A_F^* - A_F)) \\
&\quad - (T_B^S + T_F^S) \quad \text{(from (2.2.3–p) and the first line of (2.3.4))} \\
&= (\Sigma\, V_j - (T_{GG}^* - (T_{GG}^* - T_H^V - T_B^V)) - (p_L L_{GG} + p_K K_{GG}') \\
&\quad - (p_L(L_F - L_F^*) + p_A(A_F^* - A_F)) + (T_H^A + T_B^A + T_{GE}^A) \\
&\qquad\qquad \text{(from (2.2.1–T), (2.2.3–i) and (2.2.4–GG))} \\
&= p_L L + p_K K \qquad \text{(from (2.3.4))} \qquad\qquad (2.3.5)
\end{aligned}
$$

Namely, the equality between the first line and the second line of equation (2.3.5) shows the equality between value of output and factor income in the producing sector and our product and factor outlay accounts (table 2.2) are derived straightforwardly from this relation. On the other hand, the equality between the second and the third lines of (2.3.5) shows the identity between factor income and value of input services and will be used to separate capital input into price and quantity components (table 2.5).

Our second task here is to provide the conceptual basis for constructing the data for consumption goods $(q_C^*, C^*)$ and investment goods $(q_K^*, I^*)$ in our producing sector. From (2.2.3–e), the first line of (2.3.5) and (2.3.3), we get

$$
\begin{aligned}
q_C^* C^* + q_K^* I^* &= q_C(C_H + C_{GG} + C_F - C_{GG}^*) + q_K(I_H + I_B + I_{GE} + I_{GG} + I_F) \\
&\quad - (T_B^S + T_F^S) - (q_C^* C_F^* + q_K^* I_F^*). \qquad\qquad (2.3.6)
\end{aligned}
$$

Now we assume that the rate of sales tax $(t^S)$ is common to both kinds of output. Note that we will adopt the same assumption also in case of data construction in the next subsection. Then we get

$$
q_C^* = (1 - t^S)q_C, \qquad q_K^* = (1 - t^S)q_K \qquad\qquad (2.3.7)
$$

and

$$
t^S = \frac{T_B^S + T_F^S}{q_C(C_H + C_{GG} + C_F - C_{GG}^*) + q_K(I_H + I_B + I_{GE} + I_{GG} + I_F)} \qquad (2.3.8)
$$

which leads to

$$q_C^* C^* + q_K^* I^* = q_C^*(C_H + C_{GG} + C_F - C_{GG}^* - C_F^*)$$
$$+ q_K^*(I_H + I_B + I_{GE} + I_{GG} + I_F - I_F^*) . \tag{2.3.9}$$

This last relation is the explicit identity which can also be derived from (2.3.1), (2.2.1–C) and (2.2.1–I) under the condition that $q_C^*$ and $q_K^*$ are known. The essence of the separation of output, therefore, lies in how to determine the rate of sales tax (equation (2.3.8)) and the two output prices after sales tax (equation (2.3.7)).

### 2.3.2   Product and Factor Outlay Accounts for the Producing Sector

We have already described most of the basic accounting relationships for our producing sector. In this and subsequent subsections, we will provide the actual accounts and the data for some variables relevant to our analysis based on the Japanese National Income Statistics.

*Values of output = factor income.* Let us begin our discussions with the product and factor outlay accounts which show the fundamental equality between value of output and factor income in our producing sector. This accounting identity, which can be called "Gross Domestic Product and Factor Outlay for Private Sector and Government Enterprises" is shown in table 2.2. Table 2.2 is the result derived directly from equation (2.3.5) of the previous subsection. There are several points to be noted or explained concerning this table. First, value of product by general government (i.e., $q_C C_{GG}^*$) consists of "domestic product by public administration" (i.e., $p_L L_{GG}$) and "rent by general government" (i.e., $p_K K_{GG}'$). But the present National Income Statistics does not permit us to separate rental income from other property income, "interest and dividend by general government" (i.e., $p_A A_{GG}$). Therefore, we have approximated value of output in general government (i.e., $q_L C_{GG}^* + p_K K_{GG}'$) by "domestic product by public administration" plus "rent, interest and dividend by general government" minus "interest on public debt" (i.e., $p_L L_{GG} + (p_K K_{GG}' + p_A A_{GG}) - p_A A_{GG}^*$). There is, of course, no guarantee about $p_A(A_{GG} - A_{GG}^*) = 0$ and $p_A(A_{GG} - A_{GG}^*)$ should be subtracted from both sides of product and factor outlay if possible. Secondly, monopoly profit (profit from government tobacco monopoly) which belongs to the indirect tax cate-

**Table 2.2**
Gross domestic product and factor outlay for private sector and government enterprises

| | | |
|---|---|---|
| 1. | | GNP |
| 2. | − | domestic product by public administration[1] |
| 3. | − | rent, interest and dividend by general government |
| 4. | + | interest on public debt |
| 5. | − | indirect tax |
| 6. | + | monopoly profit[2] |
| 7. | + | business tax[2] |
| 8. | + | real estate acquisition tax[2] |
| 9. | + | motor vehicle tax (prefectural tax)[2] |
| 10. | + | mine-lot tax[2] |
| 11. | + | fixed estate tax (prefectural tax)[2] |
| 12. | + | fixed estate tax (municipal tax)[2] |
| 13. | + | small motor vehicle tax (municipal tax)[2] |
| 14. | + | current subsidies |
| 15. | − | net factor income received from abroad[3] |
| | | |
| 1. | | provisions for the consumption of fixed capital |
| 2. | + | statistical discrepancy |
| 3. | + | compensation for employees |
| 4. | − | domestic product by public administration |
| 5. | + | income from unincorporated enterprises |
| 6. | + | rent |
| 7. | + | interest |
| 8. | + | dividend |
| 9. | + | corporate transfer to households and institutions |
| 10. | + | direct (corporate) tax |
| 11. | + | savings of private corporation |
| 12. | + | profit from government enterprises |
| 13. | + | monopoly profit |
| 14. | + | certain indirect taxes (above, 7 + 8 + 9 + 10 + 11 + 12 + 13) |
| 15. | − | net factor income from abroad |
| 16. | − | interest on consumers' debt |

[1] NIS (1969), section 1, table 6 (pp. 30–31).
[2] Japan Statistical Yearbook (1969), 1951–1969.
[3] NIS (1969), section 1, account 6 (pp. 12–13). For the remaining items, see NIS (1969), section 1, account I (pp. 2–3) and table 2 (pp. 16–17).

gory is included as the income of the government enterprises sector in our product and factor outlay accounts without being excluded as the sales tax. Note that, according to the National Income Statistics, the government enterprises sector has the following component institutions:

the government enterprises = 3 public corporations (tobacco monopoly, national railway and telegraph and telephone company) + 5 operational enterprises (postal service, national forestry, printing, mintage, and alcohol monopoly) + some government financial institutions + other central government institutions + local government enterprises.

This definition of the GE-sector in the National Income Statistics differs a little from that in the National Wealth Survey. This difference, though small, will be allowed for in constructing the data for capital stock in order to preserve the consistency between stock data and flow data. Thirdly, motor-vehicle tax, mine-lot tax and fixed estate tax are the pure asset tax, while real property acquisition tax is the tax which is levied on the assessed value of land, houses and other dwellings purchased or constructed.[11] This difference in nature among various kinds of asset tax, together with the difference between asset and income taxes, will be allowed for in constructing the data for the service price of capital. Finally, statistical discrepancy is explicitly introduced in order to maintain accounting identities.

The value of output defined in table 2.2 must be separated into consumption goods component ($q_C^*$, $C^*$) and investment goods component ($q_K^*$, $I^*$). This separation was made based on the discussions in the previous subsection, which imply the following practical procedure:

1. By using Foreign Trade Statistics,[12] we compute value of consumption goods exports, value of investment goods export, value of consumption goods import and value of investment goods import, where consumption goods are identified with food stuffs, crude materials, fuels and light industry products, and investment goods are identified with heavy industry products and others. Note that in Foreign Trade Statistics exports are measured in terms of F.O.B. and imports in terms of C.I.F. Then we compute value shares of investment goods in total values of exports and imports ($w_{I_F}$ and $w_{I_F^*}$, respectively). The required data are not available for 1951–1952 and so the value shares of 1953 are assumed to be equal to those of 1951–1952.[13]

2. By using National Income Statistics (NIS),[14] we get $q_K I_F$ (= merchandise exports (F.O.B.) $\times w_{I_F}$), $q_C C_F$ (= exports of goods and nonfactor services $- q_K I_F$), $q_K I_F^*$ (= imports of goods and nonfactor services $\times w_{I_F^*}$) and $q_C C_F^*$ (= imports of goods and nonfactor services $- q_K I_F^*$). Since the values of $w_{I_F}$ and $w_{I_F^*}$ are based on calendar year data, some errors may arise, but they are negligible.

3. We compute $q_C (C_H + C_{GG}) - q_C C_{GG}^*$ (= private consumption expenditure + general government consumption expenditure – domestic product by public administration (= $p_L L_{GG}$) – rent, interest and dividend by general government less interest on public debt ($\div p_K K_{GG}'$)) based on NIS.

4. We get $q_K (I_H + I_B + I_{GE} + I_{GG})$ (= gross domestic capital formation) directly from NIS.

5. We compute $T_B^S + T_F^S$ (= indirect tax – monopoly profit – ... – current subsidies (item 5 ~ item 14 in the product side of table 2.1)).

6. Then we get $t^S$ (average and common rate of sales tax), i.e.,

$$t^S = (T_B^S + T_F^S) / (q_C(C_H + C_{GG} + C_F - C_{GG}^*) + q_K(I_H + I_B + I_{GE} + I_{GG} + I_F)).$$

7. We compute $q_C$ (= implicit deflator common to $C_H$ and $C_{GG}$) based on NIS and get $q_K$ (= implicit deflator for modestic capital formation) directly from NIS.[15]

8. Then we get $q_C^* = (1 - t^S)q_C$ and $q_K^* = (1 - t^S)q_K$.

9. Finally we get

$$C^* = ((1 - t^S)q_C(C_H + C_{GG} + C_F - C_{GG}^*) - q_C^* C_F^*)/q_C^*$$

and

$$I^* = ((1 - t^S)q_K(I_H + I_B + I_{GE} + I_{GG} + I_F) - q_K^* I_F^*)/q_K^* .$$

Note that by this procedure we do not attempt to separate inventories into consumption goods component and investment goods component. Namely, inventories here are regarded as investment goods and this treatment must be modified as soon as the necessary data become available. The final results obtained by the procedure mentioned above are shown in table 2.3. In this table $q_C$ and $q_K$ are the indexes of market prices (before sales tax) whose base year is 1965 *calendar* year.

**Table 2.3**
Real products and their prices

|  | $C^*$ | $I^*$ | $q_C^*$ | $q_K^*$ | $q_C$ | $q_K$ | $t^S$ |
|---|---|---|---|---|---|---|---|
| 1951 | 6927.4 | 2006.1 | 0.503 | 0.791 | 0.521 | 0.820 | 0.0348 |
| 1952 | 7703.5 | 2318.7 | 0.551 | 0.708 | 0.571 | 0.735 | 0.0357 |
| 1953 | 8143.1 | 2611.4 | 0.601 | 0.775 | 0.623 | 0.803 | 0.0347 |
| 1954 | 8614.1 | 2462.3 | 0.619 | 0.706 | 0.649 | 0.741 | 0.0465 |
| 1955 | 9278.4 | 3167.1 | 0.622 | 0.737 | 0.650 | 0.771 | 0.0433 |
| 1956 | 9456.4 | 3608.0 | 0.636 | 0.844 | 0.666 | 0.885 | 0.0458 |
| 1957 | 10174.8 | 4087.3 | 0.660 | 0.871 | 0.691 | 0.912 | 0.0450 |
| 1958 | 11241.4 | 4069.2 | 0.659 | 0.812 | 0.694 | 0.856 | 0.0505 |
| 1959 | 11957.1 | 5176.7 | 0.675 | 0.838 | 0.711 | 0.882 | 0.0497 |
| 1960 | 12913.3 | 6551.5 | 0.708 | 0.869 | 0.744 | 0.914 | 0.0488 |
| 1961 | 13672.4 | 8489.2 | 0.759 | 0.925 | 0.796 | 0.971 | 0.0473 |
| 1962 | 15329.8 | 8215.3 | 0.804 | 0.923 | 0.842 | 0.967 | 0.0450 |
| 1963 | 16398.1 | 10125.4 | 0.860 | 0.932 | 0.899 | 0.975 | 0.0433 |
| 1964 | 18127.4 | 11275.2 | 0.909 | 0.952 | 0.949 | 0.995 | 0.0425 |
| 1965 | 19129.6 | 11948.6 | 0.972 | 0.967 | 1.013 | 1.008 | 0.0401 |
| 1966 | 20563.0 | 14126.4 | 1.025 | 1.014 | 1.064 | 1.053 | 0.0367 |
| 1967 | 22304.3 | 17041.9 | 1.068 | 1.046 | 1.109 | 1.087 | 0.0370 |
| 1968 | 24589.1 | 20355.5 | 1.123 | 1.060 | 1.166 | 1.102 | 0.0373 |

($C^*$, $I^*$: billions of yen; $q_C$, $q_K$: 1965 calendar year = 1)

Therefore, $C^*$ and $I^*$ are the quantities (real values) expressed in terms of 1965 calendar year market prices.

*Factor income = value of input services.* One of the main objectives in the present paper is to measure productivity change in the producing sector (section 2.5). For this purpose, it is desirable to break down capital as much in detail as possible. The Japanese National Income Statistics permits us to allow for four types of capital, i.e., residential structures ($R$), nonresidential structures and producers' durables ($D$), inventories ($J$) and land ($S$). It is also desirable to allocate these four types of capital into various types of economic units in order to consider the effects of taxation on the price of capital service precisely. We have hitherto explicitly allowed for three types of economic units in the producing sector, i.e., households sector ($H$), private business sector ($B$) and government enterprises sector ($GE$), but we will hereafter separate private business into corporate business ($CB$) and noncorporate business ($NB$). Therefore, the capital and its corresponding service prices are classified according to the two-way classification scheme, i.e., $K_{ij}$ and $p_{ij}$ where $i = R, D, J, S$ and $j = H, CB, NB, GE$.

The effect of taxation on the service price can be seen as follows by considering the case of residential structures in the corporate business sector where all kinds of taxes can be allowed for. The relationship between service price and asset price can be derived from the equality between the asset price and the present value of the future flows of net receipts. We adopt the following notation:

$q(t)$ = the asset price in the $t$th year

$p(s)$ = the service price in the $s$th year $s \geq t$

$r$      = the after-tax rate of return

$\mu$    = the rate of depreciation (in the declining balance scheme)

$u$      = the rate of direct corporate tax

$v$      = the rate of business tax

$t_a$    = the rate of asset tax

$k$      = the rate of real estate acquisition tax

$D(s - t)$ = the depreciation scheme in the $(s - t)$th year.

Then the net receipt in the $s$th period is

$$p^*(s) - v[p^*(s) - q(t)(1 + k)D(s - t)]$$
$$- u[p^*(s) - q(t)(1 + k)D(s - t) - v(p^*(s) - q(t)(1 + k)D(s - t)]$$
$$= (1 - u)(1 - v)p^*(s) + [u + v(1 - u)]q(t)(1 + k)D(s - t)$$

where $p^*(s) = e^{-\mu(s - t)}(p(s) - t_a q(s))$. Here we note that the business tax must be included in its tax basis. In other respects, it is quite the same as the direct corporate tax. Then the equality between the asset price and the present value of future net receipts becomes

$$q(t) = \int_t^\infty e^{-r(s - t)}[e^{-\mu(s - t)}(1 - u)(1 - v)(p(s) - t_a q(s))$$
$$+ (u + v(1 - u)q(t)(1 + k)D(S - t)]\,ds - kq(t).$$

From this equation the relationship between asset price and service price can be derived, i.e.,

$$p = \frac{(1 + k)(1 - [u + v(1 - u)]Z)}{(1 - u)(1 - v)}\left[r + \mu - \frac{\dot{q}}{q}\right]q + t_a q$$

where $z = \int_t^\infty e^{-r(s-t)}D(s - t)\,ds$. The discrete expression for this formula is:[16]

$$p_t = \phi_t[q_{t-1}r_t + q_t\mu - (q_t - q_{t-1})] + q_t t_{at}$$

where

$$\phi_t = \frac{(1 + k_t)\,(1 - [u_t + v_t(1 - u_t)]\,z_t}{(1 - u_t)\,(1 - v_t)}.$$

The formula for $\phi$ of other sectors and of other types of capital can be derived from the above formula by letting the appropriate parameters be zero. The results are shown in table 2.4. As will be explained in details later, the blank squares correspond to the nonexistence of such capitals. Note that business tax in the noncorporate business sector is regarded as asset tax, because the way of taxation is very complicated within the category of noncorporate business.[17] Note also that real estate acquisition tax is neglected in case of land acquisition, because land acquisition is neglected in constructing the quantity of land series which will be explained later.[18]

The prices of various capital services are given by using the formula derived above, i.e.,

$$p_{ij,t} = \phi_{ij,t}[q_{i,t-1}\,r_{j,t} + q_{i,t}\mu_i - (q_{i,t} - q_{i,t-1})] + q_{i,t}t_{aj,t}$$

where $i = R,\ D,\ J,\ S$, and $j = H,\ C^B,\ N^B,\ GE$. Note that $r$ and $t_a$ are assumed to be constant within the $j$th sector. On the other hand, the

**Table 2.4**

$\phi_{ij}$

|   | H | CB | NB | GE |
|---|---|---|---|---|
| R | $1 + K_t$ | $\dfrac{(1 + k_t)(1 - [u_t + v_t(1 - u_t)]z_{kt})}{(1 - u_t)(1 - v_t)}$ | — | — |
| D | — | $\dfrac{1 - [u_t + v_t(1 - u_t)]z_{Dt}}{(1 - u_t)(1 - v_t)}$ | 1 | 1 |
| J | — | $\dfrac{1}{(1 - u_t)(1 - v_t)}$ | 1 | 1 |
| S | 1 | $\dfrac{1}{(1 - u_t)(1 - v_t)}$ | 1 | 1 |

quantity of capital (services) is estimated by using the perpetual inventory method which corresponds to the declining balance formula in depreciation, i.e.,

$$K_{ij,t} = I_{ij,t} + (1 - \mu_i)K_{ij,t-1} \, .$$

Then the value of services provided by the $j$th sector can be computed and must be equal to the factor income in the $j$th sector, i.e.,

$$p_{RJ}K_{Rj} + p_{Dj}K_{DJ} + p_{Jj}K_{Jj} + p_{Sj}K_{Sj}$$
$$= \text{factor income (due capital) in the } j\text{th sector } (V_{Kj}^*) \, .$$

Therefore this relationship requires allocating each component of the factor income in table 2.2 into the corresponding sectors. Table 2.5 shows the allocation and the identity between factor income and value of services in the $j$th sector. Table 2.5 also shows the same identity in the labor input, i.e.,

factor income by workers $(V_L^*)$ = value of labor services = $p_L \cdot L$ .

We neglected the real estate acquisition tax and motor-vehicle tax in the $GE$-sector, because government enterprises are not subject to fixed estate tax which occupies the dominant part in the total amount of asset taxes.

The provisions for the consumption of fixed capital ($DP$) include "damages of fixed capital by accidents" and are allocated into each sector by using the relative shares of depreciation allowance.[19] Income from unincorporated enterprises is split into two parts, compensation for capital services ($P_N$) and compensation for labor services ($W_N$). This separation is made by using the data for the number of self-employed persons ($L_s$) and the number of employees ($L_e$).[20] Namely, $W_N$ is estimated by the formula $(W_B + W_{GG}) \times (L_s/L_e)$ in table 2.5. The unpaid family workers are not considered here, because Japanese non-corporate business sector is not so efficient as the other sectors. Total interest other than that on consumers' debt (i) is allocated by using the value shares of total capital in each sector. This is a very crude way of allocation, though it is assumed that total debt is proportional to the total value of capital in each sector.[21] Real estate acquisition tax ($T_{re}$) is separated by using the relative share of new investment expenditure on residential structures in each sector. Motor-vehicle tax ($T_m$) and

**Table 2.5**
Factor income = value of input services

| Factor input | | | | Households (H) |
|---|---|---|---|---|
| | | | | $r_H, t_{aH}$ |
| | Residential Structures (R) | | $q_R$ | $P_{RH}(r_H, \mu_R, q_R, t_{aN}, \phi_{RH})$ |
| | | | $\mu_R$ | $K_{RH}(K^0_{RH}, \mu_R, I_{RH})$ |
| | Nonresidential Structures + | | $q_D$ | — |
| | Producers' Durables (D) | | $\mu_D$ | — |
| | Inventories (J) | | $q_J$ | — |
| | | | $\mu = 0$ | — |
| | Land (S) | | $q_S$ | $P_{SH}(r_H, \mu_S = 0, q_S, t_{aH}, \phi = 1)$ |
| | | | $\mu = 0$ | $K_{SH}(K^0_{SH}, \mu_S = 0, I_{SH} = 0)$ |
| Factor income | 1. provisions for the consumption of fixed capital $(DP = DP_H + DP_{CB} + DP_{NB} + DP_{GE})$ | | | $DP_H$ |
| | 2. statistical discrepancy (SD) | | | |
| | 3. compensation for employees $(W_B + W_{GG})$ | | | |
| | 4. $(-)$ domestic product by public administration $(W_{GG})$ | | | |
| | 5. income from unincorporated enterprises $(W_{NB} + P_{NB})$ | | | |
| | 6. rent (Rent) | | | Rent |
| | 7. interest other than on consumers' debt $(i = i_{CB} + i_{NB} + i_{GE})$ | | | |
| | 8. divendend (Div) | | | |
| | 9. corporate transfer (TR) | | | |
| | 10. direct corporate tax $(T_u)$ | | | |
| | 11. savings of private corporation $(S_{CB})$ | | | |
| | 12. profit from government enterprises $(P_{GE})$ | | | |
| | 13. monopoly profit (MP) | | | |
| | 14. certain indirect taxes $(T = T_H + T_{CB} + T_{NB})$ | | | $T_H$ |
| |    business taxes $(T_b = T_{bc} + T_{bN})$ | | | |
| |    real estate acquisition tax $(T_{re} = T_{reH} + T_{reC})$ | | | $T_{reH}$ |
| |    motor vehicle tax $(T_m = T_{mC} + T_{mN})$ | | | |
| |    fixed estate tax $(T_f = T_{fH} + T_{fG} + T_{fN})$ | | | $T_{fH}$ |
| |    mine-lot tax $(T_{mine})$ | | | |
| | 15. $(-)$ net factor income from abroad $(Div_f)$ | | | |
| | Total | | | $V^*_{KH}$ |

**Table 2.5 (continued)**

| Physical capital | | | Labor |
|---|---|---|---|
| Corporate business (CB) | Noncorporate business (NB) | Government enterprises (GE) | |
| $r_{CB}, t_{aCB}$ | $r_{NB}, t_{aNB}$ | $r_{GE}, t_{aGE=0}$ | |
| $P_{RCB}(r_{CB}, \mu_R, q_R, t_{aCB}, \phi_{RCB})$<br>$K_{RCB}(K_{RCB}^0, \mu_R, I_{RCB})$ | —<br>— | —<br>— | |
| $P_{DCB}(r_{CB}, \mu_D, q_D, t_{aCB}, \phi_{DCB})$<br>$K_{DCB}(K_{DCB}^0, \mu_D, I_{DCB})$ | $P_{DNB}(r_{NB}, \mu_D, q_D, t_{aNB}, \phi = 1)$<br>$K_{DNB}(K_{DNB}^0, \mu_D, I_{DNB})$ | $P_{DGE}(r_{GE}, \mu_D, q_D, t_{aGE}, \phi = 1)$<br>$K_{DGE}(K_{DGE}^0, \mu_D, I_{DGE})$ | $P_L * L$ |
| $P_{JCB}(r_{CB}, \mu_J = 0, q_J, t_{aCB}, \phi_{JCB})$<br>$K_{JCB}(K_{JCB}^0, \mu_J = 0, I_{JCB})$ | $P_{JNB}(r_{NB}, \mu_J = 0, q_J, t_{aNB}, \phi = 1)$<br>$K_{JNB}(K_{JNB}^0, \mu_J = 0, I_{JNB})$ | $P_{JGE}(r_{GE}, \mu_J = 0, q_J, t_{aGE}, \phi = 1)$<br>$K_{JGE}(K_{JGE}^0, \mu_J, I_{JGE})$ | |
| $P_{SCB}(r_{CB}, \mu_S = 0, q_S, t_{aCB}, \phi_{SCB})$<br>$K_{SCB}(K_{SCB}^0, \mu_S = 0, I_{SCB} = 0)$ | $P_{SNB}(r_{NB}, \mu_S = 0, q_S, t_{aNB}, \phi = 1)$<br>$K_{SNB}(K_{SNB}^0, \mu_S = 0, I_{SNB} = 0)$ | $P_{SGE}(r_{GE}, \mu_S = 0, q_S, t_{aGE} = 0, \phi = 1)$<br>$K_{SGE}(K_{SGE}^0, \mu_S = 0, I_{SGE} = 0)$ | |
| $DP_{CB}$ | $DP_{NB}$ | $DP_{GE}$ | |
| | SD | | |
| | | | $W_B + W_{GG}$<br>$(-)W_{GG}$ |
| | $P_{NB}$ | | $W_{NB}$ |
| $i_{CB}$<br>Div<br>TR<br>$T_u$<br>$S_{CB}$ | $i_{NB}$ | $i_{GE}$ | |
| | | $P_{GE}$<br>MP | |
| $T_{CB}$<br>  $T_{bc}$<br>  $T_{reC}$<br>  $T_{mC}$<br>  $T_{fC}$<br>  $T_{mine}$<br>  $(-)\,Div_f$ | $T_{NB}$<br>  $T_{bN}$<br><br>  $T_{mN}$<br>  $T_{fN}$ | | |
| $V_{KCB}^*$ | $V_{KNB}^*$ | $V_{KGE}^*$ | $V_L^*$ |

fixed estate tax ($T_f$) are allocated according to the value of total capital stock in each sector. Total income from capital in each sector ($V_K^{*j}$) and total income from labor ($V_L^*$) are shown in table 2.6.

### 2.3.3 Measurement of Real Capital Stocks

As it was shown above, the perpetual inventory method is employed to estimate the level of capital stock for each investment good. This method requires three basic data: (1) the investment series in constant prices ($I_{ij}$); (2) the average lifetime of capital ($n_i$); and (3) the capital stock in the benchmark year ($K_{ij}^o$).

The real investment series for each type of capital except land is obtained from the national income statistics,[22] but it must be allocated into each sector of the economy. This allocation is made by using the nominal investment series for each sector in the national income statistics.[23] Since it is impossible to separate out the investment series on residential structures in the noncorporate sector, it is incorporated

**Table 2.6**
Total capital income in each sector and total labor income

|      | $V_{KCB}^*$ | $V_{KNB}^*$ | $V_{KH}^*$ | $V_{KGE}^*$ | $V_L^*$ |
|------|---------|---------|---------|---------|---------|
| 1951 | 556.2   | 777.8   | 120.8   | 172.3   | 3446.6  |
| 1952 | 792.0   | 631.4   | 160.5   | 227.1   | 4076.7  |
| 1953 | 946.3   | 871.7   | 212.1   | 260.6   | 4629.8  |
| 1954 | 1144.8  | 446.9   | 249.0   | 227.6   | 5004.3  |
| 1955 | 1155.5  | 923.9   | 292.1   | 225.3   | 5508.4  |
| 1956 | 1546.9  | 784.9   | 347.4   | 236.6   | 6145.8  |
| 1957 | 2085.5  | 647.5   | 401.1   | 341.5   | 6800.9  |
| 1958 | 1885.2  | 800.4   | 463.5   | 348.0   | 7212.0  |
| 1959 | 2534.4  | 1018.5  | 577.4   | 358.8   | 7929.8  |
| 1960 | 3545.6  | 1022.1  | 694.5   | 440.3   | 9142.1  |
| 1961 | 4466.8  | 1624.9  | 830.2   | 584.2   | 10723.8 |
| 1962 | 4763.8  | 1220.2  | 955.7   | 581.6   | 12393.0 |
| 1963 | 5621.1  | 1817.1  | 1117.4  | 643.5   | 14319.1 |
| 1964 | 6504.8  | 2352.7  | 1328.6  | 592.6   | 16446.1 |
| 1965 | 6772.4  | 2494.1  | 1545.2  | 638.0   | 18719.8 |
| 1966 | 8375.0  | 3014.2  | 1816.6  | 809.3   | 21399.8 |
| 1967 | 10400.6 | 3554.3  | 2076.5  | 871.8   | 24869.8 |
| 1968 | 13142.7 | 4232.7  | 2379.2  | 1025.8  | 28468.8 |

(billions of yen)

entirely into that in the households sector. The allocation of factor income in table 2.5 allows for this procedure.

The asset prices can be represented by the implicit deflators which are available in the national income statistics.[24] It must be noted that the base year of implicit deflators is the calendar year of 1965. Since the implicit deflator of nonresidential structures and producers' durables is constructed separately for corporate business and government enterprise sectors, the common implicit deflator for this type of capital is constructed. Table 2.7 shows the real investment series and implicit deflator for each category. The data for land will be explained later.

The average lifetimes of residential structures and nonresidential structures and producers' durables are chosen as

$n_R = 50$ years and $n_D = 17$ years

according to K. Ohkawa, S. Yamada, S. Ishiwata and H. Seki (1966), who estimated the long-run capital stock series from the Meiji era, though the average lifetime of 17 years is that of nonresidential structures and producers' durables in the nonprimary industry. Therefore, the rates of depreciation for these two types of capital are

$\mu_R = 0.040$   and   $\mu_D = 0.117$ .

Of course the rates of depreciation for inventory and land are both zero.

The capital stocks except land in the benchmark year depend on "National Wealth Survey" which gives the data for the assessed values of various types of capital stock classified by owners at the end of calendar year 1960.[25] We must modify the raw data of "National Wealth Survey" in two respects. First, the assessed value of 1960 must be deflated by the implicit deflators in order to be consistent with the real investment series. Secondly, the values of capital stocks at the end of *fiscal* year 1960 must be obtained. For this purpose we adopt the following formula

$$K_t^{\text{fiscal year}} = K_t^{\text{calendar year}} + \frac{1}{4} I_t^{\text{fiscal year}} - \frac{1}{4} \mu K_t^{\text{calendar year}} .$$

Though the category of government enterprises in the National Wealth Survey is a little less broad than that in the National Income Statistics, its effect seems to be negligible.[26]

**Table 2.7**
Real investment and implicit deflators

| | $I_{RH}$ | $I_{RCB}$ | $I_{DCB}$ | $I_{DNB}$ | $I_{DGE}$ | $I_{JCB}$ | $I_{JNB}$ | $I_{JGE}$ | $q_R$ | $q_D$ | $q_J$ | $q_S$ |
|---|---|---|---|---|---|---|---|---|---|---|---|---|
| 1951 | 201.7 | 34.3 | 689.1 | 164.8 | 134.3 | 315.9 | 76.6 | 15.1 | 0.499 | 0.729 | 0.869 | 0.379 |
| 1952 | 298.4 | 31.5 | 735.0 | 238.2 | 173.8 | 278.7 | 11.9 | 35.1 | 0.535 | 0.746 | 0.887 | 0.404 |
| 1953 | 302.8 | 41.6 | 903.5 | 271.3 | 228.8 | 278.6 | 54.2 | -37.8 | 0.638 | 0.784 | 0.954 | 0.434 |
| 1954 | 356.1 | 39.2 | 801.6 | 295.1 | 225.8 | -65.8 | 86.8 | -6.8 | 0.635 | 0.780 | 0.909 | 0.464 |
| 1955 | 381.1 | 44.6 | 874.3 | 317.2 | 276.8 | 241.3 | 109.6 | 160.5 | 0.612 | 0.795 | 0.907 | 0.541 |
| 1956 | 419.7 | 60.8 | 1331.4 | 321.3 | 292.6 | 525.9 | -0.9 | 36.7 | 0.668 | 0.902 | 0.969 | 0.612 |
| 1957 | 467.8 | 72.5 | 1597.7 | 357.2 | 365.3 | 599.6 | 22.6 | -10.3 | 0.690 | 0.936 | 0.937 | 0.669 |
| 1958 | 513.0 | 74.9 | 1518.5 | 349.5 | 404.9 | 178.3 | 103.4 | 29.4 | 0.691 | 0.906 | 0.915 | 0.716 |
| 1959 | 598.8 | 100.5 | 1955.2 | 416.8 | 467.2 | 464.1 | 42.6 | 42.1 | 0.723 | 0.919 | 0.938 | 0.773 |
| 1960 | 683.5 | 154.6 | 2849.1 | 443.9 | 521.2 | 568.9 | 89.8 | 42.3 | 0.784 | 0.948 | 0.937 | 0.823 |
| 1961 | 749.3 | 164.0 | 3749.3 | 511.8 | 712.5 | 1373.4 | 31.7 | -27.0 | 0.897 | 0.982 | 0.951 | 0.849 |
| 1962 | 850.0 | 179.0 | 3680.4 | 628.8 | 884.3 | 250.6 | 45.5 | -19.0 | 0.921 | 0.973 | 0.961 | 0.863 |
| 1963 | 1118.1 | 199.1 | 4031.7 | 708.2 | 1030.7 | 1055.9 | 90.9 | -54.2 | 0.951 | 0.978 | 0.982 | 0.894 |
| 1964 | 1364.2 | 231.2 | 4673.6 | 824.2 | 986.8 | 617.7 | 79.6 | 61.1 | 0.983 | 0.993 | 0.995 | 0.958 |
| 1965 | 1663.6 | 203.8 | 4017.1 | 978.1 | 1195.5 | 615.2 | 74.6 | 88.9 | 1.008 | 1.003 | 1.014 | 1.014 |
| 1966 | 1832.6 | 189.7 | 4915.9 | 1129.3 | 1321.0 | 1059.8 | 114.4 | 113.6 | 1.082 | 1.044 | 1.041 | 1.076 |
| 1967 | 2140.1 | 158.1 | 6344.5 | 1330.1 | 1479.9 | 1724.4 | 36.5 | 240.4 | 1.172 | 1.060 | 1.062 | 1.154 |
| 1968 | 2445.5 | 277.5 | 7669.5 | 1664.2 | 1595.1 | 1958.0 | 16.0 | 238.2 | 1.239 | 1.068 | 1.068 | 1.245 |

($I_{RC} - I_{JG}$: billions of yen; $q_R - q_S$: 1965 calendar year = 1)

The capital stock series are shown in table 2.8.

The land data is the weakest point in this paper. Due to the lack of necessary data, we cannot help constructing a very crude series for land by using the available data as efficiently as possible. Area data for each private sector is available in the National Wealth Survey of 1955.[27] The assessed value of land in the corporate firms at the end of the 1965 fiscal year is available in the Toyokeizai Statistical Yearbook (1967).[28] Multiplying this value of land in corporate sector by the relative areas of other sectors in 1955, we estimate the 1965 value of land in each private sector.[29] The data for the value of land in the government enterprises can be found in Japan Statistical Yearbook (1965).[30] This way of estimating the land values in 1965 will result in overvaluation for noncorporate sector and undervaluation for households and government sectors.[31]

Concerning the price index for land, the data for the average price of paddy fields is available for 1955–1964,[32] and the average price index of the city land is available for 1956–1968.[33] We construct the

**Table 2.8**
Capital stock series

|  | $K_{RH}$ | $K_{RCB}$ | $K_{DCB}$ | $K_{DNE}$ | $K_{DGE}$ | $K_{JCB}$ | $K_{JNB}$ | $K_{JGE}$ |
|---|---|---|---|---|---|---|---|---|
| 1951 | 1990.6 | 234.5 | 6408.9 | 1604.3 | 799.2 | 2208.2 | 637.6 | 444.2 |
| 1952 | 2209.3 | 256.6 | 6394.1 | 1654.8 | 879.5 | 2486.9 | 649.5 | 479.3 |
| 1953 | 2423.8 | 287.9 | 6549.5 | 1732.4 | 1005.4 | 2765.5 | 703.7 | 441.5 |
| 1954 | 2682.9 | 315.6 | 6584.8 | 1824.9 | 1113.6 | 2699.7 | 790.5 | 434.7 |
| 1955 | 2956.7 | 347.6 | 6688.7 | 1928.5 | 1260.1 | 2941.0 | 900.1 | 595.2 |
| 1956 | 3258.1 | 394.5 | 7237.5 | 2024.2 | 1405.2 | 3466.9 | 899.2 | 631.9 |
| 1957 | 3595.6 | 451.2 | 7988.4 | 2144.6 | 1606.1 | 4066.5 | 921.8 | 621.6 |
| 1958 | 3964.8 | 508.1 | 8572.1 | 2243.2 | 1823.1 | 4244.8 | 1025.2 | 651.0 |
| 1959 | 4405.0 | 588.2 | 9524.3 | 2397.5 | 2077.0 | 4708.9 | 1067.8 | 693.0 |
| 1960 | 4912.3 | 719.3 | 11259.1 | 2560.9 | 2355.2 | 5277.8 | 1157.6 | 735.3 |
| 1961 | 5465.1 | 854.5 | 13691.1 | 2773.1 | 2792.1 | 6651.2 | 1189.3 | 708.3 |
| 1962 | 6096.5 | 999.3 | 15769.6 | 3077.4 | 3349.8 | 6901.8 | 1234.8 | 689.3 |
| 1963 | 6970.7 | 1158.3 | 17956.3 | 3425.6 | 3988.5 | 7957.7 | 1325.7 | 635.1 |
| 1964 | 8056.1 | 1343.3 | 20529.0 | 3949.0 | 4508.7 | 8575.4 | 1405.3 | 696.2 |
| 1965 | 9397.4 | 1493.4 | 22144.2 | 4376.7 | 5176.7 | 9190.6 | 1479.9 | 785.1 |
| 1966 | 10854.1 | 1623.4 | 24469.2 | 4994.0 | 5892.0 | 10250.4 | 1594.3 | 898.7 |
| 1967 | 12560.1 | 1716.5 | 27950.8 | 5739.8 | 6682.5 | 11977.8 | 1630.8 | 1139.1 |
| 1968 | 14503.2 | 1925.4 | 32350.1 | 6732.4 | 7495.8 | 13935.8 | 1646.8 | 1377.3 |

| 1965 | $K_{SH} = 1133.4$ | | $K_{SCB} = 2554.0$ | | $K_{SNB} = 20399.7$ | | $K_{SGE} = 136.9$ |
|---|---|---|---|---|---|---|---|
|  |  |  |  |  |  | (billions of yen) | |

land price index ($q_s$) by combining these two series using as weights the relative value shares in 1965 between the noncorporate sector and the other sectors as a whole. The missing parts of the two series are extrapolated by using the average rates of increase during the period where the data are available. The land price index thus constructed is shown in table 2.7. The quantity of land is assumed to be constant, and this may also be a strong assumption.

The value shares of each type of capital stock classified by owners are shown in table 2.9 only for the year 1965 as a reference.

### 2.3.4  Imputation of Capital Service Prices

The starting point of measuring the service prices of capital is the identity between factor income and value of services mentioned in subsection 2.3.2, i.e.,

$$p_{Rj,t} K_{Rj,t} + p_{Dj,t} K_{Dj,t} + p_{Jj,t} K_{Jj,t} + p_{Sj,t} K_{Sj,t} = V^*_{Kj,t} \quad (j = H, CB, NB, GE)$$

where

$$p_{ij,t} = \phi_{ij,t} [q_{i,t-1} r_{j,t} + q_{i,t}\mu_i - (q_{i,t} - q_{i,t-1})] + q_{i,t} t_{aj,t}$$

$$\phi_{ij,t} = \phi_{ij}(k_t, u_t, v_t, z_{RT}, z_{Dt}) \quad \begin{pmatrix} i = R, D, J, S, \\ j = H, CB, NB, GE \end{pmatrix}.$$

We now have the data for $K_{jk}$, $q_i$, $v_j$ and $\mu_i$. Therefore, all that remain to be estimated are the data for $t_{ajt}$, $k_t$, $u_t$, $v_t$, $z_{Rt}$ and $z_{Dt}$, all of which are related to the taxation structure. If all these data become available, then $r_j$ can be estimated by solving the identities and then $p_{ij}$ can be obtained.

The asset tax rate can be estimated simply by using the formula

$$t_{aj,t} = \frac{T_{aj,t}}{\sum\limits_i q_{i,t} K_{ij,t}}$$

where $T_{aj}$ is the total amount of asset tax in the $j$th sector. The formula for the rate of real estate acquisition is

$$k_t = \frac{T_{re,t}}{q_{R,t}(I_{RCB,t} + I_{RH,t})}.$$

**Table 2.9**
Relative value shares of $K_{ij}$ (1965)

|       | H     | CB    | NB    | GE    | Total |
|-------|-------|-------|-------|-------|-------|
| R     | 0.120 | 0.019 | —     | —     | 0.139 |
| D     | —     | 0.281 | 0.055 | 0.065 | 0.402 |
| J     | —     | 0.118 | 0.019 | 0.010 | 0.147 |
| S     | 0.014 | 0.032 | 0.262 | 0.002 | 0.311 |
| Total | 0.134 | 0.451 | 0.337 | 0.078 | 1.000 |

In case of corporate direct tax and business tax, we must use the effective tax rates instead of the accounting tax rates, because the services price of capital used in subsection 2.3.2 required us to add interest payments and corporate transfer to their usual tax bases. Therefore, the formulae for the effective rates of $u_t$ and $v_t$ are

$$u_t = \frac{T_u}{i_{CB} + S_{CB} + Div - Divf + TR + T_u}$$

and

$$v_t = \frac{T_{bc}}{i_{CB} + S_{CB} + Div - Divf + TR + T_u + T_{bc}}.$$

The series for $t_{jt}$, $k_t$, $u_t$ and $v_t$ are shown in table 2.10.

As to the present value of depreciation deductions, we adopt the declining balance method as the legal depreciation scheme, though the depreciation schemes in Japan are usually divided into two classes, "ordinary" and "special" depreciation, the former of which includes the straight-line method and the declining balance method.[34] The declining balance scheme in the discrete expression is

$$D_s = (1 - \alpha)^{s-1} \quad \text{and} \quad \alpha = 1 - \left( \frac{\text{scrap value}}{\text{purchase value}} \right)^{\frac{1}{n}}$$

where $s \geq 1$ and $n$ is the useful lifetime of the capital. Then the present value of depreciation deductions is

$$z = \sum_{s=1}^{n} \frac{D_s}{(1 + r)^2} = \frac{\alpha}{r + \alpha} \left[ 1 - \left( \frac{1 + \alpha}{1 + r} \right)^n \right].$$

**Table 2.10**
Rates of tax

|      | $t_{aH}$ | $t_{aC}$ | $t_{aN}$ | $k$ | $u$ | $y$ |
|------|--------|--------|--------|--------|--------|--------|
| 1951 | 0.0030 | 0.0033 | 0.0063 | 0.0000 | 0.7906 | 0.1562 |
| 1952 | 0.0040 | 0.0044 | 0.0072 | 0.0000 | 0.4918 | 0.1406 |
| 1953 | 0.0041 | 0.0045 | 0.0073 | 0.0000 | 0.4484 | 0.0961 |
| 1954 | 0.0043 | 0.0049 | 0.0070 | 0.0079 | 0.3908 | 0.0888 |
| 1955 | 0.0043 | 0.0049 | 0.0063 | 0.0199 | 0.3905 | 0.0882 |
| 1956 | 0.0039 | 0.0044 | 0.0056 | 0.0205 | 0.3630 | 0.0841 |
| 1957 | 0.0037 | 0.0043 | 0.0052 | 0.0225 | 0.3400 | 0.0774 |
| 1958 | 0.0039 | 0.0043 | 0.0053 | 0.0251 | 0.3701 | 0.0846 |
| 1959 | 0.0038 | 0.0043 | 0.0049 | 0.0211 | 0.3382 | 0.0751 |
| 1960 | 0.0036 | 0.0042 | 0.0049 | 0.0207 | 0.3196 | 0.0730 |
| 1961 | 0.0036 | 0.0042 | 0.0050 | 0.0207 | 0.3314 | 0.0768 |
| 1962 | 0.0037 | 0.0043 | 0.0051 | 0.0208 | 0.3617 | 0.0837 |
| 1963 | 0.0037 | 0.0045 | 0.0053 | 0.0163 | 0.3417 | 0.0818 |
| 1964 | 0.0037 | 0.0046 | 0.0054 | 0.0209 | 0.3509 | 0.0814 |
| 1965 | 0.0038 | 0.0049 | 0.0058 | 0.0219 | 0.3524 | 0.0805 |
| 1966 | 0.0037 | 0.0049 | 0.0059 | 0.0193 | 0.3010 | 0.0722 |
| 1967 | 0.0036 | 0.0049 | 0.0060 | 0.0186 | 0.3003 | 0.0724 |
| 1968 | 0.0035 | 0.0050 | 0.0061 | 0.0176 | 0.2785 | 0.0710 |

The ratio of scrap value to purchase value is fixed at 0.10 for most of all assets, and so we use this value.[35] We employ 50 years for $K_R$ and 17 years for $K_D$ as in the previous case, because the differences seem to be very small.[36] The rate of return is assumed to be 0.10. Then the values of $z$ for $K_R$ and $K_D$ are

$$z_R = 0.310 \quad \text{and} \quad z_D = 0.547.$$

By using the data derived up to this time, we can calculate the rates of return ($r_j$) and the prices of capital services ($p_{ij}$). The results are shown in table 2.11. The estimates of return fluctuate, reflecting the business cycles of the postwar Japanese economy. The relationship between the sizes of $r_{CB}$ and $r_{NB}$ is quite similar to that in the U.S. economy.[37] It seems that the highest values of $r_H$ among others are due to the way of imputation in estimating rental income in national income statistics.[38] We must note here that the negative values are obtained for some estimates of capital services, especially for the category of land. This is due to the extraordinary movement of land prices in the postwar Japan and due to the scarcity of data for price and quantity of land. As there is no way of improving this result

**Table 2.11**
Rates of return and prices of capital services

| | $r_H$ | $r_{CB}$ | $r_{NB}$ | $r_{GE}$ | $p_{RH}$ | $p_{RCB}$ | $p_{DCB}$ | $p_{DNB}$ | $p_{DGE}$ | $p_{JCB}$ | $p_{JNB}$ | $p_{JGE}$ | $p_{SH}$ | $p_{SCB}$ | $p_{SNB}$ | $p_{SGE}$ |
|---|---|---|---|---|---|---|---|---|---|---|---|---|---|---|---|---|
| 1952 | 0.140 | 0.021 | 0.101 | 0.159 | 0.157 | -0.004 | 0.135 | 0.149 | 0.186 | 0.005 | 0.076 | 0.120 | 0.029 | -0.035 | 0.016 | 0.035 |
| 1953 | 0.242 | 0.066 | 0.133 | 0.200 | 0.054 | -0.068 | 0.154 | 0.159 | 0.203 | -0.011 | 0.058 | 0.111 | 0.069 | -0.004 | 0.027 | 0.051 |
| 1954 | 0.088 | 0.010 | 0.069 | 0.078 | 0.088 | 0.058 | 0.145 | 0.155 | 0.157 | 0.104 | 0.117 | 0.120 | 0.010 | -0.043 | 0.003 | 0.004 |
| 1955 | 0.092 | 0.049 | 0.191 | 0.085 | 0.110 | 0.128 | 0.162 | 0.232 | 0.145 | 0.089 | 0.181 | 0.080 | -0.031 | -0.094 | 0.015 | -0.037 |
| 1956 | 0.194 | 0.140 | 0.163 | 0.163 | 0.093 | 0.089 | 0.149 | 0.133 | 0.128 | 0.115 | 0.092 | 0.085 | 0.036 | 0.010 | 0.021 | 0.017 |
| 1957 | 0.137 | 0.067 | 0.100 | 0.097 | 0.102 | 0.077 | 0.180 | 0.170 | 0.163 | 0.164 | 0.133 | 0.126 | 0.029 | -0.022 | 0.007 | 0.002 |
| 1958 | 0.110 | 0.014 | 0.080 | 0.038 | 0.108 | 0.059 | 0.202 | 0.215 | 0.171 | 0.065 | 0.101 | 0.057 | 0.029 | -0.062 | 0.010 | -0.021 |
| 1959 | 0.163 | 0.079 | 0.106 | 0.071 | 0.114 | 0.079 | 0.218 | 0.195 | 0.159 | 0.085 | 0.078 | 0.042 | 0.062 | 0.003 | 0.022 | -0.005 |
| 1960 | 0.195 | 0.101 | 0.090 | 0.085 | 0.117 | 0.066 | 0.226 | 0.169 | 0.160 | 0.156 | 0.090 | 0.081 | 0.104 | 0.048 | 0.023 | 0.016 |
| 1961 | 0.239 | 0.106 | 0.089 | 0.108 | 0.115 | 0.012 | 0.236 | 0.170 | 0.183 | 0.142 | 0.074 | 0.087 | 0.173 | 0.103 | 0.052 | 0.063 |
| 1962 | 0.132 | 0.061 | 0.047 | 0.044 | 0.137 | 0.107 | 0.246 | 0.174 | 0.166 | 0.086 | 0.040 | 0.031 | 0.110 | 0.068 | 0.031 | 0.023 |
| 1963 | 0.142 | 0.082 | 0.089 | 0.048 | 0.144 | 0.128 | 0.250 | 0.201 | 0.156 | 0.100 | 0.069 | 0.025 | 0.095 | 0.070 | 0.050 | 0.011 |
| 1964 | 0.147 | 0.088 | 0.134 | 0.029 | 0.154 | 0.141 | 0.250 | 0.238 | 0.130 | 0.128 | 0.124 | 0.016 | 0.071 | 0.029 | 0.061 | -0.037 |
| 1965 | 0.135 | 0.079 | 0.119 | 0.017 | 0.155 | 0.144 | 0.248 | 0.232 | 0.124 | 0.105 | 0.106 | -0.001 | 0.077 | 0.038 | 0.061 | -0.039 |
| 1966 | 0.177 | 0.121 | 0.137 | 0.052 | 0.154 | 0.134 | 0.258 | 0.224 | 0.133 | 0.153 | 0.118 | 0.026 | 0.121 | 0.100 | 0.064 | -0.006 |
| 1967 | 0.176 | 0.115 | 0.147 | 0.022 | 0.154 | 0.120 | 0.289 | 0.268 | 0.131 | 0.158 | 0.138 | 0.002 | 0.116 | 0.077 | 0.083 | -0.054 |
| 1968 | 0.143 | 0.121 | 0.157 | 0.017 | 0.157 | 0.175 | 0.305 | 0.289 | 0.135 | 0.195 | 0.172 | 0.017 | 0.079 | 0.078 | 0.097 | -0.071 |

significantly under the present availability of land data, we will use
the results of table 2.11 in the subsequent discussions.

## 2.4    Income, Outlay, Saving, and Wealth for the Consuming Sector

The objective of this section is to provide the wealth account for the
consuming sector which is consistent with national income statistics
for the postwar Japanese economy. The wealth of the consuming sector or the consumers' wealth is defined as the value of physical and
net financial assets held directly or indirectly by consumers who are
property owners and/or laborers. In other words, the consuming sector is identified with the integrated private sector (households sector +
private business sector) and the consumers' wealth is the net worth of
this sector. Therefore, the consumers' wealth can be called more
appropriately the *private national wealth* when it is compared with the
national wealth which is the net worth of the nation as a whole
(households sector + private business sector + government sector).
Wealth account is a stock account and so it is closely connected with
various flow accounts. In this section we will provide also the income,
outlay and saving accounts which are consistent with the wealth
account for the consuming sector. The basic idea is found in L.R.
Christensen and D.W. Jorgenson (1973b). Though one of their major
contributions is the introduction of consumer's durables and social
insurance funds into the consumers' wealth of the U.S. economy, the
latter is treated in the usual way in this section due to the lack of necessary data. On the other hand, the former is explicitly introduced
into our consumers' accounts and in this respect the content of the
present section is inconsistent with that of the previous section.[39]

### 2.4.1    Basic Accounting Relationships

In order to clarify the notion of consumers' wealth or private national
wealth, we discuss here, based on the accounting framework developed in section 2.2, the relationships between private national wealth
and national wealth, and the correspondence between wealth account
and various flow accounts, especially the saving account. The notation and assumption in this subsection are completely the same as in
section 2.2 except for the fact that the government enterprises and
the general government are integrated into the government sector

$(G = GE + GG)$. Namely, we consider here the integrated four sectors of the nation's economy according to the national balance sheet, i.e., households and nonprofit institutions sector $(H)$, private business sector $(B)$, government sector $(G)$ and foreign sector $(F)$, and we assume here again the fact that there exist in this economy only a single kind of physical asset and only a single kind of financial asset. Then the accounting identity in the balance sheet of the $j$th sector or the definition of net worth of the $j$th sector is

$$W_j = q_k K_j + q_A A_j - a_A A_j^* \qquad (j = H, B, G, F) \qquad (2.4.1)$$

where $W_j$ = net worth or wealth of the $j$th sector. Note that $K_F$ is zero and $W_F = q_A(A_F - A_F^*)$ is the net claim of foreigners. As the credit of a certain sector is always the debit of the other sectors in both cases of stock and flow, the following identities also must hold

$$\sum_j q_A A_j = \sum_j q_A A_j^* \quad \text{or} \quad \sum_j A_j = \sum_j A_j^* \qquad (j = H, B, G, F) \qquad (2.4.2)$$

and

$$\sum_j q_A \dot{A}_j = \sum_j q_A \dot{A}_j^* \quad \text{or} \quad \sum_j \dot{A}_j = \sum_j \dot{A}_j^* \qquad (j = H, B, G, F) \qquad (2.4.3)$$

which are the same equations as (2.2.1–A) and (2.2.1–$\dot{A}$).

Then the national wealth or the net worth of the nation is defined as

$$\begin{aligned} W_N &= W_H + W_B + W_G \\ &= \sum_j q_K K_J + \sum_j q_A A_j - \sum_j q_A A_j^* \qquad (j = H, B, G) \\ &= q_K K_N + q_A(A_F^* - A_F) \qquad \text{(from (2.4.2))} \end{aligned} \qquad (2.4.4)$$

where $W_N$ = national wealth and $K_N = K_H + K_B + K_G$. Namely, the national wealth is the sum of the value of domestic tangible assets and the net claims on foreigners. This is the well established relationship and has always been used in constructing the data for national wealth. On the other hand, the consumers' wealth is defined as the sum of the wealth held directly by consumers themselves in the $H$-sector and the wealth held by the property owners who are also consumers in the $B$-sector. Therefore, the consumers' wealth is the net worth of the integrated private sector ($P$) and can be called more appropriately the private national wealth.  Its symbolic expression is

$$W_P = W_H + W_B$$
$$= \sum_j q_K K_j + \sum_j q_A A_j - \sum_j q_A A_j^* \qquad (j = H, B)$$
$$= q_K K_P + q_A((A_G^* - A_G) + (A_F^* - A_F)) \qquad (2.4.5)$$

where $W_P$ = private national wealth and $K_P = K_H + K_B$.  Namely, the private national wealth is the sum of the value of private domestic tangibles assets and the net claims on government and foreigners.

So far we have been concerned with the stock relations.  Now let us turn our attention to the flow relations which are summarized in the flow of funds accounts.  The basic accounting identity of the flow side is the equality between the uses of funds and the sources of funds, i.e.,

$$q_K I_j + q_A A_j = S_j + q_A A_j^* \qquad (j = H, B, G) \qquad (2.4.6)$$

where $S_j$ = gross saving in the $j$th sector.  Saving is of course defined as the current revenue less current expenditure in each sector, i.e.,

$$S_H \equiv V_H - q_C C_H , \quad S_B \equiv V_B \quad \text{and} \quad S_G \equiv (V_{GE} + V_{GG}) - q_C C_{GG} . \qquad (2.4.7)$$

Note that the identity (2.4.6) can be derived from the definition of saving (2.4.7) and budget constraints (2.2.2–H) ~ (2.2.2–GG).  If we aggregate the identity (2.4.6) up to the national level, we get

$$\sum_j q_K I_j + \sum_j q_A A_j = \sum_j S_j + \sum_j q_A A_j^* \qquad (j = H, B, G) \qquad (2.4.8)$$

which, by allowing the identity (2.4.3), reduces to

$$q_K I_N + q_A(A_F^* - A_F) = S_N \qquad (2.4.9)$$

where $I_N + I_H + I_B + I_G$ = quantity of gross domestic investment and $S_N = S_H + S_B + S_G$ = gross national saving.  Namely, (2.4.9) shows the fact that gross domestic investment plus net foreign investment is equal to gross national saving, which is the well-known fact in the national income statistics.  On the other hand, if the aggregation is made through the private sectors only ($j = H. B.$), we obtain

$$q_K I_P + q_A(\dot{A}_G^* - \dot{A}_G) + q_A(\dot{A}_F^* - \dot{A}_F) = S_P \qquad (2.4.10)$$

where $I_P = I_H + I_B$ = quantity of gross private domestic investment and $S_P = S_H + S_B$ = *gross private national saving*. This aggregate identity (2.4.10) is the equality between the gross private national saving and the gross private domestic investment plus government deficit plus net foreign investment, and shows the uses of gross saving as in the case of (2.4.9).

Next and finally, we discuss the relationships between stock variables and flow variables. The necessary accounting (or physical) identity here is

$$\dot{K}_j = I_j - D_j \qquad (j = H, B, G) \tag{2.4.11}$$

where $D_j$ = quantity depreciated in the $j$th sector. Then the increase in national wealth becomes

$$\dot{W} = \sum_j \dot{W}_j \qquad (j = H, B, G)$$

$$= \sum (q_K \dot{K}_j) + \sum (q_A \dot{A}_j) - \sum (q_A \dot{A}_j^*) \qquad \text{(from (2.4.1))}$$

$$= \sum (q_K \dot{K}_j + \dot{q}_K K_j) + \sum (q_A \dot{A}_j + \dot{q}_A A_j) - \sum (q_A \dot{A}_j^* + \dot{q}_A A_j^*)$$

$$= \sum q_K (I_j - D_j) + \sum \dot{q}_K K_j + q_A (\dot{A}_F^* - \dot{A}_F) + \dot{q}_A (A_F^* - A_F)$$

$$\text{(from (2.4.11), (2.4.2) and (2.4.3))}$$

$$= q_K I_N + q_A (\dot{A}_F^* - \dot{A}_F) - q_K D_N + \dot{q}_K K + \dot{q}_A (A_F^* - A_F) \tag{2.4.12}$$

where

$$D_N = D_H + D_B + D_G$$

$$= S_N - q_K D + \dot{q}_K K_N + \dot{q}_A (A_F^* - A_F) \qquad \text{(from (2.4.9))}.$$

In case of the private national wealth, the same relationship becomes as follows

$$\dot{W}_P = \sum_j \dot{W}_j \qquad (j = H, B)$$

$$= q_K I_P + q_A (\dot{A}_G^* - \dot{A}_G) + q_A (\dot{A}_F^* - \dot{A}_F) - q_K D_P + \dot{q}_K K_P$$

$$\quad + \dot{q}_A (A_G^* - A_G) + \dot{q}_A (A_F^* - A_F) \tag{2.4.13}$$

where

$$D_P = D_H + D_B$$

$$= S_P - q_K D_P + \dot{q}_K K_P + \dot{q}_A ((A_G^* - A_G) + (A_F^* - A_F)).$$

Namely the change in wealth from period to period is equal to net saving (gross saving less replacement on physical capital) plus accrued capital gains in any level of aggregation or integration. By using the relation (2.4.13), we can rewrite the uses of gross private national saving expressed in the identity (2.4.10) as follows

$$S_P = \dot{W}_P + q_K D_P - \dot{q}_K K_P - \dot{q}_A((A_G^* - A_G) + (A_F^* - A_F)$$
$$= q_K D_P + (\dot{q}_K K_P) - \dot{q}_K K_P + [q_A((A_G^* - A_G) + (A_F^* - A_F))]$$
$$- \dot{q}_A((A_G^* - A_G) + (A_F^* - A_F)) \qquad \text{(from (2.4.5))} . \qquad (2.4.14)$$

The source of gross private national saving is, by definition, current revenue less current expenditure in the integrated private sector. More precisely, the gross private national saving is defined as net receipts of the $P$-sector (i.e., receipts after all kinds of payment to the $G$-sector and the $F$-sector $= V_H + V_B \equiv V_P$) less consumption expenditure of this sector $(= q_C C_H)$. Net receipts of the $P$-sector are called *gross private national income net of taxes* from the point of view of the consumer, because the integrated private sector is the sector of consumers who are property owners and/or laborers, i.e., the consuming sector. This income of the consuming sector is split into two parts, i.e.,

$$V_P = V_{LP} + V_{WP} = p_{LP} L_P + p_{WP} W_P \qquad (2.4.15)$$

where:

$V_P$    = gross private national income net of taxes
$V_{LP}$  = income from labor
$V_{WP}$  = income from wealth
$L_P$    = quantity of labor $(= L_H^*$ in section 2.2)
$p_{LP}$  = service price of labor, and
$p_{WP}$  = (imputed) service price of wealth.

Note that $p_{LP}$ and $p_{WP}$ are the service prices after every kind of tax. Service price of wealth can, of course, be expressed as (average) rate of return on wealth plus (average) rate of depreciation minus (average) rate of capitald gains. Therefore

$$r_{WP} = (V_{WP} - q_K D_P + [\dot{q}_K K_P + \dot{q}_A((A_G^* - A_G) + (A_F^* - A_F))])/W_P \quad (2.4.16)$$

were $r_{WP}$ is rate of return on wealth. Consumption expenditure of the $P$-sector is called *gross private national expenditure* and is the same concept as in the national income statistics after appropriate modifications about consumers' durables.

### 2.4.2    Income and Outlay Accounts for the Consuming Sector

We have already described most of the basic accounting relationships which are necessary in constructing the consistent wealth, income outlay and saving accounts for the consuming sector or integrated private sector. In this subsection and in subsection 2.3.3, we will discuss the actual accounts of the Japanese economy based on the National Income Statistics of Economic Planning Agency (1969) and the Flow of Funds Accounts of Bank of Japan (1969).

Let us begin our discussion with the income and outlay accounts. As was stated in the previous subsection, income of the consuming sector is called gross private national income net of taxes and defined as net receipts of the $P$-sector after all kinds of payment to the $G$-sector and the $F$-sector. This concept is, of course, closely connected with disposable income of persons in the national income statistics which is defined as net receipts of the $H$-sector. The differences between the two concepts are as follows: (1) our concept includes saving of private corporations, i.e., corporate income which is not distributed to the $H$-sector; (2) our income includes provisions for the consumption of fixed capital in the private sector and so it is the gross concept; (3) statistical discrepancy is included in our concept in order to maintain accounting identities; (4) consumers' durables are explicitly introduced and so our income includes services of consumers' durables. On the other hand, consumption expenditure of the consuming sector is the same concept as in the national income statistics except the fact that consumers consume services of consumers' durables but not consumers' durables themselves. Purchase of consumers' durables, of course, contributes to the increase in consumers' wealth. Saving is, by definition, income less consumption expenditure. Table 2.12 shows our income and outlay accounts for the consuming sector.

We must here refer to the treatment of social insurance funds. In this paper and in the usual treatment, social insurance funds are considered as belonging to the government sector.[40] In the Japanese national income statistics, the category of social insurance funds consists of the following nine components: health insurance, welfare

**Table 2.12**
Consuming sector, income and expenditure accounts

| Gross private national income net of taxes | | |
|---|---|---|
| = | (L) | Compensation of employees[1] |
| + | (L,W) | Income from unincorporated enterprises[1] |
| + | (W) | Income from property[1] |
| + | (W) | Current transfers from private corporation[1] |
| − | (W) | Interest on consumers' debt[1] |
| + | (L) | Current transfers from general government[1] |
| + | (L) | Transfers from the rest of the world[1] |
| − | (L,W) | Direct taxes and charges on persons[1] |
| − | (L) | Social insurance contributions[1] |
| − | (L) | Other current transfers to general government[1] |
| − | (L) | Transfers to the rest of the world[1] |

| Subtotal:  Disposable income of persons[1] | | |
|---|---|---|
| + | (W) | Saving of private corporations[2] |
| + | (W) | Provisions for the consumption of fixed capital[3] |
| − | (W) | Provisions for the consumption of fixed capital, government[4] |
| + | (W) | Statistical discrepancy[3] |
| + | (W) | Services of consumers' durables[5] |

| Gross private national expenditure | | |
|---|---|---|
| = | | Private consumption expenditures[1] |
| + | | Services of consumers durables[5] |
| − | | Private consumption expenditure, durables[6] |

| Gross private national saving | |
|---|---|
| = | Income – Expenditure |

[1] NIS (1969), table III, pp. 6–7.
[2] NIS (1969), table 2, pp. 16–17.
[3] NIS (1969), table I, pp. 2–3.
[4] NIS (1969), table 16, pp. 258–259.
[5] our imputation.
[6] NIS (1969), table 5, p. 236 and our estimation for 1951–1957.
(L) means income from labor
(W) means income from wealth
(L,W) means income from both labor and wealth

insurance, public personnel, mutual aid association, mariner insurance, unemployment insurance, workmens' accident compensation insurance, pensions for government employees, national health insurance and national pension. If we want to incorporate the funds of the above-mentioned social insurance accounts into the consumers' wealth, we must modify the gross private national income defined in table 2.12 and add to it the following terms:

> Social insurance contribution
>> (included in table 2.12 with negative sign)
> + Investment income in social insurance funds
>> (part of government income from property)
> + Transfers from general government to social insurance funds
> − Transfers from social insurance funds to persons
>> (part of current transfers from general government included in table 2.12 with positive sign)
> − Expenditure on goods and services in social insurance funds
>> (part of general government consumption expenditure)
> − Interest payment in social insurance funds
>> (part of interest on the public debt)
> − Gross fixed capital formation in social insurance funds
>> (part of government gross fixed capital formation)
> + Surplus of social insurance funds.

Corresponding to this modification in consumers' income, both of the government income and saving must be reduced by the same amount. This is the basic principle, but we have followed the usual treatment of social insurance funds as the available data are not enough to carry out this procedure.

The data for the variables which required computation in table 2.12 are shown in table 2.13. Concerning the data for consumers' durables, see the appendix of this section.

As was stated in the previous subsection, gross private national income net of taxes ($V_P$) can be split into two parts, income from labor ($V_{LP}$) and income from wealth ($V_{WP}$). Correspondingly in table 2.12, each item of consumers' income is identified with one of the three categories of income from labor, income from wealth and income from both labor and wealth. Therefore, in order to construct the data for both types of income, we must separate "income from unincorporated enterprises" and "direct taxes and charges on persons" into labor component and wealth component. In case of "income from unincor-

**Table 2.13**
Income and outlay accounts (data)

|      | 1 | 2 | 3 | 4 | 5 | 6 | 7 | 8 | 9 |
|------|-------|---------|---------|--------|--------|---------|---------|-------|---------|
| 1951 | 4615.1 | 3317.6 | 1297.5 | 0.0724 | 0.0520 | 3422.7 | 5715.6 | 0.598 | 1192.4 |
| 1952 | 5397.7 | 4007.8 | 1389.9 | 0.0668 | 0.0469 | 4143.2 | 6613.2 | 0.626 | 1254.5 |
| 1953 | 6509.4 | 4628.4 | 1881.0 | 0.0620 | 0.0341 | 4953.4 | 7261.3 | 0.682 | 1556.0 |
| 1954 | 6752.1 | 5144.5 | 1607.6 | 0.0557 | 0.0523 | 5301.9 | 7589.3 | 0.698 | 1450.2 |
| 1955 | 7756.5 | 5607.0 | 2149.5 | 0.0536 | 0.0368 | 5693.7 | 8256.5 | 0.689 | 2062.8 |
| 1956 | 8619.7 | 6237.7 | 2382.0 | 0.0507 | 0.0514 | 6194.9 | 8806.1 | 0.703 | 2424.8 |
| 1957 | 9637.4 | 6972.0 | 2665.4 | 0.0376 | 0.0553 | 6765.7 | 9390.4 | 0.720 | 2871.7 |
| 1958 | 10160.0 | 7414.1 | 2745.9 | 0.0359 | 0.0574 | 7290.0 | 10105.9 | 0.721 | 2870.0 |
| 1959 | 11755.8 | 8153.1 | 3602.7 | 0.0345 | 0.0413 | 8039.1 | 10953.5 | 0.733 | 3716.7 |
| 1960 | 13832.8 | 9313.0 | 4519.8 | 0.0390 | 0.0427 | 9125.5 | 11938.9 | 0.764 | 4707.3 |
| 1961 | 16903.8 | 10866.6 | 6037.2 | 0.0416 | 0.0408 | 10617.6 | 12979.7 | 0.818 | 6286.0 |
| 1962 | 18309.0 | 12521.3 | 5787.7 | 0.0436 | 0.0679 | 12041.5 | 14190.2 | 0.848 | 6267.5 |
| 1963 | 21849.9 | 14464.3 | 7385.6 | 0.0477 | 0.0558 | 14127.1 | 15630.3 | 0.903 | 7722.8 |
| 1964 | 25607.7 | 16539.8 | 9067.9 | 0.0506 | 0.0496 | 16439.3 | 17185.1 | 0.956 | 9168.4 |
| 1965 | 28306.9 | 18747.1 | 9559.8 | 0.0491 | 0.0666 | 18468.3 | 18264.3 | 1.011 | 9838.7 |
| 1966 | 33484.1 | 21440.7 | 12043.4 | 0.0467 | 0.0598 | 21117.4 | 19770.3 | 1.068 | 12366.7 |
| 1967 | 39201.6 | 24885.6 | 14316.0 | 0.0456 | 0.0615 | 24008.3 | 21693.9 | 1.106 | 15193.3 |
| 1968 | 45907.0 | 28318.2 | 17588.8 | 0.0489 | 0.0600 | 27343.5 | 23715.1 | 1.153 | 18563.5 |

1. Gross private national income ($V_P$)
2. Gross private national income, from labor ($V_{LP}$)
3. Gross private national income, from wealth ($V_{WP}$)
4. Effective rate of tax on private national income from labor ($t_L$)
5. Effective rate of tax on private national income from wealth ($t_W$)
6. Gross private national expenditure ($q_C C_P$)
7. Gross private national expenditure, at constant price ($C_P$)
8. Gross private national expenditure, implicit deflator ($q_C$)
9. Gross private national saving ($S_P$)

units: 1–3, 6, 7, 9 (billions of yen); 8 (1965 calendar year = 1) porate enterprises," this separation was made by using the data for the number of self-employed persons and the average wage rate of employees in other private sectors and government enterprises. It is, however, not so simple to separate "direct taxes and charges on persons" into labor and wealth components.

According to the Japanese national income statistics, direct taxes on persons consist of central government personal taxes ("income taxes withheld" + "income taxes not withheld" + "inheritance taxes") and local government personal taxes ("inhabitant taxes" + "motor vehicle taxes"). We first obtained the total amount of labor component $(T_L)$ by estimating the amount of labor component in each of the three tax categories, i.e., "income taxes withheld," "income taxes not withheld" and "inhabitant taxes," and then subtracted it from "direct taxes and charges on persons" to get the total amount of wealth components $(T_{WH})$. Namely, in the category of "income taxes withheld," taxes on wage and salary income and taxes on retirement income were identified with the labor component. In the category of "income taxes not withheld," the amount of labor component was estimated by multiplying the value share of assessed labor income by the total amount of "income taxes not withheld." Most of the tax payers in this category are unincorporated enterprises, and the assessed labor income in these unincorporated enterprises, which together with the assessed wage and salary income constitutes the total assessed labor income in this tax category, was estimated by using the results (labor income/ property income ratio) obtained in the separation of "income from unincorporated enterprises" mentioned above and the total amount of assessed income employed as the tax basis. By utilizing the results obtained above, the ratio between labor and wealth components in the category of central government personal taxes was computed and used to estimate the amount of labor component in the category of "inhabitant taxes." $T_L$ is the sum of the three amounts of labor component thus obtained and $T_{WH}$ is the residual obtained by subtracting $T_L$ from "direct taxes and charges on persons."[41]

The effective rate of tax on private (or personal) income from labor $(t_L)$ was computed according to the following formula

$$t_L = T_L/(V_{LP} + T_L) .$$

On the other hand, the effective rate of tax on private (not personal) income from wealth $(t_W)$ was computed by the formula

$$t_W = (T_{WH} + T_{WC})/(V_{WP} - q_K D_P + T_{WH} + T_{WC})$$

where $T_{WC}$ is the sum of direct taxes and charges on private corporations and business taxes in the corporate sector. Business taxes in the noncorporate sector were omitted, because the way of taxation is very complicated within the category of noncorporate business and it is not clear whether business taxes in this sector can be regarded as income tax or not. Note that $q_K D_P$ is not the provisions for the consumption of fixed capital in the national income statistics but the imputed value of replacement on tangible assessts which will be explained later.

Gross private national expenditure at constant prices and its implicit deflator were obtained by following the usual procedure.

### 2.4.3   Saving and Wealth Accounts for the Consuming Sector

So far we have been concerned with the actual income and outlay accounts shown in table 2.12. Now we discuss the actual saving and wealth accounts in the Japanese economy. Saving of the consuming sector which is called gross private national saving was defined as gross private national income net of taxes less gross private national expenditure. This concept of saving differs from gross (national) saving in the national income statistics in two respects: (1) our concept of saving does not include gross saving of general government, as the sector integration is made through the private sectors only; (2) our concept includes consumers' durables. These differences can clearly be seen from table 2.14, which shows the sources and uses of saving and wealth accounts. We mentioned two kinds of expression for the uses of saving in subsection 2.4.1 (see equations (2.4.10) and (2.4.14)). Correspondingly, the two ways of expression for the uses of saving are shown in table 2.14. The first way of expression makes clear the relationship between wealth (stock) account and saving (flow) account, while the second way of expression clarifies the relationship between change in wealth (change in stock) and saving (flow).

The data for variables which required computation in table 2.14 are shown in table 2.15.

In section 2.3, we have provided the data for real capital inputs in the Japanese economy for 1951–1968. There we have allowed for four types of capital, i.e., residential structures ($K_R$), nonresidential structures and producers' durables ($K_D$), inventories ($K_J$) and land ($K_S$), together with the corresponding asset prices, i.e., $q_{KR}$, $q_{KD}$, $q_{Kj}$ and

**Table 2.14**
Consuming sector, sources and uses of saving and wealth accounts

---

Sources of gross private national saving

---

=    Provisisions for the consumption of fixed capital[1]
+    Saving of private corporations[1]
+    Saving of households and private nonprofit instititutions[1]
+    Saving of general government[1]
+    Statistical discrepancy[1]

---

Subtotal: Gross (national) saving[1]

---

−    Provisions for the consumption of fixed capital, government[2]
−    Saving of general government
+    Private consumption expenditure, durables[3]

---

Uses of gross private national saving

---

=    Gross private domestic investment on tangible assets
       Gross domestic fixed capital formation, private[1]
       + Increase in stocks, private[1]
       + Private consumption expenditure, durables
+    Government deficit
       Gross domestic fixed capital formation, government[1]
       + Increase in stocks, government[1]
       − Saving of general government
       − Provisions for the consumption of fixed capital, government
+    Net lending to the rest of the world[1]
=    Replacement[4]
+    Change in the value of private domestic tangible assets
−    Capital gains accrued on private domestic tangible assets[4]
+    Change in value of net claims on government and foreigners
−    Capital gains on net claims on government and foreigners[4]

---

Private national wealth

---

=    Value of private domestic tangible assets[5]
+    Value of net claims on government and foreigners[6]

---

[1] NIS (1969), table 5, pp. 10–11.
[2] NIS (1969), table 16, pp. 258–259.
[3] NIS (1969), table 5, p. 236 and our estimation for 1951–1957.
[4] our imputation.
[5] tables 1.7 and 1.8 of our section 1.3.
[6] FFA (1).

**Table 2.15**
Saving and wealth accounts (data)

| | 1 | 2 | 3 | 4 | 5 | 6 | 7 | 8 | 9 | 10 |
|---|---|---|---|---|---|---|---|---|---|---|
| 1951 | 850.8 | — | — | — | — | 19553.0 | 19168.7 | 384.3 | 0.0664 | — |
| 1952 | 876.3 | 1273.3 | 874.9 | 24.5 | 41.9 | 20850.8 | 20422.0 | 408.8 | 0.0667 | 0.0686 |
| 1953 | 955.2 | 2176.0 | 1498.3 | 43.6 | 118.1 | 23070.3 | 22617.9 | 452.4 | 0.0815 | 0.1102 |
| 1954 | 971.9 | 835.9 | 492.6 | 16.7 | 120.9 | 23923.0 | 23453.9 | 469.1 | 0.0672 | 0.0522 |
| 1955 | 1016.8 | 2605.8 | 1876.2 | 52.1 | 267.3 | 26580.9 | 26059.7 | 521.2 | 0.0809 | 0.1233 |
| 1956 | 1225.7 | 4459.8 | 3068.5 | 89.2 | 278.3 | 31129.9 | 30519.5 | 610.4 | 0.0765 | 0.1447 |
| 1957 | 1387.9 | 3378.0 | 1620.1 | 67.6 | 338.1 | 34575.5 | 33897.5 | 678.0 | 0.0771 | 0.0936 |
| 1958 | 1441.1 | 1915.3 | 686.6 | 38.3 | -165.8 | 36529.1 | 35812.8 | 716.3 | 0.0752 | 0.0500 |
| 1959 | 1625.5 | 3787.7 | 1786.0 | 75.7 | -17.7 | 40392.5 | 39600.5 | 792.0 | 0.0892 | 0.0927 |
| 1960 | 1948.5 | 4965.1 | 1871.1 | 67.1 | 397.7 | 45424.7 | 44565.6 | 859.1 | 0.0995 | 0.1066 |
| 1961 | 2415.4 | 6662.1 | 1856.9 | 5.6 | 933.7 | 52092.4 | 51227.7 | 864.7 | 0.1159 | 0.1231 |
| 1962 | 2782.3 | 4128.9 | 468.8 | 5.8 | 181.1 | 56227.1 | 55356.6 | 870.5 | 0.1029 | 0.0650 |
| 1963 | 3244.1 | 6377.2 | 1313.8 | 535.2 | 1112.8 | 63139.5 | 61733.8 | 1405.7 | 0.1170 | 0.1040 |
| 1964 | 3796.9 | 7694.6 | 2248.1 | 615.4 | 681.5 | 71449.5 | 69428.4 | 2021.1 | 0.1269 | 0.1148 |
| 1965 | 4252.8 | 6901.2 | 2115.1 | 518.4 | 295.3 | 78869.1 | 76329.6 | 2539.5 | 0.1212 | 0.0979 |
| 1966 | 4966.7 | 10317.5 | 3779.5 | 1345.3 | 464.3 | 90531.9 | 86647.1 | 3884.8 | 0.1330 | 0.1250 |
| 1967 | 5841.1 | 13013.1 | 3893.9 | 1455.2 | 1200.0 | 105000.3 | 99660.3 | 5340.0 | 0.1363 | 0.1501 |
| 1968 | 6914.1 | 15069.1 | 3639.0 | 599.0 | 301.9 | 120668.3 | 114729.3 | 5939.0 | 0.1458 | 0.1211 |

1. Replacement $(q_K D_P)$
2. Change in value of private domestic tangible assets $((q_K \dot{K}_P))$
3. Capital gains on private domestic tangible assets $(\dot{q}_K K_P)$
4. Change in value of net claims on government and foreigners $(q_A(\dot{A}_P - A_P^*))$
5. Capital gains on net claims on government and foreigners $(\dot{q}_A(A_P - A_P^*))$
6. Private national wealth $(W_P)$
7. Value of private domestic tangible assets $(q_K K_P)$
8. Value of net claims on government and foreigners $(q_A(A_P - A_P^*))$
9. Service price of private national wealth $(P_{WP})$
10. Rate of return on private national wealth $(r_{WP})$
Units: 1–8 (billions of yen)

$q_{KS}$. Since the data for consumers' durables ($K_C$ and $q_{KC}$) are provided in the appendix of this section, we have all of the necessary data concerning the private domestic tangible assets. Namely, the value of private domestic tangible assets ($q_K K_P$) is computed as

$$q_{K,t} K_{P,t} = \sum_i q_{Ki,t} K_{i,t} \qquad (i = R, D, J, S, C) .$$

This is the value at the end of the $t$th year, since the component real capital stocks are measured at the end of the period. Then the change in the value of domestic tangible assets ($\dot{q}_K K_P$) becomes

$$q_{K,t} K_{P,t} - q_{K,t-1} K_{P,t-1} = \sum_i (q_{Ki,t} K_{i,t} - q_{Ki,t-1} K_{i,t-1}) \quad (i = R, D, J, S, C) .$$

and the capital gains on private domestic tangible assets ($\dot{q}_K K_P$) is

$$(q_{K,t} - q_{K,t-1}) K_{p,t-1} = \sum_i (q_{Ki,t} - q_{Ki,t-1}) K_{i,t-1} \qquad (i = R, D, J, S, C) .$$

We must note here that the replacement is the imputed value but not the accounting value. Since the declining balance method in depreciation is adopted in constructing the data for real capital stocks, this value ($q_K D_P$) must be

$$q_{K,t} D_{P,t} = \sum_i q_{Ki,t} \mu_i K_{i,t-1} \qquad (i = R, D, J, S, C) .$$

where $u_i$ is the rate of depreciation in the $i$th type of capital.

Our measurement of the value of net claims on government and foreigners, i.e.,

$$q_A(A_P - A_P^*) \equiv q_A \{(A_H - A_H^*) + (A_B - A_B^*)\}$$
$$= q_A\{(A_G^* - A_G) + (A_F^* - A_F)\} ,$$

is based on the Flow of Funds Accounts of Bank of Japan.[42] Namely, the data for $q_A(A_P - A_P^*)$ shown in table 2.15 is the sum of the values of *net* financial assets held by personal sector, corporate business sector and private financial institutions sector in the flow of funds accounts. Since the original data are available only for 1960–1968, a very crude series was constructed for 1951–1959 by assuming that the ratio between the value of net claims on government and foreigners and the value of domestic tangible assets (i.e., $q_A(A_P - A_P^*)/q_K K_P$) is

2 percent which is approximately the average value for the period 1960–1964, where this ratio was relatively stable. This stock variable is, of course, measured at the end of the year. Then the change in the value of net claims on government and foreigners ($\{q_A(\dot{A}_P - A_P^*)\}$) in the $t$th year is

$$q_{A,t}(A_{P,t} - A_{P,t}^*) - q_{A,t-1}(A_{P,t-1} - A_{P,t-1}^*) .$$

We must note that capital gains on net claims on government and foreigners ($\dot{q}_A(A_P - A_P^*)$) is the imputed value derived indirectly by using the identity between sources and uses of saving (see table 2.14 or equation (2.3.14) in subsection 2.3.1). Therefore, the statistical discrepancy which arises from the inconsistency between flow of funds accounts and national income statistics will be included in this category. We adopted this imputation procedure in order to maintain accounting identities and in order to avoid using the flow data in the flow of funds account which are not sufficient enough for the present purposes.

Concerning the service price of private national wealth ($p_{WP}$) and the rate of return on private national wealth ($r_{WP}$), see equations (2.3.15) and (2.3.16) in subsection 2.3.1.

## Appendix: Data for Consumers' Durables

In this section we have attempted to introduce explicitly consumers' durables into our consumers' accounts. Since the available data are far from sufficient, we could not help adopting bold simplifying assumptions in constructing the data for consumers' durables which are summarized in table 2.16. The results shown in this table were derived according to the following procedures.

1. *Purchases of consumers' durables ($q_{KC}I_C$).* — The data for 1958–1968 are available in National Income Statistics.[43] The data for 1951–1957 were extrapolated by using a log-linear expenditure function estimated by least squares methods as follows

$$\log q_{KC}I_C = -7.983 + 1.5296 \log q_C C , \qquad R^2 = 0.9785$$
$$(0.0755)$$

where $q_{KC}I_C$ is households' expenditure on consumers' durables and $q_C C$ households' total consumption expenditure.

**Table 2.16**
Consumers' durables

|      | 1      | 2      | 3     | 4      | 5      | 6      | 7     |
|------|--------|--------|-------|--------|--------|--------|-------|
| 1951 | 79.7   | 83.8   | 0.950 | 647.1  | 202.3  | 200.0  | 1.011 |
| 1952 | 109.3  | 114.0  | 0.958 | 631.6  | 199.9  | 195.2  | 1.024 |
| 1953 | 143.0  | 147.8  | 0.967 | 653.0  | 271.7  | 201.8  | 1.346 |
| 1954 | 162.3  | 176.9  | 0.917 | 699.3  | 222.6  | 216.1  | 1.030 |
| 1955 | 181.8  | 207.5  | 0.876 | 766.9  | 230.4  | 237.0  | 0.972 |
| 1956 | 205.6  | 230.2  | 0.893 | 843.7  | 279.6  | 260.8  | 1.072 |
| 1957 | 236.5  | 267.8  | 0.883 | 942.7  | 291.2  | 291.4  | 0.999 |
| 1958 | 217.8  | 257.7  | 0.845 | 1011.8 | 307.6  | 312.6  | 0.984 |
| 1959 | 306.0  | 358.7  | 0.853 | 1168.1 | 350.7  | 361.1  | 0.971 |
| 1960 | 380.7  | 436.5  | 0.872 | 1370.9 | 441.0  | 423.6  | 1.041 |
| 1961 | 501.2  | 558.7  | 0.897 | 1655.4 | 600.5  | 511.4  | 1.174 |
| 1962 | 649.2  | 700.3  | 0.927 | 2024.6 | 554.3  | 625.6  | 0.886 |
| 1963 | 868.7  | 894.6  | 0.971 | 2514.2 | 708.5  | 777.7  | 0.911 |
| 1964 | 1018.4 | 1046.6 | 0.973 | 3057.9 | 1025.3 | 944.9  | 1.085 |
| 1965 | 1048.7 | 1043.4 | 1.005 | 3489.7 | 1047.9 | 1079.1 | 0.971 |
| 1966 | 1249.6 | 1207.3 | 1.035 | 3999.0 | 1418.8 | 1235.8 | 1.148 |
| 1967 | 1518.7 | 1408.8 | 1.078 | 4608.0 | 1634.4 | 1424.9 | 1.147 |
| 1968 | 1941.8 | 1729.1 | 1.123 | 5415.5 | 1807.1 | 1674.7 | 1.079 |

1. Private consumption expenditure, durables
2. Private consumption expenditure, durables, at constant prices
3. Private consumption expenditure, deflator
4. Stock of consumers' durables
6. Services of consumers' durables, at constant prices
7. Services of consumers' durables, deflator
Units: 1,2, 4–6 (billions of yen); 3.7 (1965 calendar year = 1)

2. *Deflator or asset price of consumers' durables* ($q_{KC}$). — Tokyo Retail Price Indexes were used as the basis of our estimation.[44] Namely, $q_{KC}$ was computed by making the weighted average of "textiles" and "building materials, furniture and house furnishings." The weights are the same as in constructing retail price index as a whole in the original data source.

3. *Stock of consumers' durable* ($K_C$). — The perpetual inventory method was adopted where the rate of depreciation ($\mu_C$) was assumed to be 0.2 which is equal to the U.S. value. The 1955 stock data provided by National Wealth Survey is too large in comparison with the flow data in National Income Statistics,[45] and so the base year stock ($K_{C,1951}$) was determined in such a way that the growth rate ($g$) for

1951–1968 would be 0.12 which is the average growth rate of residential structures in the households sector. Namely,

$$K_{C,1951} = \frac{(I_{C,1968} + (1-\mu_C)I_{C,1967} + \cdots + (1-\mu_C)^{16}I_{C,1952})}{((1+g)^{17} - (1-\mu_C)^{17})}$$

which is derived from

$$K_{C,1968} - (1-\mu_C)^{17}K_{C,1951} = I_{C,1968} + (1-\mu_C)I_{C,1967} + \cdots + (1-\mu_C)^{16}I_{C,1952}$$

and

$$K_{C,1968} = (1+g)^{17}K_{C,1951} \; .$$

Note that $I_C$ is the expenditure on consumers' durables at constant prices which is defined as $q_{KC}I_C/q_{KC}$.

4. *Service price of consumers' durables* $(p_{KC})$. — In section 2.3, we derived the relationship between asset price and service price for each type of capital. We adopted the similar relationship also for consumers' durables, i.e.,

$$p_{KC} = q_{KC,-1}r + q_{KC}\mu_C - (q_{KC} - q_{KC,-1})$$

where $r$ is the rate of return on other types of capital in the households sector. By converting $p_{KC}$ into the index series with 1965 calendar year as a unit, we obtained the deflator for the services of consumers' durables $(p'_{KC})$.

5. *Services of consumers' durables at current prices and at constant prices.* — They are $p_{KC}K_C$ and $p_{KC}K_C/p'_{KC}$, respectively.

## 2.5   Measurement of Productivity Change

The purpose of this section is to measure the rate of productivity change in the Japanese economy, specifically in our producing sector for 1951–1968 within the framework of social accounting system. Special attention will be paid to the differences in quality among various types of capital, labor and output, and to the use of correctly defined prices of capital services. Though there have been a few attempts to measure the rate of productivity change (or the rate of technical progress) in the Japanese economy,[46] heterogeneity of capital, labor and output has been neglected in most cases.[47] Especially, little efforts have been made on the proper treatment of capital input. This is mainly due to the problem of how to separate social capital input into price and quantity components which is not well established in the present social accounting system. L.R. Christensen and D.W. Jorgenson (1969) provided the conceptual basis for this separation and made the measurement of real capital input in the U.S. economy for 1929–1967. Employing the same method in section 2.3, we have provided the data for real capital input and its service price in our producing sector, which makes it possible to allow for the differences in quality among various types of capital in the measurement of productivity change as the heterogeneity of capital can be reflected in the properly constructed Divisia index for capital. In section 2.3, we have provided also the data for output both of consumption goods and of investment goods. We will, therefore, allow for the heterogeneity of output in the measurement of productivity change by these two types of commodities. In case of labor input, the data for quality index of labor provided by T. Watanabe and F. Egaitsu (1968) and T. Watanabe (1972) are available for 1951–1969. We can incorporate their results into our measurement consistently, since their quality index of labor times quantity of labor (usual concept) is the Divisia index for labor under the special perfect substitutability assumption among various types of labor (see subsection 2.5.2). We will, therefore, allow for the heterogeneity of labor in the measurement of productivity change by employing their quality index of labor.

The productivity change in the national level is measured by using Divisia index which has its implicit basis on the highly aggregated production function. The concept of aggregate production function leads us to two kinds of aggregation problems, sector aggregation and factor and output aggregation. We will, therefore, start the discussions of the present section with theoretical investigations on this problem from the viewpoint of measurement of productivity change. In relation with sector aggregation, we will propose a new definition of the aggregate rate of productivity change which explicitly allows for the role of intermediate goods as factors of production. In relation with factor and output aggregation, on the other hand, we will discuss the quality indexes of capital, labor and output which correspond to the heterogeneity of those two production factors and output in the measurement of productivity change.

### 2.5.1    Aggregation Problem I (Sector Aggregation)

The measurement of rate of technical progress or rate of productivity change in the national level is implicitly or explicitly based on the aggregate production function (transformation locus) which expresses the technical relationship between net output(s) (final product(s)) and primary factor inputs. The meaning of this aggregate production function is not so clear, but one thing which can be said definitely is that there exist, under the aggregate production function, the individual production functions for each sector or industry of the economy which include in almost all sectors intermediate goods as their factors of production. In this subsection we will reconsider the analysis of productivity change in the national level under the framework of input-output system with the smooth industry production functions of neoclassical type, not of Leontief type, in which intermediate goods are explicitly included, and propose a new definition of the rate of aggregate productivity change which is a slight modification of the usual Divisia index for productivity change. The usual definition of aggregate productivity change will be shown inappropriate, because it neglects the role of intermediate goods as the factors of production, and we will emphasize the importance of explicit introduction of intermediate goods into the analysis which provides one of the reasons why a considerable proportion of output growth still remains to be explained by some sources other than primary factors inputs even after the great efforts have been made about the precise measurement of productivity change by allowing for the effects of quality changes in capital and labor, utilization rate of capital and so on.

Under the framework of input-output system,[48] the starting point of measuring the rate of productivity change in the $i$th industry is the following accounting identity

$$q_i y_i = \sum_{k=1}^{n} q_k y_{ki} + \sum_{j=1}^{m} p_j x_{ji} \qquad (i = 1, \ldots, n, \ \ j = 1, \ldots, m) \qquad (2.5.1)$$

where $y_i$ is the gross output of the industry, $y_{ki}$'s are intermediate goods, $x_{ji}$'s are primary factor inputs and $q_k$'s and $p_j$'s are prices of respective goods and services. From this identity the Divisia index for productivity change in the $i$th industry can be derived as follows

$$\frac{\dot{p}^i}{p^i} = \frac{\dot{y}_i}{y_i} = \sum_{k=1}^{n} \frac{q_k y_{ki}}{q_i y_i} \cdot \frac{\dot{y}_{ki}}{y_{ki}} + \sum_{j=1}^{m} \frac{p_j x_{ji}}{q_i y_i} \cdot \frac{\dot{x}_{ji}}{x_{ji}} . \tag{2.5.2}$$

The economic justification for using $\dot{p}^i/p^i$ as the proper measure of productivity change in the $i$th industry is based on the following industry production function

$$y_i = f^i(y_{li}, \ldots, y_{ki}, \ldots, y_{ni}; y_{li}, \ldots, x_{ji}, \ldots, x_{mi}; t) \tag{2.5.3}$$

which is assumed to be homogeneous of degree one. Shifts in this industry production function can be expressed mathematically as follows

$$\frac{\dot{f}^i}{f^i} = \frac{\dot{y}_i}{y_i} - \left( \sum_{k=1}^{n} \frac{f^i_k y_{ki}}{y_i} \cdot \frac{\dot{y}_{ki}}{y_{ki}} + \sum_{j=1}^{m} \frac{f^i_j x_{ji}}{y_i} \cdot \frac{\dot{x}_{ji}}{x_{ji}} \right) \tag{2.5.4}$$

where $\dot{f}^i = \partial f^i/\partial_t$, $f^i_k = \partial f^i/\partial y_{ki}$, and $f^i_j = \partial f^i/\partial x_{ji}$. Under the necessary conditions of producer equilibrium (of perfect competition),[49] shifts in the production function $\dot{f}^i/f^i$ can be identified with the Divisia index for productivity change $\dot{p}^i/p^i$, i.e.,

$$\dot{p}^i/p^i = \dot{f}^i/f^i . \tag{2.5.5}$$

We must note that $\dot{p}^i/p^i$ can be rewritten as follows, in terms of input coefficients ($a_{ki}$ and $b_{ji}$)

$$\frac{\dot{p}^i}{p^i} = -\left( \sum_{k=1}^{n} \frac{q_k y_{ki}}{q_i y_i} \cdot \frac{\dot{a}_{ki}}{a_{ki}} + \sum_{j=1}^{m} \frac{p_j x_{ji}}{q_i y_i} \cdot \frac{\dot{b}_{ji}}{b_{ji}} \right) \tag{2.5.6}$$

where $a_{ki} = y_{ki}/y_i$ and $b_{ji} = x_{ji}/y_i$. This is the continuous version of Leontief's definition of rate of technical progress in the $i$th industry.[50]

The following definitions are used for each goods

$$U_k = \sum_{i=1}^{n} y_{ki} \tag{2.5.7}$$

(total intermediate input of the $k$th good)

$$X_j = \sum_{i=1}^{n} x_{ji} \tag{2.5.8}$$

(total input of the $j$th primary good)

$$Y_i = y_i - U_i \qquad\qquad \text{\textemdash} \qquad\qquad (2.5.9)$$

(net output of the $i$th industry).

Then, from (2.5.1),

$$\sum_{i=1}^{n} q_i Y_i = \sum_{j=1}^{m} p_j X_j \tag{2.5.10}$$

or

$$\sum_{i=1}^{n} q_i y_i = \sum_{i=1}^{n} q_i U_i + \sum_{j=1}^{m} p_j X_j . \tag{2.5.11}$$

The most appropriate way of defining the aggregate rate of technical progress in the national economy is, judging from (2.5.6) and noting that $\sum\sum q_k y_{ki} + \sum\sum p_j x_{ji} = \sum q_i y_i$ ,

$$\frac{\dot{T}}{T} \equiv -\left( \sum_i \sum_k \frac{q_i y_{ki}}{\Sigma q_i y_i} \cdot \frac{\dot{a}_{ki}}{a_{ki}} + \sum_i \sum_j \frac{p_j x_{ji}}{\Sigma q_i y_i} \cdot \frac{\dot{b}_{ji}}{b_{ji}} \right)$$

$$= -\sum_i \frac{q_i y_i}{\Sigma q_i y_i} \left( \sum_k \frac{q_k y_{ki}}{q_i y_i} \cdot \frac{\dot{a}_{ki}}{a_{ki}} + \sum_j \frac{p_j x_{ji}}{q_i y_i} \cdot \frac{\dot{b}_{ji}}{b_{ji}} \right)$$

$$= \sum_i \frac{q_i y_i}{\Sigma q_i y_i} \cdot \frac{\dot{p}^i}{p^i}$$

$$= \sum_i \frac{q_i y_i}{\Sigma q_i y_i} \left( \frac{\dot{y}_i}{y_i} - \sum_k \frac{q_k y_{ki}}{q_i y_i} \cdot \frac{\dot{y}_{ki}}{y_{ki}} - \sum_j \frac{p_j x_{ji}}{q_i y_i} \cdot \frac{\dot{x}_{ji}}{x_{ji}} \right)$$

$$= \sum_i \frac{q_i y_i}{\Sigma q_i y_i} \cdot \frac{\dot{y}_i}{y_i} - \sum_i \sum_k \frac{q_k y_{ki}}{\Sigma q_i y_i} \cdot \frac{\dot{y}_{ki}}{y_{ki}} - \sum_i \sum_j \frac{p_j x_{ji}}{\Sigma q_i y_i} \cdot \frac{\dot{x}_{ji}}{x_{ji}}$$

$$= \sum_i \frac{q_i y_i}{\Sigma q_i y_i} \cdot \frac{\dot{y}_i}{y_i} - \frac{\Sigma q_i U_i}{\Sigma q_i y_i} \sum_k \frac{q_k U_k}{q_i U_i} \sum_i \frac{q_k y_{ki}}{q_k U_k} \cdot \frac{\dot{y}_{ki}}{y_{ki}}$$

$$\qquad - \frac{\Sigma p_j X_j}{\Sigma q_i y_i} \sum_j \frac{p_j x_j}{\Sigma p_j X_j} \sum_j \frac{p_j x_{ji}}{p_j X_j} \cdot \frac{\dot{x}_{ji}}{x_{ji}}$$

$$= \sum_i \frac{q_i y_i}{\Sigma q_i y_i} \cdot \frac{\dot{y}_i}{y_i} - \frac{\Sigma q_i U_i}{\Sigma q_i y_i} \sum_k \frac{q_k U_k}{\Sigma q_i U_i} \cdot \frac{\dot{U}_k}{U_k} - \frac{\Sigma p_j x_{ji}}{\Sigma q_i y_i} \sum_j \frac{p_j X_j}{\Sigma p_j X_j} \cdot \frac{\dot{X}_j}{X_j}$$

$(\because$ from $(2.5.7)$ and $(2.5.8))$

$$= \sum_i \frac{q_i y_i}{\Sigma q_i y_i} \cdot \frac{\dot{y}_i}{y_i} - \left[ (1-\theta) \sum_i \frac{q_i U_i}{\Sigma q_i U_i} \cdot \frac{\dot{U}_i}{U_i} + \theta \sum_j \frac{p_j X_j}{\Sigma p_j X_j} \cdot \frac{\dot{X}_j}{X_j} \right]$$

$$= \frac{\dot{y}}{y} - (1-\theta) \frac{\dot{U}}{U} - \theta \frac{\dot{X}}{X} \tag{2.5.12}$$

where

$$\theta \equiv \frac{\Sigma p_j X_j}{\Sigma q_i y_i} = \frac{\Sigma q_i Y_i}{\Sigma q_i y_i} , \qquad (1-\theta) = \frac{\Sigma q_i U_i}{\Sigma q_i y_i} ,$$

$$\frac{\dot{y}}{y} \equiv \sum \frac{q_i y_i}{\Sigma q_i y_i} \cdot \frac{\dot{y}_i}{y_i} , \qquad \frac{\dot{U}}{U} \equiv \sum \frac{q_i U_i}{\Sigma q_i U_i} \cdot \frac{\dot{U}_i}{U_i}$$

and

$$\frac{\dot{X}}{X} \sum \frac{p_j X_j}{\Sigma p_j X_j} \cdot \frac{\dot{X}_j}{X_j} .$$

The last equation corresponds to the Divisia index for productivity change derived from the identity (2.5.11). The relationship between $\dot{T}/T$ and the aggregate production function (transformation locus) will be discussed later. Note that $\dot{T}/T$ can also be defined as the weighted average of rate of technical progress of each industry as can be seen from the third equation of (2.5.12).[51] Note further that intermediate goods appear explicitly in this definition of productivity change.

The usual way of measuring the rate of technical progress in the national economy is based on the Divisia index for productivity change derived from the identity (2.5.10), which is defined as follows

$$\frac{\dot{P}}{P} \equiv \frac{\dot{Y}}{Y} - \frac{\dot{X}}{X}$$

$$= \sum_i \frac{q_i Y_i}{\Sigma q_i Y_i} \cdot \frac{\dot{Y}_i}{Y_i} - \sum_j \frac{p_j X_j}{\Sigma p_j X_j} \cdot \frac{\dot{X}_j}{X_j}$$

$$= \frac{\Sigma q_i y_i}{\Sigma q_i Y_i} \sum_i \frac{q_i (\dot{y}_i - \dot{U}_i)}{\Sigma q_i y_i} - \sum_j \frac{p_j X_j}{\Sigma p_j X_j} \cdot \frac{\dot{X}_j}{X_j}$$

$$= \frac{1}{\theta} \left( \sum_i \frac{q_i y_i}{\Sigma q_i y_i} \cdot \frac{\dot{y}_i}{y_i} - \sum_i \frac{q_i U_i}{\Sigma q_i y_i} \cdot \frac{\dot{U}_i}{U_i} - \sum_j \frac{p_j X_j}{\Sigma p_j X_j} \cdot \frac{\dot{X}_j}{X_j} \right)$$

$$= \frac{1}{\theta} \left( \sum_i \frac{q_i y_i}{\Sigma q_i y_i} \cdot \frac{\dot{y}_i}{y_i} - (1 - \theta) \sum_i \frac{q_i U_i}{\Sigma q_i U_i} \cdot \frac{\dot{U}_i}{U_i} - \theta \sum_j \frac{p_j X_j}{\Sigma p_j X_j} \cdot \frac{\dot{X}_j}{X_j} \right)$$

$$= \frac{1}{\theta} \cdot \frac{\dot{T}}{T}$$

$$= \frac{\Sigma q_i y_i}{\Sigma q_i Y_i} \sum \frac{q_i y_i}{\Sigma q_i y_i} \cdot \frac{\dot{P}^i}{P^i} = \sum \frac{q_i y_i}{\Sigma q_i Y_i} \cdot \frac{\dot{P}^i}{P^i} . \tag{2.5.13}$$

Namely $\dot{P}/P$ is the weighted sum of $\dot{P}^i/P^i$, but not the weighted average of $\dot{P}^i/P^i$ in general. Only when there exists no intermediate goods in the economy, $\dot{P}/P$ is the weighted average of $\dot{P}^i/P^i$, and can be regarded as the proper way of measuring the productivity change in the aggregate sense which reduces to $\dot{T}/T$.

The usual way of justifying the use of $\dot{P}/P$ as the proper measure of productivity change is based on the following production function

$$F(Y_1, \dots, Y_n; X_1, \dots, X_m; t) = 0 \tag{2.5.14}$$

which is assumed to be homogeneous of degree zero. Namely, first, shifts in this production function are defined in terms of appropriate weighted average rates of growth of outputs and inputs, i.e.,

$$G\dot{F} = \sum \left( \frac{F_i Y_i}{\Sigma F_i Y_i} \cdot \frac{\dot{Y}_i}{Y_i} \right) - \sum \left( \frac{F_j X_j}{\Sigma F_j X_j} \cdot \frac{\dot{X}_j}{X_j} \right) \tag{2.5.15}$$

where

$$\dot{F} = \partial F/\partial t , \quad F_i = \partial F/\partial Y_i , \quad F_j = \partial F/\partial X_j \text{ and } 1/G = -\Sigma F_i Y_i = \Sigma F_j X_j ,$$

and, next, all marginal rates of transformation between pairs of inputs and outputs are made equal to the corresponding price ratios. Then, shifts in the production function defined by (2.5.15) reduce to the Divisia index for productivity change defined by (2.5.13), i.e.,

$$G\dot{F} = \dot{P}/P .\,^{53} \tag{2.5.16}$$

The above way of justifying $\dot{P}/P$ seems, however, insufficient, because it does not provide the justification for using $G\dot{F}$ as the appropriate measure of shifts in the production function. Furthermore we can say that $G\dot{F}$ is not the appropriate measure, as far as the aggregate production function (2.5.14) is the transformation locus derived from the industry production functions of the type (2.5.3). This can be understood by considering the aggregation procedure as follows

Maximize $Y_1$

with respect to $Y_1, Y_{ki}, x_{ji}, y_i$ and $U_k$, subject to

$$y_i = f^i(y_{1i}, \ldots, y_{ki}, \ldots y_{ni}; x_{1i}, \ldots, x_{ji}, \ldots, x_{mi}; t) \qquad (i = 1 \ldots n)$$

$$U_k = \sum_{i=1}^{n} y_{ki} \qquad (k = 1 \ldots n)$$

$$Y_i = y_i - U_i \qquad (i = 1 \ldots n) \text{ and}$$

$$X_j = \sum_{i=1}^{n} x_{ji} \qquad (j = 1 \ldots m)$$

under the given $Y_2 \ldots Y_n$,     $X_1 \ldots X_m$ and $t$.

Then the Lagrangean function becomes

$$L = Y_1 + \sum_{i=1}^{n} \varepsilon_i(y_i - f^i(y_{1i} \ldots y_{ki} \ldots y_{ni}, x_{1i} \ldots x_{ji} \ldots x_{mi}; t)$$

$$+ \sum_{k=1}^{n} \eta_k\left(U_k - \sum_{i=1}^{n} y_{ki}\right)$$

$$+ \sum_{i=1}^{n} \lambda_i(y_i - U_i - Y_i)$$

$$+ \sum_{j=1}^{m} \mu_j\left(X_j - \sum x_{ji}\right). \qquad (2.5.17)$$

The first-order necessary conditions are

$$\begin{cases} 1 - \lambda_1 = 0 \\ -\varepsilon_i \partial f^i/\partial y_{ki} - \mu_k = 0 & (i = 1 \ldots n, \ k = 1 \ldots n) \\ -\varepsilon_i \partial f^i/\partial x_{ji} - \mu_j = 0 & (i = 1 \ldots n, \ j = 1 \ldots m). \\ \varepsilon_i + \lambda_i = 0 & (i = 1 \ldots n) \\ \eta_k - \lambda_k = 0 & (k = 1 \ldots n) \end{cases} \qquad (2.5.18)$$

These conditions together with the constraints of the present maximization problem determine the optimal value of $Y_1$ in terms of the parameters, i.e.,

$$Y_1 = f(Y_2, \ldots, Y_n; X_1, \ldots, X_m; t). \qquad (2.5.19)$$

If this is rewritten in the form of implicit function, the transformation locus (2.5.14) can be obtained. From the properties of the Lagrangean multipliers,[54] we can derive the following relations

$$\partial Y_1/\partial Y_i = -\lambda_i \qquad (i = 2 \ldots n)$$

$$\partial Y_1/\partial t = -\sum_{i=1}^{n} \varepsilon_i \dot{f}^i = \sum_{i=1}^{n} \lambda_i \dot{f}^i . \tag{2.5.20}$$

Therefore

$$\dot{F} = -F_1(\partial Y_1/\partial t) = -F_1 \sum_{i=1}^{n} \lambda_i \dot{f}^i = -F_1 \lambda_1 \dot{f}^1 + \sum_{i=2}^{n} F_1(\partial Y_1/\partial Y_i)\dot{f}^i$$

$$= F_1\dot{f}^1 + \sum_{i=2}^{n} (-F_i\dot{f}^i) = -\sum_{i=1}^{n} F_i\dot{f}^i$$

$$= -\sum_{i=1}^{n} F_i y_i \cdot \frac{\dot{f}^i}{f^i} . \tag{2.5.21}$$

This relationship suggests that the most appropriate way of defining the shifts in the aggregate production function (2.5.14) is

$$HF\dot{} = \sum \frac{F_i y_i}{F_i y_i} \cdot \frac{\dot{f}^i}{f^i} = \sum \frac{F_i y_i}{\Sigma F_i y_i} \cdot \frac{\dot{y}_i}{y_i}$$

$$-\left[\frac{\Sigma F_i U_i}{\Sigma F_i y_i} \sum \frac{F_i U_i}{\Sigma F_i U_i} \cdot \frac{\dot{U}_i}{U_i} + \frac{\Sigma F_j X_j}{\Sigma F_i y_i} \sum \frac{F_j X_j}{\Sigma F_j X_j} \cdot \frac{\dot{X}_j}{X_j}\right] \tag{2.5.22}$$

where $1/H = -\sum F_i y_i = \sum F_i U_i + \sum F_j X_j$. Namely $HF\dot{}$ is the weighted average of the shifts in each industry production function, and reduces to $\dot{T}/T$, i.e.,

$$HF\dot{} = \dot{T}/T , \tag{2.5.23}$$

when all marginal rates of transformation are identified with respective price ratios. On the other hand, from equation (2.5.21), we can derive

$$GF\dot{} = \sum \frac{F_i y_i}{\Sigma F_i Y_i} \cdot \frac{\dot{f}^i}{f^i} \quad \left(= \frac{\Sigma F_i y_i}{\Sigma F_i Y_i} \cdot HF\dot{}\right) \tag{2.5.24}$$

which shows that $GF\dot{}$ is the weighted sum of $\dot{f}^i/f^i$ but not the weighted average of $\dot{f}^i/f^i$ as in the case of $\dot{P}/P$. Once again we can say only when there exist no intermediate goods in the economy, $G\dot{F}$ can be regarded as a proper measure of the shifts in the aggregate production function.

It is, however, quite unrealistic to assume such an economy where the intermediate goods do not exist. As far as $\dot{P}/P$ is employed in the analysis of productivity change or as far as $G\dot{F}$ is used for the justification of $\dot{P}/P$, the rate of productivity change is surely overestimated, i.e.,[55]

$$\frac{\dot{T}}{T} = 0 \cdot \frac{\dot{P}}{P}, \tag{2.5.25}$$

or

$$H\dot{F} = \frac{\Sigma F_i Y_i}{\Sigma F_i y_i} G\dot{F}, \tag{2.5.26}$$

where $\theta = 0.481$ according to the Japanese input-output table of 1965. Therefore, all of the analyses of productivity change based on the Divisia index $P$, including R. Solow (1957), must be modified in a downward direction according to the formula (2.5.25).[56]

The unexplained part of $gross$ output can be seen by the following relations. From (2.5.12), (2.5.13) and (2.5.25), we obtain

$$\frac{\dot{Y}}{Y} = (1 - \theta) \cdot \frac{\dot{U}}{U} + \theta \cdot \frac{\dot{X}}{X} + \frac{\dot{T}}{T} = (1 - \theta) \cdot \frac{\dot{U}}{U} + \theta \left( \frac{\dot{X}}{X} + \frac{\dot{P}}{P} \right)$$

$$= (1 - \theta) \cdot \frac{\dot{U}}{U} + \theta \cdot \frac{\dot{Y}}{Y}. \tag{2.5.27}$$

Therefore,

$$\frac{\dot{T}}{T} \bigg/ \frac{\dot{y}}{y} = \left( \frac{\dot{P}}{P} \bigg/ \frac{\dot{Y}}{Y} \right) \bigg/ \left\{ \frac{1-\theta}{\theta} \left( \frac{\dot{U}}{U} \bigg/ \frac{\dot{Y}}{Y} \right) + 1 \right\} \tag{2.5.28}$$

where $(1 - \theta)/\theta = 1.08$ for $\theta = 0.481$. This relation shows, provided that both $\frac{\dot{P}}{P}$ and $\frac{\dot{Y}}{Y}$ are positive,

$$\frac{\dot{T}}{T} \bigg/ \frac{\dot{y}}{y} \overset{<}{\underset{>}{=}} \frac{\dot{p}}{p} \bigg/ \frac{\dot{Y}}{Y} \qquad \text{if} \qquad \frac{\dot{U}}{U} \overset{>}{\underset{<}{=}} 0. \tag{2.5.29}$$

Namely we can say that in growing economies the unexplained part of output growth is less (more) than that of the usual analysis, as far as the quantity of intermediate inputs in terms of Divisia index is increasing (decreasing). Though it is an empirical question and the related data are quite scarce, the case of negative $\dot{U}/U$ seems unusual in growing economies however large the degree of intermediate-goods-saving technical progress may be in those economies. We may, therefore, conclude that the explicit introduction of intermediate goods into the analysis of productivity change will reduce the unexplained part of output growth. We emphasize that the role of intermediate goods as the factors of production must not be neglected in the analysis of productivity change.

In spite of the above-mentioned conclusion and emphasis, we have not sufficient data for intermediate goods to carry out this modification in our analyses of producing sector. We will adopt $\dot{P}/P$ instead of $\dot{T}/T$ as the aggregate rate of productivity change in subsection 2.5.3 with the equations (2.5.25) and (2.5.28) in mind.

## 2.5.2 Aggregation Problem II (Factor and Output Aggregation)

In their empirical study on labor quality and economic growth in the postwar Japanese economy (1968), T. Watanabe and F. Egaitsu derived a quality index of labor based on the following three assumptions: (i) the smooth and substitutable production function which is homogeneous of degree one, (ii) the constancy of the marginal rates of substitution among different labor input, and (iii) equality between the marginal productivity of labor and wage rate. Their quality index of labor can be reinterpreted as the index of aggregation bias from the viewpoint of measurement of productivity change under more general conditions (i.e., without assuming perfect substitutabilities among various kinds of labor) and can be extended to the case of capital or output. The content of this subsection is the reinterpretation and extension of their quality index of labor and has close relations with our empirical analysis in the next subsection.

Let us first consider the economy where the true production technology is expressed by the following function

$$Y = F(K, L_1, \ldots, L_s, t) \tag{2.5.30}$$

where $Y$ is output, $K$ capital input, $L_i$ labor input of the $i$th kind and

$t$ time. $F$ is assumed to be homogeneous of degree one. Then the productivity change is measured by using the following Divisia index which is based on the production function (2.5.30) and the assumption of profit maximization under perfect competition

$$\frac{\dot{P}}{P} = \frac{\dot{Y}}{Y} - v_K \cdot \frac{\dot{K}}{K} - v_L \cdot \frac{\dot{L}}{L} \tag{2.5.31}$$

where $v_K$ = value share of capital, $v_L$ = value share of labor, $\dot{L}/L = \sum(p_{Li}L_i/p_L L) \cdot (\dot{L}_i/L_i)$, $p_L L = \sum p_{Li} L_i = V_L^*$ and $p_{Li}$ = service price (wage rate) of $L_i$. Namely, $L$ is the Divisia index for labor input. Suppose that we neglect the difference in quality among various kinds of labor and use, by mistake, the production function of the following type,

$$Y = F'(K, L', t) \tag{2.5.32}$$

where $L' = L_1 + \ldots + L_s$. Then the productivity change will be measured as

$$\frac{\dot{P}'}{P'} - \frac{\dot{Y}}{Y} - v_K \cdot \frac{\dot{K}}{K} - v_L \cdot \frac{\dot{L}'}{L'} \cdot \tag{2.5.33}$$

Therefore the aggregation bias, i.e., the bias due to the use of incorrectly aggregated quantity $L'$, becomes

$$\frac{\dot{P}'}{P'} - \frac{\dot{P}}{P} = v_L \cdot \left(\frac{\dot{L}}{L} - \frac{\dot{L}'}{L'}\right) = f_L \cdot \frac{\dot{B}}{B}, \tag{2.5.34}$$

where $B = L/L'$. Note that we have used the term "aggregation bias" in two different meanings. One is the error in the measurement of aggregate labor (i.e., $B$) and the other is the error in the measurement of productivity change (i.e., $v_L(\dot{B}/B)$). In this sense $B$ can be interpreted as the index of aggregation bias of labor in the measurement of productivity change.

By using (2.5.33) and (2.5.34) we get

$$\frac{\dot{P}}{P} = \frac{\dot{Y}}{Y} - v_K \cdot \frac{\dot{K}}{K} - v_L \cdot \left(\frac{\dot{B}}{B} + \frac{\dot{L}'}{L'}\right). \tag{2.5.35}$$

Therefore, from the point of view of measuring the productivity change, the production function (2.5.30) can be equivalently written as follows

$$Y = F(K, BL', t) .$$                                              (2.5.36)

This is the reason why $B$ can be called quality index of labor. From the definition of $B$ or $\dot{B}/B$, we obtain

$$\frac{\dot{B}}{B} = \sum \frac{p_{Li}L_i}{V_L^*} \frac{\dot{L}_i}{L_i} - \sum \frac{L_i}{L'} \cdot \frac{\dot{L}_i}{L_i} = \sum \left( \frac{p_{Li}L_i}{V_L^*} - \frac{p_L'L_i}{V_L^*} \right) \cdot \frac{\dot{L}_i}{L_i}$$    (2.5.37)

where $p_L' = V_L^*/L'$ (average wage rate). This relation shows that

$$\frac{\dot{B}}{B} = 0 \quad \text{or} \quad B = 1 \quad \text{if} \quad p_{Li} = p_L' \quad \text{or} \quad p_{Li}/p_{Lj} = 1 \quad \text{for all } i \text{ and } j .$$    (2.5.38)

Namely if all types of labor are perfect substitutes and their marginal rates of substitution are all equal to one, then there is no aggregation bias both in the measurement of labor and in the measurement of productivity change. This is clear from the fact that the production function (2.5.30) is completely equivalent to the production function (2.5.32) due to Leontief-Solow's theorem.[57] The quality index of labor derived by T. Watanabe and F. Egaitsu is our index under the special assumption that all kinds of labor are perfect substitutes but their marginal rates of substitution are different from one.[58] In this situation, the production function (2.5.30) is completely equivalent to the production function (2.5.36).

Let us next consider the more general situation where the economy's production function is expressed by

$$F(Y_1, \ldots, Y_n; K_1, \ldots, K_r; L_1, \ldots, L_s; t) = 0$$         (2.5.39)

in which various types of output and capital are also allowed for. $F$ is assumed to be homogeneous of degree zero. Based on this function, the productivity change is measured by seemingly the same formula as (2.5.31), i.e.,

$$\frac{\dot{P}}{P} = \frac{\dot{Y}}{Y} - v_K \cdot \frac{\dot{K}}{K} - v_L \cdot \frac{\dot{L}}{L}$$      (2.5.40)

where

$$\frac{\dot{Y}}{Y} = \sum \frac{q_i Y_i}{q^Y} \frac{\dot{Y}_i}{Y_i}, \quad \frac{\dot{K}}{K} = \sum \frac{p_{Ki} K_i}{p_K K} \frac{\dot{K}_i}{K_i}, \quad qY = \sum q_i Y_i,$$

$$p_K K = \sum p_{Ki} K_i = V_K^*, \quad q_i = \text{price of } Y_i$$

and $p_{li}$ = service price of $K_i$. Suppose again that we neglect the difference in quality among various types of labor, capital and output and use the production function of the following type

$$F'(Y', K', L', t) = 0 \tag{2.5.41}$$

or

$$Y' = F'(K', L', t), \tag{2.5.42}$$

where

$$Y' = \sum q_{i0} Y_i, \quad K' = \sum q_{Ki0} Ki, \quad L' = \sum p_{Li0} L_i (p_{Li0} = p'_{L0} \text{ or } 1)$$

and $q_{i0}$, $q_{ki0}$ and $p_{li0}$ are output price, *asset price* of capital and service price of labor, respectively in the base period (denoted by 0). Namely $Y'$ at the national level corresponds to GDP measured at constant prices and $K'$ is total real capital stock obtained by adding simply the component real capital stocks. Then the productivity change is measured as

$$\frac{\dot{P}'}{P'} = \frac{\dot{Y}'}{Y'} - v_K \cdot \frac{\dot{K}'}{K'} - v_L \cdot \frac{\dot{L}'}{L'} \tag{2.5.43}$$

and the aggregation bias becomes

$$\frac{\dot{P}'}{P'} - \frac{\dot{P}}{P} = v_K \left( \frac{\dot{K}}{K} - \frac{\dot{K}'}{K'} \right) + v_L \left( \frac{\dot{L}}{L} - \frac{\dot{L}'}{L'} \right) - \left( \frac{\dot{Y}}{Y} - \frac{\dot{Y}'}{Y'} \right) \tag{2.5.44}$$

$$= v_K \cdot \frac{\dot{A}}{A} + v_L \cdot \frac{\dot{B}}{B} - \frac{\dot{C}}{C}$$

where $A = K/K'$, $B = L/L'$ and $C = Y/Y'$. As in the previous case, we can interpret $A$, $B$ and $C$ as the indexes of aggregation bias in the measurement of capital, labor and output respectively. Note that the aggregation bias in the measurement of aggregate output ($C$) contributes in the opposite direction to the aggregation bias in the measurement of productivity change expressed in (2.5.44), provided that $\dot{C}/C$ is positive, which seems to be the usual case.

Combining (2.5.43) and (2.5.44), we obtain

$$\frac{\dot{P}}{P} = \left(\frac{\dot{C}}{C} + \frac{\dot{Y}'}{Y'}\right) - v_K\left(\frac{\dot{A}}{A} + \frac{\dot{K}'}{K'}\right) - v_L\left(\frac{\dot{B}}{B} + \frac{\dot{L}'}{L'}\right). \tag{2.5.45}$$

Therefore, once again, from the point of view of measuring productivity change, the production function (2.5.39) can be equivalently written as follows

$$F(CY', AK', BL', t) = 0 \tag{2.5.46}$$

or

$$CY' = F(AK', BL', t). \tag{2.5.47}$$

In this sense, $A$, $B$ and $C$ can be called the quality indexes of capital, labor and output respectively, though the true meaning of $C$ as a quality index must be derived from utility analysis. From the definition of $C$ or $\dot{C}/C$, we get

$$\frac{\dot{C}}{C} = \Sigma\left(\frac{q_iY_i}{q^Y} - \frac{q_{i0}Y_i}{Y'}\right) \cdot \frac{\dot{Y}_i}{Y_i} \tag{2.5.48}$$

and so

$$\frac{\dot{C}}{C} = 0 \quad \text{or} \quad C = 1 \quad \text{if} \quad q_i/q_j = q_{i0}/q_{j0} \quad \text{for all } i \text{ and } j. \tag{2.5.49}$$

This means that there is no aggregation bias in $Y'$ if all of the output are perfect substitutes, and correspondingly there is no aggregation bias in the measurement of productivity change caused by the measurement error in output. Similar relations in case of capital are

$$\frac{\dot{A}}{A} = \Sigma\left(\frac{p_{Ki}K_i}{p_K K} - \frac{q_{Ki0}K_i}{K'}\right) \cdot \frac{\dot{K}_i}{K_i} \tag{2.5.50}$$

and

$$\frac{\dot{A}}{A} = 0 \quad \text{or} \quad A = 1 \quad \text{if} \quad q_{Ki}/q_{Kj} = q_{Ki0}/q_{Kj0} \quad \text{for all } i \text{ and } j. \tag{2.5.51}$$

The last relation must hold, because the fact that $q_{Ki}/q_{Kj} = q_{Ki0}/q_{Kj0}$ for all $i$ and $j$ means that all of the capital goods are perfect substitutes in the output side of production and this in turn implies that they are also perfect substitutes in the input side of production. Namely, under the conditions of perfect competition and perfect substitutabilities among capital goods, the service price of the $i$th capital good must be

$$p_{Ki} = \left( r + \mu - \frac{\dot{q}_{Ki}}{q_{Ki}} \right) q_{Ki} \tag{2.5.52}$$

where $r$ is rate of interest and $\mu$ is rate of depreciation, and so the relative prices of capital services must be constant and equal to the corresponding constant relative prices of capital assets, which leads to the relationship expressed by (2.5.51). In case of labor, the same relationships have already been expressed by (2.5.37) and (2.5.38). As there exist no asset prices in case of labor except in slave economies, the discussion was rather straightforward compared to the case of capital.

From the above-mentioned relations it is clear that there exists no aggregation bias both in the measurement of capital, labor and output and in the measurement of productivity change, when perfect substitutability assumptions are valid with respect to capital, labor and output. In this case, the production function (2.5.41) or (2.5.42) is completely equivalent to the production function (2.5.39). Solow's famous work on the measurement of rate of technical progress[59] was based on the value added production function of the type (2.5.42) and so his estimates include the aggregation bias expressed by equation (2.5.44), whose direction and magnitude depend of course on the relative and absolute importance of $v_K(\dot{A}/A) + v_L(\dot{B}/B)$ and $\dot{C}/C$, i.e., the degree of perfect substitutability property.

## 2.5.3  Productivity Change in the Producing Sector

In section 2.3 we have provided all of the data except labor which are necessary in constructing the Divisia index for productivity change in the Japanese economy during the period 1951–1968. Concerning the data for labor, we have provided only the value of labor services used in production ($V_L^*$) in table 2.6. This value of labor services must be separated into quantity and price components (L and $p_L$). If the difference in quality among various types of labor is neglected, the quantity of labor is the number of workers which is defined in our producing sector as the number of employees ($L_e$) excluding that of public administration ($L_{GG}$) plus the number of self-employed persons ($L_s$), i.e.,

$$L' = L_e - L_{GG} + L_s .$$

The data for $L_e$ and $L_{GG}$ are available for 1953–1968 in National Income Statistics.[60] The data for $L_s$ and $L_e$ and $L_{GG}$ for 1951–1952 are found in Japan Statistical Yearbook.[61] The price of labor is defined as the average wage rate, i.e.,

$$p'_L = V^*_L/L' .$$

In order to measure productivity change as correctly as possible, the difference in quality among various types of labor must be allowed for. As was stated in the previous subsection, T. Watanabe and F. Egaitsu (1968) constructed the quality index of labor in the Japanese economy for 1951–1964, which was extended by T. Watanabe (1972) until 1969. They took into consideration the difference in quality among the laborers classified by age, sex and education. The estimated results of T. Watanabe and F. Egaitsu show relatively and absolutely small changes in this quality for 1951–1964 (2.1.5–3.3% per 13 years), but the extended results of T. Watanabe show a structural change in this quality (2.42–3.40% per 4 years, 1965–1969). We, therefore, employ their results in our measurement in order to allow for the difference in labor quality by age, sex and education. We choose among their various kinds of indexes, each of which corresponds to specific weights, the one which is constructed by using the 1964 wage rates as weights.[62] By using the notation $B$ for this index, the identity $V^*_L = p'_L L'$ becomes

$$V^*_L = p_L L$$

where $p_L = p'_L/B$ and $L = BL'$. $L$ is the quantity of labor measured by efficiency units which are expressed in terms of the number of workers in 1951. We must note here that the effects of difference between fiscal year and calendar year are neglected, because $B$ is based on calendar year. The series for $p'_L$, $L'$, $B$, $p_L$ and $L$ are shown in table 2.17.

**Table 2.17**
Data for labor

|      | $P_L'$ | $L'$ | $P_L$ | $L$ | $B$ |
|------|--------|------|-------|-----|-----|
| 1951 | 148.5 | 23.199 | 148.5 | 23.199 | 1.000 |
| 1952 | 170.2 | 23.941 | 169.9 | 23.988 | 1.002 |
| 1953 | 193.1 | 23.976 | 192.9 | 24.000 | 1.001 |
| 1954 | 203.3 | 24.615 | 201.4 | 24.836 | 1.009 |
| 1955 | 210.7 | 26.141 | 211.1 | 26.088 | 0.998 |
| 1956 | 224.6 | 27.353 | 224.2 | 27.407 | 1.002 |
| 1957 | 237.2 | 28.669 | 236.2 | 28.783 | 1.004 |
| 1958 | 244.1 | 29.543 | 243.3 | 29.631 | 1.003 |
| 1959 | 261.0 | 30.371 | 258.5 | 30.674 | 1.010 |
| 1960 | 289.3 | 31.599 | 285.0 | 32.073 | 1.015 |
| 1961 | 330.1 | 32.482 | 324.6 | 33.034 | 1.017 |
| 1962 | 371.6 | 33.342 | 365.4 | 33.908 | 1.017 |
| 1963 | 416.9 | 34.341 | 407.9 | 35.096 | 1.022 |
| 1964 | 464.9 | 35.372 | 452.2 | 36.362 | 1.028 |
| 1965 | 507.8 | 36.862 | 492.0 | 38.041 | 1.032 |
| 1966 | 563.1 | 38.001 | 544.6 | 39.293 | 1.034 |
| 1967 | 632.6 | 39.310 | 607.7 | 40.921 | 1.041 |
| 1968 | 718.0 | 39.648 | 683.8 | 41.634 | 1.050 |
|      | 1000 yen per person | million persons | 1000 yen per person | million persons | 1951 = 1.000 |

The productivity change in our producing sector is measured by using the Divisia index derived from the following identity

$$q_C^* C^* + q_K^* I^* = p_L L + \sum_i \sum_j p_{ij} K_{ij} \left( \begin{matrix} i = R, D, J, S \\ j = H, CB, NB, GE \end{matrix} \right)$$

or

$$q^* Y^* = pX$$

where $q * Y * = q_C^* C * + q_K^* I *$ and $pX = p_L L + \sum\sum p_{ij} K_{ij}$. Namely the Divisia index for productivity change ($P$) is defined as

$$\frac{\dot{P}}{P} = \frac{\dot{Y}^*}{Y^*} - \frac{\dot{X}}{X} \left( = \frac{\dot{p}}{p} - \frac{\dot{q}^*}{q^*} \right)$$

where

$$\frac{\dot{Y}^*}{Y^*} = \frac{q_C^* C^*}{q^* Y^*} \cdot \frac{\dot{C}^*}{C^*} + \frac{q_K^* I^*}{q^* Y^*} \cdot \frac{\dot{I}^*}{I^*}$$

$$\frac{\dot{X}}{X} = \frac{p_L L}{pX} \cdot \frac{\dot{L}}{L} + \Sigma \Sigma \frac{p_{ij} K_{ij}}{pX} \cdot \frac{\dot{K}_{ij}}{K_{ij}}$$

$$\frac{\dot{q}^*}{q^*} = \frac{q_C^* C^*}{q^* Y^*} \cdot \frac{\dot{q}_C^*}{q_C^*} + \frac{q_K^* I^*}{q^* Y^*} \cdot \frac{\dot{q}_K^*}{q_K^*}$$

and

$$\frac{\dot{p}}{p} = \frac{p_L L}{pX} \cdot \frac{\dot{p}_L}{p_L} + \Sigma \Sigma \frac{p_{ij} K_{ij}}{pX} \cdot \frac{\dot{p}_{ij}}{p_{ij}} .$$

The discrete approximation for this index is

$$\log P_t - \log P_{t-1} = (\log Y_t^* - \log Y_{t-1}^*) - (\log X_t - \log X_{t-1})$$

where

$$\log Y_t^* - \log Y_{t-1}^* = \Sigma \bar{w}_{it}(\log Y_{it}^* - \log Y_{1,t-1}^*)$$
$$\log X_t - \log X_{t-1} = \Sigma \bar{v}_{jt}(\log X_{jt} - \log X_{j,t-1})$$
$Y_{it}^* = $ the $i$th component of $Y_t^*$ in the $t$th period
$X_{jt} = $ the $j$th component of $X_t$ in the $t$th period
$\bar{w}_{it} = (w_{it} + w_{i,t-1})/2 , \qquad \bar{v}_{jt} = (v_{jt} + v_{j,t-1})/2$
$w_{it} = $ the value share of $Y_{it}^*$

and

$v_{jt} = $ the value share of $X_{jt}$ .[64]

The results of computation are shown in table 2.18. The same approximation procedure is adopted for $\dot{q}^*/q^*$. Note that the growth rates and Divisia indexes are computed without paying attention to the negative values of service prices. $\dot{p}/p$ is computed indirectly by using the approximated definitional equation, i.e.,

$$\log p_t - \log p_{t-1} = (\log P_t - \log P_{t-1}) - (\log q_t^* - \log q_{t-1}^*) .$$

The arithmetic average rate of growth and the percent of output which remains unexplained by factor input are summarized in table 2.19. Note that the proportion of output unexplained by input for the

**Table 2.18**
Growth rates and divisia indexes

| | $\dot{P}/P$ | $\dot{Y}^*/Y^*$ | $\dot{X}/X$ | $\dot{q}^*/q^*$ | $\dot{p}/p$ | $P$ | $Y^*$ | $X$ | $q^*$ | $p$ |
|------|--------|--------|-------|--------|--------|-------|-------|-------|-------|-------|
| 1951 | — | — | — | — | — | 0.578 | 0.277 | 0.479 | 0.603 | 0.349 |
| 1952 | 0.091 | 0.124 | 0.030 | 0.031 | 0.125 | 0.631 | 0.312 | 0.494 | 0.622 | 0.393 |
| 1953 | 0.065 | 0.077 | 0.011 | 0.092 | 0.163 | 0.672 | 0.336 | 0.499 | 0.679 | 0.457 |
| 1954 | −0.007 | 0.025 | 0.033 | −0.003 | −0.011 | 0.667 | 0.344 | 0.516 | 0.677 | 0.452 |
| 1955 | 0.074 | 0.131 | 0.052 | 0.015 | 0.092 | 0.717 | 0.390 | 0.543 | 0.687 | 0.493 |
| 1956 | −0.004 | 0.054 | 0.059 | 0.058 | 0.053 | 0.714 | 0.411 | 0.576 | 0.728 | 0.520 |
| 1957 | 0.026 | 0.094 | 0.065 | 0.035 | 0.063 | 0.733 | 0.450 | 0.613 | 0.754 | 0.553 |
| 1958 | 0.024 | 0.068 | 0.043 | −0.022 | 0.001 | 0.751 | 0.481 | 0.640 | 0.737 | 0.553 |
| 1959 | 0.069 | 0.129 | 0.055 | 0.027 | 0.098 | 0.803 | 0.543 | 0.676 | 0.757 | 0.608 |
| 1960 | 0.063 | 0.143 | 0.075 | 0.044 | 0.110 | 0.854 | 0.621 | 0.726 | 0.790 | 0.675 |
| 1961 | 0.064 | 0.146 | 0.077 | 0.068 | 0.137 | 0.909 | 0.712 | 0.782 | 0.844 | 0.768 |
| 1962 | 0.001 | 0.059 | 0.058 | 0.035 | 0.036 | 0.910 | 0.754 | 0.828 | 0.874 | 0.796 |
| 1963 | 0.061 | 0.131 | 0.067 | 0.045 | 0.108 | 0.965 | 0.853 | 0.883 | 0.914 | 0.883 |
| 1964 | 0.040 | 0.108 | 0.065 | 0.042 | 0.084 | 1.004 | 0.946 | 0.942 | 0.953 | 0.957 |
| 1965 | −0.004 | 0.057 | 0.061 | 0.048 | 0.044 | 1.000 | 1.000 | 1.000 | 1.000 | 1.000 |
| 1966 | 0.054 | 0.116 | 0.058 | 0.051 | 0.108 | 1.054 | 1.116 | 1.058 | 1.051 | 1.108 |
| 1967 | 0.055 | 0.133 | 0.073 | 0.037 | 0.095 | 1.113 | 1.265 | 1.136 | 1.091 | 1.215 |
| 1968 | 0.072 | 0.140 | 0.063 | 0.035 | 0.109 | 1.193 | 1.443 | 1.209 | 1.129 | 1.348 |

**Table 2.19**
Average rates of growth

|         | (1) $\dot{P}/P$ | (2) $\dot{Y}^*/Y^*$ | (3) $\dot{X}/X$ | (4) $\dot{q}^*/q^*$ | (5) $\dot{p}/p$ | (1)/(2) |
|---------|------|------|------|------|------|------|
| 1952–53 | 0.078 | 0.100 | 0.020 | 0.061 | 0.144 | 0.775 |
| 1954–57 | 0.022 | 0.076 | 0.052 | 0.026 | 0.049 | 0.292 |
| 1958–61 | 0.055 | 0.121 | 0.062 | 0.029 | 0.087 | 0.455 |
| 1962–64 | 0.033 | 0.099 | 0.063 | 0.041 | 0.076 | 0.338 |
| 1965–68 | 0.044 | 0.111 | 0.064 | 0.043 | 0.089 | 0.398 |
| 1952–53 | 0.078 | 0.100 | 0.020 | 0.061 | 0.144 | 0.775 |
| 1954–61 | 0.038 | 0.099 | 0.057 | 0.027 | 0.068 | 0.392 |
| 1962–68 | 0.039 | 0.106 | 0.064 | 0.042 | 0.084 | 0.374 |
| 1952–61 | 0.046 | 0.099 | 0.050 | 0.034 | 0.083 | 0.470 |
| 1962–68 | 0.039 | 0.106 | 0.064 | 0.042 | 0.084 | 0.374 |
| 1952–68 | 0.440 | 0.102 | 0.056 | 0.037 | 0.083 | 0.429 |

estimation period as a whole (42.9%) is a little bit greater than the result (36%) of L.R. Christensen and D.W. Jorgenson (1970) for the U.S. economy, while this proportion is smaller, to a slight extent, than the result (47.5%) of K. Yoshihara and T. Ratcliffe (1970).[65] It is frequently argued that 1961 was the turning point in the postwar Japanese economic growth. One of the reasons for the turning-point-argument was the exhaustion of backlog of new technologies accumulated in the western countries during the period of World War II and its immediate after.[66] Table 2.19 provides some evidence on this argument. Namely, when the whole estimation period is demarcated into 1952–1961 and 1962–1968, the latter period shows a tendency for decline in the growth rate of productivity change ($\dot{P}/P$) and the percentage of unexplained output growth (($\dot{P}/P)/(\dot{Y}^*/Y^*)$): This declining tendency is, however, not so conspicuous when the comparison is made between 1954–1961 and 1962–1968.

Next we discuss quality changes in capital output which can be identified with aggregation biases. As was stated in the previous subsection, the quality index of capital is defined as

$A = K/K'$

or

$$\frac{\dot{A}}{A} = \frac{\dot{K}}{K} - \frac{\dot{K'}}{K'} = \sum_{i,j} \frac{p_{ij}K_{ij}}{pK} \frac{\dot{K}_{ij}}{K_{ij}} - \sum_{i,j} \frac{K_{ij}}{K'} \frac{\dot{K}_{ij}}{K_{ij}}$$

$$= \sum_{i,j} \left( \frac{p_{ij}K_{ij}}{pK} - \frac{K_{ij}}{K'} \right) \cdot \frac{\dot{K}_{ij}}{K_{ij}}$$

where $K$ is the Divisia index for capital ($pK = \sum p_{ij}K_{ij}$) and $K'$ is the simple sum of each type of real capital ($K' = \sum K_{ij}$). It must be recalled that the quality index of labor is defined as

$$B = L/L'$$

where $L$ is the Divisia index for labor under the special perfect substitutability assumption and $L'$ is the simple sum of each type of labor ($L' = \sum L_k$). The quality index of output is defined in the same way as follows

$$C = Y^*/Y^{*'}$$

where $Y^*$ is the Divisia index for output and $Y^{*'} = C^* + I^*$. It must also be recalled that these quality indexes can be reinterpreted as those of aggregation bias from the point of view of measuring productivity change in the sense that K', and L' and Y\*' are the incorrectly aggregated quantities of capital, labor and output respectively in the measurement of productivity change.

Table 2.20 shows the quality indexes of capital corresponding to various levels of aggregation. It shows also the quality of indexes of labor and output. From this table we can see that the quality change in capital as a whole is far greater than that in labor, i.e., the growth rate of quality index per year is about 3% in capital by 0.3% in labor. This can be stated equivalently as follows: the degree of aggregation bias is far greater in capital than in labor. The reason for this fact can be understood from table 2.21, which shows the contribution of each capital to the rate of growth of quality index as a whole. From line 5 in the table we can see that the greatest contribution comes from $K_{DCB}$, i.e., nonresidential structures and producers' durables in the corporate business sector. Note that $p_{ij} K_{ij}/pK$ (line 1) shows the value share of each capital in terms of service prices and $K_{ij}/K'$ (line 2) the quantity share or the value share in terms of base year asset prices. Both shares and their gap (line 3) are quite large in category of $K_{DCB}$, and so the greatest contribution arises in this category.[67]

**Table 2.20**
Quality indexes of capital, labor and output

| | $K/K' = A$ | $K_R/K'_R$ | $K_D/K'_D$ | $K_J/K'_J$ | $K_S/K'_S$ | $K_C/K'_C$ | $K_N/K'_N$ | $K_H/K'_H$ | $K_G/K'_G$ | $L/L' = B$ | $Y/Y' = C$ |
|---|---|---|---|---|---|---|---|---|---|---|---|
| 1951 | 0.642 | 1.018 | 0.993 | 1.077 | 1.000 | 0.882 | 0.687 | 0.866 | 0.814 | 0.968 | 0.965 |
| 1952 | 0.646 | 1.019 | 0.997 | 1.038 | 1.000 | 0.860 | 0.695 | 0.879 | 0.821 | 0.970 | 0.968 |
| 1953 | 0.653 | 1.015 | 1.000 | 0.929 | 1.000 | 0.847 | 0.706 | 0.882 | 0.842 | 0.969 | 0.971 |
| 1954 | 0.663 | 1.016 | 1.002 | 0.957 | 1.000 | 0.850 | 0.730 | 0.895 | 0.852 | 0.977 | 0.967 |
| 1955 | 0.683 | 1.016 | 1.003 | 0.992 | 1.000 | 0.851 | 0.759 | 0.918 | 0.851 | 0.967 | 0.974 |
| 1956 | 0.708 | 1.015 | 1.002 | 0.976 | 1.000 | 0.866 | 0.771 | 0.936 | 0.860 | 0.970 | 0.979 |
| 1957 | 0.742 | 1.014 | 1.002 | 0.970 | 1.000 | 0.885 | 0.792 | 0.951 | 0.873 | 0.972 | 0.981 |
| 1958 | 0.768 | 1.013 | 1.000 | 0.974 | 1.000 | 0.901 | 0.817 | 0.966 | 0.886 | 0.970 | 0.977 |
| 1959 | 0.801 | 1.012 | 1.000 | 0.973 | 1.000 | 0.918 | 0.842 | 0.978 | 0.899 | 0.978 | 0.985 |
| 1960 | 0.844 | 1.008 | 1.002 | 0.975 | 1.000 | 0.941 | 0.866 | 0.984 | 0.911 | 0.983 | 0.992 |
| 1961 | 0.890 | 1.002 | 1.005 | 0.990 | 1.000 | 0.956 | 0.886 | 0.984 | 0.933 | 0.985 | 0.999 |
| 1962 | 0.926 | 0.999 | 1.004 | 0.992 | 1.000 | 0.976 | 0.914 | 0.985 | 0.958 | 0.985 | 0.995 |
| 1963 | 0.956 | 0.999 | 1.003 | 1.003 | 1.000 | 0.981 | 0.940 | 0.988 | 0.987 | 0.990 | 1.000 |
| 1964 | 0.984 | 0.999 | 1.004 | 1.002 | 1.000 | 0.995 | 0.968 | 0.993 | 0.993 | 0.996 | 1.001 |
| 1965 | 1.000 | 1.000 | 1.000 | 1.000 | 1.000 | 1.000 | 1.000 | 1.000 | 1.000 | 1.000 | 1.000 |
| 1966 | 1.015 | 1.000 | 0.997 | 0.998 | 1.000 | 1.003 | 1.028 | 1.003 | 1.002 | 1.001 | 1.001 |
| 1967 | 1.034 | 1.002 | 0.998 | 0.994 | 1.000 | 1.008 | 1.059 | 1.006 | 0.991 | 1.008 | 0.999 |
| 1968 | 1.054 | 1.002 | 1.000 | 0.991 | 1.000 | 1.013 | 1.096 | 1.010 | 0.984 | 1.017 | 0.997 |

**Table 2.21**
Why is the Growth Rate of $K/K^*$ so high?

| | $K_{RCB}$ | $K_{RH}$ | $K_{DCB}$ | $K_{DNB}$ | $K_{DGE}$ | $K_{JCB}$ | $K_{JNB}$ | $K_{JGE}$ | $K_{SCB}$ | $K_{SNB}$ | $K_{SH}$ | $K_{SGE}$ | row sum |
|---|---|---|---|---|---|---|---|---|---|---|---|---|---|
| (1) $P_{ij}K_{ij}/pK$ | 0.0105 | 0.1065 | 0.4585 | 0.1019 | 0.0694 | 0.1006 | 0.0226 | 0.0108 | -0.0057 | 0.1125 | 0.0121 | 0.0002 | 1.0000 |
| (2) $K_{ij}/K^*$ | 0.0133 | 0.0940 | 0.2228 | 0.0503 | 0.0470 | 0.0989 | 0.0195 | 0.0121 | 0.0466 | 0.3724 | 0.0207 | 0.0025 | 1.0000 |
| (3) $\dfrac{P_{ij}K_{ij}}{pK} - \dfrac{K_{ij}}{K^*}$ | -0.0028 | 0.0125 | 0.2357 | 0.0517 | 0.0225 | 0.0017 | 0.0031 | -0.0014 | -0.0523 | -0.2599 | -0.0086 | -0.0023 | 0.0000 |
| (4) $K_{ij}/K_{ij}$ (%) | 13.2500 | 12.4200 | 10.1700 | 8.8800 | 14.1000 | 11.6300 | 5.8100 | 7.5000 | 0.0000 | 0.0000 | 0.0000 | 0.0000 | — |
| (5) (3) × (4) (%) | -0.0400 | 0.1600 | 2.4000 | 0.4600 | 0.3200 | 0.0200 | 0.0200 | -0.0100 | 0.0000 | 0.0000 | 0.0000 | 0.0000 | 3.3200 |

Another finding from table 2.20 is that the aggregation through each sector of the economy for type of capital will not incur so much aggregation bias than the aggregation through each type of capital for each sector of the economy. This is based on the fact that the change in $K_i/K_i'$ ($i = R, D, J, S$) is negligible in comparison with the change in $K_j/K_j'$ ($j = H, CB, NB, GE$). This is due to the fact that the differences between the value shares and the quantity shares are quite small in the former ($p_{ij}K_{ij}/p_iK_i - K_{ij}/K_i'$) in comparison with those in the latter ($p_{ij}K_{ij}/p_jK_j - K_{ij}/K_j'$).[68]

The improvement in our measurement of productivity change, though it is not so considerable, is based on the quality change in capital rather than the quality change in labor, because the latter is quite small except for the recent periods compared with the former. Note that the quality change in output is negligible as is shown in table 2.20. More precise arguments can be made from the point of view of aggregation bias. From equation (2.5.44) in the previous subsection, we can express the bias due to the use of incorrectly aggregated quantities $K'$, $L'$ and $Y^{*'}$ as follows

$$\frac{\dot{P}'}{P'} - \frac{\dot{P}}{P} = v_K \left( \frac{\dot{K}}{K} - \frac{\dot{K}'}{K'} \right) + v_L \left( \frac{\dot{L}}{L} - \frac{\dot{L}'}{L'} \right) - \left( \frac{\dot{Y}^*}{Y^*} \frac{\dot{Y}^{*'}}{Y^{*'}} \right)$$

$$= v_K \cdot \frac{\dot{A}}{A} = v_L \cdot \frac{\dot{B}}{B} \frac{\dot{C}}{C} .$$

This relationship also shows the gains resulted from the correct measurement of capital, labor and output. Similar relation concerning the unexplained portion or output growth is, from (2.5.40), (2.5.43) and (2.5.44),

$$\frac{\dot{P}'}{P'} \bigg/ \frac{\dot{Y}^{*'}}{Y^{*'}} - \frac{\dot{P}}{P} \bigg/ \frac{\dot{Y}^*}{Y^*} - v_K \left( \frac{\dot{A}}{A} \bigg/ \frac{\dot{Y}^{*'}}{Y^{*'}} \right) + v_L \left( \frac{\dot{B}}{B} \bigg/ \frac{\dot{Y}^{*'}}{Y^{*'}} \right)$$

$$- \left( 1 - \frac{\dot{P}}{p} \bigg/ \frac{\dot{Y}^*}{Y^*} \right) \left( \frac{\dot{Y}^*}{Y^*} \bigg/ \frac{\dot{Y}^{*'}}{Y^{*'}} - 1 \right).$$

Then corresponding Japanese data show, on the average,

$$\frac{\dot{P}'}{P'} \ (5.6\%) - \frac{\dot{P}}{P} \ (4.4\%) = v_K \cdot \frac{\dot{A}}{A} \ (0.36 \times 3.3\% = 1.2\%)$$

$$+ v_L \cdot \frac{\dot{B}}{B} \ (0.64 \times 0.3\% = 0.2\%) - \frac{\dot{C}}{C} \ (0.2\%)$$

and

$$\frac{\dot{P}'}{P'} \Big/ \frac{\dot{Y}^{*\prime}}{Y^{*\prime}} \ (56.6\%) - \frac{\dot{P}}{P} \Big/ \frac{\dot{Y}^{*}}{Y^{*}} \ (42.9\%)$$

$$= v_K \left( \frac{\dot{A}}{A} \Big/ \frac{\dot{Y}^{*\prime}}{Y'} \right) (0.36 \times 33.1\% = 12.0\%)$$

$$+ v_L \left( \frac{\dot{B}}{B} \Big/ \frac{\dot{Y}^{*\prime}}{Y'} \right) (0.64 \times 2.9\% = 1.8\%)$$

$$- \left( 1 - \frac{\dot{P}}{P} \Big/ \frac{\dot{Y}^{*}}{Y^{*}} \right) \left( \frac{\dot{Y}^{*}}{Y^{*}} \Big/ \frac{\dot{Y}^{*\prime}}{Y^{*\prime}} - 1 \right) (0.57 \times 0.2\% = 0.1\%) .$$

Therefore, we can say from these two relations that the improvement in our measurement of productivity change depends exclusively upon the quality change in capital.[69]

## 2.6   Concluding Remarks

We have pursued two main objectives in the present paper. One was to provide the data and accounting basis for the theory-oriented empirical researches on macroeconomic performance in the postwar Japanese economy. The other was to measure productivity change in the producing sector based on the data and accounting framework thus provided. The methodological outcomes and empirical findings of the present paper are summarized below.

1. We have derived Walras' Law in the existing national income statistics. This means the fact that the national income statistics can be interpreted in terms of general equilibrium theory, which is an obvious but not well recognized fact. We have also shown that the present national income statistics is not precise in its treatment of general government sector, which leads to the inconsistency between national income and national wealth. (Section 2.2.)

2. We have provided the product and factor outlay accounts for the producing sector in which the key accounting identity is the equality between value of output and value of input. We have attempted to separate output into consumption goods component and investment goods component, and capital input into price and quantity components. (Section 2.3.) Concerning the consuming sector, we have constructed the income, outlay, saving and wealth accounts, and clarified the basic relationships between flow and stock variables. (Section 2.4.)

3. We have attempted to measure the productivity change in the producing sector by paying special attention to the differences in quality among various types of capital, labor and output. The final results summarized in table 2.19 are 4.4% for the average rate of productivity change and 42.9% for the average proportion of output growth which cannot be explained by factor input. The latter figure is slightly greater than the result obtained by L.R. Christensen and D.W. Jorgenson for the U.S. economy, and shows a slight improvement in comparison with other studies of productivity change in the Japanese economy. This improvement in our measurement, though small, was shown to be based exclusively on the quality improvement of capital. We have also shown in tables 2.20 and 2.21 that the quality change in capital was far greater than that in labor and that the nonresidential structures and producers' durables in the corporate business sector ($K_{DCB}$) played the most important role in this quality change. (Subsection 2.5.3.)

4. We have proposed a new definition of aggregate rate of productivity change which is a slight modification of the usual Divisia index for productivity change. The usual definition of aggregate productivity change was shown inappropriate, because it neglects the role of intermediate goods as the factors of production. We have emphasized the importance of explicit introduction of intermediate goods into the analysis which provides one of the reasons why a considerable proportion of output growth still remains to be explained by some sources other than primary factor inputs. (Subsection 2.5.1.) We have provided the theoretical basis for the quality indexes of capital, labor and output from the viewpoint of measurement of productivity change. These quality indexes were shown to be reinterpreted as indexes of aggregation bias which arises from the use of incorrectly aggregated quantities of capital, labor and output in the measurement of productivity change. (Subsection 2.5.2.)

Section 2.5 (Measurement of Productivity Change) is the result of our attempt to measure macroeconomic performance in the Japanese economy. Other attempts will be made elsewhere on the basis of the data and accounting framework provided in the present paper. Measurement of production function (based on section 2.3), measurement of consumption function (based on section 2.4) and construction of compact macroeconomic model (based on section 2.2) are now under consideration.

## Notes

1. The existing Japanese national accounting system is that of the United Nations (1970).

2. Note that the private business sector is not separated into corporate business and noncorporate business sectors. This separation will be made in section 2.3.

3. It is implicitly assumed in table 2.1 that all of the investment goods including land are reproducible.

4. The budget restriction of noncorporate business sector is quite similar to that of households sector.

5. See D. Patinkin (1965) or F. Modigliani (1963). Both of them separate the financial assets into money and other financial assets but adopt the concept of homogeneous output making no distinction between consumption goods and investment goods. Note that our formulation is completely flow equilibrium but theirs are a mixtue of flow and stock equilibria. Concerning the problems of flow and stock equilibrium, see B. Hansen (1970, ch. 7).

6. We will use the term "net product" in two different meanings. One is the output net of intermediate inputs (the first line of (2.2.3–p)) and the other is the value added in each sector (the second line of (2.2.3–p) ).

7. Concerning the latter problem, see H. Uzawa (1966).

8. If tax parameters are neglected, the competitive service prices of physical capital and money are respectively $p_K = r + \mu - \dot{q}_K/q_K$ and $p_M = r$, where $r$ is rate of return and $\mu$ is rate of depreciation. See subsection 2.3.2 for $p_K$.

9. This asymmetry still persists even when we treat money in the $H$-sector in the same way as the owner-occupied residential structures in that sector.

10. See T. Ratcliffe (1969).

11. See Japan Statistical Yearbook (1969).

12. In Foreign Trade Statistics, light industry products and heavy industry products are not separated for 1953–1957 and so the value shares of 1958 are used for the separation.

13. See NIS (1969), section 2, part 2, table 17, pp. 264–265.

14. See NIS (1969), section 1, table 5, pp. 28–29.

15. See R.E. Hall and D.W. Jorgenson (1968) and L.R. Christensen and D.W. Jorgenson (1969).

16. See T. Ratcliffe (1969).

17. If we permit land acquisition, $\phi_{ij}$'s in the last row of table 2.4 must be modified into $1 + k_t(1 + k_t)/(1 - u_t)(1 - v_t)$, $1 + k_t$, and $1 + k_t$ respectively.

18. See NIS (1969), section 2, part 2, table 16, pp. 258–259.

19. See subsection 2.5.3 of this paper.

20. Total value of capital is obtained after the quantity series of capital is computed.

21. See NIS (1969), section 1, table 4, pp. 24–25.

22. See NIS (1969), section 2, part 2, table 7, pp. 238–239. The value shares are used in allocation. The balancing item in gross private capital formation is neglected. When there are some missing data, interpolation using some appropriate ratio is made.

23. See NIS (1969), section 1, table 5, pp. 28–29.

24. See Japan Statistical Yearbook (1969). Since the National Wealth Survey of 1965 excludes the households sector, we adopt 1960 as the base year.

25. One important exception is "food control special account" which is included in the National Income Statistics but not in the National Wealth Survey. As the inventory of "food control special account," whose main component is stock of rice, occupies a large portion of inventory stock in the government enterprises sector, it is incorporated into our base year capital stock.

26. See I. Nakayama (1959).

27. The original source is "Quarterly Survey of Corporate Firms," by the Ministry of Finance.

28. The fact that "Quarterly Survey of Corporate Firms" does not include the financial sector is of course taken into consideration.

29. The year 1965 is the end year of the revaluation period.

30. See table 2.8.

31. See Japan Agricultural Yearbook (no date).

32. See Japan Statistical Yearbook (1969).

33. See T. Ratcliffe (1969).

34. See T. Ratcliffe (1969).

35. See National Wealth Survey (1955).

36. See L.R. Christensen and D.W. Jorgenson (1969).

37. The rental income for privately-owned housing is imputed by multiplying their total floor area by the average rental price per floor area of the house for rent. See NIS (1969), pp. 354–355.

38. We have not introduced explicitly consumers' durables into our producing sector, since the data for consumers' durables are obtained by using several bold assumptions. See the appendix to this section. It is a main intention of this section to show how to introduce consumers' durables into consumers' accounts.

39. The standard theories of the consumption function consider superannuation, health or unemployment insurance etc., as a part of the individual's income. See, for example, M.J. Farrel (1959). It is, therefore, more appropriate to treat social insurance funds as a part of the private wealth as in the case of L.R. Christensen and D.W. Jorgenson (1973b).

40. All of the data required for this procedure are available in Japan Statistical Yearbook (1969), but the data for the assessed wage and salary income in the category of "income taxes notwithheld" are missing for 1953–1964 and were estimated by using its shares in total assessed income linearly interpolated.

41. See Japan's Economic Statistics (no date).

42. See NIS (1969), section 2, table 5, p. 236.

43. See Japan Statistical Yearbook (1969).

44. This means the fact that $(I_C - \mu_C K_{C,-1})$ is negative around the base year of 1955.

45. They are J.C.H. Fei and G. Ranis (1965), K. Ohkawa (1968), R. Sato (1968), T. Watanabe and F. Egaitsu (1967) and K. Yoshihara and T. Ratcliffe (1970). It is needless to say that each of them deals with the problem from different viewpoints and for different time periods.

46. Ohkawa makes the most detailed treatment of the problem but does not allow for the heterogeneity of output in his aggregate analysis. Yoshihara and Ratcliffe allow for the difference in quality of labor.

47. Here we are dealing with a closed economy without international trade. The same discussion can be made about an open economy with slight modifications.

48. By the necessary conditions for producer equilibrium, we mean the following relationships between prices and marginal productivities

$$q_i \frac{\partial f^i}{\partial y_{ki}} \leq q_k \; (k = 1, \ldots, n) \text{ and } q_i \frac{\partial f^i}{\partial x_{ji}} \leq p_j \; (j = 1, \ldots, m) .$$

By conventions, the input quantity ($y_{ki}$ or $x_{ji}$) is zero when the inequality holds. There the equality (2.5.1) always holds irrespective of equality or inequality in the above relationships.

49. See W. Leontief et al. (1953).

50. Other definitions can be made about the aggregate rate of productivity change as the weighted average of $\dot{p}^i/p^i$. They are as follows

$$\frac{\dot{S}}{S} = \sum_i \frac{\sum q_k y_{ki}}{\sum_i (\sum_k q_k y_{ki})} \cdot \frac{\dot{p}^i}{p^i} \; \left( \sum q_k y_{ki} = \begin{array}{l} \text{the value of intermediate} \\ \text{input in the } i\text{th industry} \end{array} \right)$$

and

$$\frac{\dot{R}}{R} = \sum_i \frac{\sum p_i x_{ji}}{\sum_i (\sum_j p_j x_{ji})} \cdot \frac{\dot{p}^i}{p^i} \; \left( \sum p_j x_{ji} = \begin{array}{l} \text{the value added in} \\ \text{the } i\text{th industry} \end{array} \right)$$

We can easily prove the following relationship

$$\frac{\dot{T}}{T} = (1 - \theta) \frac{\dot{S}}{S} + \theta \frac{\dot{R}}{R} .$$

Note that $\dot{S}/S$ and $\dot{R}/R$ have no clear-cut relations with the aggregate production function.

51. M.K. Richter (1966) also provided the justification for $\dot{P}/P$ from the viewpoint of the invariance property of this Divisia index. As $\dot{T}/T = \theta \dot{P}/P$ (equation (2.5.25)), our modified Divisia index (for productivity change $\dot{T}/T$ also satisfies his invariance property. Only when we do not permit the "technical deterioration," i.e., negative $\dot{p}^i/p^i$, his aggregate invariance property implies the disaggregate invariance properties for each industry.

52. Let us consider the following maximization problem

Maximize $z = f (x_1 \ldots x_n)$

subject to $g^j(x_1 \ldots x_n, b_1 \ldots b_s) = 0$    $(j = 1 \ldots m)$

under the given $b_1 \ldots b_s$ .

Then we can prove easily the following relations, provided that the Lagrangean method is applicable and that the related partial derivatives exist

$$\frac{\partial z^*}{\partial b_k} = \sum_j \lambda j \frac{\partial g^j(x_1^* \ldots x_n^*, b_1 \ldots b_s)}{\partial^b k} \qquad (k = 1 \ldots s)$$

where $z^*$ and $x_i^*$'s are the optimal solutions and $\lambda_j$'s are the corresponding Lagrangean multipliers. When the constraints are of specific type, i.e.,

$$g^j(x_1 \ldots x_n, b_1 \ldots b_s) = b_j - h^j(x_1 \ldots x_n),$$

then the above relations become

$$\frac{\partial z^*}{\partial b_k} = \lambda_k \qquad (k = 1 \ldots m)$$

which are the well-known results (see, for example, G. Hadley (1964, chapter 3)).

53. E.D. Domar (1961) has derived essentially the same equation as our (2.5.25) or the last equation of our (2.5.13) by using the geometric index method, i.e., Cobb-Douglas production function (see his equation (2.2.18), p. 720). It must be, however, noted that he also considers $\dot{P}/P$ as the proper measure of the aggregate rate of technical progress. Namely according to his Rule II, "the rate of growth of the residual for the whole sector equals the sum of the growth of the $A$'s (our $\dot{P}^i/P^i$'s) of the components industries, each $A$ weighted by the ratio of the value of its product *final to the industry* (that is, used outside of the industry) to the value of the product *final to the sector* (used outside of the sector) in the base period" (p. 720). It is clear from our hitherto mentioned reasonings that his rule II is not appropriate.

54. Note that the analysis of R. Solow (1957) was based on the highly aggregated and simplified value added production function which can be derived from (2.5.14) by assuming perfect substitutabilities among various kinds of output, of capital and of labor.

55. See R. Solow (1955–1956).

56. They assume the production function of the type $Y = F(K, L_1, \ldots, L_s)$ which is rewritten by using the assumption (ii) as $Y = F(K, L)$ where

$$L = L_1 + \lambda_2 L_2 + \cdots + \lambda_s L_s \quad \text{and} \quad \lambda_i = (\partial F/\partial L_i)/(\partial F/\partial L_1) = \text{constant}.$$

By using the assumption (iii), L becomes

$$L = L_1 + \frac{p_{L2}}{p_{L1}} L_2 + \cdots + \frac{p_{Ls}}{p_{L1}} L_s.$$

Then the quality index of labor $(B)$ is defined as

$$B = L/L'.$$

Note that $L$ is the Divisia index for labor under the special perfect substitutability assumption (ii). Note further that their derivation is not made from the viewpoint of technical progress as is seen from the fact that their production function does not include the shift parameter $t$. See T. Watanabe (1972) for the detailed discussion. Notations here are ours.

57. See R. Solow (1957).

58. See NIS (1969), section 2, part 2, table 1, pp. 220–224.

59. See Japan Statistical Yearbook (1969). The original source is "Labor Force Survey" by Ministry of Labor. Japan Statistical Yearbook provides the data based on calendar year, but its effects are negligible. Precisely speaking, $L_s$ is computed by combining $L_e$ in the national income statistics and $L_s/L_e$ in Japan Statistical Yearbook. There is also a slight difference in definition between these two data sources.

60. See T. Watanabe (1972), item 2.4 in table 6 for 1951–1964 and item T.1 in table 23 for 1965–1969.

61. See L.R. Christensen and D.W. Jorgenson (1970).

62. This proportion, which is computed from table 21 of K. Ohkawa (1968), is 33.5–40.1% during the period 1952–1963 for nonprimary sector. The result of Yoshihara and Ratcliffe is 34.6% for nonprimary sector and 70.3% for primary sector. So we can see that the primary sector plays an important role in this proportion for the economy as a whole.

63. See, for example, K. Ohkawa and H. Rosovsky (1968).

64. This effect may be overestimated because the value share of $K_{DCB}$ may be overestimated, judging from the negative values which appeared partly in the estimates of service prices of the corporate land. The difference between the two shares (line 3) is quite large in $K_{SNB}$, i.e., noncorporate land which includes agricultural land. But the quantity of land is assumed to be constant and so its effect is neglected. As the agricultural land is actually decreasing, the loosening of the assumption will intensify the degree of quality improvement in capital.

65. The reason for the greatest change in $K_{NB}/K'_{NB}$ among $K_j/K'_j (j = H, CB, NB, GE)$ can be seen from the following table which has same character as table 2.21. This table shows that the greatest contribution comes from $K_{DNB}$.

| | $K_{CB}/K'_{CB}$ | | | | $K_{NB}/K'_{NB}$ | | | $K_H/K'_H$ | | $K_{GE}/K'_{GE}$ | | |
|---|---|---|---|---|---|---|---|---|---|---|---|---|
| | $K_{RCB}$ | $K_{DCB}$ | $K_{JCB}$ | $K_{SCB}$ | $K_{DNB}$ | $K_{JNB}$ | $K_{SNB}$ | $K_{RH}$ | $K_{SH}$ | $K_{DGE}$ | $K_{JGE}$ | $K_{SGE}$ |
| (1) $P_{ij}K_{ij}/p_jK_j$ | 0.0179 | 0.8246 | 0.1732 | −0.0157 | 0.4360 | 0.0942 | 0.4698 | −0.8926 | 0.1074 | 0.8865 | 0.1124 | 0.0012 |
| (2) $K_{ij}/K_j'$ | 0.0338 | 0.5770 | 0.2568 | 0.1324 | 0.1240 | 0.0461 | 0.8299 | 0.8063 | 0.1937 | 0.7416 | 0.2119 | 0.0465 |
| (3) $\dfrac{P_{ij}K_{ij}}{P_jK_j} - \dfrac{K_{ij}}{K_j}$ | −0.0159 | 0.2476 | −0.836 | −0.1481 | 0.3120 | 0.0481 | −0.3601 | 0.0863 | −0.0863 | 0.1449 | −0.0996 | −0.0453 |
| (4) $K_{ij}/K_j(\%)$ | 13.2500 | 10.1700 | | 0.0000 | 8.8800 | 5.8100 | 0.0000 | 12.4200 | 0.0000 | 14.1000 | 7.5000 | 0.0000 |
| (5) (3) × (4) (%) | −0.2100 | 2.5200 | | 0.0000 | 2.7700 | 0.2800 | 0.0000 | 1.0700 | 0.0000 | 2.0400 | −0.7500 | 0.0000 |
| (6) $\sum$(5)% | 1.33 | | | | 3.05 | | | 1.07 | | 1.30 | | |

66. Once again this effect may be overestimated due to the negative service prices of capital. See note 64.

# 3

## U.S. And Japanese Economic Growth, 1952–1974: An International Comparison

Mieko Nishimizu and
Dale W. Jorgenson

### 3.1 Introduction

The purpose of this paper is to provide an international comparison of aggregate economic growth in the United States and Japan during the period 1952–1974.[1] Throughout this period the United States has maintained its position as the world's largest economy and as the leader among industrialized countries in output *per capita*. During the period Japan has risen to its current position as the world's third largest economy behind the United States and the Soviet Union, but a substantial gap between U.S. and Japanese levels of output *per capita* remains.[2]

Our initial objective is to analyze differences between U.S. and Japanese levels of output and to allocate these differences between differences in factor input and differences in levels of technology in the two countries. Our second objective is to divide differences between levels of factor input in the United States and Japan between differences in capital and labor input. Japanese output grew rapidly relative to U.S. output during the period 1952–1960, and most of the gain was due to a substantial increase in the Japanese level of technology relative to the U.S. and Japanese labor input relative to U.S. labor input. Relative levels of capital input in the two countries remained almost unchanged until the end of the period. Capital intensity, defined as capital input per unit of labor input, rose in the United States but remained unchanged in Japan.

The last half of the 1950s and the early 1960s mark a transition in the relative growth of the U.S. and Japanese economies, involving four significant events: in 1956 the own rate of return on business capital in Japan, the marginal product of all capital in the business sector, surpassed that in the United States; in that year the share of investment goods in the value of total output in Japan overtook that in the United States; in 1957 the annual rate of growth of capital input in Japan overtook that in the United States; in 1960 the ratio of U.S. investment goods output to the Japanese output of investment goods fell below the corresponding ratio for consumption goods output.

The years 1960–1974 were a period of substantial economic growth in the United States and extremely rapid growth in Japan. During these years the average rate of growth of capital input in Japan was more than double that in the United States, running at about three times the U.S. growth rate; the own rate of return on business capital in Japan exceeded that in the United States during this period and was approximately double that in the United States. The ratio of U.S. output of investment goods to Japan fell from 7.1 in 1960 to 2.2 in 1974; the corresponding ratio for the output of consumption goods fell from 7.5 in 1960 to 4.5 in 1974.

The period 1960–1974 was characterized by average growth in labor input in the two countries at roughly similar rates. Almost all of the narrowing of the gap between U.S. and Japanese levels of output during this period was due to the increase in the relative capital intensity of production in Japan and to the rapid rise in the level of technology in Japan relative to that in the United States. The Japanese level of technology was only one-fourth of the U.S. level in 1952 and remained at less than half the corresponding U.S. level during the period 1952–1959. Beginning in 1960, the relative level of Japanese technology moved up rapidly, reaching approximately 90% of the U.S. level by 1968. Between 1968 and 1973 the gap between Japanese and U.S. technology was eliminated, so that the remaining difference in levels of output between the two countries is due to differences in levels of labor and capital input.

In 1973 the ratio of U.S. labor input to Japanese labor input was 2.4. The corresponding ratio of U.S. and Japanese capital input was 5.9, so that the capital intensity of production in the United States was more than double that in Japan in 1973. However, the year 1973 marked another milestone in the relationship of U.S. and Japanese economic growth: The ratio of investment goods output to labor input in Japan overtook that in the United States. This development suggests that the remaining gap between U.S. and Japanese output *per capita* can be closed, even in the absence of any change in relative levels of technology in the two countries.[3]

In section 3.2 we present a brief discussion of our methodology. This methodology was developed by Christensen and Jorgenson (1969, 1970, 1973a) and has been implemented by them for the United States for the period 1929–1969. Ezaki and Jorgenson (1973) have implemented this approach for Japan for the period 1951–1968. Christensen, Cummings, and Jorgenson (1980) have brought these estimates up-to-date through 1973 and have compared the results with corresponding estimates for Canada, France, Germany, Italy, Korea, the Netherlands, and the United Kingdom.

In section 3.3 we present new measures of U.S. output relative to Japanese output, purchasing power parities between the yen and the dollar in terms of output, and growth rates of output in both countries for the period 1952–1974. In section 3.4 we present corresponding measures of U.S. factor input relative to Japanese factor input, including purchasing power parities in terms of factor input and growth rates of factor input for both countries. In section 3.5 we present measures of the aggregate level of technology in the United States relative to Japan and growth rates of total factor productivity in both countries.

## 3.2 Methodology

Our first objective is to allocate differences between levels of output for the United States and Japan between differences in factor input and differences in total factor productivity. Our second objective is to separate growth in factor input from growth in total factor productivity in accounting for growth in output over time in each country. For this purpose we require comparable measures of factor input, output, and total factor productivity for the two countries. To achieve comparability in measuring output we employ purchasing power parities for the United States and Japan, based on the work of Kravis and his associates (1975). To achieve comparability in measuring factor input we develop corresponding purchasing power parities for capital and labor input for the two countries.

Our methodology is based on the economic theory of production. The point for departure for this theory is a production function giving output as a function of inputs, a dummy variable equal to one for the United States and zero for Japan, and time. We consider production under constant returns to scale, so that a proportional change in all inputs results in a proportional change in output. In analyzing differences in production patterns between the two countries and changes in production patterns over time for each country, we combine the production function with necessary conditions for producer equilibrium. We express these conditions as equalities between shares of each input in the value of output and the elasticity of output with respect to that input. The elasticities depend on inputs, the dummy variable for each country, and time, the variables that enter the production function. Under constant returns to scale the sum of the elasticities with respect to all inputs is equal to unity, so that the value shares also sum to unity.

To analyze differences in the pattern of production between countries we consider the difference in output between countries, holding all inputs and time constant. Under constant returns to scale, the necessary conditions for producer equilibrium for both countries can be combined with differences between inputs and outputs to produce an index of the difference in the level of technology that depends only on the prices and quantities of inputs and outputs in the two countries. Similarly, to analyze changes in the pattern of production for each country with time we consider the rate of technical change with respect to time for that country, defined as the rate of growth of output, holding all inputs and the country dummy variable constant. The necessary conditions for producer equilibrium for each country can be combined with growth rates of inputs and outputs for that country to provide an index of the rate of technical change for the country that depends only on the prices and quantities of its inputs and outputs.

Our methodology for productivity measurement is based on a specific form for the production function

$$
\begin{aligned}
Y = \exp\,[&\alpha_0 + \alpha_K \ln K + \alpha_L \ln L + \alpha_D D + \alpha_T T + \frac{1}{2}\beta_{KK}(\ln K)^2 \\
&+ \beta_{KL} \ln K \ln L + \beta_{KD} D \ln K + \beta_{KT} T \ln K + \frac{1}{2}\beta_{LL}(\ln L)^2 + \beta_{LD} D \ln L \\
&+ \beta_{LT} T \ln L + \frac{1}{2}\beta_{DD}D^2 + \beta_{DT} DT + \frac{1}{2}\beta_{TT}T^2],
\end{aligned}
$$

where $Y$ is output, $K$ is capital input, $L$ is labor input, $D$ is a dummy variable equal to one for the United States and zero for Japan, and $T$ is time. For this production function output is a transcendental or, more specifically, an exponential function of the logarithms of inputs. We refer to this form as *the transcendental logarithmic production function* or, more simply, the translog production function.[4] The translog production function is characterized by constant returns to scale if and only if the parameters satisfy the conditions

$$\alpha_K + \alpha_L = 1 \,, \quad \beta_{KK} + \beta_{KL} = 0 \,, \quad \beta_{KL} + \beta_{LL} = 0 \,,$$
$$\beta_{KD} + \beta_{LD} = 0 \,, \quad \beta_{KT} + \beta_{LT} = 0 \,.$$

Denoting the price of output by $q_Y$, the price of capital input by $p_K$, and the price of labor input by $p_L$, we can define the shares of capital and labor input in the value of output, say $v_K$ and $v_L$, by

$$v_K = \frac{p_K K}{q_Y Y} \,, \qquad v_L = \frac{p_L L}{q_Y Y} \,.$$

Necessary conditions for producer equilibrium are given by equalities between each value share and the elasticity of output with respect to the corresponding input

$$v_K = \frac{\partial \ln Y}{\partial \ln K} \, (K, L, D, T)$$
$$= \alpha_K + \beta_{KK} \ln K + \beta_{KL} \ln L + \beta_{KD} D + \beta_{KT} T \,;$$
$$v_L = \frac{\partial \ln Y}{\partial \ln L} \, (K, L, D, T)$$
$$= \alpha_L + \beta_{KL} \ln K + \beta_{LL} \ln L + \beta_{LD} D + \beta_{LT} T \,.$$

Under constant returns to scale the elasticities and the value shares sum to unity.

We can define the difference in technology between the two countries, say $v_D$, as the logarithmic difference between levels of output between the countries, holding capital input, labor input, and time constant

$$v_D = \frac{\partial \ln Y}{\partial T} \, (K, L, D, T)$$
$$= \alpha_D + \beta_{KD} \ln K + \beta_{LD} \ln L + \beta_{DD} D + \beta_{DT} T \,.$$

Finally, we can define the rate of technical change, say $v_T$, as the growth of output with respect to time, holding capital input, labor input, and the country dummy variable constant

$$v_T = \frac{\partial \ln Y}{\partial T} (K, L, D, T)$$

$$= \alpha_T + \beta_{KT} \ln K + \beta_{LT} \ln L + \beta_{DT} D + \beta_{TT} T .$$

## 3.3 Output

We can also consider specific forms for the functions defining aggregate output $Y$, capital input $K$, and labor input $L$. For example, the translog form for aggregate output as a function of its components is

$$Y = \exp[\alpha_1 \ln Y_1 + \alpha_2 \ln Y_2 + \cdots + \alpha_m \ln Y_m$$

$$+ \frac{1}{2} \beta_{11} (\ln Y_1)^2 + \beta_{12} \ln Y_1 \ln Y_2 + \cdots + \frac{1}{2} \beta_{mm} (\ln Y_m)^2] .$$

The translog output aggregate is characterized by constant returns to scale if and only if

$$
\begin{aligned}
\alpha_1 &+ \alpha_2 + \cdots + \alpha_m &= 1 , \\
\beta_{11} &+ \beta_{12} + \cdots + \beta_{1m} &= 0 , \\
& \cdots \\
\beta_{1m} &+ \beta_{2m} + \cdots + \beta_{mm} &= 0 .
\end{aligned}
$$

The value shares of individual outputs $\{w_{Yi}\}$ can be expressed as

$$w_{Yi} = \alpha_i + \beta_{1i} \ln Y_1 + \cdots + \beta_{mi} \ln Y_m , \qquad (i = 1, 2, \ldots, m) .$$

Considering data for the United States and Japan at a given point of time, the difference between logarithms of aggregate output for the two countries can be expressed as a weighted average of differences between logarithms of individual outputs with weights given by average value shares

$$\ln Y \ (\text{US}) - \ln Y \ (\text{JAPAN}) = \sum \hat{w}_{Yi} \ [\ln Y_i(\text{US}) - \ln Y_i(\text{JAPAN})] ,$$

where

$$\hat{w}_{Yi} = \frac{1}{2} [w_{Yi}(\text{US}) + w_{Yi}(\text{JAPAN})] , \qquad (i = 1, 2, \ldots, m) .$$

Similarly, considering data for a given country at two discrete points of time, the difference between successive logarithms of aggregate output can be expressed as a weighted average of differences between logarithms of individual outputs with weights given by average value shares

$$\ln Y(T) - \ln Y(T - 1) = \sum \bar{w}_{Yi}[\ln Y_i(T) - \ln Y_i(T - 1)] ,$$

where

$$\bar{w}_{Yi} = \frac{1}{2}[w_{Yi}(T) + w_{Yi}(T - 1)] , \qquad (i = 1, 2, \ldots, m) .$$

We refer to these expressions for aggregate output $Y$ as the *translog indexes of output*.[5]

To define price indexes corresponding to the translog indexes of aggregate output we employ the fact that the product of price and quantity indexes for the aggregate must equal the sum of the values of the components of each aggregate. The price index for aggregate output is defined as the ratio of the sum of the values of the individual outputs to the translog output index. For the United States and Japan at a given point of time the price index represents the purchasing power parity between the yen and the dollar in terms of aggregate output. If U.S. output is measured relative to Japanese output, the corresponding purchasing power parity represents the price of one dollar's worth of output in terms of yen. For a given country at different points of time the price index represents the price of aggregate output at these points of time, measured in the country's own currency. For the United States this price index provides a measure of the price of U.S. aggregate output in dollars, while for Japan it provides a measure of the price of Japanese output in yen.

The price indexes for aggregate output corresponding to translog quantity indexes can be determined solely from data on prices and quantities of the components of the aggregate. Although these prices do not have the form of translog index numbers, they are nonetheless well defined. By definition the product of price and quantity indexes for an aggregate is equal to the sum of the values of its components. Price indexes for the components of aggregate output are available from the national accounts of the United States and Japan for the period 1952–1974. Purchasing power parities for these components are available for the year 1970 from the work of Kravis and his associates (1975).

The starting point for the construction of translog indexes of output for the United States and Japan for the period 1952–1974 is the measurement of the value of total product and the value of total factor outlay for each country in current prices. The fundamental accounting identity for the production account is that the value of total product is equal to the value of total factor outlay for each country. The product and factor outlay accounts are linked through capital formation and the compensation of property. To make this link explicit we divide total output between consumption and investment goods and total factor outlay between labor and property compensation. In analyzing productive activity we have limited the scope of our production account to the private domestic sector of each country.

The production account in a complete system of national economic accounts includes the activities of the private sector, the government sector, and the rest of the world. Rest of the world production is excluded on the grounds that it can reflect a different physical and social environment for productive activity than the environment provided by the domestic sector; the government sector is also excluded from our private domestic production account. One unconventional aspect of our measure of total output is an imputation for the services of consumer durables. Our objective is to attain consistency in the treatment of owner-occupied residential structures and owner-utilized consumer durables. The services of consumer durables are included in consumption goods output while investment in consumer durables is included in investment goods output.

Given the value of total output for the United States and Japan, the remaining task is to separate these data into price and quantity components. Total product is first divided between investment and consumption goods. The value shares of investment goods products for both countries for the period 1952–1974 are presented in table 3.1. Translog indexes of consumption and investment goods output in the United States and Japan, defined as ratios between these outputs in the two countries, and annual rates of growth of consumption and investment goods output for both countries are presented in table 3.1. The quantity indexes of private domestic investment and consumption goods output can be combined into a translog quantity index of private domestic product. Translog indexes of private domestic output in the United States and Japan and annual rates of growth in both countries are presented in table 3.1. Finally, purchasing power parities between the yen and the dollar in terms of investment goods, consumption goods, and total output are given in table 3.1.

Table 3.1
Output

| Year | 1* | 2 | 3 | 4 | 5 | 6 | 7 | 8 | 9 | 10 | 11 | 12 | 13 | 14 |
|------|-----|------|-----|-----|------|------|------|-----|------|-------|------|-----|-------|-------|
| 1952 | .321 | .321 | 1.5 | 183 | — | — | 16.3 | 272 | — | — | 12.1 | 201 | — | — |
| 1953 | .317 | .292 | 9.8 | 196 | .051 | .123 | 17.0 | 282 | .033 | −.011 | 11.6 | 207 | .045 | .082 |
| 1954 | .305 | .291 | 9.2 | 191 | −.005 | .065 | 15.1 | 280 | −.019 | .099 | 10.7 | 205 | −.009 | .075 |
| 1955 | .337 | .309 | 8.9 | 183 | .036 | .075 | 15.0 | 271 | .145 | .154 | 10.5 | 205 | .071 | .099 |
| 1956 | .334 | .353 | 8.6 | 185 | .041 | .074 | 12.5 | 282 | −.009 | .174 | 9.8 | 206 | .024 | .107 |
| 1957 | .326 | .401 | 8.6 | 193 | .033 | .016 | 10.1 | 291 | −.020 | .192 | 9.2 | 213 | .016 | .082 |
| 1958 | .297 | .348 | 8.2 | 185 | .027 | .093 | 10.1 | 277 | −.059 | −.059 | 8.8 | 203 | .000 | .036 |
| 1959 | .318 | .373 | 7.8 | 190 | .033 | .072 | 9.4 | 275 | .113 | .178 | 8.3 | 205 | .057 | .110 |
| 1960 | .300 | .414 | 7.5 | 187 | .037 | .082 | 7.1 | 281 | −.013 | .264 | 7.4 | 207 | .021 | .154 |
| 1961 | .294 | .481 | 7.3 | 202 | .027 | .042 | 5.3 | 298 | .013 | .314 | 6.5 | 221 | .023 | .164 |
| 1962 | .305 | .441 | 7.2 | 215 | .041 | .053 | 5.7 | 295 | .091 | .010 | 6.6 | 235 | .056 | .033 |
| 1963 | .309 | .446 | 6.6 | 218 | .029 | .117 | 5.2 | 297 | .058 | .146 | 6.1 | 237 | .038 | .130 |
| 1964 | .310 | .450 | 6.1 | 225 | .050 | .127 | 4.7 | 301 | .059 | .167 | 5.5 | 242 | .053 | .145 |
| 1965 | .317 | .420 | 5.8 | 229 | .045 | .099 | 5.0 | 300 | .092 | .019 | 5.5 | 245 | .060 | .064 |
| 1966 | .317 | .430 | 5.6 | 236 | .057 | .080 | 4.7 | 304 | .064 | .133 | 5.3 | 249 | .059 | .102 |
| 1967 | .304 | .464 | 5.7 | 254 | .047 | .027 | 3.7 | 308 | −.017 | .216 | 4.9 | 263 | .026 | .111 |
| 1968 | .306 | .477 | 5.2 | 247 | .045 | .144 | 3.2 | 302 | .044 | .181 | 4.3 | 257 | .045 | .161 |
| 1969 | .303 | .481 | 4.9 | 240 | .030 | .087 | 2.9 | 296 | .031 | .125 | 4.0 | 253 | .031 | .105 |
| 1970 | .291 | .497 | 4.7 | 254 | .028 | .068 | 2.4 | 296 | −.054 | .161 | 3.6 | 261 | −.000 | .114 |
| 1971 | .296 | .479 | 4.4 | 254 | .022 | .093 | 2.3 | 285 | .049 | .068 | 3.4 | 259 | .034 | .081 |
| 1972 | .303 | .474 | 4.2 | 261 | .046 | .083 | 2.3 | 285 | .100 | .097 | 3.3 | 262 | .062 | .090 |
| 1973 | .306 | .500 | 4.3 | 286 | .052 | .029 | 2.2 | 310 | .085 | .135 | 3.3 | 282 | .062 | .081 |
| 1974 | .292 | .507 | 4.5 | 294 | .010 | −.033 | 2.2 | 356 | −.084 | −.066 | 3.4 | 318 | −.017 | −.050 |

* Variables:
 1. Value share of investment goods output, United States.
 2. Value share of investment goods output, Japan.
 3. Ratio between United States and Japanese consumption goods output.
 4. Purchasing power parity, consumption goods output, yen per dollar.
 5. Annual rates of growth of consumption goods output, United States.
 6. Annual rates of growth of consumption goods output, Japan.
 7. Ratio between United States and Japanese investment goods output.
 8. Purchasing power parity, investment goods output, yen per dollar
 9. Annual rates of growth of investment goods output, United States.
 10. Annual rates of growth of investment goods output, Japan.
 11. Ratio between United States and Japanese total output.
 12. Purchasing power parity, total output, yen per dollar.
 13. Annual rates of growth of total output, United States.
 14. Annual rates of growth of total output, Japan.

For the United States the share of investment goods output declined slightly from 0.321 to 0.292 over the period 1952–1974. For Japan the share of investment goods output rose dramatically from a level below that in the United States for the years 1952–1955, overtaking the share of investment goods output in the United States in 1956, and rising to 0.507, more than 50% above the U.S. share, by the end of the period in 1974. At the beginning of the period the quantity of investment goods output in the United States was more than sixteen times that in Japan; this ratio fell to 2.2 by the end of the period. The ratio of consumption goods output in the United States to that in Japan fell from 10.5 at the beginning of the period 1952–1974 to 4.5 at the end of the period. The ratio of investment goods output in the United States to that in Japan dropped below the corresponding ratio for consumption goods output in 1960. Purchasing power parities between the yen and the dollar for investment goods exhibited a very slight upward trend over the period 1952–1974. The corresponding purchasing power parities for consumption goods increased by 60%, but remained below those for investment goods throughout the period. Purchasing power parities between the yen and the dollar for total output began to rise steadily from 1958 onwards.

In 1952 total output in the United States was more than ten times that in Japan. By 1960 the ratio of U.S. to Japanese output had fallen to 7.4 and by 1969 the ratio had fallen to 4.0. By the end of the period in 1974 this ratio had fallen still further to 3.4. In both countries growth of total output accelerated between the years 1952–1960 and the years 1960–1974. The average annual rate of growth of total output in the United States rose from 2.7% for the period 1952–1960 to 3.7% for 1960–1974. For Japan the rate of growth of output rose from 9.1% for 1952–1960 to 9.5% for 1960–1974. Our first conclusion is that the acceleration in the rate of growth of Japanese output was accompanied by the rise in the share of investment goods in total output, while the corresponding acceleration in the rate of growth of U.S. output was unaccompanied by any substantial change in the investment goods share.

## 3.4   Input

If aggregate capital and labor input are translog functions of their components, we can express the differences between logarithms of aggregate inputs for the two countries in the form

$\ln K(\text{US}) - \ln K(\text{JAPAN}) = \sum \hat{v}_{Kj}[\ln K_j(\text{US}) - \ln K_j(\text{JAPAN})]$,

$\ln L(\text{US}) - \ln L(\text{JAPAN}) = \sum \hat{v}_{Lk}[\ln L_k(\text{US}) - \ln L_k(\text{JAPAN})]$,

where

$\hat{v}_{Kj} = \dfrac{1}{2}[v_{Kj}(\text{US}) + v_{Kj}(\text{JAPAN})]$,         $(j = 1, 2, \ldots, n)$,

$\hat{v}_{Lk} = \dfrac{1}{2}[v_{Lk}(\text{US}) + v_{Lk}(\text{JAPAN})]$,         $(k = 1, 2, \ldots, p)$.

Similarly, considering data for a given country at two discrete points of time, we can express the difference between successive logarithms in the form

$\ln K(T) - \ln K(T - 1) = \sum \bar{v}_{Kj}[\ln K_j(T) - \ln K_j(T - 1)]$,

$\ln L(T) - \ln L(T - 1) = \sum \bar{v}_{Lk}[\ln L_k(T) - \ln L_k(T - 1)]$,

where

$\bar{v}_{Kj} = \dfrac{1}{2}[v_{Kj}(T) + v_{Kj}(T - 1)]$,         $(j = 1, 2, \ldots, n)$,

$\bar{v}_{Lk} = \dfrac{1}{2}[v_{LK}(T) + v_{Lk}(T - 1]$,         $(k = 1, 2, \ldots, p)$.

We refer to these expressions for aggregate capital input $K$ and labor input $L$ as *translog indexes of capital and labor input.*

Price indexes for capital and labor input can be defined in a manner that is strictly analogous to the definition of price indexes for output. For the United States and Japan at a given point of time the price index for capital input represents the purchasing power parity between the yen and the dollar in terms of aggregate capital input. If U.S. capital input is measured relative to Japanese capital input, the corresponding purchasing power parity represents the price of one dollar's worth of capital input in terms of yen. Similarly, the price index for labor input represents the number of yen required to purchase one dollar's worth of labor input. For a given country at different points of time the price indexes represent the prices of aggregate capital and labor input at these points of time, measured in the country's own currency. For the United States these price indexes provide measures of prices of U.S. aggregate capital and labor input in dollars,

while for Japan they provide measures of the prices of Japanese aggregate inputs in yen.

To complete our comparison of differences in levels of output for
the two countries and sources of economic growth for each country
for the period 1952–1974, we require price indexes for the components
of capital and labor input for both countries for this period. Similarly,
we require purchasing power parities for these components. The measurement of capital input begins with data on the stock of capital for
each component of capital input. For each country the stock of capital,
say $A(T)$, is the sum of past investments, say $I(T - \tau)$, each weighted
by the relative efficiency of capital goods of each $\tau$, say $d_\tau$

$$A(T) = \sum_{\tau=0}^{\infty} d_\tau I(T - \tau) .$$

Similarly, the price of acquisition of new capital goods, say $p_I(T)$, is
the discounted value of the future prices of capital inputs, say
$p_K(T + \tau)$, each weighted by relative efficiency

$$p_I(T) = \sum_{\tau=0}^{\infty} d_\tau \prod_{S=1}^{\tau} \frac{1}{1 + r(T + S)} \, p_K(T + \tau + 1) ,$$

where $r(T)$ is the *rate of return on capital* in period $T$ and

$$\prod_{S=1}^{\tau} \frac{1}{1 + r(T + S)}$$

is the discount factor in period $T$ for future prices in period $T + \tau$.

Using data on decline in relative efficiency of capital goods with
age for each country, estimates of capital stock for that country can be
compiled from data on prices and quantities of investment in new
capital goods at each point of time by means of the perpetual inventory method.[6] We assume that relative efficiency of capital goods
declines geometrically with age,

$$d_\tau = (1 - \delta)^\tau , \qquad (\tau = 0, 1, \dots) .$$

Under this assumption capital stock at the end of each period is equal
to investment during the period less a constant proportion $\delta$ of capital
stock at the beginning of the period

$$A(T) = I(T) - \delta A(T - 1) .$$

Similarly, the price of capital input is equal to the sum of the nominal return to capital $p_I(T-1)r(T)$ and depreciation $\delta p_I(T)$, less revaluation $p_I(T) - p_I(T-1)$

$$p_K(T) = p_I(T-1)\ r(T) + \delta p_I(T) - [p_I(T) - p_I(T-1)]\ .$$

We can also express the price of capital input as the sum of the price of investment in the preceding period $p_I(T-1)$ multiplied by the *own rate of return on capital* $r(T) - [p_I(T) - p_I(T-1)]/[p_I(T-1)]$ and the current price of investment $p_I(T)$ multiplied by the rate of depreciation $\delta$

$$p_K(T) = p_I(T-1)\left[ r(T) - \frac{p_I(T) - p_I(T-1)}{p_I(T-1)} \right] + \delta p_I(T)\ .$$

Although we estimate the decline in efficiency of capital goods for each component of capital input separately for the United States and for Japan, we assume that the relative efficiency of new capital goods is the same in both countries. Accordingly, the appropriate purchasing power parity for new capital goods is the purchasing power parity for the corresponding component of investment goods output. To obtain the purchasing power parity for capital input, we first multiply the appropriate price index for investment goods in each country by the own rate of return on capital and the rate of depreciation and sum the two components to obtain the price index for capital input. We then multiply the purchasing power parity for investment goods in yen per dollar by the ratio of the price of capital services to the price of capital goods for Japan divided by the corresponding ratio for the United States

$$\frac{P_K(\text{JAPAN})}{P_K(\text{US})} = \frac{P_I(\text{JAPAN})}{P_I(\text{US})}\ \frac{P_K(\text{JAPAN})/P_I(\text{JAPAN})}{P_K(\text{US})/P_I(\text{US})}\ .$$

The resulting price index represents the purchasing power parity between the yen and the dollar in terms of aggregate capital input.

Given the value of total factor outlay for the United States and Japan, the next task is to separate these data into price and quantity components. Total factor outlay is first divided between property and labor compensation. The value shares of property compensation for both countries for the period 1952–1974 are presented in table 3.2. The

**Table 3.2**
Capital input

| Year | 1* | 2 | 3 | 4 | 5 | 6 | 7 | 8 |
|------|------|------|------|------|------|-----|------|-------|
| 1952 | .397 | .355 | .058 | .043 | 16.7 | 241 | .053 | — |
| 1953 | .380 | .295 | .052 | .019 | 18.2 | 255 | .035 | −.061 |
| 1954 | .399 | .298 | .052 | .028 | 17.7 | 252 | .039 | −.023 |
| 1955 | .402 | .329 | .060 | .054 | 18.4 | 288 | .032 | .016 |
| 1956 | .388 | .352 | .049 | .062 | 20.3 | 381 | .052 | .024 |
| 1957 | .384 | .360 | .047 | .057 | 18.9 | 406 | .042 | .072 |
| 1958 | .403 | .334 | .048 | .036 | 17.1 | 323 | .033 | .122 |
| 1959 | .398 | .357 | .051 | .048 | 16.8 | 366 | .017 | .069 |
| 1960 | .401 | .393 | .046 | .069 | 16.1 | 434 | .033 | .086 |
| 1961 | .406 | .432 | .048 | .097 | 15.2 | 540 | .030 | .120 |
| 1962 | .410 | .404 | .058 | .073 | 12.4 | 423 | .022 | .155 |
| 1963 | .413 | .404 | .060 | .078 | 11.3 | 427 | .034 | .122 |
| 1964 | .416 | .434 | .062 | .106 | 10.5 | 476 | .038 | .105 |
| 1965 | .426 | .417 | .070 | .091 | 9.7 | 418 | .043 | .117 |
| 1966 | .429 | .431 | .076 | .107 | 9.5 | 448 | .053 | .082 |
| 1967 | .421 | .444 | .067 | .129 | 9.0 | 510 | .057 | .085 |
| 1968 | .415 | .449 | .061 | .139 | 8.0 | 515 | .044 | .118 |
| 1969 | .412 | .448 | .053 | .130 | 7.5 | 409 | .046 | .137 |
| 1970 | .396 | .443 | .045 | .128 | 6.7 | 543 | .045 | .139 |
| 1971 | .406 | .415 | .047 | .098 | 5.6 | 428 | .030 | .149 |
| 1972 | .415 | .416 | .054 | .097 | 5.5 | 420 | .034 | .120 |
| 1973 | .420 | .402 | .057 | .086 | 5.9 | 465 | .045 | .109 |
| 1974 | .394 | .368 | .041 | .044 | 6.0 | 514 | .049 | .120 |

* Variables:
  1. Value share of capital input, United States.
  2. Value share of capital input, Japan.
  3. Own rate of return on business capital, United States.
  4. Own rate of return on business capital, Japan.
  5. Ratio between United States and Japanese capital input.
  6. Purchasing power parity, capital input, yen per dollar.
  7. Annual rates of growth of capital input, United States.
  8. Annual rates of growth of capital input, Japan.

starting point for the computation of a translog quantity index of capital input is a perpetual inventory estimate of the stock of each type of capital, based on past investments in constant prices. We have compiled capital stock estimates for six asset classes: consumer durables, nonresidential structures, producer durable equipment, residential structures, inventories, and land. For each of these asset classes we derive perpetual inventory estimates of the stock as follows. First, we obtain a benchmark estimate of capital stock from data on national wealth for each country in constant prices. Secondly, we deflate the investment series from the national income and product accounts for each country to obtain investment in constant prices. Thirdly, we choose an estimate of the rate of replacement from data on lifetimes of capital goods in each country.

To construct translog quantity indexes of capital input for the United States and for Japan we require value shares of individual capital inputs in total property compensation and stocks of individual assets. Property compensation for each asset is equal to the product of the price of capital input and the quantity of capital stock at the beginning of the period; in the absence of taxation property compensation is the sum of depreciation and the own rate of return on capital

$$p_K(T)K(T) = \left\{ p_I(T-1) \left[ r(T) - \frac{p_I(T) - p_I(T-1)}{p_I(T-1)} \right] + \delta p_I(T) \right\} A(T-1) .$$

Given property compensation, the stock of assets, the price of investment goods, and the rate of depreciation, we can determine the rate of return $r(T)$. In measuring the rate of return differences in the tax treatment of property compensation must be taken into account. For tax purposes the private domestic sector in each country can be divided among corporate business, noncorporate business, and households and nonprofit institutions. Households and institutions are not subject to direct taxes on property and compensation. Noncorporate business is subject to personal income taxes on property compensation, while corporate business is subject to both corporate and personal income taxes. Both households and business are subject to indirect taxes on property compensation through taxes levied in the value of property.

To allocate property compensation among individual capital inputs for the United States and Japan, we first measure property compensation for each component of the private domestic sector of each country—corporate and noncorporate business and households and nonprofit institutions. Secondly, we assume that the rate of return after taxes is the same on all assets within each sector; under this assumption we can allocate property compensation for each sector among the classes of assets utilized within the sector. We combine the price and quantity of capital for all classes of assets within each sector into a translog index of capital input for the sector. Finally, we combine these indexes for all sectors into an index of capital input for the country as a whole. We present own rates of return for the business sector, comprising corporate and noncorporate business, for the United States and Japan for the period 1952–1974 in table 3.2. Translog indexes of capital input in the two countries, defined as the difference between logarithms of these inputs in the two countries together with purchasing power parities between the yen and the dollar in terms of capital services, are also presented in table 3.2. Finally, annual rates of growth of capital input for the United States and for Japan are given in table 3.2.

For the United States the share of capital services input in the value of total factor outlay rose from 0.388 to 0.407 over the period 1952/3–1973/4. For Japan the share of capital services also rose from 0.325 to 0.385 over the same period. The capital shares in the United States and Japan were remarkable similar, fluctuating around an average of two-fifths or 40%. The own rates of return to capital of the United States follow the business cycle over the period 1952–1974. This rate of return reached a high of 7.6% in 1966 and a low of 4.1% in 1974. For the period 1952–1955 the own rate of return to capital in the business sector for Japan was comparable to or below that in the United States. Beginning in the mid–1960s, the own rate of return to capital in Japan was close to double that in the United States until it hit the low of 4.4% in 1974. This remarkable increase occurred with virtually no change in the share of property compensation in total factor outlay. Reflecting the dramatic rise in own rates of return to capital in the business sector in Japan, beginning in 1960, purchasing power parities between the yen and the dollar in terms of capital input also rose sharply over the period 1952–1974, reaching a peak of 543 yen to the dollar in 1970. These parities also reflect a much more modest increase in purchasing power parities in terms of investment goods.

The quantity of capital input in the United States was more than sixteen times that in Japan at the beginning of the period 1952–1974. By the end of the period in 1974 this ratio had dropped to 6.0. The cyclical movement of the U.S. economy is again reflected in the annual rates of growth of capital input in the United States for this period. Relatively high rates of growth characterize the beginning of the period, 1952–1954, the short-lived investment boom of 1956–1957, the more prolonged boom of 1964–1970, and the final years of the period, 1973–1974. Average annual growth rates of capital input rose modestly from 3.5% for the period 1952–1960 to 4.0% for the period 1960–1974. For Japan the annual rates of growth of capital input are well below corresponding U.S. rates of growth for the period 1952–1956. Beginning in 1957 annual rates of growth of capital input in Japan rose above U.S. levels, running at more than three times the corresponding U.S. levels during most of this remarkable period, 1957–1974. Annual growth rates of capital input increased dramatically from an average of 3.6% for the period 1952–1960 to 11.9% for 1960–1974.

To construct translog quantity indexes of labor input for the United States and Japan, it would be desirable to develop data for each country disaggregated by level of education, sex, age, occupation, and so on. Following Jorgenson and Griliches (1967) we have limited consideration to a breakdown of labor input by educational attainment. This results in indexes of the quantity of labor input for the private domestic sector of both countries. The quantity indexes of private domestic capital and labor input can be combined into a translog quantity index of private domestic factor input. Translog indexes of labor input and total factor input in the two countries, defined as the difference between logarithms of these inputs in the two countries, together with purchasing power parities between the yen and the dollars in terms of labor input and total factor input are presented in table 3.3. Finally, annual rates of growth of labor input and total factor input for the United States and Japan are given in table 3.3.

The quantity of labor input in the United States was only 2.9 times that in Japan at the beginning of the period 1952–1974. This ratio fell to a low of 2.2 in 1960 and rose toward the end of the period to a level of 2.4 in 1974. The ratio of labor input in the United States to that in Japan began at a level less than one-fifth the corresponding ratio of capital input in the two countries in 1952. The ratio of labor input in the United States to that in Japan remained at less than one-half the corresponding ratio of capital input in the two countries in 1974. Annual rates of growth of labor input in Japan fell from an average of 4.2% for the period 1952–1960 to 1.5% for the period 1960–1974. The corresponding averages for the United States are 0.8% for the period 1952–1960 and 2.0% for the period 1960–1974. Purchasing power parities between the yen and the dollar for labor input more than quadrupled over the period 1952–1974, rising from 52 to 240 yen to the dollar. These purchasing power parities remained at less than half those for capital input until 1974, the final year of the period. Most of this

**Table 3.3**
Labor and total factor input

| Year | 1* | 2 | 3 | 4 | 5 | 6 | 7 | 8 |
|------|-----|-----|-------|-------|-----|-----|-------|------|
| 1952 | 2.9 | 52 | .009 | .031 | 5.7 | 96 | — | — |
| 1953 | 2.8 | 58 | .017 | .044 | 5.4 | 100 | .024 | .010 |
| 1954 | 2.7 | 61 | −.033 | .022 | 5.3 | 104 | −.005 | .008 |
| 1955 | 2.6 | 59 | .035 | .043 | 5.4 | 110 | .033 | .035 |
| 1956 | 2.5 | 58 | .021 | .060 | 5.5 | 123 | .033 | .048 |
| 1957 | 2.4 | 59 | −.008 | .054 | 5.2 | 128 | .011 | .061 |
| 1958 | 2.3 | 61 | −.026 | .012 | 4.9 | 118 | −.002 | .050 |
| 1959 | 2.3 | 62 | .040 | .026 | 4.9 | 128 | .031 | .041 |
| 1960 | 2.2 | 66 | .013 | .046 | 4.9 | 145 | .021 | .061 |
| 1961 | 2.2 | 73 | −.004 | .019 | 4.9 | 176 | .009 | .061 |
| 1962 | 2.2 | 81 | .027 | .009 | 4.5 | 164 | .025 | .070 |
| 1963 | 2.2 | 91 | .015 | .008 | 4.4 | 176 | .023 | .054 |
| 1964 | 2.2 | 97 | .021 | .025 | 4.3 | 194 | .028 | .058 |
| 1965 | 2.3 | 105 | .037 | .018 | 4.2 | 191 | .039 | .060 |
| 1966 | 2.3 | 110 | .038 | .032 | 4.2 | 204 | .044 | .053 |
| 1967 | 2.2 | 118 | .015 | .037 | 4.1 | 226 | .033 | .058 |
| 1968 | 2.2 | 126 | .024 | .038 | 3.9 | 234 | .032 | .074 |
| 1969 | 2.3 | 135 | .032 | .016 | 3.8 | 241 | .038 | .070 |
| 1970 | 2.2 | 151 | −.011 | .003 | 3.5 | 260 | .011 | .063 |
| 1971 | 2.2 | 168 | .005 | .001 | 3.3 | 248 | .015 | .064 |
| 1972 | 2.3 | 182 | .038 | −.000 | 3.3 | 259 | .036 | .049 |
| 1973 | 2.4 | 210 | .049 | .029 | 3.5 | 293 | .047 | .062 |
| 1974 | 2.4 | 240 | .006 | −.017 | 3.4 | 322 | .023 | .035 |

* Variables:
  1. Ratio between United States and Japanes labor input.
  2. Purchasing power parity, labor input, yen per dollar.
  3. Annual rates of growth of labor input, United States.
  4. Annual rates of growth of labor input, Japan.
  5. Ratio between United States and Japanese total factor input.
  6. Purchasing power parity, total factor input, yen per dollar.
  7. Annual rates of growth of total factor input, United States.
  8. Annual rates of growth of total factor input, Japan.

dramatic rise in the purchasing power parities of labor input took place during the period 1960–1974. Purchasing power parities between the yen and the dollar for total factor input rose much more substantially than the corresponding parities for total output.

In 1952 total factor input in the United States was 5.7 times that in Japan. By 1960 the ratio of U.S. to Japanese factor input had fallen to 4.9, and by 1969 this ratio had fallen to 3.8. By 1973 this ratio had fallen to 3.5 and still further to 3.4 in 1974. The ratio of U.S. to

Japanese output reached the level only slightly above the corresponding factor input ratio in 1972, fell substantially below it in 1973 and remained so at the end of the period 1974. In both countries growth of total factor input accelerated substantially between the years 1952–1960 and the years 1960–1974. The average annual rate of growth of total factor input in the United States rose from 1.8% for the period 1952–1960 to 2.8% for 1960–1974. For Japan the rate of growth of factor input rose from 3.9% for 1952–1960 to 5.9% for 1960–1974. Our second conclusion is that acceleration in the rate of growth of Japanese factor input was accomplished with a substantial decrease in the rate of growth of labor input by a truly astonishing increase in the rate of growth of capital input, while the corresponding acceleration in the rate of growth of U.S. factor input was associated with a substantial increase in the rate of growth of labor input and much more modest increase in the rate of growth of capital input.

### 3.5 Productivity

If we consider data for both countries at a given point of time, the average difference in technology can be expressed as the difference between logarithms of output for the two countries less a weighted average of the differences between logarithms of capital and labor input for the two countries with weights given by the average value shares

$$\ln Y(\text{US}) - \ln Y(\text{JAPAN}) = \hat{v}_K [\ln K(\text{US}) - \ln K(\text{JAPAN})]$$
$$+ \hat{v}_L [\ln L(\text{US}) - \ln L(\text{JAPAN})] + \hat{v}_D ,$$

where

$$\hat{v}_K = \frac{1}{2} [v_K(\text{US}) + v_K(\text{JAPAN})] ,$$

$$\hat{v}_L = \frac{1}{2} [v_L(\text{US}) + v_L(\text{JAPAN})] ,$$

$$\hat{v}_D = \frac{1}{2} [v_D(\text{US}) + v_D(\text{JAPAN})] .$$

We refer to this expression for the average difference in technology as the *translog index of difference in technology*.

Similarly, if we consider data at any two discrete points of time for a given country, say $T$ and $T - 1$, the average rate of technical change can be expressed as the difference between successive logarithms of capital and labor input with weights given by average value shares

$$\ln Y(T) - \ln Y(T - 1) = \bar{v}_K[\ln K(T) - \ln K(T - 1)]$$
$$+ \bar{v}_L[\ln L(T) - \ln K(T - 1)] + \bar{v}_T ,$$

where

$$\bar{v}_K = \frac{1}{2}[v_K(T) + v_K(T - 1)] ,$$

$$\bar{v}_L = \frac{1}{2}[v_L(T) + v_L(T - 1)] ,$$

$$\bar{v}_T = \frac{1}{2}[v_T(T) + v_T(T - 1)] .$$

We refer to this expression for the average rate of technical change $\bar{v}_T$ as the *translog index of technical change*.

Given translog indexes of total output and total factor input we can construct translog indexes of difference in technology and technical change. The translog index of difference in technology between the United States and Japan is given in table 3.4. We also present the contributions of differences between U.S. and Japanese technology, U.S. and Japanese capital input, and U.S. and Japanese labor input in explaining differences between U.S. and Japanese output. Each of these contributions is defined as the ratio of the respective input's logarithmic difference between the United States and Japan to the difference between the logarithms of U.S. and Japanese output. Annual rates of technical change are also given for the United States and for Japan in table 3.4.

The results presented in table 3.4 describe a very remarkable closing of the gap in technology between the United States and Japan over the period 1952–1974. In 1952 the Japanese level of technology was merely one-fourth of the corresponding U.S. level. During the period 1952–1959 the difference between U.S. and Japanese technology was reduced from 75% to 51%. Beginning in 1960 the level of Japanese technology moved up sharply relative to that in the United States, reaching nearly 90% of the U.S. level by 1968. Between 1968 and 1973 the level of Japanese technology actually overtook that in the United States, so that by 1973 and also in 1974 the aggregate level of

**Table 3.4**
Productivity

| Year | 1* | 2 | 3 | 4 | 5 | 6 |
|------|------|------|------|------|------|------|
| 1952 | .757 | .303 | .426 | .270 | — | — |
| 1953 | .762 | .311 | .403 | .285 | .020 | .072 |
| 1954 | .702 | .296 | .429 | .274 | −.004 | .066 |
| 1955 | .657 | .278 | .455 | .266 | .037 | .064 |
| 1956 | .565 | .247 | .489 | .262 | −.009 | .059 |
| 1957 | .564 | .254 | .494 | .251 | .004 | .021 |
| 1958 | .585 | .269 | .484 | .246 | .003 | −.013 |
| 1959 | .517 | .243 | .503 | .252 | .026 | .069 |
| 1960 | .399 | .199 | .551 | .249 | .000 | .092 |
| 1961 | .264 | .140 | .608 | .250 | .013 | .103 |
| 1962 | .384 | .202 | .540 | .257 | .030 | −.037 |
| 1963 | .321 | .177 | .550 | .271 | .015 | .076 |
| 1964 | .240 | .140 | .582 | .277 | .024 | .086 |
| 1965 | .263 | .153 | .560 | .285 | .020 | .004 |
| 1966 | .214 | .128 | .580 | .290 | .014 | .049 |
| 1967 | .165 | .104 | .599 | .296 | −.006 | .053 |
| 1968 | .108 | .073 | .612 | .314 | .012 | .087 |
| 1969 | .061 | .043 | .618 | .337 | −.007 | .035 |
| 1970 | .015 | .011 | .619 | .368 | −.012 | .050 |
| 1971 | .047 | .038 | .572 | .389 | .018 | .016 |
| 1972 | .009 | .007 | .580 | .412 | .025 | .040 |
| 1973 | −.047 | −.039 | .609 | .429 | .014 | .018 |
| 1974 | −.012 | −.009 | .557 | .452 | −.041 | −.085 |

* Variables:
  1. Difference between U.S. and Japanese technology.
  2. Contribution of differences between U.S. and Japanese technology to differences between U.S. and Japanese output.
  3. Contribution of differences between U.S. and Japanese capital input to differences between U.S. and Japanese output.
  4. Contribution of differences between U.S. and Japanese labor input to differences between U.S. and Japanese output.
  5. Annual rates of technical change, United States.
  6. Annual rates of technical change, Japan.

technology in Japan stock ahead of that in the United States. Our third conclusion is that none of the remaining difference between U.S. and Japanese aggregate output in 1974 was due to a difference in levels of technology.

By analyzing the contributions of differences in the level of technology, capital input, and labor input to differences between U.S. and Japanese levels of output, we can obtain a different perspective on the disappearance of the gap in technology between the United States and

Japan. For the period 1952–1959 all of the reduction in the difference between U.S. and Japanese total output was due to the increase in Japanese labor input relative to U.S. labor input and to the narrowing of the technology gap between the two countries. Relative levels of capital input in the two countries remained almost unchanged. During this period capital intensity increased more rapidly in the United States than in Japan; capital intensity in Japan was almost unchanged during the period.

For the period 1960–1974 the dramatic reduction in the difference between U.S. and Japanese total output was due to the substantial increase in Japanese capital input relative to U.S. capital input and to the closing of the gap between Japanese and U.S. technology. Japanese and U.S. labor input grew at almost the same rate, whereas the average annual growth rate of capital in Japan was nearly three-fold that of the United States, and Japanese productivity grew at a rate four times that of the United States on average during this period. While the gap between U.S. and Japanese technology had closed by 1973, there still remains a substantial gap between U.S. and Japanese capital intensity of production. Our fourth conclusion is that all of the remaining difference between U.S. and Japanese output per unit of labor input is due to differences in the capital intensity of production in the two countries.

The contribution of growth in real labor input to U.S. output growth rose from 15% during the earlier period to 33% during the later period, while the contribution of real capital input fell from 49% during the earlier period to 43% in the later period. For Japan the contribution of real capital input rose from 13% during the earlier period to 51% in the later period, while the contribution of real labor input fell from 29% to 12%. Our final conclusion is that the acceleration of growth in Japan during the period 1960–1973 was due to an acceleration in the growth of capital input relative to labor input.

Our findings illustrate the correlation between initial differences in levels of technology and relative rates of growth of output that characterizes industrialized countries in the postwar period. For the period 1950–1970 Abramovitz (1977) has shown that countries that were relatively backward in the level of technology grew more rapidly. Our findings also illustrate the central role of relative growth in capital intensity in explaining relative rates of growth of output per unit of labor input in industrialized countries. For the period 1947–1973 Christensen, Cummings and Jorgenson (1980) have shown that variations in rates of growth of capital intensity are associated with variations in rates of growth of output per unit of labor input.

Our results suggest some fruitful directions for further research. Our methodology can be applied to data on the growth of output and factor input for major industrialized countries assembled by Christensen, Cummings and Jorgenson. They have already provided a comparison of patterns of economic growth for nine countries for the period 1947–1973. Our methodology could provide the basis for a comparison of relative levels of output, factor input, and technology for these countries. Growth in total factor productivity in the United States has been slower than in any other industrialized country during the postwar period. A comparison of levels of technology among industrialized countries will only likely reveal a pattern of reductivity or elimination of the gaps among levels of technology in industrialized countries comparable to that which we have found for the United States and Japan.

In view of the central role of the growth of capital input in our comparison of the United States and Japan, high priority must be given to further analysis of the growth of capital. This will require a complete accounting system, consisting of the production account we have presented in this paper, an income and expenditure account that includes savings, an accumulation account that includes capital formation, and a wealth account that includes capital stock as a component of wealth. Christensen and Jorgenson (1969, 1970, 1973a,b) have developed a system that is well adapted to the analysis of aggregate economic growth and have implemented this system for the United States for the period 1929–1969. Ezaki (1977) has implemented this system for Japan for the period 1952–1971.

Another fruitful direction for further research is the disaggregation of the production account to the level of individual industrial sectors. This will make it possible to analyze relative output, input, and productivity at the level of individual industries.[7] Gollop and Jorgenson (1980) have completed a study of U.S. economic growth for fifty-one industrial sectors for the period 1947–1973. Nishimizu (1975) and Nishimizu and Hulten (1978) have completed a study of Japanese economic growth for ten industrial sectors for the period 1955–1971. We are currently engaged in a comparative study of U.S. and Japanese economic growth for thirty industrial sectors. This study will include a comparison of levels of output, input, and productivity by industrial sector for the two countries and an analysis of industrial growth by sector in each country.

## Notes

1. A summary and comparison of studies of aggregate economic growth of Japan is given by Nishimizu and Hulten (1978).
2. A recent survey of the Japanese economy in English is presented in Patrick and Rosovsky (1976). Historical perspective on Japanese economic growth is provided by Ohkawa and Rosovsky (1973).
3. A useful discussion of future Japanese growth prospects in English is given by Patrick (1977).
4. The translog production function was introduced by Christensen, Jorgenson, and Lau (1971, 1973). The treatment of technical change outlined below is due to Diewert (1980) and to Jorgenson and Lau (1977).
5. The quantity indexes were introduced by Fisher (1922) and discussed by Törnqvist (1936), Theil (1965) and Kloek (1966). These indexes of output and input were first derived from the translog production function by Diewert (1976). The corresponding index of technical change was introduced by Christensen and Jorgenson (1970). The translog index of technical change was first derived from the form of the translog production function given above by Diewert (1980) and by Jorgenson and Lau (1977).
6. The perpetual inventory method has been employed by Goldsmith (1955). The dual to the perpetual inventory method, involving investment goods prices and capital input prices, was introduced by Christensen and Jorgenson (1969, 1973a). For further discussion of the underlying model of durable capital goods, see Jorgenson (1973a).
7. Detailed discussion of the development of Japanese technology at the level of individual industries is provided by Ozawa (1974) and by Peck and Tamura (1976).

# 4

## Economic Growth, 1947–1973: An International Comparison

Laurits R. Christensen,
Dianne Cummings, and
Dale W. Jorgenson

## 4.1 Introduction

### 4.1.1 Introduction

The purpose of this paper is to provide an international comparison of postwar patterns of aggregate economic growth for the United States and eight of its major trading partners—Canada, France, Germany, Italy, Japan, Korea, The Netherlands, and the United Kingdom. Our study covers the period 1947–1973 for the United States and as much of this period as is feasible for each of the eight remaining countries. We compare growth in real product, real factor input, and total factor productivity for all nine countries for the period 1960–1973. For all countries except Korea we compare growth during this period with growth beginning at earlier times and extending through 1960.

A complete analysis of aggregate economic growth involves the growth of real product and its sources—growth in real factor input and growth in total factor productivity. Growth in real factor input can be further divided between growth in real capital input and in real labor input. Growth in capital input involves growth in capital stock as a component of wealth through saving and capital formation. Analysis of growth in capital requires a complete accounting system, consisting of a production account, an income and expenditure account, an accumulation account, and a wealth account—all in current and constant prices.

Christensen and Jorgenson (1969, 1970, 1973a,b) have developed a complete accounting system that is well adapted to the analysis of aggregate economic growth and have implemented this system for the

United States for the period 1929–1969. In this paper we limit consideration to the production account, containing data on output and input in current and constant prices. We have extended the production account for the United States through 1973 and have implemented this account for each of the eight remaining countries. Our data on output and input are compiled in a form suitable for integration into a complete system of accounts for each country.

We first provide a brief review of previous international comparisons of patterns of aggregate economic growth that are similar in scope to this study. We discuss the selection of countries to be included and the selection of an appropriate time period for our international comparisons. In section 4.2 we present our methodology for measuring real product, real factor input, and total factor productivity. This methodology is based on the economic theory of production, beginning with a production function giving output as a function of capital input, labor input, and time. We derive index numbers of real product, real capital input, real labor input, and total factor productivity from this theory.

In section 4.3 we outline the empirical implementation of our index numbers of real product, real factor input, and total factor productivity for the nine countries included in our study. In section 4.4 we present an international comparison of patterns of economic growth for all nine countries. Our principal finding is that differences in growth rates of real product for the period 1960–1973 are associated with differences in growth rates of real factor input. An intertemporal comparison of growth rates during this period with growth rates during earlier periods ending in 1960 strongly reinforces this conclusion. Increases and decreases in growth rates of real product are associated with increases and decreases in growth rates of real factor input. We present a more detailed summary of our conclusions in section 4.5.

## 4.1.2  Alternative Methodologies

International comparisons of patterns of economic growth are no longer uncommon, but the number of studies providing real product and real factor input in both current and constant prices on an economy-wide basis is not large. We can set the stage for our detailed discussion of methodology by briefly summarizing the approaches that have been used in previous studies. In table 4.1 we present a tabular comparison among the most important of these studies for developed

**Table 4.1**
International comparisons of growth in total factor productivity

| | | | | Authors | | | |
|---|---|---|---|---|---|---|---|
| | Tinbergen (1942) | Domar (1964) | Denison (1967) | Barger (1969) | Kuznets (1971) | Bergson (1974) |
| | | | Belgium | | | | |
| | | Canada | | | Canada | | |
| | France | | Denmark | Denmark | | France | |
| | Germany | | France | France | France | Germany | |
| | | Germany | Germany | Germany | | Italy | |
| | | | Italy | Italy | | Japan | |
| | | Japan | | | | | |
| | | | Netherlands | Netherlands | | | |
| | | | Norway | Norway | Norway | | |
| | | | | Sweden | | | |
| | | | | | | U.S.S.R. | |
| | U.K. | U.K. | U.K. | U.K. | U.K. | U.K. | |
| | U.S.A. | U.S.A. | U.S.A. | U.S.A. | U.S.A. | U.S.A. | |
| Time period | 1870–1914 | 1948–60 | 1950–62 | 1950–64 | 1855–1966 | 1955–70 | |

countries.[1] The concept of total factor productivity, defined as the ratio between real product and real factor input, was introduced in a notable but neglected article by Tinbergen (1942).[2] Among the many remarkable features of Tinbergen's study is an international comparison of growth in real product, real factor input, and total factor productivity for France, Germany, the U.K. and the U.S.A. for the period 1870–1914.

The concept of total factor productivity was developed independent of Tinbergen's work by Stigler (1947). The point of departure for this development was the measurement of real factor input by weighting real capital input and real labor input by their marginal products. Important contributions to the measurement of total factor productivity were made during the 1950s by Mills (1952), Schmookler (1952), Knowles (1954, 1960), Valavanis-Vail (1955), Abramovitz (1956), Kendrick (1956), Solow (1957), and Fabricant (1959). The initial approach to total factor productivity measurement was brought to fruition by the epochal work of Kendrick (1961a). The first international comparison of growth in total factor productivity, subsequent to Tinbergen's pioneering effort, was published by Domar (1964) and five collaborators, employing the methodology of Kendrick's study for the United States. Domar's study included Canada, Germany, Japan, the U.K. and the U.S.A. and covered the period 1948–1960. A notable feature of the study was the development of separate estimates for as many as eleven sectors within each of the five countries.

Griliches (1960) and Denison (1962b) extended the original framework for the measurement of total factor productivity be applying the principle of weighting inputs by their marginal products to components of real labor input. Griliches and Jorgenson (1966) and Jorgenson and Griliches (1967) followed up this new departure in methodology by applying the same principle to components of real capital input. Christensen and Jorgenson (1969) developed a detailed methodology for weighting components of real capital input disaggregated by class of asset and by legal form of organization. This methodology incorporates data on the taxation of income from capital at both corporate and personal levels and data on rates of return and depreciation by asset class and legal form of organization.

Denison's study of U.S. economic growth (1962b) was followed in 1967 by the appearance of his volume, *Why Growth Rates Differ*, comparing U.S. economic growth for the period 1950–1962 with growth in eight European countries. Although Denison's international comparisons of growth in real product, real factor input, and total factor productivity, which he denotes output per unit of input, were limited to the nine countries listed in table 4.1, the same methodology has been employed by Walters (1968, 1970) in two studies for Canada and by Denison and Chung (1976) in a study for Japan.[3] Denison (1974) has also extended the time period of his estimates for the United States, based on the methodology of *Why Growth Rates Differ*, to include the years 1929–1969.

Concluding our brief survey of international comparisons, we can draw attention to Barger's (1969) comparison of growth for nine countries—Denison's list with Belgium being replaced by Sweden—for the period 1950–1964. This study incorporates embodied as well as disembodied sources of economic growth. Kuznets (1971) has provided a comparison of Denison's results for the postwar period with his own analysis of long-term growth trends for Canada, France, Norway, the U.K. and the U.S.A.[4] Finally, as part of a research program on Soviet economic growth, Bergson (1974) has compared the growth of Soviet real product, real factor input, and total factor productivity with that of six Western countries for the period 1955–1970.

### 4.1.3   Selection of a Methodology

In selecting an appropriate methodology for our study, Denison's approach in *Why Growth Rates Differ*, his subsequent studies of Japanese and U.S. economic growth, and the studies of Canada by Walters deserve serious consideration. For present purposes Denison's approach can be separated into three interrelated components. First, for each country Denison has measured real product, real factor input, and total factor productivity. Second, for each country Denison has analyzed the growth in output per unit of input into ten separate sources, including advances of knowledge, improved allocation of resources, balance of the capital stock, economies of scale, and a residual factor. Third, Denison has provided a comparison of productivity levels for all nine countries for the year 1960.

Our study is limited to the development of a production account within a complete accounting system, so that we focus attention on Denison's measurement of real product, real factor input, and total factor productivity. Jorgenson and Griliches (1972a) have compared Denison's results for the U.S.A. with those of Christensen and Jorgenson (1970) for the period covered by *Why Growth Rates Differ*,

*1950–1962.*[5] They conclude that the growth of real factor input accounts for a much larger proportion of growth in real product in the Christensen-Jorgenson study than in Denison's study, and that the differences in results can be traced to differences in the methodology for measuring real capital input.

Jorgenson and Griliches (1972a,b) have compared the methodology of Christensen and Jorgenson for measuring real capital input with that employed by Denison in *Why Growth Rates Differ.* They show that, by contrast with the approach of Christensen and Jorgenson, Denison's methodology fails to incorporate differences in the marginal products of capital inputs in a satisfactory way.[6] In particular, Denison fails to incorporate the effects of taxation of income from capital at both corporate and personal levels, to measure differences in rates of return and depreciation by asset class and legal form of organization, and to account properly for the impact of differences in the rate of change of the prices of different assets on rates of return. Finally, he fails to treat depreciation and replacement of capital stock in an internally consistent way.

Denison's methodology for *Why Growth Rates Differ* has been subjected to searching scrutiny from a completely different point of view by Maddison (1972). Maddison compares his own results with those of Denison as follows:

In my accounting (like that of Jorgenson and Griliches) factor input plays a much bigger role than for Denison. It explains three-quarters of growth whereas for him it represents less than half.[7]

Maddison's critique, like that of Jorgenson and Griliches, underlines the dependence of Denison's most important substantive conclusion, the unimportance of increases in capital input per unit of labor input in explaining growth in output per unit of labor input, on his methodology for the treatment of real capital input.

From our point of view the measurement of real product, real factor input, and total factor productivity is only part of the empirical study of economic growth. In addition, it is necessary to analyze the sources of growth in real factor input, especially growth in capital stock as a component of wealth and growth in capital services as a component of factor input through saving and capital formation. As we have already emphasized, in addition to a production account in current and constant prices, this necessitates accounts for income and expenditure, saving and capital formation, and wealth, also in current and constant prices. Logical inconsistencies in the treatment of real capital input would ramify into corresponding inconsistencies in the treatment of taxation and depreciation in the income and expenditure account, the treatment of revaluation and replacement in the saving and capital formation account, and the treatment of capital stock in the wealth account.

The empirical implementation of a complete accounting system necessitates an internally consistent treatment of capital in all four sets of accounts—production, income, saving, and wealth—in current and constant prices. This is a far more stringent requirement than internal consistency of the production account alone, but this requirement is met by the accounting system developed by Christensen and Jorgenson (1973a). We have adopted their methodology as the basis for our international comparisons of growth in productivity. The measurement of total factor productivity within a complete accounting system also provides a basis for overcoming a recurrent objection to conventional growth accounting. This objection is that growth of real product, real factor input, and total factor productivity are treated in isolation from other aspects of the process of economic growth, specifically from the determinants of capital formation.

### 4.1.4  Selection of Countries and Time Periods

Turning next to the selection of a sample of countries, our objective is to compare patterns of aggregate economic growth for the U.S.A. and its major trading partners. This leads immediately to the inclusion of Canada, Japan, and the four largest countries of Western Europe—France, Germany, Italy, and the U.K. Referring again to table 4.1, we find that all six international comparisons of productivity growth include the U.K. and the U.S.A. France and Germany are included in all but one of the studies. Italy is included in three of the six, while Canada and Japan are included in two of the six. Our selection of additional countries has been constrained by the resources available to us.

Our methods for analysis of sources of economic growth can be applied to data for industrialized countries such as Australia, Belgium, Denmark, Finland, The Netherlands, New Zealand, Norway, Sweden, and Switzerland. Among these countries Belgium, Denmark, The Netherlands, Norway, and Sweden have been included in one or

more of the studies listed in table 4.1. We have selected The Netherlands for inclusion in our study as the largest of these countries. Work
is currently underway on comparable studies for Belgium and Denmark. We have tested the feasibility of applying our methodology to a
developing country of importance in trade with the U.S.A. by selecting Korea as a final addition to our study. Korea also provides comparative perspective for the analysis of patterns of Japanese growth
that has proved to be very useful.

The selection of a time period for our study, like the selection of a
sample of countries, was constrained by the objectives of our study.
To provide the basis for continuing assessments of the impact of policies affecting trade and growth in each country on the pattern of
world trade and growth, we require a data base that can be readily
updated. These considerations made it necessary to limit our study to
the postwar period and to rely as much as possible on official national
accounts for the measurement of real product. The starting point for
each of our country studies was determined by the first year for which
a continuous time series running throughout the postwar period was
available. For all nine countries we were able to develop annual time
series for the period 1960–1973. For all countries except Korea we
have developed annual time series for the period 1955–1973.

## 4.2   Methodology

### 4.2.1   Introduction

Our first objective is to separate growth in real factor input from
growth in total factor productivity in accounting for growth in real
product for each of the nine countries included in our study. For this
purpose we require a methodology for measuring real factor input,
real product, and total factor productivity. Our methodology is based
on the economic theory of production and technical change. The
point of departure for this theory is a production function giving output as a function if inputs and time. We consider production under
constant returns to scale, so that a proportional change in all inputs
results in a proportional change in output.

In analyzing changes in production patterns we combine the production function with necessary conditions for producer equilibrium.
We express these conditions as equalities between shares of each input

in the value of output and the elasticity of output with respect to that input. The elasticities depend on inputs and time, the variables that enter the production function. Under constant returns to scale the sum of elasticities with respect to all inputs is equal to unity, so that value shares also sum to unity.

To analyze changes in the pattern of production with time we consider the rate of technical change, defined as the rate of growth of output, holding all inputs constant. The rate of technical change, like the elasticities of output with respect to input, depends on inputs and time. Under constant returns to scale the necessary conditions for producer equilibrium can be combined with growth rates of inputs and outputs to produce an index of the rate of technical change that depends only on the prices and quantities of inputs and outputs.

### 4.2.2    Technical Change

Our methodology for productivity measurement is based on the *production function*, $F$ characterized by constant returns to scale

$$Y = F(K, L, T),$$

where $Y$ is output, $K$ is capital input, $L$ is labor input, and $T$ is time. Denoting the price of output by $q_Y$, the price of capital input by $p_K$, and the price of labor input by $p_L$, we can define the shares of capital and labor input in the value of output, say $v_K$ and $v_L$, by

$$v_K = \frac{p_K K}{q_Y Y}, \qquad v_L = \frac{p_L L}{q_Y Y}.$$

Necessary conditions for producer equilibrium are given by equalities between each value share and the elasticity of output with respect to the corresponding input

$$v_K = \frac{\partial \ln Y}{\partial \ln K}(K, L, T),$$

$$v_L = \frac{\partial \ln Y}{\partial \ln L}(K, L, T).$$

Under constant returns to scale the elasticities and the value shares sum to unity.

The production function is defined in terms of output, capital input, and labor input. Output and the two inputs are aggregates that depend on the quantities of individual outputs and inputs. We consider aggregates that are characterized by constant returns to scale, so that proportional changes in all components of each aggregate result in proportional changes in the aggregate

$$Y = Y(Y_1, Y_2 \ldots Y_m) \,,$$
$$K = K(K_1, K_2 \ldots K_n) \,,$$
$$L = L(L_1, L_2 \ldots L_p) \,,$$

where $\{Y_i\}$ is the set of outputs, $\{K_j\}$ the set of capital inputs, and $\{L_k\}$ the set of labor inputs.

Denoting the prices of outputs by $\{q_{Yi}\}$, the prices of capital inputs by $\{p_{Kj}\}$, and the prices of labor inputs by $\{p_{Lk}\}$, we can define the shares of individual outputs in the value of output, say $\{w_{Yi}\}$; the shares of individual capital inputs in the value of capital input, say $\{v_{Kj}\}$; and the shares of individual labor inputs in the value of labor input, say $\{v_{Lk}\}$; by

$$w_{Yi} = \frac{q_{Yi} Y_i}{q_Y Y} \,, \qquad (i = 1, 2, \ldots, m) \,;$$

$$v_{Kj} = \frac{p_{Kj} K_j}{p_K K} \,, \qquad (j = 1, 2, \ldots, n) \,;$$

$$v_{Lk} = \frac{p_{Lk} L_k}{p_L L} \,, \qquad (k = 1, 2, \ldots, p) \,.$$

Necessary conditions for producer equilibrium are given by equalities between value shares and elasticities of the corresponding aggregate with respect to its individual components

$$w_{Yi} = \frac{\partial \ln Y}{\partial \ln Y_i} \,, \qquad (i = 1, 2, \ldots, m) \,;$$

$$v_{Kj} = \frac{\partial \ln K}{\partial \ln K_j} \,, \qquad (j = 1, 2, \ldots, n) \,;$$

$$v_{Lk} = \frac{\partial \ln L}{\partial \ln L_k} \,, \qquad (k = 1, 2, \ldots, p) \,.$$

Under constant returns to scale the elasticities and the value shares for each aggregate sum to unity.

Finally, we can define the rate of technical change, say $v_T$, as the growth of output with respect to time, holding capital and labor input constant

$$v_T = \frac{\partial \ln Y}{\partial T} (K, L, T) .$$

Under constant returns to scale the rate of technical change can be expressed as the rate of growth of output less a weighted average of the rates of growth of capital and labor input, where the weights are given by the corresponding value shares

$$\frac{d \ln Y}{dT} = \frac{\partial \ln Y}{\partial \ln K} \frac{d \ln K}{dT} + \frac{\partial \ln Y}{\partial \ln L} \frac{d \ln Y}{dT} + \frac{\partial \ln Y}{\partial T}$$

$$= v_K \frac{d \ln K}{dT} + v_L \frac{d \ln L}{dT} + v_T .$$

We refer to this expression for the rate of technical change $v_T$ as the *Divisia quantity index of technical change*.

The Divisia quantity index of technical change is defined in terms of aggregates for output, capital input, and labor input. The measurement of productivity begins with data for individual outputs and inputs. Under constant returns to scale the rate of growth of each aggregate can be expressed as a weighted average of its components, where the weights are given by the corresponding value shares

$$\frac{d \ln Y}{dT} = \sum w_i \frac{d \ln Y_i}{dT} ,$$

$$\frac{d \ln K}{dT} = \sum v_j \frac{d \ln K_j}{dT}$$

$$\frac{d \ln L}{dT} = \sum v_k \frac{d \ln L_k}{dT} .$$

We refer to these expressions for aggregate output, capital input, and labor input as the *Divisia indexes of output, capital input, and labor input*.[8]

If the production function $F$ gives output $Y$ as a function of aggregate input, say $X$, we can write this function in the form

$$Y = G[X(K, L), T] ,$$

where the function $G$ is homogeneous of degree one in aggregate input $X$ and aggregate input is homogeneous of degree one in capital input $K$ and labor input $L$, so that technical change is *Hicks-neutral*

$$Y = A(T) X (K,L) .$$

The rate of technical change depends only on time

$$v_T = \frac{d \ln A}{dT} ,$$

and the rate of growth of aggregate input is a weighted average of rates of growth of capital and labor input

$$\frac{d \ln X}{dT} = v_K \frac{d \ln K}{dT} + v_L \frac{d \ln L}{dT} .$$

We refer to this expression as the *Divisia index of input.*[9]

Under constant returns to scale a necessary condition for producer equilibrium is that the price of output and the prices of capital and labor inputs are consistent with equality between the value of output and the sum of the values of capital and labor input

$$q_Y Y = p_K K + p_L L .$$

Given this equality, we can express the price of output as a function, say $P$, of the prices of capital, labor input, and time

$$q_Y = P(p_K, p_L, T) .$$

We refer to this function as the *price function.*[10] Similarly, we can express the price of each aggregate as a function of the prices of its components.

We can define the rate of technical change as the negative of the growth of the price of output with respect to time, holding the prices of capital and labor input constant

$$v_T = - \frac{\partial \ln P}{\partial T} (p_K, p_L, T) .$$

We can express the rate of technical change as the rate of growth of a weighted average of input prices less the rate of growth of the price of output, where the weights are given by the corresponding value shares

$$\frac{d \ln q_T}{dT} = v_K \frac{d \ln p_K}{dT} + v_L \frac{d \ln p_L}{dT} - v_T .$$

We refer to this expression for the rate of technical change as the *Divisia price index of technical change.*

We can express each aggregate price index as a weighted average of its components

$$\frac{d \ln q_Y}{dT} = \sum w_i \frac{d \ln q_{Yi}}{dT} ,$$

$$\frac{d \ln p_K}{dT} = \sum v_j \frac{d \ln p_{Kj}}{dT} ,$$

$$\frac{d \ln p_L}{dT} = \sum v_k \frac{d \ln p_{Lj}}{dT} .$$

We refer to these expressions as *Divisia price indexes of output, capital input,* and *labor input.* If output is a function of aggregate input, the price of output can be expressed as a function of aggregate input, say $p_X$, so that

$$q_Y = \frac{p_X(p_K, p_L)}{A(T)} ,$$

and the rate of growth of the price of aggregate input is a weighted average of rates of growth of the prices of capital and labor input

$$\frac{d \ln p_X}{dT} = v_K \frac{d \ln p_K}{dT} + v_L \frac{d \ln p_L}{dT} .$$

We refer to this expression as the *Divisia price index of input.*

Divisia indexes have the property that the product of price and quantity indexes for an aggregate is equal to the sum of the values of the components of the aggregate. For example, the product of the price and quantity of aggregate output is equal to the sum of the values of the individual outputs that make up the aggregate. Divisia indexes have the reproductive property that assures consistency among subaggregates, namely, that a Divisia index of Divisia indexes is also a Divisia index. For example, if aggregate output is composed of two subaggregates such as consumption goods and investment goods, the Divisia index of output can be defined, equivalently, as a Divisia index of the components of the two subaggregates or as a Divisia index of Divisia indexes of consumption and investment goods. By duality the reproductive property holds for Divisia price indexes.

### 4.2.3   Index Numbers

Although Divisia index numbers are useful in relating data on prices and quantities to aggregate output, capital input, and labor input, and to the rate of technical change, our methodology must be extended to include data at discrete points of time. For this purpose we consider a specific form of the production function $F$

$$Y = \exp\left[\alpha_0 + \alpha_L \ln L + \alpha_K \ln K + \alpha_T T + 1/2\,\beta_{KK}(\ln K)^2 + \beta_{KL} \ln K \ln L\right.$$
$$\left. + \beta_{KT} T \cdot \ln K + 1/2\beta_{LL}(\ln L)^2 + \beta_{LT} \ln L \cdot T + 1/2\beta_{TT}T^2\right].$$

For this production function output is a transcendental or, more specifically, an exponential function of the logarithms of inputs. We refer to this form as the *transcendental logarithmic production function* or, more simply, the translog production function.[11]

The translog production function is characterized by constant returns to scale if and only if the parameters satisfy the conditions

$\alpha_K + \alpha_L = 1$ ,
$\beta_{KK} + \beta_{KL} = 0$ ,
$\beta_{KL} + \beta_{LL} = 0$ .

The value shares of capital and labor input can be expressed as

$v_K = \alpha_K + \beta_{KK} \ln K + \beta_{KL} \ln L + \beta_{KT} T$ ,
$v_L = \alpha_L + \beta_{KL} \ln K + \beta_{LL} \ln L + \beta_{LT} T$ .

Finally, the rate of technical change can be expressed as

$v_T = \alpha_T + \beta_{KT} \ln K + \beta_{LT} \ln L + \beta_{TT} T$ .

If we consider data at any two discrete points of time, say $T$ and $T - 1$, the average rate of technical change can be expressed as the difference between successive logarithms of output less a weighted average of the differences between successive logarithms of capital and labor input with weights given by average value shares

$$\ln Y(T) - \ln Y(T-1) = \bar{v}_K[\ln K(T) - \ln K(T-1)]$$
$$+ \bar{v}_L[\ln L(T) - \ln L - (T-1)] + \bar{v}_T ,$$

where

$$\bar{v}_K = 1/2[v_K(T) + v_K(T-1)] ,$$
$$\bar{v}_L = 1/2[v_L(T) + v_L(T-1)] ,$$
$$\bar{v}_T = 1/2[v_T(T) + v_T(T-1)] .$$

We refer to this expression for the average rate of technical change $v_T$ as the *translog index of technical change.*

We can also consider specific forms for the functions defining aggregate output $Y$, capital input $K$, and labor input $L$. For example, the translog form for aggregate output as a function of its components is

$$Y = \exp\left[\alpha_1 \ln Y_1 + \alpha_2 \ln Y_2 + \cdots + \alpha_m \ln Y_m \right.$$
$$\left. + 1/2\beta_{11}(\ln Y_1)^2 + \beta_{12} \ln Y_1 \ln Y_2 + \cdots + 1/2\beta_{mm}(\ln Y_m)^2 \right].$$

The translog output aggregate is characterized by constant returns to scale if and only if

$$\alpha_1 + \alpha_2 + \cdots + \alpha_m = 1 ,$$
$$\beta_{11} + \beta_{12} + \cdots + \beta_{1m} = 0 ,$$
$$\cdots \cdots \cdots \cdots \cdots$$
$$\beta_{1m} + \beta_{2m} + \cdots + \beta_{mm} = 0 .$$

The value shares of individual outputs $\{w_{Yi}\}$ can be expressed as

$$w_{Yi} = \alpha_i + \beta_{1i} \ln Y_1 + \cdots + \beta_{im} \ln Y_i , \qquad (i = 1, 2, \ldots, m) .$$

Considering data at discrete points of time, the difference between successive logarithms of aggregate output can be expressed as a weighted average of differences between successive logarithms of individual outputs with weights given by average value shares

$$\ln Y(T) - \ln Y(T-1) = \sum w_{Yi}[\ln Y_i(T) - \ln Y_i(T-1)] ,$$

where

$$\overline{w}_{Yi} = 1/2[w_{Yi}(T) + w_{Yi}(T-1)] , \qquad (i = 1, 2, \dots m) .$$

Similarly, if aggregate capital and labor input are translog functions of their components, we can express the difference between successive logarithms in the form

$$\ln K(T) - \ln K(T-1) = \sum \overline{v}_{Kj}[\ln K_j(T) - \ln K_j(T-1)] ,$$
$$\ln L(T) - \ln L(T-1) = \sum \overline{v}_{Lk}[\ln L_k(T) - \ln L_k(T-1)] ,$$

where

$$\overline{v}_{Kj} = 1/2[v_{Kj}(T) + v_{Kj}(T-1)] , \qquad (i = 1, 1, \dots, n) ;$$
$$\overline{v}_{Lk} = 1/2[v_{Lk}(T) + v_{Lk}(T-1)] , \qquad (k = 1, 2, \dots, p) .$$

We refer to these expressions for aggregate output, capital input, and labor input as *translog indexes of output, capital input*, and *labor input*.[12]

To define price indexes corresponding to translog indexes of aggregate output, capital input, and labor input, we employ the fact that the product of price and quantity indexes for each aggregate must be equal to the sum of the values of the components of the aggregate. For example, the price index for aggregate output is defined as the ratio of the sum of the values of the individual outputs to the translog output index. Price indexes for capital and labor input can be defined in a strictly analogous way. Although the resulting aggregate price indexes do not have the form of translog index numbers, these price indexes are nonetheless well defined. Each aggregate price index can be determined solely from data on prices and quantities of the components of the aggregate. By definition, the product of price and quantity indexes for an aggregate is equal to the sum of the values of its components. However, these indexes do not have the reproductive property that a translog index of translog indexes remains a translog index. The translog index for an aggregate depends on the structure of the subaggregates on which it is defined.[13]

## 4.2.4  Productivity Change

Our methodology for separating growth in real factor input from growth in total factor productivity is based on translog index numbers of aggregate output, capital input, labor input, and technical change. These index numbers provide a direct connection between the economic theory of production and technical change and data on prices and quantities of output and input at discrete points of time. We find it useful to develop further implications of our methodology for data on capital and labor input. The measurement of capital input begins with data on the stock of capital for each component of capital input. Similarly, the measurement of labor input begins with data on hours worked for each component of labor input. It is important to be explicit about the relationship between these data and the aggregates for capital and labor input defined by translog index numbers.

For a single type of capital input we first characterize the relative efficiency of capital goods of different ages by means of a sequence of nonnegtive number—$d(0)$, $d(1)$, .... . We normalize the efficiency of a new capital good at unity.

$$d(0) = 1 \, ,$$

so that the remaining elements in the sequence represent the efficiency of capital goods of every age relative to the efficiency of a new capital good. We assume that relative efficiency in nonincreasing with age, say, $\tau$, so that

$$d(\tau) - d(\tau - 1) \leq 0 \, , \qquad (\tau = 1, 2, \dots) \, ,$$

and that every capital good is eventually retired or scrapped, so that relative efficiency eventually drops to zero

$$\lim_{\tau \to \infty} d(\tau) = 0 \, .$$

The stock of capital, say $A(T)$, is the sum of past investments, say $I(T - \tau)$, each weighted by relative efficiency

$$A(T) = \sum_{\tau=0}^{\infty} d_\tau \, I(T - \tau) \, .$$

Similarly, the price of acquisition of new capital goods, say $p_I(T)$, is the discounted value of the future prices of capital input, say $p_K(T + \tau)$, weighted by relative efficiency

$$p_I(T) = \sum_{\tau=0}^{\infty} d_\tau \prod_{S=1}^{\tau} \frac{1}{1 + r(T + S)} \, p_K(T + \tau + 1) \, ,$$

where $r(T)$ is the *rate of return on capital* in period $T$ and $\displaystyle\prod_{S=1}^{\tau}$ $[1/1 + r(T + S)]$ is the discount factor in period $T$ for future prices in period $T + S$.

Using data on decline in efficiency, estimates of capital stock can be compiled from data on prices and quantities of investment in new capital goods at every point of time by means of the perpetual inventory method.[14] We assume that relative efficiency of capital goods declines geometrically with age

$$d_\tau = (1 - \delta)^\tau , \qquad (\tau = 0, 1, \dots) .$$

Under this assumption capital stock is a weighted sum of past investments with geometrically declining weights

$$A(T) = \sum_{\tau=0}^{\infty} (1 - \delta)^\tau I(T - \tau) .$$

Similarly, the price of investment goods is a weighted sum of future prices of capital input with the same weights

$$p_I(T) = \sum_{\tau=0}^{\infty} (1 - \delta)^\tau \prod_{S=1}^{\tau} \frac{1}{1 + r(T + S)} \, p_K(T + \tau + 1) .$$

Capital stock at the end of each period is equal to investment during the period less a constant proportion $\delta$ of capital stock at the beginning of the period

$$A(T) = I(T) - \delta A(T - 1) .$$

Similarly, the price of capital input is equal to the sum of the nominal return to capital $p_I(T - 1)r(T)$ and depreciation $\delta p_I(T)$, less revaluation $p_I(T) - p_I(T - 1)$

$$p_K(T) = p_I(T - 1)r(T) + \delta p_I(T) - [p_I(T) - p_I(T - 1)] .$$

We can also express the price of capital input as the sum of the price of investment $p_I(T - 1)$ multiplied by the *own rate of return on capital*

$$r(T) - \frac{p_I(T) - p_I(T - 1)}{p_I(T - 1)}$$

and depreciation

$$p_K(T) = p_I(T-1) \left[ r(T) - \frac{p_I(T) - p_I(T-1)}{p_I(T-1)} \right] + \delta p_I(T) .$$

Second, for each of the components of capital input $\{K_j(T)\}$ the flow of capital services is proportional to the stock of capital at the end of the preceding period, say $\{A_j(T-1)\}$

$$K_j(T) = Q_{Kj} A_j(T-1) , \qquad (j = 1, 2, \ldots, n) ,$$

where the constants of proportionality $\{Q_{Kj}\}$ transform capital stock into a flow of capital services per period of time. For example, the flow of capital services from a group of machines is measured as the services of the machines per period of time while the stock of capital is measured as the number of machines. The flow of capital services reflects the own rate of return to capital and the rate of depreciation, both expressed per period of time, as well as the quantity of capital stock. The flow of services per unit of stock varies from one type of capital to another, so that the constants $\{Q_{Kj}\}$ can be taken as measures of the quality of capital stock in producing capital services.

The translog index of aggregate capital input can be expressed in terms of its components or in terms of capital stocks

$$\ln K(T) - \ln K(T-1) = \sum \bar{v}_j [\ln K_j(T) - \ln K_j(T-1)] ,$$
$$= \sum \bar{v}_j [\ln A_j(T-1) - \ln A_j(T-2)] .$$

If we define the stock of capital at the beginning of the preceding time period, say $A(T-1)$, as a translog index of its components,

$$\ln A(T-1) - \ln A(T-2) = \sum \bar{v}_{Aj} [\ln A_j(T-1) - \ln A_j(T-2)] ,$$

with weights given by the value shares of the individual capital stocks $\{v_{Aj}\}$ and

$$\bar{v}_{Aj} = 1/2 [v_{Aj}(T-1) + v_{Aj}(T-2)] , \qquad (j = 1, 2, \ldots, n) .$$

We define an *index of the quality of capital stock*, say $Q_K(T)$, that transforms the translog index of capital stock into the translog index of capital input

$$K(T) = Q_K(T) A(T-1) .$$

Our index of the quality of capital stock can be expressed in the form

$$\ln Q_K(T) - \ln Q_K(T-1) = \sum \bar{v}_j [\ln A_j(T-1) - A_j(T-2)]$$
$$- [\ln A(T-1) - \ln A(T-2)] ,$$

so that this index reflects changes in the composition of capital. If all components of capital stock are growing at the same rate, quality remains unchanged. If components with higher flows of capital input per unit of stock are growing more rapidly, quality will increase. If components with lower flows per unit of stock are growing more rapidly, quality will decline.

Second, for each of the components of labor input $\{L_k(T)\}$ the flow of labor services is proportional to hours worked, say $\{H_k(T)\}$

$$L_k(T) = Q_{Lk} H_k(T) , \qquad (k = 1, 2, \ldots, p) ,$$

where the constants of proportionality $\{Q_{Lk}\}$ transform hours worked into a flow of labor services per period of time. The flow of services varies from one type of labor to another, so that the constants $\{Q_{Lk}\}$ can be taken as measures of the quality of hours worked in producing labor services.

The translog index of aggregate labor input can be expressed in terms of its components or in terms of hours worked

$$\ln L(T) - \ln L(T-1) = \sum \bar{v}_k [\ln L_k(T) - \ln L_k(T-1)]$$
$$= \sum \bar{v}_k [\ln H_k(T) - \ln H_k(T-1)] .$$

If we define hours worked, say $H(T)$, as the unweighted sum of its components,

$$H(T) = \sum H_k(T) ,$$

we can define an *index of the quality of hours worked,* say $Q_L(T)$, that transforms hours worked into the translog index of labor input

$$L(T) = Q_L(T) H(T) .$$

Our index of the quality of hours worked can be expressed in the form

$$\ln Q_L(T) - \ln Q_L(T-1) = \sum \bar{v}_k [\ln H_k(T) - \ln H_k(T-1)]$$
$$- [\ln H(T) - \ln H(T-1)] ,$$

so that this index reflects changes in the composition of hours worked. Quality remains unchanged if all components of hours worked are growing at the same rate. Quality rises if components with higher flows of labor input per hour worked are growing more rapidly and falls if components with lower flows of input per hour are growing more rapidly.

We have decomposed the rate of growth of the translog index of aggregate output into the sum of a weighted average of the rates of growth of translog indexes of aggregate capital and labor input and the rate of technical change. Using the indexes of capital and labor quality, we can decompose the rate of growth of output as follows

$$\ln Y(T) - \ln Y(T-1) = \bar{v}_k[\ln K(T) - \ln K(T-1)]$$
$$+ \bar{v}_L[\ln L(T) - \ln L(T-1)] + \bar{v}_T$$
$$= \bar{v}_K[\ln Q_K(T) - \ln Q_K(T-1)]$$
$$+ \bar{v}_K[\ln A(T-1) - \ln A(T-2)]$$
$$+ \bar{v}_L[\ln Q_L(T) - \ln Q_L(T-1)]$$
$$+ \bar{v}_L[\ln H(T) - \ln H(T-1)] + \bar{v}_T .$$

The rate of growth of output is the sum of a weighted average of the rates of growth of capital stock and hours worked, a weighted average of the rates of growth of quality of capital stock and hours worked, and the rate of technical change.

## 4.3  Production Account

### 4.3.1  Introduction

Our next objective is to identify output, capital input, labor input, and technical change with accounts for real product, real capital input, real labor input, and total factor productivity for each of the nine countries included in our study. It is important to emphasize that only the translog indexes of output, capital input, labor input, and technical change can be derived from the theoretical model of production we have presented in section 4.2. The stock of capital, the number of hours worked, and the indexes of quality of capital stock and hours worked are purely descriptive measures. Similarly, the index of total input is a descriptive measure unless we assume that technical change is Hicks-neutral. This assumption is not required in constructing production accounts for each country in this section or in the international and intertemporal comparisons given in section 4.4 below. Wherever we provide comparisons in terms of real factor input, corresponding comparisons can be provided in terms of real product and total factor productivity without using an index of total input.

In this section we outline the principles we have followed in constructing production accounts for the nine countries in our study. A description of the complete accounting system and details of its empirical implementation for the U.S.A. can be found in Christensen and Jorgenson (1973a). A brief description of the sources and methods used to construct the production account for each country is contained in the Appendix. Our summary of sources and methods is based on detailed reports on the data construction for each country. These reports are listed among our references and are available from the authors. The Appendix also includes annual time series of real product, real capital input, real labor input, and total factor productivity for each country.

### 4.3.2   Product and Factor Outlay

The starting point for the construction of translog indexes of output and technical change is the measurement of the value of total product and the value of total factor outlay in current prices. The fundamental accounting identity for the production account is that the value of total product equals the value of total factor outlay. We exclude indirect business taxes unrelated to factor outlay, such as retail sales taxes and excise taxes, from the value of total product; however, indirect business taxes which are part of the outlay on factor services, such as property taxes, are retained in the value of total factor outlay and total product. Our concept of output is intermediate between output at market prices and output at factor cost.

The production account in a complete system of national economic accounts includes the activities of the private sector, the government sector, and the rest of the world. In analyzing productive activity and its distribution between consumption and investment on the output side and between capital and labor in the input side we have limited the scope of our production account to the private domestic sector of each country. Rest of the world production is excluded on the grounds that it can reflect a different physical and social environment for productive activity than the environment provided for the domestic sector.

The boundary between private and government activity varies from country to country within our study, because of variations in the role of government enterprises. While government administration must be excluded from our private domestic production account, essentially similar economic activities—telecommunications, transportation, and public utilities—are conducted by government enterprises and by private enterprises. For some of the countries included in our study it is impossible to obtain separate accounts for government and private enterprises. For the United States, on the other hand, the government enterprises are treated in a manner that is more closely analogous to the treatment of government administration than to the treatment of private enterprises. No capital accounts are maintained for government enterprises and government administration separately. Of course, government enterprises produce an almost negligible proportion of the gross national product of the U.S.A. To provide international comparability in the scope of our product measure we have included government enterprise product for all countries.

The inclusion of government enterprises in gross private domestic product should not result in confusion since "private" gross national product includes government enterprises in the official national income and product accounts of all nine countries. One unconventional aspect of our measure of total output is an imputation for the services of consumer durables. Our objective is to attain consistency in the treatment of owner-occupied residential structures and owner-utilized consumer durable equipment. It is standard procedure for national income accounts to include an imputation for owner-occupied housing in national product but not to include an analogous imputation for consumer durables. Our measure of total input is gross private domestic factor outlay, which is equal to gross private domestic product. Table 4.A.1 gives (for each country) a complete reconciliation of gross prive domestic product and factor outlay with gross national product and national income.[15]

The product and factor outlay accounts are linked through capital formation and the compensation of property. To make this link explicit we divide total output between consumption and investment goods and total factor outlay between labor and property compensation. We include all services and nondurable goods in consumption goods; we include all structures and producer and consumer durable equipment in investment goods. Data for the U.S.A. are available for a complete separation of gross private domestic product between consumption goods and investment goods. For all nine countries it has been possible to separate gross private domestic product between consumption goods and investment goods, except for inventory investment and net exports. In table 4.A.2 we present time series for gross private domestic product. We also present time series for consumption goods product and investment goods product. Inventory investment and net exports are presented separately for countries where they could not be allocated between consumption goods and investment goods. The value shares of investment goods product for each country are presented in table 4.2.

To divide total factor outlay between labor and property compensation, it is necessary to allocate the factor outlay for self-employed persons between labor and property compensation. We have used the method of Christensen (1971) to impute labor compensation to self-employed workers. This involves assigning the estimated wage rate for employees to the self-employed. Christensen has shown that for the U.S.A. this method results in an allocation which is consistent with the assumption that after-tax rates of return are equal in the corporate and noncorporate sectors. The resulting division of gross private domestic factor outlay into labor and property compensation is presented in table 4.A.2 for all nine countries. The value shares of property compensation for each country are presented in table 4.3.

### 4.3.3  Real Capital Input

The starting point for the computation of a translog quantity index of capital input is a perpetual inventory estimate of the stock of each type of capital, based on past investments in constant prices. At each point of time the stock of each type of capital is the sum of past investments weighted by relative efficiency. Under the assumption that the efficiency of capital goods declines geometrically, the rate of replacement for the $j$th capital good, say $\delta_j$, is a constant. Capital stock at the end of each period can be estimated from investment during the period and capital stock at the beginning of the period

$$A_j(T) = I_j(T) + (1 - \delta_j)A_j(T - 1) , \qquad (j = 1, 2, \dots, n) .$$

**Table 4.2**
Value share of investment goods product, 1947–1973

| Year | Canada | France | Germany | Italy | Japan | Korea | Nether-lands | United Kingdom | United States |
|------|--------|--------|---------|-------|-------|-------|--------------|----------------|---------------|
| 1947 | .275 | | | | | | | | .281 |
| 1948 | .294 | | | | | | | | .308 |
| 1949 | .300 | | | | | | | | .290 |
| 1950 | .307 | .243 | .304 | | | | | | .340 |
| 1951 | .294 | .255 | .324 | | | | .251 | | .340 |
| 1952 | .297 | .249 | .336 | .247 | .298 | | .243 | | .321 |
| 1953 | .299 | .242 | .321 | .252 | .271 | | .272 | | .317 |
| 1954 | .296 | .249 | .339 | .258 | .274 | | .279 | | .306 |
| 1955 | .302 | .262 | .368 | .266 | .295 | | .297 | .213 | .337 |
| 1956 | .327 | .264 | .362 | .267 | .334 | | .310 | .216 | .334 |
| 1957 | .332 | .272 | .365 | .277 | .372 | | .322 | .223 | .327 |
| 1958 | .313 | .274 | .359 | .272 | .322 | | .300 | .227 | .298 |
| 1959 | .306 | .272 | .363 | .278 | .351 | | .316 | .235 | .318 |
| 1960 | .297 | .276 | .386 | .289 | .389 | .126 | .325 | .238 | .301 |
| 1961 | .292 | .287 | .391 | .300 | .450 | .133 | .326 | .238 | .295 |
| 1962 | .300 | .292 | .396 | .305 | .414 | .152 | .326 | .233 | .306 |
| 1963 | .309 | .294 | .390 | .309 | .421 | .161 | .319 | .234 | .310 |
| 1964 | .313 | .309 | .414 | .290 | .429 | .139 | .342 | .253 | .311 |
| 1965 | .326 | .311 | .422 | .269 | .408 | .169 | .341 | .251 | .318 |
| 1966 | .336 | .317 | .398 | .263 | .414 | .227 | .340 | .246 | .318 |
| 1967 | .329 | .317 | .358 | .269 | .443 | .232 | .343 | .253 | .305 |
| 1968 | .330 | .319 | .389 | .276 | .458 | .270 | .348 | .257 | .308 |
| 1969 | .324 | .326 | .412 | .281 | .463 | .282 | .334 | .250 | .304 |
| 1970 | .324 | .327 | .424 | .284 | .482 | .264 | .349 | .254 | .293 |
| 1971 | .321 | .331 | .420 | .284 | .469 | .250 | .347 | .258 | .298 |
| 1972 | .323 | .333 | .409 | .280 | .460 | .224 | .333 | .255 | .305 |
| 1973 | .323 | .333 | .405 | .281 | .486 | .265 | .329 | .264 | .308 |

**Table 4.3**
Value share of capital input, 1947–1973

| Year | Canada | France | Germany | Italy | Japan | Korea | Netherlands | United Kingdom | United States |
|------|--------|--------|---------|-------|-------|-------|-------------|----------------|---------------|
| 1947 | .346 |      |      |      |      |      |      |      | .368 |
| 1948 | .376 |      |      |      |      |      |      |      | .378 |
| 1949 | .397 |      | .340 |      |      |      |      |      | .381 |
| 1950 | .413 | .439 | .348 |      |      |      | .474 |      | .389 |
| 1951 | .406 | .387 | .368 | .419 | .382 |      | .480 |      | .403 |
| 1952 | .430 | .376 | .361 | .420 | .334 |      | .467 |      | .402 |
| 1953 | .426 | .396 | .358 | .394 | .335 |      | .469 |      | .389 |
| 1954 | .418 | .386 | .371 | .403 | .336 |      | .483 | .385 | .390 |
| 1955 | .449 | .381 | .369 | .399 | .351 |      | .482 | .370 | .401 |
| 1956 | .443 | .372 | .373 | .400 | .362 |      | .468 | .379 | .395 |
| 1957 | .423 | .377 | .369 | .402 | .346 |      | .454 | .381 | .386 |
| 1958 | .441 | .360 | .386 | .407 | .362 |      | .459 | .386 | .394 |
| 1959 | .444 | .366 | .396 | .409 | .391 | .326 | .465 | .385 | .401 |
| 1960 | .444 | .389 | .389 | .418 | .433 | .393 | .448 | .381 | .400 |
| 1961 | .447 | .385 | .379 | .415 | .401 | .385 | .443 | .378 | .404 |
| 1962 | .448 | .384 | .385 | .389 | .398 | .401 | .437 | .389 | .408 |
| 1963 | .460 | .387 | .395 | .379 | .422 | .422 | .432 | .387 | .412 |
| 1964 | .470 | .394 | .400 | .385 | .402 | .395 | .432 | .384 | .415 |
| 1965 | .467 | .398 | .400 | .396 | .415 | .383 | .416 | .383 | .421 |
| 1966 | .462 | .431 | .405 | .390 | .431 | .323 | .424 | .389 | .428 |
| 1967 | .440 | .436 | .423 | .391 | .442 | .340 | .433 | .394 | .425 |
| 1968 | .442 | .432 | .421 | .404 | .441 | .333 | .422 | .386 | .418 |
| 1969 | .436 | .441 | .413 | .374 | .436 | .355 | .413 | .371 | .414 |
| 1970 | .434 | .443 | .405 | .332 | .409 | .341 | .415 | .387 | .404 |
| 1971 | .441 | .435 | .409 | .331 | .405 | .354 | .421 | .405 | .401 |
| 1972 | .430 | .439 | .404 | .329 | .396 | .378 | .410 | .404 | .410 |
| 1973 | .470 | .439 |      |      |      |      |      |      | .418 |

We have compiled time series of capital stock estimates for seven asset classes: consumer durables, nonresidential structures, producer durable equipment, residential structures, nonfarm inventories, farm inventories, and land. For each of the seven asset classes we derive perpetual inventory estimates of the stock as follows: First, we obtain a benchmark estimate of capital stock from data on national wealth in constant prices. Second, we deflate the investment series from the national income and product accounts to obtain investment in constant prices. Third, we choose an estimate of the rate of replacement from data on lifetimes of capital goods. Finally, we estimate capital stock in every period by applying the perpetual inventory method as outlined in section 4.2 above.

Each type of capital stock can be valued in current prices by using an index of the acquisition prices for new capital goods. We employ the investment goods price indexes to convert stocks of assets in constant prices to stocks of assets in current prices. These values can be employed in estimating value shares by class of assets. The value shares and stocks can be combined to obtain a translog quantity index of aggregate capital stock. The price index of capital stock is obtained by dividing the value of all assets by the translog quantity index. The price and quantity indexes of private domestic capital stock are presented in table 4.A.3. Value shares of the seven assets in each country are presented for 1970 in table 4.4.

To construct translog price and quantity indexes of capital input we require value shares of individual capital inputs in total property compensation and stocks of individual assets. In the absence of taxation the value of the $j$th capital input is the sum of depreciation and the own return to capital, defined as the nominal return less revaluation

$$p_{Kj}(T)K_j(T) = \{ p_{Ij}(T-1)r(T) + p_{Ij}(T)\delta_j - [p_{Ij}(T) - p_{Ij}(T-1)]\}A_j(T-1),$$
$$(j = 1, 2, \ldots, n).$$

Given property compensation, the stock of assets, the price of acquisition of capital stock, and the rate of depreciation, we can determine the nominal rate of return. The nominal rate of return is equal to the ratio of property compensation less depreciation plus revaluation of assets to the value of capital stock at the beginning of the period.

In measuring the rate of return, differences in tax treatment of property compensation must be taken into account. For tax purposes

**Table 4.5**
Own rate of return to capital in the business sector, 1947–1973

| Year | Canada | France | Germany | Italy | Japan | Korea | Nether-lands | United Kingdom | United States |
|------|--------|--------|---------|-------|-------|-------|--------------|----------------|---------------|
| 1947 | .057 | | | | | | | | .078 |
| 1948 | .068 | | | | | | | | .079 |
| 1949 | .072 | | | | | | | | .063 |
| 1950 | .070 | .093 | .053 | | | | | | .066 |
| 1951 | .058 | .069 | .065 | | | | | | .071 |
| 1952 | .073 | .058 | .071 | .049 | .044 | | .057 | | .059 |
| 1953 | .066 | .066 | .065 | .057 | .030 | | .045 | | .052 |
| 1954 | .053 | .063 | .067 | .050 | .037 | | .053 | | .052 |
| 1955 | .066 | .062 | .082 | .063 | .048 | | .066 | .071 | .061 |
| 1956 | .075 | .059 | .079 | .063 | .057 | | .072 | .072 | .050 |
| 1957 | .059 | .059 | .079 | .063 | .056 | | .067 | .071 | .048 |
| 1958 | .061 | .050 | .073 | .068 | .042 | | .065 | .067 | .049 |
| 1959 | .060 | .049 | .079 | .073 | .052 | | .056 | .072 | .051 |
| 1960 | .055 | .064 | .087 | .078 | .072 | .059 | .061 | .081 | .046 |
| 1961 | .050 | .061 | .079 | .088 | .102 | .091 | .067 | .081 | .049 |
| 1962 | .055 | .062 | .069 | .086 | .079 | .083 | .057 | .073 | .059 |
| 1963 | .060 | .061 | .067 | .075 | .085 | .144 | .055 | .081 | .061 |
| 1964 | .064 | .066 | .072 | .062 | .108 | .182 | .050 | .089 | .063 |
| 1965 | .067 | .066 | .074 | .067 | .092 | .138 | .057 | .085 | .072 |
| 1966 | .066 | .081 | .069 | .077 | .107 | .137 | .054 | .078 | .077 |
| 1967 | .053 | .081 | .061 | .080 | .129 | .093 | .046 | .079 | .068 |
| 1968 | .054 | .081 | .075 | .080 | .144 | .103 | .051 | .081 | .062 |
| 1969 | .046 | .088 | .075 | .092 | .138 | .108 | .053 | .069 | .054 |
| 1970 | .049 | .085 | .079 | .074 | .137 | .098 | .051 | .057 | .046 |
| 1971 | .047 | .080 | .070 | .046 | .109 | .099 | .046 | .065 | .048 |
| 1972 | .045 | .083 | .067 | .042 | .105 | .102 | .047 | .066 | .055 |
| 1973 | .065 | .083 | .064 | .035 | .101 | .128 | .044 | .058 | .058 |

the private domestic sector can be divided into corporate business, noncorporate business, and households and nonprofit institutions. Households and institutions are not subject to direct taxes on the flow of capital services which they utilize. Noncorporate business is subject to personal income taxes on income generated from capital services, which corporate business is subject to both corporate and personal income taxes. Households and corporate and noncorporate business are subject to indirect taxes on property income through taxes levied on the value of property. In order to take these differences into account we allocate each class of assets among the four sectors. For all countries, households and institutions have been treated separately from the business sector; for some of the countries it was not possible to separate the corporate and noncorporate sectors.

Property compensation associated with assets in the household sector is not taxed directly; however, part of the income is taxed indirectly through property taxes. To incorporate property taxes into our indexes of the price and quantity of capital services we add property taxes to the return to capital and depreciation in the definition of the value of the $j$th capital input

$$p_{Kj}(T)K_j(T) = \{ p_{Ij}(T-1)r(T) + p_{Ij}(T)\delta_j - [p_{Ij}(T) - p_{Ij}(T-1)]$$
$$+ p_{Ij}(T)t_j(T)\}A_j(T-1), \qquad (j = 1, 2, \ldots, n),$$

where $t_j$ is the rate of property taxation. The nominal rate of return is the ratio of property compensation less depreciation plus revaluation of capital assets less property taxes to the value of capital stock at the beginning of the period.

Given the nominal rate of return for households and institutions, we can construct estimates of capital input prices for each class of assets held by households and institutions—land held by households and institutions, residential structures, nonresidential structures, producer durables, and consumer durables. These estimates require acquisition prices for each capital good, rates of replacement, rates of property taxation for assets held by households, and the nominal rate of return for the sector as a whole. We employ separate effective tax rates for owner-occupied residential property, both land and structures, and for consumer durables. Finally, we combine the price and quantity of capital input for each class of asset into a translog index of capital input for households and institutions.

To obtain an estimate of the noncorporate rate of return we deduct
property taxes from noncorporate property compensation, add revaluation of assets, subtract depreciation, and divide the result by the value
of noncorporate assets at the beginning of the period. The noncorporate rate of return is gross of personal income taxes on noncorporate
property compensation. Property compensation of househoulds and
institutions is not subject to the personal income tax. The value of
property compensation in the noncorporate sector is equal to the
value of the flow of capital services from residential and nonresidential structures, producer durable equipment, farm and nonfarm inventories, and land held by the sector. All farm inventories are assigned
to the noncorporate sector. Given the noncorporate rate of return, estimated from noncorporate property compensation by the method outlined above, and given data on prices of acquisition, stocks, tax rates,
and replacement rates for each class of assets, we can estimate capital
input prices for each class of assets. Price and quantity data are combined into a translog index of the quantity of capital input for the noncorporate sector.

We next consider the measurement of prices and quantities of capital input for corporate business. To obtain an estimate of the corporate rate of return we must take into account the corporate income tax.
For the U.S.A. the value of capital input for the corporate sector, modified to incorporate the corporate income tax and indirect business
taxes, becomes

$$p_{Kj}(T)K_j(T) = \left( \left[ \frac{1 - u(T)z_j(T) - k_j(T) + y_j(T)}{1 - u(T)} \right] \{ p_{Ij}(T-1)r(T) \right.$$

$$\left. + p_{Ij}(T)\delta_j - [p_{Ij}(T) - p_{Ij}(T-1)] \} + p_{Ij}(T)t_j(T) \right) A_j(T-1),$$

$$(j = 1, 2, \ldots, n),$$

where $u(T)$ is the corporate tax rate, $z_j(T)$ is the present value of
depreciation allowances on one dollar's investment, $k_j(T)$ is the
investment tax credit, and $y_j(T) = k_j(T)u(T)z_j(T)$ for 1962 and 1963
and zero for all other years. The tax credit is different from zero only
for producers' durables. Depreciation allowances are different from
zero only for producers' durables and structures. For other countries
this formula has been adopted in order to reflect the corporate tax
structure in each country.

Our method for estimating the corporate nominal rate of return is the same as for the noncorporate nominal rate of return. Property compensation in the corporate sector is the sum of the value of services from residential and nonresidential structures, producer durable equipment, nonfarm inventories, and land held by that sector. To estimate the nominal rate of return in the corporate sector we require estimates of the variables that describe the corporate tax structure—the effective corporate tax rate, the present value of depreciation allowances, and the investment tax credit. We obtain estimates of all the variables—acquisition prices and stocks of assets, rates of replacement, and variables describing the tax structure—that enter the value of capital input except, of course, for the nominal rate of return. We than determine the nominal rate of return from these variables and total corporate property compensation.

To estimate the nominal rate of return in the corporate sector our first step is to subtract property taxes from total property compensation before taxes. The second step is to subtract corporate profits tax liability. We then add revaluation of assets, subtract depreciation, and divide the result by the value of corporate assets at the beginning of the period. The corporate rate of return is gross of personal income taxes, but net of the corporate income tax. We estimate the price of capital input for each asset employed in the corporate sector by substituting the corporate rate of return into the corresponding formula for the price of capital input. These formulas also depend on acquisition prices of capital assets, rates of replacement, and variables describing the tax structure. Data on the stock of each class of assets are constructed by the perpetual inventory method. Price and quantity data of capital input by class of asset are combined into a translog index of the quantity of capital input for the corporate sector.

It is interesting to compare the rate of return on capital over time and across countries. In table 4.5 we present own rates of return for the business sector. These rates of return are computed as a weighted average of own rates of return on corporate and noncorporate assets, using the value of assets at the beginning of the period in each sector as weights. Own rates of return are adjusted for differences in rates of inflation over time and across countries. Capital input prices depend only on own rates of return. Nominal rates of return for the business sector are presented in table 4.A.3 for each country included in our study.

**Table 4.5**
Own rate of return to capital in the business sector, 1947–1973

| Year | Canada | France | Germany | Italy | Japan | Korea | Netherlands | United Kingdom | United States |
|------|--------|--------|---------|-------|-------|-------|-------------|----------------|---------------|
| 1947 | .057 | | | | | | | | .078 |
| 1948 | .068 | | | | | | | | .079 |
| 1949 | .072 | | | | | | | | .063 |
| 1950 | .070 | .093 | .053 | | | | | | .066 |
| 1951 | .058 | .069 | .065 | | | | .057 | | .071 |
| 1952 | .073 | .058 | .071 | .049 | .044 | | .045 | | .059 |
| 1953 | .066 | .066 | .065 | .057 | .030 | | .053 | | .052 |
| 1954 | .053 | .063 | .067 | .050 | .037 | | .066 | | .052 |
| 1955 | .066 | .062 | .082 | .063 | .048 | | .072 | .071 | .061 |
| 1956 | .075 | .059 | .079 | .063 | .057 | | .067 | .072 | .050 |
| 1957 | .059 | .059 | .079 | .063 | .056 | | .065 | .071 | .048 |
| 1958 | .061 | .050 | .073 | .068 | .042 | | .056 | .067 | .049 |
| 1959 | .060 | .049 | .079 | .073 | .052 | | .061 | .072 | .051 |
| 1960 | .055 | .064 | .087 | .078 | .072 | .059 | .067 | .081 | .046 |
| 1961 | .050 | .061 | .079 | .088 | .102 | .091 | .057 | .081 | .049 |
| 1962 | .055 | .062 | .069 | .086 | .079 | .083 | .055 | .073 | .059 |
| 1963 | .060 | .061 | .067 | .075 | .085 | .144 | .050 | .081 | .061 |
| 1964 | .064 | .066 | .072 | .062 | .108 | .182 | .057 | .089 | .063 |
| 1965 | .067 | .066 | .074 | .067 | .092 | .138 | .054 | .085 | .072 |
| 1966 | .066 | .081 | .069 | .077 | .107 | .137 | .046 | .078 | .077 |
| 1967 | .053 | .081 | .061 | .080 | .129 | .093 | .051 | .079 | .068 |
| 1968 | .054 | .081 | .075 | .080 | .144 | .103 | .053 | .081 | .062 |
| 1969 | .046 | .088 | .075 | .092 | .138 | .108 | .053 | .069 | .054 |
| 1970 | .049 | .085 | .079 | .074 | .137 | .098 | .051 | .057 | .046 |
| 1971 | .047 | .080 | .070 | .046 | .109 | .099 | .046 | .065 | .048 |
| 1972 | .045 | .083 | .067 | .042 | .105 | .102 | .047 | .066 | .055 |
| 1973 | .065 | .083 | .064 | .035 | .101 | .128 | .044 | .058 | .058 |

The price and quantity index numbers for capital input in the various sectors can be combined into a price and quantity index for the private domestic sector. The quantity index is a translog index number, and the price index is defined as the ratio of property compensation to the quantity index. The price and quantity indexes of private domestic capital input are presented in table 4.A.3. Growth rates of real capital input computed from quantity indexes in table 4.A.3 are presented for each country in table 4.6. The quality of capital is defined as the ratio of the quantity index of capital services to the quantity index of capital stock. The quality of capital index is also presented in table 4.A.3.

### 4.3.4   Real Product and Factor Input

To construct a quantity index of labor input, it would be desirable to use the formula for a translog labor index for a large number of skill classifications. Classifications could be defined by level of education, sex, age, occupation, and so on. Following Jorgenson and Griliches (1967), we have limited our consideration to a single skill measure—educational attainment. This results in a quality of labor index which we apply to total man-hours in the private domestic sector. In table 4.A.4 we present the components of real labor input for the private domestic sector. The first column gives total persons engaged in production. The second column gives average hours worked per person engaged. The quality index is presented in the third column. The product of the first three columns provides the quantity index for private domestic labor input. The quantity index is scaled to equal labor compensation in the base year. The ratio of labor compensation to the quantity index gives the price index for private domestic labor input. Growth rates of real labor input computed from quantity indexes in table 4.A.4 are presented in table 4.7.

The quantity indexes of private domestic capital and labor input can be combined into a translog quantity index of private domestic factor input. The price index is then computed as the ratio of the value of private domestic input to the quantity index. The price and quantity indexes are presented for each country in table 4.A.5. Growth rates of real factor input computed from the quantity indexes in table 4.A.5 are presented in table 4.8.

Given measures of total product in current prices, the remaining task is to separate these data into price and quantity components.

**Table 4.6**
Annual rates of growth of real private domestic capital input, 1947–1973

| Year | Canada | France | Germany | Italy | Japan | Korea | Netherlands | United Kingdom | United States |
|------|--------|--------|---------|-------|-------|-------|-------------|----------------|---------------|
| 1948 | .092 | | | | | | | | .067 |
| 1949 | .072 | | | | | | | | .063 |
| 1950 | .071 | | | | | | | | .042 |
| 1951 | .083 | | .043 | | | | | | .067 |
| 1952 | .073 | .054 | .052 | | | | | | .054 |
| 1953 | .066 | .042 | .070 | .019 | .014 | | | | .037 |
| 1954 | .074 | .039 | .068 | .027 | -.003 | | | | .039 |
| 1955 | .049 | .044 | .075 | .027 | .016 | | | | .032 |
| 1956 | .064 | .048 | .088 | .034 | .017 | | .026 | .053 | .052 |
| 1957 | .080 | .051 | .080 | .038 | .078 | | .004 | .035 | .042 |
| 1958 | .065 | .055 | .077 | .040 | .119 | | .021 | .040 | .034 |
| 1959 | .049 | .052 | .073 | .037 | .054 | | .052 | .044 | .018 |
| 1960 | .048 | .045 | .069 | .042 | .069 | | .055 | .051 | .034 |
| 1961 | .043 | .042 | .082 | .055 | .109 | .006 | .064 | .056 | .031 |
| 1962 | .036 | .054 | .079 | .066 | .157 | .013 | .062 | .049 | .023 |
| 1963 | .041 | .059 | .079 | .070 | .113 | .027 | .035 | .039 | .034 |
| 1964 | .045 | .064 | .067 | .078 | .089 | .039 | .041 | .046 | .039 |
| 1965 | .054 | .066 | .077 | .049 | .117 | .037 | .061 | .060 | .043 |
| 1966 | .065 | .070 | .084 | .036 | .089 | .031 | .071 | .051 | .053 |
| 1967 | .068 | .061 | .066 | .039 | .083 | .088 | .073 | .041 | .057 |
| 1968 | .054 | .064 | .041 | .052 | .117 | .113 | .063 | .043 | .044 |
| 1969 | .049 | .060 | .055 | .049 | .140 | .132 | .073 | .045 | .046 |
| 1970 | .051 | .059 | .071 | .053 | .138 | .127 | .074 | .034 | .046 |
| 1971 | .037 | .067 | .076 | .060 | .148 | .096 | .062 | .035 | .031 |
| 1972 | .044 | .064 | .073 | .049 | .123 | .090 | .057 | .047 | .035 |
| 1973 | .052 | .062 | .062 | .046 | .116 | .054 | .059 | .059 | .045 |

**Table 4.7**
Annual rates of growth of real private domestic labor input, 1947–1973

| Year | Canada | France | Germany | Italy | Japan | Korea | Nether-lands | United Kingdom | United States |
|------|--------|--------|---------|-------|-------|-------|--------------|----------------|---------------|
| 1948 | .013 |      |       |      |      |      |       |       | .016 |
| 1949 | .017 |      |       |      |      |      |       |       | -.039 |
| 1950 | -.019 |      |       |      |      |      |       |       | .038 |
| 1951 | .020 |      |       |      |      |      |       |       | .044 |
| 1952 | .011 | .016 | .030 |      |      |      |       |       | .010 |
| 1953 | .014 | -.006 | .022 | .032 | .049 |      |       |       | .017 |
| 1954 | -.005 | -.007 | .029 | .038 | .027 |      |       |       | -.034 |
| 1955 | .017 | .010 | .035 | -.001 | .040 |      |       |       | .035 |
| 1956 | .043 | .003 | .044 | -.001 | .077 |      | -.006 |       | .021 |
| 1957 | .014 | .005 | .015 | .018 | .049 |      | .024 |       | -.008 |
| 1958 | -.015 | .010 | -.014 | .002 | .035 |      | .024 | .005 | -.027 |
| 1959 | .031 | -.007 | -.009 | .009 | .046 |      | .023 | -.020 | .041 |
| 1960 | .010 | -.006 | -.006 | .027 | .059 |      | .020 | -.012 | .013 |
| 1961 | -.021 | .015 | .012 | .009 | .013 | .061 | .006 | .024 | -.005 |
| 1962 | .029 | .004 | -.000 | -.022 | .022 | .019 | -.006 | .014 | .028 |
| 1963 | .017 | .007 | -.016 | .009 | .026 | .041 | .020 | .022 | .016 |
| 1964 | .031 | .008 | .012 | -.035 | .030 | -.002 | .025 | .002 | .021 |
| 1965 | .032 | .013 | -.008 | -.069 | .043 | .106 | -.029 | .018 | .037 |
| 1966 | .027 | -.006 | -.019 | .027 | .027 | .030 | .026 | -.002 | .038 |
| 1967 | .019 | .012 | -.058 | .034 | .038 | .057 | .021 | -.013 | .015 |
| 1968 | .002 | -.002 | .018 | .013 | .034 | .079 | .013 | -.015 | .024 |
| 1969 | .019 | .017 | .016 | -.020 | .014 | .063 | .014 | -.000 | .032 |
| 1970 | -.001 | .008 | .006 | .019 | .018 | .002 | .011 | .005 | -.011 |
| 1971 | .019 | -.002 | -.022 | -.025 | .012 | .066 | -.018 | -.027 | .006 |
| 1972 | .027 | -.003 | -.016 | -.026 | .014 | .064 | .014 | -.053 | .038 |
| 1973 | .054 | .007 | -.003 | -.004 | .033 | .066 | .016 | .010 | .050 |

**Table 4.8**
Annual rates of growth of real private domestic factor input, 1947–1973

| Year | Canada | France | Germany | Italy | Japan | Korea | Netherlands | United Kingdom | United States |
|------|--------|--------|---------|-------|-------|-------|-------------|----------------|---------------|
| 1948 | .042 |      |       |       |       |      |      |      | .035 |
| 1949 | .038 |      |       |       |       |      |      |      | -.000 |
| 1950 | .017 |      |       |       |       |      |      |      | .040 |
| 1951 | .046 | .032 | .034 |       |       |      |      |      | .054 |
| 1952 | .037 | .012 | .033 |       |       |      | .009 |      | .027 |
| 1953 | .036 | .011 | .044 | .026 | .036 |      | .015 |      | .025 |
| 1954 | .028 | .023 | .047 | .034 | .017 |      | .023 |      | -.005 |
| 1955 | .031 | .020 | .055 | .010 | .032 |      | .037 |      | .034 |
| 1956 | .052 | .022 | .042 | .013 | .056 |      | .037 | .023 | .033 |
| 1957 | .043 | .027 | .021 | .026 | .059 |      | .034 | .001 | .011 |
| 1958 | .020 | .014 | .023 | .017 | .064 |      | .025 | .007 | -.003 |
| 1959 | .039 | .013 | .024 | .020 | .048 |      | .027 | .032 | .032 |
| 1960 | .027 | .025 | .034 | .033 | .063 |      | .032 | .028 | .022 |
| 1961 | .007 | .023 | .032 | .028 | .052 | .041 | .012 | .035 | .010 |
| 1962 | .032 | .027 | .021 | .015 | .078 | .017 | .046 | .020 | .026 |
| 1963 | .028 | .029 | .020 | .034 | .061 | .035 | .044 | .024 | .023 |
| 1964 | .038 | .034 | .034 | .008 | .054 | .015 | .035 | .029 | .028 |
| 1965 | .042 | .024 | .026 | -.024 | .073 | .077 | .039 | .022 | .040 |
| 1966 | .044 | .033 | .022 | .030 | .052 | .030 | .038 | .011 | .045 |
| 1967 | .041 | .027 | -.008 | .036 | .057 | .068 | .015 | .007 | .033 |
| 1968 | .025 | .022 | .028 | .028 | .071 | .090 | .032 | .017 | .033 |
| 1969 | .032 | .036 | .033 | .007 | .070 | .086 | .034 | .020 | .038 |
| 1970 | .022 | .034 | .033 | .032 | .071 | .045 | .023 | -.004 | .012 |
| 1971 | .028 | .027 | .019 | .005 | .069 | .077 | .031 | -.020 | .016 |
| 1972 | .035 | .026 | .020 | -.001 | .059 | .073 | .017 | .025 | .037 |
| 1973 | .053 | .032 | .024 | .012 | .066 | .062 | .024 | .046 | .048 |

Total product is first divided between investment goods and consumption goods. These components of total product are separated into price and quantity components using deflators from the national income and product accounts. The quantity indexes for consumption and investment goods are then combined using translog index numbers. Price indexes are constructed so that the product of price and quantity indexes equals the current dollar magnitude. Since inventory investment and net exports can be negative, quantity indexes are added to the quantity index of consumption and investment goods to obtain the quantity index of gross private domestic product. For each country the price and quantity indexes of gross private domestic product are presented in table 4.A.5. Growth rates of real product computed from quantity indexes in table 4.A.5 are presented for each country in table 4.9. Finally, an index of total factor productivity, defined as the ratio of real product to real factor input, is presented for each country in table 4.A.5. Growth rates of total factor productivity computed from the data in table 4.A.5 are presented in table 4.10.

## 4.4   International Comparisons

### 4.4.1   Introduction

Our international comparisons are based on growth of output, input, and total factor productivity for the nine countries included in our study. In section 4.3 we have presented annual rates of growth of real gross private domestic product, real gross private domestic factor input, and total factor productivity for all nine countries.[16] We have also presented rates of growth of real capital input and real labor input for these countries. In this section we first compare growth in real factor input and in total factor productivity as sources of growth in real product. We then compare growth in real capital input and in real labor input as sources of growth in real factor input. Finally, we compare our analysis of aggregate economic growth with an analysis based on measures of capital and labor input that do not incorporate changes in the quality of capital stock and the quality of hours worked.

Annual growth rates of real product, real capital input, real labor input, and total factor productivity are available for all nine countries included in our study for the period 1960–1973, so that we can com-

**Table 4.9**
Annual rates of growth of real gross private domestic product, 1947–1973

| Year | Canada | France | Germany | Italy | Japan | Korea | Nether-lands | United Kingdom | United States |
|------|--------|--------|---------|-------|-------|-------|--------------|----------------|---------------|
| 1948 | .035 |      |      |      |      |      |      |      | .054 |
| 1949 | .054 |      |      |      |      |      |      |      | .007 |
| 1950 | .097 |      |      |      |      |      |      |      | .095 |
| 1951 | .039 | .025 | .099 |      |      |      |      |      | .066 |
| 1952 | .090 | .031 | .082 |      |      |      | .015 |      | .037 |
| 1953 | .059 | .080 | .085 | .087 | .095 |      | .075 |      | .046 |
| 1954 | -.006 | .050 | .079 | .036 | .064 |      | .069 |      | -.010 |
| 1955 | .087 | .053 | .121 | .082 | .103 |      | .072 |      | .072 |
| 1956 | .095 | .046 | .081 | .047 | .043 |      | .054 | .023 | .024 |
| 1957 | .027 | .058 | .066 | .045 | .097 |      | .036 | .026 | .016 |
| 1958 | .025 | .015 | .041 | .056 | .069 |      | -.053 | .010 | .000 |
| 1959 | .042 | .050 | .076 | .065 | .069 |      | .100 | .046 | .058 |
| 1960 | .029 | .084 | .095 | .064 | .112 |      | .080 | .061 | .022 |
| 1961 | .015 | .053 | .055 | .084 | .178 | .052 | .035 | .050 | .023 |
| 1962 | .060 | .063 | .040 | .060 | .106 | .029 | .045 | .015 | .056 |
| 1963 | .055 | .058 | .041 | .047 | .109 | .097 | .033 | .039 | .039 |
| 1964 | .069 | .076 | .072 | .034 | .119 | .063 | .096 | .072 | .053 |
| 1965 | .071 | .054 | .063 | .034 | .095 | .071 | .062 | .025 | .060 |
| 1966 | .066 | .058 | .035 | .056 | .076 | .123 | .035 | .028 | .060 |
| 1967 | .029 | .050 | .000 | .073 | .114 | .084 | .049 | .031 | .027 |
| 1968 | .053 | .044 | .078 | .055 | .125 | .118 | .071 | .039 | .045 |
| 1969 | .043 | .081 | .070 | .061 | .113 | .177 | .067 | .010 | .031 |
| 1970 | .038 | .061 | .071 | .053 | .123 | .074 | .067 | .037 | -.001 |
| 1971 | .050 | .047 | .031 | -.026 | .093 | .087 | .052 | .034 | .035 |
| 1972 | .050 | .054 | .044 | .028 | .084 | .089 | .062 | .051 | .063 |
| 1973 | .066 | .067 | .060 | .061 | .081 | .191 | .050 | .068 | .063 |

**Table 4.10**
Annual rate of growth of total factor productivity

| Year | Canada | France | Germany | Italy | Japan | Korea | Netherlands | United Kingdom | United States |
|------|--------|--------|---------|-------|-------|-------|-------------|----------------|---------------|
| 1948 | -.007 |       |       |       |       |       |       |       | .018 |
| 1949 | .016  |       |       |       |       |       |       |       | .008 |
| 1950 | .080  |       |       |       |       |       |       |       | .055 |
| 1951 | -.007 | -.006 | .064 |       |       |       |       |       | .012 |
| 1952 | .053  | .019  | .050 |       |       |       | .005 |       | .010 |
| 1953 | .023  | .069  | .041 | .061 | .058 |       | .061 |       | .021 |
| 1954 | -.034 | .027  | .032 | .002 | .047 |       | .046 |       | -.004 |
| 1955 | .056  | .033  | .066 | .072 | .071 |       | .034 |       | .038 |
| 1956 | .043  | .024  | .038 | .034 | -.014 |      | .017 | -.001 | -.009 |
| 1957 | -.016 | .031  | .045 | .019 | .038 |       | .002 | .025 | .005 |
| 1958 | .005  | .001  | .018 | .039 | .004 |       | -.079 | .002 | .003 |
| 1959 | .003  | .037  | .052 | .044 | .020 |       | .073 | .014 | .026 |
| 1960 | .003  | .059  | .061 | .031 | .049 |       | .047 | .033 | .000 |
| 1961 | .008  | .030  | .023 | .056 | .125 | .011 | .022 | .015 | .014 |
| 1962 | .028  | .036  | .020 | .045 | .028 | .012 | -.002 | -.005 | .031 |
| 1963 | .027  | .029  | .021 | .013 | .048 | .062 | -.011 | .015 | .015 |
| 1964 | .032  | .043  | .038 | .026 | .065 | .048 | .061 | .043 | .025 |
| 1965 | .029  | .030  | .037 | .058 | .022 | -.006 | .022 | .003 | .021 |
| 1966 | .022  | .025  | .013 | .025 | .024 | .093 | -.003 | .016 | .015 |
| 1967 | -.012 | .023  | .008 | .037 | .057 | .016 | .034 | .025 | -.006 |
| 1968 | .029  | .021  | .051 | .027 | .054 | .028 | .038 | .023 | .013 |
| 1969 | .010  | .045  | .038 | .054 | .043 | .091 | .033 | -.010 | -.007 |
| 1970 | .016  | .027  | .038 | .020 | .053 | .029 | .044 | .041 | -.013 |
| 1971 | .023  | .019  | .013 | -.031 | .024 | .010 | .021 | .055 | .019 |
| 1972 | .016  | .029  | .024 | .029 | .025 | .015 | .045 | .026 | .026 |
| 1973 | .013  | .035  | .037 | .048 | .015 | .129 | .027 | .022 | .015 |

pare patterns of aggregate economic growth across countries for this period. For all countries except Korea annual growth rates are available for periods ending in 1960 and beginning at various times from 1947 to 1955, so that we can compare patterns of aggregate economic growth between time periods for each country except for Korea. Since the earlier periods vary in length from country to country we do not attempt to make systematic comparisons of growth patterns across countries for periods before 1960–1973.

### 4.4.2   Aggregate Economic Growth

We present average annual growth rates for real product, real factor input, total factor productivity, real capital input, and real labor input in table 4.11. This table provides average annual growth rates for all nine countries included in our study for the period 1960–1973. Our international comparisons of patterns of aggregate economic growth are based on growth in real product, real factor input, and total factor productivity for all nine countries for this period. Table 4.11 also includes average annual growth rates for all countries except for Korea for earlier periods beginning between 1947 and 1955 and ending in 1960. Our intertemporal comparisons of growth patterns are based on data for the period 1960–1973 and for the earlier periods.

During the 1960–1973 period, average growth rates of real product fell within the relatively narrow range of 4.3–5.9% for six of the nine countries included in our study. For the two North American countries, Canada and the U.S.A., average growth rates of real product were 5.1 and 4.3%, respectively. For four of the European countries—France, Germany, Italy, and The Netherlands—average growth rates were 5.9, 5.4, 4.8, and 5.6%. Growth of real product for the U.K., the fifth European country, fell below this range with an average rate of 3.8%. For the two Asian countries, Japan and Korea, growth of real product greatly exceeded this range with average rates of 10.9 and 9.7%, respectively.

Among the six countries characterized by moderate growth of real product, the range of variation in average growth rates of real factor input is the same as for real product. For France, Germany, Italy, and The Netherlands the average growth rates of real factor input are 2.9, 2.4, 1.6, and 3.0%, respectively, for the period 1960–1973. For this period the average rate of growth of real factor input for Canada is

Table 4.11
Average annual growth rates of real product, real factor input, total factor productivity, real capital input, and real labor input

|  | Canada | France | Germany | Italy | Japan | Korea | Netherlands | United Kingdom | United States |
|---|---|---|---|---|---|---|---|---|---|
|  |  |  |  |  | 1960–73 |  |  |  |  |
| Real product | .051 | .059 | .054 | .048 | .109 | .097 | .056 | .038 | .043 |
| Real factor input | .033 | .029 | .024 | .016 | .064 | .055 | .030 | .018 | .030 |
| Total factor productivity | .018 | .030 | .030 | .031 | .045 | .041 | .026 | .021 | .013 |
| Real capital input | .049 | .063 | .070 | .054 | .115 | .066 | .066 | .046 | .040 |
| Real labor input | .020 | .004 | -.007 | -.007 | .027 | .050 | .003 | .000 | .022 |
|  | 1947–60 | 1950–60 | 1950–60 | 1952–60 | 1952–60 |  | 1951–60 | 1955–60 | 1947–60 |
| Real product | .052 | .049 | .082 | .060 | .081 |  | .050 | .033 | .037 |
| Real factor input | .035 | .020 | .036 | .023 | .047 |  | .027 | .018 | .023 |
| Total factor productivity | .017 | .029 | .047 | .038 | .034 |  | .023 | .015 | .014 |
| Real capital input | .068 | .047 | .069 | .033 | .045 |  | .040 | .045 | .045 |
| Real labor input | .011 | .003 | .016 | .016 | .048 |  | .014 | .002 | .010 |

3.3% and for the U.S.A. is 3.0%. By contrast, the high-growth countries, Japan and Korea, had the highest average rates of growth of real
factor input, 6.4 and 5.5%, respectively. The low-growth country, the
U.K., had the lowest average rate of growth in real factor input at
1.8%.

Our first conclusion is that variations in average growth rates of
real product among countries during the period 1960–1973 are associated with variations in growth rates of real factor input. This conclusion is based on all possible comparisons between growth rates of real
product and real factor input for pairs of countries. For twenty-eight
of the thirty-six possible comparisons, the differences of growth rates
of real product have the same sign as the differences of growth of real
factor input. For example, a comparison of patterns of economic
growth for the period 1960–1973 for France and the U.K. reveals average rates of growth of real product of 5.9 and 3.8%, respectively.
These growth rates are associated with average rates of growth of real
factor input of 2.9 and 1.8%.

If we compare patterns of aggregate economic growth between the
period 1960–1973 and earlier periods for each country included in our
study, except for Korea, we find that average growth rates of real
product have increased for France, Japan, The Netherlands, the U.K.,
and the U.S.A., while average growth rates have decreased for
Canada, Germany, and Italy. For every country with an increased
average rate of growth of real product, the average rate of growth of
real factor input has also increased or remained the same. The most
dramatic increases are for Japan, were the average growth rate of real
product rose from 8.1% for the period 1952–1960 to 10.9% for the
period 1960–1973, while the average growth rate of real factor input
rose from 4.7% for the earlier period to 6.4% for the later period. At
the opposite end of the spectrum of growth rates in real product, the
rate of growth of real product for the U.K. rose modestly from 3.3% for
the period 1955–1960 to 3.8% for the period 1960–1973, while the rate
of growth of real factor input remained virtually unchanged at 1.8%
for both periods.

Among countries with decreases in the average rate of growth of
real product, the greatest change was for Germany with a decline from
8.2% for the period 1950–1960 to 5.4% during the period 1960–1973.
The average growth rate of real factor input dropped from 3.6–2.4%
between the two periods. For Canada the growth rate of real product

dropped from 5.2% for the period 1947–1960 to 5.1% for 1960–1973, while the growth rate of real factor input dropped from 3.5–3.3% between the two periods. For Italy the average rate of growth of real product declined from 6.0% for the period 1952–1960 to 4.8% for 1960–1973, while the growth rate of real factor input declined from 2.3% for the earlier period to 1.6% for the later period. Our second conclusion is that increases and decreases in average growth rates of real factor input between the period 1960–1973 and various earlier periods beginning from 1947 to 1955 and ending in 1960 are strongly associated with increases and decreases in average growth rates of real product for all eight countries for which data are available.

The most striking illustration of the association of growth of real factor input and growth in real product is provided by a comparison of patterns of aggregate economic growth for Germany and Japan. During the period 1950–1960 Germany had an average rate of growth of real product of 8.2%, while for the period 1952–1960 Japan had an average rate of growth of real product of 8.1%. For the period 1960–1973 the average growth rate of real product rose from the earlier period for Japan to 10.9%, while the average growth rate for Germany fell to 5.4%. For Japan the average growth rate of real factor input rose from 4.7% for the earlier period to 6.4% for the 1960–1973 period, while the average growth rate for Germany fell from 3.6–2.4%.

### 4.4.3   Growth in Capital and Labor Input

In analyzing the growth of real factor input among countries or between time periods for a given country, we first recall that the rate of growth of real factor input is a weighted average of rates of growth of real capital input and real labor input, with weights given by the value shares of each input. We give value shares for capital input together with ratios of the average weighted rate of growth of capital input, the average weighted rate of growth of labor input, and the average rate of growth of total factor productivity to the average rate of growth of real product in table 4.12. The rate of growth of each input is weighted by the value share of that input. Table 4.12 provides data for all nine countries included in our study for the period 1960–1973, and for all countries except Korea for earlier periods ending in 1960.

Value shares for capital input vary within a narrow range from .367

**Table 4.12**
Value share of capital input and contributions of growth in real capital input, real labor input and total factor productivity to growth in real product

| | Canada | France | Germany | Italy | Japan | Korea | Netherlands | United Kingdom | United States |
|---|---|---|---|---|---|---|---|---|---|
| | | | | | 1960–73 | | | | |
| Capital value share | .449 | .417 | .401 | .383 | .415 | .367 | .429 | .387 | .414 |
| Contributions of: | | | | | | | | | |
| Real capital input | .430 | .444 | .520 | .435 | .437 | .250 | .509 | .468 | .393 |
| Real labor input | .209 | .043 | -.074 | -.090 | .147 | .329 | .031 | -.006 | .306 |
| Total factor productivity | .361 | .513 | .556 | .659 | .414 | .429 | .460 | .538 | .301 |
| | 1947–60 | 1950–60 | 1950–60 | 1952–60 | 1952–60 | | 1951–60 | 1955–60 | 1947–60 |
| Capital value share | .420 | .382 | .367 | .405 | .352 | | .470 | .380 | .393 |
| Contributions of: | | | | | | | | | |
| Real capital input | .549 | .365 | .310 | .220 | .197 | | .381 | .513 | .469 |
| Real labor input | .127 | .039 | .120 | .155 | .380 | | .155 | .042 | .160 |
| Total factor productivity | .325 | .595 | .568 | .627 | .421 | | .465 | .445 | .375 |

for Korea to .449 for Canada for the period 1960–1973, so that variations in weights assigned to capital and labor input do not account for
much variation in average rates of growth of real factor input across
countries. However, average rates of growth of real capital and labor
input do vary substantially among countries as indicated in table 4.11.
For the European countries the rate of growth of labor input ranges
from a negative .7% for Italy to a positive .4% for France. Average
rates of growth of labor input for Canada and the United States are 2.0
and 2.2%, respectively, while average rates of growth of labor input
are 2.7% for Japan and 5.0% for Korea.

Comparing average rates of growth of real capital input among
countries for the period 1960–1973, we find that Japan and Germany
have the highest average rates of growth with 11.5 and 7.0%, respectively. Canada, the U.K., and the U.S.A. have relatively low average
rates of growth—4.9, 4.6, and 4.0%. For the remaining countries of
Europe the average growth rates of capital input are higher than for
the U.K. and the two North American countries, and lower than for
Japan and Germany. Averge rates of growth for France, Korea, Italy,
and The Netherlands are 6.3, 6.6, 5.4, and 6.6%.

Our third conclusion is that for the period 1960–1973 very high
average growth rates in real product are associated with high average
rates of growth of both capital and labor input, and that low average
rates of growth in real product are associated with low average rates
of growth of both inputs. Average rates of growth of real product in
the moderate range from 4.5–6%, which includes five of the nine countries in our study, can be associated either with low average growth
rates for labor and high growth rates for capital, as in Germany, or
with high average growth rates for labor and low growth rates for
capital, as in the United States. There are substantial variations
among countries in average rates of growth of both capital and labor
input, so that further analysis requires a study of the sources of
growth of capital input through the supply of saving and capital formation and the sources of growth of labor input through the supply of
work effort.

We find it useful to illustrate our third conclusion by comparing the
economic performance of the U.K. and the U.S.A. for the period
1960–1973. The average rate of growth of real product is higher for
the U.S.A. at 4.3% than for the U.K. at 3.8%. Average rates of growth
of real factor input are 3.0% for the U.S.A. and 1.8% for the U.K. Turn-

ing to average growth rates of real capital input and real labor input, we find that the difference in rates of growth of real factor input can be accounted for by the difference in average rates of growth of real labor input, zero for the U.K. and 2.2% for the U.S.A. The average rate of growth of capital input for the U.K. of 4.6% exceeded that for the U.S.A. of 4.0%. The average rate of growth of total factor productivity for the U.K. of 2.1% also exceeded that for the U.S.A. of 1.3%. The difference in average rates of growth of real labor input in the two countries accounts almost entirely for the difference in average rates of growth of real product.

If we compare the growth of real factor input between the time period 1960–1973 and earlier periods we first observe that the greatest change in value shares of capital input is to .415 for the period 1960–1973 from capital input between time periods do not account for much variation in average rates of growth of real factor input between time periods. For five of the eight countries included in our intertemporal comparisons, the value share of capital input increases between the earlier periods and the period 1960–1973. If technical change were Hicks-neutral, this would imply an average elasticity of substitution in excess of unity for these five countries, since the rate of growth of capital input exceeds the rate of growth of labor input for all countries and all periods except for Japan for the period 1952–1960.

Comparing the average rates of growth of real capital input and real labor input between time periods for a given country, we find that Japan's average rate of growth of real labor input for the period 1952–1960 was 4.8%, while the average rate of growth of real capital input was only 4.5% for this period. For the period 1960–1973 the average rate of growth of labor input declined to 2.7%, still high by international standards, while the average rate of growth of capital input jumped to 11.5%. The improvement in Japan's economic performance was due almost entirely to the increased average rate of growth of real capital input.

For Germany the decline in the average growth rate of real labor input from 1.6% during the period 1950–1960 to −.7% from 1960–1973 was as large as the decline for Japan from the period 1952–1960 to the later period. The average rate of growth of capital input rose from 6.9% for 1950–1960 to 7.0% for 1960–1973, and the average rate of growth of real product fell from 8.2% in the earlier period to 5.4% in the later period. The decline in Germany's economic performance was due primarily to the decreased average rate of growth of real labor input. The contrast with changes in Japan's economic performance between 1960–1973 and the earlier period is due to differences in the increase of the average rate of growth of capital input.

Our fourth conclusion is that a rise or fall in the average rate of growth of real labor input is associated with a fall or rise in the rate of growth of real capital input. This pattern reflects the process of substitution between capital and labor input in production. Germany and Japan provide the most striking illustrations of this pattern, with substantial changes in aggregate economic growth between 1960–1973 and the earlier periods. However, the same pattern can be seen for two countries with moderate changes in aggregate economic growth—Canada and the U.S.A. The average rate of growth of real capital input fell from 6.8–4.9% for Canada, and from 4.5–4.0% for the U.S.A. between the periods 1947–1960 and 1960–1973. Average growth rates of labor input rose from 1.1–2.0% for Canada, and from 1.0–2.2% for the U.S.A. for the same two periods. France is the only exception to the general pattern; average rates of growth of real labor input and real capital input rose from .3–.4% and from 4.7–6.3% between the periods 1950–1960 and 1960–1973.

A second illustration of our fourth conclusion involves a comparison of Korean growth for the period 1960–1973 with Japanese growth for the period 1952–1960. Average growth rates of real labor input were 4.8% for Japan and 5.0% for Korea. Korea had an average rate of growth of capital input at 6.6%, while Japan's average rate of growth was only 4.5%. Korea's average rate of growth of real product for the later period was 9.7%, compared with Japan's rate of growth of 8.1% for the earlier period. Korea's average rate of growth of total factor productivity for the later period was 4.1%, while for Japan in the earlier period the average was 3.4%. The difference in average rates of growth of capital inputs accounts for the bulk of the difference in economic performance.

### 4.4.4   Quality Change

Up to this point we have compared patterns of economic growth in terms of growth of real product, real factor input, real capital input, and real labor input. We can provide additional perspective on these results by contrasting our analysis of growth patterns and an analysis based on measures of capital and labor input that fail to incorporate changes in capital and labor quality. In table 4.13 we present average annual rates of growth of capital quality, labor quality, capital stock, and hours worked. We recall that the rate of growth of real capital input is the sum of the rates of growth of capital quality and capital stock. Similarly, the rate of growth of real labor input is the sum of the rates of growth of labor quality and hours worked.

Quality change for both capital and labor input is positive for all countries and for all time periods included in our study, except change in capital quality for Germany for the period 1952–1960. An analysis based on measures of capital and labor input that fail to incorporate changes in the quality of capital stock and hours worked would assign growth in total factor productivity a much larger role in accounting for the growth in real product. For the period 1960–1973 growth in total factor productivity is more important than growth in real factor input in accounting for growth in real product for four countries—France, Germany, Italy, and the U.K. Similarly, for earlier periods growth in total factor productivity is more important for three countries—France, Germany, and Italy.

If we were to replace our translog index of real labor input by hours worked as a measure of labor input and our translog index of real capital input by capital stock as a measure of capital input, total factor productivity would be more important than growth in factor input for every country and every time period included in our study, except for Japan during the period 1952–1960. Our fifth conclusion is that omission of changes in quality of capital stock and hours worked would result in a completely distorted view of the relative importance of growth in real factor input and growth in total factor productivity in accounting for the growth of real product.

If we compare the role of change in quality of capital stock and hours worked between the period 1960–1973 and earlier periods, we find that the differences are relatively modest except for Japan. The growth of real factor input for Japan for the period 1960–1973 is 6.4%, the highest for any country and any time period included in our study. The difference between the average rate of growth in real factor input for Japan and the average rates of growth of real factor input for the remaining countries included in our study is the most important factor in accounting for the differences in rates of growth of real product between Japan and the remaining countries. The average rate of

**Table 4.13**
Average annual growth rates of quality of capital stock, capital stock, quality of hours worked, and hours worked

| | Canada | France | Germany | Italy | Japan | Korea | Netherlands | United Kingdom | United States |
|---|---|---|---|---|---|---|---|---|---|
| | | | | | 1960–73 | | | | |
| Quality of capital stock | .011 | .012 | .005 | .004 | .030 | .027 | .020 | .004 | .010 |
| Capital stock | .038 | .051 | .066 | .050 | .085 | .039 | .046 | .042 | .030 |
| Quality of hours worked | .005 | .004 | .001 | .013 | .006 | .012 | .005 | .006 | .008 |
| Hours worked | .015 | .000 | -.010 | -.020 | .022 | .038 | -.002 | -.006 | .014 |
| | 1947–60 | 1950–60 | 1950–60 | 1952–60 | 1952–60 | | 1951–60 | 1955–60 | 1947–60 |
| Quality of capital stock | .017 | .009 | -.000 | .002 | .013 | | .009 | .010 | .009 |
| Capital stock | .051 | .038 | .070 | .031 | .033 | | .031 | .035 | .035 |
| Quality of hours worked | .006 | .005 | .001 | .002 | .002 | | .005 | .006 | .007 |
| Hours worked | .006 | -.002 | .011 | .013 | .046 | | .009 | -.004 | .003 |

growth of real product for Japan was 10.9%, also the highest for any country and any time period included in our study. Similarly, the difference between the average rate of growth of real factor input during the period 1952–1960 of 4.7% and the higher rate for the later period is an important factor in accounting for the increase in the average rate of growth form 8.1% during the earlier period.

Finally, we can analyze the role of quality change in our measures of real capital input and real labor input. Japan and Korea have the highest rates of growth of hours worked and of real labor input for the period 1960–1973. A ranking based on real labor input would coincide with a ranking based on hours worked. However, the growth of hours worked is negative or zero for all five European countries, while the growth of our translog index of real labor input is nonnegative except for Germany and Italy. Omission of change in quality of hours worked from the measurement of labor input would result in a change in sign in the average rate of growth of labor input for four of the five European countries included in our study.

Growth in the quality of capital stock for Japan during the period 1960–1973 is 3.0%, the highest for any country in our study. The rise in the average rate of growth of capital quality from 1.3% during the period 1962–1960 is an important factor in accounting for the rise in the average rate of growth of real capital input from 4.5% in the earlier period to 11.5% in the later period. Our final conclusion is that differences among countries are greater for change in capital quality than for change in labor quality, but that omission of either results in a distortion of the relative importance of growth of real capital input and real labor input in accounting for growth in real product.

## 4.5 Summary and Conclusions

In section 4.2 we have outlined a methodology for separating growth in real factor input from growth in total factor productivity, based on the transcendental logarithmic production function. Beginning with a production function that gives output as a function of capital input, labor input, and time, we have defined translog indexes of output, capital input, labor input, and technical change in terms of data on prices and quantities of output and inputs at discrete points of time. We have also introduced descriptive measures of the quality of capital stock and hours worked that transform indexes of capital stock and hours worked into translog indexes of capital and labor input. These descriptive measures are useful in comparing the results of our analysis with the results of studies that fail to incorporate quality change in measures of capital and labor input.

In section 4.3 we have identified translog indexes of output, capital input, labor input, and technical change with accounts for real product, real capital input, real labor input, and total factor productivity for each of the nine countries included in our study. For all countries we have constructed annual production accounts in current and constant prices for the period 1960–1973. For all countries except Korea we have constructed annual production accounts for various earlier periods, beginning from 1947 to 1955 and ending in 1960. Our first objective has been to assess the relative importance of growth in real factor input and in total factor productivity in accounting for patterns of aggregate economic growth for all nine countries for the period 1960–1973. Our second objective has been to assess the relative importance of changes in growth in real factor input and in total factor productivity in accounting for changes in growth of real product between earlier periods ending in 1960 and the period 1960–1973 for each country.

Our first conclusion is that variations in aggregate economic growth for the period 1960–1973 for the nine countries included in our study are associated with variations in the growth of real factor input. This conclusion is strongly reinforced by a comparison of patterns of aggregate economic growth for this period with growth during earlier periods ending in 1960 for each country except Korea. An analysis that fails to incorporate changes in the quality of capital stock and hours worked in measures of capital and labor input would assign a much larger role to variations in growth of total factor productivity in accounting for international variations in the growth of real product or for variations in growth of real product over time for a given country.

The second objective of our analysis has been to assess the role of growth in real capital input and in real labor input in accounting for aggregate economic growth. For the period 1960–1973 we find that very rapid growth of real product is associated with rapid growth of both real capital input and real labor input, and that slow growth of real product is associated with slow growth of both inputs. Moderate growth of real product can be associated with rapid growth of real capital input, rapid growth of real labor input, or moderate rates of growth of both inputs. Our intertemporal comparisons show that increases and decreases in the average rate of growth of real capital input are associated with decreases and increases, respectively, in the average rate of growth of real labor input. This finding provides evidence of substitution between capital and labor inputs in production.

Omission of changes in the quality of capital stock and hours worked from our measures of capital and labor input would obscure the role of differences in the growth of capital and labor input in accounting for differences in the growth of output among countries and between time periods for a given country. Further analysis of international and intertemporal differences in the growth of capital input and the growth of labor input requires a detailed characterization of sources of growth of these inputs. A complete system of accounts, like that developed by Christensen and Jorgenson (1973a), is essential to the analysis of sources of growth of capital input through saving, capital formation, and accumulation of wealth. An analysis of the sources of growth in labor input through the supply of work effort is also required. The analysis of sources of growth in capital and labor input remains an important objective for further research on patterns of aggregate economic growth.

## 4.6 Appendix

### 4.6.1 *Canada*

This summary is taken from Christensen and Cummings (1976).

Our principal data sources for Canada are the *National Income and Expenditure Accounts, Historial Revision, 1926–1971* and the recent annual issues of the *National Income and Expenditure Accounts*, both published by Statistics Canada. Except for the imputation for services of consumer durables, gross private domestic product and factor outlay are computed directly from these sources.

The capital stock benchmarks and replacement rates for all assets except residential structures and consumer durables are taken from Statistics Canada (1974c), *Flows and Stocks of Fixed Nonresidential Capital, Canada*. The residential structures and consumer durables benchmarks are from Gussman (1972). The replacement rate for residential structures is from Cummings and Meduna (1973), and the replacement rate for consumer durables is our estimate. We estimate the benchmark and price index for land using Danielson (1975) and Manvel (1968). Asset deflators are from the national accounts.

Our data on employment are from the *National Income and Expenditure Accounts, Historical Revision* and annual issues of the *Bank of Canada Review*. The Productivity Measures Project, Input Output Division, Statistics Canada provided us with data for average hours worked per person employed and labor income of self-employed persons. We have constructed an educational attainment index using the educational distributions in the 1941, 1951, 1961, and 1971 censuses of Canada, published by Statistics Canada.

### 4.6.2  France

This summary is taken from Brazell, Christensen, and Cummings (1975).

Our principal data sources for France are the *National Accounts Statistics* and *Les comptes de la nation 1949–1959*, both published by the Institut national de la statistique et des études économiques. Gross private domestic product and factor outlay are computed directly from these sources, except for our estimates of the inventory valuation adjustment, the services of consumer durables, and the services of institutional durables and real estate.

The nonresidential structures and producer durable equipment benchmarks are from Mairesse (1972), the residential structures benchmark is from Carré, Dubois, and Malinvaud (1972), and the inventory benchmark is from Goldsmith and Saunders (1959). We estimate the benchmark for land using Goldsmith and Saunders (1959). Our land price index is an average European land price index based on Christensen *et al.* (1975), Christensen, Cummings, and Norton (1979), Christensen, Cummings, and Schoeck (1975), and Conrad and Jorgenson (1975). The replacement rates for nonresidential structures and producers' durable equipment are from Mairesse (1972), and the consumer durables and residential structures replacement rates are our estimates. The asset deflators are from the national accounts.

The data on employment are from Carré, Dubois, and Malinvaud (1972), the Institut national de la statistique et des études économiques (*National Accounts Statistics* and "La population active par secteur d'établissement") and the Ministére des affaires sociales, *Revue francaise du travail*. Average hours worked are computed from *Annuaire statistique de la France* and various other publications of the Institut national de la statistique et des études économiques, plus information on average weeks of vacation from Carré, Dubois, and Malinvaud (1972). The educational attainment index is computed from data in the French Population Census and Carré, Dubois, and Malinvaud (1972).

### 4.6.3   Germany

This summary is taken from Conrad and Jorgenson (1975).

Our principal data source for the Federal Republic of Germany is the national income and product accounts, as published by the Statistisches Bundesamt. Except for the imputation for services of consumer durables, gross private domestic product and factor outlay are computed from these accounts.

The capital stock benchmarks are from Kirner (1968) and Stobbe (1969). The replacement rates are based on service lives estimated by Kirner (1968). The asset deflators are from the national income and product accounts.

We use estimates of man-hours compiled by the Statistisches Bundesamt. The educational attainment index is based on Denison (1967). It has been updated using information published by the Statistisches Bundesamt.

### 4.6.4   Italy

This summary is taken from Christensen, Cummings, and Norton (1979).

Our principal data source for Italy is the *Annuario di contabilita nazionale* published by the Istituto Centrale di Statistica. Except for the imputation for services of consumer durables, gross private domestic product and factor outlay are computed directly from this source.

The capital stock benchmarks for nonresidential structures, producers' durable equipment, and residential structures are from Vitali (1968); the inventory benchmark is from A. Giannone (1963); and the land benchmark is based on the work of de Meo (1973). The consumer durable benchmark and replacement rate are our estimates. The other replacement rates are from de Meo (1973). The investment deflators are from the national accounts except for land and inventories. We use a wholesale price index as the inventory deflator, and the land deflator is based on de Meo (1973).

Our data on employment are from *Annali di statistica* published by the Istituto Centrale di Statistica and *Labor Force Statistics* published by the OECD. Average hours per person employed are from *Rassegna di statistiche del lavoro* published by the Istituto Centrale di Statistica. Our educational attainment index is constructed using information from the *Ninth Census of Italy* (Istituto Centrale di Statistica, 1951), *National Policies for Education, Italy* (OECD 1960, 1963, 1966), and Denison (1967).

### 4.6.5 *Japan*

This summary is taken from Ezaki and Jorgenson (1973) and Ezaki (1974).

Our principal data source for Japan is *Annual Report on National Income Statistics* published by the Economic Planning Agency. Except for the imputation for consumer durables, gross private domestic product and factor outlay are computed from these accounts.

The capital stock benchmarks are taken from the 1955 and 1960 national wealth surveys. The replacement rates are based on services lives estimated by Ohkawa *et al.* (1966). The asset deflators are from the national income and product accounts, except for the land deflator, which is based on data from the *Japanese Statistical Yearbook*.

We use estimates of man-hours made available to us by Dr. Yoichi Okita of the Economic Planning Agency. The quality of labor index is based on the work of Watanabe (1972).

### 4.6.6 *Korea*

This summary is taken from Christensen and Cummings (1981).

Our principal data sources for Korea are the *Economic Statistics Yearbook* and the *National Income Statistics Yearbook* published by the Bank of Korea. In addition, the Bank of Korea provided us with the unpublished data which we required. Except for the imputation for services of consumer durables, gross private domestic product and factor outlay are computed directly from Bank of Korea data.

The capital stock benchmarks for nonresidential structures, producers' durable equipment, and residential structures are from the *Report on the National Wealth Survey* of the Economic Planning Board. The benchmark for land is from Mills and Song (1977). The benchmark for consumer durables and the replacement rates for all asset types are our estimates. The investment deflators are from the Economic Statistics Yearbook except for inventories and land. The inventory deflator is a wholesale price index, and the land deflator is based on the work of Mills and Song (1977).

The Economic Planning Board provided us with unpublished data on employment and average hours worked to supplement the published figures in the *Labor Statistics Yearbook*. The educational attainment index is based on data in the *Population and Housing Census* (1960, 1966, 1970) and the *Report on Wage Survey* (1967, 1970), both published by the Economic Planning Board.

### 4.6.7   *The Netherlands*

This summary is taken from Christensen, Cummings, and Schoech (1975).

Our principal data source for The Netherlands is the Centraal bureau voor de statistiek (1956, 1960, 1965, 1972) and the National Accounts (1958–1968, 1953–1969, 1960–1971, 1961–1972, 1962–1973) published by the OECD. Except for the imputation for services of consumer durables, gross private domestic product and factor outlay are computed directly from these sources.

The capital stock benchmarks, except that for consumer durables, are from Goldsmith and Saunders (1959). The capital stock benchmark for consumer durables is our estimate. The replacement rate for consumer durables is also our estimate. All other replacement rates are based on the replacement rates used by the Centraal bureau voor de statistiek. The asset deflators are all from the OECD National Accounts except for the inventory deflator which comes from *Maandschrift van het centraal bureau voor de statistiek* (1954, 1959, 1964, 1967, 1969, 1972, 1973) and the land deflator. We estimate our own land deflator using Statistical Yearbook of The Netherlands, Goldsmith and Saunders (1959), and Revell (1967).

We use the estimate of man-years compiled by the Centraal bureau voor de statistiek (1947–1966) and the Nationale rekenigen (1972–1973). The number of hours worked per week is taken from data provided by the International Labour Organization (1947 through 1973). The educational attainment index is derived from Denison (1967).

## 4.6.8    United Kingdom

This summary is taken from Christensen, Cummings, Doerner, and Singleton (1975).

Our principal data sources for the United Kingdom are *National Income and Expenditure, 1963–1973* and earlier issues of *National Income and Expenditure* (annual volumes from 1954 through 1966), both published by the Central Statistical Office (CSO). Except for the imputation for services of consumer durables, gross private domestic product and factor outlay are computed directly from these sources.

The capital stock benchmarks for nonresidential structures, residential structures, plant and machinery, vehicles, ships and aircraft, and inventories are taken from the CSO, *National Income and Expenditure* volume. The consumer durable benchmark is our estimate. The replacement rate for nonresidential structures is taken from the Inland Revenue Service. The replacement rates for plant and machinery and residential structures are the *The Stock of Fixed Capital in the United Kingdom in 1961* by Geoffrey Dean. The benchmark and price index for land are estimated using J. Revell, *The Wealth of the Nation; Inland Revenue Statistics*, published by the Board of Inland Revenue; and CSO, *Annual Abstract of Statistics*.

Our data on employment are from the CSO, *National Income and Expenditure* volumes, except for the number of self-employed, which is taken from OECD, *Labor Force Statistics*. Our average hours worked per person is taken from *British Labour Statistics, Year Books* and the *British Labour Statistics: Historical Abstract, 1886–1968*, both published by the Department of Employment. We use the rate of growth of educational attainment estimated by Matthews (1975).

## 4.6.9    United States

This summary is taken from Christensen and Jorgenson (1973a).

Our principal data source for the United States is U.S. Office of Business Economics (1966) and the Annual National Income issue (July) of the *Survey of Current Business* published by the U.S. Department of Commerce. Except for the imputations for services of durables held by consumers and institutions, gross private domestic product and factor outlay are computed directly from these sources.

The capital stock benchmarks are from Grose, Rottenberg, and

Wasson (1969) and Goldsmith (1962). The replacement rates are based on estimated service lives underlying the work by Grose, Rotterberg, and Wasson (1969). The asset deflators are all from the Bureau of Economic Analysis, except for the land deflator, which is based on Goldsmith (1962).

We use estimates of man-hours compiled by Kendrick (1973), and the index of educational attainment computed by Jorgenson and Griliches (1967). The underlying sources are the U.S. Bureau of Labor Statistics, *Special Labor Force Reports*, and the U.S. Bureau of the Census, *Census of Population and Current Population Reports*.

## Notes

1. Detailed surveys of the literature on total factor productivity have been given by Nadiri (1970) and by Kennedy and Thirlwall (1972). Nadiri (1972) has presented an international survey of estimates of growth of total factor productivity. Balassa and Bertrand (1970) have compared sources of economic growth in Eastern and Western Europe. Correa (1970) has compared sources of economic growth for Latin American countries. Patterns of economic growth have been studied from a more comprehensive perspective by Kuznets (1971) and by Chenery and Syrquin (1975).
2. The first English-language reference to Tinbergen's article that has come to our attention is by Valavanis-Vail (1955).
3. Denison's methodology is also employed in a study for Japan by Kanamori (1972).
4. Hopefully this analysis will soon be complemented by a study of long-term growth trends for France, Germany, Italy, Japan, Sweden, the U.K. and the U.S.A. by the Social Science Research Council group under the overall direction of Abramovitz and Kuznets.
5. Earlier, Denison (1969) had compared his results with estimates by Jorgenson and Griliches (1967). For Denison's reply to Jorgenson and Griliches (1972a), see Denison (1972).
6. Kendrick (1975), pp. 909–10, has drawn attention to the asymmetry in Denison's (1974) treatment of labor and capital input in his recent study of U.S. economic growth, which is based on the methodology of *Why Growth Rates Differ*.
7. Maddison (1972), p. 40.
8. These quantity indexes and the analogous price indexes discussed below were introduced by Divisia (1925, 1926). The Divisia index of technical change was introduced by Solow (1957) and discussed by Richter (1966) and by Jorgenson and Griliches (1967).
9. The definition of technical change that is neutral in the sense that it leaves the ratio of marginal products of capital and labor input unchanged is due to Hicks (1963). Hulten (1973) demonstrated that the line integral defining the Divisia index of an aggregate such as input is path independent if and only if the production function is homothetically separable in the components of the aggregate.
10. The price function was introduced by Samuelson (1953); he refers to this function as the factor-price frontier.
11. The translog production function was introduced by Christensen, Jorgenson, and Lau (1971, 1973). The treatment of technical change outlined below is due to Jorgenson and Lau (1974).

12. The quantity indexes were introduced by Fisher (1922) and discussed by Törnquist (1937), Theil (1965), and Kloek (1966). These indexes of output and input were first derived from the translog production function by Diewert (1976). The corresponding index of technical change was introduced by Christensen and Jorgenson (1970). The translog index of technical change was first derived from the form of the translog production function given above by Jorgenson (1986a). The approach developed by Jorgenson and Lau does not require the assumption of Hicks neutrality. Diewert had interpreted the ratio of translog indexes of output and input as an index of technical change under the assumption of Hicks neutrality.

13. This corrects an error in Christensen and Jorgenson (1973a), p. 261.

14. The perpetual inventory method has been employed by Goldsmith (1955) and in the BEA Capital Stock Study (1976). The dual to the perpetual inventory method, involving investment goods prices and capital input prices, was introduced by Christensen and Jorgenson (1969, 1973a). For further discussion of the underlying model of durable capital goods, see Jorgenson (1973a).

15. There are four appendix tables for each country, numbered 4.A.1 through 4.A.4. Table 4.A.1C is Table 4.A.1 for Canada, and so on.

16. All annual growth rates presented in this paper are computed as first differences of natural logarithms.

**Table 4.A.1US**
Gross private domestic product and factor outlay, 1970, United States (billions of dollars)

| | | Product | |
|---|---|---|---|
| 1. | | Private gross national product | 867.7 |
| 2. | − | Rest of the world gross national product | 4.6 |
| 3. | + | Services of consumer durables (our imputation) | 94.9 |
| 4. | + | Services of durables held by institutions (our imputation) | 2.3 |
| 5. | + | Net rent on institutional real estate (our imputation) | 0.9 |
| 6. | − | Federal indirect business tax and nontax accruals | 19.3 |
| 7. | + | Capital stock tax | — |
| 8. | − | State and local indirect business tax and nontax accruals | 74.7 |
| 9. | + | Business motor vehicle licenses | 1.4 |
| 10. | + | Business property taxes | 36.5 |
| 11. | + | Business other taxes | 3.4 |
| 12. | + | Subsidies less current surplus of federal government enterprises | 6.3 |
| 13. | + | Subsidies less current surplus of state and local government enterprises | −3.6 |
| 14. | = | Gross private domestic product | 911.2 |

| | | Factor outlay | |
|---|---|---|---|
| 1. | | Capital consumption allowances | 90.8 |
| 2. | + | Business transfer payments | 4.0 |
| 3. | + | Statistical discrepancy | −2.1 |
| 4. | + | Services of consumer durables (our imputation) | 94.9 |
| 5. | + | Services of durables held by institutions (our imputation) | 2.3 |
| 6. | + | Net rent on institutional real estate (our imputation) | 0.9 |
| 7. | + | Certain indirect business taxes (product account above, lines 8 + 10 + 11 + 12) | 41.3 |
| 8. | + | Income originating in business | 647.4 |
| 9. | + | Income originating in households and institutions | 31.6 |
| 10. | = | Gross private domestic factor outlay | 911.2 |

**Table 4.A.2US**
Private domestic capital input, 1947–1973, United States

| Year | Private domestic capital stock | | Rate of return to capital in the business sector | Services per unit of Stock | Private domestic capital input | |
|------|------------|------------|------------|------------|------------|------------|
| | price index (1) | quantity index (2) | nominal rate (3) | (4) | price index (5) | quantity index (6) |
| 1947 | .439 | 1408.58 | .249 | .115 | .532 | 155.28 |
| 1948 | .473 | 1481.72 | .164 | .118 | .567 | 166.09 |
| 1949 | .469 | 1528.20 | .051 | .119 | .516 | 176.87 |
| 1950 | .491 | 1615.26 | .116 | .121 | .587 | 184.49 |
| 1951 | .532 | 1689.55 | .162 | .122 | .639 | 197.33 |
| 1952 | .540 | 1741.48 | .072 | .123 | .623 | 208.19 |
| 1953 | .544 | 1795.36 | .057 | .124 | .601 | 215.95 |
| 1954 | .547 | 1842.30 | .064 | .125 | .622 | 224.58 |
| 1955 | .560 | 1921.90 | .086 | .126 | .656 | 231.91 |
| 1956 | .588 | 1988.56 | .107 | .127 | .631 | 244.29 |
| 1957 | .610 | 2041.74 | .093 | .128 | .624 | 254.81 |
| 1958 | .618 | 2073.27 | .065 | .129 | .650 | 263.59 |
| 1959 | .633 | 2132.93 | .078 | .129 | .675 | 268.28 |
| 1960 | .645 | 2185.66 | .069 | .130 | .690 | 277.49 |
| 1961 | .656 | 2227.54 | .067 | .131 | .698 | 286.19 |
| 1962 | .671 | 2288.67 | .083 | .131 | .739 | 292.76 |
| 1963 | .684 | 2357.66 | .084 | .132 | .754 | 302.93 |
| 1964 | .700 | 2434.23 | .091 | .134 | .781 | 314.86 |
| 1965 | .720 | 2531.43 | .105 | .135 | .837 | 328.71 |
| 1966 | .746 | 2637.08 | .120 | .137 | .876 | 346.66 |
| 1967 | .776 | 2722.34 | .109 | .139 | .850 | 367.06 |
| 1968 | .813 | 2815.00 | .111 | .141 | .866 | 383.57 |
| 1969 | .862 | 2909.54 | .113 | .143 | .898 | 401.77 |
| 1970 | .905 | 2976.91 | .103 | .145 | .845 | 420.54 |
| 1971 | .954 | 3059.12 | .105 | .146 | .908 | 433.69 |
| 1972 | 1.000 | 3167.73 | .107 | .147 | 1.000 | 449.07 |
| 1973 | 1.069 | 3293.41 | .128 | .148 | 1.097 | 469.76 |

**Table 4.A.3US**
Private domestic labor input, 1947–1973, United States

| Year | Private domestic persons engaged (1) | Private domestic hours per person (2) | Index of educational attainment (3) | Private domestic labor input price index (4) | Private domestic labor input quantity index (5) |
|------|------|------|------|------|------|
| 1947 | 52.66 | 1.132 | 0.825 | 0.316 | 436.21 |
| 1948 | 53.64 | 1.120 | 0.831 | 0.341 | 445.21 |
| 1949 | 51.92 | 1.106 | 0.836 | 0.349 | 428.17 |
| 1950 | 53.54 | 1.107 | 0.842 | 0.397 | 444.79 |
| 1951 | 55.72 | 1.105 | 0.847 | 0.396 | 465.02 |
| 1952 | 56.21 | 1.100 | 0.852 | 0.419 | 469.48 |
| 1953 | 57.21 | 1.093 | 0.857 | 0.442 | 477.71 |
| 1954 | 55.59 | 1.081 | 0.862 | 0.454 | 461.89 |
| 1955 | 57.05 | 1.085 | 0.867 | 0.471 | 478.44 |
| 1956 | 58.37 | 1.076 | 0.872 | 0.497 | 488.61 |
| 1957 | 58.37 | 1.061 | 0.878 | 0.525 | 484.59 |
| 1958 | 56.62 | 1.052 | 0.888 | 0.536 | 471.75 |
| 1959 | 57.99 | 1.058 | 0.899 | 0.557 | 491.40 |
| 1960 | 58.64 | 1.052 | 0.906 | 0.575 | 498.05 |
| 1961 | 58.32 | 1.044 | 0.913 | 0.589 | 495.62 |
| 1962 | 59.41 | 1.046 | 0.920 | 0.609 | 509.45 |
| 1963 | 59.87 | 1.047 | 0.927 | 0.626 | 517.51 |
| 1964 | 60.99 | 1.042 | 0.933 | 0.654 | 528.53 |
| 1965 | 62.80 | 1.043 | 0.940 | 0.674 | 548.68 |
| 1966 | 65.13 | 1.036 | 0.948 | 0.708 | 570.01 |
| 1967 | 66.19 | 1.026 | 0.956 | 0.740 | 578.73 |
| 1968 | 67.64 | 1.019 | 0.965 | 0.790 | 592.99 |
| 1969 | 69.53 | 1.015 | 0.974 | 0.840 | 612.54 |
| 1970 | 69.18 | 1.000 | 0.982 | 0.896 | 605.72 |
| 1971 | 69.07 | 0.998 | 0.991 | 0.946 | 609.14 |
| 1972 | 71.01 | 1.000 | 1.000 | 1.000 | 633.00 |
| 1973 | 74.15 | 0.998 | 1.009 | 1.066 | 665.43 |

**Table 4.A.4US**
Gross private domestic product and factor input, 1947–1973, United States
(constant dollars of 1958)

| Year | Gross private domestic product | | Private domestic factor input | |
|------|---------------|----------------|---------------|----------------|
| | price index (1) | quantity index (2) | price index (3) | quantity index (4) |
| 1947 | 0.543 | 407.00 | 0.388 | 568.72 |
| 1948 | 0.572 | 429.40 | 0.417 | 589.17 |
| 1949 | 0.557 | 432.53 | 0.409 | 589.03 |
| 1950 | 0.571 | 475.60 | 0.443 | 612.88 |
| 1951 | 0.611 | 507.89 | 0.480 | 646.67 |
| 1952 | 0.619 | 526.90 | 0.491 | 664.52 |
| 1953 | 0.618 | 551.54 | 0.501 | 681.24 |
| 1954 | 0.640 | 546.30 | 0.516 | 677.68 |
| 1955 | 0.644 | 586.85 | 0.539 | 701.09 |
| 1956 | 0.661 | 601.21 | 0.548 | 724.82 |
| 1957 | 0.676 | 610.95 | 0.564 | 733.00 |
| 1958 | 0.694 | 611.26 | 0.581 | 730.85 |
| 1959 | 0.702 | 647.72 | 0.603 | 754.26 |
| 1960 | 0.722 | 662.00 | 0.620 | 770.70 |
| 1961 | 0.726 | 677.43 | 0.632 | 778.09 |
| 1962 | 0.735 | 716.60 | 0.660 | 798.22 |
| 1963 | 0.742 | 744.75 | 0.676 | 817.05 |
| 1964 | 0.753 | 785.47 | 0.704 | 840.53 |
| 1965 | 0.773 | 834.43 | 0.737 | 874.65 |
| 1966 | 0.798 | 885.64 | 0.773 | 914.52 |
| 1967 | 0.814 | 909.79 | 0.783 | 945.24 |
| 1968 | 0.841 | 952.06 | 0.820 | 976.52 |
| 1969 | 0.891 | 982.31 | 0.863 | 1014.54 |
| 1970 | 0.915 | 981.43 | 0.875 | 1026.55 |
| 1971 | 0.955 | 1016.02 | 0.930 | 1042.80 |
| 1972 | 1.000 | 1082.07 | 1.000 | 1082.07 |
| 1973 | 1.063 | 1152.28 | 1.079 | 1135.16 |

**Table 4.A.1UK**
Gross private domestic product and factor outlay, 1970, United Kingdom
(billions of pounds)

| | | Product | |
|---|---|---|---|
| 1. | | Gross national product | 51.07 |
| 2. | – | Wages and salaries in general government | 5.88 |
| 3. | – | Rent from government | 1.12 |
| 4. | – | Gross trading surplus of government | 0.15 |
| 5. | – | Net property income from abroad | 0.53 |
| 6. | + | Services of consumer durables | 3.81 |
| 7. | + | Subsidies | 0.90 |
| 8. | + | Capital transfer payments | 0.80 |
| 9. | – | Indirect taxes (our definition) | 8.11 |
| 10. | + | Indirect taxes related to factor outlay | 2.95 |
| 11. | – | Selective employment tax paid by government | 0.32 |
| 12. | = | Gross private domestic product | 43.43 |

| | | Factor outlay | |
|---|---|---|---|
| 1. | | National income | 39.02 |
| 2. | + | Capital consumption allowances | 4.52 |
| 3. | + | Services of consumer durables | 3.81 |
| 4. | – | GNP originating in government | 7.15 |
| 5. | + | Taxes related to factor outlay | 2.95 |
| 6. | + | Capital transfer payments | 0.80 |
| 7. | – | GNP originating in rest of world | 0.53 |
| 8. | = | Gross private domestic product | 43.43 |

**Table 4.A.2UK**
Private domestic capital input, 1955–1973, United Kingdom

| Year | Private domestic capital stock | | Rate of return to capital in the business sector | Services per unit of Stock | Private domestic capital input | |
|---|---|---|---|---|---|---|
| | price index (1) | quantity index (2) | nominal rate (3) | (4) | price index (5) | quantity index (6) |
| 1955 | .624 | 65.51 | .071 | .129 | .770 | 8.13 |
| 1956 | .659 | 67.55 | .072 | .131 | .748 | 8.57 |
| 1957 | .683 | 69.86 | .071 | .131 | .788 | 8.88 |
| 1958 | .707 | 72.11 | .067 | .132 | .796 | 9.24 |
| 1959 | .708 | 75.00 | .072 | .134 | .812 | 9.65 |
| 1960 | .716 | 78.87 | .081 | .135 | .826 | 10.16 |
| 1961 | .733 | 82.47 | .081 | .136 | .845 | 10.74 |
| 1962 | .759 | 85.57 | .073 | .137 | .839 | 11.28 |
| 1963 | .772 | 89.17 | .081 | .137 | .885 | 11.73 |
| 1964 | .797 | 94.13 | .089 | .138 | .907 | 12.27 |
| 1965 | .828 | 98.78 | .085 | .138 | .908 | 13.03 |
| 1966 | .854 | 102.99 | .078 | .139 | .918 | 13.71 |
| 1967 | .869 | 107.42 | .079 | .139 | .949 | 14.29 |
| 1968 | .903 | 112.14 | .081 | .139 | .993 | 14.91 |
| 1969 | .936 | 116.34 | .069 | .139 | .991 | 15.59 |
| 1970 | 1.000 | 120.55 | .057 | .139 | 1.000 | 16.12 |
| 1971 | 1.098 | 124.77 | .065 | .138 | 1.130 | 16.69 |
| 1972 | 1.261 | 129.26 | .066 | .140 | 1.284 | 17.49 |
| 1973 | 1.480 | 133.67 | .058 | .144 | 1.381 | 18.56 |

**Table 4.A.3UK**
Private domestic labor input, 1955–1973, United Kingdom

| Year | Private domestic persons engaged (1) | Private domestic hours per person (2) | Index of educational attainment (3) | Private domestic labor input | |
|------|------|------|------|------|------|
| | | | | price index (4) | quantity index (5) |
| 1955 | 20.903 | 1.068 | 0.914 | 0.372 | 26.91 |
| 1956 | 21.027 | 1.062 | 0.919 | 0.404 | 27.06 |
| 1957 | 20.583 | 1.057 | 0.925 | 0.433 | 26.53 |
| 1958 | 20.382 | 1.048 | 0.931 | 0.455 | 26.20 |
| 1959 | 20.448 | 1.064 | 0.936 | 0.464 | 26.85 |
| 1960 | 20.877 | 1.050 | 0.942 | 0.492 | 27.22 |
| 1961 | 21.499 | 1.036 | 0.947 | 0.530 | 27.84 |
| 1962 | 21.596 | 1.027 | 0.953 | 0.558 | 27.88 |
| 1963 | 21.537 | 1.039 | 0.959 | 0.576 | 28.28 |
| 1964 | 21.746 | 1.041 | 0.965 | 0.613 | 28.79 |
| 1965 | 21.914 | 1.025 | 0.970 | 0.659 | 28.74 |
| 1966 | 21.939 | 1.005 | 0.976 | 0.715 | 28.37 |
| 1967 | 21.382 | 1.009 | 0.982 | 0.761 | 27.94 |
| 1968 | 21.105 | 1.016 | 0.988 | 0.815 | 27.93 |
| 1969 | 21.079 | 1.016 | 0.994 | 0.875 | 28.07 |
| 1970 | 20.711 | 1.000 | 1.000 | 1.000 | 27.31 |
| 1971 | 19.832 | 0.984 | 1.006 | 1.153 | 25.89 |
| 1972 | 19.778 | 0.991 | 1.012 | 1.260 | 26.15 |
| 1973 | 20.232 | 1.000 | 1.018 | 1.390 | 27.16 |

**Table 4.A.4UK**
Gross private domestic product and factor input, 1955–1973, United Kingdom
(constant pounds of 1958)

| Year | Gross private domestic product | | Private domestic factor input | |
| | price index (1) | quantity index (2) | price index (3) | quantity index (4) |
|---|---|---|---|---|
| 1955 | 0.624 | 26.07 | 0.491 | 33.11 |
| 1956 | 0.650 | 26.67 | 0.512 | 33.90 |
| 1957 | 0.675 | 27.36 | 0.545 | 33.93 |
| 1958 | 0.698 | 27.63 | 0.564 | 34.18 |
| 1959 | 0.702 | 28.93 | 0.575 | 35.28 |
| 1960 | 0.709 | 30.75 | 0.601 | 36.29 |
| 1961 | 0.737 | 32.34 | 0.634 | 37.59 |
| 1962 | 0.762 | 32.82 | 0.653 | 38.34 |
| 1963 | 0.781 | 34.13 | 0.679 | 39.25 |
| 1964 | 0.785 | 36.66 | 0.712 | 40.39 |
| 1965 | 0.819 | 37.58 | 0.746 | 41.29 |
| 1966 | 0.851 | 38.63 | 0.787 | 41.77 |
| 1967 | 0.874 | 39.85 | 0.829 | 42.04 |
| 1968 | 0.907 | 41.44 | 0.879 | 42.74 |
| 1969 | 0.955 | 41.86 | 0.917 | 43.62 |
| 1970 | 1.000 | 43.43 | 1.000 | 43.43 |
| 1971 | 1.083 | 44.95 | 1.144 | 42.57 |
| 1972 | 1.171 | 47.32 | 1.270 | 43.64 |
| 1973 | 1.251 | 50.65 | 1.387 | 45.71 |

**Table 4.A.1C**
Gross private domestic product and factor outlay, 1970, Canada (billions of dollars)

| | | Product | |
|---|---|---|---|
| 1. | | Gross national product | 85.69 |
| 2. | − | Wages and salaries in general government | 11.02 |
| 3. | − | Capital consumption allowances in general government | 1.23 |
| 4. | − | Net interest and miscellaneous investment income of general government (net of government enterprise remittances) | 0.80 |
| 5. | − | Net interest originating in rest of world | −1.39 |
| 6. | + | Services of consumer durables (our imputation) | 6.39 |
| 7. | − | Taxes not related to factor outlay | 7.55 |
| 8. | + | Subsidies | 0.76 |
| 9. | + | Capital assistance subsidies | 0.12 |
| 10. | − | Residual error of estimate | −0.35 |
| 11. | = | Gross private domestic product | 74.08 |

| | | Factor outlay | |
|---|---|---|---|
| 1. | | National income | 64.24 |
| 2. | + | Capital consumption allowances | 9.81 |
| 3. | + | Services of consumer durables (our imputation) | 6.39 |
| 4. | − | GNP originating in general government (2 + 3 + 4 above) | 13.05 |
| 5. | + | Capital assistance subsidies | 0.12 |
| 6. | + | Indirect taxes related to factor outlay | 4.50 |
| 7. | − | GNP originating in rest of world | −1.39 |
| 8. | − | Twice the residual error of estimate | −0.69 |
| 9. | = | Gross private domestic factor outlay | 74.08 |

**Table 4.A.2C**
Private domestic capital input, 1947–1973, Canada

| Year | Private domestic capital stock | | Rate of return to capital in the business sector | | Services per unit of Stock | Private domestic capital input | |
|---|---|---|---|---|---|---|---|
| | price index (1) | quantity index (2) | nominal rate (3) | own rate (4) | (5) | price index (6) | quantity index (7) |
| 1947 | .550 | 69.86 | .164 | .057 | .098 | .641 | 6.42 |
| 1948 | .635 | 73.38 | .217 | .068 | .101 | .748 | 7.04 |
| 1949 | .663 | 77.25 | .114 | .072 | .103 | .805 | 7.56 |
| 1950 | .700 | 82.26 | .125 | .070 | .105 | .873 | 8.12 |
| 1951 | .800 | 86.93 | .199 | .058 | .107 | .908 | 8.82 |
| 1952 | .823 | 91.29 | .103 | .073 | .109 | 1.018 | 9.49 |
| 1953 | .836 | 96.60 | .082 | .066 | .111 | 1.000 | 10.14 |
| 1954 | .836 | 100.31 | .054 | .053 | .113 | .907 | 10.92 |
| 1955 | .858 | 105.51 | .098 | .066 | .114 | 1.044 | 11.47 |
| 1956 | .902 | 112.46 | .136 | .075 | .116 | 1.072 | 12.23 |
| 1957 | .934 | 118.30 | .090 | .059 | .118 | .981 | 13.26 |
| 1958 | .950 | 123.00 | .079 | .061 | .120 | .999 | 14.15 |
| 1959 | .969 | 128.08 | .081 | .060 | .121 | 1.020 | 14.86 |
| 1960 | .989 | 132.66 | .076 | .055 | .122 | 1.021 | 15.59 |
| 1961 | 1.000 | 136.49 | .063 | .050 | .123 | 1.000 | 16.27 |
| 1962 | 1.017 | 141.10 | .077 | .055 | .124 | 1.023 | 16.87 |
| 1963 | 1.049 | 146.13 | .096 | .060 | .125 | 1.092 | 17.57 |
| 1964 | 1.090 | 152.27 | .108 | .064 | .126 | 1.173 | 18.38 |
| 1965 | 1.152 | 159.89 | .130 | .067 | .127 | 1.214 | 19.39 |
| 1966 | 1.224 | 168.12 | .134 | .066 | .129 | 1.250 | 20.69 |
| 1967 | 1.281 | 174.79 | .096 | .053 | .132 | 1.168 | 22.15 |
| 1968 | 1.309 | 181.57 | .075 | .054 | .134 | 1.194 | 23.36 |
| 1969 | 1.373 | 189.29 | .097 | .046 | .135 | 1.235 | 24.53 |
| 1970 | 1.431 | 195.13 | .098 | .049 | .136 | 1.246 | 25.81 |
| 1971 | 1.506 | 202.00 | .101 | .047 | .137 | 1.351 | 26.78 |
| 1972 | 1.602 | 209.98 | .099 | .045 | .139 | 1.366 | 27.99 |
| 1973 | 1.740 | 219.94 | .167 | .065 | .140 | 1.700 | 29.47 |

**Table 4.A.3C**
Private domestic labor input, 1947–1973, Canada

| Year | Private domestic persons engaged (1) | Private domestic hours per person (2) | Index of educational attainment (3) | Private domestic labor input price index (4) | quantity index (5) |
|------|------|------|------|------|------|
| 1947 | 4.479 | 1.100 | 0.923 | 0.440 | 17.71 |
| 1948 | 4.519 | 1.100 | 0.928 | 0.487 | 17.94 |
| 1949 | 4.611 | 1.091 | 0.932 | 0.507 | 18.24 |
| 1950 | 4.586 | 1.071 | 0.936 | 0.564 | 17.89 |
| 1951 | 4.694 | 1.062 | 0.941 | 0.643 | 18.26 |
| 1952 | 4.742 | 1.057 | 0.947 | 0.693 | 18.46 |
| 1953 | 4.785 | 1.055 | 0.952 | 0.730 | 18.71 |
| 1954 | 4.750 | 1.052 | 0.958 | 0.741 | 18.62 |
| 1955 | 4.843 | 1.043 | 0.964 | 0.775 | 18.94 |
| 1956 | 5.036 | 1.040 | 0.970 | 0.833 | 19.77 |
| 1957 | 5.136 | 1.028 | 0.976 | 0.885 | 20.04 |
| 1958 | 5.060 | 1.021 | 0.982 | 0.909 | 19.74 |
| 1959 | 5.198 | 1.018 | 0.988 | 0.931 | 20.36 |
| 1960 | 5.251 | 1.012 | 0.994 | 0.969 | 20.55 |
| 1961 | 5.172 | 1.000 | 1.000 | 1.000 | 20.13 |
| 1962 | 5.297 | 1.000 | 1.005 | 1.026 | 20.71 |
| 1963 | 5.405 | 0.992 | 1.010 | 1.068 | 21.07 |
| 1964 | 5.585 | 0.986 | 1.015 | 1.119 | 21.74 |
| 1965 | 5.789 | 0.978 | 1.019 | 1.198 | 22.45 |
| 1966 | 5.987 | 0.967 | 1.024 | 1.305 | 23.06 |
| 1967 | 6.103 | 0.961 | 1.029 | 1.402 | 23.50 |
| 1968 | 6.154 | 0.950 | 1.034 | 1.495 | 23.54 |
| 1969 | 6.305 | 0.941 | 1.039 | 1.630 | 24.00 |
| 1970 | 6.334 | 0.932 | 1.044 | 1.749 | 23.97 |
| 1971 | 6.465 | 0.926 | 1.049 | 1.875 | 24.44 |
| 1972 | 6.652 | 0.921 | 1.054 | 2.016 | 25.12 |
| 1973 | 6.986 | 0.921 | 1.059 | 2.130 | 26.51 |

**Table 4.A.4C**
Gross private domestic product and factor input, 1947–1973, Canada (constant dollars of 1961)

| Year | Gross private domestic product | | Relative share of investment goods product | Private domestic factor input | | Relative share of property compensation |
|---|---|---|---|---|---|---|
| | price index (1) | quantity index (2) | (3) | price index (4) | quantity index (5) | (6) |
| 1947 | 0.652 | 18.26 | .275 | 0.519 | 22.92 | .346 |
| 1948 | 0.740 | 18.91 | .294 | 0.586 | 23.89 | .376 |
| 1949 | 0.768 | 19.97 | .300 | 0.618 | 24.82 | .397 |
| 1950 | 0.781 | 22.01 | .307 | 0.681 | 25.24 | .413 |
| 1951 | 0.863 | 22.89 | .294 | 0.748 | 26.43 | .406 |
| 1952 | 0.897 | 25.04 | .297 | 0.819 | 27.43 | .430 |
| 1953 | 0.897 | 26.55 | .299 | 0.837 | 28.44 | .426 |
| 1954 | 0.898 | 26.40 | .296 | 0.810 | 29.26 | .418 |
| 1955 | 0.926 | 28.80 | .302 | 0.883 | 30.18 | .449 |
| 1956 | 0.934 | 31.68 | .327 | 0.830 | 31.80 | .443 |
| 1957 | 0.945 | 32.54 | .332 | 0.827 | 33.18 | .423 |
| 1958 | 0.961 | 33.37 | .313 | 0.948 | 33.84 | .441 |
| 1959 | 0.980 | 34.81 | .306 | 0.970 | 35.18 | .444 |
| 1960 | 1.000 | 35.84 | .897 | 0.992 | 36.13 | .444 |
| 1961 | 1.000 | 36.40 | .292 | 1.000 | 36.40 | .447 |
| 1962 | 0.996 | 38.65 | .300 | 1.024 | 37.58 | .448 |
| 1963 | 1.021 | 40.82 | .309 | 1.079 | 38.64 | .460 |
| 1964 | 1.049 | 43.76 | .313 | 1.144 | 40.12 | .470 |
| 1965 | 1.073 | 46.99 | .326 | 1.205 | 41.86 | .467 |
| 1966 | 1.115 | 50.20 | .336 | 1.279 | 43.76 | .462 |
| 1967 | 1.138 | 51.68 | .329 | 1.290 | 45.59 | .440 |
| 1968 | 1.157 | 54.51 | .330 | 1.350 | 46.72 | .442 |
| 1969 | 1.220 | 56.89 | .324 | 1.439 | 48.25 | .436 |
| 1970 | 1.254 | 59.07 | .324 | 1.502 | 49.31 | .434 |
| 1971 | 1.321 | 62.11 | .321 | 1.619 | 50.66 | .441 |
| 1972 | 1.361 | 65.32 | .323 | 1.695 | 52.45 | .430 |
| 1973 | 1.528 | 69.74 | .323 | 1.927 | 55.29 | .470 |

**Table 4.A.1F**
Gross private domestic product and factor outlay, 1970, France (billions of francs)

| | | Product | |
|---|---|---|---:|
| 1. | | Gross national product | 808.44 |
| 2. | – | Inventory valuation adjustment (our estimate) | −0.29 |
| 3. | – | Wages and salaries in general government | 72.17 |
| 4. | – | Capital consumption allowances in general government | 1.46 |
| 5. | – | Income originating in rest of world | 1.02 |
| 6. | + | Services of consumer durables (our imputation) | 42.92 |
| 7. | + | Services of durables held by institutions (our imputation) | 0.26 |
| 8. | + | Net rent on institutional real estate (our impuation) | 0.47 |
| 9. | – | Taxes not related to factor outlay | 26.25 |
| 10. | + | Production subsidies | 16.07 |
| 11. | + | Equipment and war damage subsidies | 8.95 |
| 12. | = | Gross private domestic product | 706.50 |

| | | Factor outlay | |
|---|---|---|---:|
| 1. | | National income | 619.30 |
| 2. | – | Inventory valuation adjustment (2 above) | −0.29 |
| 3. | + | Equipment and war damage subsidies (11 above) | 8.95 |
| 4. | + | Indirect taxes, French definition | 120.51 |
| 5. | – | Indirect taxes, our definition | 130.64 |
| 6. | + | Capital consumption allowances | 84.69 |
| 7. | + | Services of consumer durables (6 above) | 42.92 |
| 8. | + | Services of durables held by institutions (7 above) | 0.26 |
| 9. | + | Net rent on institutional real estate (8 above) | 0.47 |
| 10. | – | GNP originating in general government (3 + 4 above) | 73.63 |
| 11. | – | GNP originating in rest of world (5 above) | 1.02 |
| 12. | + | Indirect taxes related to factor outlay | 34.39 |
| 13. | = | Gross private domestic factor outlay | 706.50 |

**Table 4.A.2F**
Private domestic capital input, 1950–1973, France

| Year | Private domestic capital stock | | Rate of return to capital in the business sector | Services per unit of Stock | Private domestic capital input | |
|------|------------------------|------------------|------------------|------------------|------------------------|------------------|
| | price index (1) | quantity index (2) | nominal rate (3) | (4) | price index (5) | quantity index (6) |
| 1950 | .440 | 674.4 | .156 | .112 | .555 | 71.9 |
| 1951 | .512 | 697.8 | .228 | .113 | .535 | 75.9 |
| 1952 | .598 | 717.9 | .219 | .113 | .589 | 79.2 |
| 1953 | .607 | 744.1 | .084 | .115 | .648 | 82.3 |
| 1954 | .618 | 774.0 | .084 | .116 | .643 | 86.0 |
| 1955 | .636 | 806.4 | .094 | .117 | .652 | 90.2 |
| 1956 | .669 | 842.3 | .110 | .118 | .661 | 95.0 |
| 1957 | .723 | 877.6 | .141 | .119 | .705 | 100.3 |
| 1958 | .785 | 909.7 | .131 | .120 | .712 | 105.6 |
| 1959 | .833 | 940.9 | .107 | .121 | .767 | 110.5 |
| 1960 | .859 | 983.9 | .101 | .122 | .879 | 115.2 |
| 1961 | .895 | 1029.3 | .108 | .124 | .904 | 121.6 |
| 1962 | .938 | 1079.6 | .115 | .125 | .942 | 129.1 |
| 1963 | 1.000 | 1132.4 | .126 | .127 | 1.000 | 137.6 |
| 1964 | 1.052 | 1195.7 | .119 | .130 | 1.060 | 147.0 |
| 1965 | 1.094 | 1256.1 | .107 | .132 | 1.083 | 157.7 |
| 1966 | 1.133 | 1324.6 | .122 | .133 | 1.197 | 167.6 |
| 1967 | 1.176 | 1392.1 | .125 | .135 | 1.233 | 178.6 |
| 1968 | 1.226 | 1462.9 | .125 | .136 | 1.262 | 189.7 |
| 1969 | 1.313 | 1551.7 | .160 | .138 | 1.373 | 201.3 |
| 1970 | 1.399 | 1642.5 | .156 | .139 | 1.453 | 215.3 |
| 1971 | 1.480 | 1730.1 | .139 | .140 | 1.470 | 229.6 |
| 1972 | 1.452 | 1824.9 | .140 | .141 | 1.573 | 244.4 |
| 1973 | 1.674 | 1931.1 | .156 | .143 | 1.693 | 260.7 |

**Table 4.A.3F**
Private domestic labor input, 1950–1973, France

| Year | Private domestic persons engaged (1) | Private domestic hours per person (2) | Index of educational attainment (3) | Private domestic labor input price index (4) | Private domestic labor input quantity index (5) |
|------|------|------|------|------|------|
| 1950 | 17.613 | 1.010 | 0.937 | 0.246 | 207.4 |
| 1951 | 17.688 | 1.017 | 0.942 | 0.306 | 210.7 |
| 1952 | 17.616 | 1.010 | 0.947 | 0.370 | 209.6 |
| 1953 | 17.443 | 1.008 | 0.952 | 0.390 | 208.1 |
| 1954 | 17.458 | 1.011 | 0.957 | 0.419 | 210.1 |
| 1955 | 17.433 | 1.010 | 0.962 | 0.453 | 210.7 |
| 1956 | 17.402 | 1.012 | 0.966 | 0.500 | 211.7 |
| 1957 | 17.460 | 1.013 | 0.971 | 0.548 | 213.8 |
| 1958 | 17.395 | 1.004 | 0.976 | 0.629 | 212.2 |
| 1959 | 17.247 | 1.002 | 0.982 | 0.695 | 211.1 |
| 1960 | 17.260 | 1.011 | 0.987 | 0.742 | 214.2 |
| 1961 | 17.233 | 1.011 | 0.992 | 0.817 | 214.9 |
| 1962 | 17.301 | 1.010 | 0.996 | 0.901 | 216.5 |
| 1963 | 17.531 | 1.000 | 1.000 | 1.000 | 218.1 |
| 1964 | 17.779 | 0.995 | 1.004 | 1.084 | 221.0 |
| 1965 | 17.818 | 0.983 | 1.008 | 1.173 | 219.7 |
| 1966 | 17.888 | 0.987 | 1.013 | 1.188 | 222.5 |
| 1967 | 17.898 | 0.981 | 1.017 | 1.283 | 222.1 |
| 1968 | 17.820 | 0.974 | 1.021 | 1.430 | 220.6 |
| 1969 | 18.092 | 0.972 | 1.025 | 1.564 | 224.4 |
| 1970 | 18.318 | 0.963 | 1.030 | 1.741 | 226.1 |
| 1971 | 18.375 | 0.955 | 1.034 | 1.944 | 225.7 |
| 1972 | 18.449 | 0.944 | 1.038 | 2.181 | 225.0 |
| 1973 | 18.666 | 0.935 | 1.043 | 2.488 | 226.6 |

**Table 4.A.4F**
Gross private domestic product and factor input, 1950–1973, France (constant francs of 1963)

| Year | Gross private domestic product | | Private domestic factor input | |
|---|---|---|---|---|
| | price index (1) | quantity index (2) | price index (3) | quantity index (4) |
| 1950 | 0.498 | 182.6 | 0.338 | 269.2 |
| 1951 | 0.561 | 187.2 | 0.378 | 277.9 |
| 1952 | 0.643 | 193.1 | 0.441 | 281.4 |
| 1953 | 0.643 | 209.2 | 0.473 | 284.4 |
| 1954 | 0.652 | 219.9 | 0.492 | 291.0 |
| 1955 | 0.666 | 231.8 | 0.520 | 296.9 |
| 1956 | 0.695 | 242.7 | 0.555 | 303.6 |
| 1957 | 0.731 | 257.2 | 0.602 | 311.8 |
| 1958 | 0.799 | 261.1 | 0.660 | 316.3 |
| 1959 | 0.843 | 274.6 | 0.723 | 320.4 |
| 1960 | 0.871 | 298.6 | 0.792 | 328.5 |
| 1961 | 0.906 | 315.0 | 0.849 | 336.1 |
| 1962 | 0.943 | 335.7 | 0.916 | 345.4 |
| 1963 | 1.000 | 355.8 | 1.000 | 355.8 |
| 1964 | 1.030 | 384.1 | 1.075 | 367.9 |
| 1965 | 1.057 | 405.5 | 1.137 | 377.0 |
| 1966 | 1.082 | 429.5 | 1.194 | 389.5 |
| 1967 | 1.119 | 451.5 | 1.263 | 400.0 |
| 1968 | 1.176 | 471.7 | 1.356 | 409.0 |
| 1969 | 1.227 | 511.3 | 1.480 | 423.8 |
| 1970 | 1.300 | 543.6 | 1.611 | 438.5 |
| 1971 | 1.363 | 569.6 | 1.723 | 450.6 |
| 1972 | 1.455 | 601.4 | 1.894 | 462.2 |
| 1973 | 1.563 | 642.8 | 2.105 | 477.3 |

**Table 4.A.1G**
Gross private domestic product and factor outlay, 1970, Germany (billions of DM)

| | | Product | |
|---|---|---|---|
| 1. | | Gross national product | 685.6 |
| 2. | − | Labor compensation, government sector | 59.3 |
| 3. | − | Government contribution to legal accident insurance | 2.0 |
| 4. | − | Capital consumption, government | 3.7 |
| 5. | = | Private gross national product | 622.4 |
| 6. | + | Services of consumers' durables (our imputation) | 41.9 |
| 7. | − | Rest of world gross national product | −1.4 |
| 8. | − | Indirect taxes | 89.1 |
| 9. | + | Subsidies | 9.5 |
| 10. | + | Contribution to legal accident insurance, business and nonprofit institutions | 4.1 |
| 11. | + | Business tax | 12.1 |
| 12. | + | Real estate tax + fire protection tax (see 11) | 2.8 |
| 13. | + | Motor vehicle tax (see 11) | 3.8 |
| 14. | − | Motor vehicle tax, privatae households | 2.1 |
| 15. | = | Gross private domestic product | 606.7 |

| | | Factor outlay | |
|---|---|---|---|
| 1. | | Capital consumption allowances, business and nonprofit institutions | 71.1 |
| 2. | + | Services of consumer durables (our imputation) | 41.9 |
| 3. | + | Indirect tax on property (11 above + 12 + 13 − 14) | 16.6 |
| 4. | + | income originating in business, households, and nonprofit institutions | 473.0 |
| 5. | + | Contribution to legal accident insurance, business and nonprofit institutions (10 above) | 4.1 |
| 6. | = | Gross private domestic factor outlay | 606.7 |

**Table 4.A.2G**
Private domestic capital input, 1950–1973, Germany (billions of DM)

| Year | Private domestic capital stock | | Rate of return to capital in the business sector | Services per unit of Stock | Private domestic capital input | |
|------|-------|---------|---------|---------|-------|---------|
| | price index (1) | quantity index (2) | nominal rate (3) | (4) | price index (5) | quantity index (6) |
| 1950 | .724 | 402.4 | .046 | .132 | .593 | 50.1 |
| 1951 | .805 | 426.9 | .111 | .130 | .710 | 52.3 |
| 1952 | .839 | 455.9 | .078 | .129 | .809 | 55.1 |
| 1953 | .823 | 486.4 | .043 | .130 | .796 | 59.1 |
| 1954 | .814 | 522.3 | .049 | .130 | .798 | 63.3 |
| 1955 | .831 | 568.6 | .076 | .131 | .885 | 68.2 |
| 1956 | .843 | 615.4 | .069 | .131 | .895 | 74.5 |
| 1957 | .864 | 663.9 | .074 | .131 | .920 | 80.7 |
| 1958 | .882 | 712.9 | .067 | .131 | .905 | 87.2 |
| 1959 | .895 | 765.7 | .070 | .132 | .965 | 93.8 |
| 1960 | .923 | 829.6 | .082 | .131 | 1.035 | 100.4 |
| 1961 | .958 | 895.8 | .079 | .131 | 1.028 | 109.1 |
| 1962 | 1.000 | 963.5 | .075 | .132 | 1.000 | 118.0 |
| 1963 | 1.032 | 1026.6 | .070 | .133 | 1.006 | 127.8 |
| 1964 | 1.051 | 1103.3 | .066 | .133 | 1.064 | 136.7 |
| 1965 | 1.094 | 1188.4 | .081 | .134 | 1.095 | 147.7 |
| 1966 | 1.120 | 1263.2 | .067 | .135 | 1.074 | 160.5 |
| 1967 | 1.114 | 1318.0 | .043 | .136 | 1.022 | 171.5 |
| 1968 | 1.120 | 1390.7 | .061 | .136 | 1.131 | 178.7 |
| 1969 | 1.162 | 1482.5 | .078 | .136 | 1.182 | 188.8 |
| 1970 | 1.278 | 1584.1 | .119 | .137 | 1.236 | 202.7 |
| 1971 | 1.358 | 1685.5 | .090 | .138 | 1.241 | 218.8 |
| 1972 | 1.418 | 1786.9 | .080 | .140 | 1.280 | 235.2 |
| 1973 | 1.477 | 1888.7 | .077 | .140 | 1.323 | 250.3 |

**Table 4.A.3G**
Private domestic labor input, 1950–1973, Germany (billons of DM)

| Year | Private domestic persons engaged (1) | Private domestic hours per person (2) | Index of educational attainment (3) | Private domestic labor input price index (4) | quantity index (5) |
|------|------|------|------|------|------|
| 1950 | 19.4 | 1.146 | 0.991 | 0.344 | 168.4 |
| 1951 | 19.9 | 1.138 | 0.992 | 0.402 | 173.4 |
| 1952 | 20.3 | 1.136 | 0.992 | 0.432 | 177.3 |
| 1953 | 20.8 | 1.131 | 0.993 | 0.458 | 182.5 |
| 1954 | 21.4 | 1.132 | 0.994 | 0.480 | 188.9 |
| 1955 | 22.3 | 1.129 | 0.994 | 0.519 | 197.3 |
| 1956 | 22.9 | 1.112 | 0.995 | 0.570 | 200.3 |
| 1957 | 23.3 | 1.076 | 0.996 | 0.632 | 197.5 |
| 1958 | 23.5 | 1.057 | 0.997 | 0.688 | 195.8 |
| 1959 | 23.6 | 1.039 | 0.998 | 0.738 | 194.5 |
| 1961 | 24.0 | 1.030 | 0.999 | 0.806 | 196.9 |
| 1961 | 24.2 | 1.017 | 0.999 | 0.895 | 196.8 |
| 1962 | 24.2 | 1.000 | 1.000 | 1.000 | 193.7 |
| 1961 | 24.2 | 0.981 | 1.001 | 1.078 | 190.6 |
| 1964 | 24.1 | 0.995 | 1.001 | 1.154 | 193.0 |
| 1965 | 24.1 | 0.979 | 1.002 | 1.270 | 191.3 |
| 1966 | 24.0 | 0.967 | 1.003 | 1.378 | 187.8 |
| 1967 | 23.0 | 0.950 | 1.004 | 1.455 | 177.2 |
| 1968 | 23.0 | 0.963 | 1.005 | 1.530 | 180.5 |
| 1969 | 23.4 | 0.958 | 1.007 | 1.671 | 183.5 |
| 1970 | 23.6 | 0.950 | 1.008 | 1.930 | 184.5 |
| 1971 | 23.5 | 0.929 | 1.009 | 2.204 | 180.6 |
| 1972 | 23.4 | 0.919 | 1.010 | 2.442 | 177.8 |
| 1973 | 23.3 | 0.915 | 1.012 | 2.760 | 177.2 |

**Table 4.A.4G**
Gross private domestic product and factor input, 1950–1973, Germany
(constant DM of 1962)

| Year | Gross private domestic product | | Private domestic factor input | |
|---|---|---|---|---|
| | price index (1) | quantity index (2) | price index (3) | quantity index (4) |
| 1950 | 0.704 | 124.4 | 0.423 | 207.1 |
| 1951 | 0.779 | 137.3 | 0.499 | 214.4 |
| 1952 | 0.813 | 149.1 | 0.547 | 221.5 |
| 1953 | 0.805 | 162.3 | 0.564 | 231.4 |
| 1954 | 0.804 | 175.6 | 0.582 | 242.5 |
| 1955 | 0.821 | 198.2 | 0.636 | 256.2 |
| 1956 | 0.842 | 214.9 | 0.677 | 267.2 |
| 1957 | 0.868 | 229.6 | 0.730 | 272.8 |
| 1958 | 0.894 | 239.0 | 0.765 | 279.2 |
| 1959 | 0.908 | 257.8 | 0.819 | 285.8 |
| 1960 | 0.926 | 283.5 | 0.888 | 295.7 |
| 1961 | 0.963 | 299.5 | 0.944 | 305.4 |
| 1962 | 1.000 | 311.8 | 1.000 | 311.8 |
| 1963 | 1.028 | 325.0 | 1.050 | 318.2 |
| 1964 | 1.054 | 349.2 | 1.118 | 329.0 |
| 1965 | 1.088 | 371.9 | 1.199 | 337.6 |
| 1966 | 1.119 | 385.3 | 1.249 | 345.1 |
| 1967 | 1.124 | 385.4 | 1.265 | 342.3 |
| 1968 | 1.148 | 416.8 | 1.359 | 352.0 |
| 1969 | 1.185 | 447.2 | 1.456 | 363.7 |
| 1970 | 1.264 | 479.9 | 1.614 | 375.9 |
| 1971 | 1.352 | 495.0 | 1.748 | 382.9 |
| 1972 | 1.421 | 517.2 | 1.881 | 390.7 |
| 1973 | 1.493 | 549.5 | 2.051 | 400.1 |

**Table 4.A.1I**
Gross private domestic product and factor outlay, 1970, Italy (trillions of lire)

| | | Product | |
|---|---|---|---|
| 1. | | Gross national product | 58.26 |
| 2. | − | Wages and salaries in general government | 5.26 |
| 3. | − | Capital consumption allowances and property income of general government | 0.36 |
| 4. | − | Rest of world gross national product | 0.32 |
| 5. | + | Service of consumer durables (our imputation) | 4.00 |
| 6. | − | Taxes not related to factor outlay | 5.94 |
| 7. | + | Subsidies | 0.90 |
| 8. | = | Gross private domestic product | 51.29 |

| | | Factor outlay | |
|---|---|---|---|
| 1. | | National income, gross of capital consumption allowances | 52.21 |
| 2. | + | Services of consumer durables (our imputation) | 4.00 |
| 3. | − | GNP originating in general government (2 + 3 above) | 5.62 |
| 4. | − | Direct taxes per the national accounts | 3.56 |
| 5. | + | Direct taxes (our estimate) | 3.08 |
| 6. | + | Indirect taxes (our estimate) | 7.43 |
| 7. | − | Taxes not related to factor outlay | 5.94 |
| 8. | − | GNP originating in rest of world | 0.32 |
| 9. | = | Gross private domestic factor outlay | 51.29 |

**Table 4.A.2I**
Private domestic capital input, 1952–1973, Italy

| Year | Private domestic capital stock | | Rate of return to capital in the business sector | Services per unit of Stock | Private domestic capital input | |
|------|------------------------|------------------------|-------------------|-------------------|------------------------|------------------------|
| | price index (1) | quantity index (2) | nominal rate (3) | (4) | price index (5) | quantity index (6) |
| 1952 | .802 | 50.35 | .061 | .134 | .629 | 6.66 |
| 1953 | .802 | 51.47 | .056 | .135 | .688 | 6.79 |
| 1954 | .805 | 52.68 | .045 | .135 | .665 | 6.97 |
| 1955 | .815 | 54.51 | .073 | .136 | .727 | 7.16 |
| 1956 | .833 | 56.52 | .082 | .136 | .755 | 7.41 |
| 1957 | .858 | 58.74 | .094 | .136 | .786 | 7.70 |
| 1958 | .860 | 60.95 | .068 | .136 | .813 | 8.01 |
| 1959 | .857 | 63.54 | .064 | .136 | .844 | 8.31 |
| 1960 | .873 | 66.89 | .095 | .136 | .888 | 8.67 |
| 1961 | .892 | 71.03 | .109 | .137 | .956 | 9.15 |
| 1962 | .935 | 75.65 | .126 | .138 | 1.005 | 9.78 |
| 1963 | 1.000 | 80.81 | .144 | .139 | 1.000 | 10.49 |
| 1964 | 1.073 | 84.79 | .126 | .140 | .993 | 11.33 |
| 1965 | 1.091 | 88.10 | .090 | .140 | 1.006 | 11.91 |
| 1966 | 1.108 | 91.60 | .097 | .140 | 1.087 | 12.34 |
| 1967 | 1.136 | 96.06 | .103 | .140 | 1.138 | 12.83 |
| 1968 | 1.163 | 100.59 | .102 | .141 | 1.171 | 13.51 |
| 1969 | 1.238 | 105.92 | .151 | .141 | 1.293 | 14.18 |
| 1970 | 1.383 | 111.82 | .186 | .141 | 1.283 | 14.95 |
| 1971 | 1.468 | 116.65 | .113 | .142 | 1.136 | 15.87 |
| 1972 | 1.544 | 121.39 | .094 | .143 | 1.182 | 16.67 |
| 1973 | 1.791 | 127.17 | .196 | .144 | 1.356 | 17.46 |

**Table 4.A.3I**
Private domestic labor input, 1952–1973, Italy

| Year | Private domestic persons engaged (1) | Private domestic hours per person (2) | Index of educational attainment (3) | Private domestic labor input | |
|------|------|------|------|------|------|
| | | | | price index (4) | quantity index (5) |
| 1952 | 15.343 | 0.920 | 0.946 | 0.399 | 14.58 |
| 1953 | 15.661 | 0.938 | 0.948 | 0.429 | 15.05 |
| 1954 | 16.044 | 0.959 | 0.951 | 0.455 | 15.64 |
| 1955 | 16.096 | 0.959 | 0.953 | 0.495 | 15.62 |
| 1956 | 16.241 | 0.955 | 0.956 | 0.541 | 15.61 |
| 1957 | 16.410 | 0.968 | 0.958 | 0.570 | 15.90 |
| 1958 | 16.565 | 0.967 | 0.960 | 0.608 | 15.94 |
| 1959 | 16.497 | 0.975 | 0.963 | 0.634 | 16.09 |
| 1960 | 16.677 | 1.004 | 0.965 | 0.672 | 16.53 |
| 1961 | 16.808 | 1.001 | 0.977 | 0.731 | 16.67 |
| 1962 | 16.761 | 0.982 | 0.988 | 0.849 | 16.32 |
| 1963 | 16.667 | 1.000 | 1.000 | 1.000 | 16.47 |
| 1964 | 16.654 | 0.958 | 1.013 | 1.157 | 15.91 |
| 1965 | 16.262 | 0.903 | 1.026 | 1.289 | 14.85 |
| 1966 | 16.048 | 0.934 | 1.040 | 1.340 | 15.26 |
| 1967 | 16.281 | 0.943 | 1.053 | 1.448 | 15.78 |
| 1968 | 16.299 | 0.947 | 1.067 | 1.543 | 15.99 |
| 1969 | 16.440 | 0.915 | 1.081 | 1.723 | 15.68 |
| 1970 | 16.536 | 0.921 | 1.095 | 2.009 | 15.98 |
| 1971 | 16.496 | 0.890 | 1.110 | 2.329 | 15.58 |
| 1972 | 16.334 | 0.870 | 1.124 | 2.621 | 15.18 |
| 1973 | 16.507 | 0.849 | 1.139 | 3.200 | 15.11 |

**Table 4.A.4I**
Gross private domestic product and factor input, 1952–1973, Italy (constant lire of 1963)

| Year | Gross private domestic product | | Private domestic factor input | |
|------|-------------|----------------|-------------|----------------|
|      | price index (1) | quantity index (2) | price index (3) | quantity index (4) |
| 1952 | 0.728 | 13.73 | 0.480 | 20.85 |
| 1953 | 0.742 | 14.99 | 0.520 | 21.41 |
| 1954 | 0.756 | 15.54 | 0.531 | 22.14 |
| 1955 | 0.767 | 16.87 | 0.578 | 22.36 |
| 1956 | 0.794 | 17.69 | 0.619 | 22.66 |
| 1957 | 0.817 | 18.51 | 0.650 | 23.26 |
| 1958 | 0.827 | 19.58 | 0.684 | 23.67 |
| 1959 | 0.824 | 20.89 | 0.713 | 24.16 |
| 1960 | 0.844 | 22.27 | 0.753 | 24.98 |
| 1961 | 0.864 | 24.22 | 0.815 | 25.68 |
| 1962 | 0.921 | 25.72 | 0.909 | 26.07 |
| 1963 | 1.000 | 26.96 | 1.000 | 26.96 |
| 1964 | 1.064 | 27.89 | 1.091 | 27.19 |
| 1965 | 1.079 | 28.85 | 1.172 | 26.55 |
| 1966 | 1.110 | 30.50 | 1.237 | 27.37 |
| 1967 | 1.142 | 32.81 | 1.320 | 28.37 |
| 1968 | 1.169 | 34.66 | 1.388 | 29.18 |
| 1969 | 1.231 | 36.83 | 1.543 | 29.40 |
| 1970 | 1.321 | 38.82 | 1.689 | 30.36 |
| 1971 | 1.437 | 37.81 | 1.781 | 30.50 |
| 1972 | 1.529 | 38.89 | 1.952 | 30.46 |
| 1973 | 1.743 | 41.32 | 2.336 | 30.84 |

**Table 4.A.1J**
Gross private domestic product and factor outlay, 1970, Japan (trillions of yen)

| | | Product | |
|---|---|---|---|
| 1. | | Gross national product | 70.73 |
| 2. | − | Net factor income from abroad | −0.16 |
| 3. | + | Services of consumer durables | 2.41 |
| 4. | − | Compensation of employees by public administration (general government) | 2.16 |
| 5. | − | Rent, interest, and dividends by general government | 0.60 |
| 6. | + | Interest and dividends by general government | 0.42 |
| 7. | = | Gross private domestic product before sales tax | 70.96 |
| 8. | − | Indirect taxes | 5.31 |
| 9. | + | Monopoly profit | 0.27 |
| 10. | + | Current subsidies | 0.77 |
| 11. | + | Business tax (corporate + noncorporate) | 0.92 |
| 12. | + | Real estate acquisition tax | 0.09 |
| 13. | + | Motor vehicle tax (prefectural + municipal) | 0.19 |
| 14. | + | Mine-lot tax | 0.00 |
| 15. | + | Fixed estate tax (prefectural + municipal) | 0.52 |
| 16. | = | Gross private domestic product | 68.41 |

| | | Factor outlay | |
|---|---|---|---|
| 1. | | Provisions for the consumption of fixed capital | 9.49 |
| 2. | + | Statistical discrepancy | −0.21 |
| 3. | + | Compensation of employees | 31.02 |
| 4. | − | Compensation of employees by public administration | 2.16 |
| 5. | + | Income from unincorporated enterprises | 11.16 |
| 6. | + | Income from property, rent | 2.56 |
| 7. | + | Income from property, interest | 3.29 |
| 8. | − | Interest on consumer's debt | 0.24 |
| 9. | − | Interest on public debt | 0.42 |
| 10. | + | Income from property, dividends | 0.80 |
| 11. | + | Corporate transfers to households and nonprofit institutions | 0.10 |
| 12. | + | Direct taxes and charges on private corporations | 3.22 |
| 13. | + | Saving of private corporations | 4.71 |
| 14. | + | Profit from government enterprises | 0.09 |
| 15. | + | Monopoly profit | 0.27 |
| 16. | − | Net factor income from abroad | −0.16 |
| 17. | + | Services from consumer durables | 2.41 |
| 18. | + | Interest and dividends by general government | 0.42 |
| 19. | + | Certain indirect taxes (above 11 + 12 + 13 + 14 + 15) | 1.72 |
| 20. | = | Gross private domestic factor outlay | 68.41 |

**Table 4.A.2J**
Private domestic capital input, 1952–1973, Japan (trillions of yen)

| Year | Private domestic capital stock | | Rate of return to capital in the business sector | Services per unit of Stock | Private domestic capital input | |
|------|-------|----------|---------|---------|-------|----------|
| | price index | quantity index | nominal rate | | price index | quantity index |
| | (1) | (2) | (3) | (4) | (5) | (6) |
| 1952 | .439 | 45.96 | .102 | .145 | .349 | 6.55 |
| 1953 | .468 | 46.89 | .091 | .144 | .338 | 6.64 |
| 1954 | .483 | 47.67 | .066 | .141 | .372 | 6.62 |
| 1955 | .497 | 48.90 | .085 | .141 | .400 | 6.73 |
| 1956 | .560 | 51.02 | .193 | .140 | .465 | 6.84 |
| 1957 | .611 | 54.17 | .150 | .145 | .507 | 7.40 |
| 1958 | .624 | 56.13 | .067 | .154 | .446 | 8.33 |
| 1959 | .652 | 58.71 | .097 | .157 | .496 | 8.79 |
| 1960 | .683 | 62.76 | .121 | .160 | .603 | 9.42 |
| 1961 | .723 | 69.39 | .152 | .167 | .744 | 10.51 |
| 1962 | .736 | 74.64 | .093 | .177 | .653 | 12.29 |
| 1963 | .747 | 80.74 | .098 | .184 | .667 | 13.76 |
| 1964 | .764 | 88.25 | .129 | .186 | .771 | 15.05 |
| 1965 | .781 | 94.44 | .115 | .192 | .725 | 16.91 |
| 1966 | .815 | 101.37 | .147 | .196 | .795 | 18.48 |
| 1967 | .859 | 111.47 | .180 | .198 | .902 | 20.08 |
| 1968 | .904 | 123.92 | .199 | .203 | .977 | 22.58 |
| 1969 | .949 | 137.68 | .190 | .210 | .980 | 25.98 |
| 1970 | 1.000 | 154.29 | .190 | .217 | 1.000 | 29.84 |
| 1971 | 1.019 | 169.55 | .126 | .224 | .905 | 34.58 |
| 1972 | 1.075 | 185.02 | .157 | .231 | .909 | 39.10 |
| 1973 | 1.282 | 203.67 | .291 | .237 | .980 | 43.86 |

**Table 4.A.3J**
Private domestic labor input, 1952–1973, Japan (trillions of yen)

| Year | Private domestic persons engaged (1) | Private domestic hours per person (2) | Index of educational attainment (3) | Private domestic labor input | |
|------|------|------|------|------|------|
| | | | | price index (4) | quantity index (5) |
| 1952 | 22.72 | 1.026 | 0.936 | 0.183 | 20.23 |
| 1953 | 23.65 | 1.036 | 0.935 | 0.210 | 21.25 |
| 1954 | 24.20 | 1.031 | 0.943 | 0.224 | 21.83 |
| 1955 | 25.32 | 1.038 | 0.932 | 0.234 | 22.73 |
| 1956 | 26.61 | 1.062 | 0.936 | 0.240 | 24.54 |
| 1957 | 28.02 | 1.056 | 0.938 | 0.257 | 25.76 |
| 1958 | 29.08 | 1.055 | 0.937 | 0.264 | 26.67 |
| 1959 | 29.91 | 1.066 | 0.944 | 0.275 | 27.92 |
| 1960 | 31.15 | 1.080 | 0.949 | 0.298 | 29.61 |
| 1961 | 31.78 | 1.071 | 0.950 | 0.342 | 29.98 |
| 1962 | 33.02 | 1.054 | 0.950 | 0.391 | 30.65 |
| 1963 | 33.93 | 1.047 | 0.955 | 0.441 | 31.47 |
| 1964 | 34.91 | 1.043 | 0.960 | 0.490 | 32.43 |
| 1965 | 36.81 | 1.028 | 0.964 | 0.539 | 33.84 |
| 1966 | 37.68 | 1.029 | 0.966 | 0.596 | 34.76 |
| 1967 | 38.92 | 1.028 | 0.973 | 0.662 | 36.11 |
| 1968 | 40.02 | 1.027 | 0.981 | 0.745 | 37.38 |
| 1969 | 40.69 | 1.012 | 0.992 | 0.851 | 37.91 |
| 1970 | 41.59 | 1.000 | 1.000 | 1.000 | 38.58 |
| 1971 | 42.24 | 0.989 | 1.007 | 1.158 | 39.03 |
| 1972 | 42.80 | 0.984 | 1.014 | 1.316 | 39.59 |
| 1973 | 44.25 | 0.975 | 1.022 | 1.605 | 40.92 |

**Table 4.A.4J**
Gross private domestic product and factor input, 1952–1973, Japan (constant yen of 1970)

| Year | Gross private domestic product | | Private domestic factor input | |
|---|---|---|---|---|
| | price index (1) | quantity index (2) | price index (3) | quantity index (4) |
| 1952 | 0.533 | 11.21 | 0.241 | 24.77 |
| 1953 | 0.544 | 12.32 | 0.261 | 25.69 |
| 1954 | 0.560 | 13.13 | 0.281 | 26.13 |
| 1955 | 0.550 | 14.56 | 0.297 | 26.98 |
| 1956 | 0.597 | 15.19 | 0.318 | 28.55 |
| 1957 | 0.619 | 16.74 | 0.342 | 30.28 |
| 1958 | 0.600 | 17.93 | 0.333 | 32.30 |
| 1959 | 0.627 | 19.20 | 0.355 | 33.90 |
| 1960 | 0.676 | 21.48 | 0.402 | 36.10 |
| 1961 | 0.704 | 25.65 | 0.475 | 38.04 |
| 1962 | 0.701 | 28.53 | 0.486 | 41.14 |
| 1963 | 0.725 | 31.81 | 0.528 | 43.72 |
| 1964 | 0.768 | 35.83 | 0.596 | 46.16 |
| 1965 | 0.774 | 39.41 | 0.614 | 49.66 |
| 1966 | 0.832 | 42.54 | 0.676 | 52.33 |
| 1967 | 0.881 | 47.67 | 0.758 | 55.41 |
| 1968 | 0.924 | 54.01 | 0.840 | 59.46 |
| 1969 | 0.955 | 60.47 | 0.905 | 63.75 |
| 1970 | 1.000 | 68.41 | 1.000 | 68.41 |
| 1971 | 1.019 | 75.07 | 1.044 | 73.31 |
| 1972 | 1.074 | 81.63 | 1.128 | 77.72 |
| 1973 | 1.228 | 88.49 | 1.309 | 83.01 |

**Table 4.A.1K**
Gross private domestic product and factor outlay, 1970, Korea (billions of won)

| | | Product | |
|---|---|---|---|
| 1. | | Gross national product | 2,589.3 |
| 2. | − | Wages and salaries in general government | 186.9 |
| 3. | − | Capital consumption allowances in general government | 4.8 |
| 4. | − | General government income from property | 58.8 |
| 5. | − | Rest of world gross national product | 11.9 |
| 6. | + | Services of consumer durables | 89.4 |
| 7. | − | Taxes not related to factor outlay | 197.8 |
| 8. | + | Subsidies | 0.7 |
| 9. | − | Statistical discrepancy | −32.2 |
| 10. | = | Gross private domestic product | 2,251.5 |

| | | Factor outlay | |
|---|---|---|---|
| 1. | | National income | 2,177.7 |
| 2. | + | Capital consumption allowances | 160.2 |
| 3. | + | Services of consumer durables (our imputation) | 89.4 |
| 4. | − | GNP originating in general government (2 + 3 + 4 above) | 250.4 |
| 5. | − | Direct taxes on corporations per the national accounts | 42.7 |
| 6. | + | Direct taxes on corporations (our estimates) | 72.5 |
| 7. | − | Direct taxes on households per the national accounts | 98.9 |
| 8. | + | Direct taxes on households (our estimate) | 86.0 |
| 9. | + | Indirect taxes | 235.3 |
| 10. | − | Taxes not related to factor outlay | 197.8 |
| 11. | − | GNP originating in rest of world | 11.9 |
| 12. | − | Statistical discrepancy | −32.2 |
| 13. | = | Gross private domestic factor outlay | 2,251.5 |

**Table 4.A.2K**
Private domestic capital input, 1960–1973, Korea

| Year | Private domestic capital stock | | Rate of return to capital in the business sector | Services per unit of Stock | Private domestic capital input | |
|---|---|---|---|---|---|---|
| | price index (1) | quantity index (2) | nominal rate (3) | (4) | price index (5) | quantity index (6) |
| 1960 | .174 | 4971.0 | .152 | .087 | .159 | 433.7 |
| 1961 | .203 | 5010.8 | .306 | .088 | .237 | 436.1 |
| 1962 | .231 | 5057.9 | .239 | .088 | .267 | 442.0 |
| 1963 | .266 | 5260.9 | .312 | .090 | .381 | 453.8 |
| 1964 | .346 | 5409.4 | .407 | .090 | .564 | 472.0 |
| 1965 | .413 | 5548.6 | .267 | .091 | .580 | 489.6 |
| 1966 | .498 | 5848.8 | .273 | .091 | .689 | 505.0 |
| 1967 | .572 | 6183.4 | .203 | .094 | .651 | 551.7 |
| 1968 | .678 | 6591.1 | .227 | .100 | .750 | 618.0 |
| 1969 | .868 | 7069.2 | .243 | .107 | .843 | 704.9 |
| 1970 | 1.000 | 7483.0 | .237 | .113 | 1.000 | 800.2 |
| 1971 | 1.173 | 7894.2 | .222 | .118 | 1.033 | 880.9 |
| 1972 | 1.329 | 8192.4 | .235 | .122 | 1.234 | 964.3 |
| 1973 | 1.541 | 8709.9 | .269 | .124 | 1.613 | 1018.3 |

**Table 4.A.3K**
Private domestic labor input, 1960–1973, Korea

| Year | Private domestic persons engaged (1) | Private domestic hours per person (2) | Index of educational attainment (3) | Private domestic labor input | |
|---|---|---|---|---|---|
| | | | | price index (4) | quantity index (5) |
| 1960 | 6.785 | .982 | .887 | .155 | 920.2 |
| 1961 | 6.975 | 1.003 | .898 | .163 | 977.9 |
| 1962 | 7.170 | .982 | .909 | .190 | 996.4 |
| 1963 | 7.374 | .982 | .920 | .249 | 1038.0 |
| 1964 | 7.504 | .952 | .931 | .352 | 1036.0 |
| 1965 | 7.891 | .994 | .943 | .378 | 1151.5 |
| 1966 | 8.093 | .987 | .954 | .472 | 1186.7 |
| 1967 | 8.361 | 1.000 | .965 | .598 | 1256.8 |
| 1968 | 8.772 | 1.019 | .977 | .662 | 1359.9 |
| 1969 | 9.021 | 1.043 | .988 | .822 | 1448.5 |
| 1970 | 9.317 | 1.000 | 1.000 | 1.000 | 1451.3 |
| 1971 | 9.604 | 1.024 | 1.012 | 1.135 | 1550.5 |
| 1972 | 10.081 | 1.029 | 1.024 | 1.312 | 1653.5 |
| 1973 | 10.644 | 1.029 | 1.036 | 1.530 | 1766.6 |

**Table 4.A.4K**
Gross private domestic product and factor input, 1960–1973, Korea (constant won of 1970)

| | Gross private domestic product | | Private domestic factor input | |
|---|---|---|---|---|
| Year | price index (1) | quantity index (2) | price index (3) | quantity index (4) |
| 1960 | 0.228 | 925.8 | 0.155 | 1358.0 |
| 1961 | 0.270 | 975.2 | 0.186 | 1414.8 |
| 1962 | 0.306 | 1004.0 | 0.213 | 1438.6 |
| 1963 | 0.389 | 1106.5 | 0.289 | 1490.2 |
| 1964 | 0.535 | 1178.3 | 0.417 | 1512.8 |
| 1965 | 0.568 | 1265.2 | 0.440 | 1634.6 |
| 1966 | 0.635 | 1430.9 | 0.539 | 1685.1 |
| 1967 | 0.713 | 1556.1 | 0.615 | 1804.4 |
| 1968 | 0.778 | 1751.2 | 0.690 | 1975.0 |
| 1969 | 0.854 | 2090.4 | 0.829 | 2152.6 |
| 1970 | 1.000 | 2251.5 | 1.000 | 2251.5 |
| 1971 | 1.087 | 2456.0 | 1.098 | 2430.6 |
| 1972 | 1.252 | 2683.6 | 1.284 | 2615.7 |
| 1973 | 1.346 | 3249.5 | 1.562 | 2782.7 |

**Table 4.A.1N**
Gross private domestic product and factor outlay, 1970, Netherlands (billions of guilders)

| | | Product | |
|---|---|---|---|
| 1. | | Gross national product | 114.98 |
| 2. | − | Wages and salaries in general government | 13.48 |
| 3. | − | Capital consumption allowances in general government | 0.80 |
| 4. | − | Taxes paid by government | 0.04 |
| 5. | − | GNP originating in rest of world | 0.41 |
| 6. | + | Service of consumers durables (our imputation) | 13.58 |
| 7. | − | Taxes not related to factor outlay | 11.09 |
| 8. | + | Subsidies | 1.52 |
| 9. | = | Gross private domestic product | 104.26 |

| | | Factor outlay | |
|---|---|---|---|
| 1. | | National income | 93.70 |
| 2. | + | Capital consumption allowances | 9.73 |
| 3. | + | Services of consumer durables (our imputation) | 13.58 |
| 4. | − | National income originating in general government (2 + 3) | 14.28 |
| 5. | − | Indirect taxes considered direct by Netherlands national accounts | 0.71 |
| 6. | + | Indirect taxes related to factor outlay | 1.94 |
| 7. | − | GNP originating in rest of world | 0.41 |
| 8. | = | Gross private domestic factor outlay | 104.26 |

**Table 4.A.2N**
Private domestic capital input, 1951–1973, Netherlands

| Year | Private domestic capital stock | | Rate of return to capital in the business sector | Services per unit of Stock | Private domestic capital input | |
|------|------------------|-------------------|-------------------|-----------------|----------------|-------------------|
| | price index (1) | quantity index (2) | nominal rate (3) | (4) | price index (5) | quantity index (6) |
| 1951 | .620 | 124.21 | .199 | .098 | .796 | 11.77 |
| 1952 | .666 | 125.15 | .121 | .097 | .827 | 12.08 |
| 1953 | .656 | 127.22 | .042 | .097 | .827 | 12.13 |
| 1954 | .697 | 132.15 | .135 | .097 | .910 | 12.39 |
| 1955 | .728 | 137.68 | .115 | .099 | 1.011 | 13.05 |
| 1956 | .777 | 144.15 | .137 | .100 | 1.047 | 13.79 |
| 1957 | .826 | 150.81 | .127 | .102 | 1.034 | 14.71 |
| 1958 | .840 | 154.73 | .071 | .104 | .947 | 15.65 |
| 1959 | .842 | 159.63 | .067 | .105 | .972 | 16.20 |
| 1960 | .862 | 166.86 | .091 | .106 | 1.054 | 16.89 |
| 1961 | .881 | 174.39 | .081 | .108 | 1.013 | 17.95 |
| 1962 | .935 | 181.49 | .124 | .111 | 1.001 | 19.28 |
| 1963 | 1.000 | 188.11 | .127 | .114 | 1.000 | 20.73 |
| 1964 | 1.055 | 198.01 | .113 | .117 | 1.079 | 22.09 |
| 1965 | 1.109 | 207.95 | .108 | .120 | 1.126 | 23.75 |
| 1966 | 1.164 | 217.72 | .096 | .123 | 1.089 | 25.58 |
| 1967 | 1.179 | 228.01 | .064 | .125 | 1.131 | 27.20 |
| 1968 | 1.221 | 239.11 | .087 | .126 | 1.218 | 28.80 |
| 1969 | 1.287 | 251.19 | .104 | .128 | 1.279 | 30.56 |
| 1970 | 1.361 | 265.83 | .109 | .129 | 1.327 | 32.45 |
| 1971 | 1.496 | 278.86 | .143 | .132 | 1.392 | 35.02 |
| 1972 | 1.636 | 290.99 | .144 | .134 | 1.493 | 37.45 |
| 1973 | 1.779 | 304.25 | .133 | .137 | 1.550 | 39.83 |

**Table 4.A.3N**
Private domestic labor input, 1951–1973, Netherlands

| Year | Private domestic persons engaged (1) | Private domestic hours per person (2) | Index of educational attainment (3) | Private domestic labor input price index (4) | Private domestic labor input quantity index (5) |
|------|------|------|------|------|------|
| 1951 | 3.411 | 1.041 | 0.942 | 0.451 | 23.06 |
| 1952 | 3.367 | 1.043 | 0.946 | 0.473 | 22.92 |
| 1953 | 3.417 | 1.047 | 0.951 | 0.489 | 23.48 |
| 1954 | 3.483 | 1.047 | 0.956 | 0.530 | 24.05 |
| 1955 | 3.547 | 1.047 | 0.961 | 0.573 | 24.61 |
| 1956 | 3.602 | 1.047 | 0.966 | 0.619 | 25.12 |
| 1957 | 3.619 | 1.043 | 0.970 | 0.683 | 25.26 |
| 1958 | 3.580 | 1.043 | 0.975 | 0.711 | 25.11 |
| 1959 | 3.620 | 1.047 | 0.980 | 0.723 | 25.63 |
| 1960 | 3.692 | 1.047 | 0.985 | 0.780 | 26.27 |
| 1961 | 3.746 | 0.998 | 0.990 | 0.876 | 25.52 |
| 1962 | 3.825 | 0.998 | 0.995 | 0.926 | 26.19 |
| 1963 | 3.878 | 1.000 | 1.000 | 1.000 | 26.75 |
| 1964 | 3.952 | 0.989 | 1.005 | 1.157 | 27.10 |
| 1965 | 3.986 | 0.989 | 1.010 | 1.278 | 27.47 |
| 1966 | 4.009 | 0.989 | 1.015 | 1.408 | 27.77 |
| 1967 | 3.986 | 0.972 | 1.020 | 1.530 | 27.26 |
| 1968 | 4.021 | 0.972 | 1.025 | 1.659 | 27.64 |
| 1969 | 4.083 | 0.968 | 1.030 | 1.903 | 28.08 |
| 1970 | 4.129 | 0.948 | 1.036 | 2.188 | 27.97 |
| 1971 | 4.140 | 0.940 | 1.041 | 2.458 | 27.93 |
| 1972 | 4.082 | 0.931 | 1.046 | 2.807 | 27.43 |
| 1973 | 4.085 | 0.923 | 1.051 | 3.249 | 27.33 |

**Table 4.A.4N**
Gross private domestic product and factor input, 1951–1973, Netherlands
(constant guilders of 1963)

| Year | Gross private domestic product | | Private domestic factor input | |
|---|---|---|---|---|
| | price index (1) | quantity index (2) | price index (3) | quantity index (4) |
| 1951 | 0.728 | 27.15 | 0.586 | 33.76 |
| 1952 | 0.756 | 27.55 | 0.611 | 34.08 |
| 1953 | 0.724 | 29.71 | 0.622 | 34.57 |
| 1954 | 0.755 | 31.83 | 0.679 | 35.37 |
| 1955 | 0.799 | 34.19 | 0.744 | 36.71 |
| 1956 | 0.831 | 36.08 | 0.787 | 38.09 |
| 1957 | 0.869 | 37.39 | 0.824 | 39.39 |
| 1958 | 0.922 | 35.45 | 0.809 | 40.40 |
| 1959 | 0.875 | 39.17 | 0.826 | 41.50 |
| 1960 | 0.902 | 42.43 | 0.893 | 42.87 |
| 1961 | 0.923 | 43.92 | 0.934 | 43.39 |
| 1962 | 0.948 | 45.93 | 0.958 | 45.45 |
| 1963 | 1.000 | 47.47 | 1.000 | 47.47 |
| 1964 | 1.056 | 52.26 | 1.122 | 49.16 |
| 1965 | 1.112 | 55.58 | 1.210 | 51.12 |
| 1966 | 1.164 | 57.53 | 1.262 | 53.08 |
| 1967 | 1.199 | 60.45 | 1.344 | 53.90 |
| 1968 | 1.247 | 64.88 | 1.454 | 55.68 |
| 1969 | 1.333 | 69.40 | 1.606 | 57.63 |
| 1970 | 1.405 | 74.20 | 1.769 | 58.95 |
| 1971 | 1.503 | 78.14 | 1.932 | 60.79 |
| 1972 | 1.598 | 83.16 | 2.148 | 61.86 |
| 1973 | 1.721 | 87.46 | 2.377 | 63.33 |

# 5 Relative Productivity Levels, 1947–1973: An International Comparison

Laurits R. Christensen,
Dianne Cummings, and
Dale W. Jorgenson

## 5.1 Introduction

The purpose of this paper is to provide an international comparison of levels of output, input, and productivity for the United States and eight of its major trading partners—Canada, France, Germany, Italy, Japan, Korea, The Netherlands, and the United Kingdom. Our first objective is to compare levels of output per capita in 1970 and to allocate differences in these levels among differences in levels of capital and labor input per capita and differences in total factor productivity.[1] We present the results of this comparison in section 5.3 below.

A comparison of levels of output requires data on the relative prices of output among all the countries included in the comparison. The traditional approach of using exchange rates to estimate relative prices of output is well-known to be unsatisfactory. Reliable data for international price comparisons must be based on direct observations of prices for comparable products. Such data have been developed for sixteen countries by Kravis, Heston and Summers (1978a), who provide comparisons of relative prices and quantities of output for 1970. Except for Canada, the nine countries included in our study are among the sixteen countries analyzed by Kravis, Heston and Summers. Since relative output prices are available for the United States and Canada, we are also able to include Canada in our comparison.

Comparisons of levels of capital and labor input and levels of total factor productivity require data on relative prices for inputs. We have developed data on relative prices for capital and labor inputs for all nine countries. We obtain relative price levels of capital input among countries via relative investment goods prices, taking into account the flow of capital input per unit of capital stock in each country. We obtain relative wage levels for labor input from hourly wage rates, taking into account differences in levels of educational attainment among countries.

Our methodology for international comparisons of output, input and total factor productivity, which is presented in section 5.2, is based on the economic theory of production. We specify a flexible structure of production for all nine countries. In particular, we specify that each country has a translog production function, which permits the differences in levels of productivity among the countries to be nonneutral. We do not estimate the translog parameters econometrically; rather we use the index numbers that are exact for the translog specification. This approach was followed by Jorgenson and Nishimizu (1978), in their bilateral comparison of output, input, and productivity for the Unites States and Japan. Caves, Christensen, and Diewert (1982a), have recently derived exact translog index numbers for the multilateral case, and we adopt their procedure for our international comparison.

We find that output per capita relative to the United States in 1970 varied from 0.101 for Korea to 0.811 for Canada. For the industrialized countries except Canada the range was from 0.460 for Italy to 0.721 for Germany. Variations in capital input per capita relative to the United States were greater than for output, running from 0.082 for Korea to 0.920 for Canada. Again, excluding Canada, the range for industrialized countries was from 0.325 for Japan to 0.709 for Germany. Finally, labor input per capita ranged from 0.628 of the U.S. level for Italy to 1.346 for Japan. Labor input per capita for Japan was the only measure of output or input per capita for any country relative to the United States for 1970 that exceeded unity.

Differences between levels of total factor productivity in the United States and the eight remaining countries in 1970 were much smaller than differences in output per capita. The productivity level in Korea was 0.316 by comparison with the output level of 0.101, relative to the United States. The relative productivity level for Canada was 0.914 by comparison with the relative output of 0.811. We conclude that differences in output per capita were more closely associated with differences in levels of capital and labor inputs per capita than with differences in levels of total factor productivity.

Our second objective is to compare relative levels of output, input, and productivity among all nine countries for the period 1947–1973. The purpose of this comparison is to analyze changes in these levels over the postwar period. We provide comparisons between the United States and Canada for the whole period; we include as much of the period as possible for the seven remaining countries and provide comparisons for the period 1960–1973 for all countries. Our time series estimates are obtained by combining the rates of growth of output, input, and productivity for the individual countries with the relative levels for 1970. We present the results of our time series comparisons among countries in section 5.4.

Our time series results show that relative levels of output per capita between the United States and its eight trading partners have narrowed substantially during the postwar period. Levels of capital per capita have also narrowed throughout the postwar period for all countries relative to the United States. Patterns of relative levels of labor input per capita bear little resemblance to those for output and capital input per capita. For all countries except Korea, labor input per capita first increased and then declined relative to the United States.

Finally, relative productivity levels between the United States and its major trading partners have narrowed substantially over the postwar period. For the seven industrialized countries relative productivity levels in 1973 fell within the narrow range of 0.775 for the United Kingdom for 0.907 for Canada. For Korea the productivity gap remained very substantial; its level relative to the United States was 0.348.

This paper parallels our earlier study of patterns of economic growth over the period 1947–1973 for all nine countries.[2] We presented an analysis of sources of economic growth for each country, dividing growth in output between growth in capital and labor input and growth in total factor productivity. The main conclusion of our earlier study was that differences in growth rates of output are associated with differences in growth rates of capital and labor inputs. Our earlier paper provides detailed data and a description of data sources for each country.

## 5.2 Methodology

In this section we present our methodology for comparing levels of output, capital input, labor input, and total factor productivity for the United States and eight of its major trading partners. Following

Jorgenson and Nishimizu (1978), our methodology is based on a constant returns to scale translog production function for all nine countries,[3]

$$
\begin{aligned}
Y = \exp\Big[ & \alpha_0 + \alpha_K \ln K + \alpha_L \ln L + \alpha_T T + \sum \alpha_c D_c \\
& + 1/2\, \beta_{KK}(\ln K)^2 + \beta_{KL} \ln K \ln L + \beta_{KT} T \ln K + \sum \beta_{KC} D_C \ln K \\
& + 1/2\, \beta_{LL}(\ln L)^2 + \beta_{LT} T \ln L + \sum \beta_{LC} D_C \ln L + 1/2\, \beta_{TT} T^2 \\
& + 1/2 \sum \beta_{TC} T D_C + 1/2 \sum \beta_{CC} D_C^2 \Big],
\end{aligned}
$$

where $Y$ is output, $K$ is capital input, $L$ is labor input, $T$ is time, $D_C$ is a dummy variable equal to one for the corresponding country and zero otherwise, and $C$ is an index of countries, running over Canada, France, Germany, Italy, Japan, Korea, The Netherlands, and the United Kingdom. Since we find it useful to express levels of output, input, and productivity relative to the United States, we omit a dummy variable for the United States from the production function. Since $T$ and $D_C$ interact with capital and labor input, differences in levels of productivity across time and across countries are permitted to be nonneutral.

Denoting the price of output by $q_Y$, the price of capital input by $p_K$, and the price of labor input by $p_L$, we can define the shares of labor input in the value of output, say $v_K$ and $v_L$, by

$$
v_K = p_K K / q_Y Y, \qquad v_L = p_L L / q_Y Y.
$$

Necessary conditions for producer equilibrium in each country are given by equalities between the value shares and the elasticities of output with respect to the corresponding inputs,

$$
v_K = \frac{\partial \ln Y}{\partial \ln K}\, [K, L, T, D_C] = \alpha_K + \beta_{KK} \ln K + \beta_{KL} \ln L + \beta_{KT} T + \beta_{KC} D_C,
$$
$$
v_L = \frac{\partial \ln Y}{\partial \ln L}\, [K, L, T, D_C] = \alpha_L + \beta_{KL} \ln K + \beta_{LL} \ln L + \beta_{LT} T + \beta_{LC} D_C.
$$

Under constant returns to scale the elasticities and the value shares sum to unity for each country.

We can define the rate of productivity growth, say $v_T$, as the growth of output with respect to time, holding capital input, labor input, and the country dummy variables constant:

$$\upsilon_T = \frac{\partial \ln Y}{\partial T}[K, L, T, D_C] = \alpha_T + \beta_{KT} \ln K + \beta_{LT} \ln L + \beta_{TT} T + \beta_{TC} D_C .$$

Since we do not estimate the parameters of the production function, we must use the appropriate index number formula to estimate the rate of productivity growth. The translog rate of productivity growth between consecutive discrete data points for a given country, say $T$ and $T - 1$, is the log difference of output less a weighted average of the log differences of capital and labor input with weights given by average value shares,

$$\bar{\upsilon}_T = \ln Y(T) - \ln Y(T - 1) - \bar{\upsilon}_K[\ln K(T) - \ln K(T - 1)]$$
$$- \bar{\upsilon}_L[\ln L(T) - \ln L(T - 1)] ,$$

where

$$\bar{\upsilon}_K = 1/2[\upsilon_K(T) + \upsilon_K(T - 1)] ,$$
$$\bar{\upsilon}_L = 1/2[\upsilon_L(T) + \upsilon_L(T - 1)] ,$$
$$\bar{\upsilon}_T = 1/2(\upsilon_T(T) + \upsilon_T(T - 1)] .$$

We refer to this expression for the rate of productivity growth as the *translog index of productivity growth*.[4]

Finally, we can define the difference in productivity between any country and the United States, say $\upsilon_C$, as the logarithmic derivative of the level of output with respect to the dummy variable representing differences in productivity between the countries, holding capital input, labor input, and time constant,

$$\upsilon_C = \frac{\partial \ln Y}{\partial D_C}[K, L, T, D_C] = \alpha_C + \beta_{KC} \ln K + \beta_{LC} \ln L + \beta_{TC} T + \beta_{CC} D_C .$$

Caves, Christensen, and Diewert (1982a) have derived from the translog production function an index procedure for making transitive multilateral productivity comparisons.[5] The index that they proposed is attractive because it is base-country invariant, sacrifices only a small amount of characteristicity, and imposes no *a priori* restrictions on the structure of production.[6] Using the Caves-Christensen-Diewert approach, the difference in productivity between any two countries, say $\hat{\upsilon}_C$, can be expressed in terms of aggregate output $Y$, capital input $K$, and labor input $L$. For example, expressing differences in productivity relative to the United States,

$$\hat{v}_C = \ln Y(C) - \ln Y(US) - \hat{v}_K(C)[\ln K(C) - \overline{\ln K}]$$
$$+ \hat{v}_K(US)[\ln K(US) - \overline{\ln K}] - \hat{v}_L(C)[\ln L(C) - \overline{\ln L}]$$
$$+ \hat{v}_L(US)[\ln L(US) - \overline{\ln L}],$$

where

$$\hat{v}_K(C) = 1/2\left[v_K(C) + \frac{1}{n}\sum v_K\right], \qquad \hat{v}_L(C) = 1/2\left[v_L(C) + \frac{1}{n}\sum v_L\right],$$

and a bar indicates the average over all $n$ countries. We refer to these expressions for differences in productivity as *translog multilateral indexes of differences in productivity.*[7]

To complete our methodology for comparing levels of output, capital input, labor input, and levels of productivity between the United States and eight of its major trading partners, we require specific forms for the functions defining aggregate output $Y$, capital input $K$, and labor input $L$. We specify aggregate output as a constant returns to scale translog function of its components for all nine countries,

$$Y = \exp[\alpha_1 \ln Y_1 + \alpha_2 \ln Y_2 + \cdots + \alpha_m \ln Y_m$$
$$+ 1/2\beta_{11}(\ln Y_1)^2 + \beta_{12} \ln Y_1 \ln Y_2 + \cdots + 1/2\beta_{mm}(\ln Y_m)^2],$$

where $\{Y_i\}$ is the set of components of aggregate output.

Denoting the prices of the components of aggregate output by $\{q_{Yi}\}$, we can define the shares of these components in the value of output say $\{w_{Yi}\}$, by

$$w_{Yi} = q_{Yi}Y_i/q_Y Y, \qquad i = 1, 2, \ldots, m.$$

The value shares of individual outputs can be expressed as

$$w_{Yi} = \alpha_i + \beta_{1i} \ln Y_1 + \cdots + \beta_{mi} \ln Y_m, \qquad i = 1, 2, \ldots, m.$$

Since aggregate output is a translog function of its components, the difference between successive logarithms of aggregate output can be expressed as a weighted average of differences between logarithms of individual outputs with weights given by average value shares,

$$\ln Y(T) - \ln Y(T - 1) = \sum \bar{w}_{Yi}[\ln Y_i(T) - \ln Y_i(T - 1)],$$

where

$$\bar{w}_{Yi} = 1/2[w_{Yi}(T) + w_{Yi}(T - 1)] , \qquad i = 1, 2, \ldots, m .$$

We refer to these expressions for aggregate output as *translog indexes of output*.[8]

Similarly, considering data for all nine countries at a given point of time, the differences between logarithms of aggregate output for any two countries can be expressed as the difference between weighted averages of differences between aggregate output for each country and the geometric average of output for all nine countries. For example, expressing differences relative to the United States,

$$\ln Y(C) - \ln Y(US) = \sum \hat{w}_i(C)[\ln Y_i(C) - \overline{\ln Y_i}]$$
$$- \sum \hat{w}_i(US)[\ln Y_i(US) - \overline{\ln Y_i}] ,$$

where

$$\hat{w}_i(C) = \frac{1}{2}\left[ w_i(C) + \frac{1}{n} \sum w_i \right], \qquad \overline{\ln Y_i} = \frac{1}{n} \sum \ln Y_i , \qquad i = 1, 2, \ldots, m .$$

We refer to these expressions for relative output as *translog multilateral indexes of relative output*.[9]

To define price indexes corresponding to the translog multilateral indexes of relative output we employ the fact that the product of price and quantity indexes for the aggregate must equal the sum of the values of the components of each aggregate. The price index for aggregate output is defined as the ratio of the sum of the values of the individual outputs to the translog multilateral index of relative output. Such a price index is often referred to as the purchasing power parity of the currencies of the two countries.[10] If output is measured relative to the United States, the corresponding purchasing power parity represents the price of one unit of domestic currency's worth of output in terms of dollars.

The price indexes for aggregate output corresponding to the translog multilateral indexes of relative output can be determined solely from data on prices and quantities of the components of the aggregate. Although these price indexes do not have the form of translog multilateral index numbers, they are nonetheless well defined. By definition the product of price and quantity indexes for an aggregate is equal to the sum of the values of its components. Price indexes for the components of aggregate output are available from the national accounts for each country described in our previous paper. Purchasing power parities for these components are available for the year 1970 from Kravis, Heston and summers (1978a) for all countries except Canada; we have constructed purchasing power parities for Canada by methods described in appendix A.

If aggregate capital and labor input are translog functions of their components for all nine countries, we can express the difference between successive logarithms of aggregate capital and labor inputs for a given country in the form

$$\ln K(T) - \ln K(T-1) = \sum \overline{v}_{Kj} [\ln K_j(T) - \ln K_j(T-1)] ,$$
$$\ln L(T) - \ln L(T-1) = \sum \overline{v}_{Lk} [\ln L_k(T) - \ln L_k(T-1)] ,$$

where $\{K_j\}$ is the set of components of aggregate capital input, $\{L_k\}$ the set of components of aggregate labor input, and

$$\overline{v}_{Kj} = 1/2[v_{Kj}(T) + v_{Kj}(T-1)] , \qquad j = 1, 2, \ldots, p ,$$
$$\overline{v}_{Lk} = 1/2[v_{Lk}(T) + v_{Lk}(T-1)] , \qquad k = 1, 2, \ldots, q ,$$

where $\{v_{Kj}\}$ are the shares of the components of capital input in the value of aggregate input and $\{v_{Lk}\}$ are the shares of components of labor input in the value of aggregate labor input.

Similarly, we can express the differences between logarithms of aggregate capital and labor input for any two countries relative to the United States in the form

$$\ln K(C) - \ln K(US) = \sum \hat{v}_{Kj}(C)[\ln K_j(C) - \overline{\ln K_j}]$$
$$- \sum \hat{v}_{Kj}(US)[\ln K_j(US) - \overline{\ln K_j}] ,$$
$$\ln L(C) - \ln L(US) = \sum \hat{v}_{Lk}(C)[\ln L_k(C) - \overline{\ln L_k}]$$
$$- \sum \hat{v}_{Lk}(US)[\ln L_k(US) - \overline{\ln L_k}] ,$$

where

$$\hat{v}_{Kj}(C) = 1/2 \left[ v_{Kj}(C) + \frac{1}{n} \sum v_{Kj} \right], \qquad \overline{\ln K_j} = \frac{1}{n} \sum \ln K_j , \qquad j = 1, 2, \ldots, p,$$

$$\hat{v}_{Lk}(C) = 1/2 \left[ v_{Lk}(C) + \frac{1}{n} \sum v_{Lk} \right], \qquad \overline{\ln L_k} = \frac{1}{n} \sum \ln L_k , \qquad k = 1, 2, \ldots, q.$$

We refer to these expressions for relative capital and labor inputs as *translog multilateral indexes of relative capital and labor inputs.*[11]

Price indexes for capital and labor input can be defined in a manner that is strictly analogous to the definition of price indexes for output. For any two countries at a given point of time the price index for capital input represents the purchasing power parity between the domestic currencies of the two countries in terms of aggregate capital input. For example, if capital input is measured relative to the United States, the corresponding purchasing power parity represents the price of one unit of domestic currency's worth of capital input in terms of dollars. Similarly, the price index for labor input represents the price of one unit of domestic currency's worth of labor input in terms of dollars.

To complete our comparison of differences in capital input and labor input for the United States and eight of its major trading partners, we require price indexes for the components of capital and labor input for all nine countries. Similarly, we require purchasing power parities for these components. The measurement of capital input begins with data on the stock of capital for each component of capital input, based on past investments in constant prices. At each point of time the stock of the $j$th type of capital, say $A_j(T)$, is the sum of past investments, say $I_j(T - \tau)$, weighted by the relative efficiencies of capital goods of each age $\tau$, say $d_{j\tau}$,

$$A_j(T) = \sum_{\tau=0}^{\infty} d_{j\tau} I_j(T - \tau), \qquad j = 1, 2, \ldots, p.$$

Similarly, the price of acquisition of the $j$th new capital good, say $P_{Ij}(T)$, is the discounted value of future prices of the $j$th capital input, say $P_{Kj}(T - \tau)$, each weighted by relative efficiency,

$$p_{Ij}(T) = \sum_{\tau=0}^{\infty} \prod_{S=1}^{\tau} \frac{1}{1 + r(T + S)} \, p_{Kj}(T + \tau + 1), \qquad j = 1, 2, \ldots, p,$$

where $r(T)$ is the nominal rate of return on capital in period $T$, and

$$\prod_{S=1}^{\tau} 1/(1 + r(T + S))$$

is the discount factor in period $T$ for future prices in period $T + \tau + 1$.

Using data on decline in relative efficiency with age for all nine

countries, estimates of capital stock of each type can be compiled from
data on prices and quantities of investment in new capital goods of
each type at each point of time by the perpetual inventory method.[12]
We assume that the relative efficiency of the $j$th capital good declines
geometrically with age,

$$d_{j\tau} = (1 - \delta_j)^\tau, \qquad \tau = 0, 1, \ldots, \qquad j = 1, 2, \ldots, p.$$

Under this assumption the rate of replacement for the $j$th capital
good, say $\delta_j$, is a constant. Capital stock at the end of each period can
be estimated from investment during the period and capital stock at
the beginning of the period,

$$A_j(T) = I_j(T) + (1 - \delta_j)A_j(T - 1), \qquad j = 1, 2, \ldots, p.$$

Similarly, the price of the $j$th capital good is equal to the sum of the
nominal return to capital $p_{Ij}(T - 1)r(T)$ and depreciation $\delta_j P_{Tj}(T)$, less
revaluation $p_{Ij}(T) - p_{Ij}(T - 1)$,

$$p_{Kj}(T) = p_{Ij}(T - 1)r(T) + \delta_j p_{Ij}(T) - [p_{Ij}(T) - p_{Ij}(T - 1)], \qquad j = 1, 2, \ldots, p.$$

We can also express the price of the $j$th capital input as the sum of the
price of investment in the preceding period $P_{Ij}(T - 1)$ multiplied by
the own rate of return on capital $r(T) - [P_{Ij}(T) - p_{Ij}(T - 1)]/p_{Ij}(T - 1)$
and the current price of investment $p_{Ij}(T)$ multiplied by the rate of
depreciation $\delta_j$,

$$p_{Kj}(T) = p_{Ij}(T - 1)\left[ r(T) - \frac{p_{Ij}(T) - p_{Ij}(T - 1)}{p_{Ij}(T - 1)} \right] + \delta_j p_{Ij}(T), \qquad j = 1, 2, \ldots, p.$$

Although we estimate the decline in efficiency of capital goods for
each component of capital input separately for all nine countries, we
assume that the relative efficiency of new capital goods is the same in
all countries. Accordingly, the appropriate purchasing power parity
for new capital goods is the purchasing power parity for the corresponding component of investment goods output. To obtain the purchasing power parities for capital input, we multiply the purchasing
power parity for investment goods for any two countries by the ratio
of the price of capital input to the price of investment goods for one

country relative to that of the other;[13] for example, expressing the purchasing power parity for capital input in dollars,

$$\frac{p_{Kj}(\text{US})}{p_{Kj}(\text{C})} = \frac{p_{Ij}(\text{US})}{p_{Ij}(\text{C})} \cdot \frac{p_{Kj}(\text{US})/p_{Ij}(\text{US})}{p_{Kj}(\text{C})/p_{Ij}(\text{C})} , \qquad j = 1, 2, \ldots, p .$$

In constructing translog multilateral indexes of relative labor input for the United States and eight of its major trading partners we assume that the relative efficiency of an hour worked is the same for a given type of labor input in all nine countries. We distinguish among workers that differ in educational attainment for all countries. Labor input for each country is the product of employment, average hours worked, and an index of educational attainment. The indexes of educational attainment employed in constructing indexes of relative labor input are described in detail in appendix B. To obtain purchasing power parities for labor input, we multiply the relative hourly wage rates for any two countries by the ratio of labor input per hour worked for the two countries.[14] Hourly wage rates are obtained by dividing labor compensation for employees and self-employed workers in each country by the product of employment and average hours worked.

All the comparisons reported in this paper are base-country invariant, but they are not base-year invariant. We use 1970 as the base year for all of our time series comparisons. The principal reason for this approach is the fact that the detailed international price comparisons of Kravis, Heston and Summers (1978a), on which we rely, are available only for 1970. This being the case, it is necessary to construct price indexes for other years by chain-linking them to 1970. Thus we did not have the option, recommended by Caves, Christensen and Diewert (1982a), of constructing comparisons that are both base-country and base-year invariant.

### 5.3    Multilateral Comparisons for 1970

The starting point for the construction of multilateral translog indexes of relative output for the United States and eight of its major trading partners for 1970 is the measurement of the value of total product and the value of total factor outlay for each country in current prices. The fundamental accounting identity for the production account is that the value of total product is equal to the value of total factor outlay for each country. The product and factor outlay accounts are linked through capital formation and the compensation of property. To make this link explicit, we divide total output between consumption and investment goods and total factor outlay between labor and property compensation. In analyzing productive activity we have limited the scope of our production account to the private domestic sector of each country.

All nine countries include government enterprises in the private domestic sector of their national accounts. A case could be made for excluding government enterprises in a study such as ours, but the data are not available to do so. The U.S. accounts do not recognize any capital input for government enterprises. This lack of comparability is not important, however, since U.S. government enterprises produce an almost negligible portion of U.S. private domestic product.

An unconventional aspect of our measure of total output is an imputation for the services of consumer durables. Our objective is to attain consistency in the treatment of owner-occupied residential structures and owner-utilized consumer durables. The services of consumer durables are included in consumption goods output, while investment in consumer durables is included in investment goods output. For all nine countries it has been possible to separate gross private domestic product between consumption goods and investment goods, except for inventory investment and net exports. We obtain quantity indexes for nondurable consumption goods and services, consumer durable equipment, producer durable equipment, residential structures, nonresidential structures, inventory investment, and net exports.

Our first step in constructing translog multilateral indexes of relative capital input for the United States and eight of its major trading partners is to divide total factor outlay between labor and property compensation. We have used the method of Christensen (1971) to impute labor compensation to self-employed workers. For the United States, Christensen has shown that this method results in equal after-tax rates of return in the corporate and noncorporate sectors. We have compiled capital stock estimates of six asset classes: consumer durables, producer durable equipment, residential structures, nonresidential structures, inventories, and land. Given property compensation, the stock of assets, the price of acquisition of new capital goods, and the rate of depreciation, we can determine the nominal rate of return.

The nominal rate of return is equal to the ratio of property compensation less depreciation plus revaluation of assets to the value of capital stock at the beginning of the period. In measuring the rate of return, differences in tax treatment of property compensation must be taken into account. For tax purposes the private domestic sector of each country can be divided among corporate business, noncorporate business, and households and nonprofit institutions. Households and institutions are not subject to direct taxes on the capital input they use. Noncorporate business is subject to personal income taxes, while corporate business is subject both to corporate and personal income taxes.

We proceed to compute relative levels of output per capita for 1970 and to allocate the differences in these levels among differences in capital and labor input per capita and differences in levels of productivity. In table 5.1 we present translog multilateral indexes of output, capital input, and labor input for all countries relative to the United States for the year 1970. We also present these indexes in per capita terms.[15] Finally, we present translog multilateral indexes of differences in productivity between each country and the United States and the share of labor compensation in the value of output for each country in 1970. Since the United States had nearly double the population of Japan and almost four times the population of France, Germany, Italy, or the United Kingdom in 1970, we find it useful to focus on comparisons among countries in per capita terms.

In 1970 the level of output per capita for Canada relative to the United States was higher than for any other country at 0.811. Germany was highest among European countries with a relative level of 0.721. Output per capita relative to the United States for the European countries ranged from Germany's 0.721 down to Italy's 0.460. Relative output per capita for the United Kingdom was next lowest at 0.546 with relative output for The Netherlands at 0.623 and France at 0.675. Relative output per capita for Japan at 0.583 fell above the levels of Italy and the United Kingdom, but below the levels of France, Germany, and The Netherlands. Korea, the only newly industrialized country included in our study, had a level of output per capita relative to the United States of 0.101.

**Table 5.1**
Output, inputs, population and productivity relative to the United States and labor's share in the value of output, 1970

|  | United States | Canada | France | Germany | Italy | Japan | Korea | Netherlands | United Kingdom |
|---|---|---|---|---|---|---|---|---|---|
| Output | | .084 | .167 | .213 | .120 | .295 | .016 | .040 | .148 |
| Capital input | | .096 | .174 | .210 | .105 | .164 | .013 | .040 | .146 |
| Labor input | | .088 | .239 | .252 | .164 | .680 | .115 | .053 | .246 |
| Output p.c.[a] | | .811 | .675 | .721 | .460 | .583 | .101 | .623 | .546 |
| Capital input p.c.[a] | | .920 | .702 | .709 | .403 | .325 | .082 | .633 | .540 |
| Labor input p.c.[a] | | .846 | .966 | .850 | .628 | 1.346 | .749 | .841 | .907 |
| Population | | .104 | .248 | .296 | .261 | .505 | .154 | .064 | .271 |
| Total factor productivity | | .914 | .788 | .909 | .876 | .779 | .316 | .828 | .742 |
| | | | | *Labor's share in the value of output* | | | | | |
| | .604 | .566 | .557 | .587 | .626 | .558 | .645 | .587 | .632 |

[a]p.c. = per capita.

Relative levels of output between any two countries can be expressed in terms of relative levels of capital and labor input and differences in levels of productivity. Focussing attention on capital input per capita relative to the United States we find Canada again in the lead with a level of 0.920. Germany again leads European countries with a relative level of 0.709. Capital input per capita for Italy relative to the United States was the lowest among European countries at 0.403. Relative capital input for the United Kingdom was next lowest at 0.540, while The Netherlands had a level of 0.633 and France had a level of 0.702. Relative capital input for Japan at 0.325 fell outside the range of European countries; Korea had the lowest level of capital input per capita relative to the United States at 0.082.

Turning to levels of labor input per capita, we find that Japan rather than Canada had the highest level relative to the United States at an astonishing 1.346. Among European countries, the highest level was for France at 0.966 and the lowest was for Italy at 0.628. The remaining European countries had relative levels of 0.841 for The Netherlands, 0.850 for Germany, and 0.907 for the United Kingdom. Canada fell within the range for European countries at 0.846, as did Korea at 0.0749. Below we provide a more detailed analysis of labor input per capita.

Our final comparison among the United States and eight of its major trading partners for 1970 is for relative levels of productivity. The level of productivity relative to the United States was highest for Canada at 0.914, followed by Germany at 0.909. Somewhat surprisingly, Italy is found to have had the second highest level of productivity among the European countries (0.876). The U.K. had the lowest productivity level among the European countries (0.742); France (0.788) and The Netherlands (0.828) fell in the mid-range of the European countries—as did Japan (0.778). Finally, Korea's level of productivity (0.316), was substantially below that of the other countries.

Our next objective is to analyze relative levels of labor input per capita in more detail. In table 5.2 we present levels of employment per capita, hours worked per employee, and quality of labor input, defined as labor input per hour worked, for all countries relative to the United States for the year 1970. The translog multilateral indexes of relative labor input per capita given in table 5.1 are the products of these three measures of labor input. Our analysis of relative levels of

**Table 5.2**
Decomposition of per capita labor input relative to the United States

|  | Canada | France | Germany | Italy | Japan | Korea | Netherlands | United Kingdom |
|---|---|---|---|---|---|---|---|---|
| Employment | 0.880 | 1.069 | 1.152 | 0.977 | 1.226 | 0.874 | 0.938 | 1.105 |
| Hours worked | 1.043 | 1.114 | 1.112 | 1.091 | 1.201 | 1.284 | 1.191 | 1.090 |
| Quality | 0.922 | 0.811 | 0.663 | 0.589 | 0.915 | 0.667 | 0.752 | 0.753 |

labor input is based on a decomposition of the indexes of relative labor input per capita among these three components.

Our translog multilateral indexes of relative labor input in table 5.1 reveal that Japan had almost thirty-five percent more labor input per capita than the United States in 1970. The results presented in table 5.2 show that this was made up of twenty-three percent greater employment per capita, twenty percent greater hours worked per employee, and eight and a half percent less labor input per hour worked or labor quality—all relative to the United States. We find that Japan was at or close to the upper end of the range of variation among the seven remaining countries for each of the three components that make up relative labor input per capita.

Specifically, we find that Japan's per capita employment (1.226) was the highest of any country—the next highest being Germany at 1.152. Japan's hours worked per employee (1.201) was above every country except Korea (1.240), but The Netherlands was very close at 1.191. Finally, Japan's level of labor quality (0.915) was above that of all countries other than Canada (0.922) relative to the U.S. Thus we see that Japan's high level of per capita labor input resulted from her high position in all three of the components. We conclude that the quantity and quality of labor input was a very important source of Japan's level of output per capita relative to the United States.

Just as Japan is notable for having a very high level of per capita labor input relative to the U.S., Italy is notable for her very low level of labor input, which was thirty-seven percent below the U.S. in 1970. This can be traced principally to Italy's level of labor quality, which was below that of Korea as well as those of all the other industrial countries. In addition to the low quality index, Italy had relatively low levels of employment per capita and hours worked per employee.

Considering all nine countries included in our study we find that the United States was in the middle of the range of employment per capita with Japan (1.220), Germany (1.152), the United Kingdom (1.105), and France (1.069), above the United States and Italy (0.977), The Netherlands (0.938), Canada (0.880), and Korea (0.874), below the United States. All countries had higher levels of hours worked per employee than the United States, ranging from Canada at 1.043 to Japan at 1.201. Finally, the United States had the highest relative level of labor quality. Canada and Japan were the closest to the United States with European countries considerably below beginning with

France (0.811), followed by the United Kingdom (0.753), The Netherlands (0.752), Germany (0.663), and Italy (0.589). Korea was within the
European range at 0.667.

Comparing capital input per capita with labor input per capita in
table 5.1, we find that labor input per capita is more similar to the
United States than capital input per capita for all countries except
Canada. In table 5.3 we present an analysis of the capital-labor ratio
relative to the United States in terms of employment, hours worked,
and labor input as a whole. Only Canada had a higher level of capital
input relative to any measure of labor input than the United States.
On any of the three measures, Germany, France, and The Netherlands
had capital-labor ratios below the U.S. and Canada, but above the
other four countries. The capital-labor ratio in Japan was substantially
below all the countries except that of Korea.

## 5.4    Relative Levels of Output, Inputs, and Productivity, 1947–1973

In this section our objective is to compare relative levels of output,
capital input, and labor input per capita and relative levels of productivity for the United States and eight of its major trading partners for
the period 1947–1973. We are able to provide comparisons between
the United States and Canada for the entire period; we include as
much of the period was possible for the seven remaining countries,
including Germany and France for 1950–1973, The Netherlands for
1951–1973, Italy and Japan for 1952–1973, the United Kingdom for
1955–1973, and Korea for 1960–1973. These comparisons are based on
translog multilateral index numbers of relative output, input, and productivity for 1970, which are extended forward and backward in time
via time series translog index numbers of output, input, and productivity for the individual countries.

In table 5.4 we present levels of output per capita for all countries
relative to the United States. The relative levels of output per capita
have narrowed substantially over the postwar period. The most dramatic gain in output was for Japan, with a doubling of output per
capita relative to the United States from 1952 to 1963 and a further
increase amounting to slightly less than a doubling between 1963 and
1973. Germany is the only other country that doubled its output rela-

**Table 5.3**
Capital-labor ratio relative to the United States

| | Canada | France | Germany | Italy | Japan | Korea | Netherlands | United Kingdom |
|---|---|---|---|---|---|---|---|---|
| Capital input/ employment | 1.046 | .657 | .616 | .413 | .266 | .094 | .674 | .488 |
| Capital input/ hours worked | 1.003 | .589 | .554 | .378 | .221 | .073 | .566 | .448 |
| Capital input/ labor input | 1.008 | .727 | .835 | .642 | .242 | .110 | .751 | .595 |

**Table 5.4**
Per capita output relative to the United States

|      | Canada | France | Germany | Italy | Japan | Korea | Nether-lands | United Kingdom |
|------|--------|--------|---------|-------|-------|-------|--------------|----------------|
| 1947 | .701   |        |         |       |       |       |              |                |
| 1948 | .687   |        |         |       |       |       |              |                |
| 1949 | .718   |        |         |       |       |       |              |                |
| 1950 | .717   | .421   | .320    |       |       |       |              |                |
| 1951 | .692   | .409   | .338    |       |       |       | .422         |                |
| 1952 | .722   | .413   | .363    | .265  | .169  |       | .417         |                |
| 1953 | .723   | .432   | .378    | .280  | .175  |       | .432         |                |
| 1954 | .718   | .463   | .432    | .296  | .188  |       | .470         |                |
| 1955 | .724   | .458   | .473    | .303  | .192  |       | .472         | .485           |
| 1956 | .771   | .472   | .498    | .314  | .209  |       | .489         | .491           |
| 1957 | .767   | .495   | .522    | .327  | .226  |       | .501         | .502           |
| 1958 | .780   | .505   | .545    | .349  | .236  |       | .475         | .513           |
| 1959 | .763   | .505   | .561    | .355  | .248  |       | .498         | .512           |
| 1960 | .765   | .541   | .618    | .375  | .285  | .069  | .530         | .537           |
| 1961 | .758   | .560   | .642    | .402  | .331  | .070  | .537         | .556           |
| 1962 | .758   | .559   | .635    | .408  | .326  | .067  | .531         | .537           |
| 1963 | .768   | .572   | .612    | .415  | .355  | .071  | .530         | .544           |
| 1964 | .779   | .586   | .636    | .407  | .385  | .070  | .552         | .553           |
| 1965 | .780   | .585   | .644    | .393  | .386  | .070  | .552         | .539           |
| 1966 | .779   | .585   | .619    | .393  | .403  | .074  | .537         | .525           |
| 1967 | .775   | .601   | .586    | .414  | .436  | .077  | .549         | .531           |
| 1968 | .777   | .601   | .632    | .420  | .487  | .082  | .563         | .530           |
| 1969 | .783   | .633   | .675    | .434  | .523  | .095  | .583         | .522           |
| 1970 | .811   | .675   | .721    | .460  | .583  | .101  | .623         | .546           |
| 1971 | .822   | .684   | .716    | .434  | .603  | .106  | .632         | .550           |
| 1972 | .809   | .678   | .700    | .420  | .615  | .108  | .631         | .547           |
| 1973 | .807   | .680   | .695    | .418  | .622  | .122  | .622         | .552           |

tive to the United States over our sample period; the doubling occurred between 1950 and 1961.

Although Japan began the postwar period with a lower level of output per capita relative to the United States than any other industrialized country, it surpassed Italy in 1966 and the United Kingdom in 1969 and caught up to The Netherlands in 1973. By the end of the period of our study in 1973, Japan's level of output per capita relative to the United States stood at 0.622; by comparison, the relative level of output for France was 0.680 and for Germany was 0.695. Canada was the country closest to the United States in output per capita at the beginning of the postwar period and maintained its lead over other countries throughout the period, ending with a level of output per capita relative to the United States of 0.807 in 1973, a substantial gain over the level of 0.701 in 1947.

All of the countries in our sample had substantially higher levels of real output per capita relative to the U.S. in 1973 than they had in the early postwar period. But for most countries the recent gains have not been as large as the early gains. In fact Italy and the U.K. had virtually the same levels of real output per capita relative to the U.S. in 1973 as they had in 1960. Also, Canada, France, Germany, and The Netherlands did not gain on the U.S. after 1970. But projection of this short-term trend beyond 1973 is probably not warranted since these countries did not experience the severe recession in 1970 and the strong recovery through 1973 that was experienced by the U.S. Although Korea continued to gain on the U.S. level of output per capita in the 1970s, her level is still very low.

Turning to capital input relative to the United States, we present levels of capital input per capita for all eight trading partners in table 5.5. The patterns of change for relative capital input are similar to those for relative output for the postwar period, but there are important differences. The most dramatic gain in capital input, as for output, is for Japan with a doubling of capital input per capita relative to the United States from 1957 to 1966. Japan's gains were small for the period 1952 to 1957; by contrast her gains in relative output per capita over the period 1952 to 1957 were substantial. Germany doubled its capital input per capita relative to the United States over the period 1950–1972; by contrast it doubled relative output per capita between 1950 and 1961.

Japan began the postwar period with a lower level of capital input per capita than any other industrialized country and it has yet to overtake any of the five European countries included in our study. Levels of capital input per capita relative to the United States in 1973 were closely comparable for Japan at 0.417 and for Italy at 0.422. Relative levels of capital input in 1973 were 0.566 for the United Kingdom, 0.692 for The Netherlands, 0.761 for France and 0.789 for Germany. Canada was the closest to the United States in capital input per capita at the beginning of the postwar period at 0.719 in 1947 and has gained steadily since then, ending with a relative level of capital input per capita of 0.931 in 1973.

Focussing on labor input per capita relative to the United States, we present relative levels of labor input for all countries in table 5.6. The

**Table 5.5**
Per capita capital input relative to the United States

|      | Canada | France | Germany | Italy | Japan | Korea | Nether-lands | United Kingdom |
|------|--------|--------|---------|-------|-------|-------|--------------|----------------|
| 1947 | .719   |        |         |       |       |       |              |                |
| 1948 | .736   |        |         |       |       |       |              |                |
| 1949 | .740   |        |         |       |       |       |              |                |
| 1950 | .758   | .481   | .379    |       |       |       |              |                |
| 1951 | .764   | .480   | .373    |       |       |       | .469         |                |
| 1952 | .771   | .482   | .375    | .318  | .128  |       | .461         |                |
| 1953 | .785   | .488   | .390    | .315  | .120  |       | .449         |                |
| 1954 | .804   | .495   | .405    | .315  | .116  |       | .443         |                |
| 1955 | .812   | .507   | .425    | .317  | .116  |       | .454         | .436           |
| 1956 | .815   | .511   | .444    | .316  | .116  |       | .458         | .443           |
| 1957 | .833   | .521   | .463    | .318  | .121  |       | .470         | .445           |
| 1958 | .854   | .534   | .486    | .323  | .133  |       | .484         | .453           |
| 1959 | .875   | .552   | .516    | .333  | .142  |       | .494         | .470           |
| 1960 | .884   | .560   | .537    | .339  | .150  | .076  | .500         | .483           |
| 1961 | .892   | .576   | .566    | .351  | .165  | .073  | .517         | .499           |
| 1962 | .902   | .592   | .600    | .371  | .188  | .071  | .543         | .516           |
| 1963 | .904   | .612   | .608    | .387  | .206  | .070  | .566         | .524           |
| 1964 | .908   | .629   | .624    | .402  | .219  | .069  | .579         | .527           |
| 1965 | .909   | .649   | .649    | .402  | .236  | .067  | .595         | .541           |
| 1966 | .913   | .656   | .671    | .397  | .244  | .065  | .607         | .543           |
| 1967 | .917   | .663   | .682    | .392  | .252  | .067  | .609         | .538           |
| 1968 | .921   | .676   | .685    | .396  | .272  | .071  | .617         | .539           |
| 1969 | .918   | .686   | .691    | .399  | .297  | .077  | .624         | .542           |
| 1970 | .920   | .702   | .709    | .403  | .325  | .082  | .632         | .540           |
| 1971 | .924   | .727   | .743    | .417  | .361  | .087  | .660         | .546           |
| 1972 | .930   | .747   | .773    | .424  | .392  | .091  | .681         | .555           |
| 1973 | .931   | .761   | .789    | .422  | .417  | .092  | .692         | .566           |

patterns bear little resemblance to those for relative levels of output and capital input per capita. For all countries except Korea, labor input per capita first increased and then decreased relative to the United States over the postwar period. The peak in relative labor input per capita was reached for Canada in 1949 at 1.050; the peaks for France, Germany, and The Netherlands were reached in 1958 at levels of 1.130, 1.154 and 0.965, respectively. The peaks for the United Kingdom and Italy were reached in 1961 and 1963 at 1.067 and 0.727, respectively. Finally, the peak for Japan was reached in 1971 at 1.348.

Labor input per capita relative to the U.S. fell substantially following postwar peaks, except for Japan and Korea. The largest decline was for Germany from a high of 1.154 in 1958 to 0.747 in 1973. Japan's relative labor input per capita did not change much over the period

**Table 5.6**
Per capita labor input relative to the United States

|  | Canada | France | Germany | Italy | Japan | Korea | Nether-lands | United Kingdom |
|---|---|---|---|---|---|---|---|---|
| 1947 | 1.001 | | | | | | | |
| 1948 | 0.997 | | | | | | | |
| 1949 | 1.050 | | | | | | | |
| 1950 | 0.988 | 1.087 | 1.000 | | | | | |
| 1951 | 0.956 | 1.068 | 0.993 | | | | .866 | |
| 1952 | 0.947 | 1.067 | 1.015 | .564 | 0.886 | | .862 | |
| 1953 | 0.932 | 1.053 | 1.032 | .578 | 0.934 | | .872 | |
| 1954 | 0.950 | 1.110 | 1.113 | .624 | 0.998 | | .930 | |
| 1955 | 0.926 | 1.084 | 1.130 | .612 | 0.969 | | .923 | 1.000 |
| 1956 | 0.938 | 1.075 | 1.130 | .606 | 1.065 | | .927 | 0.999 |
| 1957 | 0.944 | 1.101 | 1.128 | .637 | 1.134 | | .944 | 1.000 |
| 1958 | 0.948 | 1.130 | 1.154 | .665 | 1.196 | | .965 | 1.027 |
| 1959 | 0.933 | 1.086 | 1.108 | .660 | 1.213 | | .949 | 1.020 |
| 1960 | 0.925 | 1.095 | 1.111 | .693 | 1.266 | .646 | .964 | 1.030 |
| 1961 | 0.908 | 1.110 | 1.117 | .722 | 1.316 | .681 | .943 | 1.067 |
| 1962 | 0.906 | 1.077 | 1.073 | .712 | 1.302 | .666 | .943 | 1.046 |
| 1963 | 0.904 | 1.071 | 1.006 | .727 | 1.316 | .674 | .950 | 1.056 |
| 1964 | 0.912 | 1.063 | 0.994 | .686 | 1.315 | .648 | .941 | 1.052 |
| 1965 | 0.898 | 1.023 | 0.955 | .609 | 1.282 | .686 | .817 | 1.021 |
| 1966 | 0.882 | 1.000 | 0.904 | .605 | 1.281 | .674 | .891 | 0.977 |
| 1967 | 0.879 | 0.987 | 0.847 | .622 | 1.335 | .696 | .861 | 0.953 |
| 1968 | 0.854 | 0.959 | 0.848 | .623 | 1.340 | .728 | .852 | 0.934 |
| 1969 | 0.840 | 0.946 | 0.835 | .602 | 1.309 | .744 | .836 | 0.914 |
| 1970 | 0.845 | 0.966 | 0.850 | .628 | 1.346 | .749 | .841 | 0.907 |
| 1971 | 0.855 | 0.960 | 0.827 | .615 | 1.348 | .790 | .834 | 0.861 |
| 1972 | 0.844 | 0.921 | 0.785 | .584 | 1.304 | .803 | .786 | 0.841 |
| 1973 | 0.842 | 0.881 | 0.747 | .556 | 1.279 | .811 | .745 | 0.835 |

1960–1973. Korea's labor input per capita rose fairly steadily relative to the U.S. from 1960 to 1973.

Given the perspective provided by our analysis of per capita labor input relative to the United States over the postwar period, the behavior of relative labor input for Japan seems less surprising. Relative labor input for Japan began at a level of 0.886 in 1952 and rose to a 1971 peak of 1.348. From 1971 to 1973 her relative level of input fell rapidly, in line with patterns for other industrialized countries during this same period. The 1973 level of 1.279 is not far out of line from the peak levels for France and Germany of 1.130 and 1.154 in 1958. Still, labor input per capita for Japan has been and remains very high by international standards, reflecting high employment per capita, hours worked per employee, and labor input per hour worked as indicated in table 5.2.

Finally, in table 5.7 we present levels of total factor productivity relative to the United States for all eight major trading partners. Patterns of relative productivity levels are similar to relative levels of output and capital input per capita, but there are some important contrasts. Productivity levels relative to the United States have narrowed substantially for all countries over the postwar period. The most dramatic gains in relative productivity have been for Germany and Japan. While Germany more than doubled its levels of output and capital input per capita relative to the United States, it less than doubled its relative level of productivity. Similarly, Japan doubled its capital

**Table 5.7**
Total factor productivity relative to the United States

|  | Canada | France | Germany | Italy | Japan | Korea | Nether-lands | United Kingdom |
|---|---|---|---|---|---|---|---|---|
| 1947 | .812 | | | | | | | |
| 1948 | .793 | | | | | | | |
| 1949 | .800 | | | | | | | |
| 1950 | .820 | .531 | .462 | | | | | |
| 1951 | .804 | .521 | .493 | | | | .644 | |
| 1952 | .840 | .526 | .522 | .590 | .434 | | .641 | |
| 1953 | .841 | .552 | .531 | .615 | .443 | | .667 | |
| 1954 | .817 | .570 | .571 | .621 | .465 | | .702 | |
| 1955 | .832 | .567 | .609 | .641 | .482 | | .700 | .668 |
| 1956 | .876 | .586 | .631 | .670 | .494 | | .718 | .673 |
| 1967 | .859 | .601 | .652 | .674 | .507 | | .716 | .687 |
| 1958 | .860 | .600 | .660 | .698 | .496 | | .660 | .686 |
| 1959 | .841 | .606 | .681 | .705 | .505 | | .691 | .678 |
| 1960 | .843 | .643 | .737 | .716 | .551 | .240 | .724 | .700 |
| 1961 | .838 | .654 | .748 | .740 | .601 | .239 | .731 | .701 |
| 1962 | .836 | .658 | .742 | .740 | .564 | .235 | .708 | .677 |
| 1963 | .846 | .667 | .740 | .730 | .588 | .246 | .690 | .677 |
| 1964 | .851 | .679 | .768 | .731 | .621 | .252 | .715 | .689 |
| 1965 | .859 | .685 | .785 | .762 | .613 | .245 | .716 | .677 |
| 1966 | .864 | .692 | .770 | .770 | .631 | .265 | .704 | .678 |
| 1967 | .859 | .713 | .752 | .801 | .658 | .271 | .733 | .699 |
| 1968 | .873 | .719 | .810 | .808 | .708 | .275 | .751 | .706 |
| 1969 | .868 | .757 | .869 | .851 | .740 | .303 | .782 | .704 |
| 1970 | .914 | .788 | .909 | .876 | .779 | .316 | .828 | .742 |
| 1971 | .916 | .789 | .900 | .830 | .768 | .313 | .829 | .769 |
| 1972 | .909 | .791 | .892 | .827 | .773 | .310 | .845 | .770 |
| 1973 | .907 | .806 | .906 | .849 | .772 | .348 | .855 | .775 |

input per capita relative to the United States from 1957 to 1967, doubled its output per capita relative to the United States from 1957 to 1963, and almost doubled relative output again from 1963 to 1973, but it less than doubled its relative total factor productivity over the period 1952 to 1973.

Japan began the postwar period with a lower level of total factor productivity relative to the United States than any other industrialized country. Japan caught up to the United Kingdom in 1966 and had drawn close to France by the end of our period of study in 1973. Germany began the postwar period with the lowest relative level of total factor productivity of any European country, but had overtaken France in 1954, the United Kingdom in 1959, Italy and The Netherlands in 1960, and had drawn abreast of Canada by 1973. Canada was the country closest to the United States in relative productivity at the beginning of the postwar period and remained closest to the United States in 1973, having gained substantially in relative productivity throughout the postwar period.

The time pattern of changes in differences of productivity level relative to the U.S. is mixed. Germany, Italy, and Japan experienced greater gains early in the postwar period than in recent years. On the other hand, Canada, Korea, The Netherlands, and the U.K. have had their most rapid gains on the U.S. in recent years. By 1973 the range of levels of total factor productivity relative to the United States for industrialized countries had narrowed significantly—from 0.775 for the United Kingdom to 0.907 for Canada. By contrast the level of total factor productivity for Korea relative to the United States was 0.348 in 1973.

We have presented all of our time series comparisons in tables 5.4–5.7 with the U.S. level normalized to 1.000 for each year. This facilitates comparisons for any single year, but it makes it impossible to compare relative levels in different years. For example, table 5.7 does not provide enough information to infer answers to questions such as: What was Korea's level of productivity in 1973 relative to Japan's level of productivity in 1952? Such comparisons are of obvious interest, and they can be constructed by making use of time series indexes for the United States. We provide these comparisons in tables 5.8–5.11. In each of these tables the U.S. indexes are normalized to 1.000 in 1970. The entries for all the other countries are obtained by multiplying the U.S. entries by all the figures in the corresponding

**Table 5.8**
Per capita output relative to the 1970 level for the United States

|      | Canada | France | Germany | Italy | Japan | Korea | Nether-lands | United Kingdom | United States |
|------|--------|--------|---------|-------|-------|-------|--------------|----------------|---------------|
| 1947 | .408 |      |      |      |      |      |      |      | 0.583 |
| 1948 | .416 |      |      |      |      |      |      |      | 0.606 |
| 1949 | .431 |      |      |      |      |      |      |      | 0.600 |
| 1950 | .465 | .273 | .208 |      |      |      |      |      | 0.649 |
| 1951 | .471 | .278 | .230 |      |      |      | .287 |      | 0.681 |
| 1952 | .499 | .286 | .251 | .184 | .117 |      | .289 |      | 0.692 |
| 1953 | .515 | .307 | .269 | .199 | .124 |      | .308 |      | 0.712 |
| 1954 | .498 | .321 | .299 | .205 | .131 |      | .326 |      | 0.693 |
| 1955 | .530 | .335 | .346 | .221 | .140 |      | .345 | .355 | 0.731 |
| 1956 | .567 | .347 | .367 | .231 | .154 |      | .360 | .361 | 0.736 |
| 1957 | .564 | .364 | .383 | .240 | .166 |      | .368 | .369 | 0.735 |
| 1958 | .564 | .366 | .394 | .252 | .171 |      | .344 | .371 | 0.723 |
| 1959 | .575 | .381 | .423 | .268 | .187 |      | .375 | .386 | 0.754 |
| 1960 | .580 | .410 | .468 | .284 | .216 | .052 | .402 | .407 | 0.758 |
| 1961 | .578 | .428 | .490 | .307 | .252 | .054 | .410 | .425 | 0.763 |
| 1962 | .603 | .445 | .505 | .324 | .259 | .054 | .422 | .427 | 0.795 |
| 1963 | .626 | .466 | .498 | .338 | .289 | .057 | .432 | .443 | 0.815 |
| 1964 | .665 | .500 | .543 | .347 | .328 | .060 | .471 | .472 | 0.853 |
| 1965 | .699 | .524 | .578 | .352 | .346 | .063 | .494 | .483 | 0.896 |
| 1966 | .733 | .551 | .583 | .370 | .379 | .069 | .505 | .494 | 0.941 |
| 1967 | .741 | .574 | .560 | .396 | .417 | .074 | .525 | .507 | 0.956 |
| 1968 | .770 | .595 | .626 | .416 | .482 | .082 | .558 | .525 | 0.990 |
| 1969 | .792 | .640 | .683 | .439 | .529 | .096 | .589 | .528 | 1.012 |
| 1970 | .811 | .675 | .721 | .460 | .583 | .101 | .623 | .546 | 1.000 |
| 1971 | .842 | .700 | .734 | .445 | .617 | .109 | .648 | .564 | 1.024 |
| 1972 | .875 | .733 | .757 | .455 | .665 | .116 | .682 | .591 | 1.082 |
| 1973 | .923 | .777 | .795 | .477 | .711 | .139 | .712 | .631 | 1.143 |

Table 5.9
Per capita capital input relative to the 1970 level for the United States

| | Canada | France | Germany | Italy | Japan | Korea | Netherlands | United Kingdom | United States |
|---|---|---|---|---|---|---|---|---|---|
| 1947 | 0.373 | | | | | | | | 0.519 |
| 1948 | 0.402 | | | | | | | | 0.547 |
| 1949 | 0.424 | | | | | | | | 0.572 |
| 1950 | 0.445 | .283 | .222 | | | | | | 0.587 |
| 1951 | 0.472 | .297 | .230 | | | | .289 | | 0.617 |
| 1952 | 0.492 | .307 | .240 | .203 | .081 | | .294 | | 0.638 |
| 1953 | 0.510 | .318 | .254 | .205 | .078 | | .292 | | 0.651 |
| 1954 | 0.534 | .329 | .269 | .209 | .077 | | .294 | | 0.665 |
| 1955 | 0.548 | .342 | .287 | .214 | .078 | | .306 | .294 | 0.674 |
| 1956 | 0.569 | .357 | .310 | .220 | .081 | | .320 | .309 | 0.698 |
| 1957 | 0.596 | .373 | .331 | .227 | .086 | | .337 | .319 | 0.715 |
| 1958 | 0.621 | .388 | .353 | .235 | .097 | | .352 | .330 | 0.728 |
| 1959 | 0.638 | .402 | .376 | .242 | .103 | | .360 | .342 | 0.729 |
| 1960 | 0.655 | .415 | .398 | .252 | .112 | .056 | .371 | .358 | 0.742 |
| 1961 | 0.671 | .434 | .426 | .264 | .124 | .055 | .389 | .375 | 0.752 |
| 1962 | 0.684 | .449 | .455 | .281 | .143 | .054 | .412 | .391 | 0.758 |
| 1963 | 0.699 | .473 | .470 | .299 | .159 | .054 | .437 | .405 | 0.773 |
| 1964 | 0.725 | .502 | .498 | .321 | .175 | .055 | .462 | .421 | 0.798 |
| 1965 | 0.749 | .535 | .535 | .331 | .195 | .056 | .490 | .446 | 0.824 |
| 1966 | 0.785 | .564 | .576 | .341 | .210 | .056 | .521 | .467 | 0.859 |
| 1967 | 0.825 | .596 | .614 | .352 | .227 | .060 | .548 | .484 | 0.900 |
| 1968 | 0.857 | .629 | .638 | .369 | .253 | .066 | .575 | .502 | 0.931 |
| 1969 | 0.887 | .662 | .667 | .385 | .287 | .074 | .603 | .523 | 0.966 |
| 1970 | 0.920 | .702 | .709 | .403 | .325 | .082 | .632 | .540 | 1.000 |
| 1971 | 0.943 | .741 | .758 | .425 | .369 | .089 | .674 | .557 | 1.020 |
| 1972 | 0.974 | .782 | .810 | .444 | .411 | .096 | .713 | .582 | 1.048 |
| 1973 | 1.013 | .827 | .858 | .459 | .454 | .100 | .752 | .615 | 1.088 |

**Table 5.10**
Per capita labor input relative to the 1970 level for the United States

| | Canada | France | Germany | Italy | Japan | Korea | Nether-lands | United Kingdom | United States |
|---|---|---|---|---|---|---|---|---|---|
| 1947 | 1.017 | | | | | | | | 1.017 |
| 1948 | 1.014 | | | | | | | | 1.017 |
| 1949 | 1.010 | | | | | | | | 0.962 |
| 1950 | 0.971 | 1.068 | 0.983 | | | | | | 0.983 |
| 1951 | 0.966 | 1.078 | 1.003 | | | | .875 | | 1.010 |
| 1952 | 0.945 | 1.066 | 1.013 | .563 | 0.885 | | .861 | | 0.999 |
| 1953 | 0.932 | 1.052 | 1.031 | .577 | 0.933 | | .872 | | 0.999 |
| 1954 | 0.902 | 1.054 | 1.057 | .593 | 0.948 | | .882 | | 0.949 |
| 1955 | 0.895 | 1.047 | 1.092 | .591 | 0.937 | | .891 | .966 | 0.966 |
| 1956 | 0.909 | 1.042 | 1.095 | .588 | 1.032 | | .898 | .968 | 0.969 |
| 1957 | 0.891 | 1.040 | 1.066 | .602 | 1.071 | | .892 | .945 | 0.945 |
| 1958 | 0.857 | 1.022 | 1.044 | .601 | 1.082 | | .873 | .929 | 0.904 |
| 1959 | 0.865 | 1.006 | 1.027 | .611 | 1.124 | | .880 | .945 | 0.927 |
| 1960 | 0.854 | 1.012 | 1.026 | .640 | 1.170 | .597 | .891 | .952 | 0.924 |
| 1961 | 0.821 | 1.004 | 1.010 | .653 | 1.191 | .616 | .853 | .965 | 0.905 |
| 1962 | 0.830 | 0.987 | 0.983 | .652 | 1.192 | .610 | .863 | .958 | 0.916 |
| 1963 | 0.830 | 0.983 | 0.923 | .667 | 1.207 | .619 | .871 | .969 | 0.917 |
| 1964 | 0.849 | 0.989 | 0.925 | .639 | 1.224 | .603 | .876 | .979 | 0.931 |
| 1965 | 0.858 | 0.977 | 0.912 | .581 | 1.224 | .655 | .876 | .975 | 0.955 |
| 1966 | 0.865 | 0.981 | 0.887 | .593 | 1.257 | .661 | .874 | .958 | 0.981 |
| 1967 | 0.866 | 0.972 | 0.835 | .613 | 1.315 | .686 | .848 | .939 | 0.985 |
| 1968 | 0.854 | 0.958 | 0.847 | .623 | 1.339 | .727 | .851 | .934 | 0.999 |
| 1969 | 0.858 | 0.967 | 0.853 | .615 | 1.338 | .761 | .855 | .934 | 1.022 |
| 1970 | 0.845 | 0.966 | 0.850 | .628 | 1.346 | .749 | .841 | .907 | 1.000 |
| 1971 | 0.851 | 0.955 | 0.823 | .612 | 1.341 | .786 | .830 | .857 | 0.995 |
| 1972 | 0.865 | 0.944 | 0.805 | .599 | 1.337 | .823 | .806 | .863 | 1.025 |
| 1973 | 0.901 | 0.942 | 0.799 | .595 | 1.368 | .867 | .797 | .894 | 1.070 |

**Table 5.11**
Total factor productivity relative to the 1970 level for the United States

| | Canada | France | Germany | Italy | Japan | Korea | Netherlands | United Kingdom | United States |
|---|---|---|---|---|---|---|---|---|---|
| 1947 | .608 | | | | | | | | 0.749 |
| 1948 | .604 | | | | | | | | 0.762 |
| 1949 | .614 | | | | | | | | 0.768 |
| 1950 | .665 | .431 | .375 | | | | | | 0.812 |
| 1951 | .661 | .428 | .405 | | | | .529 | | 0.822 |
| 1952 | .697 | .436 | .433 | .490 | .360 | | .532 | | 0.829 |
| 1953 | .713 | .468 | .450 | .521 | .375 | | .565 | | 0.847 |
| 1954 | .689 | .480 | .481 | .524 | .392 | | .592 | | 0.843 |
| 1955 | .728 | .496 | .533 | .561 | .422 | | .613 | .585 | 0.876 |
| 1956 | .760 | .508 | .548 | .581 | .429 | | .623 | .584 | 0.868 |
| 1957 | .749 | .524 | .568 | .588 | .442 | | .624 | .599 | 0.872 |
| 1958 | .753 | .525 | .577 | .610 | .434 | | .577 | .600 | 0.875 |
| 1959 | .755 | .545 | .612 | .633 | .453 | | .621 | .609 | 0.898 |
| 1960 | .757 | .578 | .663 | .644 | .495 | .215 | .651 | .629 | 0.898 |
| 1961 | .763 | .596 | .682 | .674 | .547 | .218 | .666 | .639 | 0.911 |
| 1962 | .785 | .618 | .697 | .695 | .530 | .221 | .665 | .636 | 0.939 |
| 1963 | .806 | .636 | .706 | .696 | .561 | .235 | .658 | .646 | 0.953 |
| 1964 | .832 | .664 | .751 | .715 | .607 | .246 | .699 | .674 | 0.977 |
| 1965 | .857 | .684 | .783 | .760 | .611 | .245 | .715 | .676 | 0.998 |
| 1966 | .875 | .701 | .780 | .779 | .639 | .268 | .713 | .687 | 1.013 |
| 1967 | .865 | .718 | .757 | .806 | .663 | .273 | .737 | .704 | 1.007 |
| 1968 | .890 | .733 | .826 | .824 | .722 | .280 | .766 | .720 | 1.020 |
| 1969 | .900 | .767 | .880 | .862 | .749 | .307 | .792 | .713 | 1.013 |
| 1970 | .914 | .788 | .909 | .876 | .779 | .316 | .828 | .742 | 1.000 |
| 1971 | .936 | .804 | .917 | .846 | .783 | .319 | .845 | .784 | 1.019 |
| 1972 | .950 | .827 | .933 | .865 | .809 | .324 | .884 | .805 | 1.046 |
| 1973 | .963 | .856 | .962 | .901 | .819 | .369 | .908 | .823 | 1.062 |

previous table. For example, the output per capita figures in table 5.8 are obtained by multiplying all the entries in table 5.4 by the U.S. output per capita time series. All the figures in these tables are directly comparable. For example, in table 5.11 Korea's level of productivity in 1973 (0.369) can be directly compared with Japan's level in 1952 (0.360) to infer that Japan's 1952 level was 0.976 times Korea's 1973 level.

## 5.5   Concluding Remarks

Our estimated relative levels of real output per capita for 1970 can be compared with those reported by Kravis, Heston and Summers. We present this comparison in table 5.12. The figures for all countries are taken from Kravis, Heston, and Summers (1978a), except for Canada, which is taken from Kravis, Heston, and Summers (1978b). The results of our study are quite similar to those of Kravis, Heston, and Summers, given the differences in the scope of the product measures employed in the two studies and differences in methodology.

Relative levels of real output per capita and productivity have previously been reported for a subset of the countries in our sample for 1960. Denison (1967) provided estimates for France, Germany, Italy, The Netherlands, and the U.K., relative to the U.S.; and Walters (1968) provided comparison of the U.S. and Canada. In table 5.13 we present the 1960 relative levels of real national income per capita and total

**Table 5.12**
Alternative estimates of per capita output relative to the United States, 1970

|  | Kravis, Heston, Summers[a] | Christensen, Cummings, Jorgenson[b] |
| --- | --- | --- |
| Canada | .819 | .811 |
| France | .732 | .675 |
| Germany | .782 | .721 |
| Italy | .492 | .460 |
| Japan | .592 | .583 |
| Korea | .121 | .101 |
| Netherlands | .687 | .623 |
| United Kingdom | .635 | .546 |

[a] All countries except Canada are from Kravis, Heston, and Summers (1978a).
[b] Table 5.1 above.

**Table 5.13**
Alternative estimates of per capita output and productivity relative to the
United States, 1960

|  | Output per capita | | Productivity | |
|---|---|---|---|---|
|  | Denison and Walters[a] | Christensen, Cummings, Jorgenson[b] | Denison and Walters[b] | Christensen, Cummings, Jorgenson[b] |
| Canada | .726 | .765 | .826 | .843 |
| France | .656 | .541 | .661 | .643 |
| Germany | .729 | .618 | .683 | .737 |
| Italy | .429 | .375 | .497 | .716 |
| Netherlands | .613 | .530 | .658 | .724 |
| United Kingdom | .724 | .537 | .656 | .700 |

[a] Canada is from Walters (1968); the remaining countries from Denison (1967).
[b] Tables 4.4 and 4.7 above.

factor productivity from the Denison and Walters studies. For comparison we present our own estimates for 1960 from tables 5.4 and 5.7 above. The results of our study are fairly similar to those of Denison and Walters. but our estimates of relative output per capita differ more widely from those of Denison and Walters for 1960 than from those of Kravis, Heston, and Summers for 1970, reflecting more substantial differences in the scope of the product measures and differences in methodology. Our estimates of relative productivity levels for 1960 are similar to those of Denison and Walters, except for Italy.[16]

We can compare our results for Japan with those of Denison and Chung (1967) and those of Jorgenson and Nishimizu (1978). Since Denison and Chung provide relative levels of output per capita and productivity for 1970, we compare estimates for this year from all three studies. Denison and Chung estimated Japan's levels of real national income and productivity relative to the United States to be 0.676 and 0.619, respectively. Our corresponding figures are 0.583 and 0.778, indicating lower real product but higher productivity for Japan relative to the U.S. Our estimate of relative real output per capita is very similar to that of Jorgenson and Nishimizu (0.550), but our estimate of Japan's relative productivity is much lower than theirs (0.985). This difference can be traced to the treatment of real labor input. Jorgenson and Nishimizu assumed that the relative wages of government workers in the United States and Japan, as reported by Kravis,

Heston, and Summers, were appropriate for the private sector as well. Consequently, they used this ratio to deflate the ratio of labor compensation in the United States and Japan to obtain the relative quantity of labor input. We do not believe that such a treatment is appropriate, and we have constructed a direct comparison of real labor input for all the countries in our study— including the United States and Japan.

It would be worthwhile to update our results in order to analyze the impact of the oil crisis beginning in 1973 on relative levels of output per capita, capital and labor input per capita, and total factor productivity. It would also be valuable to incorporate additional countries into this study, especially newly industrialized countries similar to Korea. Finally, it would be interesting to model changes in capital and labor input and relative levels of total factor productivity by estimating the parameters of the economic model described in section 5.2. This would permit inferences with respect to the elasticity of substitution between capital and labor and with respect to differences among countries as to the nature of their growth in total factor productivity.

## 5.6    Appendix A: Price Comparisons between Canada and the United States

Segal and Pratt (1967) provide price comparisons for individual components of consumer durables and nondurables in 1965. We have updated these comparisons to 1970 using data on prices from the Bureau of Economic Analysis (1977) for the United States and Statistics Canada (1975) for Canada. We obtain price ratios for consumer durables and for consumer nondurables by weighting price ratios of individual components by average value shares for these components for the two countries. The Canadian value shares are taken from Statistics Canada (1973); the U.S. value shares are taken from Bureau of Labor Statistics (1978).

The remainder of our output and capital input price comparisons for Canada and the United States are based on estimates contained in Walters (1968). Walters' estimates are for 1966; we update these estimates using data from the national accounts. Walters provides a single price relative for structures, which we use for both residential and nonresidential structures.

### 5.7 Appendix B: Methods and Data Sources for Relative Labor Input

Total labor compensation and total employment for each country are taken from Christensen, Cummings, and Jorgenson (1980). Labor input is computed as the product of employment, average hours worked, and an index of educational attainment relative to the United States. Christensen, Cummings, and Jorgenson provide indexes of average hours worked which are comparable across time for each country. With the exception of the United States, Japan, and Korea, actual hours worked cannot be inferred from the indexes, so that it is necessary to obtain the level of hours worked for a base year for the remaining countries. Our estimates of the level of average hours worked are as follows: France, Germany, Italy, The Netherlands, and the United States—estimates for 1960 from Denison (1967); Canada—1960 estimate from Walters (1968).

Indexes of educational attainment cannot be developed on a multi-lateral basis since data for the various countries are not available for the same year on the same educational classification. However, the U.S. data base is sufficiently rich that a binary comparison can be constructed between the United States and each of the eight remaining countries for a single base year. These estimates are updated to 1970 using the rates of growth of educational attainment from Christensen, Cummings, and Jorgenson (1980). Table 5.14 indicates the source of the data on educational attainment and earnings for each country.

**Table 5.14**
Sources of data on educational attainment and earnings

| Canada | Statistics Canada (1974a) and (1975), for 1971 |
|---|---|
| France | Carré, Dubois and Malinvaud (1972), for 1968 |
| Germany | Denison (1967) for 1964 |
| Italy | OECD (1966) for 1966 educational attainment, and Denison (1967) for earnings |
| Japan | Denison and Chung (1976), for 1970 |
| Korea | Economic Planning Board (1973), for 1970 |
| Netherlands | Central Statistical Bureau (1977), for 1971 |
| United Kingdom | Central Statistical Office (1975), for 1972 |
| United States | Bureau of the Census (1966), for comparison with Italy and Germany |
| | Bureau of the Census (1973), for comparison with Canada, France, Korea, the Netherlands, and the U.S. |
| | Denison and Chung (1970), for comparison with Japan |

# Notes

1. Paper presented at the International Seminar on Macroeconomics, Oxford, June 23–24, 1980. The authors are grateful to Douglas W. Caves for helpful discussions, and to Linda Borucki and Irene Powell for research assistance.
2. A survey of international comparisons of output and productivity is given by Kravis (1976).
3. See Christensen, Cummings and Jorgenson (1980). We present a survey of international comparisons of patterns of economic growth on pp. 596–599. We describe patterns of growth in productivity for all nine countries in Christensen, Cummings and Jorgenson (1978).
4. The translog production function was introduced by Christensen, Jorgenson and Lau (1971, 1973).
5. The translog index of productivity growth was introduced by Christensen and Jorgenson (1970). See Caves, Christensen, and Diewert (1982a), Diewert (1980), and Jorgenson and Lau (1980), for derivations of this index from the translog production function and for further discussion.
6. By transitivity we mean that all pairs of comparisons pass the following test: $I_{kl} = I_{kn}/I_{ln}$, where $I_{ij}$ is an index comparing countries $i$ and $j$. In the index number literature this condition is often referred to as circularity.

7. Base-country invariance means that all countries are treated symmetrically, regardless of the order in which they are compared. The term characteristicity was coined by Dreschler (1973); it indicates the degree to which index number weights reflect the economic conditions that are specific to the two entities being compared. Other than constant returns to scale, the comparison technique is free of restrictions such as neutrality of differences in productivity over time or across countries.

8. The translog index of differences in productivity was introduced by Jorgenson and Nishimizu (1978). Jorgenson and Nishimizu derived this and index from the translog production function for two countries. Caves, Christensen, and Diewert (1982a) have pointed out that the translog multilateral productivity index specializes to the Jorgenson-Nishimizu index in the two-country case.

9. The translog quantity indexes were introduced by Fisher (1922) and discussed by Törnqvist (1936), Theil (1965), and Kloek (1966). These indexes of input and output were derived from the translog production function by Diewert (1976).

10. For further discussion of multilateral translog quantity index and a comparison with alternative methodologies, see Caves, Christensen, and Diewert (1982a).

11. Purchasing power parities for output and comparisons of output per capita have been presented for sixteen countries by Kravis, Heston and Summers (1978a). Kravis, Heston and Summers (1978b) have presented comparisons of output per capita for 100 countries, based on an extrapolation of their detailed results for sixteen countries. Earlier references to data on purchasing power parities are Gilbert and Kravis (1954), Gilbert et al. (1958), and Kravis, Kenessey, Heston and Summers (1975).

12. The translog multilateral index for input comparisons was introduced by Caves, Christensen, and Diewert (1982a).

13. The perpetual inventory method is employed by Goldsmith (1955). The dual to the perpetual inventory method, involving the prices of investment goods and capital services, was introduced by Christensen and Jorgenson (1969, 1973a,b). The perpetual inventory method and its dual were employed in Christensen, Cummings, and Jorgenson (1980). For a more detailed discussion of the underlying model of durable capital goods, see Jorgenson (1973).

14. This approach to purchasing power parities for capital input was introduced by Jorgenson and Nishimizu (1978).

15. This approach to purchasing power parities for labor input is similar to that of Denison (1967) and Krueger (1968). Denison's method has also been employed by Denison and Chung (1976).

16. The population data are from the Organization for Economic Cooperation and Development (1977) and Bank of Korea (1977). The 1970 U.S. population was 204.879 million.

17. Different indexes of the quality of labor in Italy account for most of the difference in the estimated levels of productivity.

# 6

## Sectoral Productivity Gaps Between the United States, Japan and Germany, 1960–1979

Klaus Conrad and
Dale W. Jorgenson

### 6.1 Introduction

The purpose of this paper is to look quantitatively at structural problems in the German economy by comparing sectoral differences in the pattern of production for 28 industrial sectors of the U.S. and Japanese economy relative to the German economy. Our objective is to shed some light on the ongoing discussion of the international competitiveness of the German economy and the future of its position as the western world's third largest economy behind the United States and Japan. For this purpose we compare levels of output, capital, labor and intermediate inputs for U.S. and Japanese industries relative to the German industries. We also present levels of sectoral total factor productivity and growth in total factor productivity for U.S. and Japan relative to Germany.

Christensen *et al.* (1981) present at the macro-level differences between levels of total factor productivity in the United States and eight other countries for the period 1952–1973. They find that the productivity level in Germany was 0.522 in 1952 and 0.906 in 1973 relative to the United States. In 1960 it was 0.737 and Denison (1967) found for the same year a gap of 0.683. The productivity level in Japan relative to the U.S. was 0.434 in 1952 and 0.772 in 1973. Christensen *et al.* (1981) concluded that productivity gaps between the United States and its major trading partners have narrowed substantially over the postwar period. A Japan-U.S. comparison on the aggregate level by Jorgenson and Nishimizu (1978) showed an even more remarkable narrowing of the productivity gap over the period 1952–1974.

Disaggregated analysis of the differences in the pattern of production at the industry level will facilitate a better understanding of the anatomy of findings at the macro-level. In this paper we analyze, for each industrial sector, differences between U.S. and German levels of output and between Japanese and German levels of output, and we allocate these differences to the differences in factor input and the differences in levels of productivity in the sector in the two countries in question.

## 6.2 Methodology

Our methodology for a comparison of output and input levels and of total factor productivity (TFP) for Germany (G) to its trading partners U.S. (U) and Japan (J) is based on a production function for all three countries with common properties in the production process of the corresponding product[1]

$$x = F(v, D_J, D_U, t),$$  (6.1)

where $x$ is the sectoral output, $v$ is the vector of inputs, $t$ is time as a representation for technical change, and $D_U$ and $D_J$ are dummy variables for the United States and Japan. As we express levels of output, input and total factor productivity relative to Germany, we omit a dummy variable for Germany from the production function. The dummy variables catch the country-specific deviation from the joint production process as given in (6.1). If we want to derive the difference in the level of output between Germany and Japan at a given point of time, we differentiate (6.1) totally with respect to $D_J$

$$\frac{dx}{dD_J} = \sum_{i=1}^{n} F_{v_i} \frac{dv_i}{dD_J} + \frac{\partial F}{\partial D_J}.$$  (6.2)

In terms of logarithmic derivatives (6.2) is equivalent to

$$\frac{d \ln x}{dD_J} = \sum_{i=1}^{n} \frac{\partial \ln x}{\partial \ln v_i} \frac{d \ln v_i}{dD_J} + \frac{\partial \ln x}{\partial D_J}.$$  (6.3)

The difference in productivity between any country and Germany, say $w_{DJ}$ in the case of Japan, is defined as follows

$$w_{DJ} = \frac{\partial \ln x}{\partial D_J} = \frac{d \ln x}{dD_J} - \sum \frac{\partial \ln x}{\partial \ln v_i} \frac{d \ln v_i}{dD_J}.$$  (6.4)

The difference in productivity of a sector between two countries, $w_{DJ}$, is the logarithmic difference in the sectors' output levels between countries, holding factor input and time constant. This is the economic interpretation of the partial derivative $\partial \ln x / \partial D_J$. For calculating the difference in productivity we use (6.4) with weights depending on the assumptions made with respect to firms' behavior and price determination. Under the assumption of perfect competition we obtain

$$\frac{\partial \ln x}{\partial \ln v_i} = \frac{q_i v_i}{p \cdot x} =: w_i , \qquad (i = 1, \ldots, n) , \tag{6.5}$$

where $p$ and $q_i (i = 1, \ldots, n)$ are the prices of output and inputs, respectively. In this case, the difference in productivity (6.4) can be calculated as

$$w_{DJ} = \frac{d \ln x}{dD_J} - \sum_{i=1}^{n} w_i \frac{d \ln v_i}{dD_J} . \tag{6.6}$$

The advantage of measuring differences in productivity by means of a Divisia index (6.6) is that the production function need not be specified. Since measurement is based on discrete data points we have to approximate the continuous Divisia index by a discrete index. In order to make the resulting approximation error as small as possible we make sure that the index is "exact."[2] An index is defined to be exact if the following relation holds for a production function $x = F(v)$

$$F(v(T))/F(v(0)) = I(q(T), q(0), v(T), v(0)) ,$$

where $q$ is the vector of input prices. If the index $I$ is known, it is possible in such cases to determine exactly the value of the production function at time $T$ from the value at time 0. However, any discrete index is only exact with respect to certain types of production functions. Therefore the choice for a discrete index also implies the fixation on a certain production function. If we select a discrete approximation of the Divisia index we must pay attention to the implication that the implied production function should be compatible with the data observed for the production process.

For measuring productivity differences we choose as a discrete approximation of the Divisia index the Törnqvist-index. In this case

(6.6) becomes an expression for differences in productivity referred to as *translog index of differences in productivity*[3]

$$\bar{w}_{DJ} = \ln x(G) - \ln x(J) - \sum_i \bar{w}_i(\ln v_i(G) - \ln v_i(J)) , \qquad (6.7)$$

where $\bar{w}_i$ is an average of the cost shares of both countries:

$$\bar{w}_i = 1/2(w_i(J) + w_i(G)) .$$

As mentioned above, it is of interest to know the type of production function for which the Törnqvist-index is exact. In his quadratic approximation lemma Diewert (1976) has shown that the Törnqvist index is exact if and only if the production function is homogeneous and translog (Christensen *et al.*, 1971; 1973), a production function of a very flexible functional form. The conclusion is that the Törnqvist or translog index is superior to the traditional indexes like Paasche or Laspeyres, a geometric mean, or Fisher's ideal index. Those indexes are exact only if the production function is of one of the following restrictive types: Leontief, Cobb-Douglas or a quadratic function, respectively. The reasons for the increasing number of empirical studies using the Törnqvist index are: (i) the implied production function is of a flexible form, (ii) the parameters of the production function need not be known, (iii) derivatives of the first order are sufficient for an exact determination of the difference in productivity (see (6.5)).

Similarly to the translog index of differences in productivity (Jorgenson and Nishimizu 1978) we can define the translog index of productivity growth (Christensen and Jorgenson, 1970). For this reason we do not determine differences in output and productivity between two countries but between two points in time. Instead of (6.3) we obtain

$$\frac{d \ln x}{dt} = \sum_i \frac{\partial \ln x}{\partial \ln v_i} \frac{d \ln v_i}{dt} + \frac{\partial \ln x}{\partial t} , \qquad (6.8)$$

where $w_t := \partial \ln x/\partial t$ is the rate of productivity growth defined as the growth of output with respect to time, holding factor inputs and the country dummy variables constant. Similarly as above, the *translog index of productivity growth* between consecutive discrete data points for a given country is

$$\bar{w}_t = \ln x(t) - \ln x(t-1) - \sum_i \bar{w}_i(\ln v_i(t) - \ln v_i(t-1)) \qquad (6.9)$$

where $\bar{w}_i := 1/2(w_i(t) + w_i(t-1))$ is an average of the countries cost shares.

For making multilateral productivity comparisons we cannot use the bilateral index discussed above as those indexes are not base-country invariant. Bilateral indexes do not satisfy the circularity condition, but all pairs of comparisons should pass the following circularity condition: $I_{km} = I_{kn}/I_{mn}$ where $I_{ij}$ is an index comparing countries $i$ and $j$. Caves $et$ $al.$ (1982a) have derived a translog multilateral index of productivity which satisfies the circularity condition, and imposes no $a$ $priori$ restrictions on the structure of production. To achieve circularity they construct a hypothetical country $H$ with output $\overline{\ln x}$, inputs $\overline{\ln v_i}$ and cost shares $\bar{w}_i$, where a bar indicates the average over all three countries. The difference in productivity between, say Japan, and this hypothetical country $H$ is

$$\bar{w}_{J,It} = \ln x(J) - \overline{\ln x} - 1/2 \sum_i (w_i(J) + \bar{w}_i)(\ln v_i(J) - \overline{\ln v_i}) .$$

Similarly, the differences in productivity between Germany and country $H$ is

$$\bar{w}_{G,II} = \ln x(G) - \overline{\ln x} - 1/2 \sum_i (w_i(G) + \bar{w}_i)(\ln v_i(G) - \overline{\ln v_i}) .$$

A circular multilateral index of differences in productivity can be derived by defining

$$\bar{w}_{G,J} = \bar{w}_{G,H} - \bar{w}_{J,H} ,$$

i.e., with C = Japan or U.S.

$$\bar{w}_{G,C} = \ln x(G) - \ln x(C)$$
$$- 1/2 \sum_i (w_i(G) + \bar{w}_i)(\ln v_i(G) - \overline{\ln v_i})$$
$$+ 1/2 \sum_i (w_i(C) + \bar{w}_i)(\ln v_i(C) - \overline{\ln v_i}) . \qquad (6.10)$$

This expression for differences in productivity, the $translog$ $multilateral$ $index$ $of$ $differences$ $in$ $productivity$, is base-country invariant (circular), i.e., $\bar{w}_{G,J} = \bar{w}_{G,U} - \bar{w}_{J,U}$, and specializes to the bilateral index in the two-country case.[4]

For input comparisons we can employ similar expressions for relative inputs. If $V$ is the input aggregate, the bilateral translog index between Japan and the hypothetical country $H$ is

$$\ln V\,(J) - \overline{\ln V} = 1/2 \sum_i (\overline{w}_{vi}(J) + \overline{w}_{vi})\,(\ln v_i(J) - \overline{\ln v_i}) \,. \tag{6.11}$$

Similarly for Germany

$$\ln V(G) - \overline{\ln V} = 1/2 \sum_i (\overline{w}_{vi}(G) + \overline{w}_{vi})\,(\ln v_i(G) - \overline{\ln v_i}) \,. \tag{6.12}$$

If we subtract (6.11) from (6.12), we obtain the circular *translog multilateral indexes of relative factor inputs*,[5] in our case relative to Germany

$$\ln V(G) - \ln V(C) = 1/2 \sum_i (w_{vi}(G) + \overline{w}_i)(\ln v_i(G) - \overline{\ln v_i})$$
$$- 1/2 \sum_i (w_{vi}(C) + \overline{w}_i)(\ln v_i(C) - \overline{\ln v_i}) \,, \tag{6.13}$$

where the bar indicates the average of input $i$ over all three countries, and $C = J$ or $U$.

### 6.3   Data and Purchasing Power Parities

A comparison of levels of output, inputs and levels of total factor productivity requires data on the relative prices of output and for inputs among all the countries included in the comparison. The traditional approach of using exchange rates to estimate relative prices of output is well-known to be unsatisfactory. Reliable data for international price comparisons must be based on direct observations of prices for comparable products. Such data have been developed by Kravis *et al.* (1982) who provide comparisons of relative prices and quantities of output for 1975. To obtain relative price levels of capital and labor input for 1975 we follow Jorgenson and Nishimizu (1978) in constructing purchasing power parities for labor and capital input.

The starting point for the analysis of differences in the sectoral pattern of production between countries is the production account for each sector in each country. The value of output, defined from the producer's point of view, includes the value of labor and capital input as well as the value of intermediate input. It also includes subsidies as they are considered part of producer's income, but excludes all indirect taxes on output as they are not part of production costs. The value of labor input includes all taxes levied on labor and all costs incurred by the producers in employment of labor such as various insurances, etc. The value of capital input includes all taxes levied on the ownership and the utilization of capital. Output and factor input have been measured so that the value of output is equal to the value of all factor inputs in each sector.

We employ the sectoral production accounts developed for the United States by Gollop and Jorgenson (1980), for Japan by Jorgenson and Nishimizu (1979), and for Germany by Conrad and Unger (1984). Leaving the details of the accounts to these studies, the main characteristics of the data base can be summarized here. The production accounts are prepared for 51 industries in the U.S., 30 industries in Japan and 46 industries in Germany. We maintain strict sectoral correspondence and consistency between the three countries in terms of 28 sectors, which are the aggregates over the original accounts. Price and quantity indexes of labor input for every sector in each country are measured on the basis of labor compensation and man-hours worked, classified at least by workers, employees, self-employed and family workers. Labor input for each country is the product of employment, average hours worked, and an index of educational attainment. Hourly wage rates are obtained by dividing labor compensation for employees, workers and self-employed in each country by the corresponding labor input. Price and quantity indexes of sectoral capital input in each country are measured on the basis of property compensation and capital stocks, estimated by asset types (structures, producers' durable equipments, inventory) within each sector. Flow of capital input is assumed proportional to the level of capital stocks in each sector. Under the assumption that the relative efficiency of the $j$th capital good declines geometrically with age, the rate of replacement, say $\delta_j$, is a constant. Capital stock at the end of each period, say $A_j(t)$, has been estimated from investment $I_j(t)$ during the period and capital stock at the beginning of the period.

$$A_j(t) = I_j(t) + (1 - \delta_i) A_j(t - 1) \tag{6.14}$$

$j$ = structures, equipment, inventory .

The dual to the perpetual inventory method (6.14), involving the prices $p_I$ of investment goods and of capital services $q_K$, implies that the price $q_{Kj}$ of the $j$th capital input can be expressed as

$$q_{Kj}(t) = p_{Ij}(t-1) \left\{ r(t) - \frac{p_{Ij}(t) - p_{Ij}(t-1)}{p_{Ij}(t-1)} \right\} + \delta_j P_{Ij}(t) , \qquad (6.15)$$

where $r(t)$ is the sector's nominal rate of return on capital. Corrected by the rate of inflation we obtain the own rate of return on capital. Price and quantity indexes of sectoral intermediate input in each country are measured on the basis of interindustry transaction matrices estimated annually for each country.

To achieve comparability in sectoral accounts between the three countries, we develop purchasing power parities (PPPs) based on the work of Kravis *et al.* (1982). They provide PPPs for detailed components of aggregate consumption goods output and investment goods output for the year 1975 between the yen and the dollar, and between the DM and the dollar. We construct the PPPs for sectoral output and intermediate input by mapping the Kravis *et al.*'s classification system and our industry classification system. To obtain PPPs for capital input in 1975, we take the ratio of the price of capital input for one country relative to that of the other.

$$\frac{q_{K,t}(C)}{q_{K,t}(US)} = \frac{p_{I,t-1}(C)\bar{r}_t(C) + \delta(C)p_{I,t}(C)}{p_{I,t-1}(US)\bar{r}_t(US) + \delta(US)p_{I,t}(US)} , \qquad (6.16)$$

where $\bar{r}$ is the own rate of return on capital specified in (6.15). We next rewrite (6.16) to make use of the PPP for investment goods output as an appropriate PPP for new capital goods. This gives us the PPP for capital input in dollars,

$$\frac{q_{K,t}(C)}{q_{K,t}(US)} = \frac{p_{I,t}(C)}{p_{I,t}(US)} \frac{\left\{ \dfrac{p_{I,t-1}(C)}{p_{I,t}(C)} \bar{r}_t(C) + \delta(C) \right\}}{\left\{ \dfrac{p_{I,t-1}(US)}{p_{I,t}(US)} \bar{r}_t(US) + \delta(US) \right\}} . \qquad (6.17)$$

If the rate of inflation, the rate of return and the rate of replacement are the same in two countries, the PPP for capital input in 1975 is equal to the PPP for investment goods output. To obtain PPPs for labor input, we multiply the relative hourly wage rates for any two countries by the ratio of labor input per hour worked for the two countries. This ratio adjusts man-hours worked in Germany and Japan in the base year to achieve equivalence with American and

Japanese man-hours. For the Germany-U.S. comparison we take such a quality index from Denison (1967, pp. 70–77). His quality adjustment index on the aggregate level for all employed persons is 94.8 compared to 100 for the U.S. On this basis one should expect output per man-hour to be 5.2 percent lower in Germany than in the U.S. For the Japan-U.S. comparison Denison and Chung (1976, p. 103) have calculated an index of 95.2 (U.S. = 100) as an appropriate factor for the education component of Japanese labor input.

All the comparisons reported in the paper are base-country invariant, but they are not base-year invariant. As the Kravis *et al.* (1982) study is only available for 1970 and 1975, we use 1975 as the base year and construct price indexes for other years by chain-linking them to 1975. In symbols we employ

$$PPPX = PPPX_0 \, (p^G/p^{US}) \,, \tag{6.18}$$

where $PPPX_0$ is the PPP for sectoral output in DM for 1975, $p^G$ is the German output deflator, and $p^{US}$ is the U.S. output deflator. Similarly, PPPs for factor inputs are

$$PPP_i = PPP_{i0} \, (q_i^G/q_i^{US}) \,, \qquad i = K, L, M \,, \tag{6.19}$$

where the meaning of the variables is analogous to (6.18) and $M$ is intermediate inputs.

## 6.4   Empirical Results

Our results are summarized in tables 6.1 and 6.2. Table 6.1 shows indexes of total factor productivities for each of the 28 industries. The indexes are normalized to unity in 1960 with rates of growth of total factor productivity (TFP) accumulated up to 1979. There is no industry in Germany and U.S. with an average growth rate of TFP of 3 percent and more per year (at least 1.76 in 1979), but three in Japan (transportation equipment, electrical machinery, finance). Industries with an average growth rate of TFP between 2 and 3 percent (1.46 to 1.76) are four in Germany (utilities, electrical machinery, trade, transportation), only two in the U.S. (electrical machinery, textile), but six in Japan (chemicals, fabricated metal, precision instruments, miscellaneous manufacturing, apparel, transportation). There are, however, 22 industries in the U.S. with an average growth rate of TFP of less than

**Table 6.1**
Indexes of total factor productivity (normalized to 1.0 in 1960) by industry
and country

| Industry | Germany | | U.S. | | Japan | |
|---|---|---|---|---|---|---|
| | 1970 | 1979 | 1970 | 1979 | 1970 | 1979 |
| Agriculture | 1.09 | 1.22 | 1.18 | 1.25 | 0.92 | 0.94 |
| Utilities | 1.36 | 1.52 | 1.16 | 1.00 | 1.20 | 1.19 |
| Mining | 1.18 | 1.35 | 1.07 | 0.54 | 1.21 | 1.34 |
| Chemicals | 1.13 | 1.27 | 1.18 | 1.19 | 1.49 | 1.60 |
| Petroleum | 1.34 | 1.16 | 1.23 | 0.56 | 0.89 | 0.63 |
| Rubber, plastic | 1.24 | 1.39 | 1.11 | 1.18 | 1.17 | 1.21 |
| Stone, clay, glass | 1.15 | 1.25 | 1.06 | 1.04 | 1.33 | 1.26 |
| Primary metal | 1.03 | 1.06 | 0.98 | 0.92 | 1.11 | 1.18 |
| Nonferrous metal | 1.04 | 1.09 | 1.04 | 0.95 | 0.99 | 1.01 |
| Fabricated metal | 1.13 | 1.22 | 1.09 | 1.11 | 1.32 | 1.48 |
| Transportation equipment | 0.94 | 1.16 | 1.07 | 1.09 | 2.16 | 1.80 |
| Machinery | 1.14 | 1.17 | 1.09 | 1.14 | 1.26 | 1.25 |
| Motor vehicles | 1.06 | 1.25 | 1.08 | 1.17 | 1.02 | 1.07 |
| Electrical machinery | 1.29 | 1.55 | 1.20 | 1.46 | 1.44 | 1.89 |
| Precision instruments | 1.20 | 1.35 | 1.10 | 1.16 | 1.25 | 1.65 |
| Miscellaneous manufacturing | 1.10 | 1.14 | 1.09 | 0.99 | 1.26 | 1.58 |
| Lumber, wood, furniture | 1.26 | 1.42 | 1.06 | 0.96 | 1.27 | 1.45 |
| Paper, etc. | 1.15 | 1.26 | 1.09 | 1.09 | 1.17 | 1.17 |
| Printing, etc. | 1.12 | 1.15 | 1.01 | 1.21 | 1.08 | 0.89 |
| Leather | 1.04 | 1.12 | 1.04 | 0.97 | 1.13 | 1.15 |
| Textile mill | 1.10 | 1.28 | 1.25 | 1.49 | 1.06 | 1.09 |
| Apparel, etc. | 1.12 | 1.21 | 1.04 | 1.23 | 1.26 | 1.47 |
| Food, etc. | 1.03 | 1.07 | 1.03 | 1.00 | 0.99 | 0.82 |
| Construction | 1.03 | 1.21 | 0.99 | 0.87 | 0.90 | 0.87 |
| Trade | 1.42 | 1.61 | 1.12 | 1.19 | 1.29 | 1.28 |
| Transportation and communication | 1.30 | 1.56 | 1.09 | 1.21 | 1.35 | 1.61 |
| Finance, insurance | 1.16 | 1.39 | 1.00 | 1.08 | 1.53 | 2.19 |
| Services | 1.01 | 1.02 | 0.93 | 0.95 | 1.13 | 1.00 |

one percent (less than 1.20) against 10 industries in Germany and 14 in
Japan. All three countries have experienced relative high productivity·
growth in electrical machinery, precision instruments, and transportation and communication. Industries with low or no productivity
growth in all three countries are primary metal, nonferrous metal,
food, construction and services. The service sector with its growing
weight in national output is often claimed to be one reason for the current decline in productivity growth.

Table 6.2 summarizes our results of the existence or nonexistence of

**Table 6.2**
Summary of the results

| Industry | Germany–U.S. | Germany–Japan | U.S.–Japan |
|---|---|---|---|
| Agriculture | + | + | + |
| Utilities | 1974 (−) | + | + |
| Mining | 1973 (−) | + | 1973 (+) |
| Chemicals | — | 1967 (+) | 1974 (+) |
| Petroleum | * | * | + |
| Rubber, plastic | 1963 (−) | + | + |
| Stone, clay, glass | 1979 (−) | + − | + − |
| Primary metal | 1975 (−) | 1971 (+) | 1975 (+) |
| Nonferrous metal | * | * | 1972 (+) |
| Fabricated metal | 1966 (−) | + | + − |
| Transportation equipment | 1971 (−) | + − | + − |
| Machinery | — | 1969 (+) | 1973 (+) |
| Motor vehicles | — | + − | + − |
| Electrical machinery | − | 1971 (+) | 1973 (+) |
| Precision instruments | 1979 (−) | 1967 (+) | 1973 (+) |
| Miscellaneous manufacturing | — | 1965 (+) | 1977 (+) |
| Lumber, wood, furniture | 1964 (−) | + | 1977 (+) |
| Paper, etc. | — | − | 1965 (+) |
| Printing, etc. | − | + | + |
| Leather | 1969 (−) | 1967 (+) | 1967 (+) |
| Textile mill | − | 1971 (+) | + |
| Apparel, etc. | 1968 (−) | 1973 (+) | 1970 (+) |
| Food, etc. | − | + | + |
| Construction | 1977 (−) | + | + |
| Trade | 1975 (−) | + | + − |
| Transportation and communication | — | − | − |
| Finance, insurance | + | + − | 1971 (+) |
| Services | 1965 (+) | + | + |

| | |
|---|---|
| — | Productivity gap closing, |
| − | Productivity gap not closing, |
| Year (−) | Productivity gap closed in year mentioned, |
| + − | Productivity advantage losing by the first country, |
| + | Productivity advantage not losing by the first country, |
| Year (+) | Productivity advantage lost by the first country in the year mentioned, |
| * | Negative profits in several years; methodology not applicable. |

productivity gaps and their narrowing or closing. A Germany-U.S. comparison shows that all manufacturing industries in Germany were behind their U.S. counterparts in their levels of technology at the beginning of the period 1960–1979. German industries with a gradual but continuous narrowing of the gap are chemicals, machinery, motor vehicles, miscellaneous manufacturing, paper, and transportation and communication. They even remain behind the U.S. in 1979. Industries which have caught up with the U.S. in the sixties are rubber and plastic, fabricated metal, lumber, leather, and apparel. Industries which have caught up in the seventies are utilities, mining, stone, primary metal, transportation equipment, precision instruments, construction, and trade. Industries which do not show any tendency to catch up to the U.S. levels of technology are electrical machinery, printing textile, and food.

A German-Japanese comparison shows that most Japanese industries were behind their German counterparts in the levels of technology in the early sixties. However, nine German industries which belong to the manufacturing sector, have lost their productivity advantage between 1965 and 1978. In the sixties chemicals, machinery, precision instruments, miscellaneous manufacturing, and leather lost their productivity advantage and in the seventies the same happened to primary metal, electrical machinery, textile, and apparel. No closing of the Japanese productivity gap can be found in 11 industries, and in 4 industries we observe a catching up by the Japanese industries. Those industries are stone, transportation equipment, motor vehicles, and finance. German industries with a productivity gap to their Japanese counterparts are paper, and transportation and communication.

Finally, a U.S.-Japanese comparison shows a similar picture as a U.S.-Germany comparison. In all industries except transportation we find a U.S. productivity advantage in the early sixties. In 13 industries the U.S. lost their productivity advantage between 1965 and 1978. Whereas in the sixties only 2 industries (paper, leather) have caught up with the U.S., most of the productivity advantage was lost in the seventies. Furthermore, 5 industries show a tendency to lose their productivity advantage in the near future. There are, however, still 9 out of 26 sectors where the U.S. stands ahead of Japan since 1960 although those industries belong mainly to the light manufacturing sector or to the nonmanufacturing sector.

The result of this study can be summarized by concluding that the catching-up process by the Japanese economy is a challenge to most of the industries of the manufacturing sector of the U.S. and German economy. In the near future the diffusion of technology and living standards should eliminate the gaps in levels of sectoral technologies so that the remaining differences in levels of output between the countries is only due to differences in levels of factor input. This will be, however, as our results show, no smooth process of convergency.

## Notes

1. The methodological concept was first derived by Jorgenson and Nishimizu (1978; 1979) and has been extended by Denny and Fuss (1983a) and Caves et al. (1982a).

2. See Diewert (1976) and Lau (1979) for exact indexes in the economic theory of index numbers.

3. The translog index of differences in productivity was introduced by Jorgenson and Nishimizu (1978).

4. For an application of translog multilateral indexes of differences in productivity see Christensen et al. (1981).

5. The translog multilateral index for input comparisons was introduced by Caves et al. (1982a) and applied by Christensen et al. (1981).

# 7    Japan—U.S. Industry-Level Productivity Comparisons, 1960–1979

Dale W. Jorgenson,
Masahiro Kuroda, and
Mieko Nishimizu

This article presents a comparison between patterns of growth in Japanese and U.S. industries during the period 1960–1979. During the period of rapid economic growth in Japan, 1960–1970, annual growth rates of productivity in Japan were substantially higher than those in the United States. Since 1970, productivity growth rates have decreased in the Japanese economy and interindustry variation in productivity performance has increased dramatically. For 9 of 30 industries included in the study the productivity gap between Japan and the United States closed during the period 1960–1979. For 19 industries there remain some significant differences in productivity levels in 1979.

## 7.1    Introduction

The purpose of this chapter is to provide an international comparison between patterns of growth in Japanese and U.S. industries during the period 1960–1979. Throughout the period 1960–1979, the United States has maintained its position as the world's largest economy and the leader among industrialized countries in output per capita. During this period Japan has become the world's third largest economy behind the United States and the Soviet Union, but a substantial gap between Japanese and U.S. levels of output per capita has remained.

Starting with the sudden increase in oil prices in 1973, Japan and the United States have experienced a dramatic deterioration in rates of economic growth. The primary objective of this chapter is to characterize patterns of growth for each of 30 industrial sectors in the two countries and to assess the impact of the oil crisis on both countries. A secondary objective is to anlayze the differences in the sectoral levels of productivity between the two countries during the period 1960–1979.

Our methodology for international comparisons is based on the economic theory of production. This methodology was developed by Jorgenson and Nishimizu (1978) and applied to aggregate comparisons of economic growth in Japan and the United States during the period 1952–1974. Christensen *et al.* (1980, 1981) have extended these comparisons to nine countries, including Japan and the United States, during the period 1947–1973. These Japan-U.S. comparisons are based on earlier studies of economic growth in the United States by Christensen and Jorgenson (1970, 1973a) and in Japan by Ezaki and Jorgenson (1973) and by Nishimizu and Hulten (1978).

Christensen *et al.* (1980) found that the years 1960–1973 were a period of substantial economic growth in the United States and of extremely rapid growth in Japan. Christensen *et al.* (1981) analyzed relative levels of output, capital input, labor input, and productivity in the two countries. They concluded that the narrowing of the gap between levels of output during this period was due to (1) the increase in the relative capital intensity of production in Japan, and (2) the rapid rise in the level of productivity in Japan relative to the United States. An analysis of sectoral patterns of production will facilitate a better understanding of these findings at the aggregate level.

The plan of this chapter is as follows. We discuss the theoretical framework for international comparisons in section 7.2. Section 7.3 presents a brief discussion of the data for the measurement of output and inputs by industry and summarizes our empirical findings about patterns of growth in Japan and the United States. Section 7.4 discusses the estimation of the purchasing power parities for output and inputs required for international comparisons. Section 7.5 presents our empirical findings on differences in productivity levels by industry between Japan and the United States. Concluding remarks are given in section 7.6.

## 7.2   Theoretical Framework

Our methodology is based on the economic theory of production. We find it convenient to regard the data on production patterns in Japan and the United States as separate sets of observations. However, we assume that these observations are generated by bilateral models of production for each industrial sector. We can describe the implications of the theory of production in terms of production functions for each sector. These functions give output as a function of capital, labor, and intermediate inputs, a dummy variable equal to one for Japan and zero for the United States, and time as an index of technology.

To represent our models of production we first require some notation. There are $I$ industrial sectors, indexed by ($I = 1, 2, \ldots, I$). In our application $I$ is equal to 30 industries in Japan and the United States. We denote the quantities of outputs by $\{Z_i\}$ and the quantities of capital, labor, and intermediate inputs by $\{K_i, L_i, M_i\}$. Similarly, we denote the output prices by $\{q_i\}$ and the input prices by $\{p_K^i \ p_L^i \ p_M^i\}$. We can represent the shares of inputs in the value of output by

$$v_K^i = \frac{p_K^i K_i}{q_i Z_i} \ , \qquad v_L^i = \frac{p_L^i L_i}{q_i Z_i} \ , \qquad v_M^i = \frac{p_M^i M_i}{q_i Z_i} \ , \qquad (i = 1, 2, \ldots, I) \ .$$

Outputs are valued in producers' prices, while inputs are valued in purchasers' prices.

In addition, we require the notation:

$v_i = (v_K^i, v_L^i, v_M^i)$

vector of value shares of the $i$th industry ($i = 1, 2, \ldots, I$).

$\ln X_i = (\ln K_i, \ln L_i, \ln M_i)$

vector of logarithms of input quantities of the
    $i$th industry ($i = 1, 2, \ldots, I$).

$T$ time as an index of technology.

$D$ dummy variable, equal to one for Japan and zero for the
    United States.

We assume that the $i$th industry allocates the value of its output among the three inputs in accord with the production function

$$\ln Z_i = \ln X_i' \alpha_X^i + \alpha_T^i \cdot T + \alpha_D^i \cdot D + 1/2 \ln X_i' B_{XX}^i \ln X_i + \ln X_i' \beta_{XT}^i \cdot T$$
$$+ \ln X_i' \beta_{XD}^i \cdot D + 1/2 \beta_{TT}^i \cdot T^2 + \beta_{TD}^i \cdot T \cdot D + 1/2 \beta_{DD}^i \cdot D^2 \ ,$$
$$(i = 1, 2, \ldots, I) \ . \tag{7.1}$$

For these production functions, outputs are transcendental or, more specifically, exponential functions of the logarithms of the inputs. We refer to these forms as *transcendental logarithmic production functions* or, more simply, translog production functions, indicating the role of the variables.

The translog production function (7.1) was introduced by Christensen *et al.* (1971, 1973). In this representation the scalars $\{\alpha_T^i, \alpha_D^i, \beta_{TT}^i, \beta_{TD}^i, \beta_{DD}^i\}$, the vectors $\{\alpha_X^i, \beta_{XT}^i, \beta_{XD}^i\}$, and the matrices $\{B_{XX}^i\}$ are constant parameters. These parameters differ among industries, reflecting differences among technologies. Within each industry differences in technology among time periods are represented by time as an index of technology. Differences in technology between Japan and the United States are represented by a dummy variable, equal to one for Japan and zero for the United States.

We consider production under constant returns to scale, so that a proportional change in all inputs results in a proportional change in output. In analyzing differences in each industry's production patterns between the two countries, we combine the production function with necessary conditions for producer equilibrium. We express these conditions as equalities between shares of each input in the value of the output of the industry and the elasticity of output with respect to that input. The elasticities depend on input levels, the dummy variable for each country, and time. Under constant returns to scale the sum of the elasticities with respect to all inputs is equal to unity, so that the value shares also sum to unity.

The value shares of the $i$th industry are equal to the logarithmic derivatives of the production function with respect to logarithms of the inputs

$$v_i \frac{\partial \ln Z_i}{\partial \ln X_i}, \qquad (i = 1, 2, \ldots, I) . \tag{7.2}$$

Applying this relationship to the translog production function, we obtain the system of value shares

$$v_i = \alpha_X^i + B_{XX}^i \ln X_i + \beta_{XT}^i \cdot T + \beta_{XD}^i \cdot D , \qquad (i = 1, 2, \ldots, I) . \tag{7.3}$$

We can define *rates of technical change*, say $\{v_T^i\}$, as rates of growth of outputs with respect to time, holding the inputs constant

$$v_T^i = \frac{\partial \ln Z_i}{\partial T}, \qquad (i = 1, 2, \ldots, I) . \tag{7.4}$$

For the translog production function this relationship takes the form

$$v_T^i = \alpha_T^i + B_{XT}^{i'} \ln X_i + \beta_{TT}^i \cdot T + \beta_{TD}^i \cdot D , \qquad (i = 1, 2, \ldots, I) . \tag{7.5}$$

Similarly, we can define *differences in technology* between Japan and the United States, say $\{v_D^i\}$, as the rates of growth of outputs with respect to the dummy variable, holding the inputs constant

$$v_D^i = \frac{\partial \ln Z_i}{\partial D} , \qquad (i = 1, 2, \ldots, I) . \tag{7.6}$$

For the translog production function this relationship is

$$v_D^i = \alpha_D^i + B_{XD}^{i'} \ln X_i + \beta_{TD}^i \cdot T + \beta_{DD}^i \cdot D , \qquad (i = 1, 2, \ldots, I) . \tag{7.7}$$

The outputs $\{Z_i\}$, inputs $\{K_i, L_i, M_i\}$, and prices $\{q_i, p_K^i, p_L^i, p_M^i\}$ are observable for all time periods in both countries. The value shares $\{v^i\}$ can be derived from the prices and quantities and are also directly observable. Although the rates of technical change $\{v_T^i\}$ are not directly observable, average rates of technical change in any two points of time, say $T$ and $T - 1$, can be expressed as the difference between the growth rate of output and a weighted average of the growth rates of inputs,

$$\overline{v}_T^i = \ln Z_i(T) - \ln Z_i(T - 1) - \overline{v}_i^i [\ln X_i(T) - \ln X_i(T - 1)] ,$$
$$(i = 1, 2, \ldots, I) , \tag{7.8}$$

where the average rates of technical change are

$$\overline{v}_T^i = 1/2 \, [v_T^i(T) - v_T^i(T - 1)] ,$$

and the weights are given by the average value shares

$$\overline{v}_i = 1/2 \, [v_i(T) - v_i(T - 1)] , \qquad (i = 1, 2, \ldots, I) .$$

We refer to the index numbers (7.8) as *translog quantity indexes of the rates of technical change*.[1]

Similarly, the differences in technology $\{v_D^i\}$ are not directly observable. However, the average of these differences for Japan and the United States can be expressed as the differences between logarithms of the outputs, less a weighted average of the differences between the logarithms of the inputs,

$$\hat{v}_D^i = \ln Z_i(\text{JAPAN}) - \ln Z_i(\text{U. S.}) - \hat{v}_i^i [\ln X_i(\text{JAPAN}) - \ln X_i(\text{U. S.})] ,$$
$$(i = 1, 2, \ldots, I) , \tag{7.9}$$

where the average differences in technology

$$\hat{v}^i_D = 1/2\,[v^i_D(\text{JAPAN}) + v^i_D(\text{U.S.})]\,,$$

and the weights are given by the average value shares

$$\hat{v}_i = 1/2\,[v_i(\text{JAPAN}) + v_i(\text{U.S.})]\,, \qquad (i = 1, 2, \ldots, J)\,.$$

We refer to the index numbers (7.9) as *translog quantity indexes of differences in technology*.[2]

In our bilateral models of production the capital, labor, and intermediate inputs are aggregates that depend on the quantities of individual capital inputs, labor inputs, and intermediate inputs into the sector. We can extend our bilateral models of production by expressing the inputs as functions of their components. For this purpose we require some additional notation. We denote the quantities of capital inputs by $\{K_{ki}\}$, labor inputs by $\{L_{li}\}$, and intermediate inputs by $\{M_{mi}\}$. Similarly, we denote the prices of these inputs by $\{p^i_{Kk}, p^i_{Ll}, p^i_{Mm}\}$. We can represent the shares of the individual inputs in the value of the corresponding aggregate by

$$v^i_{Kk} = \frac{p^i_{Kk}K_{ki}}{p^i_K K_i}\,, \qquad (i = 1, 2, \ldots, I\,;\quad k = 1, 2, \ldots, K)\,,$$

$$v^i_{Ll} = \frac{p^i_{Ll}K_{li}}{p^i_L L_i}\,, \qquad (i = 1, 2, \ldots, I\,;\quad l = 1, 2, \ldots, L)\,,$$

$$v^i_{Mm} = \frac{p^i_{Mm}K_{mi}}{p^i_M M_i}\,, \qquad (i = 1, 2, \ldots, I\,;\quad m = 1, 2, \ldots, M)\,,$$

Inputs are valued in purchasers' prices.

$v^K_i = (v^i_{K1}, v^i_{K2}, \ldots, v^i_{KK})$        vector of value shares of capital inputs in the $i$th industry ($i = 1, 2, \ldots, I$).

$v^L_i = (v^i_{L1}, v^i_{L2}, \ldots, v^i_{LL})$        vector of value shares of labor inputs in the $i$th industry ($i = 1, 2, \ldots, I$).

$v^M_i = (v^i_{M1}, v^i_{M2}, \ldots, v^i_{MM})$        vector of value shares of intermediate inputs in the $i$th industry ($i = 1, 2, \ldots, I$).

$\ln K^i = (\ln K_{1i}, \ln K_{2i}, \ldots,$     vector of logarithms of capital input
$\ln K_{Ki})$     quantities of the $i$th industry ($i = 1, 2, \ldots, I$).

$\ln L^i = (\ln L_{1i}, \ln L_{2i}, \ldots,$     vector of logarithms of labor input
$\ln L_{Li})$     quantities of the $i$th industry ($i = 1, 2, \ldots, I$).

$\ln M^i = (\ln M_{1i}, \ln M_{2i}, \ldots,$     vector of logarithms of intermediate
$\ln M_{Mi})$     input quantities of the $i$th industry ($i = 1, 2, \ldots, I$).

We assume that the $i$th industry allocates the values of capital, labor, and intermediate inputs among the components of each aggregate in accord with the functions

$$\ln K_i = \ln K^{i\prime} \alpha^i_K + 1/2 \ln K^{i\prime} B^i_{KK} \ln K^i ,$$

$$\ln L_i = \ln L^{i\prime} \alpha^i_L + 1/2 \ln L^{i\prime} B^i_{LL} \ln L^i , \qquad\qquad (7.10)$$

$$\ln M_i = \ln M^{i\prime} \alpha^i_M + 1/2 \ln M^{i\prime} B^i_{MM} \ln M^i , \qquad (i = 1, 2, \ldots, I) .$$

Each input is a transcendental logarithmic or translog function of its components. In these representations the vectors $\{\alpha^i_K, \alpha^i_L, \alpha^i_M\}$ and the matrices $\{B^i_{KK}, B^i_{LL}, B^i_{MM}\}$ are constant parameters. These parameters differ among industries, reflecting differences in technologies. For a given industry the parameters are the same for both countries in all time periods.

Under constant returns to scale a proportional change in all the components of a given input results in a proportional change in that input. In analyzing the differences in each industry's production patterns between the two countries, we employ necessary conditions for producer equilibrium. We express these conditions as equalities between shares of each component in the value of the input and the elasticity of the input with respect to that component. The elasticities depend only on the input levels. Under constant returns the sum of the elasticities is equal to unity, so that the value shares also sum to unity.

The individual inputs $\{K_{ki}, L_{li}, M_{mi}\}$ and their prices $\{p^i_{Kk}, p^i_{Ll}, p^i_{Mm}\}$ are observable for all time periods in both countries. The value shares $\{v^i_{Kk}, v^i_{Ll}, v^i_{Mm}\}$ can be derived from the prices and quanities. The average rates of growth of the inputs between any two points of time, say $T$ and $T - 1$, can be expressed as weighted averages of the growth rates of their components,

$$\ln K_i(T) - \ln K_i(T-1) = \bar{v}_i^{K'} [\ln K^i(T) - \ln K^i(T-1)] ,$$

$$\ln L_i(T) - \ln L_i(T-1) = \bar{v}_i^{L'} [\ln L^i(T) - \ln L^i(T-1)] , \qquad (7.11)$$

$$\ln M_i(T) - \ln M_i(T-1) = \bar{v}_i^{M'} [\ln M^i(T) - \ln M^i(T-1)] , \qquad (i = 1, 2, \ldots, I) ,$$

where

$$\bar{v}_i^K = 1/2 [v_i^K(T) + v_i^K(T-1)] ,$$

$$\bar{v}_i^L = 1/2 [v_i^L(T) + v_i^L(T-1)] ,$$

$$\bar{v}_i^M = 1/2 [v_i^M(T) + v_i^M(T-1)] , \qquad (i = 1, 2, \ldots, I) .$$

We refer to the index numbers (7.11) as *translog quantity indexes of capital, labor, and intermediate inputs.*

Similarly, average logarithmic differences between Japan and the United States can be expressed as weighted averages of the logarithmic differences of the components,

$$\ln K_i(\text{JAPAN}) - \ln K_i(\text{U. S.}) = \hat{v}_i^{K'} [\ln K^i(\text{JAPAN}) - \ln K^i(\text{U. S.})] ,$$

$$\ln L_i(\text{JAPAN}) - \ln L_i(\text{U. S.}) = \hat{v}_i^{L'} [\ln L^i(\text{JAPAN}) - \ln L^i(\text{U. S.})] , \qquad (7.12)$$

$$\ln M_i(\text{JAPAN}) - \ln M_i(\text{U. S.}) = \hat{v}_i^{M'} [\ln M^i(\text{JAPAN}) - \ln M^i(\text{U. S.})] ,$$

$$(i = 1, 2, \ldots, I) .$$

We refer to the index numbers (7.12) as *translog quantity indexes of differences in capital, labor, and intermediate inputs.*[3]

The product of price and quantity indexes must equal the sum of the values of the components of each aggregate. Price indexes corresponding to the translog indexes of capital, labor, and intermediate inputs can be defined as ratios of the sum of the values of the individual components to the corresponding translog quantity index. For Japan and the United States at a given point in time, the price indexes represent purchasing power parities between the yen and the dollar for output and inputs in each industry. If U.S. labor input is measured relative to Japanese labor input, for example, the corresponding purchasing power parity represents the price of one dollar's worth of labor input in terms of yen. The price indexes corresponding to translog quantity indexes can be determined solely from data on prices and quantities of the individual components.

## 7.3    An International Comparison of Sectoral Patterns of Growth

The starting point of our analysis of sectoral patterns of production between Japan and the United States is the production account for each industry in both countries. The measurement of output and inputs must conform to the fundamental identity that the value of output is equal to the value of all inputs in each industry. We define the value of output from the point of view of the producer in each industry. This value includes the value of labor and capital input as well as the value of intermediate input. The value of output from the producers' point of view also includes subsidies, since they are included in producer income. This value excludes all indirect taxes on output as well as trade and transportation margins incurred in deliveries of output to other sectors, since they are not part of production costs.

Similarly, the value of each input is defined from the purchasers' point of view. The value of labor input includes all taxes levied on labor and all costs incurred in employment of labor such as insurance, meals, and transportation costs. The value of capital input includes all taxes levied on the ownership and the utilization of capital. It also includes costs of transportation and installation incurred in the deliveries of capital goods to the users, since these expenses are reflected in utilization costs. The value of intermediate input also includes all taxes and trade and transportation margins associated with taking the deliveries of intermediate input from other sectors.

We employ the industry production accounts for the United States originated by Gollop and Jorgenson (1980) and updated by Jorgenson *et al.* (1986). For Japan we estimate sectoral production accounts including annual input-output tables. These input-output tables are compiled using the Lagrangian method developed by Kuroda (1988),[4] rather than the well-known RAS method. The production accounts were prepared for 31 industries in Japan, and 35 industries for the United States, as shown in table 7.1.[5] Accounts for these industries are consolidated into accounts for the 30 industries used in our study.

Price and quantity indexes of labor input for each industry in both countries are measured on the basis of labor compensation and hours worked, disaggregated by age, education, occupation, class of employment, and sex.[6] Price and quantity indexes of sectoral capital input in each country are measured on the basis of property compensation and capital stocks. Capital input is disaggregated by asset

**Table 7.1**
List of industries

| Japan | United States |
| --- | --- |
| 1. Agriculture, forestry, and fisheries | 1. Agricultural production, agricultural |
| 2. Mining | services |
| 3. Construction | 2. Metal mining |
| 4. Food and kindred products | 3. Coal mining |
| 5. Textile mill products | 4. Crude petrolem and natural gas |
| 6. Apparel and other fabricated textile | 5. Nonmetallic mining |
| products | 6. Contract construction |
| 7. Lumber and wood products, except | 7. Food and kindred products |
| furniture | 8. Tobacco manufacturing |
| 8. Furniture and fixtures | 9. Textile mill products |
| 9. Paper and allied products | 10. Apparel and other fabricated textiles |
| 10. Printing, publishing, and allied products | 11. Lumber and wood products |
| 11. Chemical and allied products | 12. Furniture and fixtures |
| 12. Petroleum refiner and related industries | 13. Paper and allied products |
| 13. Rubber and miscellaneous plastic | 14. Printing and publishing |
| products | 15. Chemicals and allied products |
| 14. Leather and leather products | 16. Petroleum and coal products |
| 15. Stone, clay, and glass products | 17. Rubber and miscellaneous plastic |
| 16. Iron and steel | products |
| 17. Nonferrous metal | 18. Leather and leather products |
| 18. Fabricated metal products | 19. Stone, clay, and glass products |
| 19. Machinery | 20. Primary metal products |
| 20. Electric machinery | 21. Fabricated metal products |
| 21. Motor vehicles and equipment | 22. Machinery except electrical |
| 22. Transportation equipment except motor | 23. Electric machinery equipment and |
| vehicles | supplies |
| 23. Precision instruments | 24. Motor vehicles and equipment |
| 24. Miscellaneous manufacturing | 25. Transportation equipment except motor |
| 25. Transportation and communication | 26. Professional photo equipment and |
| 26. Electric utility, gas and water supply | watches |
| 32. Wholesale and retail trade | 27. Miscellaneous manufacturing |
| 33. Finance and insurance | 28. Railroad and rail express service, |
| 29. Real estate | street rail, bus lines and taxi, trucking |
| 30. Services | services and warehousing, water |
| 31. Government services | transportation, air transportation, |
| | and transportation service |
| | 29. Telephone, telegraph, miscellaneous |
| | radio broadcasting, and TV |
| | 30. Electric utility |
| | 31. Gas utility, water supply, and |
| | sanitary services |
| | 32. Wholesale trade |
| | 33. Retail trade, finance, insurance, and |
| | real estate |
| | 34. Services except private households |
| | 35. Government service |

type—residential structures, nonresidential structures, producer's durable equipment, inventories, and land—and by the legal form of organization, corporate and noncorporate, within each industry.

The flow of capital input for each asset type is assumed to be proportional to the corresponding level of capital stock. The price of capital services is imputed on the basis of the correspondence between asset prices and service prices implicit in the equality of the value of an asset to the discounted flow of its future services.[7] Service prices of capital assets depend on the tax structure, necessitating a distinction between different legal forms of organization. Price and quantity indexes of intermediate input in each country are measured on the basis of interindustry transaction matrices estimated annually for each country, using a set of benchmark matrices.

Table 7.2 presents average annual growth rates of output and input during the period 1960–1979 in U.S. and Japanese industries. The average productivity growth rate over the entire period is 1.12% per year in Japan and 0.26% per year in the United States at the economy-wide level. Output in Japan grew by 8.46% annually during the period, while capital input, labor input, and intermediate input grew by 9.96, 2.71, and 8.50% per year, respectively. The growth rate of capital input was higher than that of output by more than 1%, which means that capital productivity was decreasing gradually during the postwar period. On the other hand, the growth rate of labor input was less than that of gross output by nearly 6%, which implies that labor productivity improved significantly during the period. During the same period in the United States, output grew by 3.48% annually, while, capital, labor, and intermediate inputs grew by 3.75, 1.47, and 4.08% per year, respectively. U.S. labor productivity improved gradually, but at a slower rate than that in Japan, while U.S. capital productivity decreased during the period.

Structural change in the distribution of inputs and outputs by sectors can be observed by analyzing the differences in growth rates among sectors. Figure 7.1 shows the average annual growth rate in gross output, capital, labor, and intermediate inputs in each industry during the period 1960–1979. The number on the horizontal line stands for the industry according to the list of industries given in table 7.1. The height of each pole represents the average annual growth rate for each measure in Japan, while the dotted line represents the corresponding measure for the United States.

**Table 7.2**
Average annual growth rates of output, inputs, and productivity in Japan and the United States, 1960–1979 (percent per year)

| Industry | United States | | | | | Japan | | | | |
|---|---|---|---|---|---|---|---|---|---|---|
| | Productivity (1) | Output (2) | Capital (3) | Labor (4) | Intermediate (5) | Productivity (1) | Output (2) | Capital (3) | Labor (4) | Intermediate (5) |
| 1. Agriculture | 1.32 | 2.21 | 3.31 | -2.93 | 2.32 | -0.78 | 1.31 | 5.54 | -3.33 | 2.91 |
| 2. Mining | -3.02 | 2.11 | 3.92 | 2.50 | 6.59 | 2.17 | 3.43 | 3.58 | -7.47 | 4.68 |
| 3. Construction | -0.74 | 1.48 | 3.11 | 2.70 | 1.82 | -1.39 | 8.09 | 13.46 | 6.70 | 9.66 |
| 4. Foods | 0.05 | 2.58 | 3.06 | -0.003 | 3.03 | -1.23 | 5.89 | 10.61 | 3.67 | 6.25 |
| 5. Textiles | 2.12 | 3.93 | 2.81 | -0.03 | 2.44 | 0.29 | 3.44 | 5.28 | -1.68 | 3.18 |
| 6. Fabricated textiles | 1.11 | 2.50 | 4.77 | 0.39 | 1.65 | 1.01 | 10.15 | 8.76 | 6.08 | 9.91 |
| 7. Lumber | -0.51 | 3.27 | 3.01 | 1.14 | 5.76 | 1.88 | 5.78 | 5.71 | 0.10 | 4.77 |
| 8. Furniture | 0.35 | 3.94 | 4.61 | 1.44 | 4.77 | 1.01 | 8.67 | 9.25 | 3.12 | 9.34 |
| 9. Paper | 0.47 | 3.80 | 2.64 | 1.11 | 4.38 | 0.88 | 7.61 | 10.16 | 1.83 | 6.73 |
| 10. Printing | 0.98 | 2.75 | 2.51 | 1.34 | 1.97 | -0.08 | 6.56 | 8.67 | 2.80 | 8.57 |
| 11. Chemicals | 0.91 | 5.35 | 4.73 | 1.93 | 5.24 | 2.45 | 10.16 | 10.09 | 1.60 | 8.08 |
| 12. Petroleum, Coal | -3.10 | 3.63 | 2.03 | 0.84 | 7.86 | -3.16 | 10.53 | 12.44 | 3.44 | 14.12 |
| 13. Rubber | 0.86 | 5.32 | 6.09 | 3.66 | 4.76 | 0.59 | 7.02 | 13.02 | 1.43 | 6.61 |
| 14. Leather | -0.15 | -0.53 | 1.29 | -1.97 | 0.37 | 0.67 | 7.30 | 9.13 | 2.25 | 7.22 |
| 15. Stone, clay | 0.22 | 2.83 | 2.66 | 1.15 | 3.61 | 1.20 | 9.30 | 12.17 | 2.79 | 8.66 |
| 16. Iron, steel | -0.44 | 2.48 | 1.45 | 0.76 | 3.86 | 0.90 | 9.07 | 11.62 | 0.68 | 8.20 |

**Table 7.2 (continued)**

| Industry | United States | | | | | Japan | | | | |
|---|---|---|---|---|---|---|---|---|---|---|
| | Productivity (1) | Output (2) | Capital (3) | Labor (4) | Intermediate (5) | Productivity (1) | Output (2) | Capital (3) | Labor (4) | Intermediate (5) |
| 17. Nonferrous metal | 0.57 | 3.33 | 3.95 | 1.71 | 3.38 | 0.12 | 7.87 | 10.38 | 2.28 | 7.40 |
| 18. Fabricated metal | 0.72 | 5.19 | 4.76 | 3.09 | 5.59 | 1.91 | 11.21 | 16.52 | 3.95 | 10.48 |
| 19. Machinery | 1.99 | 5.75 | 5.76 | 2.13 | 4.67 | 1.29 | 10.16 | 13.16 | 2.73 | 9.70 |
| 20. Electric machinery | 0.84 | 4.28 | 4.62 | 1.78 | 3.95 | 3.28 | 13.28 | 12.37 | 4.90 | 10.67 |
| 21. Motor vehicles | | | | | | 0.59 | 11.82 | 14.06 | 6.81 | 11.78 |
| 22. Transportation equipment | 0.44 | 3.14 | 3.33 | 0.92 | 3.71 | 3.07 | 9.36 | 11.00 | -0.21 | 7.46 |
| 23. Precision instruments | 0.78 | 5.60 | 5.54 | 2.91 | 7.00 | 2.63 | 10.94 | 13.76 | 4.22 | 8.44 |
| 24. Miscellaneous manufacturing | -0.25 | 2.63 | 2.80 | 0.61 | 4.11 | 2.89 | 12.77 | 14.55 | 3.93 | 10.86 |
| 25. Transportation, communication | 1.03 | 3.77 | 5.79 | 1.48 | 2.54 | 2.64 | 8.54 | 7.18 | 3.28 | 8.74 |
| 26. Utility | -0.11 | 4.51 | 5.41 | 1.73 | 5.16 | 0.91 | 8.86 | 10.88 | 2.21 | 9.32 |
| 27. Trade | 0.93 | 3.58 | 4.22 | 1.74 | 3.39 | 0.83 | 8.46 | 10.07 | 5.93 | 7.16 |
| 28. Finance | 0.41 | 4.67 | 2.23 | 3.51 | 5.23 | 4.08 | 12.08 | 9.15 | 5.05 | 9.64 |
| 29. Real estate | -0.20 | 4.23 | 4.62 | 3.29 | 5.08 | 4.21 | 11.17 | 5.45 | 10.16 | 15.41 |
| 30. Services | | | | | | -0.11 | 8.84 | 10.83 | 6.51 | 8.79 |
| Average | 0.26 | 3.48 | 3.75 | 1.43 | 4.08 | 1.12 | 8.46 | 9.96 | 2.71 | 8.50 |

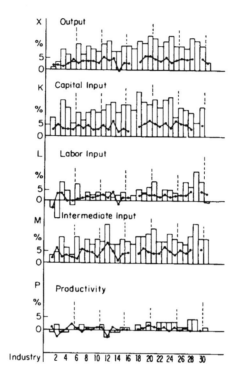

**Figure 7.1.** Skyline of average annual growth rates of output, input, and productivity, 1960–1979. The height of each pole stands for average annual growth rate of gross output, input, and productivity during the period 1960–1979 in Japan. Dotted lines stand for the corresponding measure in the United States.

Average annual growth rates of output in Japan during the period 1960–1979 were higher than those of the United States for almost all of the industries—except agriculture-forestry-fisheries and textile products. One of the remarkable features of the economic growth in Japan is an extraordinarily high growth of capital input. In all industries except the mining industry, the growth rates of capital input in Japan were more than double those in the United States. On the other hand, differences in the growth rates of labor input between Japan and the United States were not so pronounced. Another interesting feature of Japanese economic growth is the high growth rate of intermediate input, which implies an increasing role for interindustry transactions. The last "skylines" in figure 7.1 show that average annual growth rates of productivity in Japan were higher than those in the United

States in almost all of the industries, althoug the growth rates among industries were fairly diverse.

Average annual growth rates of output by industry in Japan and the United States are presented in figure 7.2 during the following four subperiods: 1960–1965, 1965–1970, 1970–1973, and 1973–1979. In the first and second subperiods, the growth rates of output in Japan were substantially higher than those in the United States except for primary industry. Differences of the growth rates by industry between the two countries were particularly remarkable in the second subperiod, when the Japanese economy reached the peak of its postwar economic growth, while the U.S. economy was experiencing the social and economic impacts of the Vietnam War. In the third subperiod, following the oil crisis, the growth pattern by industry in Japan changed dramatically, and average annual growth rates of output by industry became quite similar between Japan and the United States.

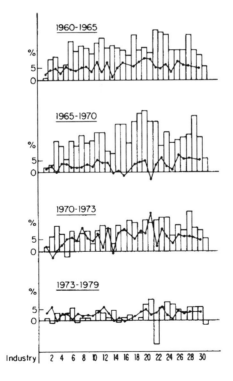

**Figure 7.2.** Skyline of average annual growth rates of output by industry.

Figure 7.3 presents average annual growth rates of capital input by industry during four subperiods. High rates of growth of capital input in the Japanese economy have characterized each subperiod, especially until the third subperiod. During the first subperiod, 1960–1965, annual growth rates of capital input in Japan were about three times those in the United States. Annual growth rates of capital input in the United States increased during the second subperiod compared with the first period, in spite of the deterioration in the growth of output. During the third subperiod the growth of capital input in the United States slowed in spite of the recovery of the U.S. economy. In the Japanese economy a high rate of capital formation continued until the end of the third subperiod in spite of the gradual slowdown of the growth of output in this period. After the oil crisis the Japanese economy experienced dramatic changes in the growth of the capital input in almost all industries.

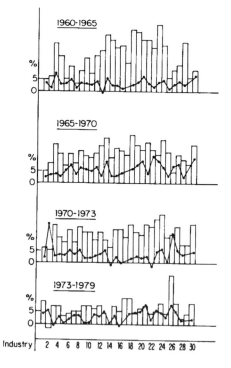

**Figure 7.3.** Skyline of average annual growth rates of capital input by industry.

Figure 7.4 presents average annual growth rates of labor input by industry during each subperiod. During the first subperiod, 1960–1965, the Japanese industries experienced high growth rates of labor input, significantly higher than those in the U.S. industries, except for primary industry and government service. Starting in the second subperiod, 1965–1970, annual growth rates of labor input slowed down in almost all industries in Japan. In the third and fourth periods, some manufacturing industries in Japan experienced negative growth of labor input. Labor input growth rates in the Japanese industries were not significantly different from those in the United States.

Figure 7.5 presents average annual growth rates of intermediate input by industry. During the first and second subperiods, annual growth rates of intermediate input in Japanese industries were significantly higher than those in the United States. Starting in the third sub-

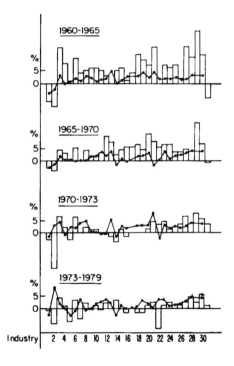

**Figure 7.4.** Skyline of average annual growth rates of labor input by industry.

period the annual growth rates of intermediate input in the Japanese economy declined dramatically, while in the United States these growth rates increased in some industries compared with those in the previous subperiods.

Finally, figure 7.6 presents average annual growth rates of productivity by industry. During the high economic growth period, 1960–1970, annual growth rates of productivity in Japan were significantly higher than those in the United States. Since 1970, growth rates of productivity have decreased in the Japanese economy and the interindustry variation in productivity performance has increased dramatically. Especially after the oil crisis, there were no significant differences between annual growth rates of productivity in Japanese and U.S. industries. Variations of annual growth rates of productivity among industries were also remarkably similar between the U.S. and Japanese economies after the oil crisis.

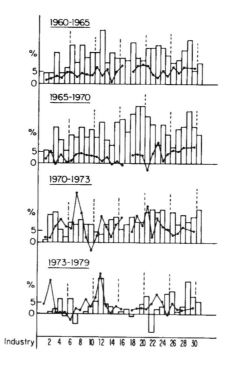

**Figure 7.5.** Skyline of average annual growth rates of intermediate input by industry.

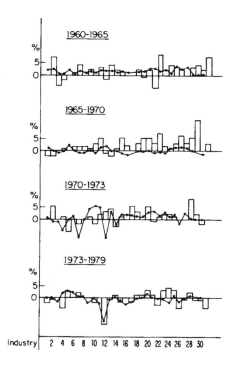

**Figure 7.6.** Skyline of average annual growth rates of productivity by industry.

## 7.4    Estimation of Purchasing Power Parity Indexes

As discussed in section 7.2, price indexes corresponding to the translog indexes of differences in output and inputs represent the purchasing power parities between the yen and the dollar. To achieve comparability in industry accounts between the two countries, we develop purchasing power parities based on the work by Kravis and his associates (1975, 1978a). Kravis and his associates provide purchasing power parities between the yen and the dollar for a detailed breakdown of consumption goods and investment goods production for the year 1970.

We construct purchasing power parities for industry outputs and intermediate inputs by mapping the Kravis classifications system into our industry classification system. Unfortunately, a complete corre-

spondence between the two systems is impossible since not all intermediate deliveries by different sectors are covered in the Kravis system. We correct for the gap between the two systems by including
close substitutes to a given industry's intermediate deliveries as well
as deliveries to final demand.

To obtain the purchasing power parity for industry output from the
producer's point of view, we adjust the results by "peeling off" the
indirect taxes and trade and transportation margins for each industry.
To obtain the purchasing power parity for industry output, we aggregate these results in translog forms by using nominal shares in com-
modity-mix of the 1970 "V Table" in Japan as weights. To obtain the
purchasing power parity for intermediate input components in each
industry, we aggregate commodity-based purchasing power parities
in translog form by using deliveries of intermediate input from other
industries in the 1970 "U Table" in Japan as weights.

Although we estimate the decline in efficiency of capital goods for
each component of industry capital input separately for Japan and the
United States, we assume that the relative efficiency of new capital
goods in a given industry is the same in both countries. Accordingly,
the appropriate purchasing power parity for new capital goods is the
purchasing power parity for the corresponding component of investment goods output. To obtain the purchasing power parity for capital
input, we adjust the purchasing power parity for investment goods in
yen per dollar by the ratio of the price of capital services to the price of
capital goods for Japan relative to the corresponding ratio for the
United States for each industry by asset type. The resulting price
index represents the purchasing power parity between the yen and
the dollar in terms of capital input. Given the detailed classification of
labor input for each industry in our data base, we construct our own
purchasing power parities for labor input on the basis of the relative
wage levels between the yen and the dollar for each component of
labor input in every industry.

Final results of purchasing power parities for industry output and
capital, labor, and intermediate inputs in 1970 are shown in table 7.3.
According to our purchasing power parities for industry output in
1970, prices in Japan are higher than those in United States in only
seven sectors; agriculture-forestry-fisheries, construction, food and
kindred products, petroleum refinery products, rubber products, electricity and gas products, and real estate. The purchasing power

**Table 7.3**
The Japanese price index transformed by the purchasing power parity index
at 1970 (U.S. price = 1.0000)

| Industry | Output price | Labor input price | Capital input price | Intermediate input price |
|---|---|---|---|---|
| 1. Agriculture | 1.04556 | .60588 | .90835 | 0.93388 |
| 2. Mining | 0.72125 | .21263 | .88095 | 0.96271 |
| 3. Construction | 1.03487 | .18607 | .92127 | 0.76498 |
| 4. Foods | 1.03569 | .21894 | .92190 | 0.90049 |
| 5. Textiles | 0.77898 | .24099 | .90871 | 0.78202 |
| 6. Fabricated textiles | 0.76952 | .18975 | .86037 | 0.76056 |
| 7. Lumber | 0.79154 | .22805 | .84363 | 0.91618 |
| 8. Furniture | 0.67944 | .22952 | .84214 | 0.76835 |
| 9. Paper | 0.58858 | .22170 | .89567 | 0.69511 |
| 10. Printing | 0.78107 | .21251 | .86742 | 0.70800 |
| 11. Chemicals | 0.66210 | .25039 | .91711 | 0.79106 |
| 12. Petroleum, coal | 1.59952 | .21846 | .89588 | 0.93331 |
| 13. Rubber | 1.06186 | .24042 | .86013 | 0.78726 |
| 14. Leather | 0.71273 | .23569 | .82076 | 0.83144 |
| 15. Stone, clay | 0.69603 | .23083 | .89998 | 0.79475 |
| 16. Iron, steel | 0.82840 | .25200 | .91586 | 0.86336 |
| 17. Nonferrous metal | 0.74743 | .25200 | .89579 | 0.81615 |
| 18. Fabricated metal | 0.81514 | .21072 | .90205 | 0.80720 |
| 19. Machinery | 0.61327 | .22564 | .92020 | 0.72993 |
| 20. Electrical machinery | 0.68127 | .22308 | .92036 | 0.72860 |
| 21. Motor vehicles | 0.78627 | .18581 | .91647 | 0.77580 |
| 22. Transportation equipment | 0.94794 | .21944 | .87722 | 0.77478 |
| 23. Precision instruments | 0.71912 | .23150 | .86402 | 0.74613 |
| 24. Miscellaneous manufacturing | 0.69473 | .22549 | .88034 | 0.73974 |
| 25. Transportation, communication | 0.47247 | .22713 | .91027 | 0.85350 |
| 26. Utility | 1.02936 | .26605 | .90389 | 1.06311 |
| 27. Trade | 0.66155 | .26889 | .93094 | 0.82322 |
| 28. Finance | 0.63356 | .30796 | .84372 | 0.75604 |
| 29. Real estate | 1.02034 | .30796 | .73650 | 0.94961 |
| 30. Services | 0.56751 | .25592 | .91719 | 0.78941 |

parities for labor input in 1970 represent lower costs of labor input in Japan relative to the United States. In that year hourly wages in Japan were 30% or less of U.S. hourly wages, except for agriculture-forestry-fisheries. The purchasing power parities for capital input in 1970 are also less than unity. The cost of capital input in Japan averaged 80% of that in the United States.

## 7.5 International Comparison of Productivity Levels

Our empirical results on the productivity gap between Japan and the United States are summarized in table 7.4. There are 9 industries in which productivity gaps between the two countries closed during the period 1960–1979. In 19 industries there remain some differences in productivity levels in 1979. An inspection of our summary table gives an interesting interpretation of Japanese industrial structure and development. Wit the exception of 3 industries—lumber and wood products, precision instruments, and other miscellaneous manufacturing industry—all the Japanese manufacturing industries which had not closed their productivity gap with the United States belong to either light consumer goods industries or investment goods industries.

Most of the Japanese manufacturing industries that had closed the gap by 1979 belong to the raw material processing industries or intermediate goods industries. With respect to the primary sector, agriculture-forestry-fisheries has still had a fairly large difference in productivity. On the other hand the productivity gap of the mining sector had closed by 1971. With respect to the tertiary sector—except for utilities, trade, and other services—the productivity gap had closed by 1979. These findings may reflect a logical sequence of industrial development and structural change for an economy such as that of Japan.

The productivity gap in agriculture-forestry-fisheries has been increasing between the United States and Japan. Average annual growth rates of productivity during the period 1960–1973 were 1.63 and −0.82 in the United States and Japan, respectively; those after 1974 were 0.63 and −0.68. Although the productivity growth rate in this sector deteriorated with the impact of the oil shock in the United States more than in Japan, the productivity gap has been growing because of the continued negative productivity growth rate in Japan.

**Table 7.4**
Technology gap between the United States and Japan

| Industry | Technology gap closed (year) | Technology gap not closing |
|---|---|---|
| 1. Agriculture | | × |
| 2. Mining | × (1972) | |
| 3. Construction | | × |
| 4. Foods | | × |
| 5. Textiles | | × |
| 6. Fabricated textiles | | × |
| 7. Lumber | × (1975) | |
| 8. Furniture | | × |
| 9. Paper | | × |
| 10. Printing | | × |
| 11. Chemicals | × (1975) | |
| 12. Petroleum, coal | | × |
| 13. Rubber | | × |
| 14. Leather | | × |
| 15. Stone, clay | | × |
| 16. Primary Metal | × (1979) | |
| 18. Fabricated metal | × (1973) | |
| 19. Machinery | | × |
| 20. Electric machinery | | × |
| 21. Motor vehicles | | × |
| 22. Transportation equipment | | × |
| 23. Precision instruments | × (1967) × (1974) | |
| 24. Miscellaneous manufacturing | × (1978) | |
| 25. Transportation, communication | × (1968) | |
| 26. Utility | | × |
| 27. Trade | | × |
| 28. Finance and real estate | × (1971) | |
| 30. Services | | × |

In the mining sector the productivity gap closed by 1971, but the growth rates of productivity after 1974 became negative in both the United States and Japan. One must be careful in interpreting the productivity gap in the mining sector, due to major differences in the commodity composition of this industry between the two countries. Production in the Japanese mining sector is mainly gravel and building stone. The impact of the oil price change is therefore much greater in the U.S. mining sector than in Japan.

The productivity gap in construction between the United States and Japan has continued to be fairly large, although the difference has been closing gradually since 1973. Average annual productivity growth rates in construction were negative in both countries, indicating declining efficiency in construction over the period. In some of the light manufacturing industries, such as food and kindred products, apparel products, furniture and fixtures, and rubber products, productivity gaps between the two countries have not been closed. Before 1973, productivity gaps were reduced, but this trend was reversed after 1974, indicating that the impact of the economic change in 1974 in those sectors was greater in Japan than in the United States.

In the textile industry the productivity gap between the United States and Japan has been increasing over the period. After 1974 the average annual growth rates of productivity are 2.97 and 2.85% in the United States and Japan, respectively, implying that the productivity gap has been increasing recently with more rapid progress of productive efficiency in the United States. In the printing and publishing industry the U.S. productivity advantage has also been increasing. Since the impact of 1974 was larger in Japan than in the United States, these productivity gaps are expected to continue to expand in the future.

In three of the light manufacturing industries, namely, lumber and wood products, miscellaneous manufacturing industries, and precision instruments, as well as raw material manufacturing such as chemical products, primary metal products, and fabricated metal products, productivity gaps between the two countries were closed during the period 1960 to 1979. In these industries, average annual growth rates of productivity in Japan exceed those in the United States, implying that the techniological advantage in Japan is expected to continue in the future.

In some light manufacturing industries, such as leather products, and investment goods manufacturing, such as machinery, electric machinery, and motor vehicles, there remain some productivity gaps. In these industries, however, average annual growth rates of productivity in Japan are fairly high relative to those in the United States, so that productivity gaps in these industries could be closed in the near future. In stone and clay and other transportation equipment industries, the growth rate of productivity in Japan before 1973 was fairly large. The technology gaps were closing before 1973. Since the impact of the oil crisis was considerable in Japan, however, the technology gaps began to increase the U.S. advantage after 1974.

Petroleum refining is the industry which suffered the most serious impact of economic change in 1974. Average annual growth rates of productivity before 1973 are –0. 17 and –0. 18% in the United States and Japan, while after 1974 the growth rates are –9. 41 and –9. 62%, respectively. The economic change seems to have affected the petroleum refinery industry equally in the United States and Japan. Negative growth rates of productivity in both countries imply that productive efficiency in this industry is gradually deteriorating over the period. The productivity gap between the two countries remains basically unchanged over the period.

Transportation and communication and finance and insurance in the tertiary sector in Japan had a higher growth rate of productivity during the period. Productivity gaps in these industries were closed in 1968 and 1971, respectively. After 1974, productivity growth rates were higher in Japan relative to the United States. Productivity gaps in both sectors have continued to expand to the advantage of Japan. In the utility sector, gas and electricity supply, the productivity level in the United States continues to show a fairly large advantage over Japan. Both in Japan and in the United States this industry suffered from the oil crises and average annual growth rates of productivity after 1974 are –2. 30 and –3. 62% in the United States and Japan, respectively.

Finally, productivity gaps in wholesale and retail and other service sectors have not been closed by 1979. The average annual growth rate of productivity in the wholesale and retail sector of the United States is slightly higher than that of Japan over the period 1960–1979, so that the productivity gap between the two countries has been increasing gradually. On the other hand, the productivity gap in other service sectors continued to narrow until 1973. After 1974, however, the gap began to expand.

Future patterns of the technology gap between the United States and Japan are summarized in table 7.5. Industries are divided into seven categories. Type I through Type VI include industries in which U.S. technology still had an advantage at the 1979 level. Type I includes four industries—agriculture-forestry-fisheries, textiles, printing and publishing, and trade industries—in which technology gaps are expected to continue to expand in the future. Type II represents industries in which the technology gaps were closing before 1973 but are expanding after 1973. These industries include food and kindred

## Table 7.5
Types of technology gap between the United States and Japan and expected pattern of technology gap

| Type of technology gap | Industry | Technology gap in 1979 | Average annual growth rate of productivity (%) | | | |
|---|---|---|---|---|---|---|
| | | | 1960–1973 | | 1973–1979 | |
| | | | U.S. | Japan | U.S. | Japan |
| **Type I** U.S. had still taken an advantage in the 1979 technology. The technology gaps are expected to continue to expand in the future. | (1) Agriculture | U.S. > Japan | 1.630 | −0.824 | 0.633 | −0.680 |
| | (5) Textile | U.S. > Japan | 1.717 | −0.892 | 2.974 | 2.847 |
| | (10) Printing | U.S. > Japan | 1.515 | 0.690 | −0.192 | −1.767 |
| | (27) Trade | U.S. > Japan | 1.408 | 1.506 | −0.121 | −0.639 |
| **Type II** U.S. had an advantage in the 1979 technology. The technology gaps were closing before 1973. The technology gaps, however, were expanding after 1973 and are expected to expand in the future. | (4) Food and kindred products | U.S. > Japan | −0.934 | −0.162 | 2.189 | −3.544 |
| | (6) Apparel | U.S. > Japan | 0.560 | 1.301 | 2.292 | 0.378 |
| | (8) Furniture | U.S. > Japan | 0.195 | 1.484 | 0.697 | −0.020 |
| | (13) Rubber | U.S. > Japan | 1.491 | 1.493 | −0.513 | −1.390 |
| | (15) Stone and clay | U.S. > Japan | 0.928 | 2.449 | −1.327 | −1.492 |
| | (22) Other transportation equipment | U.S. > Japan | 0.944 | 6.020 | −0.647 | −3.320 |
| | (26) Utility | U.S. > Japan | 0.896 | 3.000 | −2.303 | −3.612 |
| | (30) Service | U.S. > Japan | −0.433 | 0.377 | 0.300 | −0.115 |
| **Type III** U.S. had an advantage in the 1979 technology. The technology gaps are expected to close in the near future. | (14) Leather | U.S. > Japan | −0.200 | 0.348 | −0.028 | 1.381 |
| | (19) Machinery | U.S. > Japan | 0.976 | 1.545 | 0.154 | 0.744 |
| | (20) Electric machinery | U.S. > Japan | 2.073 | 3.516 | 1.804 | 2.780 |
| | (21) Motor vehicles | U.S. > Japan | 1.313 | 0.188 | −0.173 | 1.410 |

**Table 7.5 (continued)**

| Type of technology gap | Industry | Technology gap in 1979 | Average annual growth rate of productivity (%) | | | |
|---|---|---|---|---|---|---|
| | | | 1960–1973 | | 1973–1979 | |
| | | | U.S. | Japan | U.S. | Japan |
| **Type IV**<br>U.S. had an advantage in the 1979 technology. Although the technology gaps were expanding before 1973, those after 1973 were closing and expected to close in the future | (9) Paper | U.S. > Japan | 1.594 | 1.401 | −1.972 | −0.343 |
| **Type V**<br>U.S. had an advantage in the 1979 technology. The technology gaps were mostly constant during the period 1960–1973. | (12) Petroleum | U.S. > Japan | −0.173 | −0.177 | −9.411 | −9.615 |
| **Type VI**<br>U.S. had an advantage in the 1979 technology. Productivity growth rates are negative in both countries. The technology gap, however, is expected to close in the future | (3) Construction | U.S. > Japan | −0.278 | −1.916 | −1.766 | −0.247 |
| **Type VII**<br>Japan had an advantage in the 1979 technology. The technology gaps are expected to continue to expand in the future. | (2) Mining | U.S. < Japan | 0.450 | 3.369 | −10.506 | −0.434 |
| | (7) Lumber | U.S. < Japan | −1.112 | 1.641 | 0.794 | 2.424 |
| | (11) Chemicals | U.S. < Japan | 2.445 | 3.580 | −2.419 | −0.018 |
| | (16) Primary Metal | U.S. < Japan | 0.305 | 1.130 | −0.205 | 0.400 |
| | (18) Fabricated metal | U.S. < Japan | 0.954 | 2.510 | −0.262 | 0.584 |
| | (23) Precision instruments | U.S. < Japan | 1.522 | 2.260 | −0.839 | 3.426 |
| | (24) Miscellaneous manufacturing | U.S. < Japan | 0.955 | 2.355 | −2.855 | 4.073 |
| | (25) Transportation and communication | U.S. < Japan | 1.030 | 2.564 | 1.019 | 2.801 |
| | (28) Finance and real estate | U.S. < Japan | 0.171 | 4.973 | 0.929 | 2.109 |

products, apparel, furniture, rubber, stone and clay, other transportation equipment, utilities, and other services. Type III includes leather and investment goods industries such as machinery, electrical machinery, and motor vehicles, in which the technology gaps are expected to close in the near future, although the United States still has an advantage at the 1979 technology level. Paper and allied products are classified in Type IV; U.S. technology expanded its advantage before 1973, but the technology gap is decreasing after 1974, due to the deterioration of the U.S. industry. Petroleum with a constant technology gap in favor of the United States and construction with negative growth rates of productivity in both countries are classified as Type V and Type VI, respectively.

Finally, Type VII includes nine industries in which Japan took an advantage in the 1979 technology level. The Japanese advantage is expected to continue to expand in the future. These include mining, lumber, chemical, primary metal, fabricated metal, precision instruments, miscellaneous manufacturing, transportation and communication, and finance and insurance.

## 7.6  Conclusion

In an earlier comparison of aggregate economic growth patterns in Japan and the United States, Christensen et al. (1981) concluded that the differences in productivity at the aggregate level between the two countries had declined until the early 1970s. Important differences in levels of output between the two countries were due to differences in the level of capital input. Our industry results provide further confirmation of this catching-up process by the Japanese economy. Patrick and Rosovsky (1976) present an overview of the process.

From the viewpoint of an international comparison of the pattern of economic growth by industry during the period 1960–1979, we can point out the following features of economic growth in Japan relative to the United States: (1) Economic growth in Japan has been accompanied by an extraordinarily high growth of capital input. In all industries except the mining industry, growth rates of capital input in Japan were as much as double those in the United States. (2) Differences in the growth rates of labor input between the two countries were not as pronounced during the period. (3) Another interesting feature in Japanese economic growth has the high growth of intermediate input.

(4) Finally, average annual growth rates of productivity in Japan were higher than those in the United States in almost all industries. Since 1970, however, not only did growth rates of productivity decline dramatically in Japan, but also the interindustry variation in productivity performance increased substantially.

According to our purchasing power parities for industry output in 1970, the industry output prices in Japan were higher than those in the United States in only seven sectors. The purchasing power parities for labor input in 1970 represent the relatively low cost of labor input in Japan; the hourly wage in Japan was less than 30% of that in the United States. On the other hand, the purchasing power parities for capital input in 1970 show that the cost of capital in Japan was about 80% of that in the United States.

With respect to the comparison of the productivity levels by industry between Japan and the United States we can conclude with some observations on Japanese industrial structure and development. With some exceptions, those Japanese manufacturing industries that had not closed their productivity gap with the United States belong to either light consumer goods industries or investment goods industries. Most of the Japanesse manufacturing industries that had closed the gap by 1979 belong to the raw material processing industries or intermediate goods manufacturing industries.

In three light manufacturing industries—lumber and wood products, miscellaneous manufacturing industries, and precision instruments—productivity gaps were closed by 1979 and the technological advantages in Japan are expected to continue in the near future. In some of the light manufacturing and investment goods manufacturing, there remain some productivity gaps between the two countries. In these industries, however, we can expect that productivity gaps will be reduced in the near future. Our results indicate that Japan has already entered a new era in its economic history. Japan is no longer a late comer, running faster in order to catch up.

## Notes

1. The translog index of technical change was introduced by Christensen and Jorgenson (1970) and derived from the translog production function by Jorgenson and Nishimizu (1978).

2. The bilateral difference in productivity levels was introduced by Jorgenson and Nishimizu (1978). Multilateral differences were considered by Caves et al. (1982a, b); see Denny and Fuss (1983b) for an alternative approach.

3. Translog quantity indexes were introduced by Fisher (1922) and discussed by Törnqvist (1936), Theil (1965), and Kloek (1966). These indexes were first derived from the translog production function by Diewert (1976, 1980). Translog quantity indexes of differences in output, input, and productivity were first derived from the translog production function by Jorgenson and Nishimizu (1978).

4. The transaction matrix of the Japanese input-output tables represents transactions on a commodity-by-commodity classification, while the U.S. table represents an industry-by-industry classification. For an international comparison, we first compiled a time series of Japanese input-output tables, using consistent concepts and definitions over the period 1960–1979 and employing published Japanese input-output tables in 1960, 1965, 1970, and 1975 as benchmarks. We then converted these tables, classified by commodity, into transaction tables on an industry basis on the assumption of the industry technology. The converted tables for Japan are comparable to the U.S. input-output tables.

5. Time series data on nominal output at the 31-industry level in Japan and the output deflators, which are used in input-output tables as control totals by sector, are estimated mainly from the following three sources: (1) nominal output series of the 28-commodity order during the period 1960–1974, prepared for the econometric model for the *New Economic and Social Seven-Year Plan* is the Japanese Government in 1976; (2) time series commodity output series of the 2000-commodity classification in constant prices of 1970 during the period 1955–1968, prepared by a joint project of Nikkei Data Center and Keio Economic Observatory; (3) time series commodity output during the period 1970–1979 in the *New System of National Accounts* by the Economic Planning Agency. Our estimates of nominal output and output deflators for the period 1960–1979 are constructed from these three sources by a linkage procedure. Since commodity classification in the above sources do not match precisely, we use *Census of Manufacturers, Report by Commodity* to decompose textile mill products into our 5th and 6th industries and transportation equipment into our 21st and 22nd industries.

6. In estimating labor input in Japan, we rely mainly on the *Basic Wage Structures Survey*, which includes data for total labor compensation, the number of employees, and hours worked, disaggregated by age, education, occupation, class of employment, and sex. The industry classifications in certain years such as 1959, 1962, 1963, and 1974 are not well matched in our classification. Decomposition on the industry classification is accomplished by subsidiary data sources such as *Census of Manufacturers, Report by Industry, Report on Labor Force Survey* and *Establishment Census*. Labor input from temporary employees, day laborers, the self-employed, and unpaid family workers are classified only by sex and industry. These estimates are based mainly on the *Report on Labor Force Survey*; industries not matched with our classification have to be decomposed by using *Census of Manufactures, Report of Industry, Establishment Census*, and *Employment Status Survey*.

7. Time series of capital stocks by asset type are constructed for Japan by the double benchmark perpetual inventory method. We used gross capital stocks by asset type, by industry, and by legal form of organization in the 1955 and 1970 *National Wealth Survey* as benchmarks. Property compensation by industry is available in the input-output table. The flow of captial input is assumed proportional to the level of capital stock for each asset in each industry. From the asset price and service price correspondence implied by equality between the value of an asset and the discounted value of its flow of future services, we can estimate the rate of return on capital stock and impute the capital service price.

# 8 Productivity and Economic Growth in Japan and the United States

Dale W. Jorgenson

During the period from 1960 to 1973, the economic growth rate in Japan was at the rate of 10 or 11 percent per year. Japan was not the only country that grew rapidly during that period. France and Germany grew at 5.9 and 5.4 percent per year between 1960 and 1973 and Italy grew at 4.8 percent per year between 1960 and 1973 and Italy grew at 4.8 percent per year. Even the United Kingdom grew at a respectable 3.8 percent per year. The United States grew at 4.3 percent per year during this period. To fill out the roster of the seven major industrialized countries, Canada grew at 5.1 percent per year.[1]

After the first oil crisis in 1973, and even more so after the second oil crisis in 1978–1979, there was a dramatic decline of economic growth among industrialized countries. Growth in the OECD countries dipped to 2.6 percent per year between 1973 and 1979. Japanese growth dropped from the double-digit levels of the 1960s and the early 1970s to 3.8 percent per year from 1973 to 1979. In the United States, the growth rate dropped to slightly above the OECD average at 2.8 percent per year. The rate of economic growth in Germany dropped to 2.4 percent and in France to 3.1 percent. In every major industrialized country there was a precipitous fall in the rate of economic growth.

The sources of economic growth in Japan and the United States over the whole period from 1960 to 1979 are given in table 8.1. If we compare Japan and the United States during the period 1960–1979, we see that the growth of output over the whole period was 8.3 percent in Japan and only 3.5 percent in the United States. We can allocate this growth in output in the two countries among its three sources, namely, the contribution of capital input, the contribution of labor input and the rate of technical change. By far, the most important contributor to economic growth in both countries is the growth of capital

**Table 8.1**
Sources of economic growth, Japan and the United States, 1960–1979

|  | 1960–79 | | 1973–79 | |
|---|---|---|---|---|
|  | Japan | U.S. | Japan | U.S. |
| **Average annual growth rate** | | | | |
| Net output | .083 | .035 | .038 | .028 |
| Capital input | .096 | .040 | .060 | .038 |
| Labor input | .031 | .020 | .015 | .017 |
| **Annual rate of contribution to growth** | | | | |
| Capital input | .050 | .015 | .029 | .014 |
| Labor input | .015 | .012 | .008 | .011 |
| Technical change | .020 | .007 | .001 | .003 |
| Quality change of capital input | .018 | .004 | .005 | .003 |
| Quantity change of capital input | .032 | .012 | .024 | .011 |
| Quality change of labor input | .010 | .002 | .005 | .001 |
| Hours worked change | .005 | .010 | .004 | .010 |
| Weighted average of sector technical change | .007 | .004 | −.012 | −.007 |
| **Contribution of allocational changes** | | | | |
| Net output | .004 | .002 | .014 | .009 |
| Capital input | .009 | .001 | .005 | −.000 |
| Labor input | .001 | .000 | −.005 | .002 |

Sources: Jorgenson, Gollup, Fraumeni (1987) and
Jorgenson, Kuroda, and Nishimizu (1987).

input. This growth source accounts for about 5 percentage points of the Japanese economic growth rate and about 1.5 percentage points of the U.S. economic growth rate. This amounts to 60 percent of Japanese growth and 40 percent of U.S. growth.

Labor input in the two countries is a major contributor to economic growth, accounting for 1.5 percent of the Japanese growth rate and 1.2 percent of the U.S. growth rate. The rate of technical change is an important contributor as well, at nearly 2 percent in Japan and 0.7 percent in the United States. I conclude that by far the most important contributor to economic growth in the two countries is the growth of capital input. The relative importance of capital input is much greater in Japan than in the United States.

Focusing attention on the period from 1973 to 1979 after the energy crisis, we can see that capital input retained its lead as a source of economic growth in both countries. However, the decline in the growth of capital input in Japan was much greater than in the United States. The contribution of capital dropped from 5.0 percent in Japan to 2.8 percent in the period 1973–1979. The contribution of labor declined as well, from 1.5 to 0.8 percent, and the rate of technical change dropped rom approximately 2 percent to a mere one-tenth of 1 percent, 0.13 percent to be more precise, during the period from 1973 to 1979.

If we consider the corresponding figures for the United States, we see that there was an almost negligible decline in the contribution of capital input from 1.5 to 1.4 percent per year. The same is true of the contribution of labor. Therefore, the impact of the oil crisis on U.S. economic growth has to be traced to the decline in the rate of technical change, the so-called "unexplained residual," which declined from 0.7 to 0.3 percent per year.

During short periods of time, it is possible for output growth to exceed the sustainable level by increasing the proportion of the national product devoted to capital formation. That is the mechanism at work in the very rapid growth in the Japanese economy during the 1960s and the early 1970s. Referring again to table 8.1, capital input grew 1.3 percent more rapidly than output in Japan during the period 1960–1979. This was the consequence of the increase in the proportion of the national product that was devoted to capital formation.

Was the decline in the growth of output that took place in the period from 1973 to 1979 due to the fall in the growth of capital? Since capital is so important to Japanese economic growth, this is a potential explanation of the slowdown. In table 8.1 we see that the decline in output was 4.5 percent. But capital declined only 3.6 percent. Therefore, after the energy crisis as well as before, the growth rate of capital input was higher than that of output. Rather than causing the slowdown, the growth of capital after the energy crisis contributed to the continued growth of output at unsustainable levels. My first conclusion is that the decline in the growth rate of capital is not the cause of the slowdown in Japanese economic growth.

Turning to the United States, we see that the output growth rate declined by about six-tenths of 1 percent while the capital growth rate declined by only two-tenths of 1 percent. Despite the fact that capital is the most important source of U.S. growth, the decline in the growth rate of capital was not the cause of the slowdown in the growth of output. In the United States as in Japan the growth of output was maintained at unsustainably high levels during the period after the energy crisis. The growth of capital did not account for the slowdown that took place in the United States.

There was a decline in the growth rate of labor input in Japan from an average of 3.1 percent for the period 1960–1979 to 1.5 percent for the period 1973–1979. If we consider the period 1973–1979, we see that hours worked have continued to grow in Japan, but that the upgrading of the labor force has declined by about 50 percent. Labor quality change is a very important growth source and is part of the story of the slowdown in economic growth in Japan. I have now identified one factor that is clearly responsible for part of the decline in the growth in Japan—the decline in the change of quality of labor input.

The contribution of labor quality in the United States dropped from 0.22 to 0.06 percent between the period 1960–1979 and the period 1973–1979. Hours worked in the United States have grown at rates almost double those in Japan throughout the period 1960–1979. This remained the case during the period 1973–1979. Hours worked grew even more rapidly during the period after the energy crisis than before. My second conclusion is that the reduction in the rate of upgrading of the labor force was an important factor in the decline of economic growth in both countries.

Finally, let us turn our attention to the rate of technical change. The decline from 1960–1979 was 1.9 percent in Japan and 0.4 percent in the United States. It is clear the decline in the rate of technical change must play the predominant role in explaining the slowdown. The next question is: how is it possible to link the rate of technical change to energy prices? There is an element of truth in the idea that the growth of output at the aggregate level cannot be traced directly to the change in energy prices, since energy itself is a small proportion of aggregate output.[2] This is true in both Japan and the United States. However, this point of view ignores the fact that aggregate growth is the result of the growth of individual industrial sectors.

At this point I introduce a very important distinction. At the aggregate level, output is produced from capital and labor inputs. At the level of individual sectors, we find a role for capital and labor inputs, but also for inputs of energy and other intermediate goods. Rather than carrying over measures of output appropriate for economic aggregates to the sectoral level, we can define the value of output for each industrial sector to include the value of capital, labor, energy, and other intermediate inputs. In table 8.1, I have weighted the sectoral rates of technical change at the individual sectors by the total output of the sector, divided by the deliveries of output to final demand.

The other components that link technical change at the sectoral level to technical change at the aggregate level include the redistributions of output, capital input, and labor input among sectors. If we consider the period from 1960 to 1979, we see that the decomposition of the rate of technical change in Japan of 2.0 percent allocates 0.7 percent to rates of technical change at the sectoral level, 0.4 percent to the redistribution of outputs among sectors, 0.9 percent to the redistribution of capital input, and 0.1 percent to the redistribution of labor input.

In table 8.1 we see that sectoral technical change accounts for only about a third of the aggregate technical change in Japan. The remaining two-thirds correspond to gains in efficiency that are not sustainable. These gains in efficiency result from the redistribution of the basic factors of production and the output of the different sectors. Redistributional gains are not sustainable since there is an upper limit to the amount of reallocation that can take place.

If we now consider the period from 1973 to 1979 we find that the weighted sum of sectoral rates of technical change in Japan went from a positive 0.7 percent to a negative 1.2 percent. In other words, the rate of technical change from 1973 to 1979 was negative in the average Japanese industry. In the United States, rates of technical change at the sectoral level declined from 0.4 to a negative 0.7 percent. This is a paradox, and it deserves an explanation.

In both Japan and the United States, production methods reverted to vintages of technological development that existed before the energy crisis—perhaps in the middle 1060s in Japan and the early 1960s in the United States. These earlier technological strata were appropriate to the new energy price situation. I conclude that it is perfectly consistent with a theory of economic growth to have negative rates of technical change, like the ones we see in table 8.1 for the period 1973 to 1979.

We now have an even deeper mystery than before. The rate of technical change in Japan and the United States at the aggregate level is an unexplained residual and the same is true at the sectoral level. We find that dramatic changes in the rate of technical change at the sectoral level are behind the growth slowdown that we have observed. These changes are in the nature of unexplained residuals at the level of individual industries. At this point, I will use the concept of biased technical change to analyze the changes in economic growth that we have seen both in Japan and in the United States. In table 8.2, I have classified industries in Japan by the pattern of biases of technical change. Four basic types of biases are related to capital, labor, energy, and materials inputs. We now require a more precise definition of the notion of a bias.[3]

The bias of technical change is the change in the relative share in the value of the output of a particular input as technology evolves. If we take energy as an example, we can say that if the share of energy in the value of the output of an industry is independent of the level of technology, then technical change is unbiased or neutral with respect to energy. If the share of energy declines, we say that technical change is energy saving. If the share increases, technical change is energy using. We have a threefold classification of technical change with respect to each input—capital, labor, energy, and materials—input using, input saving and neutral.

**Table 8.2**
Classification of Japanese industries by biases of productivity growth

---

*Capital Using, Labor Using, Energy Using, Material Saving*
  Agriculture, mining, construction, textiles,
  fabricated metal, transportation equipment,
  services

*Capital Saving, Labor Using, Energy Saving, Material Saving*
  Machinery, finance and insurance

*Capital Saving, Labor Using, Energy Using, Material Using*
  Food, petroleum

*Capital Saving, Labor Using, Energy Using, Material Saving*
  Apparel, lumber, furniture, paper, printing,
  chemicals, rubber, leather, stone, clay, and
  glass, iron and steel, nonferrous metal,
  motor vehicles, instruments, miscellaneous
  manufacturing, transportation and communication,
  utilities, trade, real estate

---

Source: Kuroda, Yoshioka, and Jorgenson (1984).

One aspect of biased technical change relates to the direction of changes in the use of various inputs as technology evolves. For example, if a sector uses more capital, labor and energy and saves materials, we have the pattern that is described in the first panel of table 8.2. This pattern characterizes a substantial number of industries in Japan. However, there is a completely different implication of biased technical change. If technical change is energy using, then the rate of technical change declines when the price of energy increases. This provides the link between changes in energy prices and changes in the rate of technical change at the sectoral level.

Among all Japanese industries, only 3 out of the 30 listed in table 8.2 are characterized by energy-saving technical change. In the other 27 industries, technical change is energy using. With unchanged input prices, the evolution of technology results in the use of more and more energy and a reduction in the use of the other inputs. The other implication of energy-using technical change is that if we have an increase in energy prices there must be a corresponding reduction in the rate of technical change. In 27 out of the 30 Japanese industries, we have a direct link between energy prices and the rate of technical change through the energy using bias.

To make the link between sectoral rates of technical change more explicit, the typical Japanese industry described in table 8.2 is characterized by energy-using technical change. This implies that when energy prices increase, as they did in 1973 and again in 1978, there will be a reduction in the rate of technical change in the average industry. We have already seen a decline in the weighted sum of sectoral rates of technical change for Japanese industries in the period 1973–1979 in table 8.1. I have identified this decline as the major explanatory factor in the slowdown of Japanese economic growth.

The weighted sum of sectoral rates at technical change dropped from 0.7 percent per year in Japan for the period 1960–1979 to a negative 1.2 percent during the period 1973–1979. The decrease of 1.9 percentage points more than accounts for the decline in the aggregate rate of technical change in Japan. This decline is the most important source of the slowdown in economic growth that occurred after 1973.

In table 8.3, I consider the implications of biased technical change for the slowdown in U.S. economic growth. In the first panel of this table, observe that the character of technical change in the United States is predominantly capital using, labor using, energy using, and

Table 8.3
Classification of U.S. industries by biases of productivity growth

---

*Capital Using, Labor Using, Energy Using, Material Saving*
  Agriculture, metal mining, crude petroleum and
  natural gas, nonmetallic mining, textiles,
  apparel, lumber, furniture, printing, leather,
  fabricated metals, electrical machinery, motor
  vehicles, instruments, miscellaneous manufacturing,
  transportation, trade, finance, insurance
  and real estate, services

*Capital Using, Labor Using, Energy Saving, Material Saving*
  Coal mining, tobacco manufactures, communications,
  government enterprises

*Capital Using, Labor Saving, Energy Saving, Material Saving*
  Petroleum refining

*Capital Using, Labor Saving, Energy Saving, Material Using*
  Constructior

*Capital Saving, Labor Saving, Energy Using, Material Saving*
  Electric utilities

*Capital Saving, Labor Using, Energy Saving, Material Saving*
  Primary metals

*Capital Saving, Labor Using, Energy Using, Material Saving*
  Paper, chemicals, rubber, stone, clay, and glass,
  machinery except electrical, transportation
  equipment and ordnance, gas utilities

*Capital Saving, Labor Saving, Energy Using, Material Using*
  Food

---

Source: Dale W. Jorgenson (1983).

material saving. By contrast, the character of technical change in Japan is predominantly capital saving, labor using, energy using, and material saving. In both countries, technical change is characterized by using more energy. But in the United States, technical change also uses more capital as well as more labor, whereas in Japan, technical change uses less capital, less materials, and more labor along with more energy.

I have now arrived at the final explanation of the slowdown in U.S. and Japanese economic growth. I have emphasized that there are important sources of the slowdown in Japan associated with the falloff in upgrading of the labor force. However, the most important single factor in the Japanese slowdown is the sharp decline in the rate of technical change. I have now succeeded in linking that decline directly to energy prices through the energy using bias of technical change in Japan.

In the United States, the character of technical change is similar to that in Japan in the use of energy. The effect of higher energy prices in the United States was to slow economic growth. Of course, there are two additional facts that should be kept in mind. First, economic growth in the United States was a good deal less rapid than in Japan before the energy crisis. Second, energy prices increased much less substantially in the United States than in Japan. This is why the weighted sum of rates of technical change at the sectoral level decreased in the United States by 1 percent, whereas in Japan, the decrease was nearly 2 percent.

My overall conclusion is that there was a dramatic impact of energy prices on economic growth during the energy crisis. The economic impact was very strongly negative in both the United States and Japan. The impact of higher energy prices was pervasive in the sense that it affected almost every industry in both economies. Almost every industry experienced a slowdown in the rate of technical change. This can be traced to the relationship between higher energy prices and the rate of technical change at the sectoral level in both countries.

## Notes

1. Comparisons of patterns of economic growth in industrialized countries are given by Christensen, Cummings, and Jorgenson (1980, 1981). Comparisons between Japan and the United States are given by Jorgenson and Nishimizu (1978), Jorgenson with Kuroda and Nishimizu (1987), and Jorgenson with Sakuramoto, Yoshioka, and Kuroda (1988).
2. An excellent analysis of the slowdown in economic growth in industrialized countries is presented by Lindbeck (1983). A leading proponent of the view that energy prices have no impact on economic growth is Denison (1984).
3. Biases of technical change are discussed in Jorgenson (1983, 1984b), and Kuroda *et al* (1984).

# 9 Productivity and International Competitiveness in Japan and the United States, 1960–1985

Dale W. Jorgenson and
Masahiro Kuroda

## 9.1 Introduction

The political relationship between Japan and the United States has become increasingly preoccupied with "trade frictions." These disputes over trade issues have accompanied the massive expansion of Japanese exports to the United States. Explanations for the resulting trade imbalance must include variations in the yen-to-dollar exchange rate, changes in the relative prices of capital and labor in the two countries, and the relative growth of productivity in Japanese and U.S. industries. We analyze the role of each of these factors in explaining the rise in competitiveness of Japanese industries relative to their U.S. counterparts.

At the outset of our discussion it is essential to define a measure of international competitiveness. Our measure of international competitiveness is the price of an industry's output in Japan relative to the price in the United States. Japanese exports are generated by U.S. purchases from Japanese industries, while U.S. exports result from Japanese purchases from U.S. industries. The relative price of an industry's output enters the decisions of purchasers in both countries and the rest of the world. In order to explain changes in international competitiveness we must account for changes in the determinants of this relative price.

The starting point for our analysis of the competitiveness of Japanese and U.S. industries is the yen-to-dollar *exchange rate*. This is simply the number of yen required to purchase one U.S. dollar in the market for foreign exchange. Variations in the yen-to-dollar exchange rate are easy to document and are often used to characterize movements in relative prices in the two countries. However, movements in these relative prices of goods and services do not coincide with variations in the exchange rate. To account for changes in international competitiveness a measure of the relative prices of specific goods and services is required.

To assess the international competitiveness of Japanese and U.S. industries it is necessary to carry out price comparisons for industry outputs in the two countries. These comparisons are hampered by the fact that the makeup of a given industry may differ substantially between Japan and the United States. For example, the steel industry produces an enormous range of different steel products. The relative importance of different types of steel differs between the two countries. The composition of the output of the steel industry in each country also changes over time. These differences must be taken into account in comparing the relative prices of steel between Japan and the United States.

Relative prices between Japanese and U.S. industries can be summarized by means of purchasing power parities. The purchasing power parity for a specific industry's output is the number of yen required in Japan to purchase an amount of the industry's output that would cost one dollar in the United States. The dimensions of purchasing power parities are the same as the yen-to-dollar exchange rate, namely, yen per dollar. However, the purchasing power parities reflect the relative prices of goods and services that make up the industry's output in both countries.

The most familiar application of the notion of purchasing power parity is to the relative prices of such aggregates as the gross domestic product. This application has been the focus of the landmark studies of Kravis, Heston, and Sumers (1978a). As a consequence of their research, it is now possible to compare the relative prices of gross domestic product for a wide range of countries, including Japan and the United States. Kravis, Heston, and Summers have based their purchasing power parities for gross domestic product on relative prices for 153 commodity groups.

In this study we estimate purchasing power parities for 29 industries in Japan and the United States for the period 1960–1985. These are relative prices of the outputs of each industry in the two countries in terms of yen per dollar. We divide the relative price of each industry's output by the yen-to-dollar exchange rate to translate purchasing power parities into relative prices in terms of dollars.[1] We find it convenient to employ relative prices in dollars as measures of international competitiveness. Variations in the exchange rate are reflected in the relative prices of outputs for all 29 industries.

To account for changes in international competitiveness between Japanese and U.S. industries, we have compiled purchasing power parities for the inputs into each industry. By analogy with outputs, the purchasing power parities for inputs are based on the relative prices of the goods and services that make up the inputs of each industry. We have disaggregated inputs among capital and labor services, which are primary factors of production, and energy and other intermediate goods, which are produced by one industry and consumed by other industries. We can translate purchasing power parities for inputs into relative prices in dollars by dividing by the yen-to-dollar exchange rate. We describe purchasing power parities for output and inputs in 29 industries of the United States and Japan in section 9.2 below.

Our final step in accounting for international competitiveness between Japanese and U.S. industries is to measure relative levels of productivity for all 29 industries. For this purpose we employ a model of production for each industry. This model enables us to express the price of output in each country as a function of the prices of inputs and the level of productivity in that country. We can account for the relative prices of output between Japan and the United States by allowing input prices and levels of productivity to differ between countries. We have compiled data on relative productivity levels in Japan and the United States for the period 1960–1985. For this purpose we have revised and extended the estimates for 1960–1979 reported by Jorgenson, Kuroda, and Nishimizu (1987).

The methodology for our study was originated by Jorgenson and Nishimizu (1978). They provided a theoretical framework for productivity comparisons based on bilateral production function at the aggregate level. They employed this framework in comparing aggregate output, input, and productivity for Japan and the United States.[2] This methodology was extended to the industry level by Jorgenson and Nishimizu (1981) and employed in international comparisons between Japanese and U.S. industries. The industry-level methodology introduced models of production for individual industries based on bilateral production functions for each industry. This methodology was used in Jorgenson, Kuroda, and Nishimizu (1987), which involved comparisons between Japan and the United States at the industry level for the period 1960–1979.[3] We discuss the theoretical framework for international comparisons briefly in the appendix to this paper.

We present comparisons of productivity levels between the United States and Japan by industry in section 9.3. Jorgenson, Kuroda, and Nishimizu (1987) have presented a taxonomy of Japanese and U.S. industries, based on the development of relative productivity levels over the period 1960–1979. They have used this taxonomy to project the likely development of relative productivity levels for each industry. We can now assess the validity of these projections on the basis of developments during the period 1960–1985. We find that the taxonomy has been very useful in forming expectations about future developments in productivity. Finally, we employ changes in relative productivity levels and relative prices of inputs in accounting for changes in international competitiveness between Japanese and U.S. industries over the period 1960–1985. Section 9.4 provides a summary and conclusion.

## 9.2 Purchasing Power Parities

We treat data on production patterns in Japan and the United States as separate sets of observations. We assume that these observations are generated by bilateral models of production for each industrial sector presented in detail in the appendix. We can describe the implications of the theory of production in terms of production functions for each industry. These production functions give industry outputs as functions of capital, labor, energy, and other intermediate inputs, a dummy variable equal to one for Japan and zero for the United States, and time as an index of technology.

In our bilateral models of production, the capital, labor, energy, and other intermediate input prices are aggregates that depend on the prices of individual capital inputs, labor inputs, energy inputs, and other intermediate inputs in Japan and the United States. The product of price and quantity indices must equal the value of all the components of each aggregate. We define price indices corresponding to each aggregate as ratios of the value of the components of the aggregate to the corresponding quantity index. In international comparisons, the price indices represent purchasing power parities between the yen and the dollar. For example, the price index for labor input represents the Japanese price in yen for labor input costing one in the United States.

Our methodology for estimating purchasing power parities is based on linking time-series data sets on prices in Japan and the United States. Suppose that we observe the price of the output of the $i$th industry in Japan and the United States, say $q_i(\text{JAPAN})$ and $q_i(\text{U.S.})$, in the base period, where these prices are evaluated in terms of yen and dollars, respectively. We can define the *purchasing power parity* for the output of the $i$th industry, say $\text{PPP}_i$, as follows:

$$\text{PPP}_i = \frac{q_i(\text{JAPAN})}{q_i(\text{U.S.})}, \quad (i = 1, 2, \dots, I).$$ (9.1)

The purchasing power parity gives the number of yen required in Japan to purchase an amount of the output of the $i$th industry costing one dollar in the United States in the base period.

To estimate purchasing power parities for outputs of all industries in Japan and the United States, we first construct a time series of prices for the output of each industry in both countries in domestic currency. To obtain price indices for industry outputs in the United States, we normalize the price index for each industry, say $q_i(\text{U.S.}, T)$, at unity in the base period. We normalize the corresponding price index for Japan, say $q_i(\text{JAPAN}, T)$, at the purchasing power parity in the base period. We obtain estimates of purchasing power parities for all years, say $\text{PPP}_i(T)$, from these price indices and the purchasing power parity for the base period from the equation

$$\text{PPP}_i(T) = \text{PPP}_i(0) \frac{q_i(\text{JAPAN}, T)}{q_i(\text{JAPAN}, 0)} \frac{q_i(\text{U.S.}, 0)}{q_i(\text{U.S.}, T)}, \quad (i = 1, 2, \dots, I),$$ (9.2)

where $\text{PPP}_i(0)$ is the purchasing power parity in the base period and $q_i(\text{JAPAN}, 0)$ and $q_i(\text{U.S.}, 0)$ are the prices of outputs of the $i$th industry in Japan and the U.S. in the base period.

Finally, we define the *relative price* of the output of the $i$th industry in Japan and the United States in dollars, say $p_i(\text{JAPAN}, \text{U.S.})$, as the ratio of the purchasing power parity for that industry to the yen-to-dollar exchange rate, say $E$

$$p_i(\text{JAPAN}, \text{U.S.}) = \frac{\text{PPP}_i}{E}, \quad (i = 1, 2, \dots, I).$$ (9.3)

The relative price of the output of the $i$th industry in Japan and the United States is the ratio of the number of dollars required in Japan to purchase an amount of the industry's output costing one dollar in the United States. This index is our measure of international competitiveness between the Japanese industry and its U.S. counterpart.

In order to construct purchasing power parities and the corresponding relative prices between Japanese and U.S. industries, we require an estimate of the purchasing power parity for each industry in the base period. For this purpose we have developed purchasing power parities for industry outputs based on the results of Kravis, Heston, and Summers (1978a). They have provided purchasing power parities between the yen and the dollar for 153 commodity groups for the year 1970. These commodity groups are components of the gross domestic product of each country, corresponding to deliveries to final demand at purchasers' prices.

We construct purchasing power parities for industry outputs, energy inputs, and other intermediate inputs by mapping the 153 commodity groups employed by Kravis, Heston, and Summers (1978a) into the industry classification system shown in table 9.1. Unfortunately, a complete correspondence between the two systems is impossible, since not all intermediate goods delivered by the different industrial sectors are included among the 153 commodity groups delivered to final demand. We have eliminated the gap between the two systems by utilizing the purchasing power parities of close substitutes for a given industry's deliveries to intermediate demand.

To obtain purchasing power parities for industry outputs from the producer's point of view, we adjust the price indices for commodity groups in Japan and the United States by "peeling off" the indirect taxes paid and trade and transportation margins for each industry. We estimate these margins from the interindustry transactions table for 1970 for each country. To obtain the purchasing power parities for industry outputs, we aggregate the results for commodity groups, using as weights the relative shares of each commodity in the value of industry output from the 1970 interindustry transactions tables. Similarly, to obtain purchasing power parities for components of intermediate input in each industry, we aggregate purchasing power parities for goods and services delivered by that industry to other industries. We employ relative shares in the value of deliveries of intermediate input from other industries from the 1970 interindustry transaction tables as weights.

For both Japan and the United States, capital stocks are divided among seven types of depreciable assets and two types of nondepre-

**Table 9.1**
List of industries

| Number | Industries | Abbreviation |
|---|---|---|
| 1. | Agriculture, forestry & fisheries | Agric. |
| 2. | Mining | Mining |
| 3. | Construction | Construct. |
| 4. | Food & kindred products | Foods |
| 5. | Textile mill products | Textiles |
| 6. | Apparel & other fabricated textile | Apparel |
| 7. | Lumber & wood products, except furniture | Lumber |
| 8. | Furniture & fixtures | Furniture |
| 9. | Paper & allied products | Paper |
| 10. | Printing, Publishing & allied products | Printing |
| 11. | Chemical & allied products | Chemical |
| 12. | Petroleum refinery & coal products | Petroleum |
| 13. | Rubber & miscellaneous plastic products | Rubber |
| 14. | Leather & leather products | Leather |
| 15. | Stone, clay & glass products | Stone |
| 16. | Primary metal products | Prim. Metal |
| 17. | Fabricated metal products | Fab. Metal |
| 18. | Machinery | Machinery |
| 19. | Electric machinery | Elec. Mach. |
| 20. | Motor vehicles & equipment | Mot. Veh. |
| 21. | Transportation equipment, except motors | Trsp. Eqpt. |
| 22. | Precision instruments | Prec. Inst. |
| 23. | Miscellaneous manufacturing | Mfg. Misc. |
| 24. | Transportation & communication | Trsp. Comm. |
| 25. | Electric utility & gas supply | Utilities |
| 26. | Wholesale & retail trade | Trade |
| 27. | Finance, insurance & real estate | Finance |
| 28. | Other service | Service |
| 29. | Government services | Gov. Serv. |

ciable assets for each industry. These assets are further subdivided among legal forms of organization. We employ the equality between the price of an asset and the discounted flow of future capital services to derive service prices for capital input. Although we estimate the decline in efficiency of capital goods for each component of capital input separately for Japan and the United States, we assume that the relative efficiency of new capital goods in a given industry is the same in both countries. The appropriate purchasing power parity for new capital goods is the purchasing power parity for the corresponding component of investment goods output. To obtain the purchasing power parity for capital input, we multiply the purchasing power parity for investment goods by the ratio of the price of capital goods for Japan relative to the United States. The resulting price index represents the purchasing power parity for capital input.

For both Japan and the United States, labor inputs are cross-classified by employment status, sex, age, education, and occupation. Given the detailed classification of labor input for each industry in our data base, we construct purchasing power parities for labor input on the basis of relative wage levels for each component of labor input in each industry. Purchasing power parities for industry output, capital, labor, energy, and other intermediate inputs in 1970 are shown in table 9.2.

According to our purchasing power parities for industry output in 1970, prices in Japan were higher than those in United States in only six sectors—agriculture-forestry-fisheries, construction, food and kindred products, petroleum refinery and coal products, rubber products, and electricity and gas. The purchasing power parities for labor input in 1970 represent substantially lower costs of labor input in Japan relative to the United States. In that year, hourly wages in Japan were 30 percent or less of U.S. hourly wages. By contrast, the cost of capital in Japan averaged about 80 percent of that in the United States in 1970. The purchasing power parities for intermediate inputs are calculated as a weighted average of the purchasing power parities of industry outputs. The cost of intermediate inputs in Japan, other than energy, was between 60–90 percent of the cost in the United States in 1970. On the other hand, the purchasing power parities for energy inputs in 1970 are greater than unity, implying that the cost of energy in Japan was higher than that in the United States.

We have estimated purchasing power parities between the yen and the dollar in 1970 for the 29 industries listed in table 9.1 above. We have also compiled price indices for industry outputs and inputs in both countries for the period of 1960–1985. We obtain indices of prices of outputs and inputs for each industry in Japan relative to those in the United States for each year from equation (2) above. Table 9.3 presents time series for price indices of value added and capital and labor inputs for the period 1960–1985 in Japan and the United States. Column 1 of the table represents the yen-dollar exchange rate. The second and third columns represent price indices for for Japan. The second column gives the domestic price index with base equal to the purchasing power parity in 1970. The third column gives this price index, divided by an index of the yen-dollar exchange rate, equal to

**Table 9.2**
The Japanese price index transformed by purchasing power parity index at 1970 (United States price = 1.000)

| Industry | Output price | Capital price | Labor price | Energy price | Material price |
|---|---|---|---|---|---|
| Agric. | 1.04556 | 0.90835 | 0.21352 | 1.48236 | 0.91204 |
| Mining | 0.72125 | 0.88095 | 0.21263 | 1.44013 | 0.70573 |
| Construct. | 1.03487 | 0.92127 | 0.18607 | 1.42641 | 0.72203 |
| Foods | 1.03569 | 0.92190 | 0.21894 | 1.26554 | 0.88483 |
| Textiles | 0.77898 | 0.90871 | 0.24099 | 1.18329 | 0.76975 |
| Apparel | 0.76952 | 0.86037 | 0.18975 | 1.24298 | 0.74821 |
| Lumber | 0.79154 | 0.84363 | 0.22805 | 1.22680 | 0.90165 |
| Furniture | 0.67945 | 0.84214 | 0.22952 | 1.22178 | 0.74429 |
| Paper | 0.58858 | 0.89567 | 0.22170 | 1.18606 | 0.65664 |
| Printing | 0.78107 | 0.86742 | 0.21251 | 1.12482 | 0.65975 |
| Chemical | 0.66210 | 0.91711 | 0.25039 | 1.33630 | 0.71200 |
| Petroleum | 1.59952 | 0.89588 | 0.21846 | 1.31298 | 0.88291 |
| Rubber | 1.06186 | 0.86013 | 0.24042 | 1.22499 | 0.76731 |
| Leather | 0.71273 | 0.82076 | 0.23569 | 1.31561 | 0.81086 |
| Stone | 0.69603 | 0.89998 | 0.23083 | 1.31627 | 0.72567 |
| Prim. Metal | 0.81706 | 0.91205 | 0.25200 | 1.37079 | 0.80318 |
| Fab. Metal | 0.81514 | 0.90205 | 0.21072 | 1.32346 | 0.77507 |
| Machinery | 0.61327 | 0.92020 | 0.22564 | 1.28346 | 0.71093 |
| Elec. Mach. | 0.68127 | 0.92036 | 0.22308 | 1.24327 | 0.71054 |
| Mot. Veh. | 0.78627 | 0.91647 | 0.18581 | 1.17290 | 0.76428 |
| Trsp. Eqpt. | 0.94794 | 0.87722 | 0.21944 | 1.24063 | 0.76549 |
| Prec. Inst. | 0.71912 | 0.86402 | 0.23150 | 1.22607 | 0.71774 |
| Mfg. Misc. | 0.69473 | 0.88034 | 0.22549 | 1.27395 | 0.71238 |
| Trsp. Comm. | 0.47247 | 0.91027 | 0.22713 | 1.43624 | 0.68624 |
| Utilities | 1.02936 | 0.90389 | 0.26605 | 1.49490 | 0.78528 |
| Trade | 0.66155 | 0.93094 | 0.25889 | 1.35118 | 0.73683 |
| Finance | 0.86176 | 0.83300 | 0.30796 | 1.14490 | 0.77297 |
| Service | 0.56751 | 0.91719 | 0.25592 | 1.22718 | 0.73724 |
| Gov. Serv. | 0.30797 | 0.00000 | 0.19482 | 1.35489 | 0.68436 |

Note: See table 9.1 for key to industry abbreviations.

**Table 9.3**
Comparison of trend of value-added price index between Japan and the United States

| Year | (1) Exchange rate | (2) Value-added Japan (1) | (3) Value-added Japan (2) | (4) Value-added United States |
|------|------|------|------|------|
| 1960 | 360    | 0.49401 | 0.49401 | 0.78454 |
| 1961 | 360    | 0.53183 | 0.53183 | 0.79409 |
| 1962 | 360    | 0.55298 | 0.55298 | 0.80279 |
| 1963 | 360    | 0.57685 | 0.57685 | 0.80636 |
| 1964 | 360    | 0.59492 | 0.59492 | 0.81563 |
| 1965 | 360    | 0.61978 | 0.61978 | 0.83047 |
| 1966 | 360    | 0.64779 | 0.64779 | 0.86174 |
| 1967 | 360    | 0.67604 | 0.67604 | 0.88078 |
| 1968 | 360    | 0.69657 | 0.69657 | 0.91007 |
| 1969 | 360    | 0.72318 | 0.72318 | 0.95491 |
| 1970 | 360    | 0.75878 | 0.75878 | 1.00000 |
| 1971 | 348    | 0.77834 | 0.80517 | 1.04760 |
| 1972 | 303.1  | 0.80947 | 0.96143 | 1.09325 |
| 1973 | 271.7  | 0.92428 | 1.22466 | 1.16623 |
| 1974 | 292.1  | 0.87190 | 1.07460 | 1.29731 |
| 1975 | 296.8  | 0.99093 | 1.20194 | 1.42734 |
| 1976 | 296.5  | 1.05665 | 1.28294 | 1.49954 |
| 1977 | 268.3  | 1.10367 | 1.48088 | 1.60448 |
| 1978 | 210.1  | 1.18892 | 2.03717 | 1.73642 |
| 1979 | 219.5  | 1.21565 | 1.99378 | 1.89859 |
| 1980 | 203    | 1.27198 | 2.25573 | 2.09651 |
| 1981 | 219.9  | 1.30588 | 1.13787 | 2.29653 |
| 1982 | 235    | 1.34193 | 1.05572 | 2.43595 |
| 1983 | 232.2  | 1.36365 | 2.11418 | 2.51156 |
| 1984 | 251.1  | 1.37795 | 1.97556 | 2.59771 |
| 1985 | 224.05 | 1.38862 | 2.23121 | 2.66754 |

Note: Col. 1 is the observed exchange rate (yen/dollar); col. 2 is the Japanese price index transformed by the purchasing power parity (PPP) index; col. 3 is the Japanese PPP-based price index denominated by exchange rate; col. 4 is the U.S. corresponding price index.

one in 1970. The fourth column gives the corresponding price index in the United States with base equal to one in 1970.

According to the results presented in table 9.4, the price deflator for aggregate value-added in Japan was 0.49401 in 1960, while that in the United States was 0.78454 in that year. This implies that the Japanese aggregate price index in 1960 was only 63 percent of that in the United States. Under the fixed yen-dollar exchange rate of 360 yen to the dollar that prevailed until 1970, the ratio of the Japanese price index to

**Table 9.4**
Comparison of trend of capital input prices between Japan and the United States

| Year | (1) Exchange rate | (2) Capital Japan (1) | (3) Capital Japan (2) | (4) Capital United States |
|------|------|------|------|------|
| 1960 | 360 | 0.62499 | 0.62499 | 0.79723 |
| 1961 | 360 | 0.70010 | 0.70010 | 0.80034 |
| 1962 | 360 | 0.64268 | 0.64268 | 0.87577 |
| 1963 | 360 | 0.62544 | 0.62544 | 0.91310 |
| 1964 | 360 | 0.68795 | 0.68795 | 0.96814 |
| 1965 | 360 | 0.68865 | 0.68865 | 1.05671 |
| 1966 | 360 | 0.71741 | 0.71741 | 1.08764 |
| 1967 | 360 | 0.78290 | 0.78290 | 1.06235 |
| 1968 | 360 | 0.86281 | 0.86281 | 1.07711 |
| 1969 | 360 | 0.88634 | 0.88634 | 1.09371 |
| 1970 | 360 | 0.89842 | 0.89842 | 1.00000 |
| 1971 | 348 | 0.81956 | 0.8478206 | 1.07581 |
| 1972 | 303.1 | 0.83773 | 0.9949943 | 1.16855 |
| 1973 | 271.7 | 0.92240 | 1.2221715 | 1.22005 |
| 1974 | 292.1 | 0.99464 | 1.2258486 | 1.12504 |
| 1975 | 296.8 | 0.92340 | 1.1200269 | 1.29908 |
| 1976 | 296.5 | 0.94393 | 1.1460870 | 1.42287 |
| 1977 | 268.3 | 0.96151 | 1.2901364 | 1.63368 |
| 1978 | 210.1 | 1.15219 | 1.9742427 | 1.78198 |
| 1979 | 219.5 | 1.21611 | 1.9945312 | 1.82541 |
| 1980 | 203 | 1.00809 | 1.7877458 | 1.85044 |
| 1981 | 219.9 | 0.98245 | 1.6083765 | 2.00438 |
| 1982 | 235 | 1.04394 | 1.5992272 | 1.96229 |
| 1983 | 232.2 | 1.06156 | 1.6458294 | 2.13698 |
| 1984 | 251.1 | 1.10386 | 1.5825949 | 2.43909 |
| 1985 | 224.05 | 1.15020 | 1.8481231 | 2.46379 |

Note: Col. 1 is the observed exchange rate (yen/dollar); col. 2 is the Japanese price index transformed by the purchasing power parity (PPP) index; col. 3 is the Japanese PPP-based price index denominated by exchange rate; col. 4 is the U.S. corresponding price index.

the U.S. price index rose to 76 percent in 1970. With the collapse of the fixed-exchange-rate regime in 1970 and the beginning of the energy crisis in 1973, the price index in Japan, denominated in dollars, exceeded the corresponding U.S. price index. This was a consequence of more rapid inflation in Japan and a substantial appreciation of the yen through 1973. The competitiveness of U.S. industries relative to their Japanese counterparts reached a temporary peak in that year.

After 1979 the U.S. inflation rate continued at a high level, while Japan underwent a severe deflation, accompanied by depreciation of the yen. This had the short-run effect of restoring the competitiveness of Japanese industries. Inflation resumed in Japan after 1974, and the yen was allowed to appreciate again, reaching an exchange rate of 210 yen to the dollar in 1978. Once again, Japanese prices, denominated in terms of dollars, exceeded U.S. prices. This situation continued until 1980 as inflation in the United States continued at high rates. In the 1980s U.S. prices rose to well above the level of Japanese prices due to the rapid appreciation of the U.S. dollar relative to the Japanese yen. By 1985 the Japanese price level in dollars was only 83 percent of the U.S. price, which implies that Japanese industries had a substantial competitive advantage relative to their U.S. counterparts.

According to the international comparison of capital input prices shown in table 9.4, the cost of capital in Japan in 1960 was almost 78 percent of that in the United States and gradually rose to 89 percent of the U.S. level by 1970. After the energy crisis in 1973 the cost of capital in Japan increased relative to the United States, exceeding the U.S. level by almost 11 percent in 1978. The appreciation of the U.S. dollar reversed this trend. By 1985 the relative cost of capital in Japan had fallen to only 75 percent of the U.S. level, which is lower than the level that prevailed almost a quarter century earlier, in 1960. The rise in the cost of capital in Japan relative to that in the United States after the energy crisis was a consequence of the appreciation of the yen. The fall of this relative price in the 1980s resulted from the appreciation of the dollar.

Finally, a comparison of labor input prices in table 9.5 shows that the Japanese wage rate in 1960 was only 11 percent the U.S. wage rate. By 1970 the Japanese wage rate had reached 23 percent of the U.S. level. Rapid wage increases in Japan during the 1970s and the sharp appreciation of the yen raised wage rates in Japan to 60 percent of the U.S. level in 1980. The subsequent appreciation of the dollar and rapid wage increases in the United States resulted in a decline in

**Table 9.5**
Comparison of trend of labor input prices between Japan and the United States

| Year | (1) Exchange rate | (2) Labor Japan (1) | (3) Labor Japan (2) | (4) Labor United States |
|------|-------------------|---------------------|---------------------|-------------------------|
| 1960 | 360 | 0.06759 | 0.06759 | 0.60926 |
| 1961 | 360 | 0.07795 | 0.07795 | 0.64391 |
| 1962 | 360 | 0.08871 | 0.08871 | 0.65408 |
| 1963 | 360 | 0.10203 | 0.10203 | 0.66726 |
| 1964 | 360 | 0.10864 | 0.10864 | 0.68739 |
| 1965 | 360 | 0.12425 | 0.12425 | 0.70308 |
| 1966 | 360 | 0.13732 | 0.13732 | 0.74533 |
| 1967 | 360 | 0.15215 | 0.15215 | 0.79066 |
| 1968 | 360 | 0.17714 | 0.17714 | 0.8549 |
| 1969 | 360 | 0.20104 | 0.20104 | 0.90917 |
| 1970 | 360 | 0.23211 | 0.23211 | 1 |
| 1971 | 348 | 0.26643 | 0.2756172 | 1.07431 |
| 1972 | 303.1 | 0.30113 | 0.3576601 | 1.14898 |
| 1973 | 271.7 | 0.38076 | 0.5045034 | 1.24142 |
| 1974 | 292.1 | 0.46834 | 0.5772078 | 1.36978 |
| 1975 | 296.8 | 0.55019 | 0.6673463 | 1.49983 |
| 1976 | 296.5 | 0.59518 | 0.7226468 | 1.62713 |
| 1977 | 268.3 | 0.6492 | 0.8710846 | 1.73529 |
| 1978 | 210.1 | 0.67337 | 1.1537991 | 1.84918 |
| 1979 | 219.5 | 0.70365 | 1.1540501 | 2.00071 |
| 1980 | 203 | 0.75423 | 1.3375507 | 2.21758 |
| 1981 | 219.9 | 0.79732 | 1.3052987 | 2.39774 |
| 1982 | 235 | 0.8339 | 1.2774638 | 2.54319 |
| 1983 | 232.2 | 0.83456 | 1.2938914 | 2.64133 |
| 1984 | 251.1 | 0.85129 | 1.2204874 | 2.73005 |
| 1985 | 224.05 | 0.89202 | 1.4332836 | 2.864 |

Note: Col. 1 is the observed exchange rate (yen/dollar); col. 2 is the Japanese price index transformed by the purchasing power parity (PPP) index; col. 3 is the Japanese PPP-based price index denominated by exchange rate; col. 4 is the U.S. corresponding price index.

Japanese wage rates relative to the United States. The relative price of labor input in Japan was only 50 percent of the U.S. level in 1985.

Our international comparisons of relative prices of aggregate output and inputs show, first, that the Japanese economy has been more competitive than the U.S. economy throughout the period 1960–1985, except for 1973 and 1978–1979. Second, lower wage rates have contributed to Japan's international competitiveness throughout the period, especially before the energy crisis in 1973. Lower costs of capital have also contributed to Japan's international competitiveness for most of the same period with important exceptions in 1973 and 1978–1980.

We turn next to international competitiveness of Japanese and U.S. industries. Exchange rates play the same role in relative price comparisons at the industry level as at the aggregate level. However, industry inputs include energy and other intermediate goods as well as the primary factors of production—capital and labor inputs. The price of energy inputs in each industrial sector is an aggregate of inputs of petroleum and coal products and electricity and gas products. The relative prices of the outputs of these two industries in Japan and the United States are given in the following table 9.6.

The energy crisis of 1973 had an enormous impact on the prices of energy in both Japan and the United States. Prices of petroleum and coal products in Japan were almost double those in the United States, while prices of electricity and gas were about 1.3 times those in the United States in 1985. By comparison petroleum and coal products in Japan were only 1.6 times as expensive as those in the United States in

**Table 9.6**
Relative prices of outputs in two energy industries

|  | Petroleum & coal | | Electricity & gas | |
|---|---|---|---|---|
| Year | Japan | United States | Japan | United States |
| 1960 | 1.71118 | 0.97477 | 0.83247 | 0.94299 |
| 1965 | 1.51919 | 0.94523 | 1.00311 | 0.96430 |
| 1970 | 1.59952 | 1.00000 | 1.02936 | 1.00000 |
| 1975 | 5.34666 | 2.51780 | 2.26813 | 1.78555 |
| 1980 | 14.75987 | 6.46713 | 5.99713 | 3.45804 |
| 1985 | 13.28313 | 5.98764 | 6.25211 | 5.04334 |

**Table 9.7**
Annual growth rate of prices

| Period | Source | Price increase (%) | |
| --- | --- | --- | --- |
| | | Japan | Unites States |
| 1960–1970 | Capital service | 2.8435 | 2.2153 |
| | Labor service | 12.2062 | 4.5325 |
| | Energy input | 0.5881 | 0.4513 |
| | Material input | 2.1515 | 2.0432 |
| 1970–1980 | Capital service | −0.5899 | 6.3782 |
| | Labor service | 11.6868 | 8.0232 |
| | Energy input | 13.8936 | 15.1777 |
| | Material input | 7.7005 | 8.1342 |
| 1980–1985 | Capital service | 0.0777 | 5.9044 |
| | Labor service | 3.8273 | 5.2741 |
| | Energy input | 1.2662 | 4.3062 |
| | Material input | 0.5704 | 3.2437 |

Note: Annual growth rates of each price are estimated in terms of a simple average of an annual growth rate by industry in each item.

1970, while electricity and gas were only slightly more expensive in Japan than in the United States in that year.

Table 9.7 gives average annual growth rates of input prices in Japan and the United States in the 1960s, 1970s and 1980s at the industry level. Differences in the growth rates of the cost of capital between Japan and the United States were negligible in the 1960s. Since 1970 average rates of growth in the United States have been considerably higher. The rates of growth of wage rates in Japan were substantially higher than those in the U.S. rates throughout in the 1960s and 1970s. During the 1980s, however, annual rates of growth of wages in the United States exceeded those in Japan by about 1.5 percent per year.

The movements of energy input prices were similar in the two countries in the 1960s. We have already described these movements during the energy crisis of the 1970s. Rates of growth of energy prices in the United States during the 1980s were about three percent per year higher than those in Japan. This implies that differences between energy prices in the two countries have been decreasing since 1980, in spite of the relatively high level of energy prices in Japan. The growth rates of other intermediate input prices in the United States were also higher than those in Japan after 1980. The higher growth rates of input prices in the United States since 1980—including capital, labor, energy, and other intermediate inputs—have resulted in a substantial deterioration of international competitiveness of U.S. industries relative to their Japanese counterparts.

## 9.3   Relative Productivity Levels

In this section we estimate relative levels of productivity in Japan and the United States for each of the 29 industries included in our study. Jorgenson, Kuroda, and Nishimizu (1987) have reported relative productivity levels for the two countries for the period 1960–1979. All Japanese industries had lower levels of productivity than their U.S. counterparts in 1960. However, there were nine industries in which productivity gaps between the two countries had closed during the period 1960–1979. In 19 industries differences in productivity levels between Japan and the United States remained in 1979.

Jorgenson, Kuroda, and Nishimizu (1987) have divided Japanese and U.S. industries into seven categories. Type 1 included four industries in which productivity gaps between Japan and the United States were expected to increase in the future—agriculture-forestry-fisheries, textiles, printing and publishing, and trade. Type 2 includes industries in which the productivity gaps were decreasing before 1973, but increasing after 1973. These industries were food and kindred products, apparel, furniture, rubber, stone and clay, other transportation equipment, utilities, and other services. Type 3 includes industries in which the United States had an advantage in productivity in 1979, but productivity gaps between Japan and the United States were expected to close in the near future. This category contains investment-goods industries such as nonelectrical machinery, electrical machinery, and motor vehicles.

Paper and allied products constitute type 4; in this industry U.S. productivity levels increased relative to those in Japan before 1973, but the productivity gap was decreasing afterward due to deterioration of productivity in the U.S. industry. Petroleum and coal products with a constant productivity gap, favoring the United States, and construction with negative growth rates of productivity in both countries are classified as type 5 and type 6, respectively. Finally, type 7 includes the nine industries in which Japan had a productivity advantage in 1979.

The Japanese advantage was expected to increase in the future. These include mining, lumber, chemicals, primary metals, fabricated metals, precision instruments, miscellaneous manufacturing, transportation and communication, and finance and insurance.

In order to assess the validity of this taxonomy in projecting future patterns of relative productivity growth in Japan and the U.S. we consider additional observations for the period 1979–1985. However, we must take note of the following revisions in the data base. First, we have revised U.S. intermediate input measures by constructing a time series of interindustry transactions tables for the period 1947–1985. The methodology is consistent with the approach used for constructing a time series of Japanese interindustry transaction tables for the period 1960–1985.[4] Second, we were able to obtain more detailed information on wage differentials between full-time employees and other employees in Japan. We used this information to improve our estimates of labor compensation for temporary employees, day laborers, and unpaid family workers in Japan.

The earlier estimates of purchasing power parities for labor input were based on the relative wage levels for full-time workers in Japan and the United States. In the agricultural sector in Japan, however, there is a substantial number of irregular and part-time workers, especially unpaid family workers. Taking the labor compensation of these workers into account, we find that we overestimated the purchasing power parity of labor input in the agricultural sector in our earlier work. We have revised the purchasing power parity index of labor input in the agriculture-forestry-fisheries industry in 1970 from 0.60588 to 0.21352, as shown in table 9.2. This is much closer to results for other industries, where we only take account of ordinary full-time employees in estimating the purchasing power parity index for labor input.

The three revisions in the data base have resulted in two substantial changes in the taxonomy of industries presented for the period 1960–1979 in Jorgenson, Kuroda, and Nishimizu (1987). The fabricated metal products industry was moved to type 1 from the type 7 classification of Jorgenson, Kuroda, and Nishimizu (1987). Second, the trade sector was classified in type 1 and is now classified in type 7 in the revised version. The remaining 26 industries were classified in the same way as in the industrial taxonomy of the earlier paper.

A new industrial taxonomy, based on our revised data base for the period 1960–1985, is given in table 9.8. Industries in which the United

**Table 9.8**
An industrial taxonomy in terms of technology gap

| Type of technology | Industry | Technology gaps 1980 | Average annual growth rate of productivity | | | | | | Technology gaps 1985 |
|---|---|---|---|---|---|---|---|---|---|
| | | | 1960–1970 | | 1970–1980 | | 1980–1985 | | |
| | | | Japan | United States | Japan | United States | Japan | United States | |
| Type 1 | (1) Agric. | U > J | 0.452 | 1.178 | -1.641 | 0.673 | -0.274 | 4.431 | U > J |
| | (3) Construct. | U > J | 0.854 | 0.228 | 0.717 | -1.070 | -1.707 | 0.516 | U > J |
| | (4) Foods | U > J | -0.155 | 0.556 | 0.370 | 0.208 | -0.917 | 0.800 | U > J |
| | (5) Textiles | U > J | 0.526 | 1.437 | -1.220 | 0.187 | 0.188 | 0.309 | U > J |
| | (10) Printing | U > J | 0.858 | 0.647 | -1.469 | 0.218 | 0.020 | 0.979 | U > J |
| | (12) Petroleum | U > J | -1.358 | 1.616 | -3.889 | -4.560 | -1.290 | 3.422 | U > J |
| | (17) Fab. Metal | U > J | 2.668 | 0.293 | 0.837 | 0.618 | 0.009 | 0.376 | U > J |
| Type 2 | (8) Furniture | U > J | 1.405 | 0.030 | 1.364 | 0.792 | 1.020 | 1.475 | U > J |
| | (13) Rubber | U > J | 1.499 | 0.868 | 0.550 | 0.981 | 2.623 | 3.502 | U > J |
| | (15) Stone | U > J | 2.794 | 0.339 | -1.248 | 0.555 | 0.414 | 2.443 | U > J |
| | (20) Mot. Veh. | J > U | 0.086 | 0.155 | 0.512 | 0.282 | -1.286 | 2.553 | U > J |
| | (21) Trsp. Eqpt. | U > J | 6.649 | 1.395 | 0.706 | -4.260 | 2.107 | 3.456 | U > J |
| Type 3 | (6) Apparel | U > J | 2.294 | 0.625 | 1.414 | 1.160 | 0.420 | 0.203 | U > J |
| | (28) Service | U > J | 1.378 | 0.700 | -3.033 | 0.018 | 0.502 | -1.179 | U > J |
| | (27) Finance | U > J | 1.810 | 0.535 | 0.150 | 0.181 | 3.311 | -1.179 | U > J |
| Type 5 | (25) Utilities | U > J | 3.222 | 2.111 | -2.991 | -1.497 | 0.603 | -1.668 | U > J |

**Table 9.8 (continued)**

| Type of technology | Industry | Technology gaps 1980 | Average annual growth rate of productivity | | | | | | Technology gaps 1985 |
|---|---|---|---|---|---|---|---|---|---|
| | | | 1960–1970 | | 1970–1980 | | 1980–1985 | | |
| | | | Japan | United States | Japan | United States | Japan | United States | |
| Type 7 | (2) Mining | J > U | 1.662 | 1.084 | 1.722 | -5.584 | 0.301 | 0.045 | J > U |
| | (7) Lumber | J > U | 2.781 | 0.965 | 2.032 | 0.738 | 3.522 | 1.211 | J > U |
| | (9) Paper | J > U | 1.616 | 0.338 | 0.505 | 0.233 | 1.982 | 1.207 | J > U |
| | (11) Chemical | J > U | 3.343 | 1.501 | 0.731 | -1.517 | 2.671 | 1.630 | J > U |
| | (14) Leather | U > J | 0.926 | 0.452 | 0.713 | 1.066 | 0.552 | -4.352 | J > U |
| | (16) Prim. Metal | J > U | 0.915 | 0.088 | 0.781 | 0.534 | 0.624 | -2.294 | J > U |
| | (18) Machinery | J > U | 2.212 | 0.809 | 0.377 | 0.693 | -1.073 | 0.785 | J = U |
| | (19) Elec. Mach. | J > U | 3.304 | 0.093 | 3.663 | 0.693 | 3.222 | 0.500 | J > U |
| | (22) Prec. Inst. | J > U | 1.943 | 0.729 | 3.626 | 0.130 | 1.513 | 3.105 | J > U |
| | (23) Mfg. Misc. | J > U | 1.741 | 0.647 | 1.257 | 0.795 | 0.252 | 0.230 | J > U |
| | (24) Trsp. Comm. | J > U | 3.056 | 1.085 | 0.490 | 0.995 | 1.186 | 0.251 | J > U |
| | (26) Trade | J > U | 2.507 | 0.077 | 0.838 | 0.316 | 0.607 | 2.600 | J = U |

Note: For industry abbreviations, see table 9.1 above. U = Unites States; J = Japan. Type 1: the United States had still an advantage in the 1980 technology. The technology gaps are expected to continue to expand in the future. Type 2: the United States had an advantage in the 1980 technology. Before 1980, the technology gaps partly were closing. But they, however, were expanding in 1980s and are expected to expand in the future. Type 3: the United States had an advantage in the 1980 technology. The technology gaps are expected to close in the near future. Type 5: The United States had an advantage in the 1980 technology. The technology gaps were mostly constant during the period 1960–1985. Type 7: Japan had an advantage in the 1980 technology. The technology gaps are expected to continue to expand in the future.

States has a substantial advantage in productivity in 1980 and productivity gaps between Japan and the United States are expected to persist into the future include agriculture-forestry-fisheries, textile products, and printing and publishing industries. These industries coincide with type 1 in Jorgenson, Kuroda, and Nishimizu (1987). Productivity growth since 1980 has added three industries to this category—petroleum and coal products, construction, and food and kindred products. These industries were classified in types 2, 5, and 6 in the earlier paper.

Type 2 includes those industries in which the United States had a productivity advantage in 1980 after productivity gaps had been closed during the 1960s and 1970s, but the U.S. productivity advantage was expected to grow in the future. The industries in this category in the 1987 paper included furniture and fixtures, rubber products, stone, clay and glass and other transportation equipment. Motor vehicles was added to this category in the 1980s. In the previous paper this industry was classified as type 3, where the technology gaps were expected to close in the near future.

According to new evidence on the productivity gap in the motor vehicle industry during the period 1980–1985, the gap between Japan and the United States had closed by 1982, as we expected from our earlier observations. After 1983, however, the gap increased again due to rapid productivity growth in the U.S. industry. The index of productivity in motor vehicles in Japan and the U.S. during the period 1979–1985 is given in table 9.9.

Type 3 includes industries in which productivity gaps are expected to close in the near future, even though the United States had a productivity advantage in 1980. Three industries included in this

**Table 9.9**
Index of productivity in motor vehicles

| Year | Japan | United States |
| --- | --- | --- |
| 1979 | 0.91639 | 0.97490 |
| 1980 | 0.91050 | 0.53853 |
| 1981 | 0.89246 | 0.88842 |
| 1982 | 0.86165 | 0.84402 |
| 1983 | 0.85502 | 0.95674 |
| 1984 | 0.85545 | 1.02915 |
| 1985 | 0.85379 | 0.98393 |

category in Jorgenson, Kuroda, and Nishimizu (1987)—leather, non-electrical machinery, and electrical machinery—had already attained U.S. levels of productivity by 1980, as we expected. In table 9.8 we have reclassified these industries in type 7. Industries added to type 3 in the 1980s were apparel, miscellaneous manufacturing, and finance, insurance, and real estate, previously classified as type 2 and type 7. These are three industries in which we were unable to project relative trends in productivity during the 1980s. Finally, type 7 includes industries in which Japan had a productivity advantage that we expected to increase in the future. Three industries previously classified in type 3 were added to this category in the 1980s, so that 12 industries of the 29 are included in type 7.

In evaluating the usefulness of the industrial taxonomy presented in Jorgenson, Kuroda, and Nishimizu (1987), we find only four industries in which the trend of technology gaps was not projected. The U.S. productivity advantage was expected to increase in apparel and miscellaneous manufacturing. The Japanese advantage was expected to increase in motor vehicles and finance. We conclude that the predictive power of the Jorgenson-Kuroda-Nishimizu taxonomy is substantial. We can also draw attention to the findings from new observations during the period 1980–1985. According to table 9.9 industries with a clear advantage in productivity in Japan or the United States fall into two groups. Type 1 includes seven industries with a U.S. advantage, while type 7 includes 12 industries with a Japanese advantage.

To analyze the trend of productivity differences between Japan and the United States, we have estimated the mean and variance of relative productivity by industry during the period 1960–1985. The results are shown in figures 9.1 and 9.2. The mean of relative productivity levels between the two countries remained fairly stable until 1973 and then rose through the 1970s. This movement peaked in 1980. Since that time, the trend has reversed with gains in productivity levels for the United States during the 1980s. The variance of the relative productivity levels shown in figure 9.2 was stable until the oil crisis in 1973 and has expanded rapidly since.

We conclude that the energy crisis had a very substantial impact on patterns of productivity growth by industry. Both the mean and the variance of relative productivity levels between Japan and the United States expanded during the period 1974–1980. In the 1980s the mean of the relative productivity level has fallen, while the variance has increased rapidly. This implies that the relative productivity levels in

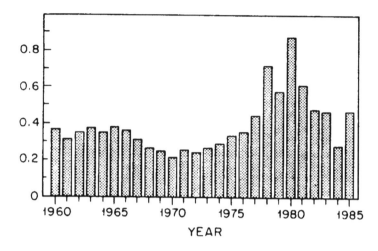

**Figure 9.1.** Average of proportional gap of the technology between the United States and Japan.

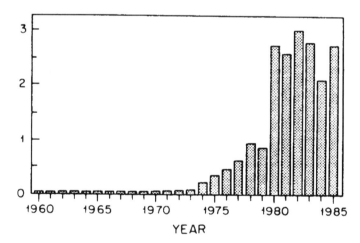

**Figure 9.2.** Variance of proportional gap of the technology between the United States and Japan.

the two countries have tended to differ substantially among industries, as shown in table 9.9.

Finally, we turn to international competitiveness between Japan and the United States. We can account for movements in the relative prices of industry outputs in the two countries by changes in relative input prices and changes in relative productivity levels. Figures 9.3a and 9.3b show the relative prices of industry outputs between Japan and the United States in terms of dollars. We have expressed these prices in logarithmic form so that a negative difference implies that the U.S. output price is below the Japanese price, while a positive difference implies the Japanese price is below the U.S. price.

Figure 9.3a includes plots of the relative prices of industries in which the United States has a higher level of productivity in 1985. In the 1960s the Japanese output prices were relatively low, due primarily to lower labor costs. Although lower relative wage rates in Japan helped to reduce relative prices of output, they were almost totally offset by the lower levels of productivity in Japan during the 1960s.

After the energy crisis of 1973, U.S. output prices in the industries plotted in figure 9.3a fell relative to Japanese prices until 1980 due to much greater increase in energy prices in Japan and appreciation of the yen relative to the dollar. During the 1980s the international competitiveness of Japanese industries has been increasing in spite of the productivity gains in the United States. This is because of the more rapid increase in U.S. wage rates and costs of capital and the appreciation of the dollar. It is especially interesting that output prices in textile products, motor vehicles, and fabricated metals industries have been almost the same in Japan and the United States since 1980, notwithstanding the increasing U.S. productivity advantage in these industries.

In figures 9.3a–9.3b, we present plots of the relative output prices of industries in which Japan had a productivity advantage in 1985. The time trends of relative prices in these industries during the period 1960–1985 are very similar to those of industries in which the United States had a productivity advantage. However, the price levels are lower in Japan, so that Japan has a clear advantage in international competitiveness. These features are especially evident in industries classified as type 7 in our industrial taxonomy.

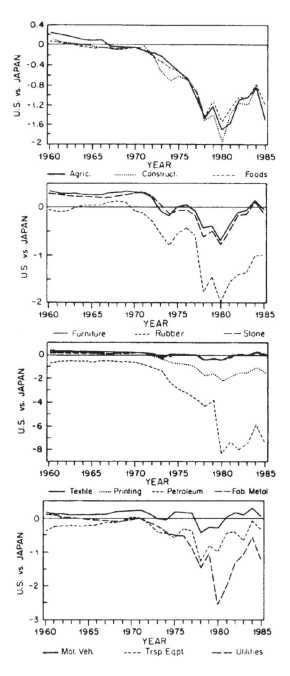

**Figure 9.3a.** Trends of proportional gap of denominated output prices.

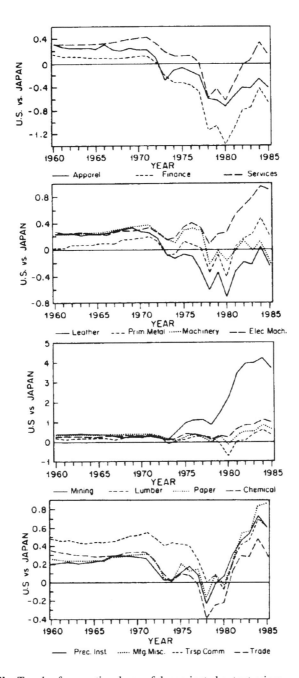

**Figure 9.3b.** Trends of proportional gap of denominated output prices.

## 9.4   Conclusion

Jorgenson (1988a) has recently summarized the results of international comparisons between Japan and the United States. The period 1960–1973 was characterized by substantial economic growth in the United States and very rapid economic growth in Japan. Capital input was by far the most important source of growth in both countries, accounting for about 40 percent of U.S. economic growth and 60 percent of Japanese growth. The period 1973–1979 was dominated by the energy crisis, which began with drastic increases in petroleum prices in 1973. Growth slowed significantly in the United States and declined dramatically in Japan during this period. The growth of capital input remained the most important source of economic growth in both countries, but productivity growth at the sectoral level essentially disappeared.

During the period 1960–1973 productivity growth in Japan exceeded that in the United States for almost all industries. After the energy crisis in 1973, there were very few significant differences between growth rates of productivity in Japanese and U.S. industries. In this paper we have extended these observations through 1985. An important focus for our work has been the assessment of longer-term trends in productivity growth. In particular, we have tried to establish whether or not the slowdown in productivity growth in Japan and the United States after the energy crisis has become permanent. For this purpose we have focused on productivity growth in both countries since 1979.

The second issue we have considered is the trend of industry-level productivity differences between the two countries. Jorgenson, Kuroda, and Nishimizu (1987) showed that almost every Japanese industry had a lower level of productivity that its U.S. counterpart in 1960. By the end of the period 1960–1979 there were nine industries in which productivity gaps between the two countries had closed. These industries were primarily concentrated in producer's goods manufacturing and were focused on export-oriented industries. In the remaining 19 industries productivity gaps between Japan and the United States remained in 1979. In this paper we have reexamined these findings in light of the experience accumulated during the period 1979–1985.

We can summarize our conclusions as follows: After 1970 productivity growth deteriorated substantially in both Japan and the United States. An important issue is whether the productivity slowdown is a permanent feature of both economies. To resolve this issue we can consider average productivity growth rates in Japanese and U.S. industries over the period 1960–1985, as shown in table 9.10. We conclude that productivity growth in Japan and the United States has revived slightly since 1980. However, the growth rates for the period 1980–1985 are well below those for the period 1960–1973, especially in Japan.

A second issue is whether productivity levels in Japan and the United States have tended to converge. While the mean of relative productivity levels between Japan and the United States has fallen since 1980, the variance has expanded rapidly. This implies that convergence of Japanese and U.S. levels of productivity during the 1960s has given way to sharply divergent trends in relative productivity by industry during the 1970s and, especially, during the 1980s. Figures 9.3a–9.3b provide our results on international competitiveness between Japan and the United States. The competitiveness of U.S. industries has been declining since 1980, due to more rapid growth of input prices in the United States and the appreciation of the dollar relative to the yen.

The industrial taxonomy presented by Jorgenson, Kuroda, and Nishimizu (1987) has proved to be relatively robust. The productivity trends by industry that was projected on the basis of our earlier results have materialized with only a few exceptions. While the United States retains an overall advantage in relative productivity levels, there is a substantial number of industries where Japan has gained an advan-

**Table 9.10**
Average productivity growth rates in Japan and the United States

|           | Japan (%) | United States (%) |
|-----------|-----------|-------------------|
| 1960–1965 | 1.478     | 1.993             |
| 1965–1970 | 1.946     | −0.985            |
| 1970–1973 | 0.686     | 0.941             |
| 1973–1975 | −1.481    | −3.064            |
| 1975–1980 | 0.178     | −1.058            |
| 1980–1985 | 0.760     | 0.448             |

tage and seems likely to increase it. Perhaps equally important, the increase in the variance of relative productivity levels among industries has created opportunities for both countries to benefit from the great expansion in Japan-U.S. trade that has already taken place. However, this increase is also an important source of "trade frictions" and will require continuing efforts at coordination of trade policies in the two countries.

## 9.5  Appendix

The industries in our data base for Japan are classified into 31 industrial sectors. For the United States, the industries are classified into 35 industrial sectors.[5] For international comparison we have aggregated these industries to the 29 sectors given in table 9.1. To represent our bilateral models of production we require the following notation:

$q_i$ — price of the output of the $i$th industry;

$p_{Ki}, p_{Li}, p_{Ei}, p_{Mi}$ — prices of capital, labor, energy, and other intermediate inputs in the $i$th industry.

$v_{Ki}, v_{Li}, v_{Ei}, v_{Mi}$ — value shares of capital, labor, energy and other intermediate inputs in the $i$th industry.

We represent the vector of value shares of the $i$th industry by $v_i$. Similarly, we represent the vector of logarithms of input prices of the $i$th industry by $\ln p_i$. We employ a time trend $T$ as an index of technology and a dummy variable $D$, equal to one for Japan and zero for the United States, to represent differences in technology between the two countries. Under competitive conditions we can represent technology by a price function that is dual to the production function relating each industry's output to the corresponding inputs, the level of technology, and differences in technology between the two countries.

$$\ln q_i = \ln p_i{'}\alpha^i + \alpha_t^i\, T + \alpha_d^i\, D + 1/2 \ln p_i{'}B^i \ln p_i + \ln p_i{'}\beta_t^i\, T + \ln p_i{'}\beta_d^i\, D$$
$$+ 1/2\, \beta_{tt}^i\, T^2 + \beta_{td}^i\, T\, D + 1/2\, \beta_{dd}^i\, D^2\, ,\quad (i = 1, 2, \ldots, I)\, . \qquad \text{(A1)}$$

For each industry the price of output is a transcendental or, more specifically, an exponential function of the logarithms of the input prices. We refer to these functions as *translog price functions*.[6] In this representation the scalars—$\alpha_t^i$, $\alpha_d^i$, $\beta_{tt}^i$, $\beta_{dd}^i$—the vectors—$\alpha^i$, $\beta_t^i$, $\beta_d^i$—and the matrices, $B^i$, are constant parameters that differ among industries. These parameters reflect differences in technology among industries. Within each industry differences in technology among time periods are represented by time as an index of technology. Differences in technology between Japan and the U.S. are represented by a dummy variable, equal to one for Japan and zero for the United States.

In analyzing differences in each industry's production patterns between Japan and the United States, we combine the price function with demand functions for inputs. We can express these functions as equalities between shares of each input in the value of the output of the industry and the elasticity of the output price with respect to the price of that input. These elasticities depend on input prices, dummy variables for each country, and time as an index of technology. The sum of the elasticities with respect to all inputs is equal to unity, so that the value shares also sum to unity.

For each industry the value shares are equal to the logarithmic derivatives of the price function with respect to logarithms of the input prices

$$v_i = \alpha^i + B^i \ln p_i + \beta_t^i \, T + \beta_d^i \, D \, , \quad (i = 1, 2, \ldots, I) \, . \tag{A2}$$

We can define *rates of productivity growth*, say $v_{Ti}$, as the negative of rates of growth of the price of output with respect to time, holding the input prices constant

$$-v_{Ti} = \alpha_t^i + \beta_t^{i\prime} \ln p_i + \beta_{tt}^i \, T + \beta_{dt}^i \, D \, , \quad (i = 1, 2, \ldots, I) \, . \tag{A3}$$

Similarly, we can define *differences in technology* between Japan and the United States, say $v_{Ti}$, as the negative of rates of growth of the price of output with respect to the dummy variable, holding the input prices constant

$$-v_{Di} = \alpha_d^i + \beta_d^{i\prime} \ln p_i + \beta_{td}^i \, T + \beta_{dd}^i \, D \, , \quad (i = 1, 2, \ldots, I) \, . \tag{A4}$$

The price of output, the prices of inputs, and the value shares for all four inputs are observable for each industry in the period 1960–1985 in both countries. The rates of productivity growth are not directly observable, but average rates of productivity growth between two points of time, say $T$ and $T - 1$, can be expressed as the difference between a weighted average of growth rates of input prices and the growth rates of the price of output for each industry

$$-\bar{v}_{Ti} = \ln q_i(T) - \ln q_i(T-1) - \bar{v}_i' \left[ \ln p_i(T) - \ln p_i(T-1) \right],$$

$$(i = 1, 2, \ldots, I), \tag{A5}$$

where the average rates of technical change are

$$\bar{v}_{Ti} = 1/2[v_{Ti}(T) + v_{Ti}(T-1)],$$

and the weights are given by the average value shares

$$\bar{v}_i = 1/2[v_i(T) + v_i(T-1)].$$

We refer to the index numbers (A.5) as *translog price indices* of the rates of productivity growth.[7]

Similarly, differences in productivity $v_{Di}$ are not directly observable. However, the average of these differences for Japan and the United States can be expressed as a weighted average of differences between the logarithms of the input prices, less the difference between logarithms of the output price

$$-\hat{v}_{Di} = \ln q_i(\text{JAPAN}) - \ln q_i(\text{U. S.}) - \hat{v}_i'[\ln p_i(\text{JAPAN}) - \ln p_i(\text{U. S.})],$$

$$(i = 1, 2, \ldots, I), \tag{A6}$$

where the average differences in productivity are

$$\hat{v}_{Di} = 1/2[v_{Di}(\text{JAPAN}) + v_{Di}(\text{U. S.})],$$

and the weights are given by the average value shares

$$\hat{v}_i = 1/2[v_i(\text{JAPAN}) + v_i(\text{U. S.})].$$

We refer to the index numbers (A.6) as *translog price indices* of differences in productivity.

## Notes

1. Equivalently, these prices could be expressed in terms of yen.
2. Christensen, Cummings, and Jorgenson (1980, 1981) have compared aggregate outputs, inputs, and productivity levels for nine countries, including Japan and the United States. Their estimates of relative productivity levels are based on the methodology for multilateral comparisons developed by Caves, Christensen, and Diewert (1982a, b). An alternative approach is presented by Denny and Fuss (1983b).
3. A similar approach is employed by Conrad and Jorgenson (1985) in comparisons for 1960–1979 among the Federal Republic of Germany, Japan, and the United States. This methodology is also used by Nishimizu and Robinson (1986) in comparisons among manufacturing industries in Japan, Koreau, Turkey, and Yugoslavia.

4. The methodology was originated by Kuroda (1988).

5. This classification is a consolidation of that used by Jorgenson, Gollop, and Fraumeni (1987).

6. The translog price function was introduced by Christensen, Jorgenson, and Lau (1971, 1973).

7. Diewert (1976) showed that the index numbers employed by Christensen and Jorgenson (1973a) are exact for the translog price function of Christensen, Jorgenson, and Lau (1971, 1973).

# References

Abramovitz, Moses. 1956. Resources and Output Trends in the United States since 1870. *American Economic Review* 46, no. 2 (May): 5–23.

———. 1962. Economic Growth in the United States (A Review Article). *American Economic Review* 52, no. 4 (September): 762–782.

———. 1977. Rapid Growth Potential and its Realization: The Experience of Capitalist Economics in the Postwar Period. *Memorandum* 211. Stanford University: Center for Research in Economic Growth.

Abramovitz, Moses, and Paul A. David. 1973a. Economic Growth in America: Historical Parables and Realities. *De Economist* 121, no. 3: 251–272.

———. 1973b. Reinterpreting Economic Growth: Parables and Realities. *American Economic Review* 63, no. 2 (May): 428–439.

Alchian, Armen. 1963. Reliability of Progress Curves in Airframe Production. *Econometrica* 31, no. 4 (October): 679–693.

Armstrong, Alan. 1974. *Structural Change in The British Economy 1948–1968*. A Programme for Growth, 12. London: Chapman and Hall.

Arrow, Kenneth J. 1962a. The Measurement of Real Value Added. In *Nations and Households in Economic Growth*, eds. Paul A. David and Melvyn W. Reder, 3–20. New York: Academic Press.

———. 1962b. The Economic Implications of Learning by Doing. *Review of Economic Studies* 29, no. 3, no. 86 (June): 155–173.

———. 1964. Optimal Capital Policy, the Cost of Capital, and Myopic Decision Rules. *Annals of the Institute of Statistical Mathematics* 16, nos. 1/2: 16–30.

———. 1974. The Measurement of Real Value Added. In *Nations and Households in Economic Growth*, ed. Paul A. David and Melvyn W. Reder, 3–20. New York: Academic Press.

Arrow, Kenneth J., Hollis B. Chenery, Bagicha S. Minhas, and Robert M. Solow. 1961. Capital-Labor Substitution and Economic Efficiency. *Review of Economics and Statistics* 63, no. 3 (August): 225–247.

Baily, Martin N. 1981. Productivity and the Services of Capital and Labor. *Brookings Papers on Economic Activity*, no. 1: 1–50.

———. 1982. The Productivity Slowdown by Industry. *Brookings Papers on Economic Activity*, no. 2: 423–454.

———. 1986. What Has Happened to Productivity Growth? *Science* 234, no. 4775 (October): 443–451.

Baily, Martin N., and Alok K. Chakrabarti. 1988. *Innovation and the Productivity Crisis*. Washington, DC: The Brookings Institution.

Baily, Martin N., and Robert J. Gordon. 1988. Measurement Issues, the Productivity Slowdown, and the Explosion of Computer Power. *Brookings Papers on Economic Activity*, no. 2: 1–45.

Balassa, Bela, and Trent J. Bertrand. 1970. Growth Performance of Eastern European Economies and Comparable Western European Countries. *American Economic Review* 60, no. 2 (May): 314–320.

Bank of Canada. Various dates. *Bank of Canada Review*. Ottawa: Queen's Printer.

Bank of Japan. Various dates. *Japan's Economic Statistics*.

Bank of Korea. 1972. *National Income Statistics Yearbook, 1972*. Seoul: Bank of Korea.

———. 1973. *Economic Statistics Yearbook, 1973*. Seoul: Bank of Korea.

———. 1977. *Economic Statistics Yearbook, 1977*. Seoul: Bank of Korea.

Barger, Harold. 1969. Growth in Developed Nations. *Review of Economics and Statistics* 51, no 2 (May): 143–148.

Baumol, William J., and Edward N. Wolff. 1984. On Interindustry Differences in Absolute Productivity. *Journal of Political Economy* 92, no. 6 (December): 1017–1034.

BEA. *See* Bureau of Economic Analysis.

Beckmann, Martin, and Ryuzo Sato. 1969. Aggregate Production Functions and Types of Technical Progress: A Statistical Analysis. *American Economic Review* 59, no. 1 (March): 88–101.

Beidleman, Carl R. 1976. Economic Depreciation in a Capital Goods Industry. *National Tax Journal* 29, no. 4 (December): 379–390.

Bentzel, Ragnar. 1978. A Vintage Model of Swedish Economic Growth from 1870 to 1975. In *The Importance of Technology and the Permanence of Structure in Industrial Growth*, eds. Bo Carlsson, Gunnar Eliasson, and Mohammed I. Nadiri, 13–50. Stockholm: Industrial Institute for Economic and Social Research.

Bergman, Lars. 1985. Extensions and Applications of the MSG-Model: A Brief Survey. In *Production, Multi-sectoral Growth and Planning*, eds. Finn R. Forsund, Michael Hoel, and Svein Longva, 127–161. Amsterdam: North-Holland.

————. 1990. The Development of Computable General Equilibrium Modeling. In *General Equilibrium Modeling and Economic Policy Analysis*, eds. Lars Bergman, Dale W. Jorgenson, and Erno Zalai, 3–30. Oxford: Basil Blackwell.

Bergson, Abram. 1961. *The Real National Income of the Soviet Union since 1928.* Cambridge, MA: Harvard University Press.

————. 1974. Soviet Postwar Economic Development. *Wicksell Lectures 1974.* Stockholm: Almqvist and Wicksell.

————. 1975. Index Numbers and the Computation of Factor Productivity. *Review of Income and Wealth*, ser. 21, no. 3 (September): 259–278.

————. 1978. *Productivity and the Social System—the USSR and the West.* Cambridge, MA: Harvard University Press.

————. 1987. Comparative Productivity: The USSR, Eastern Europe, and the West. *American Economic Review* 77, no. 3 (June): 342–357.

Berndt, Ernst R., and Laurits R. Christensen. 1973. The Translog Function and the Substitution of Equipment, Structures, and Labor in U.S. Manufacturing 1929–1968. *Journal of Econometrics* 1, no. 1 (March): 81–113.

————. 1974. Testing for the Existence of a Consistent Aggregate Index of Labor Input. *American Economic Review* 64, no 3. (June): 391–404.

Berndt, Ernst R., and Melvyn Fuss. 1986. Editor's Introduction. *Journal of Econometrics* 33, nos. 1/2 (October/November): 1–5.

Berndt, Ernst R., and Dale W. Jorgenson. 1973. Production Structures. In *U.S. Energy Resources and Economic Growth*, eds. Dale W. Jorgenson and Hendrik S. Houthakker, ch. 3. Washington, DC: Energy Policy Project.

Berndt, Ernst R., Shunseke Mori, Takamitsu Sawa, and David O. Wood. 1990. Energy Price Shocks and Productivity Growth in the Japanese and U.S. Manufacturing Industry. In *Productivity Growth in Japan and the United States*, ed. Charles R. Hulten. NBER Studies in Income and Wealth, vol. 53. Chicago: University of Chicago Press.

Berndt, Ernst R., and David O. Wood. 1975. Technology, Prices, and the Derived Demand for Energy. *Review of Economics and Statistics* 56, no. 3 (August): 259–268.

Binswanger, Hans P. 1978. Issues in Modeling Induced Technical Change. In *Induced Innovation*, eds. Hans P. Binswanger and Vernon W. Ruttan, 128–163. Baltimore, MD: Johns Hopkins University Press.

Bishop, Yvonne M.M., Steven E. Fienberg, and Paul W. Holland. 1975. *Discrete Multivariate Analysis.* Cambridge, MA: MIT Press.

Blackorby, Charles, Daniel Primont, and Robert R. Russell. 1977. On Testing Separability Restrictions with Flexible Functional Forms. *Journal of Econometrics* 5, no. 2 (March): 195–209.

BLS. *See* Bureau of Labor Statistics.

Brazell, D.W., Laurits R. Christensen, and Dianne Cummings. 1975. *Real Product, Real Factor Input, and Productivity in France, 1951–1973*. Social Systems Research Institute: University of Wisconsin, Discussion Paper no. 7527.

Brown, Murray. 1980. The Measurement of Capital Aggregates: A Postreswitching Problem. In *The Measurement of Capital*, ed. Dan Usher, 377–420. Chicago, IL: University of Chicago Press.

Bruno, Michael. 1978. Duality, Intermediate Inputs, and Value Added. In *Production Economics: A Dual Approach to Theory and Applications*, eds. Melvyn Fuss and Daniel McFadden, 2: 3–16. Amsterdam: North-Holland.

————. 1984. Raw Materials, Profits, and the Productivity Slowdown. *Quarterly Journal of Economics* 99, no. 1 (February): 1–30.

Bureau of the Census. Various dates. *Census of Population*. Washington, DC: U.S. Department of Commerce.

————. Various dates. *Current Population Reports*. Washington, DC: U.S. Department of Commerce.

————. 1966. *Current Population Reports, Population Characteristics*, series P-60, no. 157. Washington, DC: U.S. Government Printing Office.

————. 1972. *Census of Population: 1970, Occupation by Industry*. Final Report PC(2)-7C. Washington, DC: U.S. Department of Commerce.

————. 1973a. *Census of Population: 1970, Earnings by Occupation and Education*. Final Report PC(2)-8B. Washington, DC: U.S. Department of Commerce.

————. 1973b. *Census of Population: 1970, Industrial Characteristics*. Final Report PC(2)-7B. Washington, DC: U.S. Department of Commerce.

————. 1973c. *Census of Population: 1970, Occupational Characteristics*. Final Report PC(2)-7A. Washington, DC: U.S. Department of Commerce.

————. 1973d. *Census of Population, 1970, Subject Reports*, Final report PC (2)-5B, Educational Attainment. Washington, DC: U.S. Government Printing Office.

————. 1985. *Census of Population and Housing: 1980*. One Percent Sample Computer Tape. Washington, DC: U.S. Department of Commerce.

Bureau of Economic Analysis. Various monthly issues. *Survey of Current Business*. Washington, DC: U.S. Department of Commerce.

————. Various years. *Input-Output Transactions Tables*. Computer Tape. Washington, DC: U.S. Department of Commerce.

————. 1976. Fixed Nonresidential Business and Residential Capital in the United States, 1925–1975, pp. 253–725. Washington, DC: U.S. Department of Commerce, National Technical Information Service.

————. 1977. *The National Income and Product Accounts of the United States, 1929–1974: Statistical tables*. Washington, DC: U.S. Government Printing Office.

———. 1984. The Input-Output Structure of the U.S. Economy, 1977. *Survey of Current Business* 64, no. 5 (May): 42–79.

———. 1986. *The National Income and Product Accounts of the United States, 1929–1982: Statistical Tables*. Washington, DC: U.S. Government Printing Office.

———. 1987a. *Fixed Reproducible Tangible Wealth in the United States, 1925–1985*. Washington, DC: U.S. Government Printing Office.

———. 1987b. *Gross National Product Originating by Industry for 14 Income Components*. Computer Tape. Washington, DC: U.S. Department of Commerce.

Bureau of Labor Statistics. Various dates. *Special Labor Force Reports*. Washington, DC: U.S. Department of Labor.

———. 1963. *Manufacturing Industries 1962: Employer Expenditures for Selected Supplementary Compensation Practices for Production and Related Workers*. Bulletin no. 1428 Washington, DC: U.S. Department of Labor.

———. 1971. *BLS Handbook of Methods for Surveys and Studies*. Bulletin no. 1711. Washington, DC: U.S. Department of Labor

———. 1978. *Consumer Expenditure Survey: Interview Survey, 1972–1973*. Washington, DC: U.S. Government Printing Office.

———. 1983. *Trends in Multifactor Productivity, 1948–1981*, Bulletin no. 2178. Washington, DC: U.S. Department of Labor.

———. 1987. *Time Series on Output, Prices, and Employment*. Computer Tape. Washington, DC: U.S. Department of Labor, Office of Economic Growth.

Bureau of Statistics. 1975. *Japanese Statistical Yearbook*. Tokyo: Office of the Prime Minister.

Burgess, David F. 1974. A Cost Minimization Approach to Import Demand Equations. *Review of Economics and Statistics* 56, no. 2 (May): 224–234.

Burmeister, Edwin. 1980a. *Capital Theory and Dynamics*. Cambridge: Cambridge University Press.

———. 1980b. Comment. In *The Measurement of Capital*, ed. Dan Usher, 421–431. Chicago, IL: University of Chicago Press.

Campbell, Beth, and Janice Peskin. 1979. Expanding Economic Accounts and Measuring Economic Welfare: A Review of Proposals. Washington, DC: Bureau of Economic Analysis, U.S. Department of Commerce, October.

Carré, Jean-Jacques, Paul Dubois, and Edmond Malinvaud. 1972. *La croissance français*. Paris: Editions du Sevil; English trans. by Pohn P. Hatfield, *French Economic Growth*. Stanford: Stanford University Press (1975).

———. 1975. *French Economic Growth*. Stanford, CA: Stanford University Press.

Caves, Douglas W., Laurits R. Christensen, and Erwin W. Diewert. 1982a. Multilateral Comparisons of Output, Input, and Productivity Using Superlative Index Numbers. *Economic Journal* 92, no. 365 (March): 73–86.

———. 1982b. The Economic Theory of Index Numbers and the Measurement of Input, Output, and Productivity. *Econometrica* 50, no. 6 (November): 1393–1414.

Caves, Douglas W., Laurits R. Christensen, and Michael W. Trethaway. 1984. Economies of Density versus Economies of Scale: Why Trunk and Local Service Airline Costs Differ. *Rand Journal of Economics* 15, no. 4, Winter): 471–489.

Caves, Douglas W., Laurits R. Christensen, Michael W. Trethaway, and Robert Windle. 1985. Network Effects and the Measurement of Returns to Scale and Density for U.S. Railroads. In *Analytical Studies in Transport Economics*, ed. Andrew F. Daughety, 97–120. Cambridge: Cambridge University Press.

Census of Population. See Bureau of the Census.

Centraal Bureau voor de Statistiek. 1967. *Arbeidsvolume in geregistrede arbeidsreserve, 1947–1966*. The Hague: Staatsuitgeverij.

———. *Jaarcijfers voor Nederland*, 1963–1964, 1967–1968, 1974. The Hague: Staatsuitgeverij.

———. *Maandschrift van het Centraal Bureau voor de Statistiek*, 1954, 1959, 1964, 1967, 1969, 1972, 1973, 1974. The Hague: Staatsuitgiverij.

———. *National rekeningen*, 1956, 1960, 1965, 1972, 1973, 1974. The Hague: Staatsuitgeverij.

Central Statistical Bureau. 1977. *Statistical Yearbook of The Netherlands*. The Hague: Staatsuitgeverij.

Central Statistical Office. Various dates. *Annual Abstract of Statistics*. London: Her Majesty's Stationery Office.

———. Annual Volumes from 1954 through 1966. *National Income and Expenditure*. London: Her Majesty's Stationery Office.

———. 1974. *National Income and Expenditure, 1963–1973*. London: Her Majesty's Stationary Office.

———. 1975. *General Household Survey, 1972*. London: Her Majesty's Stationery Office.

Chenery, Hollis, and Moises Syrquin. 1975. *Patterns of Development 1950–1970*. New York: Oxford University Press.

Chinloy, Peter T. 1980. Sources of Quality Change in Labor Input. *American Economic Review* 70, no. 1 (March): 108–119.

———. 1981. *Labor and Productivity*. Cambridge, MA: Abt Books.

Chirinko, Robert S. 1988. Will 'The' Neoclassical Theory of Investment Please Rise? In *The Impact of Taxation on Business Investment*, eds. Jack Mintz and Douglas Purvis, 107–167. Ottawa, Ontario: John Deutsch Institute.

Christensen, Laurits R. 1971. Entrepreneurial Income: How Does It Measure Up? *American Economic Review* 61, no. 4 (September): 575–585.

Christensen, Laurits R., and Dianne Cummings. 1976. Real Product, Real Factor Input, and Productivity in Canada, 1947–1973. Social Systems Research Institute: University of Wisconsin, Discussion Paper no. 7604.

―――. 1981. Real Product, Real Factor Input, and Productivity in Korea, 1960–1973. *Journal of Development Economics* 8, no.3 (June): 285–302.

Christensen, Laurits R., Dianne Cummings, and Dale W. Jorgenson. 1978. Productivity Growth, 1947–1973: An International Comparison. In *The Impact of International Trade and Investment on Employment*, ed. W. Dewald, 211–233. Washington, DC: U.S. Government Printing Office.

―――. 1980. Economic Growth, 1947–1973: An International Comparison. In *New Developments in Productivity Measurement*, eds. John W. Kendrick and Beatrice Vaccara, 595–698. NBER Studies in Income and Wealth, vol. 41. New York: Columbia University Press.

―――. 1981. Relative Productivity Levels, 1947–1973: An International Comparison. *European Economic Review* 16, no. 1 (May): 61–94.

Christensen, Laurits R., Dianne Cummings, and Brien E. Norton. 1979. Real Product, Real Factor Input, and Productivity in Italy, 1952–1973. Social Systems Research Institute: University of Wisconsin, Discussion Paper no. 7918.

Christensen, Laurits R., Dianne Cummings, and P. Schoeck. 1975. Real Product, Real Factor Input, and Productivity in The Netherlands, 1951–1973. Social Systems Research Institute: University of Wisconsin, Discussion Paper no 7529.

Christensen, Laurits R., Dianne Cummings, D. Doerner, and Kenneth Singleton, 1975. Real Product, Real Factor Input, and Productivity in the United Kingdom, 1955–1973. Social Systems Research Institute: University of Wisconsin, Discussion Paper no. 7530.

Christensen, Laurits R., and William H. Greene. 1976. Economies of Scale in U.S. Electric Power Generation. *Journal of Political Economy* 84, no. 4 (August): 655–676.

Christensen, Laurits R., and Dale W. Jorgenson. 1969. The Measurement of U.S. Real Capital Input, 1929–1967. *Review of Income and Wealth*, ser. 15, no. 4 (December): 293–320.

―――. 1970. U.S. Real Product and Real Factor Input, 1929–1967. *Review of Income and Wealth*, ser. 16, no. 1 (March): 19–50.

―――. 1973a. Measuring Economic Performance in the Private Sector. In *The Measurement of Economic and Social Performance*, ed. Milton Moss, 233–251. NBER Studies in Income and Wealth, vol. 37. New York: Columbia University Press.

―――. 1973b. U.S. Income, Saving and Wealth, 1929–1969. *Review of Income and Wealth*, ser. 19, no. 4 (December): 329–362.

Christensen, Laurits R., Dale W. Jorgenson, and Lawrence J. Lau. 1971. Conjugate Duality and the Transcendental Logarithmic Production Function. *Econometrica* 39, no. 4 (July): 255–256.

―――. 1973. Transcendental Logarithmic Production Frontiers. *Review of Economics and Statistics* 55, no. 1 (February): 28–45.

Cobb, Charles W., and Paul H. Douglas. 1928. A Theory of Production. *American Economic Review* 18, no. 1 (March): 139–165.

Coen, Robert. 1975. Investment Behavior, the Measurement of Depreciation, and Tax Policy. *American Economic Review* 65, no. 1 (March): 59–74.

―――. 1980. Depreciation, Profits, and Rates of Return in Manufacturing Industries. In *The Measurement of Capital*, ed. Dan Usher, 121–152. Chicago, IL: University of Chicago Press.

Cole, Rosanne, Y.C. Chen, Joan A. Barquin-Stolleman, Ellen Dulberger, Nurhan Helvacian, and James H. Hodge. 1986. Quality-Adjusted Price Indexes for Computer Processors and Selected Peripheral Equipment. *Survey of Current Business* 66, no. 1 (January): 41–50.

Conrad, Klaus. 1985. *Produktivitätslücken nach Wirtschaftszweigen in internationalen Vergleich*. Berlin: Springer-Verlag.

Conrad, Klaus and Dale W. Jorgenson. 1975. *Measuring Performance in the Private Economy of the Federal Republic of Germany, 1950–1973*. Tübingen: J.C.B. Mohr.

―――. 1977. Tests of a Model of Production for the Federal Republic of Germany, 1950–1973. *European Economic Review* 10, no. 1 (October): 51–75.

―――. 1978. The Structure of Technology: Nonjointness and Commodity Augmentation, Federal Republic of Germany, 1950–1973. *Empirical Economics* 3, no. 2: 91–113.

―――. 1985. Sectoral Productivity Gaps between the United States, Japan, and Germany, 1960–1979. In *Probleme und Perspektiven der weltwirtschaftlichen Entwicklung*, ed. Herbert Giersch, 335–347. Berlin: Duncker and Humbolt.

Conrad, Klaus, and Ralph Unger. 1984. Dynamische Allokation von Produktionsfaktoren: Produktivitätsentwicklung und Produktionsfaktoren in 28 Produktbereichen, 1960–1978. Paper Presented at the Symposium on Intertemporal Allocation, University of Mannheim, 1984.

Correa, Hector. 1970. Sources of Economic Growth in Latin America. *Southern Economic Journal* 37, no. 1 (July): 17–31.

Court, Andrew T. 1939. Hedonic Price Indexes with Automotive Examples. In *The Dynamics of Automobile Demand*, 99–117. New York: General Motors Corporation.

Cowing, Thomas G., and V. Kerry Smith. 1978. The Estimation of a Production Technology: A Survey of Econometric Analyses of Steam Electric Generation. *Land Economics* 54, no. 2 (May): 158–168.

Cowing, Thomas G., and Rodney E. Stevenson, eds. 1981. *Productivity Measurement in Regulated Industries.* New York: Academic Press.

Cummings, Dianne, and L. Meduna. 1973. *The Canadian Consumer Accounts.* Ottawa: Research Projects Group, Strategic Planning and Research, Department of Manpower and Immigration.

Danielson, R. S. 1975. *Output and Input Data for Canadian Agriculture, 1926–1970.* Ottawa: Research Projects Group, Strategic Planning and Research, Department of Manpower and Immigration.

Dean, Geoffrey. 1964. The Stock of Fixed Capital in the United Kingdom in 1961. *Journal of the Royal Statistical Society,* ser. A [General], vol 127, pt. 3: 327–352.

Deaton, Angus, and John Muellbauer. 1980. *Economics and Consumer Behavior.* Cambridge: Cambridge University Press.

Debreu, Gerard. 1951. The Coefficient of Resource Utilization. *Econometrica* 19, no. 3 (July): 273–292.

———. 1954. Numerical Representations of Technological Change. *Metroeconomica* 6, no. 3 (August): 45–54.

de Leeuw, Frank. 1989. Gross Product by Industry: Comments on Recent Criticisms. *Survey of Current Business* 68, no. 7 (July): 132–133.

de Meo, Giuseppe. 1973. Sintesi statistica du un ventennio di vita economica italiana. *Annali di statistica,* ser. 8, vol.27.

Denison, Edward F. 1957. Theoretical Aspects of Quality Change, Capital Consumption, and Net Capital Formation. In *Problems of Capital Formation,* 215–261. NBER Studies in Income and Wealth. Princeton: Princeton University Press.

———. 1961. Measurement of Labor Input: Some Questions of Definition and the Adequacy of Data. In *Output, Input, and Productivity Measurement,* 347–372. NBER Studies in Income and Wealth vol. 25. Princeton, NJ: Princeton University Press.

———. 1962a. How to Raise the High-Employment Growth Rate by One Percentage Point. *American Economic Review* 52, no. 2 (May): 67–75.

———. 1962b. *Sources of Economic Growth in the United States and the Alternative Before Us.* New York: Committee for Economic Development.

———. 1964a. Capital Theory and the Rate of Return (A Review Article). *American Economic Review* 54, no. 5 (September): 721–725.

———. 1964b. The Unimportance of the Embodied Question. *American Economic Review* 54, no. 1 (March): 90–4.

————. 1966. Discussion. *American Economic Review* 66, no. 2 (May): 76–78.

————. 1967. *Why Growth Rates Differ.* Washington, DC: The Brookings Institution.

————. 1969. Some Major Issues in Productivity Analysis: An Examination of Estimates by Jorgenson and Griliches. *Survey of Current Business* 49, no. 5, pt. 2 (May): 1–27.

————. 1971. Welfare Measurement and the GNP. *Survey of Current Business* 51, no. 1 (January): 13–16, 39.

————. 1972. Final Comments. *Survey of Current Business* 52, no. 5, pt. 2 (May): 95–110.

————. 1974. *Accounting for United States Economic Growth, 1929 to 1969.* Washington, DC: The Brookings Institution.

————. 1979. *Accounting for Slower Economic Growth: The United States in the 1970s.* Washington, DC: The Brookings Institution.

————. 1983. The Interruption of Productivity Growth in the United States. *Economic Journal* 93, no. 369 (March): 56–77.

————. 1984. Accounting for Slower Economic Growth: An Update. In *International Comparisons of Productivity and Causes of the Slowdown*, ed. John W. Kendrick, 1–45. Cambridge, MA: Ballinger.

————. 1985. *Trends in American Economic Growth, 1929–1982*, Washington, DC: The Brookings Institution.

————. 1989. *Estimates of Productivity Change by Industry.* Washington, DC: The Brookings Institution.

Denison, Edward F., and William K. Chung. 1976. *How Japan's Economy Grew So Fast.* Washington, DC: The Brookings Institution.

Denny, Michael, and Melvyn Fuss. 1977. The Use of Approximation Analysis to Test for Separability and the Existence of Consistent Aggregates. *American Economic Review* 67, no. 3 (June): 404–418.

————. 1983a. Intertemporal Changes in the Levels of Regional Labor Productivity in Canadian Manufacturing. In *Developments in Econometric Analyses of Productivity*, ed. Ali Dogramaci, 17–34. Boston, MA.

————. 1983b. A General Approach to Intertemporal and Interspatial Productivity Comparisons. *Journal of Econometrics* 23, no. 3 (December): 315–330.

Denny, Michael, Melvyn Fuss, and Leonard Waverman. 1981a. The Measurement and Interpretation of Total Factor Productivity in Regulated Industries, with an Application to Canadian Telecommunications. In *Productivity Measurement in Regulated Industries*, eds. Thomas G. Cowing and Rodney E. Stevenson, 179–218. New York: Academic Press.

————. 1981b. The Substitution Possibilities for Energy: Evidence from

U.S. and Canadian Manufacturing Industries. In *Modeling and Measuring Natural Resource Substitution*, eds. Ernst R. Berndt and Barry C. Field, 230–258. Cambridge, MA: MIT Press.

Denny, Michael, and Cheryl Pinto. 1978. An Aggregate Model with Multi-Product Technologies. In *Production Economics: A Dual Approach to Theory and Applications*, ed. Melvyn Fuss and Daniel McFadden, 2, 17–52. Amsterdam: North-Holland.

Department of Agriculture and Forestry (Government of Japan). *Japan Agricultural Yearbook*.

Department of Employment. 1971. *British Labour Statistics: Historical Abstract 1886–68*. London: Her Majesty's Stationery Office.

Department of Employment. Annual volumes from 1969 through 1973. *British Labour Statistics Yearbook*. London: Her Majesty's Stationery Office.

Dholakis, Bankul H. 1974. *The Sources of Economic Growth in India*. New Delhi: Good Companions.

Diewert, W. Erwin. 1971. An Application of the Shephard Duality Theorem, A Generalized Leontief Production Function. *Journal of Political Economy* 79, no. 3 (May/June): 481–507.

———. 1973. Functional Forms for Profit and Transformation Functions. *Journal of Economic Theory* 6, no. 3 (June): 284–316.

———. 1976. Exact and Superlative Index Numbers. *Journal of Econometrics* 4, no. 2 (May): 115–146.

———. 1978. Hicks' Aggregation Theorem and the Existence of a Real Value-added Function. In *Production Economics: A Dual Approach to Theory and Applications*, eds. Melvyn Fuss and Daniel McFadden, 2: 17–52. Amsterdam: North-Holland.

———. 1980. Aggregation Problems in the Measurement of Capital. In *The Measurement of Capital*, ed. Dan Usher, 433–528. Chicago, IL: University of Chicago Press.

———. 1981. The Theory of Total Factor Productivity Measurement in Regulated Industries. In *Productivity Measurement in Regulated Industries*, eds. Thomas G. Cowing and Rodney E. Stevenson, 17–44. New York: Academic Press.

Divisia, François. 1925. L'indice monétaire et la théorie de la monnaie. *Revue d'Economie Politique* 39: 842–61, 980–1008, 1121–51.

Divisia, François. 1926. L'indice monétaire et la théorie de la monnaie. *Revue d'Economie Politique* 40, no. 1: 49–81.

Domar, Evsey. 1961. On the Measurement of Technological Change. *Economic Journal* 71, no. 284 (December): 709–729.

———. 1962. On Total Factor Productivity and All That. *Journal of Political Economy* 70, no. 6 (December): 597–606.

————. 1963. Total Productivity and the Quality of Capital. *Journal of Political Economy* 71, no. 6 (December): 586–588.

Domar, Evsey, Scott M. Eddie, Bruce H. Herrick, Paul M. Hohenberg, Michael D. Intriligator, and Michizo Miyamato. 1964. Economic Growth and Productivity in the United States, Canada, United Kingdom, Germany and Japan in the Postwar Period. *Review of Economics and Statistics* 46, no. 1 (February): 33–40.

Dominion Bureau of Statistics. 1946. *Census of Canada, 1941.* Ottawa: Queen's Printer.

Dominion Bureau of Statistics. 1953. *Census of Canada, 1951.* Ottawa: Queen's Printer.

Dominion Bureau of Statistics. 1963. *Census of Canada, 1961.* Ottawa: Queen's Printer.

Douglas, Paul H. 1948. Are There Laws of Production? *American Economic Review* 38, no. 1 (March): 1–41.

————. 1967. Comments on the Cobb-Douglas Production Function. In *The Theory and Empirical Analysis of Production*, ed. Murray Brown, 15–22. New York: Columbia University Press.

————. 1976. The Cobb-Douglas Production Function Once Again: Its History, Its Testing, and Some Empirical Values. *Journal of Political Economy* 84, no. 5 (October): 903–916.

Dreschler, László. 1973. Weighting of Index Numbers in Multilateral International Comparisons. *Review of Income and Wealth* 19, no. 1 (March): 17–34.

Dulberger, Ellen. 1989. The Application of a Hedonic Model to a Quality-Adjusted Price Index for Computer Processors. In *Technology and Capital Formation*, eds. Dale W. Jorgenson and Ralph Landau, 37–76. Cambridge, MA: MIT Press.

Economic Planning Agency (Government of Japan). 1953. *Annual Report on National Income Statistics.* Tokyo: Government of Japan.

Economic Planning Agency (Government of Japan). 1955. *National Wealth Survey.*

Economic Planning Agency (Government of Japan). 1969. *Revised Report on National Income Statistics (1951–1967)* (August).

Economic Planning Board. 1963. *1960 Population and Housing Census of Korea, 20% Sample Tabulation Report, 11–1 Whole Country.* Seoul: Government of Korea.

Economic Planning Board. 1967. *Report on Wage Survey, 1967.* Seoul: Government of Korea.

Economic Planning Board. 1969. *1966 Population Census Report of Korea, 12–1 Whole Country.* Seoul: Government of Korea.

Economic Planning Board. 1973. *1970 Population and Housing Census Report, vol. 2, 10% Sample Survey, 4–1 Economic Activity.* Seoul: Government of Korea.

Economic Planning Board. 1973. *Report on the National Wealth Survey.* Seoul: Government of Korea.

Eisner, Robert. 1972. Components of Capital Expenditures: Replacement and Modernization. *Review of Economics and Statistics* 54, no. 3 (August): 297–305.

———. 1978. Total Incomes in the United States, 1959 and 1969. *Review of Income and Wealth,* ser. 24, no. 1 (March): 41–70.

———. 1985. The Total Incomes System of Accounts. *Survey of Current Business* 65, no. 1 (January): 24–48.

———. 1988. Extended Accounts for National Income and Product. *Journal of Economic Literature* 24: 1611–1684.

———. 1989. *The Total Incomes System of Accounts.* Chicago, IL: University of Chicago Press.

Elias, Victor J. 1978. Sources of Economic Growth in Latin American Countries. *Review of Economics and Statistics* 60, no. 3 (August): 362–370.

Engerman, Stanley, and Sherwin Rosen. 1980. New Books on the Measurement of Capital. In *The Measurement of Capital,* ed. Dan Usher, 153–170. Chicago, IL: University of Chicago Press.

Englander, A. Steven, and Axel Mittelstadt. 1988. Total Factor Productivity: Macroeconomic and Structural Aspects of the Slowdown. *OECD Economic Studies* 10 (Spring): 7–56.

Epstein, Larry G., and Michael Denny. 1980. Endogenous Capital Utilization in a Short-Run Production Model: Theory and an Empirical Application. *Journal of Econometrics* 12, no. 2 (February): 189–207.

Epstein, Larry G., and Adonis Yatchew. 1985. The Empirical Determination of Technology and Expectations: A Simplified Procedure. *Journal of Econometrics* 27, no. 2 (February): 235–258.

Ezaki, Mitsuo. 1974. Quantitative Study of Japan's Economic Growth, 1952–1980: An Approach from the System of National Accounts. Ph.D. Thesis, Harvard University.

———. 1977. *Nihon Keizai no Moderu Bunseki Kokumin Keizai Keisan Kara no Sekkin (An Analysis of Japanese Economy: An Approach from the System of National Accounts).* Tokyo: Sobun-Sha.

———. 1978. Growth Accounting of Postwar Japan: The Input Side. *Economic Studies Quarterly* 29, no. 2 (June): 193–215.

———. 1985. Growth Accounting Based on Input-Output Tables. In *Input-Output Models,* ed. Shamsher Ali, 325–370. Tokyo: Institute of Developing Economies.

Ezaki, Mitsuo, and Dale W. Jorgenson. 1973. Measurement of Macroeconomic Performance in Japan, 1951–1968. In *Economic Growth: The Japanese Experience since the Meiji Era*, vol. 1, eds. Kazushi Ohkawa and Yujiro Hayami, 286–361. Tokyo: Japan Economic Research Center.

Fabricant, Solomon. 1959. *Basic Facts on Productivity Change*, Occasional Paper no. 63. New York: National Bureau of Economic Research.

Farrell, Michael J. 1959. The New Theories of the Consumption Function. *Economic Journal* 69 (December): 678–696.

Fei, John C., and Gustav Ranis. 1965. Innovation Intensity and Factor Bias in the Theory of Growth. *International Economic Review* 6, no. 2 (May): 182–198.

Feldstein, Martin S., and David K. Foot. 1974. The Other Half of Gross Investment: Replacement and Modernization Expenditures. *Review of Economics and Statistics* 56, no. 1 (February): 49–58.

Fisher, Franklin M. 1971. Aggregate Production Functions and the Explanation of Wages: A Simulation Experiment. *Review of Economics and Statistics* 53, no. 4 (November): 305–326.

———. 1982. On Perfect Aggregation in the National Output Deflator and Generalized Rybczynski Theorems. *International Economic Review* 23, no. 1 (February): 43–60.

Fisher, Franklin M., and Karl Shell. 1972. The Pure Theory of the National Output Deflator. In *The Economic Theory of Price Indexes*, eds. Franklin M. Fisher and Karl Shell, 49–113. New York: Academic Press.

Fisher, Franklin M., Robert M. Solow, and James M. Kearl. 1977. Aggregate Production Functions: Some CES Experiments. *Review of Economic Studies* 44(2), no. 137 (June): 305–320.

Fisher, Irving. 1922. *The Making of Index Numbers*. Boston: Houghton-Mifflin.

Forsund, Finn R., and Lennart Hjalmarsson. 1979. Frontier Production Functions and Technical Progress: A Study of General Milk Processing Swedish Dairy Plants. *Econometrica* 47, no. 4 (July): 883–901.

———. 1983. Technical Progress and Structural Change in the Swedish Cement Industry 1955–1979. *Econometrica* 51, no. 5 (September): 1449–1467.

———. 1987. *Analyses of Industrial Structure: A Putty-Clay Approach*. Stockholm: Almqvist and Wiksell International.

Forsund, Finn R. and Eilev S. Jansen. 1983. Technical Progress and Structural Change in the Norwegian Primary Aluminum Industry. *Scandinavian Journal of Economics* 85, no. 2: 113–126.

Franco, M. I. 1973. *Rassegna di statistiche del lavoro*, vol.1. Rome: Istituto centrale di statistica.

Fraumeni, Barbara M., and Dale W. Jorgenson. 1980. The Role of Capital in U.S. Economic Growth, 1948–1976. In *Capital, Efficiency and Growth*, ed. George M. von Furstenberg, 9–25. Cambridge: Ballinger.

———. 1986. The Role of Capital in U.S. Economic Growth, 1948–1979.

In *Measurement Issues and Behavior of Productivity Variables*, ed. Ali Dogramaci, 161–244. Boston, MA: Martinus Nijhoff.

Friede, Gerhard. 1979. *Investigation of Producer Behavior in the Federal Republic of Germany Using the Translog Price Function*. Cambridge, MA: Oelgeschlager, Gunn, and Hain.

Frohn, Joachim, Rolf Krengel, Peter Kuhbier, Karl H. Oppenlander, Luitpold Uhlmann. 1973. *Der Technische Fortschritt in der Industrie*. Berlin: Duncker and Humbolt.

Fuss, Melvyn. 1977. The Structure of Technology over Time: A Model for Testing the 'Putty-Clay' Hypothesis. *Econometrica* 45, no. 8 (November): 1797–1821.

———. 1978. Factor Substitution in Electricity Generation: A Test of the Putty-Clay Hypothesis. In *Production Economics: A Dual Approach to Theory and Applications*, eds. Melvyn Fuss and Daniel McFadden, 2: 187–214. Amsterdam: North-Holland.

———. 1983. A Survey of Recent Results in the Analysis of Production Conditions in Telecommunications. In *Economic Analysis of Telecommunications*, eds. Leon Courville, Alain de Fontenay, and A. Rodney Dobell, 3–26. Amsterdam: North-Holland.

Geary, Robert C. 1961. Productivity Aspects of Accounts Deflation. In *Studies in Social and Financial Accounting*. Income and Wealth, ser. 9, ed. Phyllis Deane, 31–45. London: Bowes and Bowes.

Giannone, A. 1963. Evaluations of Italian National Wealth in the Last Fifty Years. *Banca Nazionale del Lavoro Quarterly Review* 16 nos. 64–67 (December): 421–436.

Giersch, Herbert, and Frank Wolter. 1983. Towards an Explanation of the Productivity Slowdown: An Acceleration-Deceleration Hypothesis. *Economic Journal* 93, no. 369 (March): 35–55.

Gilbert, M. and Associates. 1958. *Comparative National Products and Price Levels: A Study of Western Europe and the United States*. Paris: Organization for European Economic Cooperation.

Gilbert, M. and Irving B. Kravis. 1954. *An International Comparison of National Products and the Purchasing Power of Currencies*. Paris: Organization for European Economic Cooperation.

Goldsmith, Raymond W. 1955. *A Study of Saving in the United States*. Princeton, NJ: Princeton University Press.

———. 1962. *The National Wealth of the United States in the Postwar Period*. New York: National Bureau of Economic Research.

Goldsmith, Raymond W., and Christopher Saunders, eds. 1959. *The Measurement of National Wealth*. Chicago: Quadrangle Books.

Gollop, Frank M. 1979. Accounting for Intermediate Input: The Link Between Sectoral and Aggregate Measures of Productivity Growth. In *The Measurement and Interpretation of Productivity Growth*, 318–333. Washington, DC: National Academy of Sciences.

————. 1983. Growth Accounting in an Open Economy. In *Developments in Econometric Analyses of Productivity*, ed. Ali Dogramaci, 35–62. Boston, MA: Kluwer-Nijhoff.

————. 1985. Analysis of the Productivity Slowdown: Evidence for a Sector-Biased or Sector-Neutral Industrial Strategy. In *Productivity Growth and U.S. Competitiveness*, eds. William J. Baumol and Kenneth McLennan, 160–186. New York: Oxford University Press.

Gollop, Frank M., and Dale W. Jorgenson. 1980. U.S. Productivity Growth by Industry, 1947–1973. In *New Developments in Productivity Measurement and Analysis*, eds. John W. Kendrick and Beatrice Vaccara, 41: 17–136. Chicago, IL: University of Chicago Press.

————. 1983. Sectoral Measures of Labor Cost for the United States, 1948–1978. In *The Measurement of Labor Cost*, ed. Jack E. Triplett, 185–235, 503–520. NBER Studies in Income and Wealth, vol. 44. Chicago, IL: University of Chicago Press.

Gollop, Frank M. and Mark J. Roberts. 1981. The Sources of Economic Growth in the U.S. Electric Power Industry. In *Productivity Measurement in Regulated Industries*, eds. Thomas G. Cowing and Rodney E. Stevenson, 107–145. New York: Academic Press.

Gordon, Robert J. 1989. The Postwar Evolution of Computer Prices. In *Technology and Capital Formation*, eds. Dale W. Jorgenson and Ralph Landau, 77–126. Cambridge, MA: MIT Press.

————. 1990. *The Measurement of Durable Goods Prices* Chicago, IL: University of Chicago Press.

Gorman, John A., John C. Musgrave, Gerald Silverstein, and Kathy A. Comins. 1985. Fixed Private Capital in the United States. *Survey of Current Business* 65, no. 7 (July): 36–59.

Green, H.A. John. 1966. Embodied Progress, Investment, and Growth. *American Economic Review* 56, no. 1 (March): 138–151.

Greene, William H. 1983. Simultaneous Estimation of Factor Substitution, Economies of Scale, Productivity, and Non-Neutral Technical Change. In *Developments in Econometric Analyses of Productivity*, ed. Ali Dogramaci, 121–144. Boston, MA: Kluwer-Nijhoff.

Griliches, Zvi. 1960. Measuring Inputs in Agriculture: A Critical Survey. *Journal of Farm Economics* 42, no. 5 (December): 1411–27.

————. 1961a. Discussion. *American Economic Review* 51, no. 2 (May): 127–130.

————. 1961b. Hedonic Price Indexes for Automobiles: An Econometric Analysis of Quality Change. In *The Price Statistics of the Federal Government*, 137–196. New York: National Bureau of Economic Research.

————. 1964. Notes on the Measurement of Price and Quality Changes. In *Models of Income Determination*, 301–404. NBER Studies in Income and Wealth, vol. 28. Princeton, NJ: Priceton University Press.

————. 1967. Production Functions in Manufacturing: Some Empirical Results. In *The Theory and Empirical Analysis of Production*, ed. Murray Brown, 275–322. New York: Columbia University Press.

————. 1971a. Hedonic Price Indexes Revisited. In *Price Indexes and Quality Change*, ed. Zvi Griliches, 3–15. Cambridge, MA: Harvard University Press.

————, ed. 1971b. *Price Indexes and Quality Change*. Cambridge, MA: Harvard University Press.

————. 1984. Introduction. In *R&D, Patents, and Productivity*, ed. Zvi Griliches, 1–20. Chicago, IL: University of Chicago Press.

————. 1988a. Postscript on Hedonics. In *Technology, Education, and Productivity*, ed. Zvi Griliches, 119–122. Oxford: Basil Blackwell.

————. 1988b. Productivity Puzzles and R&D: Another Nonexplanation. *Journal of Economic Perspectives* 2, no. 4 (Fall): 9–21.

Griliches, Zvi, and Dale W. Jorgenson. 1966. Sources of Measured Productivity Change: Capital Input. *American Economic Review* 56, no. 2 (May): 50–61.

Groes, Nils, and Peter Bjerregaard. 1978. *Real Product, Real Factor Input and Productivity in Denmark*. Copenhagen: Institute of Economics, University of Copenhagen.

Grose, Lawrence, Irving Rottenberg, and Robert Wasson. 1966. New Estimates of Fixed Business Capital in the United States, 1925–1965. *Survey of Current Business* 46, no. 12 (December): 34–40.

Gullickson, William, and Michael J. Harper. 1987. Multifactor Productivity in U.S. Manufacturing, 1949–1983. *Monthly Labor Review* 110, no. 10 (October): 18–28.

Gussman, T. K. 1972. *The Demand for Durables, Nondurables, Services and the Supply of Labour in Canada: 1946–1969*. Ottawa: Research Projects Group, Strategic Planning and Research, Department of Manpower and Immigration.

Haavelmo, Trygve. 1960. *A Study in the Theory of Investment*. Chicago, IL: University of Chicago Press.

Hadley, George. 1964. *Nonlinear and Dynamic Programming*. Reading, MA: Addison-Wesley.

Hall, Robert E. 1968. Technical Change and Capital from the Point of View of the Dual. *Review of Economic Studies* 35(1), no. 101 (January): 35–46.

————. 1971. The Measurement of Quality Change from Vintage Price Data. In *Price Indexes and Quality Change*, ed. Zvi Griliches, 240–271. Cambridge, MA: Harvard University Press.

————. 1973. The Specification of Technology with Several Kinds of Output. *Journal of Political Economy* 81, no. 4 (July/August): 878–892.

————. 1986. Market Structure and Macroeconomic Fluctuations. *Brookings Papers on Economic Activity*, no. 2: 285–322.

————. 1987. Productivity and the Business Cycle. *Carnegie-Rochester Conference Series on Public Policy* 28: 421–444.

————. 1988. The Relation between Price and Marginal Cost in U.S. Industry. *Journal of Political Economy* 96, no. 5 (October): 921–947.

Hall, Robert E., and Dale W. Jorgenson. 1967. Tax Policy and Investment Behavior. *American Economic Review* 57, no. 3 (June): 391–414.

————. 1968. The Quantitative Impact of Tax Policy in Investment Expenditures, Working Paper 136. Berkeley, CA: Institute of Business and Economic Research. University of California, July.

————. 1969. Tax Policy and Investment Behavior: Reply and Further Results. *American Economic Review* 59, no. 3 (June): 388–401.

————. 1971. Applications of the Theory of Optimum Capital Accumulation. In *Tax Incentives and Capital Spending*, ed. Gary Fromm, 9–60. Washington, DC: The Brookings Institution.

Hansen, Bert. 1970. *A Survey of General Equilibrium Systems.* New York: McGraw-Hill.

Hansen, Lars P., and Thomas J. Sargent. 1980. Formulating and Estimating Linear Rational Expectations Models. *Journal of Economic Dynamics and Control* 2, no. 1 (February): 7–46.

————. 1981. Linear Rational Expectations Models for Dynamically Interrelated Variables. In *Rational Expectations and Econometric Practice*, eds. Robert E. Lucas and Thomas J. Sargent, 1: 127–156. Minneapolis, MN: University of Minnesota Press.

Harper, Michael J., Ernst R. Berndt, and David O. Wood. 1989. Rates of Return and Capital Aggregation Using Alternative Rental Prices. In *Technology and Capital Formation*, eds. Dale W. Jorgenson and Ralph Landau, 331–372. Cambridge, MA: MIT Press.

Hayashi, Fumio. 1982. Tobin's Marginal $q$ and Average $q$. *Econometrica* 50, no. 1 (January): 213–224.

Heady, Earl O., and John L. Dillon. 1961. *Agricultural Production Functions.* Ames, IO: Iowa State University Press.

Hicks, John R. 1946. *Value and Capital*, 2nd ed. Oxford: Oxford University Press (1st ed., 1939).

————. 1963. *The Theory of Wages* 2nd ed. London: Macmillan (1st ed., 1932).

Hildenbrand, Werner. 1981. Short-Run Production Functions Based on Microdata. *Econometrica* 49, no. 5 (September): 1095–1125.

Ho, Mun S., and Dale W. Jorgenson. 1993. *Trade Policy and U.S. Economic Growth. Journal of Policy Modeling* 15, no. 2 (June).

Hotelling, Harold S. 1925. A General Mathematical Theory of Depreciation. *Journal of the American Statistical Association* 20, no. 151 (September): 340–353.

Houthakker, Hendrik S. 1955–1956. The Pareto Distribution and the Cobb-Douglas Production Function in Activity Analysis. *Review of Economic Studies* 23(1), no. 60: 27–31.

Hudson, Edward A., and Dale W. Jorgenson. 1974. U.S. Energy Policy and Economic Growth, 1975–2000. *Bell Journal of Economics and Management Science* 5, no. 2 (Autumn): 461–514.

Hulten, Charles R. 1973. Divisia Index Numbers. *Econometrica* 41, no. 6 (November): 1017–1026.

———. 1978. Growth Accounting with Intermediate Inputs. *Review of Economic Studies* 45(3), no. 141 (October): 511–518.

Hulten, Charles R., James W. Robertson, and Frank C. Wykoff. 1989. Energy, Obsolescence, and the Productivity Slowdown. In *Technology and Capital Formation*, eds. Dale W. Jorgenson and Ralph Landau, 225–258. Cambridge, MA: MIT Press.

Hulten, Charles R. and Frank C. Wykoff. 1981a. Economic Depreciation and the Taxation of Structures in United States Manufacturing Industries: An Empirical Analysis. In *The Measurement of Capital*, ed. Dan Usher, 83–120. Chicago, IL: University of Chicago Press.

———. 1981b. The Estimation of Economic Depreciation Using Vintage Asset Prices: An Application of the Box-Cox Power Transformation. *Journal of Econometrics* 15, no. 3 (April): 367–396.

———. 1981c. The Measurement of Economic Depreciation. In *Depreciation, Inflation, and the Taxation of Income from Capital*, ed. Charles R. Hulten, 81–125. Washington, DC: The Urban Institute Press.

Inland Revenue. 1969. *Report of the Commissioner of Her Majesty's Inland Revenue for the Year Ended 31 March 1969, the 112th Report*. London: Her Majesty's Stationery Office.

———. *Inland Revenue Statistics*. London: Her Majesty's Stationery Office.

International Labour Organization. Annual Volumes from 1947 to 1973. *Yearbook of Labour Statistics*. Geneva: International Labour Organization.

Institut national de la statistique et des études économiques. 1961. *Annuaire statistique de la France*, vol. 67. Paris: Institut national de la statistique et des études économique.

———. 1963. Les comptes de la nation 1949–1959. *Études et Conjoncture* 18, no. 12 (December): 1105–1257.

————. 1964a. *Annuaire statistique de la France*, vol. 70. Paris: Institut national de la statistique et des études économique.

————. 1964b. La population active par secteur d'établissement. *Études et conjoncture* 19, no. 3 (March): 9–22.

————. 1970a. *Les comptes de la nation, base 1962: résultats d'ensemble des comptes, séries 1959–1966*. Les Collections de l'I.N.S.E.E., série C, no. 7 (May).

————. 1970b. *Rapport sur les comptes de la nation, 1969*. Les Collections de l'I.N.S.E.E., série C, no. 8 (June).

————. 1971a. *Les comptes de la nation, base 1962: les comptes de biens et services, séries 1959–1966*. Les Collections del'I.N.S.E.E., série C, no. 10 (May).

————. 1971b. *Rapport sur les comptes de la nation 1970*. Les Collections de l'I.N.S.E.E., série C, no. 11 (June).

————. 1972a. *Les comptes de la nation, base 1962: les comptes des années 1949–1959*. Les Collections de l'I.N.S.E.E., série C, no. 13 (April).

————. 1972b. *Rapport sur les comptes de la nation 1971*. Les Collections de l'I.N.S.E.E., série C, no. 15 (June).

————. 1973a. *Rapport sur les comptes de la nation 1972*. Les Collections de l'I.N.S.E.E., série C, no. 15 (June).

————. 1973b. *Annuaire statistique de la France*, vol. 78. Paris: Institut national de la statistique et des études économique.

————. 1974. *Rapport sur les comptes de la nation 1973*. Les Collections de l'I.N.S.E.E., série C, no. 29–30 (June).

Istituto centrale di statistica. *Annali di statistica*. ser. 8, vol. 15–27.

————. 1958. *Ninth Census of Italy*, 1951, vol. 7. Rome: Istituto centrale di statistica.

————. 1973a. *Annuario di contabilita nazionale*, vol. 111, tome 1 and 2.

————. 1973b. *Il valore della lire dal 1861 al 1972*. Rome: Istituto centrale di statistica.

Johansen, Leif. 1972. *Production Functions*. Amsterdam: North-Holland.

————. 1976. *A Multi-Sectoral Study of Economic Growth*, 2nd ed. (1st ed. 1960). Amsterdam: North-Holland.

Jorgenson, Dale W. 1963. Capital Theory and Investment Behavior. *American Economic Review* 53, no. 2 (May): 247–259.

————. 1965. Anticipations and Investment Behavior. In *The Brookings Quarterly Econometric Model of the United States*, eds. James S. Duesenberry, Gary Fromm, Lawrence R. Klein, and Edwin Kuh, 35–92. Chicago, IL: Rand McNally.

————. 1966. The Embodiment Hypothesis. *Journal of Political Economy* 74, no. 1 (February): 1–17.

———. 1967. The Theory of Investment Behavior. In *The Determinants of Investment Behavior*, ed. Robert Ferber, 129–156. New York: Columbia University Press.

———. 1968. Industry Changes in Nonlabor Costs: Comment. In *The Industrial Composition of Income and Product*, ed. John W. Kendrick, 176–184. NBER Studies in Income and Wealth, vol. 32. New York: Columbia University Press.

———. 1972. Issues in Growth Accounts: Final Reply. *Survey of Current Business* 52, no. 5, pt. 2 (May): 111.

———. 1973a. The Economic Theory of Replacement and Depreciation. In *Econometrics and Economic Theory*, ed. Willy Sellekaerts, 189–221. New York: Macmillan.

———. 1973b. Technology and Decision Rules in the Theory of Investment Behavior. *Quarterly Journal of Economics* 87, no. 4 (November): 523–543.

———. 1974. Investment and Production: A Review. In *Frontiers in Quantitative Economics*, eds. Michael D. Intriligator and David A. Kendrick, 2: 341–366. Amsterdam: North-Holland.

———. 1980. Accounting for Capital. In *Capital, Efficiency and Growth*, ed. George M. von Furstenberg, 251–319. Cambridge: Ballinger.

———. 1981. International Differences in Levels of Technology: A Comparison Between U.S. and Japanese Industries. In *International Roundtable Congress Proceedings*, eds. Institute of Statistical Mathematics. Tokyo: Institute of Statistical Mathematics.

———. 1982. Econometric and Process Analysis Models for the Analysis of Energy Policy. In *Perspectives on Resource Policy Modeling: Energy and Minerals*, eds. Rafi Amit and Mordecai Avriel, 9–62. Cambridge, MA: Ballinger.

———. 1983. Modeling Production for General Equilibrium Analysis. *Scandinavian Journal of Economics* 85, no. 2: 101–112.

———. 1984a. Econometric Methods for Applied General Equilibrium Analysis. In *Applied General Equilibrium Analysis*, eds. Herbert E. Scarf and John B. Shoven, 139–203. Cambridge: Cambridge University Press.

———. 1984b. The Role of Energy in Productivity Growth. In *International Comparisons of Productivity and Causes of the Slowdown*, ed. John W. Kendrick, 270–323. Cambridge, MA: Ballinger. Earlier, less detailed versions of this material appeared in *American Economic Review* 74, no. 2 (May 1978): 26–30; and in *The Energy Journal* 5, no. 3 (July 1984): 11–25.

———. 1986a. Econometric Methods for Modeling Producer Behavior. In *Handbook of Econometrics*, eds. Zvi Griliches and Michael D. Intriligator, 3: 1841–1915. Amsterdam: North-Holland.

———. 1986b. The Great Transition: Energy and Economic Change. *Energy Journal* 7, no. 3: 1–11.

————. 1988a. Productivity and Economic Growth in Japan and the U.S.. *American Economic Review* 78, no. 2 (May): 217–222.

————. 1988b. Productivity and Postwar U.S. Economic Growth. *Journal of Economic Perspectives* 2, no. 4 (Fall): 23–41.

————. 1989. Capital as a Factor of Production. In *Technology and Capital Formation*, eds. Dale W. Jorgenson and Ralph Landau, 1–36. Cambridge, MA: MIT Press.

————. 1990. Productivity and Economic Growth. In *Fifty Years of Economic Measurement*, eds. E. R. Berndt and J. Triplett, 19–118. Chicago, IL: University of Chicago Press.

Jorgenson, Dale W., and Barbara M. Fraumeni. 1981. Relative Prices and Technical Change. In *Modeling and Measuring Natural Resource Substitution*, eds. Ernst R. Berndt and Barry C. Field, 17–47. Cambridge, MA: MIT Press.

————. 1989. The Accumulation of Human and Nonhuman Capital, 1948–1984. In *The Measurement of Saving, Investment, and Wealth*, eds. Robert E. Lipsey and Helen S. Tice, 227–282. Chicago, IL: University of Chicago Press.

————. 1992. The Output of the Education Sector. In *Output Measurement in the Services Sector*, ed. Zvi Griliches. Chicago, IL: University of Chicago Press.

Jorgenson, Dale W., Frank M. Gollop, and Barbara M. Fraumeni. 1986. Productivity and Sectoral Output Growth in the United States. In *Interindustry Differences in Productivity Growth*, ed. John W. Kendrick. Cambridge, MA: Ballinger.

————. 1987. *Productivity and U.S. Economic Growth*. Cambridge, MA: Harvard University Press.

Jorgenson, Dale W., and Zvi Griliches. 1967. The Explanation of Productivity Change. *Review of Economic Studies* 34(3), no. 99 (July): 249–280.

————. 1971. Divisia Index Numbers and Productivity Measurement. *Review of Income and Wealth*, ser. 17, no. 2 (June): 53–55.

————. 1972a. Issues in Growth Accounting: A Reply To Edward F. Denison. *Survey of Current Business* 52, no. 5, pt. 2 (May): 65–94.

————. 1972b. Issues in Growth Accounting: Final Reply. *Survey of Current Business* 52, no. 5, pt. 2 (May): 111.

Jorgenson, Dale W., Masahiro Kuroda, and Mieko Nishimizu. 1987. Japan-U.S. Industry-Level Productivity Comparisons, 1969–1979. *Journal of the Japanese and International Economies* 1, no. 1 (March): 1–30.

Jorgenson, Dale W., and Lawrence J. Lau. 1974. The Duality of Technology and Economic Behavior. *Review of Economic Studies* 41(2), no. 126 (April): 181–200.

————. 1975. The Structure of Consumer Preferences. *Annals of Social and Economic Measurement* 4, no. 1 (January): 49–101.

Jorgenson, Dale W., and Mieko Nishimizu. 1978. U.S. and Japanese Economic Growth, 1952–1974: An International Comparison. *The Economic Journal* 88, no. 352 (December): 707–726.

———. 1979. Sectoral Differences in Levels of Technology: An International Comparison Between the United States and Japan, 1955–1972. Paper Presented at the North American Summer Meeting of the Econometric Society, Montreal, June 27–30, 1979.

———. 1981. International Differences in Levels of Technology: A Comparison Between U.S. and Japanese Industries. In *International Roundtable Congress Proceedings*. Tokyo: Institute of Statistical Mathematics.

Jorgenson, Dale W., and Peter J. Wilcoxen. 1990. Environmental Regulation and U.S. Economic Growth. *Rand Journal of Economics* 21, no. 2 (Summer): 314–340.

Jorgenson, Dale W., and Kun-Young Yun. 1986. The Efficiency of Capital Allocation. *Scandinavian Journal of Economics* 88, no. 1: 85–107.

———. 1991. *Tax Reform and the Cost of Capital*. New York: Oxford University Press.

Jorgenson, Dale W., et al. 1988. Bilateral Models of Production for Japanese and U.S. Industries. In *Productivity in the U.S. and Japan*, eds. Charles R. Hulten and J. R. Norsworthy. NBER Studies in Income and Wealth, vol. 51. Chicago, IL: University of Chicago Press.

Kanamori, Hisao. 1972. What Accounts for Japan's High Rate of Growth? *Review of Income and Wealth*, ser. 18, no. 2 (June): 155–172.

Katz, Arnold J. 1988. Conceptual Issues in the Measurement of Economic Depreciation, Capital Input, and the Net Capital Stock. Discussion Paper no. 30 (July). Washington, DC: Bureau of Economic Analysis, U.S. Department of Commerce.

Kendrick, John W. 1956. Productivity Trends: Capital and Labor. *Review of Economics and Statistics* 38, no. 3 (August): 248–257.

———. 1961a. *Productivity Trends in the United States*. Princeton, NJ: Princeton University Press.

———. 1961b. Some Theoretical Aspects of Capital Measurement. *American Economic Review* 51, no. 2 (May): 102–111.

———. 1968. Industry Changes in Nonlabor Costs. In *The Industrial Composition of Income and Product*, ed. John W. Kendrick. NBER Studies in Income and Wealth, vol. 32. New York: Columbia University Press.

———. 1973. *Postwar Productivity Trends in the United States, 1948–1969*. New York: National Bureau of Economic Research.

———. 1975. Review of Edward F. Denison's "Accounting for United

States Economic Growth, 1929–1969." *Journal of Economic Literature* 13, no. 3 (September): 909–910.

———. 1976. *The Formation and Stocks of Total Capital.* New York: Columbia University Press.

———. 1979. Expanding Imputed Values in the National Income and Product Accounts. *Review of Income and Wealth,* ser. 25, no. 4 (December): 349–364.

———. 1983a. *Interindustry Differences in Productivity Growth.* Washington, DC: American Enterprise Institute.

———. 1983b. International Comparisons of Recent Productivity Trends. In *Energy, Productivity, and Economic Growth,* eds. Sam H. Schurr, Sidney Sonenblum, and David O. Wood, 71–120. Cambridge, MA: Oelgeschlager, Gunn, and Hain.

———. 1984. International Comparisons of Productivity Trends. In *Measuring Productivity,* 95–140. Japan Productivity Center. New York: UNIPUB.

Kendrick, John W., and Elliot S. Grossman. 1980. *Productivity in the United States: Trends and Cycles.* Baltimore: The Johns Hopkins University Press.

Kendrick, John W., and Ryuzo Sato. 1963. Factor Prices, Productivity, and Growth. *American Economic Review* 53, no. 5 (December): 974–1003.

Kennedy, Charles. 1964. Induced Bias in Innovation and the Theory of Distribution. *Economic Journal* 74, no. 298 (September): 541–547.

Kennedy, Charles, and A.P. Thirlwall. 1972. Technical Progress: A Survey. *Economic Journal* 82, no. 325 (March): 11–72.

Kim, Kwang S., and Joon K. Park. 1985. *Sources of Economic Growth in Korea: 1963–1982.* Seoul: Korea Development Institute.

Kirner, Wolfgang. 1968. Zeitreihen für das Anlagevermögen der Wirtschaftsbereiche in der Bundesrepublik Deutschland. *DIW — Beiträge zur Strukturforschung.* Berlin: Deutsches Institut für Wirtschaftsforschung, vol. 5.

Kloek, Tuun. 1966. *Indexcijfers: Enige methodologisch aspecten.* The Hague: Pasmans.

Knowles, James C. 1954. *Potential Economic Growth of the United States during the Next Decade.* Joint Committee on the Economic Report, 83rd Congress, Second Session. Washington, DC: U.S. Government Printing Office.

———. 1960. *The Potential Economic Growth in the United States.* Study Paper 20, Joint Economic Committee, 86th Congress, Second Session. Washington, DC: U.S. Government Printing Office.

Kohli, Ulrich R. 1981. Nonjointness and Factor Intensity in U.S. Production. *International Economic Review* 22, no. 1 (February): 3–18.

———. 1983. Non-joint Technologies. *Review of Economic Studies* 50(1), no. 160 (January): 209–219.

Koopmans, Tjalling C. 1977. Examples of Production Relations Based on

Microdata. In *The Microeconomic Foundations of Macroeconomics*, ed. Geoffrey C. Harcourt, 144–171. London: Macmillan.

Kravis, Irving B. 1959. Relative Income Shares in Fact and Theory. *American Economic Review* 49, no. 5 (December): 917–949.

———. 1976. A Survey of International Comparisons of Productivity. *Economic Journal* 86, no. 341 (March): 1–44.

Kravis, Irving B., Alan W. Heston, and Robert Summers. 1978a. *United Nations International Comparison Project: Phase II. International Comparison of Real Product and Purchasing Power*. Baltimore, MD: Johns Hopkins University Press.

———. 1978b. Real GDP Per Capita for More Than One Hundred Countries. *Economic Journal* 88, no. 350 (June): 215–242.

———. 1982. *World Product and Income: International Comparisons of Real Gross Product*. Baltimore, MD.

Kravis, Irving B., Z. Kenessey, Alan Heston, and Robert Summers. 1975. *A System of International Comparisons of Gross Product and Purchasing Power*. Baltimore: Johns Hopkins University.

Krueger, Anne O. 1968. Factor Endowments and Per Capita Income Differences Among Countries. *Economic Journal* 78, no. 311 (September): 641–659.

Kunze, Kent. 1979. Evaluation of Work-Force Composition Adjustment. In *Measurement and Interpretation of Productivity*, National Research Council, 334–362. Washington, DC: National Academy of Sciences.

———. 1988. Method of Estimation for Updating the Transactions Matrix in Input-Ouput Relationships. In *Statistical Data Bank Systems*, eds. K. Uno and S. Shishido. Amsterdam: North-Holland.

Kuroda, Masahrio, Kanji Yoshioka, and Dale W. Jorgenson. 1984. Relative Price Changes and Biases of Technical Change in Japan. *Economic Studies Quarterly* 35, no. 2 (August): 116–138.

Kuznets, Simon. 1961. *Capital in the American Economy*. Princeton, NJ: Princeton University Press.

———. 1971. *Economic Growth of Nations*. Cambridge: Harvard University Press.

Lau, Lawrence J. 1969. Duality and the Structure of Utility Functions. *Journal of Economic Theory* 1, no. 4 (December): 374–396.

———. 1978. Applications of Profit Functions. In *Production Economics: A Dual Approach to Theory and Applications*, eds. Melvyn Fuss and Daniel McFadden, 1: 133–216. Amsterdam: North-Holland.

———. 1979. On Exact Index Numbers. *The Review of Economics and Statistics* 61, no. 1: 73–82.

Leontief, Wassily. 1936. Composite Commodities and the Problem of Index Numbers. *Econometrica* 4, no. 1 (January): 39–59.

————. 1947a. Introduction to a Theory of the Internal Structure of Functional Relationships. *Econometrica* 15, no. 4 (October): 361–373.

————. 1947b. A Note on the Interrelation of Subsets of Independent Variables of a Continuous Function with Continuous First Derivatives. *Bulletin of the American Mathematical Society* 53, no. 4 (April): 343–350.

————. 1951. *The Structure of the American Economy, 1919–1939*, 2nd ed. (1st ed. 1941). New York: Oxford University Press.

————. 1953a. Dynamic Analysis. In *Studies in the Structure of the American Economy*, ed. Wassily Leontief, 53–90. New York: Oxford University Press.

————. 1953b. Structural Change. In *Studies in the Structure of the American Economy*, ed. Wassily Leontief, 17–52. New York: Oxford University Press.

Leontief, Wassily, *et al.* 1953. *Studies in the Structure of the American Economy*, 17–90. New York: Oxford University Press.

Lindbeck, Assar. 1983. The Recent Slowdown of Productivity Growth. *Economic Journal* 93, no. 369 (March): 13–34.

Link, Albert N. 1987. *Technological Change and Productivity Growth*. New York: Harwood Academic Publishers.

Liviatan, Nissan. 1966. The Concept of Capital in Professor Solow's Model. *Econometrica* 34, no. 1 (January): 220–224.

Longva, Svein, and Oystein Olsen. 1983. Producer Behaviour in the MSG Model. In *Analysis of Supply and Demand of Electricity in the Norwegian Economy*, eds. Olav Bjerkholt, Svein Longva, Oystein Olsen, and Steinar Strom, 52–83. Oslo: Central Statistical Bureau.

Lucas, Robert E. 1967. Adjustment Costs and the Theory of Supply. *Journal of Political Economy* 75, no. 4, part 1 (August): 321–334.

Machlup, Fritz. 1962. *The Production and Distribution of Knowledge in the United States*. Princeton, NJ: Princeton University Press.

Maddison, Angus. 1972. Explaining Economic Growth. *Banca Nazionale del Lavoro Quarterly Review*, no. 102 (September): 3–54.

————. 1987. Growth and Slowdown in Advanced Capitalist Economies: Techniques of Quantitative Assessment. *Journal of Economic Literature* 25, no. 2 (June): 649–698.

Mairesse, Jacques. 1972. *L'evaluation du capital fixe productif: méthodes et résultats*. Collections de l'I.N.S.E.E., série C, nos. 18–19 (November).

Majer, Helge. 1973. *Die "Technologische Lücke" zwischen der Bundesrepublik Deutschland und den Vereinigten Staaten von Amerika*. Tübingen.

Malpezzi, Stephen, Larry Ozanne, and Thomas Thibodeau. 1987. Microeconomic Estimates of Housing Depreciation. *Land Economics* 63, no. 4 (November): 372–385.

Mansfield, Edwin. 1984. R&D and Innovation: Some Empirical Findings. In *R&D, Patents, and Productivity*, ed. Zvi Griliches, 127–148. Chicago, IL: University of Chicago Press.

Manvel, Allen D. 1968. Trends in the Value of Real Estate and Land, 1956–1966. *Three Land Research Studies.* The National Commission on Urban Problems. Washington, DC: U.S. Government Printing Office.

Massell, Benton F. 1961. A Disaggregated View of Technical Change. *Journal of Political Economy* 69, no. 6 (December): 547–557.

Matthews, Robin C.O. 1975. Private correspondence.

Matthews, Robin C.O., Charles H. Feinstein, and J.C. Odling-Smee. 1982. *British Economic Growth.* Standford, CA: Stanford University Press.

McFadden, Daniel. 1963. Further Results on CES Production Functions. *Review of Economic Studies* 30(2), no. 83 (June): 73–83.

McGuckin, Robert H., and George A. Pascoe, Jr. 1988. The Longitudinal Research Database (LRD): Status and Research Possibilities, Discussion Paper CES 88–2 (July). Washington, DC: Center for Economic Studies, U.S. Bureau of the Census.

Meese, Richard. 1980. Dynamic Factor Demand Schedules for Labor and Capital under Rational Expectatons. *Journal of Econometrics* 14, no. 1 (September): 141–158.

Meyer, John, and Edwin Kuh. 1957. *The Investment Decision.* Cambridge, MA: Harvard University Press.

Mills, E.S. and B.N. Song. 1977. Korea's Urbanization and Urban Problems, 1945–1975. Korea Dvelopment Institute, Working Paper 7701.

Mills, Frederick C. 1952. *Productivity and Economic Progress.* Occasional Paper 38. New York: National Bureau of Economic Research.

Ministère des Affaires Sociales. 1952. *Revue française du travail,* vol. 7, nos. 1–3 (January-March).

———. 1954. *Revue française du travail,* vol. 9, no. 1 (January).

———. 1956. *Revue française du travail,* vol. 10., no. 1 (January).

Modigliani, Franco. 1963. The Monetary Mechanism and its Interaction with Real Phenomena. *Review of Economics and Statistics* 45, no. 1, pt. 2 (February): 79–107.

Mohr, Michael F. 1986. The Theory and Measurement of the Rental Price of Capital in Industry-Specific Productivity Analysis. In *Measurement Issues and Behavior of Productivity Variables,* ed. Ali Dogramaci, 99–159. Boston, MA: Kluwer-Nijhoff.

———. 1988a. Capital Depreciation and Related Issues: Definitions, Theory, and Measurement, Discussion Paper 28 (June). Washington, DC: Bureau of Economic Analysis, U.S. Department of Commerce.

———. 1988b. Capital Inputs and Capital Aggregation in Production, Discussion Paper 31 (August). Washington, DC: Bureau of Economic Analysis, U.S. Department of Commerce.

————. 1988c. The Rental Price of Capital: Two Views. Discussion Paper 34 (September). Washington, DC: Bureau of Economic Analysis, U.S. Department of Commerce.

Moorsteen, Richard H. 1961. On Measuring Productive Potential and Relative Efficiency. *Quarterly Journal of Economics* 75, no. 3 (August): 451–467.

Morrison, Catherine J., and Ernst R. Berndt. 1981. Short-run Labor Productivity in a Dynamic Model. *Journal of Econometrics* 16, no. 3 (August): 339–366.

Muellbauer, John. 1975. The Cost of Living and Taste and Quality Change. *Journal of Economic Theory* 10, no. 3 (June): 269–283.

Musgrave, John C. 1986. Fixed Reproducible Tangible Wealth in the United States. *Survey of Current Business* 66, no. 1 (January): 51–75.

Nadiri, Mohammed Ishaq. 1970. Some Approaches to the Theory and Measurement of Total Factor Productivity: A Survey. *Journal of Economic Literature* 8, no. 4 (December): 1137–1178.

————. 1972. International Studies of Factor Inputs and Total Factor Productivity: A Brief Survey. *Review of Income and Wealth*, ser. 18, no. 2 (June): 129–154.

Nakamura, Shinichiro. 1984. *An Inter-Industry Translog Model of Prices and Technical Change for the West German Economy.* Berlin: Springer-Verlag.

Nakayama, Ichiro. 1959. *Nippon no Kokufu Kozo (Structure of National Wealth in Japan).*

National Research Council. 1979. *Measurement and Interpretation of Productivity.* Washington, DC: National Academy of Sciences (Rees Report).

NBER. *See* National Bureau of Economic Research.

Nelson, Richard R. 1981. Research on Productivity Growth and Productivity Differences: Dead Ends and New Departures. *Journal of Economic Literature* 19, no. 3 (September 1981): 1029–1064.

Nerlove, Marc L. 1967. Recent Empirical Studies of the CES and Related Production Functions. In *The Theory and Empirical Analysis of Production*, ed. Murray Brown, 55–122. New York: Columbia University Press.

Nishimizu, Mieko. 1975. Total Factor Production Analysis: A Disaggregated Study of the Postwar Japanese Economy with Explicit Consideration of Intermediate Inputs, and Comparison with the United States. Ph.D. Dissertation. Baltimore: Johns Hopkins University.

Nishimizu, Mieko, and Charles R. Hulten. 1978. The Sources of Japanese Economic Growth: 1955–1971. *Review of Economics and Statistics* 60, no. 3 (August): 351–361.

Nishimizu, Mieko, and Sherman Robinson. 1986. Productivity Growth in Manufacturing. In *Industrialization and Growth*, eds. Hollis B. Chenery, Sherman Robinson, and Moshe Syrquin, 283–308. Oxford: Oxford University Press.

Norsworthy, J. Randolph. 1984a. Capital Input Measurement: Options and Inaccuracies. In *Measuring Productivity*, 93–94. Japan Productivity Center. New York: UNIPUB.

————. 1984b. Growth Accounting and Productivity Measurement. *Review of Income and Wealth* ser. 30, no. 3 (September): 309–329.

Norsworthy, J. Randolph, and Michael Harper. 1981. The Role of Capital Formation in the Recent Slowdown in Productivity Growth. In *Aggregate and Industry-Level Productivity Analyses*, eds. Ali Dogramaci and Nabil R. Adam, 122–148. Boston, MA: Kluwer-Nijhoff.

Norsworthy, J. Randolph, Michael Harper, and Kent Kunze. 1979. The Slowdown in Productivity Growth: Analysis of Some Contributing Factors. *Brookings Papers on Economic Activity*, no. 2 (Fall): 387–421.

Office of Business Economics. 1966. *Capital Stock Study*. Washington, DC: U.S. Department of Commerce.

————. 1966. *The National Income and Product Accounts of the United States, 1929–1965, A Supplement to the Survey of Current Business*. Washington, DC: U.S. Department of Commerce.

Office of Industrial Economics. 1975. *Business Building Statistics*. Washington, DC: U.S. Department of the Treasury.

Office of Labor Affairs. 1974. *Yearbook of Labor Statistics*. Seoul: Office of Labor Affairs.

Office of the Prime Minister (Government of Japan). 1969. *Japan Statistical Yearbook*.

Ohkawa, Kazushi. 1968. Nihon Keizai no Seisan to Bunpai, 1905–1963 (The Output and Distribution of the Japanese Economy, 1905–1963). *Keizai Kenkyu* (April).

Ohkawa, Kazushi, and Henry Rosovsky. 1968. Postwar Japanese Growth in Historical Perspective: A Second Look. In *Economic Growth: The Japanese Experience since the Meiji Era*, eds. Lawrence Klein and Kazushi Ohkawa.

————. 1973. *Japanese Economic Growth*. Stanford, CA: Stanford University Press.

Ohkawa, Kazushi, S. Yamada, S. Ishiwata, and H. Seki. 1966. *Shihon Stokku (Capital Stock)*. Tokyo: Toyo Heizai Shinposha Showa 41.

Organization for Economic Cooperation and Development. Various annual issues. *National Accounts, 1950–1968, 1953–1969, 1960–1971, 1961–1972, 1962–1973*. Paris: O.E.C.D.

————. Various annual issues. *Labor Force Statistics, 1956–1966, 1962–1973*. Paris: O.E.C.D.

————. Various annual issues. *Reviews of National Policies for Education, Italy, 1960, 1963, 1966*. Paris: O.E.C.D.

————. 1966. Reviews of National Policies for Education, Italy. Paris: Organization for Economic Cooperations and Development.

————. 1977. Main Economic Indicators: Historical Statistics. Paris: Organization for Economic Cooperations and Development.

Ozawa, Terutomo. 1974. *Japan's Technological Challenge to the West, 1950–1974.* Cambridge, MA: MIT Press.

Patinkin, Don. 1965. *Money, Interest and Prices,* 2nd edition. New York: Harper and Row.

Patrick, Hugh. 1977. The Future of the Japanese Economy: Output and Labor Productivity. *The Journal of Japanese Studies* 3, no. 2 (Summer): 219–249.

Patrick, Hugh, and Henry Rosovsky, eds. 1976. *Asia's New Giant.* Washington, DC: The Brookings Institution.

Peck, Merton J., with the collaboration of Shuji Tamura. 1976. Technology. Chapter 8 in *Asia's New Giant,* eds. Hugh Patrick and Henry Rosovsky, 525–586. Washington, DC: The Brookings Institution.

Pindyck, Robert S., and Julio J. Rotemberg. 1983a. Dynamic Factor Demands and the Effects of Energy Price Shocks. *American Economic Review* 73, no. 5 (December): 1066–1079.

————. 1983b. Dynamic Factor Demands under Rational Expectations. *Scandinavian Journal of Economics* 85, no. 2: 223–239.

Ramm, Wolfhard. 1970. Measuring the Services of Household Durables: The Case of Automobiles. *Proceedings of the Business and Economic Statistics Section of the American Statistical Association*: 149–158.

Ratcliffe, Tait. 1969. Tax Policy and Investment Behavior in Japan. Ph.D. Dissertation. Berkeley: University of California.

Revell, Jack. 1967. *The Wealth of the Nation.* Cambridge: Cambridge University Press.

Richter, Marcel K. 1966. Invariance Axioms and Economic Indexes. *Econometrica* 34, no. 4 (October): 239–255.

Robinson, Sherman. 1989. Multisectoral Models. In *Handbook of Development Economics,* eds. Hollis B. Chenery and T. N. Srinivasan, 2, 885–947. Amsterdam: North-Holland.

Romer, Paul M. 1987. Crazy Explanations for the Productivity Slowdown. In *NBER Macroeconomics Annual 1987,* ed. Stanley Fischer, 163–201. Cambridge, MA: MIT Press.

Rosen, Sherwin. 1974. Hedonic Prices and Implicit Markets: Product Differentiation in Pure Competition. *Journal of Political Economy* 82, no. 1 (January-February): 34–55.

Ruggles, Nancy, and Richard Ruggles. 1970. *The Design of Economic Accounts.* New York: Columbia University Press.

————. 1973. A Proposal for a System of Economic and Social Accounts. In *The Measurement of Social and Economic Performance*, ed. Milton Moss, 111–145. New York: Columbia University Press.

————. 1982. Integrated Economic Accounts for the United States, 1947–1980. *Survey of Current Business* 62, no. 5 (May): 1–53.

Samuelson, Paul A. 1951. Abstract of a Theorem Concerning Substitutability in Open Leontief Models. In *Activity Analysis of Production and Allocation*, ed. Tjalling C. Koopmans, 142–146. New York: Wiley.

————. 1953. Prices of Factors and Goods in General Equilibrium. *Review of Economic Studies* 21(1), no. 54: 1–20.

————. 1962. Parable and Realism in Capital Theory: The Surrogate Production Function. *Review of Economic Studies* 29(3) no. 86 (June): 193–206.

————. 1965. A Theory of Induced Innovation along Kennedy-Weizsäcker Lines. *Review of Economics and Statistics* 47, no. 4 (November): 343–356.

————. 1979. Paul Douglas's Measurement of Production Functions and Marginal Productivities. *Journal of Political Economy* 87, no. 5, pt. 1 (October): 923–939.

Samuelson, Paul A., and Subramanian Swamy. 1974. Invariant Economic Index Numbers and Canonical Duality: Survey and Synthesis. *American Economic Review* 64, no. 4 (September): 566–593.

Sargent, Thomas J. 1978. Estimation of Dynamic Labor Demand Schedules under Rational Expectations. *Journal of Political Economy* 86, no. 6 (December): 1009–1045.

Sato, Kazuo. 1975. *Production Functions and Aggregation*. Amsterdam: North-Holland.

————. 1976. The Meaning and Measurement of the Real Value Added Index. *Review of Economic Statistics* 58, no. 4 (November): 434–442.

Sato, Ryuzo. 1968. Technical Progress and the Aggregate Production Function of Japan (1930–1960). *The Economic Studies Quarterly* 19, no. 1 (March).

Sato, Ryuzo, and Martin Beckmann. 1968. Neutral Inventions and Production Functions. *Review of Economic Studies* 35(1), no. 101 (January): 57–66.

Segal, Herbert, and Frances Pratt. 1967 *Comparative Urban Consumer Price Levels in the U.S. and Canada*. Ottawa: Prices Division, Dominion Bureau of Statistics.

Schmookler, Jacob 1952. The Changing Efficiency of the American Economy, 1869–38. *Review of Economics and Statistics* 39, no. 3 (August): 214–231.

Schultz, Theodore W. 1961. Investment in Human Capital. *American Economic Review* 41, no. 1 (March): 1–17.

Shephard, Ronald W. 1953. *Cost and Production Functions*. Princeton, NJ: Princeton University Press.

————. 1970. *Theory of Cost and Production Functions*. Princeton, NJ: Princeton University Press.

Shoven, John B., and John Whalley. 1984. Applied General-Equilibrium Models of Taxation and Trade. *Journal of Economic Literature* 22, no. 3 (September): 1007–1051.

Sims, Christopher. 1969. Theoretical Basis for a Double-Deflated Index of Real Value Added. *Review of Economics and Statistics* 51, no. 4 (November): 470–471.

————. 1977. Remarks on Real Value Added. *Annals of Social and Economic Measurement* 6, no. 1 (Winter): 127–132.

Solow, Robert M. 1955. The Production Function and the Theory of Capital. *Review of Economic Studies* 23(2), no. 61: 101–8.

————. 1956. A Contribution to the Theory of Economic Growth. *Quarterly Journal of Economics* 70, no. 1 (February): 65–94.

————. 1957. Technical Change and the Aggregate Production Function. *Review of Economics and Statistics* 39, no. 3 (August): 312–320.

————. 1960. Investment and Technical Progress. In *Mathematical Methods in the Social Sciences, 1959*, eds. Kenneth J. Arrow, Samuel Karlin, and Patrick Suppes, 89–104. Stanford, CA: Stanford University Press.

————. 1962. Technical Progress, Capital Formation, and Economic Growth. *American Economic Review* 52, no. 2 (May): 76–86.

————. 1963a. *Capital Theory and the Rate of Return*. Amsterdam: North-Holland.

————. 1963b. Heterogeneous Capital and Smooth Production Functions: An Experimental Study. *Econometrica* 31, no. 4 (October): 623–645.

————. 1964. Capital, Labor, and Income in Manufacturing. In *The Behavior of Income Shares*, 101–128. NBER Studies in Income and Wealth. Princeton, NJ: Princeton University Press.

————. 1967. Some Recent Developments in the Theory of Production. In *The Theory and Empirical Analysis of Production*, ed. Murray Brown, 25–50. New York: Columbia University Press.

————. 1970. *Growth Theory*. Oxford: Oxford University Press.

————. 1988. Growth Theory and After. *American Economic Review* 78, no. 3 (June): 307–317.

Sono, Masazo. 1961. The Effect of Price Changes on the Demand and Supply of Separable Goods. *International Economic Review*, 2, no. 3 (September): 239–271.

Star, Spencer 1974. Accounting for the Growth of Output. *American Economic Review* 64, no. 1 (March): 123–135.

Statistical Office of the United Nations. 1968. A System of National Accounts. *Studies in Methods*, ser. F, no. 2, rev. 3. New York: Department of Economics and Social Affairs, United Nations.

————. 1973. *Family Expenditure in Canada, 1969.* Ottawa: Information Canada.

Statistics Canada. 1974a. *1971 Census of Canada.* Labor Force and Individual Income. Ottawa: Information Canada.

————. 1974b. *National Income and Expenditure Accounts, Historical Revision, 1926–1971.* Ottawa: Gross National Product Division.

————. 1974c. Flows and Stocks of Fixed Nonresidential Capital, Canada. Ottawa: Information Canada.

————. 1975. *1971 Census of Canada.* Income of Individuals. Ottawa: Information Canada.

————. 1976. *National Income and Expenditure Accounts,* vol. 1, 1926–1974. Ottawa: Information Canada.

Statistisches Bundesamt. *Fachserie N, Volkswirtschaftliche Gesamtrechnungen.* Reihe 1, Konten und Standardtabellen, 1969, 1970, 1971, 1972 and Vorbericht 1973. Mainz: Verlag W. Kohlhammer.

————. *Statistisches Jahrbuch für die Bundesrepublik Deutschland.* Jahrgänge 1952 bis 1973. Mainz: Verlag W. Kohlhammer.

Stigler, George J. 1947. *Trends in Output and Employment.* New York: National Bureau of Economic Research.

Stobbe, Alfred. 1969. *Volkswirtschaftliches Rechnungswegen.* Berlin: Springer-Verlag.

Stone, Richard. 1956. *Quantity and Price Indexes in National Accounts.* Paris: Organization for European Economic Cooperation.

Summers, Lawrence H. 1981. Taxation and Corporate Investment: A $q$-Theory Approach. *Brookings Papers on Economic Activity,* no. 1: 67–127.

Taubman, Paul, and Robert Rasche. 1969. Economic and Tax Depreciation of Office Buildings. *National Tax Journal* 22, no. 3 (September): 334–346.

Taylor, Lance. 1975. Theoretical Foundations and Technical Implications. In *Economy-Wide Models and Development Planning,* ed. Charles K. Blitzer, Peter B. Clark, and Lance Taylor, 33–109. Oxford: Oxford University Press.

Terborgh, George. 1954. *Realistic Depreciation Policy,* Washington, DC: Machinery and Allied Products Institute.

Theil, Henri. 1965. The Information Approach to Demand Analysis. *Econometrica* 33, no. 1 (January): 67–87.

Thirtle, Colin G., and Vernon W. Ruttan. 1987. *The Role of Demand and Supply in the Generation and Diffusion of Technical Change.* New York: Harwood Academic Publishers.

Thor, Carl G., George E. Sadler, and Elliot S. Grossman. 1984. Comparison of Total Factor Productivity in Japan and the United States. In *Measuring Productivity,* 57–72. Japan Productivity Center. New York: UNIPUB.

Tinbergen, Jan. 1942. Zur Theorie der langfristigen Wirtschaftsentwicklung, *Weltwirtschaftliches Archiv*, 55, no. 1, pp. 511–549; English translation (1959), "On the Theory of Trend Movements," in *Jan Tinbergen, Selected Papers*, eds. Leo H. Klaassen, Leendert M. Koyck, and Hendrikus J. Witteveen, 182–221. Amsterdam: North-Holland.

Tobin, James. 1969. A General Equilibrium Approach to Monetary Theory. *Journal of Money, Credit, and Banking* 1, no. 1 (February): 15–29.

Törnqvist, Leo. 1936. The Bank of Finland's Consumption Price Index. *Bank of Finland Monthly Bulletin*, no. 10: 1–8.

Toyokeizaishinpo-sha. 1967. *Keizai Tokei Nenkan (Economic Statistical Yearbook)*.

Triplett, Jack E. 1975. The Measurement of Inflation: A Survey of Research on the Accuracy of Price Indexes. In *Analysis of Inflation*, ed. Paul H. Earl, 19–82. Lexington, MA: Heath.

———. 1983a. Concepts of Quality in Input and Output Price Measures: A Resolution of the User-Value Resource-Cost Debate. In *The U.S. National Income and Product Accounts: Selected Topics*, ed. Murray F. Foss, 296–311. Chicago, IL: University of Chicago Press.

———. 1983b. Introduction: An Essay on Labor Cost. In *The Measurement of Labor Cost*, ed. Jack E. Triplett, 1–60. Chicago, IL: University of Chicago Press.

———. 1986. The Economic Interpretation of Hedonic Methods. *Survey of Current Business* 66, no. 1 (January): 36–40.

———. 1987. Hedonic Functions and Hedonic Indexes. In *The New Palgrave: A Dictionary of Economics*, eds. John Eatwell, Murray Milgate, and Peter Newman, 2: 630–634. New York: Stockton.

———. 1989. Price and Technological Change in a Capital Good: Survey of Research on Computers. In *Technology and Capital Formation*, eds. Dale W. Jorgenson and Ralph Landau, 127–213. Cambridge, MA: MIT Press.

———. 1990. Two Views on Computer Prices, Discussion Paper no. 45 (February). Bureau of Economic Analysis, U.S. Department of Commerce.

United Nations. 1964. *System of National Accounts and Supporting Tables*. Studies in Method, ser. F, no. 2 (January): 3rd edition.

Uzawa, Hirofumi. 1962. Production Functions with Constant Elasticity of Substitution. *Review of Economic Studies* 29(4), no. 81 (October): 291–299.

———. 1966. On a Neoclassical Model of Economic Growth. *Economic Studies Quarterly* 17, no. 1 (September): 1–14.

———. 1969. Time Preference and the Penrose Effect in a Two-Class Model of Economic Growth. *Journal of Political Economy* 77, no. 4, pt. 2 (July/August): 628–652.

Valavanis-Vail, Stefan. 1955. An Econometric Model of Growth, U.S.A., 1869–1953. *American Economic Review* 45, no. 2 (May): 208–221.

Vitali, Ornello. 1968. *La formazione del capitale in Italia.* Milan: E.N.I. Pubblicazione della Scuola Enrico Mattei di Studi Superiori sugli Idrocarburi.

von Weizsäcker, C. Christian. 1962. A New Technical Progress Function. Cambridge, MA: Department of Economics, MIT, unpublished.

Walderhaug, Albert J. 1973. The Composition of Value Added in the 1963 Input-Output Study. *Survey of Current Business* 53, no. 4 (April): 34–44.

Waldorf, William H., Kent Kunze, Larry S. Rosenblum, and Michael B. Tannen. 1986. New Measures of the Contribution of Education and Experience to U.S. Productivity Growth. Washington, DC: U.S. Department of Labor.

Walras, Leon. 1954. *Elements of Pure Economics,* trans. William Jaffe, from the French Edition Definitive, 1926 (1st ed. 1877). Homewood, NJ: Irwin.

Walters, Alan. 1963. Production and Cost Functions: An Econometric Survey. *Econometrica* 31, no. 1 (January-April): 1–66.

Walters, Dorothy. 1968. *Canadian Income Levels and Growth: An International Perspective.* Staff Study no. 23. Ottawa: Economic Council of Canada.

———. 1970. *Canadian Growth Revisited, 1950–1967.* Staff Study no. 28. Ottawa: Economic Council of Canada.

Watanabe, Tsunehiko. 1971. A Note on Measuring Sectoral Input Productivity. *Review of Income and Wealth* ser. 17, no. 4 (December): 335–340.

———. 1972. Improvements of Labor Quality and Economic Growth — Japan's Postwar Experience. *Economic Development and Cultural Change* 21, no. 1 (October): 33–53.

Watanabe, Tsunehiko, and Fumio Egaitsu. 1967. Gijutsu Shinpo to Keizai Seicho (Technical Progress and Economic Growth). In *Keizai Seicho to Shigen Haibun (Economic Growth and Resource Allocation),* ed. Motoo Kaji.

———. 1968. Rodoryoku no Shitsu to Keizai Seicho (Improvement of Labor Quality and Economic Growth — Japan's Postwar Experience). *Economic Studies Quarterly* 19, no. 1 (March).

Waugh, Frederick V. 1929. *Quality as a Determinant of Vegetable Prices.* New York: Columbia University Press.

Weitzman, Martin L. 1983. On the Meaning of Comparative Factor Productivity. In *Marxism, Central Planning, and the Soviet Economy,* ed. Padma Desai, 166–170. Cambridge, MA: MIT Press.

Winston, Clifford. 1985. Conceptual Developments in the Economics of Transportation: An Interpretive Survey. *Journal of Economic Literature* 23, no. 1 (March): 57–94.

Wolff, Edward N. 1985a. Industrial Composition, Interindustry Effects, and the U.S. Productivity Slowdown. *Review of Economics and Statistics* 67, no. 2 (May): 268–277.

————. 1985b. The Magnitude and Causes of the Recent Productivity Slowdown in the United States: A Survey of Recent Studies. In *Productivity Growth and U.S. Competitiveness*, eds. William J. Baumol and Kenneth McLennan, 160–186. New York: Oxford University Press.

Woodland, Alan D. 1978. On Testing Weak Separability. *Journal of Econometrics* 8, no. 3 (December): 383–398.

Wykoff, Frank C. 1989. Economic Depreciation and the User Cost of Business-Leased Automobiles. In *Technology and Capital Formation*, eds. Dale W. Jorgenson and Ralph Landau, 259–292. Cambridge, MA: MIT Press.

Yoshihara, Kunio, and Tait Ratcliffe. 1970. Productivity Change in the Japanese Economy, 1905–1965. *Discussion Paper* 8. The Center for Southeast Asian Studies: Kyoto University.

Young, Allan. 1989. BEA's Measurement of Computer Output. *Survey of Current Business* 69, no. 7 (July): 108–115.

Young, Allan, and John C. Musgrave. 1980. Estimation of Capital Stock in the United States. In *The Measurement of Capital*, ed. Dan Usher, 23–58. Chicago, IL: University of Chicago Press.

# Index

Accounting relationships, in the
  producing sector, 110–112
ACMS (Arrow, Chenery, Minhas, and
  Solow), 76, 88
Aggregate economic growth (1952–1974),
  U.S. and Japan, 179–202
  input, 180, 188–197
  methodology for, 181–184
  output, 180, 184–188
  productivity, 197–201
Aggregate economic growth, international
  comparison, 203–295, 377
  alternative methodologies, 204–207
  country, selecting, 209–210
  methodology for, 210–223
  methodology for, selecting, 207–209
  timeframe, selecting, 209–210
Aggregate growth accounts, 69–70
Aggregate input, 4
  Japan and U.S., 188–197
  measuring, 60–61
  value of, 62
Aggregate output, 3–5, 8
  data sources for, 61–65
  defined, 62
  growth rate (1947–1985), 4
  Japan and U.S., 184–188
  measuring, 57–61
  methods for, 61–65
  sectoral output and, 71
  value of, 62
Aggregate production account, 61–62
Aggregate production function, 1–7,
  57–61, 71
  constant elasticity of substitution, 76

measuring productivity change and,
  147, 148
neo-classical, 148
Aggregate production models, 75–81
  alternative models, 81–87
  compensation and, 63
  disaggregated data set vs., 9, 16–17
  economic growth and, 9, 16, 17
  limitations of, 9, 76–77, 86
  over sectors, 59–61
  property compensation and, 64
  sectoral model vs., 76
  traditional approach, 75–77
  validating, 71
Aggregate productivity, 16
  aggregate production account and, 61
  alternative sources for, 65–72
  Christensen and Jorgenson's analysis
    of, 65–66
  data sources for, 61–65
  in foreign countries, 66–67
  growth rate, 4, 8
  integrated with sectoral productivity,
    71
  Kendrick's analysis of, 53
  measuring, 57–61
  methods for, 61–65
  rate of technical progress, 150–151
Aggregate value added, 62–63
  unweighted vs. weighted measures, 70
Aggregation bias, 156, 158, 159, 160
  capital, 170
  capital vs. labor, 167
  conclusions concerning, 161
  meanings of, 157

Aggregation bias (*cont.*)
    productivity change and, 167
Aggregation problem I, 148–156
    aggregate productivity change, 148
    Divisia index, for productivity change,
        151–152
    input-output system, 148–149
    measuring productivity change,
        148–156
    shifts in aggregate production function,
        154–155
Aggregation problem II, 156–161
Asset price, 117–118
    implicit deflators and, 123–124
Asset tax rate, formula for, 126
Australia, 209

Bank of Japan, Flow of Funds Accounts,
    135
    net claims on government and
        foreigners, 143–144
Belgium, 209
Bias, 382
    defined, 382
    in measurement of sectoral output, 56
Biased technical change, 382–384
    energy prices and, 383
    slowdown in U.S. economic growth
        and, 383–384
Bilateral indexes, 337
Box-Cox rates, 29, 31
Budget restrictions, in Japanese economy,
    102–104
Buildings, vintage price functions for,
    29–30
Bureau of Labor Statistics (BLS), 328
    data on output, 48
    measurement of capital input, 38, 40, 43
    measurement of labor input, 23
    measurement of value added, 67

Canada, 209
    aggregate economic growth, 242–245
    capital input per capita, 317–318, 323
    capital input, value share of, 228
    capital-labor ratio, 315
    capital stock by asset class, value shares
        of, 230
    data sources for, 254–255
    decomposition of per capita labor
        input, 312–313

gross private domestic product and
    factor input, 273
gross private domestic product and
    factor outlay, 270
investment goods product, value share
    of, 227
labor input per capita, 319, 324
output per capita, 314, 316–317, 322
own rate of return to capital, 234
price comparison with U.S., 328
private domestic capital input, 271
private domestic labor input, 272
quality change, 251
real capital and labor input, 246–247,
    249
real gross private domestic product,
    240
real private domestic capital input, 236
real private domestic factor input, 238
real private domestic labor input, 237
total factor productivity, 241
    1947–1973, 320–321, 325
Capital, 140, 143
    cost of, in Japan and U.S., 398
    quality change in, 168, 170–172
    quality indexes of, 167, 168
Capital goods, 29
    mortality rates for, 39
Capital input, 4–6
    aggregate, 4, 64–65
    alternative data sources, 37–44
    alternative sources and methods for,
        37–44
    annual growth rate for Japan, 357–360,
        362
    annual growth rate for U.S., 357–360,
        362
    Bureau of Labor statistics methodology,
        38, 40, 43
    comparison of Japanese and U.S. prices,
        397
    data sources, 34–37
    decline in, 379
    Dennison's measures, 68–69
    Dennison's methodology, 37, 38, 40–42,
        43
    depreciation and, 46–47
    as factor in economic growth, 4–6, 15,
        377–378
    index of, 36–37, 43

international (1947–1973), 228
in Japanese economy, 140, 179–180, 189,
    191–195, 200–201
Kendrick's methodology, 37, 38, 42–44
measuring, 28–34
methods for, 34–37
perpetual inventory method and, 38–40
price of, 191
purchasing power parities for, 393–394
real, 208, 209, 223, 226–235, 245–249
reallocation of, 8
real private domestic, annual rates of
    growth by country, 236
relative prices for, 297
rental price of, 28–29
sectoral measures of, 34–37
separation of, 172
social, 147
symmetric, 73
in U.S. economy, 179–180, 189, 191–195,
    200–201
value of, 339
"Capital input method," 67–68
Capital input per capita (1947–1973),
    317–319, 323
by country, 318
U.S. level in 1970, 323
Capital input per capita (1970), 298, 299
by country, 310–311
Capital intensity, defined, 179
Capital-labor ratio, relative to U.S.,
    314–315
Capital services, 126–130
estimating quantity of, 119
share of, U.S. vs. Japan, 194
Capital stock, 6, 7
aggregate, 65
by asset class, international value
    shares of (1970), 230
capital input and, 6, 7, 28, 40–44
estimates for asset classes, 192–193, 229
in Japan and U.S., 190, 392–393
Kendrick's methodology, 42–44, 143
measurement of real, 122–130
sectoral measures of capital input and,
    35, 37
series, 125
Caves, Christensen, and Diewert, 301
*Census of Population*, 21
Christensen–Greene model, 83–84, 85

Christensen, Laurits R., 100, 226, 308, 348
economic growth patterns in Japan and
    U.S., 374
translog production function and, 349
Christensen, Laurits R. and D.W.
    Jorgenson, 181, 209, 224, 254
accounting system for aggregate
    economic growth, 203–204
analysis of aggregate growth, 201
consumer wealth and, 130
growth rate and, 166, 172
real capital input and, 206
rental prices for capital goods, 28–29
separation of social capital input, 147
vs. Denison, 207–208
Circular multilateral index of differences
    in productivity, 337
Cobb-Douglas functional form, 2, 16, 336
limitations of, 76, 86
sectoral productivity and, 61, 73
Compensation, 21
aggregate production model and, 63
data on, 21
for Japanese agriculture workers, 403
Japanese wage rate, 398–401
male vs. female, 25–26
pattern of hourly earnings, 27
property, 28, 35–36, 40
self-employed workers and, 21, 26–27
U.S. wage rate, 398–401
Competitiveness, international, Japan and
    U.S., 387–417
comparison of capital input prices, 397
conclusions, 412–414
economic competitiveness, 400
effect of inflation, 398
effect on input prices, 401–402
exchange rate, 387–389
gap of output prices, 409–411
industrial competitiveness, 400–402
industry classification system, 392–393
industry outputs, 409–411
Japanese price index, 395
labor input prices, 398–400
measure of, 387, 391–192
methodology for, 389–390
productivity gaps, 402–411
purchasing power parities and, 388–402
relative prices, 388–389
relative productivity, 389, 402–411

Competitiveness (*cont.*)
  value-added price index, 396
Conference on Research in Income and
    Wealth, 1, 88–89
Constant elasticity of substitution (CES),
    76
Consumer expenditure accounts, 136, 144,
    172
  *See also* Consumers' durables
Consumer income, 135–140, 172
  accounts, 136
  defined, 135
  different concepts of, 135
Consumer saving accounts, 140–144, 172
  data, 142
  sources and uses of, 141
Consumers' durables, 143, 144
  asset price of, 145
  data for, 144–146
  imputation for services of, 225, 186
  NIS data for, 144–145
  service price of, 146
  services of, 146
  stock of, 145–146
Consumer wealth, 130–144
  defined, 130, 131–132
Consumer wealth accounts, 130, 140–144,
    172
  data, 142
  sources and uses of, 141

Decomposition of per capita labor input,
    relative to U.S., 311–314
Denison, Edward F., 7, 15, 23, 24, 27, 341
  capital input method, 67–68
  decline in economic growth and, 80
  labor input and, 24–26
  measurement of aggregate
      productivity, 67–68
  measurement of capital input, 37–38
  measurement of total factor
      productivity, 205–207
  relative levels of real output per capita,
      326–327
  vs. Christensen and Jorgenson, 207–208
  *Why Growth Rates Differ*, 206–208
Denmark, 209
Depreciation, 28
  of commercial and industrial buildings,
      30–31

declining balance method, 127
defined, 28, 39, 67
discounted value definition of, 68
energy prices and, 31
geometric, 34
Japanese schemes for, 127
"one-hoss shay" pattern, 41–42, 46
"ordinary," 127
sectoral output and, 46–48
"special," 127
straight-line pattern, 41–42, 127
Depreciation rates, for business assets,
    31–34
"Direct taxes and charges on persons,"
    137, 139
Distribution in production, 105–109
  defined, 105
Divisia indexes, 157, 215–216
  aggregate production function and, 147
  for capital, 147
  of capital input, 213, 215
  for differences in productivity, 335
  growth rates and, 165
  of input, 214
  for labor, 147, 157
  of labor input, 213, 215
  of output, 213, 215
  price index of technical change, 215
  for productivity change, 149, 151–152,
      161, 163–164
  quantity index of technical change, 213
  reproductive quality of, 215–216
Divisia index numbers, 216
Domar, Evsey, 61, 205, 206
Domestic product, real gross private,
    international growth of, 249
Douglas, Paul H., 2, 3, 16
  traditional approach to aggregate
      production model, 75
Durables. *See* Consumers' durables;
    Producers' durables

Econometric model for vintage price
    functions, 29–31
Econometric modeling of production,
    72–73, 76, 77–78, 87–89
  Bell Canada, 84
  constant returns to scale in, 83
  difficulty of, 74
  electric power industry, 83–84

embodied technical change and, 82–83
  influence of Hicks, 88
  nonsubstitution theorem and, 74
  sectoral production models and, 85
  translog production functions in, 74–75
  vs. noneconometric modeling, 74
Economic growth, 3–6
  aggregate, 242–245
  aggregate, international comparison of,
    203–295, 377
  aggregate production model and, 9, 16
  biased technical change and, 383–384
  capital input and, 4–6, 8, 15, 377–378,
    412
  Christensen and Jorgenson's analysis
    of, 65–66
  consumer behavior as factor in, 87
  decline in, 9, 77, 347
  decline in Japanese, 379–380
  decline in U.S., 379–380
  energy prices and, 80
  investment boom in U.S., 194
  Japan and U.S.
    1952–1974, 179–202
    1960–1973, 348–375
    1960–1979, 377–385, 412
  labor input and, 4–6, 9, 15
  modeling, 16–17, 87
  neoclassical theory of, 2, 87
  productivity and, 1–98
  rank of Japan, 179
  rank of U.S., 179
  sources of, Japan and U.S., 377–378, 412
  sources of, U.S., 3–17
  within industries, 10–15, 16, 368–374
  See also Aggregate productivity;
    Sectoral productivity
Economic theory of production, 181, 298,
    348
  measuring total factor productivity,
    204
  production function of, 181–182
Economic theory of production and
    technical change, 210
Educational attainment and earnings, 329
  data sources, 330
Efficiency, 2
  geometric decline in, 29
  patterns of decline in, 46–47
  See also Depreciation

Energy crisis, 378–379
  economic growth and, 385, 412
  price of energy and, 400–401
  production methods and, 381
  productivity patterns and, 407–409
  rate of technical change and, 385
Energy, price of, productivity growth and,
    81
Energy, price of in Japan and U.S., 80
  electricity and gas, 400
  growth rates, 401
  petroleum and coal, 400
Exchange rate, yen-to-dollar, 387–389,
    394–395
Ezaki and Jorgenson, 181, 348

Factor and Output Aggregation. See
    Aggregation problem II
Factor income, value of input services
    and, 120–121
Factor input, real private domestic,
    international annual growth of, 238
Foreign Trade Statistics, 114
France, 209
  aggregate economic growth, 242–244
  capital input per capita, 317–318, 323
  capital input, value share of, 228
  capital-labor ratio, 315
  capital stock by asset class, value shares
    of, 230
  data sources for, 255–256
  decomposition of per capita labor
    input, 312–313
  gross private domestic product and
    factor input, 277
  gross private domestic product and
    factor outlay, 274
  investment goods product, value share
    of, 227
  labor input per capita, 319, 324
  output per capita, 316–317, 322
  own rate of return to capital, in
    business sector, 234
  private domestic capital input, 275
  private domestic labor input, 276
  quality change, 250–251
  real capital and labor input, 246–247
  real gross private domestic product,
    240
  real gross private factor input, 238

France (cont.)
    real private domestic capital input,
        annual growth of, 236
    real private domestic labor input,
        annual growth of, 237
    total factor productivity (1947–1973),
        320–321, 325
    total factor productivity, 241

General equilibrium production model,
    16–17, 104
General equilibrium theory, 101–109
    national income statistics and, 171
Germany, 209
    aggregate economic growth, 242–245
    capital input per capita, 317–318, 323
    capital input, value share of, 228
    capital-labor ratio, 315
    capital stock by asset class, value shares
        of, 230
    data sources for, 256
    decomposition of per capita labor
        input, 312–313
    gross private domestic product and
        factor input, 281
    gross private domestic product and
        factor outlay, 278
    index of total factor productivity,
        342–343
    investment goods product, value share
        of, 227
    labor input per capita, 319, 324
    output per capita, 314, 316–317, 322
    own rate of return to capital, in
        business sector, 234
    private domestic capital input, 279
    private domestic labor input, 280
    quality change, 250–252
    real capital and labor input, 246–249
    real gross private domestic product,
        240
    real private domestic capital input, 236
    real private domestic factor input, 238
    real private domestic labor input, 237
    sectoral productivity gaps with U.S.
        and Japan, 333–376
    total factor productivity, 241
    1947–1973, 320–321, 325
Government enterprises sector, 114
    gross product and factor outlay for,
        113–114

"National Wealth Survey" vs. National
    Income Statistics (NIS), 123
Gross domestic product (GDP), 104
    imputational equations in, 106–107, 108
Gross national product (GNP), 225
    defined as income, 104–105
    defined as output, 104
    imputational equations in, 106–107, 108
Gross private domestic product and factor
    input, 273
    for Canada, 273
    for France, 277
    for Germany, 281
    for Italy, 285
    for Japan, 289
    for The Netherlands, 295
    for U.K., 269
    for U.S., 265
Gross private domestic product and factor
    outlay, 270
    for Canada, 270
    for France, 274
    for Germany, 278
    for Italy, 282
    for Japan, 286
    for Korea, 290, 292
    for The Netherlands, 292
    for U.K., 266
    for U.S., 262
Gross private national expenditure,
    134–135
Gross private national income net of
    taxes, 134, 136
    additions to, 137
Gross private national saving, 132–133,
    136
    defined, 140
    differences from national income
        statistics, 140
Growth rates, 166
    Divisia indexes and, 165
    K/K, 169

"Hedonic technique", for price
    measurement, 29, 83
Hulten and Wykoff, 29–31, 32, 37
Hulten-Wykoff geometric rates, 40

Imputation of capital service prices,
    126–130

Imputation on physical capital, 105–109
  computing GDP and, 106–107, 108
  computing GNP and, 106–107
  money and, 109
  problems with, 107–109
  sales tax and, 107
Income accounts (data), 138
Income, consumer, 135–140
Income from unincorporated enterprises,
  137, 139, 303
Indexes of quality
  capital stock, 221–222
  hours worked, 222–223
  labor, 235
Indexes of total factor productivity, 342
  summary of, 341–345
Industries, 344–348
  aggregated, 414
  classification system, 392–393
  list of Japanese, 356
  list of U.S., 356
  relative productivity of, 412–413
  revised taxonomy, 403–407
  taxonomy for Japanese and U.S.,
    402–407
  type 1, 402, 403, 404–406
  type 2, 402, 404–406
  type 3, 402, 404–407, 412–413
  type 4, 402, 404
  type 5, 402, 404
  type 6, 402
  type 7, 402–403, 404–407, 409
  See also Sectoral output
Industry productivity comparisons, Japan
  and U.S., 347–376, 402–411
  industrial taxonomies for, 402–407
  theoretical framework, 347–354
Inflation, 398
Input prices, growth of in Japan and U.S.,
  401–402
Intermediate goods, 172
Intermediate input, 10–12, 17–20
  alternative sources and methods for,
    51–57
  annual growth rate for Japan, 357–360,
    363–364
  annual growth rate for U.S., 357–360,
    363–364
  constructing sectoral data on, 48–50
  data sources, 48–51

growth rate (1947–1969), 53–56
measuring, 44–51
in measuring sectoral productivity,
  44–45, 51
methods for, 38–51
purchasing power parities for, 392
sectoral output and, 45–46, 48–50,
  56–57
symmetric, 73
unweighted index by sector, 49–50
International comparison of economic
  growth (1947–1973), 203–295
Intertemporal production model, 81–82
Investment goods
  output, Japan and U.S., 188
  price indexes, 229
  product, 226
  product, international (1947–1973), 227
Italy, 209
  aggregate economic growth, 242–245
  capital input per capita, 317–318, 323
  capital input, value share of, 228
  capital-labor ratio, 315
  capital stock by asset class, value shares
    of, 230
  data sources for, 256–257
  decomposition of per capita labor
    input, 312–313
  gross private domestic product and
    factor input, 285
  gross private domestic product and
    factor outlay, 282
  investment goods product, value share
    of, 227
  labor input per capita, 319, 324
  output per capita, 316, 322
  own rate of return to capital, in
    business sector, 234
  private domestic capital input, 283
  private domestic labor input, 284
  quality change, 250–252
  real capital and labor input, 246–247
  real gross private domestic product,
    240
  real private domestic capital input, 236
  real private domestic factor input, 238
  real private domestic labor input, 237
  total factor productivity (1947–1973),
    320–321, 325
  total factor productivity, 241

Japan
   accounting framework for economy,
      101–109
   aggregate economic growth, 242–245
   annual growth rate of capital input,
      357–360, 362
   annual growth rate of labor input,
      357–360, 363
   annual growth rate of output, 357–360,
      357–361
   annual productivity growth, 357–360,
      364–365
   capital input per capita, 317–319, 323
   capital input, value share of, 228
   capital-labor ratio, 315
   capital stock by asset class, value shares
      of, 230
   data sources for, 257
   decline in capital input (1973–1979),
      379
   decline in change of quality of labor
      input, 380
   decline in economic growth, 379–380
   decline in output, 379
   decomposition of per capita labor
      input, 312–313
   distribution in production, 105–109
   economic growth (1960–1979), 347–376,
      377–385
   economic sectors, 101–102, 103
   gross private domestic product and
      factor input, 289
   gross private domestic product and
      factor outlay, 286
   imputation on capital in economy,
      106–107
   income, outlay, saving, and wealth, for
      consuming sector, 130–144
   index of total factor productivity,
      342–343
   industrial classification by biases of
      productivity growth, 382
   investment goods product, value share
      of, 227
   labor input per capita, 319–320, 324
   macroeconomic performance
      (1951–1968), 99–169
   national economy, 99
   output per capita, 314, 316–317, 322,
      326
      own rate of return to capital, in
         business sector, 234
   private domestic capital input, 287
   private domestic labor input, 288
   product and factor outlay, for
      producing sector, 109–130
   production account for, 355–356
   productivity change in economy,
      146–171
   quality change, 250–252
   rate of growth of output (1960–1974),
      188
   real capital and labor input, 246–249
   real gross private domestic product,
      240
   real private domestic capital input, 236
   real private domestic factor input, 238
   real private domestic labor input,
      annual growth of, 237
   sectoral productivity gaps with U.S.
      and Germany, 333–376
   total factor productivity, 241
   1947–1973, 320–321, 325
   See also U.S. vs. Japanese economic
      growth (1952–1974)
Japanese national accounting system, 100
   equality in, 104
Japanese National Income Statistics (NIS),
      99, 100, 106, 112
   consumer durables, data for, 144–145
   consumption, computing, 115
   data on labor, 162
   definition of GE sector, 114
   exports and imports, computing, 115
   general equilibrium theory and, 171
   implicit deflators in, 123, 124
   types of capital, 116
   Walras' Law and, 171
Japan Statistical Yearbook, 162, 257
Jorgenson and Nishimizu, 298, 300, 327,
      412
   methodology for international
      comparisons, 348, 389
   productivity gap, Japan and U.S.,
      333
   sectoral production accounts, 339
Jorgenson, D.W., 100
   industry production accounts, 355
   summary of international comparison,
      Japan and U.S., 412

Jorgenson, Kuroda, and Nishimizu, 389, 407
  relative productivity levels, Japan and U.S., 402
  taxonomy of industries, 390, 402–403, 407, 413

Kendrick, John W., 2–3, 6, 23, 27, 86
  definition of sectoral output, 46–47
  labor input and, 24
  measurement of aggregate productivity, 70
  measurement of capital input and, 37–38, 42–44
  measurement of sectoral productivity, 48, 51, 52–53, 56–57
  measurement of total factor productivity, 205, 206
K/K growth rate, 169
Korea, 210
  aggregate economic growth, 242–244
  capital input per capita, 318–319, 323
  capital input, value share of, 228
  capital-labor ratio, 315
  capital stock by asset class, value shares of, 230
  data sources for, 257–258
  decomposition of per capita labor input, 312–313
  gross private domestic product and factor outlay, 290, 292
  investment goods product, value share of, 227
  labor input per capita (1947–1973), 319, 324
  output per capita, 309, 316–317, 322, 326
  own rate of return to capital, in business sector, 234
  private domestic capital input, 291
  private domestic labor input, 291
  quality change, 251–252
  real capital and labor input, 246–247, 249
  real gross private domestic product, 240
  real private domestic capital input, 236
  real private domestic factor input, 238
  real private domestic labor input, 237

total factor productivity, 241
  1947–1973, 320–321, 325
Kravis, 181
  international price comparisons, 338
  purchasing power parities, 185, 340–341, 365–366
Kravis, Heston, and Summers, 297, 327, 328
  commodity groups, 392
  international price comparisons, 307
  purchasing power parities for GDP, 388
  real output per capita, 326
Kuznets, Simon, 1, 3, 87, 88
  international growth trends and, 207

Labor input
  aggregate index, 63–64
  alternative data sources, 22–27
  alternative methods for, 22–27
  annual growth rate for Japan, 357–360, 363
  annual growth rate for U.S., 357–360, 363
  data sources, 20–22
  as factor in economic growth, 4–6, 15, 378
  heterogeneous measures of, 6, 7
  Japanese and U.S., 179, 180, 195–196, 198–200, 398–400
  Japanese decline in change of quality of, 380
  measuring, 17–22
  methods for, 22
  purchasing power parities for, 195–196, 307, 366–368, 394, 403
  real, 204, 223, 245–249
  reallocation of, 8
  real private domestic, annual growth rates of (1947–1973), 237
  relative, data sources, 329
  relative wage levels for, 298
  sectoral measures of, 21–22
  symmetric, 73
  U.S. decline in change of quality of, 380
  value of, 338–339
Labor input per capita (1947–1973), 319–320
  by country, 319
  U.S. level in 1970, 324

Labor input per capita (1970), 298, 299
  by country, 310–311
  decomposition of, 311–314
Labor, quality change in, 162, 168, 170, 172
Labor, quality index of (Watanabe and
    Egaitsu), 156, 158, 167, 168
  data for, 163
  producer productivity change and, 162
"Learning by doing" model (Arrow), 85
Leontief-Solow theorem, 158
Leontief, Wassily, 148
  input-output models, 73
  production function, 336
  rate of technical progress, definition of,
    149
  study of sectoral productivity, 51, 52
Linear logarithmic form. See Cobb-
    Douglas functional form

Macroeconomic performance in Japan
    (1951–1968), 99–169
  aggregation problem I, 148–156
  aggregation problem II, 156–161
  basic accounting framework, 101–109
  consumers' durables, data for, 144–146
  distribution in production, 105–109
  imputation of capital service prices,
    126–130
  income and outlay accounts, 135–140
  private national wealth, 130–135
  product and factor outlay, 109–126
  productivity change, 161–171
  measurement of, 148
  saving and wealth accounts, 140–144
  social accounting system and, 99
Macroeconomic theories, 99
Modeling strategies, economic growth
    and, 16–17
Myopic decision rules, 82

National Income Statistics of Economic
    Planning Agency, 135, 257
National wealth, 131
National Wealth Survey, 123, 145
  modification of data, 123
Net claims, on governments and
    foreigners, 143–144
Netherlands, The, 209–210
  aggregate economic growth, 242–244
  capital input per capita, 317–318, 323
  capital input, value share of, 228

capital-labor ratio, 315
capital stock by asset class, value shares
    of, 230
data sources for, 258
decomposition of per capita labor
    input, 312–313
gross private domestic product and
    factor outlay, 292, 295
investment goods product, value share
    of, 227
labor input per capita, 319, 324
output per capita, 316–317, 322
own rate of return to capital, in
    business sector, 234
private domestic capital input, 293
private domestic labor input, 294
quality change, 251
real capital and labor input, 246–247
real gross private domestic product,
    240
real private domestic capital input, 236
real private domestic factor input, 238
real private domestic labor input, 237
total factor productivity (1947–1973),
    320–321, 325
total factor productivity, 241
Nonsubstitution theorem (Samuelson), 74
Norway, 209

Outlay, consumer, 135–140
  accounts (data), 139
Outlay, producing sector, 109–112
Output
  aggregate, 3–5, 8, 57–61
  alternative sources and methods for,
    51–57
  annual growth rate for Japan, 357–361
  annual growth rate for U.S., 357–361
  data sources, 48–51
  in government sector, 51
  investment goods, Japan and U.S., 188
  in Japanese economy, 101, 179–180,
    184–188
  measuring, 44–51
  methods for, 48–51
  in private sector, 51
  purchasing power parities for, 391, 392
  relative prices of, 296, 387, 391–392,
    409–411
  sales tax and, 112

separation of, 172
translog indexes of, 185, 186–187, 303
in U.S. economy, 179, 184–188
value of, 338
*See also* Sectoral output
Output per capita (1947–1973), 314–317,
    322
    alternatives, 326–328
    by country, 316
    U.S. level in 1970, 322
Output per capita (1970), 298, 299
    by country, 309–310
Output, quality index of, 167, 168
Own rate of return to capital,
    international, in business sector, 234

Perpetual inventory method, 28, 31
    capital stock estimates and, 192–193
    measuring capital input and, 28–29,
        38–40
    measuring capital stock and, 122
    quantity of capital services and, 119
    stock of consumer durables and,
        145–146
Population, relative to the U.S., 310
Price comparisons, 297, 328
    Canada and U.S., 328
    data for international, 338–341
    Japan and U.S., 388
Price functions, 214
Price indexes, 303–304
    aggregate, Japan and U.S., 397–398
    for aggregate output, 303–304
    for capital and labor input, 305
    Japanese, transformed by purchasing
        power parities, 394–395
    value added, Japan and U.S., 396
Private domestic capital input, 271
    for Canada, 271
    for France, 275
    for Germany, 279
    for Italy, 283
    for Japan, 287
    for Korea, 291
    for The Netherlands, 293
    for U.K., 267
    for U.S., 263
Private domestic labor input, 272
    for Canada, 272
    for France, 276

for Germany, 280
for Italy, 284
for Japan, 288
for Korea, 291
for The Netherlands, 294
for U.K., 268
for U.S., 264
Private national wealth. *See* Consumer
    wealth
Producers' durables, 172
Producing sector, 109
    accounting framework for, 110–112
    consumption and investment goods,
        data for, 111–112
    economic units in, 116–117
    product and factor outlay accounts for,
        112–122
    productivity change in, 161–171, 172
    value of output and input services,
        110–111, 112, 172
Product and factor outlay, 224–226
Product and factor outlay, for producing
    sector, 109–112, 113–114
    accounts, 112–122
    equality of output and input value, 172
    real products and prices, 116
    U.S. vs. Japan, 186
Production account, 223–239, 224–225
    government vs. private, 225
    for industries in Japan, 355–356
    for industries in U.S., 355–356
    private domestic, 225
Production functions, 1–7
    aggregate, 1–7, 57–61, 71
    disaggregated, 72–73
    distribution in production and, 105–106
    output as function of inputs and time,
        210
    productivity change and, 149
    sectoral, 17–20, 45–46
    translog, 19–20, 22, 182–183
    U.S. vs. Japan, 181–182
Production models, 81–87
    econometric, 72–81
    induced technical change, 81
    intertemporal, 81–82
    sectoral, 73–75, 77–79, 86
Production patterns, Japan and U.S.,
    181–182
    analyzing changes in, 182, 210–211

Production patterns (*cont.*)
  analyzing differences in, 181–182, 425
Productivity, 4–6
  alternative sources and methods for,
    51–57
  annual growth rates in Japan, 357–360,
    364–365, 375
  change in, 146–171, 172
  decline in, 9
  economic growth and, 1–98
  as factor in economic growth, 15
  gaps in, Japan and U.S., 368–375,
    402–411
  growth, biases of, 78–79
  growth rates for Japan and U.S., 413
  industrial, in Japan and U.S., 402–403
  and international competitiveness,
    387–417
  Japan and U.S., 197–201, 368–374,
    377–385, 387–417
  measuring, 17–22, 44–51, 211–212
  role of technology in, 199–201
  total factor, international annual
    growth of, 241
  total factor, in U.S., 201
  translog multilateral indexes of
    differences in, 302
Productivity change, 218–223
Productivity change, in Japanese
    economy, 146–171
  aggregate production function and, 148
  aggregation bias and, 161
  aggregation problem I, 148–156
  aggregation problem II, 156–161
  capital input and, 146–147
  comparison of productivity levels,
    368–375, 409–411
  Divisia index and, 147, 148–149
  input-output system and, 148–149
  intermediate goods and, 156
  measuring, 146–171
  postwar growth, 166
  in producing sector, 161–171
  quality change in capital and, 168,
    170–171
  quality change in labor and, 162, 168,
    170
  quality change in output and, 168, 170
  quality index of labor and, 156–161
  relative productivity levels, 402–411

  various types capital, 158–159
  various types output, 158–159
  vs. U.S., methodology for, 181–188
Productivity change, in producing sector,
    161–171, 172
  aggregate rate of, 172
  aggregation bias and, 167, 170–171
  average growth rates, 166
  Divisia indexes and, 163–165
  postwar growth, 166
  quality change in capital and, 168,
    170–171
  quality change in output and, 168, 170
  quality index of labor and, 162, 168, 170
  value of labor services, 161–162
Productivity gap, U.S. and Japan, 368–375,
    402–411, 412
  in agriculture-forestry-fisheries,
    368–370, 402, 406
  in apparel, 402
  in construction, 406
  in finance and insurance, 369, 371, 403
  in food, 402, 406
  in furniture, 402, 406
  in investment-goods industries, 402
  in leather, 406–407
  in light manufacturing, 369–370
  in machinery, 406–407
  in mining and manufacturing, 403
  in motor vehicles, 406
  in paper and allied products, 402
  in petroleum refining, 369, 371, 402, 406
  in printing and publishing, 402, 406
  proportional gap of output prices,
    409–411
  in service sector, 369, 371
  technology gaps and, 371–374
  in textile industry, 369–370, 402, 406
  in trade, 402
  in transportation and communication,
    369, 371, 403
  in utilities, 402
Productivity growth, 78–79
  biases of, 78–79, 382–384
  classification of industries by, 79
  comparison of levels of, 368–375
  Japan and U.S., 357–360, 364–365,
    368–375, 413
Productivity levels, Japan and U.S.,
    347–376, 389

Productivity levels, relative, international comparison of, 297–331
  by country, 310–311
*Productivity Trends in the U.S.*, 2
Purchasing power parities, 340–341
  Japanese price index and, 394–395
Purchasing power parities, Japan and U.S., 181, 185, 186–187, 365–385, 388–402
  for agriculture, 403
  for capital goods, 191, 306, 366
  for capital input, 191, 194, 306–307, 366–368, 393–394
  for consumption goods, 188
  estimating indexes of, 365–368
  for industry output, 366–367, 391, 392
  for intermediate input, 367, 394
  for intermediate input components, 366, 392
  for investment goods, 188, 194, 306, 366
  for labor input, 195–196, 307, 366–368, 394, 403
  methodology for estimating, 391–394
  yen-to-dollar exchange rate and, 388–389

Quality change, international, 249–252
Quality indexes, 167
  capital, 167, 168
  labor, 156, 162, 163, 167, 168
  output, 167, 168
Quantity index of labor input, 235

Rates of productivity growth, 415
Rates of return, 128–129, 191
  corporate, 232
  corporate nominal, 233
  Japan and U.S., 193
  noncorporate, 232
  noncorporate nominal, 233
Real capital input, 208, 209, 223, 226–235, 250
  aggregate economic growth and, 253–254
  international growth of, 245–249
Real factor input, 203, 204
  aggregate economic growth and, 253
  analyzing, 245

Real labor input, 204, 223, 250
  aggregate economic growth and, 253–254
  international growth of, 245–249
Real product, 204, 208, 223
  aggregate economic growth and, 203, 242–245, 253–254
  prices and, 116
  sources of, 203
Rees Report (National Research Council), 3, 22–23
  measurement of capital input, 37
  measurement of intermediate input, 51
Relative efficiencies, 42–43
  constant, 42–43
  "one-hoss shay" pattern, 43
  straight-line pattern, 43
Relative productivity levels, international comparison of, 297–331
  methodology, 299–307
Relative productivity levels, Japan and U.S., 389, 402–411
  methodology, 389–390
  productivity gaps in, 402
Rental price concept, 15, 28
  capital services and, 39
Rental prices, 28–29, 34

Saving accounts, 140–144
  data, 142
  sources and uses of, 141
Sector aggregation. *See* Aggregation problem I
Sectoral growth, 9
  Japan and U.S., 355–365
  sources of, 9–15
Sectoral measures of capital input, 34–37
  capital stock and, 35
  Kendrick vs. Jorgenson, 44
  perpetual inventory method and, 38–40
Sectoral output, 9–15, 16, 27
  bias in measurement of, 56–57
  depreciation and, 46–47
  growth rate (1947–1969), 53–56
  intermediate input and, 45–46, 48–50, 56–57
  measuring, 44–45
  *See also* Sectoral productivity

Sectoral production model, 73–75, 77–79
    economic growth and, 86
    vs. aggregate model, 76
Sectoral productivity, 8
    aggregate models and, 59, 60
    construction of data on, 51
    decline in, 9, 77, 80
    energy prices and, 80
    gaps in, 333–345
    index of, 50, 57
    Kendrick's measurement of, 48, 51,
        52–53, 56–57
    labor input and, 21–22
    Leontief study, 51, 52
    measuring, 17–22, 44–45, 51
    in public and private sectors, 51
Sectoral productivity gaps, U.S., Japan,
        and Germany, 333–345
    data, 338–341
    methodology for, 324–338
    purchasing power parities, 340
    results, 341–345
Social accounting system, 99
Social insurance funds, 135
    in Japanese national income statistics,
        135, 137
Solow, Robert M., 3, 57, 85
    embodied technical change and, 82–83
    rate of technical progress and, 161
Stigler, George J., 2
    total factor productivity and, 206
Sweden, 209

Taxes, 113–114
    asset tax rate, formula for, 126
    corporate business sector, 309
    corporate income, 232
    direct, on persons in Japan, 139
    effect on service price, 117
    formulae for effective rate on private
        income, 139–140
    formulae for effective rates, 127
    gross private national income net of,
        134
    "income taxes not withheld," 139
    "income taxes withheld," 139
    noncorporate business sector, 193, 309
    private domestic sector, 193, 309
    pure asset, 114
    real property acquisition, 114

Technical change, 380–385
    biased, 382–383
    decline in economic growth and, 383
    energy use and, 382–385
    sectoral, 383
Technical change, rate of, 197–198,
        214–215, 216–217
    aggregate, 381
    decline in, 379–380
    defined, 350
    Divisia quantity index of technical
        change, 213
    energy prices and, 380, 383, 385
    as factor in economic growth, 378
    sectoral, 378, 381–383
    translog index of technical change and,
        198, 217
Technology, Japan and U.S., 179, 180,
        197–201, 371–374
    closing of gap, 198–200, 344–345, 348,
        406
    differences in, 350–351
    gaps in, 371–374, 406–409
    industrial taxonomy, technology gap
        and, 404–405
    other industrialized nations and, 201
    rate of technical change, 198, 350
    translog index of difference in
        technology, 197–199
    translog index of technical change, 198
    translog quantity indexes of differences
        in technology, 352
    translog quantity indexes of rates of
        technical change, 351
Tinbergen, Jan, 2, 6, 16, 57, 59
    aggregate production function and, 76,
        86
    international comparisons, 205, 206
    measurement of sectoral output, 56
    neoclassical model of economic growth,
        86–87
    total factor productivity and, 205,
        206
Tokyo Retail Price Indexes, 145
Tövrnqvist-index, 335–336
    vs. traditional indexes, 336
Total capital income, by sector, 122
Total factor input (1952–1974), Japan and
        U.S., 196–197
Total factor outlay, 226

Total factor productivity, 204, 223
  defined, 206
  German output and input, 334
  international, 250
  international comparisons of, 298,
    309–310, 320–321
  relative to U.S., 298, 310, 320–321
Total labor income, by sector, 122
Toyokeizai Statistical Yearbook, 125
Trade imbalance, Japan and U.S., 387
Transcendental logarithmic production
    function. See Translog production
    functions
Translog indexes
  of capital stock, 221
  of difference in technology, 197–199
  of differences in productivity, 336
  of productivity growth, 301, 336
  of technical change, 198, 224
Translog indexes of capital input, 189–190,
    192–193, 218
  for business sector, 194
  quantity index, 226, 229
Translog indexes of labor input, 189–190,
    218
  by education, 195
Translog indexes of output, 185–187, 218,
    303
  product and factor outlay and, 224
Translog index numbers, 218–219
  for labor input, 22
Translog multilateral indexes
  of differences in productivity, 302, 309,
    337
  of relative capital and labor inputs,
    305
  of relative capital input, 305, 308–309
  of relative factor inputs, 338
  of relative labor input, 305, 313
  of relative output, 303, 307–308
Translog price functions, 414
Translog price indexes
  of differences in productivity, 416
  of rates of productivity growth, 416
Translog production functions, 19–20, 22,
    182–183, 216, 349
Translog quantity indexes
  of aggregate capital stock, 229
  of capital, labor, and intermediate
    inputs, 354

of differences in capital, labor, and
    intermediate inputs, 354
of differences in technology, 352
of rates of technical change, 351

Unexplained residual, 379
United Kingdom, 209
  aggregate growth rate, 242–244
  capital input per capita, 317–318, 323
  capital input, value share of, 228
  capital-labor ratio, 315
  capital stock by asset class, value shares
    of, 230
  data sources for, 259
  decomposition of per capita labor
    input, 312–313
  gross private domestic product and
    factor input, 269
  gross private domestic product and
    factor outlay, 266
  investment goods product, value share
    of, 227
  labor input per capita, 319, 324
  output per capita, 316–317, 322
  own rate of return to capital, in
    business sector, 234
  private domestic capital input, 267
  private domestic labor input, 268
  quality change, 250–251
  real capital and labor input, 246–248
  real gross private domestic product,
    240
  real private domestic capital input, 236
  real private domestic factor input, 238
  real private domestic labor input, 237
  total factor productivity, 241
  1947–1973, 320–321, 325
United States, 209
  aggregate growth rate, 242–244
  annual growth rate of capital input,
    357–360, 362
  annual growth rate of labor input,
    357–360, 363
  annual growth rate of output, 357–360,
    357–361
  annual productivity growth, 357–360,
    364–365
  capital input per capita, 1970 level, 323
  capital input, value share of, 228

United States (*cont.*)
  capital stock by asset class, value shares
      of, 230
  data sources for, 259–260
  decline in capital input, 379
  decline in change of quality of labor
      input, 380
  decline in economic growth, 379–380
  decline in output, 379–380
  economic growth in, 374–375
  gross private domestic product and
      factor outlay, 262, 265
  index of total factor productivity,
      342–343
  industrial classification by biases of
      productivity growth, 384
  investment goods product, value share
      of, 227
  labor input per capita, 1970 level, 324
  output per capita, 1970 level, 321
  own rate of return to capital, in
      business sector, 234
  price comparison with Canada, 328
  private domestic capital input, 263
  private domestic labor input, 264
  production account for, 355–356
  quality change, 251
  real capital and labor input, 246–249
  real gross private domestic product,
      240
  real private domestic capital input, 236
  real private domestic factor input, 238
  real private domestic labor input, 237
  sectoral productivity gaps with Japan
      and Germany, 333–376
  total factor productivity, 1970 level, 325
  total factor productivity, 241
U.S. vs. Japanese economic growth
    (1952–1974), 179–295
  aggregate input, 188–197
  aggregate output, 184–188
  capital input, 179–180, 189, 191–195,
      200–201
  capital services, share of, 194
  capital stock and, 190
  effect of, of technology, 180, 198–201
  investment goods output, 180, 188
  labor input, 180, 195–196, 198–200
  methodology, 181–184
  output, 184–188, 196–197
  output of consumption goods, 180, 188

  output of investment goods, 188
  own rate of return, 194
  per capita gap, 179, 180
  price indexes, 185, 189–190
  productivity, 197–201
  property compensation and, 193
  purchasing power parities, 181,
      185–187, 365–385
  total factor input, 196–197
  transition in, 179–180
  translog indexes of output, 185,
      185–187
  translog index of difference in
      technology, 197–199

Valuation, 51
Value added, 3–5
  aggregate, 62–63
  depreciation and, 46–48
  gross, defined, 48
  as measurement of sectoral
      productivity, 44–45, 52–53
  national income as measure of, 67
  net, defined, 48
  reallocation of, 8, 9
  sectoral index, 62–63
  sectoral output and, 45–48
Vintage price functions, 29–30
  alternatives to, 34
  for commercial and industrial
      buildings, 29–30
  correction of bias in, 31
  depreciation and, 31, 34
  for trucks, 29

Walras' Law, 104
  national income statistics and, 171
Watanabe, T. and F. Egaitsu, 147
  quality index of labor, 156, 158, 162, 163
Wealth accounts, 130, 140–144
  data, 142
  sources and uses of, 141
Wealth, Japanese consumer, 130–144
*Why Growth Rates Differ*, 206–208
  vs. Christensen and Jorgenson results,
      207–208

Yen-to-dollar exchange rate, 387–388,
    394–395
  defined, 387
  purchasing power parities and, 388–389
Yoshihara, K. and T. Ratcliffe, 166